T0177154

Foundations of Data Science

This book provides an introduction to the mathematical and algorithmic foundations of data science, including machine learning, high-dimensional geometry, and analysis of large networks. Topics include the counterintuitive nature of data in high dimensions, important linear algebraic techniques such as singular value decomposition, the theory of random walks and Markov chains, the fundamentals of and important algorithms for machine learning, algorithms, and analysis for clustering, probabilistic models for large networks, representation learning including topic modeling and nonnegative matrix factorization, wavelets, and compressed sensing. Important probabilistic techniques are developed including the law of large numbers, tail inequalities, analysis of random projections, generalization guarantees in machine learning, and moment methods for analysis of phase transitions in large random graphs. Additionally, important structural and complexity measures are discussed such as matrix norms and VC-dimension. This book is suitable for both undergraduate and graduate courses in the design and analysis of algorithms for data.

Avrim Blum is Chief Academic Officer at the Toyota Technological Institute at Chicago and formerly Professor at Carnegie Mellon University. He has over 25,000 citations for his work in algorithms and machine learning. He has received the AI Journal Classic Paper Award, ICML/COLT 10-Year Best Paper Award, Sloan Fellowship, NSF NYI award, and Herb Simon Teaching Award, and is a fellow of the Association for Computing Machinery.

John Hopcroft is the IBM Professor of Engineering and Applied Mathematics at Cornell University. He is a member National Academy of Sciences and National Academy of Engineering, and a foreign member of the Chinese Academy of Sciences. He received the Turing Award in 1986, was appointed to the National Science Board in 1992 by President George H. W. Bush, and was presented with the Friendship Award by Premier Li Keqiang for his work in China.

Ravindran (Ravi) Kannan is Principal Researcher for Microsoft Research, India. He was the recipient of the Fulkerson Prize in Discrete Mathematics (1991) and the Knuth Prize (ACM) in 2011. He is a distinguished alumnus of Indian Institute of Technology, Bombay, and his past faculty appointments include Massachusetts Institute of Technology, Carnegie-Mellon University, Yale University, and the Indian Institute of Science.

Foundations of Data Science

Avrim Blum

Toyota Technological Institute at Chicago

John Hopcroft

Cornell University, New York

Ravindran Kannan

Microsoft Research, India

Shaftesbury Road, Cambridge CB2 8EA, United Kingdom

One Liberty Plaza, 20th Floor, New York, NY 10006, USA

477 Williamstown Road, Port Melbourne, VIC 3207, Australia

314–321, 3rd Floor, Plot 3, Splendor Forum, Jasola District Centre,
New Delhi – 110025, India

103 Penang Road, #05–06/07, Visioncrest Commercial, Singapore 238467

Cambridge University Press is part of Cambridge University Press & Assessment,
a department of the University of Cambridge.

We share the University's mission to contribute to society through the pursuit of
education, learning and research at the highest international levels of excellence.

www.cambridge.org
Information on this title: www.cambridge.org/9781108485067
DOI: 10.1017/9781108755528

First published 2020 (version 3, February 2023)

Printed in the United Kingdom by TJ Books Limited, Padstow Cornwall

A catalogue record for this publication is available from the British Library

Library of Congress Cataloging-in-Publication data
Names: Blum, Avrim, 1966– author. | Hopcroft, John E., 1939– author. |
Kannan, Ravindran, 1953– author.
Title: Foundations of data science / Avrim Blum, Toyota Technological Institute at Chicago,
John Hopcroft, Cornell University, New York, Ravindran Kannan, Microsoft Research, India.
Description: First edition. | New York, NY : Cambridge University Press, 2020. |
Includes bibliographical references and index.
Identifiers: LCCN 2019038133 (print) | LCCN 2019038134 (ebook) |
ISBN 9781108485067 (hardback) | ISBN 9781108755528 (epub)
Subjects: LCSH: Computer science. | Statistics. | Quantitative research.
Classification: LCC QA76 .B5675 2020 (print) | LCC QA76 (ebook) | DDC 004–dc23
LC record available at https://lccn.loc.gov/2019038133
LC ebook record available at https://lccn.loc.gov/2019038134

ISBN 978-1-108-48506-7 Hardback

Contents

1	**Introduction**	*page* 1
2	**High-Dimensional Space**	4
	2.1 Introduction	4
	2.2 The Law of Large Numbers	4
	2.3 The Geometry of High Dimensions	8
	2.4 Properties of the Unit Ball	8
	2.5 Generating Points Uniformly at Random from a Ball	13
	2.6 Gaussians in High Dimension	15
	2.7 Random Projection and Johnson-Lindenstrauss Lemma	16
	2.8 Separating Gaussians	18
	2.9 Fitting a Spherical Gaussian to Data	20
	2.10 Bibliographic Notes	21
	2.11 Exercises	22
3	**Best-Fit Subspaces and Singular Value Decomposition (SVD)**	29
	3.1 Introduction	29
	3.2 Preliminaries	31
	3.3 Singular Vectors	31
	3.4 Singular Value Decomposition (SVD)	34
	3.5 Best Rank-k Approximations	36
	3.6 Left Singular Vectors	37
	3.7 Power Method for Singular Value Decomposition	39
	3.8 Singular Vectors and Eigenvectors	42
	3.9 Applications of Singular Value Decomposition	42
	3.10 Bibliographic Notes	53
	3.11 Exercises	54
4	**Random Walks and Markov Chains**	62
	4.1 Stationary Distribution	65
	4.2 Markov Chain Monte Carlo	67
	4.3 Areas and Volumes	71
	4.4 Convergence of Random Walks on Undirected Graphs	73
	4.5 Electrical Networks and Random Walks	81
	4.6 Random Walks on Undirected Graphs with Unit Edge Weights	85

4.7   Random Walks in Euclidean Space   92
4.8   The Web as a Markov Chain   95
4.9   Bibliographic Notes   98
4.10 Exercises   99

5   Machine Learning   109

5.1   Introduction   109
5.2   The Perceptron Algorithm   110
5.3   Kernel Functions and Nonlinearly Separable Data   111
5.4   Generalizing to New Data   113
5.5   VC-Dimension   118
5.6   VC-Dimension and Machine Learning   126
5.7   Other Measures of Complexity   127
5.8   Deep Learning   128
5.9   Gradient Descent   134
5.10 Online Learning   138
5.11 Boosting   145
5.12 Further Current Directions   148
5.13 Bibliographic Notes   152
5.14 Exercises   152

6   Algorithms for Massive Data Problems: Streaming, Sketching, and Sampling   159

6.1   Introduction   159
6.2   Frequency Moments of Data Streams   160
6.3   Matrix Algorithms Using Sampling   169
6.4   Sketches of Documents   177
6.5   Bibliographic Notes   178
6.6   Exercises   179

7   Clustering   182

7.1   Introduction   182
7.2 k-Means Clustering   185
7.3 k-Center Clustering   189
7.4   Finding Low-Error Clusterings   189
7.5   Spectral Clustering   190
7.6   Approximation Stability   197
7.7   High-Density Clusters   199
7.8   Kernel Methods   201
7.9   Recursive Clustering Based on Sparse Cuts   202
7.10 Dense Submatrices and Communities   202
7.11 Community Finding and Graph Partitioning   205
7.12 Spectral Clustering Applied to Social Networks   208
7.13 Bibliographic Notes   210
7.14 Exercises   210

8   Random Graphs   215

8.1   The $G(n, p)$ Model   215

8.2 Phase Transitions 222

8.3 Giant Component 232

8.4 Cycles and Full Connectivity 235

8.5 Phase Transitions for Increasing Properties 239

8.6 Branching Processes 241

8.7 CNF-SAT 246

8.8 Nonuniform Models of Random Graphs 252

8.9 Growth Models 254

8.10 Small-World Graphs 261

8.11 Bibliographic Notes 266

8.12 Exercises 266

9 **Topic Models, Nonnegative Matrix Factorization, Hidden Markov Models, and Graphical Models** 274

9.1 Topic Models 274

9.2 An Idealized Model 277

9.3 Nonnegative Matrix Factorization 279

9.4 NMF with Anchor Terms 281

9.5 Hard and Soft Clustering 282

9.6 The Latent Dirichlet Allocation Model for Topic Modeling 283

9.7 The Dominant Admixture Model 285

9.8 Formal Assumptions 287

9.9 Finding the Term-Topic Matrix 290

9.10 Hidden Markov Models 295

9.11 Graphical Models and Belief Propagation 298

9.12 Bayesian or Belief Networks 299

9.13 Markov Random Fields 300

9.14 Factor Graphs 301

9.15 Tree Algorithms 301

9.16 Message Passing in General Graphs 303

9.17 Warning Propagation 310

9.18 Correlation between Variables 311

9.19 Bibliographic Notes 315

9.20 Exercises 315

10 **Other Topics** 318

10.1 Ranking and Social Choice 318

10.2 Compressed Sensing and Sparse Vectors 322

10.3 Applications 325

10.4 An Uncertainty Principle 327

10.5 Gradient 330

10.6 Linear Programming 332

10.7 Integer Optimization 334

10.8 Semi-Definite Programming 334

10.9 Bibliographic Notes 336

10.10 Exercises 337

11 Wavelets   341

  11.1 Dilation   341
  11.2 The Haar Wavelet   342
  11.3 Wavelet Systems   345
  11.4 Solving the Dilation Equation   346
  11.5 Conditions on the Dilation Equation   347
  11.6 Derivation of the Wavelets from the Scaling Function 350
  11.7 Sufficient Conditions for the Wavelets to Be Orthogonal 353
  11.8 Expressing a Function in Terms of Wavelets   355
  11.9 Designing a Wavelet System   356
  11.10 Applications   357
  11.11 Bibliographic Notes   357
  11.12 Exercises   357

12 Background Material   360

  12.1 Definitions and Notation   360
  12.2 Useful Relations   361
  12.3 Useful Inequalities   365
  12.4 Probability   372
  12.5 Bounds on Tail Probability   380
  12.6 Applications of the Tail Bound   386
  12.7 Eigenvalues and Eigenvectors   387
  12.8 Generating Functions   400
  12.9 Miscellaneous   404
  12.10 Exercises   407

References   411
Index   421

CHAPTER ONE

Introduction

Computer science as an academic discipline began in the 1960s. Emphasis was on programming languages, compilers, operating systems, and the mathematical theory that supported these areas. Courses in theoretical computer science covered finite automata, regular expressions, context-free languages, and computability. In the 1970s, the study of algorithms was added as an important component of theory. The emphasis was on making computers useful. Today, a fundamental change is taking place and the focus is more on a wealth of applications. There are many reasons for this change. The merging of computing and communications has played an important role. The enhanced ability to observe, collect, and store data in the natural sciences, in commerce, and in other fields calls for a change in our understanding of data and how to handle it in the modern setting. The emergence of the web and social networks as central aspects of daily life presents both opportunities and challenges for theory.

While traditional areas of computer science remain highly important, increasingly researchers of the future will be involved with using computers to understand and extract usable information from massive data arising in applications, not just how to make computers useful on specific well-defined problems. With this in mind we have written this book to cover the theory we expect to be useful in the next 40 years, just as an understanding of automata theory, algorithms, and related topics gave students an advantage in the last 40 years. One of the major changes is an increase in emphasis on probability, statistics, and numerical methods.

Early drafts of the book have been used for both undergraduate and graduate courses. Background material needed for an undergraduate course has been put into a background chapter with associated homework problems.

Modern data in diverse fields such as information processing, search, and machine learning is often advantageously represented as vectors with a large number of components. The vector representation is not just a book-keeping device to store many fields of a record. Indeed, the two salient aspects of vectors – geometric (length, dot products, orthogonality, etc.) and linear algebraic (independence, rank, singular values, etc.) – turn out to be relevant and useful. Chapters 2 and 3 lay the foundations of geometry and linear algebra, respectively. More specifically, our intuition from two- or three-dimensional space can be surprisingly off the mark when it comes to high dimensions. Chapter 2 works out the fundamentals needed to understand the differences. The emphasis of the chapter, as well as the book in general, is to get across the intellectual ideas and the mathematical foundations rather than focus on particular applications, some of which are briefly described. Chapter 3 focuses on singular value decomposition (SVD) a central tool to deal with matrix data. We give a from-first-principles description of the mathematics and algorithms for SVD. Applications of singular value decomposition include principal component analysis, a widely used technique we touch on, as well as modern applications to statistical mixtures of probability densities, discrete optimization, etc., which are described in more detail.

Exploring large structures like the web or the space of configurations of a large system with deterministic methods can be prohibitively expensive. Random walks (also called Markov chains) turn out often to be more efficient as well as illuminative. The stationary distributions of such walks are important for applications ranging from web search to the simulation of physical systems. The underlying mathematical theory of such random walks, as well as connections to electrical networks, forms the core of Chapter 4 on Markov chains.

One of the surprises of computer science over the last two decades is that some domain-independent methods have been immensely successful in tackling problems from diverse areas. Machine learning is a striking example. Chapter 5 describes the foundations of machine learning, both algorithms for optimizing over given training examples as well as the theory for understanding when such optimization can be expected to lead to good performance on new, unseen data. This includes important measures such as the Vapnik–Chervonenkis dimension; important algorithms such as the Perceptron Algorithm, stochastic gradient descent, boosting, and deep learning; and important notions such as regularization and overfitting.

The field of algorithms has traditionally assumed that the input data to a problem is presented in random access memory, which the algorithm can repeatedly access. This is not feasible for problems involving enormous amounts of data. The streaming model and other models have been formulated to reflect this. In this setting, sampling plays a crucial role and, indeed, we have to sample on the fly. In Chapter 6 we study how to draw good samples efficiently and how to estimate statistical and linear algebra quantities with such samples.

While Chapter 5 focuses on supervised learning, where one learns from labeled training data, the problem of unsupervised learning, or learning from unlabeled data, is equally important. A central topic in unsupervised learning is clustering, discussed in Chapter 7. Clustering refers to the problem of partitioning data into groups of similar objects. After describing some of the basic methods for clustering, such as the k-means algorithm, Chapter 7 focuses on modern developments in understanding these, as well as newer algorithms and general frameworks for analyzing different kinds of clustering problems.

Central to our understanding of large structures, like the web and social networks, is building models to capture essential properties of these structures. The simplest model is that of a random graph formulated by Erdös and Renyi, which we study in detail in Chapter 8, proving that certain global phenomena, like a giant connected component, arise in such structures with only local choices. We also describe other models of random graphs.

Chapter 9 focuses on linear-algebraic problems of making sense from data, in particular topic modeling and nonnegative matrix factorization. In addition to discussing well-known models, we also describe some current research on models and algorithms with provable guarantees on learning error and time. This is followed by graphical models and belief propagation.

Chapter 10 discusses ranking and social choice as well as problems of sparse representations such as compressed sensing. Additionally, Chapter 10 includes a brief discussion of linear programming and semidefinite programming. Wavelets, which are an important method for representing signals across a wide range of applications, are discussed in Chapter 11 along with some of their fundamental mathematical properties. Chapter 12 includes a range of background material.

A word about notation in the book. To help the student, we have adopted certain notations and, with a few exceptions, adhered to them. We use lowercase letters for scalar variables and functions, boldface lowercase for vectors, and uppercase letters for matrices. Lowercase near the beginning of the alphabet tend to be constants; in the middle of the alphabet, such as i, j, and k, are indices in summations; n and m for integer sizes; and x, y, and z for variables. If A is a matrix, its elements are a_{ij} and its rows are $\mathbf{a_i}$. If $\mathbf{a_i}$ is a vector, its coordinates are a_{ij}. Where the literature traditionally uses a symbol for a quantity, we also used that symbol, even if it meant abandoning our convention. If we have a set of points in some vector space, and work with a subspace, we use n for the number of points, d for the dimension of the space, and k for the dimension of the subspace.

The term "almost surely" means with probability tending to one. We use $\ln n$ for the natural logarithm and $\log n$ for the base two logarithm. If we want base ten, we will use $\log_{10}$. To simplify notation and to make it easier to read, we use $E^2(1 - x)$ for $\left(E(1 - x)\right)^2$ and $E(1 - x)^2$ for $E\left((1 - x)^2\right)$. When we say "randomly select" some number of points from a given probability distribution, independence is always assumed unless otherwise stated.

CHAPTER TWO

High-Dimensional Space

2.1. Introduction

High-dimensional data has become very important. However, high-dimensional space is very different from the two- and three-dimensional spaces we are familiar with. Generate n points at random in d-dimensions where each coordinate is a zero mean, unit variance Gaussian. For sufficiently large d, with high probability, the distances between all pairs of points will be essentially the same. Also the volume of the unit ball in d-dimensions, the set of all points $\mathbf{x}$ such that $|\mathbf{x}| \leq 1$, goes to zero as the dimension goes to infinity. The volume of a high-dimensional unit ball is concentrated near its surface and is also concentrated at its equator. These properties have important consequences that we will consider.

2.2. The Law of Large Numbers

If one generates random points in d-dimensional space using a Gaussian to generate coordinates, the distance between all pairs of points will be essentially the same when d is large. The reason is that the square of the distance between two points $\mathbf{y}$ and $\mathbf{z}$,

$$|\mathbf{y} - \mathbf{z}|^2 = \sum_{i=1}^{d} (y_i - z_i)^2,$$

can be viewed as the sum of d independent samples of a random variable x that is the squared difference of two Gaussians. In particular, we are summing independent samples $x_i = (y_i - z_i)^2$ of a random variable x of bounded variance. In such a case, a general bound known as the Law of Large Numbers states that with high probability, the average of the samples will be close to the expectation of the random variable. This in turn implies that with high probability, the sum is close to the sum's expectation.

Specifically, the Law of Large Numbers states that

$$\text{Prob}\left(\left|\frac{x_1 + x_2 + \cdots + x_n}{n} - E(x)\right| \geq \epsilon\right) \leq \frac{Var(x)}{n\epsilon^2}. \tag{2.1}$$

The larger the variance of the random variable, the greater the probability that the error will exceed ϵ. Thus the variance of x is in the numerator. The number of samples n is in the denominator, since the more values that are averaged, the smaller the probability that the difference will exceed ϵ. Similarly the larger ϵ is, the smaller the probability that the difference will exceed ϵ and hence ϵ is in the denominator. Notice that squaring ϵ makes the fraction a dimensionless quantity.

We use two inequalities to prove the Law of Large Numbers. The first is Markov's inequality that states that the probability that a nonnegative random variable exceeds a is bounded by the expected value of the variable divided by a.

Theorem 2.1 (Markov's inequality) *Let x be a nonnegative random variable. Then for $a > 0$,*

$$Prob(x \geq a) \leq \frac{E(x)}{a}.$$

Proof For a continuous nonnegative random variable x with probability density p,

$$E(x) = \int_0^\infty xp(x)dx = \int_0^a xp(x)dx + \int_a^\infty xp(x)dx$$

$$\geq \int_a^\infty xp(x)dx \geq a \int_a^\infty p(x)dx = a Prob(x \geq a).$$

Thus, $Prob(x \geq a) \leq \frac{E(x)}{a}$. ∎

The same proof works for discrete random variables with sums instead of integrals.

Corollary 2.2 $Prob(x \geq bE(x)) \leq \frac{1}{b}$

Markov's inequality bounds the tail of a distribution using only information about the mean. A tighter bound can be obtained by also using the variance of the random variable.

Theorem 2.3 (Chebyshev's inequality) *Let x be a random variable. Then for $c > 0$,*

$$Prob\left(|x - E(x)| \geq c\right) \leq \frac{Var(x)}{c^2}.$$

Proof $Prob(|x - E(x)| \geq c) = Prob(|x - E(x)|^2 \geq c^2)$. Note that $y = |x - E(x)|^2$ is a nonnegative random variable and $E(y) = Var(x)$, so Markov's inequality can be applied giving:

$$Prob(|x - E(x)| \geq c) = Prob\left(|x - E(x)|^2 \geq c^2\right) \leq \frac{E(|x - E(x)|^2)}{c^2} = \frac{Var(x)}{c^2}.$$

∎

The Law of Large Numbers follows from Chebyshev's inequality together with facts about independent random variables. Recall that:

$$E(x + y) = E(x) + E(y),$$
$$Var(x - c) = Var(x),$$
$$Var(cx) = c^2 Var(x).$$

Also, if x and y are independent, then $E(xy) = E(x)E(y)$. These facts imply that if x and y are independent, then $Var(x + y) = Var(x) + Var(y)$, which is seen as follows:

$$Var(x + y) = E(x + y)^2 - E^2(x + y)$$
$$= E(x^2 + 2xy + y^2) - \left(E^2(x) + 2E(x)E(y) + E^2(y)\right)$$
$$= E(x^2) - E^2(x) + E(y^2) - E^2(y) = Var(x) + Var(y),$$

where we used independence to replace $E(2xy)$ with $2E(x)E(y)$.

Theorem 2.4 (**Law of Large Numbers**) *Let* $x_1, x_2, \ldots, x_n$ *be* n *independent samples of a random variable* x. *Then*

$$Prob\left(\left|\frac{x_1 + x_2 + \cdots + x_n}{n} - E(x)\right| \geq \epsilon\right) \leq \frac{Var(x)}{n\epsilon^2}$$

Proof $E(\frac{x_1 + x_2 + \cdots + x_n}{n}) = E(x)$ and thus

$$\mathrm{Prob}\left(\left|\frac{x_1 + x_2 + \cdots + x_n}{n} - E(x)\right| \geq \epsilon\right) = \mathrm{Prob}\left(\left|\frac{x_1 + x_2 + \cdots + x_n}{n}\right.\right.$$
$$\left.\left. - E\left(\frac{x_1 + x_2 + \cdots + x_n}{n}\right)\right| \geq \epsilon\right)$$

By Chebyshev's inequality,

$$\mathrm{Prob}\left(\left|\frac{x_1 + x_2 + \cdots + x_n}{n} - E(x)\right| \geq \epsilon\right) = \mathrm{Prob}\left(\left|\frac{x_1 + x_2 + \cdots + x_n}{n}\right.\right.$$
$$\left.\left. - E\left(\frac{x_1 + x_2 + \cdots + x_n}{n}\right)\right| \geq \epsilon\right)$$
$$\leq \frac{Var\left(\frac{x_1 + x_2 + \cdots + x_n}{n}\right)}{\epsilon^2}$$
$$= \frac{1}{n^2\epsilon^2} Var(x_1 + x_2 + \cdots + x_n)$$
$$= \frac{1}{n^2\epsilon^2}\left(Var(x_1) + Var(x_2) + \cdots + Var(x_n)\right)$$
$$= \frac{Var(x)}{n\epsilon^2}.$$

∎

The Law of Large Numbers is quite general, applying to any random variable x of finite variance. Later we will look at tighter concentration bounds for spherical Gaussians and sums of 0–1 valued random variables.

One observation worth making about the Law of Large Numbers is that the size of the universe does not enter into the bound. For instance, if you want to know what fraction of the population of a country prefers tea to coffee, then the number n of people you need to sample in order to have at most a δ chance that your estimate is off by more than ϵ depends only on ϵ and δ and not on the population of the country.

As an application of the Law of Large Numbers, let $\mathbf{z}$ be a d-dimensional random point whose coordinates are each selected from a zero mean, $\frac{1}{2\pi}$ variance Gaussian.

Table 2.1: Table of tail bounds. The Higher Moments bound is obtained by applying Markov to x^r. The Chernoff, Gaussian Annulus, and Power Law bounds follow from Theorem 2.5 which is proved in Chapter 12.

	Condition	Tail bound
Markov	$x \geq 0$	$\text{Prob}(x \geq a) \leq \frac{E(x)}{a}$
Chebyshev	Any x	$\text{Prob}(\lvert x - E(x)\rvert \geq a) \leq \frac{\text{Var}(x)}{a^2}$
Chernoff	$x = x_1 + x_2 + \cdots + x_n$ $x_i \in [0, 1]$ i.i.d. Bernoulli;	$\text{Prob}(\lvert x - E(x)\rvert \geq \varepsilon E(x))$ $\leq 3e^{-c\varepsilon^2 E(x)}$
Higher Moments	r positive even integer	$\text{Prob}(\lvert x\rvert \geq a) \leq E(x^r)/a^r$
Gaussian Annulus	$x = \sqrt{x_1^2 + x_2^2 + \cdots + x_n^2}$ $x_i \sim N(0,1); \beta \leq \sqrt{n}$ indep.	$\text{Prob}(\lvert x - \sqrt{n}\rvert \geq \beta) \leq 3e^{-c\beta^2}$
Power Law for x_i; order $k \geq 4$	$x = x_1 + x_2 + \cdots + x_n$ x_i i.i.d.; $\varepsilon \leq 1/k^2$	$\text{Prob}(\lvert x - E(x)\rvert \geq \varepsilon E(x))$ $\leq (4/\varepsilon^2 k n)^{(k-3)/2}$

We set the variance to $\frac{1}{2\pi}$ so the Gaussian probability density equals one at the origin and is bounded below throughout the unit ball by a constant.[1] By the Law of Large Numbers, the square of the distance of $\mathbf{z}$ to the origin will be $\Theta(d)$ with high probability. In particular, there is vanishingly small probability that such a random point $\mathbf{z}$ would lie in the unit ball. This implies that the integral of the probability density over the unit ball must be vanishingly small. On the other hand, the probability density in the unit ball is bounded below by a constant. We thus conclude that the unit ball must have vanishingly small volume.

Similarly if we draw two points $\mathbf{y}$ and $\mathbf{z}$ from a d-dimensional Gaussian with unit variance in each direction, then $\lvert\mathbf{y}\rvert^2 \approx d$ and $\lvert\mathbf{z}\rvert^2 \approx d$. Since for all i,

$$E(y_i - z_i)^2 = E(y_i^2) + E(z_i^2) - 2E(y_i z_i) = Var(y_i) + Var(z_i) - 2E(y_i)E(z_i) = 2,$$

$\lvert\mathbf{y} - \mathbf{z}\rvert^2 = \sum_{i=1}^{d}(y_i - z_i)^2 \approx 2d$. Thus by the Pythagorean theorem, the random d-dimensional $\mathbf{y}$ and $\mathbf{z}$ must be approximately orthogonal. This implies that if we scale these random points to be unit length and call $\mathbf{y}$ the North Pole, much of the surface area of the unit ball must lie near the equator. We will formalize these and related arguments in subsequent sections.

We now state a general theorem on probability tail bounds for a sum of independent random variables. Tail bounds for sums of Bernoulli, squared Gaussian, and Power Law distributed random variables can all be derived from this. Table 2.1 summarizes some of the results.

---

[1] If we instead used variance 1, then the density at the origin would be a decreasing function of d, namely $(\frac{1}{2\pi})^{d/2}$, making this argument more complicated.

Theorem 2.5 **(Master Tail Bounds Theorem)** *Let* $x = x_1 + x_2 + \cdots + x_n$, *where* $x_1, x_2, \ldots, x_n$ *are mutually independent random variables with zero mean and variance at most* σ^2. *Let* $0 \le a \le \sqrt{2}n\sigma^2$. *Assume that* $|E(x_i^s)| \le \sigma^2 s!$ *for* $s = 3, 4, \ldots, \lfloor (a^2/4n\sigma^2) \rfloor$. *Then,*

$$Prob\,(|x| \ge a) \le 3e^{-a^2/(12n\sigma^2)}.$$

The proof of Theorem 2.5 is elementary. A slightly more general version, Theorem 12.5, is given in Chapter 12. For a brief intuition of the proof, consider applying Markov's inequality to the random variable x^r where r is a large even number. Since r is even, x^r is nonnegative, and thus $\text{Prob}(|x| \ge a) = \text{Prob}(x^r \ge a^r) \le E(x^r)/a^r$. If $E(x^r)$ is not too large, we will get a good bound. To compute $E(x^r)$, write $E(x)$ as $E(x_1 + \cdots + x_n)^r$ and expand the polynomial into a sum of terms. Use the fact that by independence $E(x_i^{r_i} x_j^{r_j}) = E(x_i^{r_i})E(x_j^{r_j})$ to get a collection of simpler expectations that can be bounded using our assumption that $|E(x_i^s)| \le \sigma^2 s!$. For the full proof, see Chapter 12.

2.3. The Geometry of High Dimensions

An important property of high-dimensional objects is that most of their volume is near the surface. Consider any object A in R^d. Now shrink A by a small amount ϵ to produce a new object $(1 - \epsilon)A = \{(1 - \epsilon)x | x \in A\}$. Then the following equality holds:

$$\text{volume}\big((1 - \epsilon)A\big) = (1 - \epsilon)^d \text{volume}(A).$$

To see that this is true, partition A into infinitesimal cubes. Then, $(1 - \varepsilon)A$ is the union of a set of cubes obtained by shrinking the cubes in A by a factor of $1 - \varepsilon$. When we shrink each of the $2d$ sides of a d-dimensional cube by a factor f, its volume shrinks by a factor of f^d. Using the fact that $1 - x \le e^{-x}$, for any object A in R^d we have:

$$\frac{\text{volume}\big((1 - \epsilon)A\big)}{\text{volume}(A)} = (1 - \epsilon)^d \le e^{-\epsilon d}.$$

Fixing ϵ and letting $d \to \infty$, the above quantity rapidly approaches zero. This means that nearly all of the volume of A must be in the portion of A that does not belong to the region $(1 - \epsilon)A$.

Let S denote the unit ball in d-dimensions, that is, the set of points within distance one of the origin. An immediate implication of the above observation is that at least a $1 - e^{-\epsilon d}$ fraction of the volume of the unit ball is concentrated in $S \setminus (1 - \epsilon)S$, namely in a small annulus of width ϵ at the boundary. In particular, most of the volume of the d-dimensional unit ball is contained in an annulus of width $O(1/d)$ near the boundary. This is illustrated in Figure 2.1. If the ball is of radius r, then the annulus width is $O\left(\frac{r}{d}\right)$.

2.4. Properties of the Unit Ball

We now focus more specifically on properties of the unit ball in d-dimensional space. We just saw that most of its volume is concentrated in a small annulus of width $O(1/d)$ near the boundary. Next we will show that in the limit as d goes to infinity,

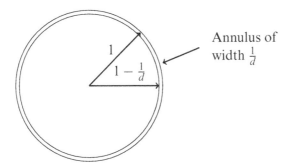

Figure 2.1: Most of the volume of the d-dimensional ball of radius r is contained in an annulus of width $O(r/d)$ near the boundary.

the volume of the ball goes to zero. This result can be proven in several ways. Here we use integration.

2.4.1. Volume of the Unit Ball

To calculate the volume $V(d)$ of the unit ball in R^d, one can integrate in either Cartesian or polar coordinates. In Cartesian coordinates the volume is given by

$$V(d) = \int_{x_1=-1}^{x_1=1} \int_{x_2=-\sqrt{1-x_1^2}}^{x_2=\sqrt{1-x_1^2}} \cdots \int_{x_d=-\sqrt{1-x_1^2-\cdots-x_{d-1}^2}}^{x_d=\sqrt{1-x_1^2-\cdots-x_{d-1}^2}} dx_d \cdots dx_2 dx_1.$$

Since the limits of the integrals are complicated, it is easier to integrate using polar coordinates. In polar coordinates, $V(d)$ is given by

$$V(d) = \int_{S^d} \int_{r=0}^{1} r^{d-1} dr d\Omega.$$

Since the variables Ω and r do not interact,

$$V(d) = \int_{S^d} d\Omega \int_{r=0}^{1} r^{d-1} dr = \frac{1}{d} \int_{S^d} d\Omega = \frac{A(d)}{d}$$

where $A(d)$ is the surface area of the d-dimensional unit ball. For instance, for $d = 3$ the surface area is 4π and the volume is $\frac{4}{3}\pi$. The question remains how to determine the surface area $A(d) = \int_{S^d} d\Omega$ for general d.

Consider a different integral,

$$I(d) = \int_{-\infty}^{\infty} \int_{-\infty}^{\infty} \cdots \int_{-\infty}^{\infty} e^{-(x_1^2+x_2^2+\cdots x_d^2)} dx_d \cdots dx_2 dx_1.$$

Including the exponential allows integration to infinity rather than stopping at the surface of the sphere. Thus, $I(d)$ can be computed by integrating in both Cartesian and polar coordinates. Integrating in polar coordinates will relate $I(d)$ to the surface area $A(d)$. Equating the two results for $I(d)$ allows one to solve for $A(d)$.

First, calculate $I(d)$ by integration in Cartesian coordinates.

$$I(d) = \left[\int_{-\infty}^{\infty} e^{-x^2} dx \right]^d = \left(\sqrt{\pi} \right)^d = \pi^{\frac{d}{2}}.$$

Here, we have used the fact that $\int_{-\infty}^{\infty} e^{-x^2} dx = \sqrt{\pi}$. For a proof of this, see Section 12.2 of Chapter 12. Next, calculate $I(d)$ by integrating in polar coordinates. The volume of the differential element is $r^{d-1} d\Omega dr$. Thus,

$$I(d) = \int_{S^d} d\Omega \int_0^{\infty} e^{-r^2} r^{d-1} dr.$$

The integral $\int_{S^d} d\Omega$ is the integral over the entire solid angle and gives the surface area, $A(d)$, of a unit sphere. Thus, $I(d) = A(d) \int_0^{\infty} e^{-r^2} r^{d-1} dr$. Evaluating the remaining integral gives

$$\int_0^{\infty} e^{-r^2} r^{d-1} dr = \int_0^{\infty} e^{-t} t^{\frac{d-1}{2}} \left(\frac{1}{2} t^{-\frac{1}{2}} dt \right) = \frac{1}{2} \int_0^{\infty} e^{-t} t^{\frac{d}{2}-1} dt = \frac{1}{2} \Gamma \left(\frac{d}{2} \right),$$

and hence, $I(d) = A(d) \frac{1}{2} \Gamma \left(\frac{d}{2} \right)$ where the Gamma function $\Gamma(x)$ is a generalization of the factorial function for non-integer values of x. $\Gamma(x) = (x-1)\Gamma(x-1), \Gamma(1) = \Gamma(2) = 1$, and $\Gamma \left(\frac{1}{2} \right) = \sqrt{\pi}$. For integer $x, \Gamma(x) = (x-1)!$.

Combining $I(d) = \pi^{\frac{d}{2}}$ with $I(d) = A(d) \frac{1}{2} \Gamma \left(\frac{d}{2} \right)$ yields

$$A(d) = \frac{\pi^{\frac{d}{2}}}{\frac{1}{2} \Gamma \left(\frac{d}{2} \right)},$$

establishing the following lemma.

Lemma 2.6 *The surface area $A(d)$ and the volume $V(d)$ of a unit-radius ball in d-dimensions are given by*

$$A(d) = \frac{2\pi^{\frac{d}{2}}}{\Gamma(\frac{d}{2})} \quad and \quad V(d) = \frac{2\pi^{\frac{d}{2}}}{d \, \Gamma(\frac{d}{2})}.$$

To check the formula for the volume of a unit ball, note that $V(2) = \pi$ and $V(3) = \frac{2}{3} \frac{\pi^{\frac{3}{2}}}{\Gamma(\frac{3}{2})} = \frac{4}{3} \pi$, which are the correct volumes for the unit balls in two and three dimensions. To check the formula for the surface area of a unit ball, note that $A(2) = 2\pi$ and $A(3) = \frac{2\pi^{\frac{3}{2}}}{\frac{1}{2} \sqrt{\pi}} = 4\pi$, which are the correct surface areas for the unit ball in two and three dimensions. Note that $\pi^{\frac{d}{2}}$ is an exponential in $\frac{d}{2}$ and $\Gamma \left(\frac{d}{2} \right)$ grows as the factorial of $\frac{d}{2}$. This implies that $\lim_{d \to \infty} V(d) = 0$, as claimed.

2.4.2. Volume near the Equator

An interesting fact about the unit ball in high dimensions is that most of its volume is concentrated near its "equator." In particular, for any unit-length vector $\mathbf{v}$ defining "north," most of the volume of the unit ball lies in the thin slab of points whose dot-product with $\mathbf{v}$ has magnitude $O(1/\sqrt{d})$. To show this fact, it suffices by symmetry to fix $\mathbf{v}$ to be the first coordinate vector. That is, we will show that most of the volume of the unit ball has $|x_1| = O(1/\sqrt{d})$. Using this fact, we will show that two random points in the unit ball are with high probability nearly orthogonal, and also give an alternative proof from the one in Section 2.4.1 that the volume of the unit ball goes to zero as $d \to \infty$.

Theorem 2.7 *For $c \geq 1$ and $d \geq 3$, at least a $1 - \frac{2}{c}e^{-c^2/2}$ fraction of the volume of the d-dimensional unit ball has $|x_1| \leq \frac{c}{\sqrt{d-1}}$.*

Proof By symmetry we just need to prove that at most a $\frac{2}{c}e^{-c^2/2}$ fraction of the half of the ball with $x_1 \geq 0$ has $x_1 \geq \frac{c}{\sqrt{d-1}}$. Let A denote the portion of the ball with $x_1 \geq \frac{c}{\sqrt{d-1}}$ and let H denote the upper hemisphere (see Figure 2.2). We will then show that the ratio of the volume of A to the volume of H goes to zero by calculating an upper bound on volume(A) and a lower bound on volume(H) and proving that

$$\frac{\text{volume}(A)}{\text{volume}(H)} \leq \frac{\text{upper bound volume}(A)}{\text{lower bound volume}(H)} = \frac{2}{c}e^{-\frac{c^2}{2}}.$$

To calculate the volume of A, integrate an incremental volume that is a disk of width dx_1 and whose face is a ball of dimension $d - 1$ and radius $\sqrt{1 - x_1^2}$. The surface area of the disk is $(1 - x_1^2)^{\frac{d-1}{2}} V(d - 1)$ and the volume above the slice is

$$\text{volume}(A) = \int_{\frac{c}{\sqrt{d-1}}}^{1} (1 - x_1^2)^{\frac{d-1}{2}} V(d - 1) dx_1$$

To get an upper bound on the above integral, use $1 - x \leq e^{-x}$ and integrate to infinity. To integrate, insert $\frac{x_1 \sqrt{d-1}}{c}$, which is greater than one in the range of integration, into the integral. Then

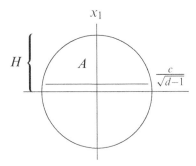

Figure 2.2: Most of the volume of the upper hemisphere of the d-dimensional ball is below the plane $x_1 = \frac{c}{\sqrt{d-1}}$.

$$\text{volume}(A) \le \int_{\frac{c}{\sqrt{d-1}}}^{\infty} \frac{x_1\sqrt{d-1}}{c} e^{-\frac{d-1}{2}x_1^2} V(d-1) dx_1$$

$$= V(d-1)\frac{\sqrt{d-1}}{c} \int_{\frac{c}{\sqrt{d-1}}}^{\infty} x_1 e^{-\frac{d-1}{2}x_1^2} dx_1$$

Now

$$\int_{\frac{c}{\sqrt{d-1}}}^{\infty} x_1 e^{-\frac{d-1}{2}x_1^2} dx_1 = -\frac{1}{d-1}e^{-\frac{d-1}{2}x_1^2}\Big|_{\frac{c}{\sqrt{(d-1)}}}^{\infty} = \frac{1}{d-1}e^{-\frac{c^2}{2}}$$

Thus, an upper bound on volume(A) is $\frac{V(d-1)}{c\sqrt{d-1}}e^{-\frac{c^2}{2}}$.

The volume of the hemisphere below the plane $x_1 = \frac{1}{\sqrt{d-1}}$ is a lower bound on the entire volume of the upper hemisphere, and this volume is at least that of a cylinder of height $\frac{1}{\sqrt{d-1}}$ and radius $\sqrt{1 - \frac{1}{d-1}}$. The volume of the cylinder is $V(d-1)(1 - \frac{1}{d-1})^{\frac{d-1}{2}}\frac{1}{\sqrt{d-1}}$. Using the fact that $(1-x)^a \ge 1 - ax$ for $a \ge 1$, the volume of the cylinder is at least $\frac{V(d-1)}{2\sqrt{d-1}}$ for $d \ge 3$.

Thus,

$$\text{ratio} \le \frac{\text{upper bound above plane}}{\text{lower bound total hemisphere}} = \frac{\frac{V(d-1)}{c\sqrt{d-1}}e^{-\frac{c^2}{2}}}{\frac{V(d-1)}{2\sqrt{d-1}}} = \frac{2}{c}e^{-\frac{c^2}{2}}.$$

∎

One might ask why we computed a lower bound on the total hemisphere, since it is one-half of the volume of the unit ball, which we already know. The reason is that the volume of the upper hemisphere is $\frac{1}{2}V(d)$, and we need a formula with $V(d-1)$ in it to cancel the $V(d-1)$ in the numerator.

Near Orthogonality

One immediate implication of the above analysis is that if we draw two points at random from the unit ball, with high probability their vectors will be nearly orthogonal to each other. Specifically, from our previous analysis in Section 2.3, with high probability both will be close to the surface and will have length $1 - O(1/d)$. From our analysis earlier, if we define the vector in the direction of the first point as "north," with high probability the second will have a projection of only $\pm O(1/\sqrt{d})$ in this direction, and thus their dot product will be $\pm O(1/\sqrt{d})$. This implies that with high probability the angle between the two vectors will be $\pi/2 \pm O(1/\sqrt{d})$. In particular, we have the following theorem that states that if we draw n points at random in the unit ball, with high probability all points will be close to unit length and each pair of points will be almost orthogonal.

Theorem 2.8 *Consider drawing n points* $\mathbf{x}_1, \mathbf{x}_2, \ldots, \mathbf{x}_n$ *at random from the unit ball. With probability* $1 - O(1/n)$

1. $|\mathbf{x}_i| \ge 1 - \frac{2 \ln n}{d}$ *for all i, and*

2. $|\mathbf{x}_i \cdot \mathbf{x}_j| \le \frac{\sqrt{6 \ln n}}{\sqrt{d-1}}$ *for all* $i \neq j$.

Proof For the first part, for any fixed i by the analysis of Section 2.3, the probability that $|\mathbf{x_i}| < 1 - \epsilon$ is less than $e^{-\epsilon d}$. Thus

$$\text{Prob}\left(|\mathbf{x_i}| < 1 - \frac{2\ln n}{d}\right) \le e^{-(\frac{2\ln n}{d})d} = 1/n^2.$$

By the union bound, the probability there exists an i such that $|\mathbf{x_i}| < 1 - \frac{2\ln n}{d}$ is at most $1/n$.

For the second part, Theorem 2.7 states that for a component of a Gaussian vector the probability $|x_i| > \frac{c}{\sqrt{d-1}}$ is at most $\frac{2}{c}e^{-\frac{c^2}{2}}$. There are $\binom{n}{2}$ pairs i and j, and for each such pair, if we define $\mathbf{x_i}$ as "north," the probability that the projection of $\mathbf{x_j}$ onto the "north" direction is more than $\frac{\sqrt{6\ln n}}{\sqrt{d-1}}$ is at most $O(e^{-\frac{6\ln n}{2}}) = O(n^{-3})$. Thus, the dot product condition is violated with probability at most $O\left(\binom{n}{2}n^{-3}\right) = O(1/n)$ as well. ∎

Alternative Proof That Volume Goes to Zero
Another immediate implication of Theorem 2.7 is that as $d \to \infty$, the volume of the ball approaches zero. Specifically, consider a small box centered at the origin of side length $\frac{2c}{\sqrt{d-1}}$. Using Theorem 2.7, we show that for $c = 2\sqrt{\ln d}$, this box contains over half of the volume of the ball. On the other hand, the volume of this box clearly goes to zero as d goes to infinity, since its volume is $O((\frac{\ln d}{d-1})^{d/2})$. Thus the volume of the ball goes to zero as well.

By Theorem 2.7, with $c = 2\sqrt{\ln d}$, the fraction of the volume of the ball with $|x_1| \ge \frac{c}{\sqrt{d-1}}$ is at most:

$$\frac{2}{c}e^{-\frac{c^2}{2}} = \frac{1}{\sqrt{\ln d}}e^{-2\ln d} = \frac{1}{d^2\sqrt{\ln d}} < \frac{1}{d^2}.$$

Since this is true for each of the d dimensions, by a union bound, at most a $O(\frac{1}{d}) \le \frac{1}{2}$ fraction of the volume of the ball lies outside the cube, completing the proof.

Discussion
One might wonder how it can be that nearly all the points in the unit ball are very close to the surface and yet at the same time nearly all points are in a box of side-length $O(\frac{\ln d}{d-1})$. The answer is to remember that points on the surface of the ball satisfy $x_1^2 + x_2^2 + \cdots + x_d^2 = 1$, so for each coordinate i, a typical value will be $\pm O(\frac{1}{\sqrt{d}})$. In fact, it is often helpful to think of picking a random point on the sphere as very similar to picking a random point of the form $(\pm\frac{1}{\sqrt{d}}, \pm\frac{1}{\sqrt{d}}, \pm\frac{1}{\sqrt{d}}, \ldots \pm\frac{1}{\sqrt{d}})$. A schematic illustration of the relationship between the unit-radius sphere and unit-volume cube is given in Figure 2.3.

2.5. Generating Points Uniformly at Random from a Ball

Consider generating points uniformly at random on the surface of the unit ball. For the two-dimensional version of generating points on the circumference of a unit-radius circle, independently generate each coordinate uniformly at random from the interval $[-1, 1]$. This produces points distributed over a square that is large enough

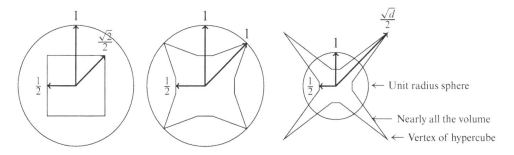

Figure 2.3: Illustration of the relationship between the sphere and the cube in 2, 4, and d-dimensions.

to completely contain the unit circle. Project each point onto the unit circle. The distribution is not uniform, since more points fall on a line from the origin to a vertex of the square than fall on a line from the origin to the midpoint of an edge of the square due to the difference in length. To solve this problem, discard all points outside the unit circle and project the remaining points onto the circle.

In higher dimensions, this method does not work, since the fraction of points that fall inside the ball drops to zero and all of the points would be thrown away. The solution is to generate a point each of whose coordinates is an independent Gaussian variable. Generate $x_1, x_2, \ldots, x_d$, using a zero mean, unit variance Gaussian, namely $\frac{1}{\sqrt{2\pi}} \exp(-x^2/2)$ on the real line.[2] Thus, the probability density of $\mathbf{x}$ is

$$p(\mathbf{x}) = \frac{1}{(2\pi)^{\frac{d}{2}}} e^{-\frac{x_1^2 + x_2^2 + \cdots + x_d^2}{2}}$$

and is spherically symmetric. Normalizing the vector $\mathbf{x} = (x_1, x_2, \ldots, x_d)$ to a unit vector, namely $\frac{\mathbf{x}}{|\mathbf{x}|}$, gives a distribution that is uniform over the surface of the sphere. Note that once the vector is normalized, its coordinates are no longer statistically independent.

To generate a point $\mathbf{y}$ uniformly over the ball (surface and interior), scale the point $\frac{\mathbf{x}}{|\mathbf{x}|}$ generated on the surface by a scalar $\rho \in [0, 1]$. What should the distribution of ρ be as a function of r? It is certainly not uniform, even in two dimensions. Indeed, the density of ρ at r is proportional to r for $d = 2$. For $d = 3$, it is proportional to r^2. By similar reasoning, the density of ρ at distance r is proportional to r^{d-1} in d dimensions. Solving $\int_{r=0}^{r=1} c r^{d-1} dr = 1$ (the integral of density must equal 1), one should set $c = d$. Another way to see this formally is that the volume of the radius r ball in d dimensions is $r^d V(d)$. The density at radius r is exactly $\frac{d}{dr}(r^d V_d) = d r^{d-1} V_d$. So, pick $\rho(r)$ with density equal to $d r^{d-1}$ for r over $[0, 1]$.

---

[2]One might naturally ask: "How do you generate a random number from a 1-dimensional Gaussian?" To generate a number from any distribution given its cumulative distribution function P, first select a uniform random number $u \in [0, 1]$ and then choose $x = P^{-1}(u)$. For any $a < b$, the probability that x is between a and b is equal to the probability that u is between $P(a)$ and $P(b)$, which equals $P(b) - P(a)$ as desired. For the two-dimensional Gaussian, one can generate a point in polar coordinates by choosing angle θ uniform in $[0, 2\pi]$ and radius $r = \sqrt{-2\ln(u)}$ where u is uniform random in $[0, 1]$. This is called the Box-Muller transform.

We have succeeded in generating a point

$$y = \rho \frac{\mathbf{x}}{|\mathbf{x}|}$$

uniformly at random from the unit ball by using the convenient spherical Gaussian distribution. In the next sections, we will analyze the spherical Gaussian in more detail.

2.6. Gaussians in High Dimension

A one-dimensional Gaussian has its mass close to the origin. However, as the dimension is increased, something different happens. The d-dimensional spherical Gaussian with zero mean and variance σ^2 in each coordinate has density function

$$p(\mathbf{x}) = \frac{1}{(2\pi)^{d/2}\sigma^d} \exp\left(-\frac{|\mathbf{x}|^2}{2\sigma^2}\right).$$

The value of the density is maximum at the origin, but there is very little volume there. When $\sigma^2 = 1$, integrating the probability density over a unit ball centered at the origin yields almost zero mass, since the volume of such a ball is negligible. In fact, one needs to increase the radius of the ball to nearly $\sqrt{d}$ before there is a significant volume and hence significant probability mass. If one increases the radius much beyond $\sqrt{d}$, the integral barely increases even though the volume increases, since the probability density is dropping off at a much higher rate. The following theorem formally states that nearly all the probability is concentrated in a thin annulus of width $O(1)$ at radius $\sqrt{d}$.

Theorem 2.9   (Gaussian Annulus Theorem) *For a d-dimensional spherical Gaussian with unit variance in each direction, for any $\beta \leq \sqrt{d}$, all but at most $3e^{-c\beta^2}$ of the probability mass lies within the annulus $\sqrt{d} - \beta \leq |\mathbf{x}| \leq \sqrt{d} + \beta$, where c is a fixed positive constant.*

For a high-level intuition, note that $E(|\mathbf{x}|^2) = \sum_{i=1}^{d} E(x_i^2) = dE(x_1^2) = d$, so the mean squared distance of a point from the center is d. The Gaussian Annulus Theorem says that the points are tightly concentrated. We call the square root of the mean squared distance, namely $\sqrt{d}$, the radius of the Gaussian.

To prove the Gaussian Annulus Theorem, we make use of a tail inequality for sums of independent random variables of bounded moments (Theorem 12.5).

Proof (Gaussian Annulus Theorem) Let $\mathbf{x} = (x_1, x_2, \ldots, x_d)$ be a point selected from a unit variance Gaussian centered at the origin, and let $r = |\mathbf{x}|$. $\sqrt{d} - \beta \leq |\mathbf{x}| \leq \sqrt{d} + \beta$ is equivalent to $|r - \sqrt{d}| \geq \beta$. If $|r - \sqrt{d}| \geq \beta$, then multiplying both sides by $r + \sqrt{d}$ gives $|r^2 - d| \geq \beta(r + \sqrt{d}) \geq \beta\sqrt{d}$. So, it suffices to bound the probability that $|r^2 - d| \geq \beta\sqrt{d}$.

Rewrite $r^2 - d = (x_1^2 + \cdots + x_d^2) - d = (x_1^2 - 1) + \cdots + (x_d^2 - 1)$ and perform a change of variables: $y_i = x_i^2 - 1$. We want to bound the probability that $|y_1 + \cdots + y_d| \geq \beta\sqrt{d}$. Notice that $E(y_i) = E(x_i^2) - 1 = 0$. To apply Theorem 12.5, we need to bound the sth moments of y_i.

For $|x_i| \leq 1$, $|y_i|^s \leq 1$ and for $|x_i| \geq 1$, $|y_i|^s \leq |x_i|^{2s}$. Thus,

$$|E(y_i^s)| = E(|y_i|^s) \leq E(1 + x_i^{2s}) = 1 + E(x_i^{2s})$$

$$= 1 + \sqrt{\frac{2}{\pi}} \int_0^\infty x^{2s} e^{-x^2/2} dx.$$

Using the substitution $2z = x^2$,

$$|E(y_i^s)| = 1 + \frac{1}{\sqrt{\pi}} \int_0^\infty 2^s z^{s-(1/2)} e^{-z} dz$$

$$\leq 2^s s!.$$

The last inequality is from the Gamma integral.

Since $E(y_i) = 0$, $Var(y_i) = E(y_i^2) \leq 2^2 2 = 8$. Unfortunately, we do not have $|E(y_i^s)| \leq 8s!$ as required in Theorem 12.5. To fix this problem, perform one more change of variables, using $w_i = y_i/2$. Then, $Var(w_i) \leq 2$ and $|E(w_i^s)| \leq 2s!$, and our goal is now to bound the probability that $|w_1 + \cdots + w_d| \geq \frac{\beta\sqrt{d}}{2}$. Applying Theorem 12.5 where $\sigma^2 = 2$ and $n = d$, this occurs with probability less than or equal to $3e^{-\frac{\beta^2}{96}}$. ∎

In the next sections we will see several uses of the Gaussian Annulus Theorem.

2.7. Random Projection and Johnson-Lindenstrauss Lemma

One of the most frequently used subroutines in tasks involving high-dimensional data is nearest neighbor search. In nearest neighbor search we are given a database of n points in $\mathbf{R}^d$ where n and d are usually large. The database can be preprocessed and stored in an efficient data structure. Thereafter, we are presented "query" points in $\mathbf{R}^d$ and are asked to find the nearest or approximately nearest database point to the query point. Since the number of queries is often large, the time to answer each query should be very small, ideally a small function of $\log n$ and $\log d$, whereas preprocessing time could be larger, namely a polynomial function of n and d. For this and other problems, dimension reduction, where one projects the database points to a k-dimensional space with $k \ll d$ (usually dependent on $\log d$), can be very useful so long as the relative distances between points are approximately preserved. We will see, using the Gaussian Annulus Theorem, that such a projection indeed exists and is simple.

The projection $f : \mathbf{R}^d \to \mathbf{R}^k$ that we will examine (many related projections are known to work as well) is the following. Pick k Gaussian vectors $\mathbf{u}_1, \mathbf{u}_2, \ldots, \mathbf{u}_k$ in $\mathbf{R}^d$ with unit-variance coordinates. For any vector $\mathbf{v}$, define the projection $f(\mathbf{v})$ by:

$$f(\mathbf{v}) = (\mathbf{u}_1 \cdot \mathbf{v}, \mathbf{u}_2 \cdot \mathbf{v}, \ldots, \mathbf{u}_k \cdot \mathbf{v}).$$

The projection $f(\mathbf{v})$ is the vector of dot products of $\mathbf{v}$ with the $\mathbf{u}_i$. We will show that with high probability, $|f(\mathbf{v})| \approx \sqrt{k}|\mathbf{v}|$. For any two vectors $\mathbf{v}_1$ and $\mathbf{v}_2$, $f(\mathbf{v}_1 - \mathbf{v}_2) = f(\mathbf{v}_1) - f(\mathbf{v}_2)$. Thus, to estimate the distance $|\mathbf{v}_1 - \mathbf{v}_2|$ between two vectors $\mathbf{v}_1$ and $\mathbf{v}_2$ in $\mathbf{R}^d$, it suffices to compute $|f(\mathbf{v}_1) - f(\mathbf{v}_2)| = |f(\mathbf{v}_1 - \mathbf{v}_2)|$ in the k-dimensional space, since the factor of $\sqrt{k}$ is known and one can divide by it. The reason distances increase when we project to a lower-dimensional space is that the vectors $\mathbf{u}_i$ are not unit length. Also notice that the vectors $\mathbf{u_i}$ are not orthogonal. If we had required them to be orthogonal, we would have lost statistical independence.

Theorem 2.10 (The Random Projection Theorem) *Let $\mathbf{v}$ be a fixed vector in $\mathbf{R}^d$ and let f be defined as above. There exists constant $c > 0$ such that for $\varepsilon \in (0, 1)$,*

$$Prob\left(\left||f(\mathbf{v})| - \sqrt{k}|\mathbf{v}|\right| \geq \varepsilon\sqrt{k}|\mathbf{v}|\right) \leq 3e^{-ck\varepsilon^2},$$

where the probability is taken over the random draws of vectors $\mathbf{u_i}$ used to construct f.

Proof By scaling both sides of the inner inequality by $|\mathbf{v}|$, we may assume that $|\mathbf{v}| = 1$. The sum of independent normally distributed real variables is also normally distributed where the mean and variance are the sums of the individual means and variances. Since $\mathbf{u_i} \cdot \mathbf{v} = \sum_{j=1}^{d} u_{ij}v_j$, the random variable $\mathbf{u_i} \cdot \mathbf{v}$ has Gaussian density with zero mean and unit variance, in particular,

$$Var(\mathbf{u_i} \cdot \mathbf{v}) = Var\left(\sum_{j=1}^{d} u_{ij}v_j\right) = \sum_{j=1}^{d} v_j^2 Var(u_{ij}) = \sum_{j=1}^{d} v_j^2 = 1.$$

Since $\mathbf{u_1} \cdot \mathbf{v}, \mathbf{u_2} \cdot \mathbf{v}, \ldots, \mathbf{u_k} \cdot \mathbf{v}$ are independent Gaussian random variables, $f(\mathbf{v})$ is a random vector from a k-dimensional spherical Gaussian with unit variance in each coordinate, and so the theorem follows from the Gaussian Annulus Theorem (Theorem 2.9) with d replaced by k. ∎

The random projection theorem establishes that the probability of the length of the projection of a single vector differing significantly from its expected value is exponentially small in k, the dimension of the target subspace. By a union bound, the probability that any of $O(n^2)$ pairwise differences $|\mathbf{v_i} - \mathbf{v_j}|$ among n vectors $\mathbf{v_1}, \ldots, \mathbf{v_n}$ differs significantly from their expected values is small, provided $k \geq \frac{3}{c\varepsilon^2} \ln n$. Thus, this random projection preserves all relative pairwise distances between points in a set of n points with high probability. This is the content of the Johnson-Lindenstrauss Lemma.

Theorem 2.11 (Johnson-Lindenstrauss Lemma) *For any $0 < \varepsilon < 1$ and any integer n, let $k \geq \frac{3}{c\varepsilon^2} \ln n$ with c as in Theorem 2.9. For any set of n points in $\mathbf{R}^d$, the random projection $f : R^d \rightarrow R^k$ defined above has the property that for all pairs of points $\mathbf{v_i}$ and $\mathbf{v_j}$, with probability at least $1 - 3/2n$,*

$$(1 - \varepsilon)\sqrt{k}\,|\mathbf{v_i} - \mathbf{v_j}| \leq |f(\mathbf{v_i}) - f(\mathbf{v_j})| \leq (1 + \varepsilon)\sqrt{k}\,|\mathbf{v_i} - \mathbf{v_j}|.$$

Proof Applying the Random Projection Theorem (Theorem 2.10), for any fixed $\mathbf{v_i}$ and $\mathbf{v_j}$, the probability that $|f(\mathbf{v_i} - \mathbf{v_j})|$ is outside the range

$$\left[(1 - \varepsilon)\sqrt{k}|\mathbf{v_i} - \mathbf{v_j}|, (1 + \varepsilon)\sqrt{k}|\mathbf{v_i} - \mathbf{v_j}|\right]$$

is at most $3e^{-ck\varepsilon^2} \leq 3/n^3$ for $k \geq \frac{3\ln n}{c\varepsilon^2}$. Since there are $\binom{n}{2} < n^2/2$ pairs of points, by the union bound, the probability that any pair has a large distortion is less than $\frac{3}{2n}$. ∎

17

Remark It is important to note that the conclusion of Theorem 2.11 asserts for all $\mathbf{v_i}$ and $\mathbf{v_j}$, not just for most of them. The weaker assertion for most $\mathbf{v_i}$ and $\mathbf{v_j}$ is typically less useful, since our algorithm for a problem such as nearest neighbor search might return one of the bad pairs of points. A remarkable aspect of the theorem is that the number of dimensions in the projection is only dependent logarithmically on n. Since k is often much less than d, this is called a dimension reduction technique. In applications, the dominant term is typically the $1/\varepsilon^2$ term.

For the nearest neighbor problem, if the database has n_1 points and n_2 queries are expected during the lifetime of the algorithm, take $n = n_1 + n_2$ and project the database to a random k-dimensional space, for k as in Theorem 2.11. On receiving a query, project the query to the same subspace and compute nearby database points. The Johnson Lindenstrauss Lemma says that with high probability this will yield the right answer whatever the query. Note that the exponentially small in k probability was useful here in making k only dependent on $\ln n$, rather than n.

2.8. Separating Gaussians

Mixtures of Gaussians are often used to model heterogeneous data coming from multiple sources. For example, suppose we are recording the heights of individuals age 20–30 in a city. We know that on average, men tend to be taller than women, so a natural model would be a Gaussian mixture model $p(x) = w_1 p_1(x) + w_2 p_2(x)$, where $p_1(x)$ is a Gaussian density representing the typical heights of women, $p_2(x)$ is a Gaussian density representing the typical heights of men, and w_1 and w_2 are the *mixture weights* representing the proportion of women and men in the city. The *parameter estimation problem* for a mixture model is the problem: given access to samples from the overall density p (e.g., heights of people in the city, but without being told whether the person with that height is male or female), reconstruct the parameters for the distribution (e.g., good approximations to the means and variances of p_1 and p_2, as well as the mixture weights).

There are taller women and shorter men, so even if one solved the parameter estimation problem for heights perfectly, given a data point, one couldn't necessarily tell which population it came from. That is, given a height, one couldn't necessarily tell if it came from a man or a woman. In this section, we will look at a problem that is in some ways easier and in some ways harder than this problem of heights. It will be harder in that we will be interested in a mixture of two Gaussians in high dimensions as opposed to the $d = 1$ case of heights. But it will be easier in that we will assume the means are quite well separated compared to the variances. Specifically, our focus will be on a mixture of two spherical unit-variance Gaussians whose means are separated by a distance $\Omega(d^{1/4})$. We will show that at this level of separation, we can with high probability uniquely determine which Gaussian each data point came from. The algorithm needed to do so will actually be quite simple. Calculate the distance between all pairs of points. Points whose distance apart is smaller are from the same Gaussian, whereas points whose distance is larger are from different Gaussians. Later, we will see that with more sophisticated algorithms, even a separation of $\Omega(1)$ suffices.

First, consider just one spherical unit-variance Gaussian centered at the origin. From Theorem 2.9, most of its probability mass lies on an annulus of width $O(1)$

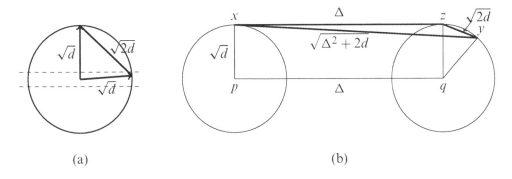

(a)   (b)

Figure 2.4: (a) indicates that two randomly chosen points in high dimension are surely almost nearly orthogonal. (b) indicates the distance between a pair of random points from two different unit balls approximating the annuli of two Gaussians.

at radius $\sqrt{d}$. Also $e^{-|\mathbf{x}|^2/2} = \prod_i e^{-x_i^2/2}$ and almost all of the mass is within the slab $\{\mathbf{x} \mid -c \leq x_1 \leq c\}$, for $c \in O(1)$. Pick a point $\mathbf{x}$ from this Gaussian. After picking $\mathbf{x}$, rotate the coordinate system to make the first axis align with $\mathbf{x}$. Independently pick a second point $\mathbf{y}$ from this Gaussian. The fact that almost all of the probability mass of the Gaussian is within the slab $\{\mathbf{x} \mid -c \leq x_1 \leq c, c \in O(1)\}$ at the equator implies that $\mathbf{y}$'s component along $\mathbf{x}$'s direction is $O(1)$ with high probability. Thus, $\mathbf{y}$ is nearly perpendicular to $\mathbf{x}$. So, $|\mathbf{x} - \mathbf{y}| \approx \sqrt{|\mathbf{x}|^2 + |\mathbf{y}|^2}$. See Figure 2.4(a). More precisely, since the coordinate system has been rotated so that $\mathbf{x}$ is at the North Pole, $\mathbf{x} = (\sqrt{d} \pm O(1), 0, \ldots, 0)$. Since $\mathbf{y}$ is almost on the equator, further rotate the coordinate system so that the component of $\mathbf{y}$ that is perpendicular to the axis of the North Pole is in the second coordinate. Then $\mathbf{y} = (O(1), \sqrt{d} \pm O(1), 0, \ldots, 0)$. Thus,

$$(\mathbf{x} - \mathbf{y})^2 = d \pm O(\sqrt{d}) + d \pm O(\sqrt{d}) = 2d \pm O(\sqrt{d})$$

and $|\mathbf{x} - \mathbf{y}| = \sqrt{2d} \pm O(1)$ with high probability.

Consider two spherical unit variance Gaussians with centers $\mathbf{p}$ and $\mathbf{q}$ separated by a distance Δ. The distance between a randomly chosen point $\mathbf{x}$ from the first Gaussian and a randomly chosen point $\mathbf{y}$ from the second is close to $\sqrt{\Delta^2 + 2d}$, since $\mathbf{x} - \mathbf{p}, \mathbf{p} - \mathbf{q}$, and $\mathbf{q} - \mathbf{y}$ are nearly mutually perpendicular. Pick $\mathbf{x}$ and rotate the coordinate system so that $\mathbf{x}$ is at the North Pole. Let $\mathbf{z}$ be the North Pole of the ball approximating the second Gaussian. Now pick $\mathbf{y}$. Most of the mass of the second Gaussian is within $O(1)$ of the equator perpendicular to $\mathbf{z} - \mathbf{q}$. Also, most of the mass of each Gaussian is within distance $O(1)$ of the respective equators perpendicular to the line $\mathbf{q} - \mathbf{p}$. See Figure 2.4 (b). Thus,

$$|\mathbf{x} - \mathbf{y}|^2 \approx \Delta^2 + |\mathbf{z} - \mathbf{q}|^2 + |\mathbf{q} - \mathbf{y}|^2$$
$$= \Delta^2 + 2d \pm O(\sqrt{d}).$$

Ensuring that two points picked from the same Gaussian are closer to each other than two points picked from different Gaussians requires that the upper limit of the distance between a pair of points from the same Gaussian is at most the lower limit of distance between points from different Gaussians. This requires that $\sqrt{2d} + O(1) \leq \sqrt{2d + \Delta^2} - O(1)$ or $2d + O(\sqrt{d}) \leq 2d + \Delta^2$, which holds when $\Delta \in \omega(d^{1/4})$. Thus, mixtures of spherical Gaussians can be separated in this way, provided their centers are separated by $\omega(d^{1/4})$. If we have n points and want to correctly separate all of them with high probability, we need our individual high-probability statements to hold with probability $1 - 1/poly(n)$,[3] which means our $O(1)$ terms from Theorem 2.9 become $O(\sqrt{\log n})$. So we need to include an extra $O(\sqrt{\log n})$ term in the separation distance.

> **Algorithm for Separating Points from Two Gaussians** Calculate all pairwise distances between points. The cluster of smallest pairwise distances must come from a single Gaussian. Remove these points. The remaining points come from the second Gaussian.

One can actually separate Gaussians where the centers are much closer. In the next chapter we will use singular value decomposition to separate points from a mixture of two Gaussians when their centers are separated by a distance $O(1)$.

2.9. Fitting a Spherical Gaussian to Data

Given a set of sample points, $x_1, x_2, \ldots, x_n$, in a d-dimensional space, we wish to find the spherical Gaussian that best fits the points. Let f be the unknown Gaussian with mean μ and variance σ^2 in each direction. The probability density for picking these points when sampling according to f is given by

$$c \, \exp\left(-\frac{(x_1 - \mu)^2 + (x_2 - \mu)^2 + \cdots + (x_n - \mu)^2}{2\sigma^2}\right)$$

where the normalizing constant c is the reciprocal of $\left[\int e^{-\frac{|x-\mu|^2}{2\sigma^2}} dx\right]^n$. In integrating from $-\infty$ to ∞, one can shift the origin to μ and thus c is $\left[\int e^{-\frac{|x|^2}{2\sigma^2}} dx\right]^{-n} = \frac{1}{(2\pi)^{\frac{n}{2}}}$ and is independent of μ.

The *Maximum Likelihood Estimator* (MLE) of f, given the samples $x_1, x_2, \ldots, x_n$, is the f that maximizes the above probability density.

> **Lemma 2.12** *Let $\{x_1, x_2, \ldots, x_n\}$ be a set of n d-dimensional points. Then $(x_1 - \mu)^2 + (x_2 - \mu)^2 + \cdots + (x_n - \mu)^2$ is minimized when μ is the centroid of the points $x_1, x_2, \ldots, x_n$, namely $\mu = \frac{1}{n}(x_1 + x_2 + \cdots + x_n)$.*

> ***Proof*** Setting the gradient of $(x_1 - \mu)^2 + (x_2 - \mu)^2 + \cdots + (x_n - \mu)^2$ with respect to μ to zero yields
>
> $$-2(x_1 - \mu) - 2(x_2 - \mu) - \cdots - 2(x_n - \mu) = 0.$$
>
> Solving for μ gives $\mu = \frac{1}{n}(x_1 + x_2 + \cdots + x_n)$. ∎

To determine the maximum likelihood estimate of σ^2 for f, set μ to the true centroid. Next, show that σ is set to the standard deviation of the sample. Substitute $v = \frac{1}{2\sigma^2}$ and $a = (x_1 - \mu)^2 + (x_2 - \mu)^2 + \cdots + (x_n - \mu)^2$ into the formula for the probability of picking the points $x_1, x_2, \ldots, x_n$. This gives

---

[3] poly(n) means bounded by a polynomial in n.

$$\frac{e^{-av}}{\left[\int_x e^{-x^2v}dx\right]^n}.$$

Now, a is fixed and v is to be determined. Taking logs, the expression to maximize is

$$-av - n\ln\left[\int_x e^{-vx^2}dx\right].$$

To find the maximum, differentiate with respect to v, set the derivative to zero, and solve for σ. The derivative is

$$-a + n\frac{\int_x |x|^2 e^{-vx^2}dx}{\int_x e^{-vx^2}dx}.$$

Setting $y = |\sqrt{v}\mathbf{x}|$ in the derivative, yields

$$-a + \frac{n}{v}\frac{\int_y y^2 e^{-y^2}dy}{\int_y e^{-y^2}dy}.$$

Since the ratio of the two integrals is the expected distance squared of a d-dimensional spherical Gaussian of standard deviation $\frac{1}{\sqrt{2}}$ to its center, and this is known to be $\frac{d}{2}$, we get $-a + \frac{nd}{2v}$. Substituting σ^2 for $\frac{1}{2v}$ gives $-a + nd\sigma^2$. Setting $-a + nd\sigma^2 = 0$ shows that the maximum occurs when $\sigma = \frac{\sqrt{a}}{\sqrt{nd}}$. Note that this quantity is the square root of the average coordinate distance squared of the samples to their mean, which is the standard deviation of the sample. Thus, we get the following lemma.

Lemma 2.13 *The maximum likelihood spherical Gaussian for a set of samples is the Gaussian with center equal to the sample mean and standard deviation equal to the standard deviation of the sample from the true mean.*

Let $\mathbf{x}_1, \mathbf{x}_2, \ldots, \mathbf{x}_n$ be a sample of points generated by a Gaussian probability distribution. Then $\mu = \frac{1}{n}(\mathbf{x}_1 + \mathbf{x}_2 + \cdots + \mathbf{x}_n)$ is an unbiased estimator of the expected value of the distribution. However, if in estimating the variance from the sample set we use the estimate of the expected value rather than the true expected value, we will not get an unbiased estimate of the variance, since the sample mean is not independent of the sample set. One should use $\tilde{\mu} = \frac{1}{n-1}(\mathbf{x}_1 + \mathbf{x}_2 + \cdots + \mathbf{x}_n)$ when estimating the variance. See Section 12.4.10 in Chapter 12.

2.10. Bibliographic Notes

The vector space model was introduced by Salton [SWY75]. There is vast literature on the Gaussian distribution, its properties, drawing samples according to it, etc. The reader can choose the level and depth according to his/her background. The Master Tail Bounds theorem and the derivation of Chernoff and other inequalities from it are from [Kan09]. The original proof of the Random Projection Theorem by Johnson and Lindenstrauss was complicated. Several authors used Gaussians to simplify the proof. The proof here is due to Dasgupta and Gupta [DG99]. See [Vem04] for details and applications of the theorem. [MU05] and [MR95b] are textbooks covering much of the material touched upon here.

2.11. Exercises

Exercise 2.1

1. Let x and y be independent random variables with uniform distribution in $[0, 1]$. What is the expected value $E(x)$, $E(x^2)$, $E(x - y)$, $E(xy)$, and $E(x - y)^2$?
2. Let x and y be independent random variables with uniform distribution in $[-\frac{1}{2}, \frac{1}{2}]$. What is the expected value $E(x)$, $E(x^2)$, $E(x-y)$, $E(xy)$, and $E(x-y)^2$?
3. What is the expected squared distance between two points generated at random inside a unit d-dimensional cube?

Exercise 2.2 Randomly generate 30 points inside the cube $[-\frac{1}{2}, \frac{1}{2}]^{100}$ and plot distance between points and the angle between the vectors from the origin to the points for all pairs of points.

Exercise 2.3 Show that for any $a \geq 1$ there exist distributions for which Markov's inequality is tight by showing the following:

1. For each $a = 2, 3$, and 4 give a probability distribution $p(x)$ for a nonnegative random variable x where $\text{Prob}(x \geq a) = \frac{E(x)}{a}$.
2. For arbitrary $a \geq 1$ give a probability distribution for a nonnegative random variable x where $\text{Prob}(x \geq a) = \frac{E(x)}{a}$.

Exercise 2.4 Show that for any $c \geq 1$ there exist distributions for which Chebyshev's inequality is tight, in other words, $Prob(|x - E(x)| \geq c) = Var(x)/c^2$.

Exercise 2.5 Let x be a random variable with probability density $\frac{1}{4}$ for $0 \leq x \leq 4$ and zero elsewhere.

1. Use Markov's inequality to bound the probability that $x \geq 3$.
2. Make use of $\text{Prob}(|x| \geq a) = \text{Prob}(x^2 \geq a^2)$ to get a tighter bound.
3. What is the bound using $\text{Prob}(|x| \geq a) = \text{Prob}(x^r \geq a^r)$?

Exercise 2.6 Consider the probability distribution $p(x = 0) = 1 - \frac{1}{a}$ and $p(x = a) = \frac{1}{a}$. Plot the probability that x is greater than or equal to a as a function of a for the bound given by Markov's inequality and by Markov's inequality applied to x^2 and x^4.

Exercise 2.7 Consider the probability density function $p(x) = 0$ for $x < 1$ and $p(x) = c\frac{1}{x^4}$ for $x \geq 1$.

1. What should c be to make p a legal probability density function?
2. Generate 100 random samples from this distribution. How close is the average of the samples to the expected value of x?

Exercise 2.8 Let U be a set of integers and X and Y be subsets of U whose symmetric difference $X \triangle Y$ is 1/10 of U. Prove that the probability that none of the elements selected at random from U will be in $X \triangle Y$ is less than $e^{-0.1n}$.

Exercise 2.9 Let G be a d-dimensional spherical Gaussian with variance $\frac{1}{2}$ in each direction, centered at the origin. Derive the expected squared distance to the origin.

Exercise 2.10 Consider drawing a random point $\mathbf{x}$ on the surface of the unit sphere in R^d. What is the variance of x_1 (the first coordinate of $\mathbf{x}$)? See if you can give an argument without doing any integrals.

Exercise 2.11 How large must ε be for 99% of the volume of a 1000-dimensional unit-radius ball to lie in the shell of ε-thickness at the surface of the ball?

Exercise 2.12 Prove that $1 + x \le e^x$ for all real x. For what values of x is the approximation $1 + x \approx e^x$ within 0.01?

Exercise 2.13 For what value of d does the volume, $V(d)$, of a d-dimensional unit ball take on its maximum? Hint: Consider the ratio $\frac{V(d)}{V(d-1)}$.

Exercise 2.14 A three-dimensional cube has vertices, edges, and faces. In a d-dimensional cube, these components are called faces. A vertex is a zero-dimensional face, an edge a one-dimensional face, etc.

1. For $0 \le k \le d$, how many k-dimensional faces does a d-dimensional cube have?
2. What is the total number of faces of all dimensions? The d-dimensional face is the cube itself, which you can include in your count.
3. What is the surface area of a unit cube in d-dimensions (a unit cube has a side-length of 1 in each dimension)?
4. What is the surface area of the cube if the length of each side is 2?
5. Prove that the volume of a unit cube is close to its surface.

Exercise 2.15 Consider the portion of the surface area of a unit radius, three-dimensional ball with center at the origin that lies within a circular cone whose vertex is at the origin. What is the formula for the incremental unit of area when using polar coordinates to integrate the portion of the surface area of the ball that is lying inside the circular cone? What is the formula for the integral? What is the value of the integral if the angle of the cone is $36°$? The angle of the cone is measured from the axis of the cone to a ray on the surface of the cone.

Exercise 2.16 Consider a unit radius, circular cylinder in three-dimensions of height 1. The top of the cylinder could be a horizontal plane or half of a circular ball. Consider these two possibilities for a unit radius, circular cylinder in four dimensions. In four dimensions the horizontal plane is three-dimensional and the half circular ball is four-dimensional. In each of the two cases, what is the surface area of the top face of the cylinder? You can use $V(d)$ for the volume of a unit radius, d-dimension ball, and $A(d)$ for the surface area of a unit radius, d-dimensional ball. An infinite-length, unit radius, circular cylinder in 4-dimensions would be the set $\{(x_1, x_2, x_3, x_4) | x_2^2 + x_3^2 + x_4^2 \le 1\}$ where the coordinate x_1 is the axis.

Exercise 2.17 Given a d-dimensional circular cylinder of radius r and height h,

1. What is the surface area in terms of $V(d)$ and $A(d)$?
2. What is the volume?

Exercise 2.18 How does the volume of a ball of radius 2 behave as the dimension of the space increases? What if the radius was larger than 2 but a constant independent of d? What function of d would the radius need to be for a ball of radius r to have approximately constant volume as the dimension increases? Hint: You may want to use Stirling's approximation, $n! \approx \left(\frac{n}{e}\right)^n$, for factorial.

Exercise 2.19 If $\lim\limits_{d \to \infty} V(d) = 0$, the volume of a d-dimensional ball for sufficiently large d must be less than $V(3)$. How can this be if the d-dimensional ball contains the three-dimensional ball?

Exercise 2.20

1. Write a recurrence relation for $V(d)$ in terms of $V(d-1)$ by integrating over x_1. Hint: At $x_1 = t$, the $(d-1)$-dimensional volume of the slice is the volume of a $(d-1)$-dimensional sphere of radius $\sqrt{1-t^2}$. Express this in terms of $V(d-1)$ and write down the integral. You need not evaluate the integral.
2. Verify the formula for $d = 2$ and $d = 3$ by integrating and comparing with $V(2) = \pi$ and $V(3) = \frac{4}{3}\pi$.

Exercise 2.21 Consider a unit ball A centered at the origin and a unit ball B whose center is at distance s from the origin. Suppose that a random point x is drawn from the mixture distribution: "with probability $1/2$, draw at random from A; with probability $1/2$, draw at random from B." Show that a separation $s \gg 1/\sqrt{d-1}$ is sufficient so that $\text{Prob}(x \in A \cap B) = o(1)$; i.e., for any $\epsilon > 0$ there exists c such that if $s \geq c/\sqrt{d-1}$, then $\text{Prob}(x \in A \cap B) < \epsilon$. In other words, this extent of separation means that nearly all of the mixture distribution is identifiable.

Exercise 2.22 Consider the upper hemisphere of a unit-radius ball in d dimensions. What is the height of the maximum-volume cylinder that can be placed entirely inside the hemisphere? As you increase the height of the cylinder, you need to reduce the cylinder's radius so that it will lie entirely within the hemisphere.

Exercise 2.23 What is the volume of the maximum-size d-dimensional hypercube that can be placed entirely inside a unit radius d-dimensional ball?

Exercise 2.24 Calculate the ratio of area above the plane $x_1 = \epsilon$ to the area of the upper hemisphere of a unit radius ball in d dimensions for $\epsilon = 0.001, 0.01, 0.02, 0.03, 0.04, 0.05$ and for $d = 100$ and $d = 1,000$.

Exercise 2.25 Almost all of the volume of a ball in high dimensions lies in a narrow slice of the ball at the equator. However, the narrow slice is determined by the point on the surface of the ball that is designated the North Pole. Explain how this can be true if several different locations are selected for the location of the North Pole giving rise to different equators.

Exercise 2.26 Explain how the volume of a ball in high dimensions can simultaneously be in a narrow slice at the equator and also be concentrated in a narrow annulus at the surface of the ball.

Exercise 2.27 Generate 500 points uniformly at random on the surface of a unit radius ball in 50 dimensions. Then randomly generate five additional points. For each of the five new points, calculate a narrow band of width $\frac{2}{\sqrt{50}}$ at the equator, assuming the point was the North Pole. How many of the 500 points are in each band corresponding to one of the five equators? How many of the points are in all five bands? How wide do the bands need to be for all points to be in all five bands?

Exercise 2.28 Place 100 points at random on a d-dimensional unit-radius ball. Assume d is large. Pick a random vector and let it define two parallel hyperplanes on opposite sides of the origin that are equal distance from the origin. How close can the hyperplanes be moved and still have at least a .99 probability that all of the 100 points land between them?

Exercise 2.29 Let $\mathbf{x}$ and $\mathbf{y}$ be d-dimensional, zero-mean, unit variance Gaussian vectors. Prove that $\mathbf{x}$ and $\mathbf{y}$ are almost orthogonal by considering their dot product.

Exercise 2.30 Prove that with high probability, the angle between two random vectors in a high-dimensional space is at least $45°$. Hint: Use Theorem 2.8.

Exercise 2.31 Project the volume of a d-dimensional ball of radius $\sqrt{d}$ onto a line through the center. For large d, give an intuitive argument that the projected volume should behave like a Gaussian.

Exercise 2.32

1. Write a computer program that generates n points uniformly distributed over the surface of a unit-radius d-dimensional ball.
2. Generate 200 points on the surface of a sphere in 50 dimensions.
3. Create several random lines through the origin and project the points onto each line. Plot the distribution of points on each line.
4. What does your result from (3) say about the surface area of the sphere in relation to the lines, i.e., where is the surface area concentrated relative to each line?

Exercise 2.33 If one generates points in d-dimensions with each coordinate a unit variance Gaussian, the points will approximately lie on the surface of a sphere of radius $\sqrt{d}$.

1. What is the distribution when the points are projected onto a random line through the origin?
2. If one uses a Gaussian with variance four, where in d-space will the points lie?

Exercise 2.34 Randomly generate a 100 points on the surface of a sphere in 3-dimensions and in 100-dimensions. Create a histogram of all distances between the pairs of points in both cases.

Exercise 2.35 We have claimed that a randomly generated point on a ball lies near the equator of the ball, independent of the point picked to be the North Pole. Is the same claim true for a randomly generated point on a cube? To test this claim, randomly generate 10 ± 1 valued vectors in 128 dimensions. Think of these 10 vectors as 10 choices for the North Pole. Then generate some additional ± 1 valued vectors. To how many of the original vectors is each of the new vectors close to being perpendicular; that is, how many of the equators is each new vector close to?

Exercise 2.36 Define the equator of a d-dimensional unit cube to be the hyperplane $\left\{ \mathbf{x} \mid \sum_{i=1}^{d} x_i = \frac{d}{2} \right\}$.

1. Are the vertices of a unit cube concentrated close to the equator?

2. Is the volume of a unit cube concentrated close to the equator?

3. Is the surface area of a unit cube concentrated close to the equator?

Exercise 2.37 Consider a non-orthogonal basis $e_1, e_2, \ldots, e_d$. The e_i are a set of linearly independent unit vectors that span the space.

1. Prove that the representation of any vector in this basis is unique.

2. Calculate the squared length of $z = \left(\frac{\sqrt{2}}{2}, 1 \right)_e$ where z is expressed in the basis $e_1 = (1, 0)$ and $e_2 = \left(-\frac{\sqrt{2}}{2}, \frac{\sqrt{2}}{2} \right)$

3. If $y = \sum_i a_i e_i$ and $z = \sum_i b_i e_i$, with $0 < a_i < b_i$, is it necessarily true that the length of z is greater than the length of y? Why or why not?

4. Consider the basis $e_1 = (1, 0)$ and $e_2 = \left(-\frac{\sqrt{2}}{2}, \frac{\sqrt{2}}{2} \right)$.
    (a) What is the representation of the vector $(0, 1)$ in the basis (e_1, e_2)?

    (b) What is the representation of the vector $\left(\frac{\sqrt{2}}{2}, \frac{\sqrt{2}}{2} \right)$?

    (c) What is the representation of the vector $(1, 2)$?

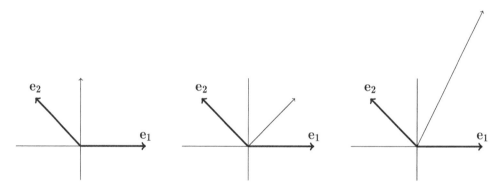

Exercise 2.38 Generate 20 points uniformly at random on a 900-dimensional sphere of radius 30. Calculate the distance between each pair of points. Then, select a method of projection and project the data onto subspaces of dimension $k = 100$, 50, 10, 5, 4, 3, 2, 1 and calculate the difference between $\sqrt{k}$ times the original distances and the new pairwise distances. For each value of k what is the maximum difference as a percent of $\sqrt{k}$?

Exercise 2.39 What happens in high dimension to a lower-dimensional manifold? To see what happens, consider a sphere of dimension 100 in a 1,000-dimensional space when the 1,000-dimensional space is projected to a random 500-dimensional space. Will the sphere remain essentially spherical? Given an intuitive argument justifying your answer.

Exercise 2.40 In d-dimensions there are exactly d-unit vectors that are pairwise orthogonal. However, if you wanted a set of vectors that were almost orthogonal, you might squeeze in a few more. For example, in two dimensions, if almost orthogonal meant at least 45 degrees apart, you could fit in three almost orthogonal vectors. Suppose you wanted to find 1,000 almost orthogonal vectors in 100 dimensions. Here are two ways you could do it:

1. Begin with 1,000 orthonormal 1,000-dimensional vectors, and then project them to a random 100-dimensional space.

2. Generate 1,000 100-dimensional random Gaussian vectors.

Implement both ideas and compare them to see which does a better job.

Exercise 2.41 Suppose there is an object moving at constant velocity along a straight line. You receive the GPS coordinates corrupted by Gaussian noise every minute. How do you estimate the current position?

Exercise 2.42

1. What is the maximum-size rectangle that can be fitted under a unit-variance Gaussian?
2. What unit area rectangle best approximates a unit-variance Gaussian if one measures goodness of fit by the symmetric difference of the Gaussian and the rectangle?

Exercise 2.43 Let $x_1, x_2, \ldots, x_n$ be independent samples of a random variable x with mean μ and variance σ^2. Let $m_s = \frac{1}{n}\sum_{i=1}^{n} x_i$ be the sample mean. Suppose one estimates the variance using the sample mean rather than the true mean, that is,

$$\sigma_s^2 = \frac{1}{n}\sum_{i=1}^{n}(x_i - m_s)^2.$$

Prove that $E(\sigma_s^2) = \frac{n-1}{n}\sigma^2$ and thus one should have divided by $n - 1$ rather than n.

> **Hint.** First calculate the variance of the sample mean and show that $\text{var}(m_s) = \frac{1}{n}\text{var}(x)$. Then calculate $E(\sigma_s^2) = E[\frac{1}{n}\sum_{i=1}^{n}(x_i - m_s)^2]$ by replacing $x_i - m_s$ with $(x_i - m) - (m_s - m)$.

Exercise 2.44 Generate 10 values by a Gaussian probability distribution with zero mean and variance 1. What is the center determined by averaging the points? What is the variance? In estimating the variance, use both the real center and the estimated center. When using the estimated center to estimate the variance, use both $n = 10$ and $n = 9$. How do the three estimates compare?

Exercise 2.45 Suppose you want to estimate the unknown center of a Gaussian in d-space that has variance 1 in each direction. Show that $O(\log d/\varepsilon^2)$ random samples from the Gaussian are sufficient to get an estimate m_s of the true center μ, so that with probability at least 99%,

$$\|\mu - m_s\|_\infty \le \varepsilon.$$

How many samples are sufficient to ensure that with probability at least 99%

$$\|\mu - m_s\|_2 \le \varepsilon?$$

Exercise 2.46 Use the probability distribution $\frac{1}{3\sqrt{2\pi}}e^{-\frac{1}{2}\frac{(x-5)^2}{9}}$ to generate 10 points.

(a) From the 10 points estimate μ. How close is the estimate of μ to the true mean of 5?

(b) Using the true mean of 5, estimate σ^2 by the formula $\sigma^2 = \frac{1}{10}\sum_{i=1}^{10}(x_i - 5)^2$. How close is the estimate of σ^2 to the true variance of 9?

(c) Using your estimate m of the mean, estimate σ^2 by the formula $\sigma^2 = \frac{1}{10} \sum_{i=1}^{10} (x_i - m)^2$. How close is the estimate of σ^2 to the true variance of 9?

(d) Using your estimate m of the mean, estimate σ^2 by the formula $\sigma^2 = \frac{1}{9} \sum_{i=1}^{10} (x_i - m)^2$. How close is the estimate of σ^2 to the true variance of 9?

Exercise 2.47 Create a list of the five most important things that you learned about high dimensions.

Exercise 2.48 Write a short essay whose purpose is to excite a college freshman to learn about high dimensions.

CHAPTER THREE

Best-Fit Subspaces and Singular Value Decomposition (SVD)

3.1. Introduction

In this chapter, we examine the *singular value decomposition* (SVD) of a matrix. Consider each row of an $n \times d$ matrix A as a point in d-dimensional space. The singular value decomposition finds the best-fitting k-dimensional subspace for $k = 1, 2, 3, \ldots$, for the set of n data points. Here, "best" means minimizing the sum of the squares of the perpendicular distances of the points to the subspace, or equivalently, maximizing the sum of squares of the lengths of the projections of the points onto this subspace.[1] We begin with a special case where the subspace is one-dimensional, namely a line through the origin. We then show that the best-fitting k-dimensional subspace can be found by k applications of the best-fitting line algorithm, where on the ith iteration we find the best-fit line perpendicular to the previous $i - 1$ lines. When k reaches the rank of the matrix, from these operations we get an exact decomposition of the matrix called the *singular value decomposition*.

In matrix notation, the singular value decomposition of a matrix A with real entries (we assume all our matrices have real entries) is the factorization of A into the product of three matrices, $A = UDV^T$, where the columns of U and V are orthonormal[2] and the matrix D is diagonal with positive real entries. The columns of V are the unit length vectors defining the best-fitting lines described above (the ith column being the unit length vector in the direction of the ith line). The coordinates of a row of U will be the fractions of the corresponding row of A along the direction of each of the lines.

The SVD is useful in many tasks. Often a data matrix A is close to a low-rank matrix, and it is useful to find a good low-rank approximation to A. For any k, the singular value decomposition of A gives the best rank-k approximation to A in a well-defined sense.

---

[1]This equivalence is due to the Pythagorean Theorem. For each point, its squared length (its distance to the origin squared) is exactly equal to the squared length of its projection onto the subspace plus the squared distance of the point to its projection; therefore, maximizing the sum of the former is equivalent to minimizing the sum of the latter. For further discussion, see Section 3.2.

[2]A set of vectors is orthonormal if each is of length one and they are pairwise orthogonal.

If $\mathbf{u_i}$ and $\mathbf{v_i}$ are columns of U and V, respectively, then the matrix equation $A = UDV^T$ can be rewritten as

$$A = \sum_i d_{ii}\mathbf{u_i}\mathbf{v_i}^T.$$

Since $\mathbf{u_i}$ is a $n \times 1$ matrix and $\mathbf{v_i}$ is a $d \times 1$ matrix, $\mathbf{u_i}\mathbf{v_i}^T$ is an $n \times d$ matrix with the same dimensions as A. The ith term in the above sum can be viewed as giving the components of the rows of A along direction $\mathbf{v_i}$. When the terms are summed, they reconstruct A.

This decomposition of A can be viewed as analogous to writing a vector $\mathbf{x}$ in some orthonormal basis $\mathbf{v_1}, \mathbf{v_2}, \ldots, \mathbf{v_d}$. The coordinates of $\mathbf{x} = (\mathbf{x} \cdot \mathbf{v_1}, \mathbf{x} \cdot \mathbf{v_2} \ldots, \mathbf{x} \cdot \mathbf{v_d})$ are the projections of $\mathbf{x}$ onto the $\mathbf{v_i}$'s. For SVD, this basis has the property that for any k, the first k vectors of this basis produce the least possible total sum of squares error for that value of k.

In addition to the singular value decomposition, there is an eigenvalue decomposition. Let A be a square matrix. A vector $\mathbf{v}$ such that $A\mathbf{v} = \lambda\mathbf{v}$ is called an eigenvector and λ the eigenvalue. When A is symmetric, the eigenvectors are orthogonal and A can be expressed as $A = VDV^T$ where the eigenvectors are the columns of V and D is a diagonal matrix with the corresponding eigenvalues on its diagonal. For a symmetric matrix A, the singular values are the absolute values of the eigenvalues. Some eigenvalues may be negative, but all singular values are positive by definition. If the singular values are distinct, then A's right singular vectors and eigenvectors are identical up to scalar multiplication. The left singular vectors of A are identical with the right singular vectors of A when the corresponding eigenvalues are positive and are the negative of the right singular vectors when the corresponding eigenvalues are negative. If a singular value has multiplicity d greater than one, the corresponding singular vectors span a subspace of dimension d, and any orthogonal basis of the subspace can be used as the eigenvectors or singular vectors.[3]

The singular value decomposition is defined for all matrices, whereas the more familiar eigenvector decomposition requires that the matrix A be square and certain other conditions on the matrix to ensure orthogonality of the eigenvectors. In contrast, the columns of V in the singular value decomposition, called the *right-singular vectors* of A, always form an orthogonal set with no assumptions on A. The columns of U are called the *left-singular vectors* and they also form an orthogonal set (see Section 3.6). A simple consequence of the orthonormality is that for a square and invertible matrix A, the inverse of A is $VD^{-1}U^T$.

Eigenvalues and eignevectors satisfy $A\mathbf{v} = \lambda\mathbf{v}$. We will show that singular values and vectors satisfy a somewhat analogous relationship. Since $A\mathbf{v_i}$ is a $n \times 1$ matrix (vector), the matrix A cannot act on it from the left. But A^T, which is a $d \times n$ matrix, can act on this vector. Indeed, we will show that

$$A\mathbf{v_i} = d_{ii}\mathbf{u_i} \quad \text{and} \quad A^T\mathbf{u_i} = d_{ii}\mathbf{v_i}.$$

In words, A acting on $\mathbf{v_i}$ produces a scalar multiple of $\mathbf{u_i}$ and A^T acting on $\mathbf{u_i}$ produces the same scalar multiple of $\mathbf{v_i}$. Note that $A^TA\mathbf{v_i} = d_{ii}^2\mathbf{v_i}$. The ith singular vector of A is the ith eigenvector of the square symmetric matrix A^TA.

---

[3]When $d = 1$, there are actually two possible singular vectors, one the negative of the other. The subspace spanned is unique.

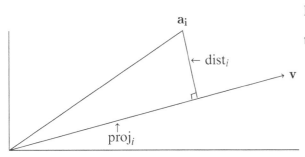

Minimizing $\sum_i \text{dist}_i^2$ is equivalent to maximizing $\sum_i \text{proj}_i^2$

Figure 3.1: The projection of the point $\mathbf{a_i}$ onto the line through the origin in the direction of $\mathbf{v}$.

3.2. Preliminaries

Consider projecting a point $\mathbf{a_i} = (a_{i1}, a_{i2}, \ldots, a_{id})$ onto a line through the origin. Then

$$a_{i1}^2 + a_{i2}^2 + \cdots + a_{id}^2 = (\text{length of projection})^2 + (\text{distance of point to line})^2.$$

This holds by the Pythagorean Theorem (see Figure 3.1). Thus,

$$(\text{distance of point to line})^2 = a_{i1}^2 + a_{i2}^2 + \cdots + a_{id}^2 - (\text{length of projection})^2.$$

Since $\sum_{i=1}^n \left(a_{i1}^2 + a_{i2}^2 + \cdots + a_{id}^2 \right)$ is a constant independent of the line, minimizing the sum of the squares of the distances to the line is equivalent to maximizing the sum of the squares of the lengths of the projections onto the line. Similarly for best-fit subspaces, maximizing the sum of the squared lengths of the projections onto the subspace minimizes the sum of squared distances to the subspace.

Thus, we have two interpretations of the best-fit subspace. The first is that it minimizes the sum of squared distances of the data points to it. This first interpretation and its use are akin to the notion of least-squares fit from calculus.[4] The second interpretation of best-fit subspace is that it maximizes the sum of projections squared of the data points on it. This says that the subspace contains the maximum content of data among all subspaces of the same dimension. The choice of the objective function as the sum of squared distances seems a bit arbitrary, and in a way it is. But the square has many nice mathematical properties. The first of these, as we have just seen, is that minimizing the sum of squared distances is equivalent to maximizing the sum of squared projections.

3.3. Singular Vectors

We now define the *singular vectors* of an $n \times d$ matrix A. Consider the rows of A as n points in a d-dimensional space. Consider the best-fit line through the origin. Let $\mathbf{v}$ be

---

[4]But there is a difference: here we take the perpendicular distance to the line or subspace, whereas, in the calculus notion, given n pairs, $(x_1, y_1), (x_2, y_2), \ldots, (x_n, y_n)$, we find a line $l = \{(x, y) | y = mx + b\}$ minimizing the vertical squared distances of the points to it, namely, $\sum_{i=1}^n (y_i - mx_i - b)^2$.

a unit vector along this line. The length of the projection of $\mathbf{a_i}$, the ith row of A, onto $\mathbf{v}$ is $|\mathbf{a_i} \cdot \mathbf{v}|$. From this we see that the sum of the squared lengths of the projections is $|A\mathbf{v}|^2$. The best-fit line is the one maximizing $|A\mathbf{v}|^2$ and hence minimizing the sum of the squared distances of the points to the line.

With this in mind, define the *first singular vector* $\mathbf{v_1}$ of A as

$$\mathbf{v_1} = \arg \max_{|\mathbf{v}|=1} |A\mathbf{v}|.$$

Technically, there may be a tie for the vector attaining the maximum, and so we should not use the article "the"; in fact, $-\mathbf{v_1}$ is always as good as $\mathbf{v_1}$. In this case, we arbitrarily pick one of the vectors achieving the maximum and refer to it as "the first singular vector," avoiding the more cumbersome "one of the vectors achieving the maximum." We adopt this terminology for all uses of arg max.

The value $\sigma_1(A) = |A\mathbf{v_1}|$ is called the *first singular value* of A. Note that $\sigma_1^2 = \sum_{i=1}^{n}(\mathbf{a_i} \cdot \mathbf{v_1})^2$ is the sum of the squared lengths of the projections of the points onto the line determined by $\mathbf{v_1}$.

If the data points were all either on a line or close to a line, intuitively, $\mathbf{v_1}$ should give us the direction of that line. It is possible that data points are not close to one line, but lie close to a two-dimensional subspace or more generally a low-dimensional space. Suppose we have an algorithm for finding $\mathbf{v_1}$ (we will describe one such algorithm later). How do we use this to find the best-fit two-dimensional plane or more generally the best-fit k-dimensional space?

The greedy approach begins by finding $\mathbf{v_1}$ and then finding the best two-dimensional subspace containing $\mathbf{v_1}$. The sum of squared distances helps. For every two-dimensional subspace containing $\mathbf{v_1}$, the sum of squared lengths of the projections onto the subspace equals the sum of squared projections onto $\mathbf{v_1}$ plus the sum of squared projections along a vector perpendicular to $\mathbf{v_1}$ in the subspace. Thus, instead of looking for the best two-dimensional subspace containing $\mathbf{v_1}$, look for a unit vector $\mathbf{v_2}$ perpendicular to $\mathbf{v_1}$ that maximizes $|A\mathbf{v}|^2$ among all such unit vectors. Using the same greedy strategy to find the best three- and higher-dimensional subspaces defines $\mathbf{v_3}, \mathbf{v_4}, \ldots$ in a similar manner. This is captured in the following definitions. There is no a priori guarantee that the greedy algorithm gives the best fit. But in fact, the greedy algorithm does work and yields the best-fit subspaces of every dimension as we will show.

The *second singular vector*, $\mathbf{v_2}$, is defined by the best-fit line perpendicular to $\mathbf{v_1}$:

$$\mathbf{v_2} = \arg \max_{\substack{\mathbf{v} \perp \mathbf{v_1} \\ |\mathbf{v}|=1}} |A\mathbf{v}|.$$

The value $\sigma_2(A) = |A\mathbf{v_2}|$ is called the *second singular value* of A. The *third singular vector* $\mathbf{v_3}$ and the *third singular value* are defined similarly by

$$\mathbf{v_3} = \arg \max_{\substack{\mathbf{v} \perp \mathbf{v_1}, \mathbf{v_2} \\ |\mathbf{v}|=1}} |A\mathbf{v}|$$

and

$$\sigma_3(A) = |A\mathbf{v_3}|,$$

and so on. The process stops when we have found singular vectors $\mathbf{v}_1, \mathbf{v}_2, \ldots, \mathbf{v}_r$, singular values $\sigma_1, \sigma_2, \ldots, \sigma_r$, and

$$\max_{\substack{\mathbf{v} \perp \mathbf{v}_1, \mathbf{v}_2, \ldots, \mathbf{v}_r \\ |\mathbf{v}|=1}} |A\mathbf{v}| = 0.$$

The greedy algorithm found the $\mathbf{v}_1$ that maximized $|A\mathbf{v}|$ and then the best-fit two-dimensional subspace containing $\mathbf{v}_1$. Is this necessarily the best-fit two-dimensional subspace overall? The following theorem establishes that the greedy algorithm finds the best subspaces of every dimension.

Theorem 3.1 (The Greedy Algorithm Works) *Let A be an $n \times d$ matrix with singular vectors $\mathbf{v}_1, \mathbf{v}_2, \ldots, \mathbf{v}_r$. For $1 \le k \le r$, let V_k be the subspace spanned by $\mathbf{v}_1, \mathbf{v}_2, \ldots, \mathbf{v}_k$. For each k, V_k is the best-fit k-dimensional subspace for A.*

Proof The statement is obviously true for $k = 1$. For $k = 2$, let W be a best-fit two-dimensional subspace for A. For any orthonormal basis $(\mathbf{w}_1, \mathbf{w}_2)$ of W, $|A\mathbf{w}_1|^2 + |A\mathbf{w}_2|^2$ is the sum of squared lengths of the projections of the rows of A onto W. Choose an orthonormal basis $(\mathbf{w}_1, \mathbf{w}_2)$ of W so that $\mathbf{w}_2$ is perpendicular to $\mathbf{v}_1$. If $\mathbf{v}_1$ is perpendicular to W, any unit vector in W will do as $\mathbf{w}_2$. If not, choose $\mathbf{w}_2$ to be the unit vector in W perpendicular to the projection of $\mathbf{v}_1$ onto W. This makes $\mathbf{w}_2$ perpendicular to $\mathbf{v}_1$.[5] Since $\mathbf{v}_1$ maximizes $|A\mathbf{v}|^2$, it follows that $|A\mathbf{w}_1|^2 \le |A\mathbf{v}_1|^2$. Since $\mathbf{v}_2$ maximizes $|A\mathbf{v}|^2$ over all $\mathbf{v}$ perpendicular to $\mathbf{v}_1$, $|A\mathbf{w}_2|^2 \le |A\mathbf{v}_2|^2$. Thus,

$$|A\mathbf{w}_1|^2 + |A\mathbf{w}_2|^2 \le |A\mathbf{v}_1|^2 + |A\mathbf{v}_2|^2.$$

Hence, V_2 is at least as good as W and so is a best-fit two-dimensional subspace.

For general k, proceed by induction. By the induction hypothesis, V_{k-1} is a best-fit k-1–dimensional subspace. Suppose W is a best-fit k-dimensional subspace. Choose an orthonormal basis $\mathbf{w}_1, \mathbf{w}_2, \ldots, \mathbf{w}_k$ of W so that $\mathbf{w}_k$ is perpendicular to $\mathbf{v}_1, \mathbf{v}_2, \ldots, \mathbf{v}_{k-1}$. Then

$$|A\mathbf{w}_1|^2 + |A\mathbf{w}_2|^2 + \cdots + |A\mathbf{w}_{k-1}|^2 \le |A\mathbf{v}_1|^2 + |A\mathbf{v}_2|^2 + \cdots + |A\mathbf{v}_{k-1}|^2$$

since V_{k-1} is an optimal $k-1$ dimensional subspace. Since $\mathbf{w}_k$ is perpendicular to $\mathbf{v}_1, \mathbf{v}_2, \ldots, \mathbf{v}_{k-1}$, by the definition of $\mathbf{v}_k$, $|A\mathbf{w}_k|^2 \le |A\mathbf{v}_k|^2$. Thus,

$$|A\mathbf{w}_1|^2 + |A\mathbf{w}_2|^2 + \cdots + |A\mathbf{w}_{k-1}|^2 + |A\mathbf{w}_k|^2$$
$$\le |A\mathbf{v}_1|^2 + |A\mathbf{v}_2|^2 + \cdots + |A\mathbf{v}_{k-1}|^2 + |A\mathbf{v}_k|^2,$$

proving that V_k is at least as good as W and hence is optimal. ■

Note that the n-dimensional vector $A\mathbf{v}_i$ is a list of lengths (with signs) of the projections of the rows of A onto $\mathbf{v}_i$. Think of $|A\mathbf{v}_i| = \sigma_i(A)$ as the *component* of the matrix A along $\mathbf{v}_i$. For this interpretation to make sense, it should be true that adding up the squares of the components of A along each of the $\mathbf{v}_i$ gives the square of the "whole content of A". This is indeed the case and is the matrix analogy of decomposing a vector into its components along orthogonal directions.

---

[5]This can be seen by noting that $\mathbf{v}_1$ is the sum of two vectors that each are individually perpendicular to $\mathbf{w}_2$, namely the projection of $\mathbf{v}_1$ to W and the portion of $\mathbf{v}_1$ orthogonal to W.

Consider one row, say $\mathbf{a_j}$, of A. Since $\mathbf{v_1}, \mathbf{v_2}, \ldots, \mathbf{v_r}$ span the space of all rows of A, $\mathbf{a_j} \cdot \mathbf{v} = 0$ for all $\mathbf{v}$ perpendicular to $\mathbf{v_1}, \mathbf{v_2}, \ldots, \mathbf{v_r}$. Thus, for each row $\mathbf{a_j}$, $\sum_{i=1}^{r} (\mathbf{a_j} \cdot \mathbf{v_i})^2 = |\mathbf{a_j}|^2$. Summing over all rows j,

$$\sum_{j=1}^{n} |\mathbf{a_j}|^2 = \sum_{j=1}^{n} \sum_{i=1}^{r} (\mathbf{a_j} \cdot \mathbf{v_i})^2 = \sum_{i=1}^{r} \sum_{j=1}^{n} (\mathbf{a_j} \cdot \mathbf{v_i})^2 = \sum_{i=1}^{r} |A\mathbf{v_i}|^2 = \sum_{i=1}^{r} \sigma_i^2(A).$$

But $\sum_{j=1}^{n} |\mathbf{a_j}|^2 = \sum_{j=1}^{n} \sum_{k=1}^{d} a_{jk}^2$, the sum of squares of all the entries of A. Thus, the sum of squares of the singular values of A is indeed the square of the "whole content of A," i.e., the sum of squares of all the entries. There is an important norm associated with this quantity, the Frobenius norm of A, denoted $||A||_F$ defined as

$$||A||_F = \sqrt{\sum_{j,k} a_{jk}^2}.$$

Lemma 3.2 *For any matrix A, the sum of squares of the singular values equals the square of the Frobenius norm. That is, $\sum \sigma_i^2(A) = ||A||_F^2$.*

Proof By the preceding discussion. ∎

The vectors $\mathbf{v_1}, \mathbf{v_2}, \ldots, \mathbf{v_r}$ are called the *right-singular vectors*. The vectors $A\mathbf{v_i}$ form a fundamental set of vectors, and we normalize them to length 1 by

$$\mathbf{u_i} = \frac{1}{\sigma_i(A)} A\mathbf{v_i}.$$

Later we will show that $\mathbf{u}_i$ similarly maximizes $|\mathbf{u}^T A|$ over all $\mathbf{u}$ perpendicular to $\mathbf{u}_1, \ldots, \mathbf{u}_{i-1}$. These $\mathbf{u}_i$ are called the *left-singular vectors*. Clearly, the right-singular vectors are orthogonal by definition. We will show later that the left-singular vectors are also orthogonal.

3.4. Singular Value Decomposition (SVD)

Let A be an $n \times d$ matrix with singular vectors $\mathbf{v_1}, \mathbf{v_2}, \ldots, \mathbf{v_r}$ and corresponding singular values $\sigma_1, \sigma_2, \ldots, \sigma_r$. The left-singular vectors of A are $\mathbf{u_i} = \frac{1}{\sigma_i} A\mathbf{v_i}$ where $\sigma_i \mathbf{u_i}$ is a vector whose coordinates correspond to the projections of the rows of A onto $\mathbf{v_i}$. Each $\sigma_i \mathbf{u_i} \mathbf{v_i}^T$ is a rank one matrix whose rows are the "$\mathbf{v_i}$ components" of the rows of A, i.e., the projections of the rows of A in the $\mathbf{v_i}$ direction. We will prove that A can be decomposed into a sum of rank one matrices as

$$A = \sum_{i=1}^{r} \sigma_i \mathbf{u_i} \mathbf{v_i}^T.$$

Geometrically, each point is decomposed in A into its components along each of the r orthogonal directions given by the $\mathbf{v_i}$. We will also prove this algebraically. We begin with a simple lemma that two matrices A and B are identical if $A\mathbf{v} = B\mathbf{v}$ for all $\mathbf{v}$.

Lemma 3.3 *Matrices A and B are identical if and only if for all vectors $\mathbf{v}$, $A\mathbf{v} = B\mathbf{v}$.*

Proof Clearly, if $A = B$, then $A\mathbf{v} = B\mathbf{v}$ for all $\mathbf{v}$. For the converse, suppose that $A\mathbf{v} = B\mathbf{v}$ for all $\mathbf{v}$. Let $\mathbf{e_i}$ be the vector that is all zeros except for the ith component, which has value 1. Now $A\mathbf{e_i}$ is the ith column of A, and thus $A = B$ if for each i, $A\mathbf{e_i} = B\mathbf{e_i}$. ∎

Theorem 3.4 *Let A be an $n \times d$ matrix with right-singular vectors $\mathbf{v_1}, \mathbf{v_2}, \ldots, \mathbf{v_r}$, left-singular vectors $\mathbf{u_1}, \mathbf{u_2}, \ldots, \mathbf{u_r}$, and corresponding singular values $\sigma_1, \sigma_2, \ldots, \sigma_r$. Then*

$$A = \sum_{i=1}^{r} \sigma_i \mathbf{u_i} \mathbf{v_i}^T.$$

Proof We first show that multiplying both A and $\sum_{i=1}^{r} \sigma_i \mathbf{u_i} \mathbf{v_i}^T$ by $\mathbf{v_j}$ results in equality.

$$\sum_{i=1}^{r} \sigma_i \mathbf{u_i} \mathbf{v_i}^T \mathbf{v_j} = \sigma_j \mathbf{u_j} = A \mathbf{v_j}.$$

Since any vector $\mathbf{v}$ can be expressed as a linear combination of the singular vectors plus a vector perpendicular to the $\mathbf{v_i}$, $A\mathbf{v} = \sum_{i=1}^{r} \sigma_i \mathbf{u_i} \mathbf{v_i}^T \mathbf{v}$ for all $\mathbf{v}$ and by Lemma 3.3, $A = \sum_{i=1}^{r} \sigma_i \mathbf{u_i} \mathbf{v_i}^T$. ∎

The decomposition $A = \sum_i \sigma_i \mathbf{u_i} \mathbf{v_i}^T$ is called the *singular value decomposition, SVD*, of A. We can rewrite this equation in matrix notation as $A = UDV^T$ where $\mathbf{u_i}$ is the ith column of U, $\mathbf{v_i}^T$ is the ith row of V^T, and D is a diagonal matrix with σ_i as the ith entry on its diagonal (see Figure 3.2). For any matrix A, the sequence of singular values is unique, and if the singular values are all distinct, then the sequence of singular vectors is unique up to signs. However, when some set of singular values are equal, the corresponding singular vectors span some subspace. Any set of orthonormal vectors spanning this subspace can be used as the singular vectors.

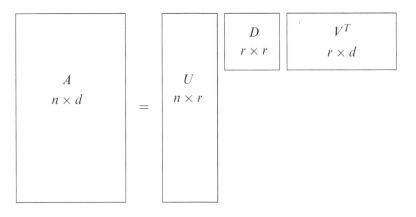

Figure 3.2: The SVD decomposition of an $n \times d$ matrix.

3.5. Best Rank-k Approximations

Let A be an $n \times d$ matrix and think of the rows of A as n points in d-dimensional space. Let

$$A = \sum_{i=1}^{r} \sigma_i \mathbf{u_i} \mathbf{v_i}^T$$

be the SVD of A. For $k \in \{1, 2, \ldots, r\}$, let

$$A_k = \sum_{i=1}^{k} \sigma_i \mathbf{u_i} \mathbf{v_i}^T$$

be the sum truncated after k terms. It is clear that A_k has rank k. We show that A_k is the best rank-k approximation to A, where error is measured in the Frobenius norm. Geometrically, this says that $\mathbf{v_1}, \ldots, \mathbf{v_k}$ define the k-dimensional space minimizing the sum of squared distances of the points to the space. To see why, we need the following lemma.

Lemma 3.5 *The rows of A_k are the projections of the rows of A onto the subspace V_k spanned by the first k singular vectors of A.*

Proof Let $\mathbf{a}$ be an arbitrary row vector. Since the $\mathbf{v_i}$ are orthonormal, the projection of the vector $\mathbf{a}$ onto V_k is given by $\sum_{i=1}^{k} (\mathbf{a} \cdot \mathbf{v_i}) \mathbf{v_i}^T$. Thus, the matrix whose rows are the projections of the rows of A onto V_k is given by $\sum_{i=1}^{k} A \mathbf{v_i} \mathbf{v_i}^T$. This last expression simplifies to

$$\sum_{i=1}^{k} A \mathbf{v_i} \mathbf{v_i}^T = \sum_{i=1}^{k} \sigma_i \mathbf{u_i} \mathbf{v_i}^T = A_k.$$

∎

Theorem 3.6 *For any matrix B of rank at most k*

$$\|A - A_k\|_F \le \|A - B\|_F$$

Proof Let B minimize $\|A - B\|_F^2$ among all rank k or less matrices. Let V be the space spanned by the rows of B. The dimension of V is at most k. Since B minimizes $\|A - B\|_F^2$, it must be that each row of B is the projection of the corresponding row of A onto V: Otherwise, replace the row of B with the projection of the corresponding row of A onto V. This still keeps the row space of B contained in V, and hence the rank of B is still at most k. But it reduces $\|A - B\|_F^2$, contradicting the minimality of $\|A - B\|_F$.

Since each row of B is the projection of the corresponding row of A, it follows that $\|A - B\|_F^2$ is the sum of squared distances of rows of A to V. Since A_k minimizes the sum of squared distance of rows of A to any k-dimensional subspace, from Theorem 3.1, it follows that $\|A - A_k\|_F \le \|A - B\|_F$. ∎

In addition to the Frobenius norm, there is another matrix norm of interest. Consider an $n \times d$ matrix A and a large number of vectors where for each vector x we wish to compute $A\mathbf{x}$. It takes time $O(nd)$ to compute each product $A\mathbf{x}$, but if we approximate A by $A_k = \sum_{i=1}^{k} \sigma_i \mathbf{u_i} \mathbf{v_i}^T$ and approximate $A\mathbf{x}$ by $A_k\mathbf{x}$, it requires only k dot products of d-dimensional vectors, followed by a sum of k n-dimensional vectors, and takes time $O(kd + kn)$, which is a win provided $k \ll \min(d, n)$. How is the error measured? Since $\mathbf{x}$ is unknown, the approximation needs to be good for every $\mathbf{x}$. So we take the maximum over all $\mathbf{x}$ of $|(A_k - A)\mathbf{x}|$. Since this would be infinite if $|\mathbf{x}|$ could grow without bound, we restrict the maximum to $|\mathbf{x}| \leq 1$. Formally, we define a new norm of a matrix A by

$$||A||_2 = \max_{|\mathbf{x}| \leq 1} |A\mathbf{x}|.$$

This is called the 2-norm or the spectral norm. Note that it equals $\sigma_1(A)$.

As an application consider a large database of documents that form rows of an $n \times d$ matrix A. There are d terms, and each document is a d-dimensional vector with one component for each term, which is the number of occurrences of the term in the document. We are allowed to "preprocess" A. After the preprocessing, we receive queries. Each query $\mathbf{x}$ is an d-dimensional vector that specifies how important each term is to the query. The desired answer is an n-dimensional vector that gives the similarity (dot product) of the query to each document in the database, namely $A\mathbf{x}$, the "matrix-vector" product. Query time is to be much less than preprocessing time, since the idea is that we need to answer many queries for the same database. There are many other applications where one performs many matrix vector products with the same matrix. This technique is applicable to these situations as well.

3.6. Left Singular Vectors

The left singular vectors are also pairwise orthogonal. Intuitively if $\mathbf{u_i}$ and $\mathbf{u_j}, i < j$, were not orthogonal, one would suspect that the right singular vector $\mathbf{v_j}$ had a component of $\mathbf{v_i}$, which would contradict that $\mathbf{v_i}$ and $\mathbf{v_j}$ were orthogonal. Let i be the smallest integer such that $\mathbf{u_i}$ is not orthogonal to all other $\mathbf{u_j}$. Then to prove that $\mathbf{u_i}$ and $\mathbf{u_j}$ are orthogonal, we add a small component of $\mathbf{v_j}$ to $\mathbf{v_i}$, normalize the result to be a unit vector

$$\mathbf{v'_i} = \frac{\mathbf{v_i} + \epsilon \mathbf{v_j}}{|\mathbf{v_i} + \epsilon \mathbf{v_j}|}$$

and show that $|A\mathbf{v'_i}| > |A\mathbf{v_i}|$, a contradiction.

Theorem 3.7 *The left singular vectors are pairwise orthogonal.*

Proof Let i be the smallest integer such that $\mathbf{u_i}$ is not orthogonal to some other $\mathbf{u_j}$. Without loss of generality, assume that $\mathbf{u_i}^T \mathbf{u_j} = \delta > 0$. If $\mathbf{u_i}^T \mathbf{u_j} < 0$, then just replace $\mathbf{u_i}$ with $-\mathbf{u_i}$. Clearly $j > i$, since i was selected to be the smallest such index. For $\varepsilon > 0$, let

$$\mathbf{v'_i} = \frac{\mathbf{v_i} + \epsilon \mathbf{v_j}}{|\mathbf{v_i} + \epsilon \mathbf{v_j}|}.$$

Notice that $\mathbf{v'_i}$ is a unit length vector.

$$A\mathbf{v'_i} = \frac{\sigma_i \mathbf{u_i} + \varepsilon \sigma_j \mathbf{u_j}}{\sqrt{1 + \varepsilon^2}}$$

has length at least as large as its component along $\mathbf{u_i}$ which is

$$\mathbf{u_i^T}\left(\frac{\sigma_i\mathbf{u_i} + \varepsilon\sigma_j\mathbf{u_j}}{\sqrt{1+\varepsilon^2}}\right) > \left(\sigma_i + \varepsilon\sigma_j\delta\right)\left(1 - \tfrac{\varepsilon^2}{2}\right) > \sigma_i - \tfrac{\varepsilon^2}{2}\sigma_i + \varepsilon\sigma_j\delta - \tfrac{\varepsilon^3}{2}\sigma_j\delta > \sigma_i,$$

for sufficiently small ϵ, a contradiction, since $\mathbf{v_i} + \varepsilon\mathbf{v_j}$ is orthogonal to $\mathbf{v_1}, \mathbf{v_2}, \ldots, \mathbf{v_{i-1}}$, since $j > i$ and σ_i is defined to be the maximum of $|A\mathbf{v}|$ over such vectors. ∎

Next we prove that A_k is the best rank-k, 2-norm approximation to A. We first show that the square of the 2-norm of $A - A_k$ is the square of the $(k+1)^{st}$ singular value of A. This is essentially by definition of A_k; that is, A_k represents the projections of the rows in A onto the space spanned by the top k singular vectors, and so $A - A_k$ is the remaining portion of those rows, whose top singular value will be σ_{k+1}.

Lemma 3.8 $\|A - A_k\|_2^2 = \sigma_{k+1}^2.$

Proof Let $A = \sum_{i=1}^{r} \sigma_i \mathbf{u_i}\mathbf{v_i}^T$ be the singular value decomposition of A. Then $A_k = \sum_{i=1}^{k} \sigma_i\mathbf{u_i}\mathbf{v_i}^T$ and $A - A_k = \sum_{i=k+1}^{r} \sigma_i\mathbf{u_i}\mathbf{v_i}^T$. Let $\mathbf{v}$ be the top singular vector of $A - A_k$. Express $\mathbf{v}$ as a linear combination of $\mathbf{v_1}, \mathbf{v_2}, \ldots, \mathbf{v_r}$. That is, write $\mathbf{v} = \sum_{j=1}^{r} c_j\mathbf{v_j}$. Then

$$|(A - A_k)\mathbf{v}| = \left|\sum_{i=k+1}^{r} \sigma_i\mathbf{u_i}\mathbf{v_i}^T\sum_{j=1}^{r} c_j\mathbf{v_j}\right| = \left|\sum_{i=k+1}^{r} c_i\sigma_i\mathbf{u_i}\mathbf{v_i}^T\mathbf{v_i}\right|$$

$$= \left|\sum_{i=k+1}^{r} c_i\sigma_i\mathbf{u_i}\right| = \sqrt{\sum_{i=k+1}^{r} c_i^2\sigma_i^2},$$

since the $\mathbf{u_i}$ are orthonormal. The $\mathbf{v}$ maximizing this last quantity, subject to the constraint that $|\mathbf{v}|^2 = \sum_{i=1}^{r} c_i^2 = 1$, occurs when $c_{k+1} = 1$ and the rest of the c_i are zero. Thus, $\|A - A_k\|_2^2 = \sigma_{k+1}^2$, proving the lemma. ∎

Finally, we prove that A_k is the best rank-k, 2-norm approximation to A:

Theorem 3.9 *Let A be an $n \times d$ matrix. For any matrix B of rank at most k,*

$$\|A - A_k\|_2 \leq \|A - B\|_2.$$

Proof If A is of rank k or less, the theorem is obviously true, since $\|A - A_k\|_2 = 0$. Assume that A is of rank greater than k. By Lemma 3.8, $\|A - A_k\|_2^2 = \sigma_{k+1}^2$. The null space of B, the set of vectors $\mathbf{v}$ such that $B\mathbf{v} = 0$, has dimension at least $d - k$. Let $\mathbf{v_1}, \mathbf{v_2}, \ldots, \mathbf{v_{k+1}}$ be the first $k + 1$ singular vectors of A. By a dimension argument, it follows that there exists a $\mathbf{z} \neq 0$ in

$$\text{Null}\,(B) \cap \text{Span}\,\{\mathbf{v_1}, \mathbf{v_2}, \ldots, \mathbf{v_{k+1}}\}.$$

Scale $\mathbf{z}$ to be of length 1.

$$\|A - B\|_2^2 \geq |(A - B)\,\mathbf{z}|^2.$$

Since $Bz = 0$,

$$\|A - B\|_2^2 \geq |Az|^2 .$$

Since $\mathbf{z}$ is in the Span $\{\mathbf{v}_1, \mathbf{v}_2, \ldots, \mathbf{v}_{k+1}\}$,

$$|A\mathbf{z}|^2 = \left| \sum_{i=1}^{n} \sigma_i \mathbf{u_i} \mathbf{v_i}^T \mathbf{z} \right|^2 = \sum_{i=1}^{n} \sigma_i^2 \left(\mathbf{v_i}^T \mathbf{z} \right)^2$$

$$= \sum_{i=1}^{k+1} \sigma_i^2 \left(\mathbf{v_i}^T \mathbf{z} \right)^2 \geq \sigma_{k+1}^2 \sum_{i=1}^{k+1} \left(\mathbf{v_i}^T \mathbf{z} \right)^2 = \sigma_{k+1}^2 .$$

It follows that $\|A - B\|_2^2 \geq \sigma_{k+1}^2$, proving the theorem. ∎

For a square symmetric matrix A and eigenvector $\mathbf{v}$, $A\mathbf{v} = \lambda\mathbf{v}$. We now prove the analog for singular values and vectors we discussed in the introduction.

Lemma 3.10 (**Analog of eigenvalues and eigenvectors**)

$$A\mathbf{v_i} = \sigma_i \mathbf{u_i} \text{ and } A^T \mathbf{u_i} = \sigma_i \mathbf{v_i}.$$

Proof The first equation follows from the definition of left singular vectors. For the second, note that from the SVD, we get $A^T \mathbf{u_i} = \sum_j \sigma_j \mathbf{v_j} \mathbf{u_j}^T \mathbf{u_i}$, where since the $\mathbf{u_j}$ are orthonormal, all terms in the summation are zero except for $j = i$. ∎

3.7. Power Method for Singular Value Decomposition

Computing the singular value decomposition is an important branch of numerical analysis in which there have been many sophisticated developments over a long period of time. The reader is referred to numerical analysis texts for more details. Here we present an "in-principle" method to establish that the approximate SVD of a matrix A can be computed in polynomial time. The method we present, called the *power method*, is simple and is in fact the conceptual starting point for many algorithms. Let A be a matrix whose SVD is $\sum_i \sigma_i \mathbf{u_i} \mathbf{v_i}^T$. We wish to work with a matrix that is square and symmetric. Let $B = A^T A$. By direct multiplication, using the orthogonality of the $\mathbf{u_i}$'s that was proved in Theorem 3.7,

$$B = A^T A = \left(\sum_i \sigma_i \mathbf{v_i} \mathbf{u_i}^T \right) \left(\sum_j \sigma_j \mathbf{u_j} \mathbf{v_j}^T \right)$$

$$= \sum_{i,j} \sigma_i \sigma_j \mathbf{v_i} (\mathbf{u}_i^T \cdot \mathbf{u_j}) \mathbf{v}_j^T = \sum_i \sigma_i^2 \mathbf{v_i} \mathbf{v_i}^T .$$

The matrix B is square and symmetric, and has the same left-singular and right-singular vectors. In particular, $B\mathbf{v_j} = (\sum_i \sigma_i^2 \mathbf{v_i} \mathbf{v}_i^T)\mathbf{v_j} = \sigma_j^2 \mathbf{v_j}$, so $\mathbf{v_j}$ is an eigenvector of B with eigenvalue σ_j^2. If A is itself square and symmetric, it will have the same right-singular and left-singular vectors, namely $A = \sum_i \sigma_i \mathbf{v_i} \mathbf{v_i}^T$, and computing B is unnecessary.

Now consider computing B^2.

$$B^2 = \left(\sum_i \sigma_i^2 \mathbf{v_i} \mathbf{v_i}^T \right) \left(\sum_j \sigma_j^2 \mathbf{v_j} \mathbf{v_j}^T \right) = \sum_{ij} \sigma_i^2 \sigma_j^2 \mathbf{v_i} (\mathbf{v_i}^T \mathbf{v_j}) \mathbf{v_j}^T.$$

When $i \neq j$, the dot product $\mathbf{v_i}^T \mathbf{v_j}$ is zero by orthogonality.[6] Thus, $B^2 = \sum_{i=1}^{r} \sigma_i^4 \mathbf{v_i} \mathbf{v_i}^T$. In computing the kth power of B, all the cross-product terms are zero and

$$B^k = \sum_{i=1}^{r} \sigma_i^{2k} \mathbf{v_i} \mathbf{v_i}^T.$$

If $\sigma_1 > \sigma_2$, then the first term in the summation dominates, so $B^k \to \sigma_1^{2k} \mathbf{v_1} \mathbf{v_1}^T$. This means a close estimate to $\mathbf{v_1}$ can be computed by simply taking the first column of B^k and normalizing it to a unit vector.

3.7.1. A Faster Method

A problem with the above method is that A may be a very large, sparse matrix, say a $10^8 \times 10^8$ matrix with 10^9 non-zero entries. Sparse matrices are often represented by just a list of non-zero entries, say a list of triples of the form (i, j, a_{ij}). Though A is sparse, B need not be and in the worse case may have all 10^{16} entries non-zero[7] and it is then impossible to even write down B, let alone compute the product B^2. Even if A is moderate in size, computing matrix products is costly in time. Thus, a more efficient method is needed.

Instead of computing B^k, select a random vector $\mathbf{x}$ and compute the product $B^k \mathbf{x}$. The vector $\mathbf{x}$ can be expressed in terms of the singular vectors of B augmented to a full orthonormal basis as $\mathbf{x} = \sum_{i=1}^{d} c_i \mathbf{v_i}$. Then

$$B^k \mathbf{x} \approx (\sigma_1^{2k} \mathbf{v_1} \mathbf{v_1}^T) \left(\sum_{i=1}^{d} c_i \mathbf{v_i} \right) = \sigma_1^{2k} c_1 \mathbf{v_1}.$$

Normalizing the resulting vector yields $\mathbf{v_1}$, the first singular vector of A. The way $B^k \mathbf{x}$ is computed is by a series of matrix vector products, instead of matrix products. $B^k \mathbf{x} = A^T A \ldots A^T A \mathbf{x}$, which can be computed right-to-left. This consists of $2k$ vector times sparse matrix multiplications.

To compute k singular vectors, one selects a random vector $\mathbf{r}$ and finds an orthonormal basis for the space spanned by $\mathbf{r}, A\mathbf{r}, \ldots, A^{k-1}\mathbf{r}$. Then compute A times each of the basis vectors, and find an orthonormal basis for the space spanned by the resulting vectors. Intuitively, one has applied A to a subspace rather than a single vector. One repeatedly applies A to the subspace, calculating an orthonormal basis after each application to prevent the subspace collapsing to the one-dimensional subspace spanned by the first singular vector. The process quickly converges to the first k singular vectors.

An issue occurs if there is no significant gap between the first and second singular values of a matrix. Take for example the case when there is a tie for the first singular vector and $\sigma_1 = \sigma_2$. Then, the above argument fails. We will overcome this hurdle.

---

[6] The "outer product" $\mathbf{v_i} \mathbf{v_j}^T$ is a matrix and is not zero even for $i \neq j$.
[7] E.g., suppose each entry in the first row of A is non-zero and the rest of A is zero.

Theorem 3.11 below states that even with ties, the power method converges to some vector in the span of those singular vectors corresponding to the "nearly highest" singular values. The theorem assumes it is given a vector $\mathbf{x}$, which has a component of magnitude at least δ along the first right singular vector $\mathbf{v}_1$ of A. We will see in Lemma 3.12 that a random vector satisfies this condition with fairly high probability.

Theorem 3.11 *Let A be an $n \times d$ matrix and $\mathbf{x}$ a unit length vector in $\mathbf{R}^d$ with $|\mathbf{x}^T \mathbf{v}_1| \geq \delta$, where $\delta > 0$. Let V be the space spanned by the right singular vectors of A corresponding to singular values greater than $(1 - \varepsilon)\sigma_1$. Let $\mathbf{w}$ be the unit vector after $k = \frac{\ln(1/\varepsilon\delta)}{2\varepsilon}$ iterations of the power method, namely*

$$\mathbf{w} = \frac{\left(A^T A\right)^k \mathbf{x}}{\left|\left(A^T A\right)^k \mathbf{x}\right|}.$$

Then $\mathbf{w}$ has a component of at most ε perpendicular to V.

Proof Let

$$A = \sum_{i=1}^{r} \sigma_i \mathbf{u}_i \mathbf{v}_i^T$$

be the SVD of A. If the rank of A is less than d, then for convenience complete $\{\mathbf{v}_1, \mathbf{v}_2, \ldots \mathbf{v}_r\}$ into an orthonormal basis $\{\mathbf{v}_1, \mathbf{v}_2, \ldots \mathbf{v}_d\}$ of d-space. Write $\mathbf{x}$ in the basis of the $\mathbf{v}_i$'s as

$$\mathbf{x} = \sum_{i=1}^{d} c_i \mathbf{v}_i.$$

Since $(A^T A)^k = \sum_{i=1}^{d} \sigma_i^{2k} \mathbf{v}_i \mathbf{v}_i^T$, it follows that $(A^T A)^k \mathbf{x} = \sum_{i=1}^{d} \sigma_i^{2k} c_i \mathbf{v}_i$. By hypothesis, $|c_1| \geq \delta$.

Suppose that $\sigma_1, \sigma_2, \ldots, \sigma_m$ are the singular values of A that are greater than or equal to $(1 - \varepsilon)\sigma_1$ and that $\sigma_{m+1}, \ldots, \sigma_d$ are the singular values that are less than $(1 - \varepsilon)\sigma_1$. Now,

$$|(A^T A)^k \mathbf{x}|^2 = \left| \sum_{i=1}^{d} \sigma_i^{2k} c_i \mathbf{v}_i \right|^2 = \sum_{i=1}^{d} \sigma_i^{4k} c_i^2 \geq \sigma_1^{4k} c_1^2 \geq \sigma_1^{4k} \delta^2.$$

The component of $|(A^T A)^k \mathbf{x}|^2$ perpendicular to the space V is

$$\sum_{i=m+1}^{d} \sigma_i^{4k} c_i^2 \leq (1 - \varepsilon)^{4k} \sigma_1^{4k} \sum_{i=m+1}^{d} c_i^2 \leq (1 - \varepsilon)^{4k} \sigma_1^{4k},$$

since $\sum_{i=1}^{d} c_i^2 = |\mathbf{x}| = 1$. Thus, the component of $\mathbf{w}$ perpendicular to V has squared length at most $\frac{(1-\varepsilon)^{4k}\sigma_1^{4k}}{\sigma_1^{4k}\delta^2}$ and so its length is at most

$$\frac{(1 - \varepsilon)^{2k}\sigma_1^{2k}}{\delta\sigma_1^{2k}} = \frac{(1 - \varepsilon)^{2k}}{\delta} \leq \frac{e^{-2k\varepsilon}}{\delta} = \varepsilon,$$

since $k = \frac{\ln(1/\epsilon\delta)}{2\epsilon}$. ∎

Lemma 3.12 *Let* $\mathbf{y} \in \mathbf{R}^n$ *be a random vector with the unit-variance spherical Gaussian as its probability density. Normalize y to be a unit length vector by setting* $\mathbf{x} = \mathbf{y}/|\mathbf{y}|$. *Let* $\mathbf{v}$ *be any unit length vector. Then*

$$Prob\left(|\mathbf{x}^T\mathbf{v}| \leq \frac{1}{20\sqrt{d}}\right) \leq \frac{1}{10} + 3e^{-d/96}.$$

Proof Proving for the unit length vector $\mathbf{x}$ that $\text{Prob}(|\mathbf{x}^T\mathbf{v}| \leq \frac{1}{20\sqrt{d}}) \leq \frac{1}{10} + 3e^{-d/96}$ is equivalent to proving for the unnormalized vector $\mathbf{y}$ that $\text{Prob}(|\mathbf{y}| \geq 2\sqrt{d}) \leq 3e^{-d/96}$ and $\text{Prob}(|\mathbf{y}^T\mathbf{v}| \leq \frac{1}{10}) \leq 1/10$. That $\text{Prob}(|\mathbf{y}| \geq 2\sqrt{d})$ is at most $3e^{-d/96}$ follows from Theorem 2.9 with $\sqrt{d}$ substituted for β. The probability that $|\mathbf{y}^T\mathbf{v}| \leq \frac{1}{10}$ is at most $1/10$ because $\mathbf{y}^T\mathbf{v}$ is a random, zero mean, unit-variance Gaussian with density at most $1/\sqrt{2\pi} \leq 1/2$ in the interval $[-1/10, 1/10]$, so the integral of the Gaussian over the interval is at most $1/10$. ∎

3.8. Singular Vectors and Eigenvectors

For a square matrix B, if $B\mathbf{x} = \lambda\mathbf{x}$, then $\mathbf{x}$ is an *eigenvector* of B and λ is the corresponding *eigenvalue*. We saw in Section 3.7, if $B = A^T A$, then the right singular vectors $\mathbf{v_j}$ of A are eigenvectors of B with eigenvalues σ_j^2. The same argument shows that the left singular vectors $\mathbf{u_j}$ of A are eigenvectors of AA^T with eigenvalues σ_j^2.

The matrix $B = A^T A$ has the property that for any vector $\mathbf{x}, \mathbf{x}^T B\mathbf{x} \geq 0$. This is because $B = \sum_i \sigma_i^2 \mathbf{v_i}\mathbf{v_i}^T$ and for any $\mathbf{x}$, $\mathbf{x}^T\mathbf{v_i}\mathbf{v_i}^T\mathbf{x} = (\mathbf{x}^T\mathbf{v_i})^2 \geq 0$. A matrix B with the property that $\mathbf{x}^T B\mathbf{x} \geq 0$ for all $\mathbf{x}$ is called *positive semi-definite*. Every matrix of the form $A^T A$ is positive semi-definite. In the other direction, any positive semi-definite matrix B can be decomposed into a product $A^T A$, and so its eigenvalue decomposition can be obtained from the singular value decomposition of A. The interested reader should consult a linear algebra book.

3.9. Applications of Singular Value Decomposition

3.9.1. Centering Data

Singular value decomposition is used in many applications, and for some of these applications it is essential to first center the data by subtracting the centroid of the data from each data point.[8] If you are interested in the statistics of the data and how it varies in relationship to its mean, then you would center the data. On the other hand, if you are interested in finding the best low-rank approximation to a matrix, then you do not center the data. The issue is whether you are finding the best-fitting subspace or the best-fitting affine space. In the latter case you first center the data and then find the best-fitting subspace. See Figure 3.3.

We first show that the line minimizing the sum of squared distances to a set of points, if not restricted to go through the origin, must pass through the centroid of the points. This implies that if the centroid is subtracted from each data point, such a

---

[8] The centroid of a set of points is the coordinate-wise average of the points.

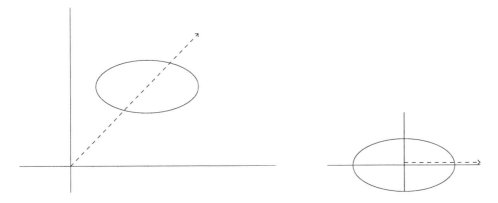

Figure 3.3: If one wants statistical information relative to the mean of the data, one needs to center the data. If one wants the best low-rank approximation, one would not center the data.

line will pass through the origin. The best-fit line can be generalized to k dimensional "planes." The operation of subtracting the centroid from all data points is useful in other contexts as well. We give it the name *centering data*.

Lemma 3.13 *The best-fit line (minimizing the sum of perpendicular distances squared) of a set of data points must pass through the centroid of the points.*

Proof Subtract the centroid from each data point so that the centroid is $\mathbf{0}$. After centering the data, let ℓ be the best-fit line and assume for contradiction that ℓ does not pass through the origin. The line ℓ can be written as $\{\mathbf{a} + \lambda \mathbf{v} | \lambda \in \mathbf{R}\}$, where $\mathbf{a}$ is the closest point to $\mathbf{0}$ on ℓ and $\mathbf{v}$ is a unit length vector in the direction of ℓ, which is perpendicular to $\mathbf{a}$. For a data point $\mathbf{a_i}$, let $dist(\mathbf{a_i}, \ell)$ denote its perpendicular distance to ℓ. By the Pythagorean theorem, we have $|\mathbf{a_i} - \mathbf{a}|^2 = dist(\mathbf{a_i}, \ell)^2 + (\mathbf{v} \cdot \mathbf{a_i})^2$, or equivalently, $dist(\mathbf{a_i}, \ell)^2 = |\mathbf{a_i} - \mathbf{a}|^2 - (\mathbf{v} \cdot \mathbf{a_i})^2$. Summing over all data points:

$$\sum_{i=1}^{n} dist(\mathbf{a_i}, \ell)^2 = \sum_{i=1}^{n} \left(|\mathbf{a_i} - \mathbf{a}|^2 - (\mathbf{v} \cdot \mathbf{a_i})^2 \right) = \sum_{i=1}^{n} \left(|\mathbf{a_i}|^2 + |\mathbf{a}|^2 - 2\mathbf{a_i} \cdot \mathbf{a} - (\mathbf{v} \cdot \mathbf{a_i})^2 \right)$$

$$= \sum_{i=1}^{n} |\mathbf{a_i}|^2 + n|\mathbf{a}|^2 - 2\mathbf{a} \cdot \left(\sum_i \mathbf{a_i} \right) - \sum_{i=1}^{n} (\mathbf{v} \cdot \mathbf{a_i})^2$$

$$= \sum_i |\mathbf{a_i}|^2 + n|\mathbf{a}|^2 - \sum_i (\mathbf{v} \cdot \mathbf{a_i})^2,$$

where we used the fact that since the centroid is $\mathbf{0}$, $\sum_i \mathbf{a_i} = \mathbf{0}$. The above expression is minimized when $\mathbf{a} = \mathbf{0}$, so the line $\ell' = \{\lambda \mathbf{v} : \lambda \in \mathbf{R}\}$ through the origin is a better fit than ℓ, contradicting ℓ being the best-fit line. ∎

A statement analogous to Lemma 3.13 holds for higher-dimensional objects. Define an *affine space* as a subspace translated by a vector. So an affine space is a set of the form

$$\left\{ \mathbf{v_0} + \sum_{i=1}^{k} c_i \mathbf{v_i} | c_1, c_2, \ldots, c_k \in \mathbf{R} \right\}.$$

Here, $\mathbf{v}_0$ is the translation and $\mathbf{v}_1, \mathbf{v}_2, \ldots, \mathbf{v}_k$ form an orthonormal basis for the subspace.

Lemma 3.14 *The k-dimensional affine space that minimizes the sum of squared perpendicular distances to the data points must pass through the centroid of the points.*

Proof We only give a brief idea of the proof, which is similar to the previous lemma. Instead of $(\mathbf{v} \cdot \mathbf{a_i})^2$, we will now have $\sum_{j=1}^{k}(\mathbf{v_j} \cdot \mathbf{a_i})^2$, where the $\mathbf{v_j}, j = 1, 2, \ldots, k$ are an orthonormal basis of the subspace through the origin parallel to the affine space. ∎

3.9.2. Principal Component Analysis

The traditional use of SVD is in principal component analysis (PCA). PCA is illustrated by a movie recommendation setting where there are n customers and d movies. Let matrix A with elements a_{ij} represent the amount that customer i likes movie j. One hypothesizes that there are only k underlying basic factors that determine how much a given customer will like a given movie, where k is much smaller than n or d. For example, these could be the amount of comedy, drama, and action, the novelty of the story, etc. Each movie can be described as a k-dimensional vector indicating how much of these basic factors the movie has, and each customer can be described as a k-dimensional vector indicating how important each of these basic factors is to that customer. The dot product of these two vectors is hypothesized to determine how much that customer will like that movie. In particular, this means that the $n \times d$ matrix A can be expressed as the product of an $n \times k$ matrix U describing the customers and a $k \times d$ matrix V describing the movies (see Figure 3.4). Finding the best rank-k approximation A_k by SVD gives such a U and V. One twist is that A may not be exactly equal to UV, in which case $A - UV$ is treated as noise. Another issue is that SVD gives a factorization with negative entries. Nonnegative matrix factorization (NMF) is more appropriate in some contexts where we want to keep entries nonnegative. NMF is discussed in Chapter 9.

In the above setting, A was available fully, and we wished to find U and V to identify the basic factors. However, in a case such as movie recommendations, each

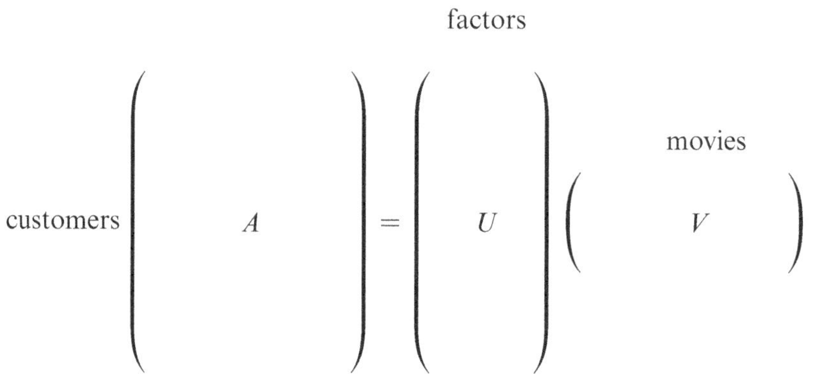

Figure 3.4: Customer-movie data

customer may have seen only a small fraction of the movies, so it may be more natural to assume that we are given just a few elements of A and wish to estimate A. If A were an arbitrary matrix of size $n \times d$, this would require $\Omega(nd)$ pieces of information and cannot be done with a few entries. But again, hypothesize that A is a small-rank matrix with added noise. If now we also assume that the given entries are randomly drawn according to some known distribution, then there is a possibility that SVD can be used to estimate the whole of A. This area is called *collaborative filtering* and one of its uses is to recommend movies or to target an ad to a customer based on one or two purchases. We do not describe it here.

3.9.3. Clustering a Mixture of Spherical Gaussians

Clustering is the task of partitioning a set of points into k subsets or clusters where each cluster consists of nearby points. Different definitions of the quality of a clustering lead to different solutions. Clustering is an important area that we will study in detail in Chapter 7. Here we will see how to solve a particular clustering problem using singular value decomposition.

Mathematical formulations of clustering tend to have the property that finding the highest-quality solution to a given set of data is NP-hard. One way around this is to assume stochastic models of input data and devise algorithms to cluster data generated by such models. Mixture models are a very important class of stochastic models. A mixture is a probability density or distribution that is the weighted sum of simple component probability densities. It is of the form

$$f = w_1 p_1 + w_2 p_2 + \cdots + w_k p_k,$$

where $p_1, p_2, \ldots, p_k$ are the basic probability densities and $w_1, w_2, \ldots, w_k$ are positive real numbers called *mixture weights* that add up to one. Clearly, f is a probability density and integrates to one.

The *model-fitting problem* is to fit a mixture of k basic densities to n independent, identically distributed samples, each sample drawn according to the same mixture distribution f. The class of basic densities is known, but various parameters such as their means and the component weights of the mixture are not. Here, we deal with the case where the basic densities are all spherical Gaussians. There are two equivalent ways of thinking of the hidden sample generation process:

1. Pick each sample according to the density f on $\mathbf{R}^d$.
2. Pick a random i from $\{1, 2, \ldots, k\}$ where probability of picking i is w_i. Then, pick a sample according to the density p_i.

One approach to the model-fitting problem is to break it into two subproblems:

1. First, cluster the set of samples into k clusters $C_1, C_2, \ldots, C_k$, where C_i is the set of samples generated according to p_i (see (2) above) by the hidden generation process.
2. Then fit a single Gaussian distribution to each cluster of sample points.

The second problem is relatively easier, and indeed we saw the solution in Chapter 2, where we showed that taking the empirical mean (the mean of the sample) and the empirical standard deviation gives us the best-fit Gaussian. The first problem is harder, and this is what we discuss here.

If the component Gaussians in the mixture have their centers very close together, then the clustering problem is unresolvable. In the limiting case where a pair of component densities are the same, there is no way to distinguish between them. What condition on the inter-center separation will guarantee unambiguous clustering? First, by looking at one-dimensional examples, it is clear that this separation should be measured in units of the standard deviation, since the density is a function of the number of standard deviation from the mean. In one dimension, if two Gaussians have inter-center separation at least six times the maximum of their standard deviations, then they hardly overlap. This is summarized in the question: How many standard deviations apart are the means? In one dimension, if the answer is at least six, we can easily tell the Gaussians apart. What is the analog of this in higher dimensions?

We discussed in Chapter 2 distances between two sample points from the same Gaussian as well the distance between two sample points from two different Gaussians. Recall from that discussion that:

- If $\mathbf{x}$ and $\mathbf{y}$ are two independent samples from the same spherical Gaussian with standard deviation[9] σ, then

$$|\mathbf{x} - \mathbf{y}|^2 \approx 2(\sqrt{d} \pm O(1))^2 \sigma^2.$$

- If $\mathbf{x}$ and $\mathbf{y}$ are samples from different spherical Gaussians each of standard deviation σ and means separated by distance Δ, then

$$|\mathbf{x} - \mathbf{y}|^2 \approx 2(\sqrt{d} \pm O(1))^2 \sigma^2 + \Delta^2.$$

To ensure that points from the same Gaussian are closer to each other than points from different Gaussians, we need

$$2(\sqrt{d} - O(1))^2 \sigma^2 + \Delta^2 > 2(\sqrt{d} + O(1))^2 \sigma^2.$$

Expanding the squa res, the high-order term $2d$ cancels and we need that

$$\Delta > cd^{1/4}$$

for some constant c. While this was not a completely rigorous argument, it can be used to show that a distance-based clustering approach (see Chapter 2 for an example) requires an inter-mean separation of at least $cd^{1/4}$ standard deviations to succeed, thus unfortunately not keeping with mnemonic of a constant number of standard deviations separation of the means. Here, indeed, we will show that $\Omega(1)$ standard deviations suffice provided the number k of Gaussians is $O(1)$.

The central idea is the following. Suppose we can find the subspace spanned by the k centers and project the sample points to this subspace. The projection of a spherical Gaussian with standard deviation σ remains a spherical Gaussian with standard deviation σ (Lemma 3.15). In the projection, the inter-center separation remains the same. So in the projection, the Gaussians are distinct provided the inter-center separation in the whole space is at least $ck^{1/4}\sigma$, which is less than $cd^{1/4}\sigma$

---

[9]Since a spherical Gaussian has the same standard deviation in every direction, we call it the *standard deviation of the Gaussian.*

for $k \ll d$. Interestingly, we will see that the subspace spanned by the k-centers is essentially the best-fit k-dimensional subspace that can be found by singular value decomposition.

Lemma 3.15 *Suppose p is a d-dimensional spherical Gaussian with center $\boldsymbol{\mu}$ and standard deviation σ. The density of p projected onto a k-dimensional subspace V is a spherical Gaussian with the same standard deviation.*

Proof Rotate the coordinate system so V is spanned by the first k coordinate vectors. The Gaussian remains spherical with standard deviation σ, although the coordinates of its center have changed. For a point $\mathbf{x} = (x_1, x_2, \ldots, x_d)$, we will use the notation $\mathbf{x}' = (x_1, x_2, \ldots x_k)$ and $\mathbf{x}'' = (x_{k+1}, x_{k+2}, \ldots, x_n)$. The density of the projected Gaussian at the point $(x_1, x_2, \ldots, x_k)$ is

$$ce^{-\frac{|\mathbf{x}'-\boldsymbol{\mu}'|^2}{2\sigma^2}} \int\limits_{\mathbf{x}''} e^{-\frac{|\mathbf{x}''-\boldsymbol{\mu}''|^2}{2\sigma^2}} \, d\mathbf{x}'' = c'e^{-\frac{|\mathbf{x}'-\boldsymbol{\mu}'|^2}{2\sigma^2}} .$$

This implies the lemma. ∎

We now show that the top k singular vectors produced by the SVD span the space of the k centers. First, we extend the notion of best fit to probability distributions. Then we show that for a single spherical Gaussian whose center is not the origin, the best-fit one-dimensional subspace is the line though the center of the Gaussian and the origin. Next, we show that the best-fit k-dimensional subspace for a single Gaussian whose center is not the origin is any k-dimensional subspace containing the line through the Gaussian's center and the origin. Finally, for k spherical Gaussians, the best-fit k-dimensional subspace is the subspace containing their centers. Thus, the SVD finds the subspace that contains the centers (see Figure 3.5).

Recall that for a set of points, the best-fit line is the line passing through the origin that maximizes the sum of squared lengths of the projections of the points onto the line. We extend this definition to probability densities instead of a set of points.

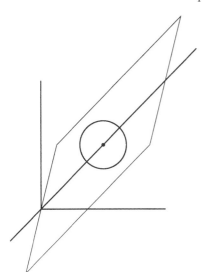

1. The best fit 1-dimension subspace to a spherical Gaussian is the line through its center and the origin.
2. Any k-dimensional subspace containing the line is a best fit k-dimensional subspace for the Gaussian.
3. The best fit k-dimensional subspace for k spherical Gaussians is the subspace containing their centers.

Figure 3.5: Best fit subspace to a spherical Gaussian.

Definition 3.1 *If p is a probability density in d space, the best-fit line for p is the line in the $\mathbf{v}_1$ direction where*

$$\mathbf{v}_1 = \arg\max_{|\mathbf{v}|=1} \ E_{\mathbf{x}\sim p}\left[(\mathbf{v}^T\mathbf{x})^2\right].$$

For a spherical Gaussian centered at the origin, it is easy to see that any line passing through the origin is a best-fit line. Our next lemma shows that the best-fit line for a spherical Gaussian centered at $\boldsymbol{\mu} \neq 0$ is the line passing through $\boldsymbol{\mu}$ and the origin.

Lemma 3.16 *Let the probability density p be a spherical Gaussian with center $\boldsymbol{\mu} \neq 0$. The unique best-fit one-dimensional subspace is the line passing through $\boldsymbol{\mu}$ and the origin. If $\boldsymbol{\mu} = 0$, then any line through the origin is a best-fit line.*

Proof For a randomly chosen $\mathbf{x}$ (according to p) and a fixed unit length vector $\mathbf{v}$,

$$
\begin{aligned}
E_{\mathbf{x}\sim p}\left[(\mathbf{v}^T\mathbf{x})^2\right] &= E_{\mathbf{x}\sim p}\left[vv^T\,(\mathbf{x}-\boldsymbol{\mu}) + \mathbf{v}^T\boldsymbol{\mu})^2\right] \\
&= E_{\mathbf{x}\sim p}\left[(\mathbf{v}^T\,(\mathbf{x}-\boldsymbol{\mu}))^2 + 2(\mathbf{v}^T\boldsymbol{\mu})(\mathbf{v}^T\,(\mathbf{x}-\boldsymbol{\mu})) + (\mathbf{v}^T\boldsymbol{\mu})^2\right] \\
&= E_{\mathbf{x}\sim p}\left[(\mathbf{v}^T\,(\mathbf{x}-\boldsymbol{\mu}))^2\right] + 2(\mathbf{v}^T\boldsymbol{\mu})E\left[\mathbf{v}^T\,(\mathbf{x}-\boldsymbol{\mu})\right] + (\mathbf{v}^T\boldsymbol{\mu})^2 \\
&= E_{\mathbf{x}\sim p}\left[(\mathbf{v}^T\,(\mathbf{x}-\boldsymbol{\mu}))^2\right] + (\mathbf{v}^T\boldsymbol{\mu})^2 \\
&= \sigma^2 + (\mathbf{v}^T\boldsymbol{\mu})^2
\end{aligned}
$$

where the fourth line follows from the fact that $E[\mathbf{v}^T(\mathbf{x}-\boldsymbol{\mu})] = 0$, and the fifth line follows from the fact that $E[(\mathbf{v}^T(\mathbf{x}-\boldsymbol{\mu}))^2]$ is the variance in the direction $\mathbf{v}$. The best-fit line $\mathbf{v}$ maximizes $E_{\mathbf{x}\sim p}[(\mathbf{v}^T\mathbf{x})^2]$ and therefore maximizes $(\mathbf{v}^T\boldsymbol{\mu})^2$. This is maximized when $\mathbf{v}$ is aligned with the center $\boldsymbol{\mu}$. To see uniqueness, just note that if $\boldsymbol{\mu} \neq 0$, then $\mathbf{v}^T\boldsymbol{\mu}$ is strictly less when $\mathbf{v}$ is not aligned with the center. ∎

We now extend Definition 3.1 to k-dimensional subspaces.

Definition 3.2 *If p is a probability density in d-space then the best-fit k-dimensional subspace V_k is*

$$V_k = \operatorname*{argmax}_{\substack{V \\ dim(V)=k}} E_{\mathbf{x}\sim p}\left(|\operatorname{proj}(\mathbf{x}, V)|^2\right),$$

where proj(x, V) is the orthogonal projection of x onto V.

Lemma 3.17 *For a spherical Gaussian with center $\boldsymbol{\mu}$, a k-dimensional subspace is a best-fit subspace if and only if it contains $\boldsymbol{\mu}$.*

Proof If $\boldsymbol{\mu} = \mathbf{0}$, then by symmetry any k-dimensional subspace is a best-fit subspace. If $\boldsymbol{\mu} \neq \mathbf{0}$, then the best-fit line must pass through $\boldsymbol{\mu}$ by Lemma 3.16. Now, as in the greedy algorithm for finding subsequent singular vectors, we would project perpendicular to the first singular vector. But after the projection, the mean of the Gaussian becomes $\mathbf{0}$, and any vectors will do as subsequent best-fit directions. ∎

This leads to the following theorem.

Theorem 3.18 *If p is a mixture of k spherical Gaussians, then the best-fit k-dimensional subspace contains the centers. In particular, if the means of the Gaussians are linearly independent, the space spanned by them is the unique best-fit k-dimensional subspace.*

Proof Let p be the mixture $w_1 p_1 + w_2 p_2 + \cdots + w_k p_k$. Let V be any subspace of dimension k or less. Then,

$$\mathop{E}_{\mathbf{x} \sim p} \left(|\mathrm{proj}(\mathbf{x}, V)|^2 \right) = \sum_{i=1}^{k} w_i \mathop{E}_{\mathbf{x} \sim p_i} \left(|\mathrm{proj}(\mathbf{x}, V)|^2 \right).$$

If V contains the centers of the densities p_i, by Lemma 3.17, each term in the summation is individually maximized, which implies the entire summation is maximized, proving the theorem. ∎

For an infinite set of points drawn according to the mixture, the k-dimensional SVD subspace gives exactly the space of the centers. In reality, we have only a large number of samples drawn according to the mixture. However, it is intuitively clear that as the number of samples increases, the set of sample points will approximate the probability density, and so the SVD subspace of the sample will be close to the space spanned by the centers. The details of how close it gets as a function of the number of samples are technical, and we do not carry this out here.

3.9.4. Ranking Documents and Web Pages

An important task for a document collection is to rank the documents according to their intrinsic relevance to the collection. A good candidate definition of "intrinsic relevance" is a document's projection onto the best-fit direction for that collection, namely the top left-singular vector of the term-document matrix. An intuitive reason for this is that this direction has the maximum sum of squared projections of the collection and so can be thought of as a synthetic term-document vector best representing the document collection.

Ranking in order of the projection of each document's term vector along the best-fit direction has a nice interpretation in terms of the power method. For this, we consider a different example, that of the web with hypertext links. The World Wide Web can be represented by a directed graph whose nodes correspond to web pages and directed edges to hypertext links between pages. Some web pages, called *authorities*, are the most prominent sources for information on a given topic. Other pages, called *hubs*, are ones that identify the authorities on a topic. Authority pages are pointed to by many hub pages and hub pages point to many authorities. One is led to what seems like a circular definition: a hub is a page that points to many authorities and an authority is a page that is pointed to by many hubs.

One would like to assign hub weights and authority weights to each node of the web. If there are n nodes, the hub weights form an n-dimensional vector $\mathbf{u}$ and the authority weights form an n-dimensional vector $\mathbf{v}$. Suppose A is the adjacency matrix representing the directed graph. Here a_{ij} is 1 if there is a hypertext link from page i to page j and 0 otherwise. Given hub vector $\mathbf{u}$, the authority vector $\mathbf{v}$ could be computed by the formula

$$v_j \propto \sum_{i=1}^{d} u_i a_{ij},$$

since the right hand side is the sum of the hub weights of all the nodes that point to node j. In matrix terms,

$$\mathbf{v} = A^T \mathbf{u}/|A^T \mathbf{u}|.$$

Similarly, given an authority vector $\mathbf{v}$, the hub vector $\mathbf{u}$ could be computed by $\mathbf{u} = A\mathbf{v}/|A\mathbf{v}|$. Of course, at the start, we have neither vector. But the above discussion suggests a power iteration. Start with any $\mathbf{v}$. Set $\mathbf{u} = A\mathbf{v}$, then set $\mathbf{v} = A^T\mathbf{u}$, then renormalize and repeat the process. We know from the power method that this converges to the left-singular and right-singular vectors. So after sufficiently many iterations, we may use the left vector $\mathbf{u}$ as the hub weights vector and project each column of A onto this direction and rank columns (authorities) in order of this projection. But the projections just form the vector $A^T\mathbf{u}$ that equals a multiple of $\mathbf{v}$. So we can just rank by order of the v_j. This is the basis of an algorithm called the HITS algorithm, which was one of the early proposals for ranking web pages.

A different ranking called *pagerank* is widely used. It is based on a random walk on the graph described above. We will study random walks in detail in Chapter 4.

3.9.5. An Illustrative Application of SVD

A deep neural network in which inputs images are classified by category such as cat, dog, or car maps an image to an activation space. The dimension of the activation space might be 4,000, but the set of cat images might be mapped to a much lower-dimensional manifold. To determine the dimension of the cat manifold, we could construct a tangent subspace at an activation vector for a cat image. However, we only have 1,000 cat images and they are spread far apart in the activation space. We need a large number of cat activation vectors close to each original cat activation vector to determine the dimension of the tangent subspace. To do this we want to slightly modify each cat image to get many images that are close to the original. One way to do this is to do a singular value decomposition of an image and zero out a few very small singular values. If the image is 1,000 by 1,000, there will be 1,000 singular values. The smallest 100 will be essentially zero, and zeroing out a subset of them should not change the image much and produce images whose activation vectors are very close. Since there are $\binom{100}{10}$ subsets of 10 singular values, we can generate, say, 10,000 such images by zeroing out 10 singular values. Given the corresponding activation vectors, we can form a matrix of activation vectors and determine the rank of the matrix, which should give the dimension of the tangent subspace to the original cat activation vector.

To determine the rank of the matrix of 10,000 activation vectors, we again do a singular value decomposition. To determine the actual rank, we need to determine a cutoff point below which we conclude the remaining singular values are noise.

We might consider a sufficient number of the largest singular values so that their sum of squares is 95% of the square of the Frobenius norm of the matrix or look to see where there is a sharp drop in the singular values.

3.9.6. An Application of SVD to a Discrete Optimization Problem

In clustering a mixture of Gaussians, SVD was used as a dimension reduction technique. It found a k-dimensional subspace (the space of centers) of a d-dimensional space and made the Gaussian clustering problem easier by projecting the data to the subspace. Here, instead of fitting a model to data, we consider an optimization problem where applying dimension reduction makes the problem easier. The use of SVD to solve discrete optimization problems is a relatively new subject with many applications. We start with an important NP-hard problem, the maximum cut problem for a directed graph $G(V, E)$.

The maximum cut problem is to partition the nodes of an n-node directed graph into two subsets S and $\bar{S}$ so that the number of edges from S to $\bar{S}$ is maximized. Let A be the adjacency matrix of the graph. With each vertex i, associate an indicator variable x_i. The variable x_i will be set to 1 for $i \in S$ and 0 for $i \in \bar{S}$. The vector $\mathbf{x} = (x_1, x_2, \ldots, x_n)$ is unknown, and we are trying to find it or, equivalently, the cut, so as to maximize the number of edges across the cut. The number of edges across the cut is precisely

$$\sum_{i,j} x_i(1 - x_j)a_{ij}.$$

Thus, the maximum cut problem can be posed as the optimization problem:

$$\text{Maximize} \sum_{i,j} x_i(1 - x_j)a_{ij} \quad \text{subject to } x_i \in \{0, 1\}.$$

In matrix notation,

$$\sum_{i,j} x_i(1 - x_j)a_{ij} = \mathbf{x}^T A(\mathbf{1} - \mathbf{x}),$$

where $\mathbf{1}$ denotes the vector of all 1's. So, the problem can be restated as

$$\text{Maximize } \mathbf{x}^T A(\mathbf{1} - \mathbf{x}) \quad \text{subject to } x_i \in \{0, 1\}. \tag{3.1}$$

This problem is NP-hard. However we will see that for dense graphs – that is, graphs with $\Omega(n^2)$ edges and therefore whose optimal solution has size $\Omega(n^2)$[10] – we can use the SVD to find a near-optimal solution in polynomial time. To do so we will begin by computing the SVD of A and replacing A by $A_k = \sum_{i=1}^{k} \sigma_i \mathbf{u_i v_i}^T$ in (3.1) to get

$$\text{Maximize } \mathbf{x}^T A_k(\mathbf{1} - \mathbf{x}) \quad \text{subject to } x_i \in \{0, 1\}. \tag{3.2}$$

Note that the matrix A_k is no longer a 0-1 adjacency matrix.

We will show that:

1. For each 0-1 vector $\mathbf{x}$, $\mathbf{x}^T A_k(\mathbf{1} - \mathbf{x})$ and $\mathbf{x}^T A(\mathbf{1} - \mathbf{x})$ differ by at most $\frac{n^2}{\sqrt{k+1}}$. Thus, the maxima in (3.1) and (3.2) differ by at most this amount.

---

[10] Any graph of m edges has a cut of size at least $m/2$. This can be seen by noting that the expected size of the cut for a *random* $\mathbf{x} \in \{0, 1\}^n$ is exactly $m/2$.

2. A near-optimal $\mathbf{x}$ for (3.2) can be found in time $n^{O(k)}$ by exploiting the low rank of A_k, which is polynomial time for constant k. By Item 1 this is near optimal for (3.1) where near optimal means with additive error of at most $\frac{n^2}{\sqrt{k+1}}$.

First, we prove Item 1. Since $\mathbf{x}$ and $\mathbf{1} - \mathbf{x}$ are 0-1 n-vectors, each has length at most $\sqrt{n}$. By the definition of the 2-norm, $|(A - A_k)(\mathbf{1} - \mathbf{x})| \leq \sqrt{n}||A - A_k||_2$. Now since $\mathbf{x}^T(A - A_k)(\mathbf{1} - \mathbf{x})$ is the dot product of the vector $\mathbf{x}$ with the vector $(A - A_k)(\mathbf{1} - \mathbf{x})$,

$$|\mathbf{x}^T(A - A_k)(\mathbf{1} - \mathbf{x})| \leq n||A - A_k||_2.$$

By Lemma 3.8, $||A - A_k||_2 = \sigma_{k+1}(A)$. The inequalities,

$$(k + 1)\sigma_{k+1}^2 \leq \sigma_1^2 + \sigma_2^2 + \cdots \sigma_{k+1}^2 \leq ||A||_F^2 = \sum_{i,j} a_{ij}^2 \leq n^2$$

imply that $\sigma_{k+1}^2 \leq \frac{n^2}{k+1}$, and hence $||A - A_k||_2 \leq \frac{n}{\sqrt{k+1}}$, proving Item 1.

Next we focus on Item 2. It is instructive to look at the special case when $k=1$ and A is approximated by the rank one matrix A_1. An even more special case when the left and right-singular vectors $\mathbf{u}$ and $\mathbf{v}$ are identical is already NP-hard to solve exactly because it subsumes the problem of whether for a set of n integers, $\{a_1, a_2, \ldots, a_n\}$, there is a partition into two subsets whose sums are equal. However, for that problem, there is an efficient dynamic programming algorithm that finds a near-optimal solution. We will build on that idea for the general rank k problem.

For Item 2, we want to maximize $\sum_{i=1}^k \sigma_i(\mathbf{x}^T\mathbf{u_i})(\mathbf{v_i}^T(\mathbf{1} - \mathbf{x}))$ over 0-1 vectors $\mathbf{x}$. A piece of notation will be useful. For any $S \subseteq \{1, 2, \ldots n\}$, write $\mathbf{u_i}(S)$ for the sum of coordinates of the vector $\mathbf{u_i}$ corresponding to elements in the set S, that is, $\mathbf{u}_i(S) = \sum_{j \in S} u_{ij}$, and similarly for $\mathbf{v_i}$. We will find S to maximize $\sum_{i=1}^k \sigma_i\mathbf{u}_i(S)\mathbf{v}_i(\bar{S})$ using dynamic programming.

For a subset S of $\{1, 2, \ldots, n\}$, define the $2k$-dimensional vector,

$$\mathbf{w}(S) = \big(\mathbf{u_1}(S), \mathbf{v_1}(\bar{S}), \mathbf{u_2}(S), \mathbf{v_2}(\bar{S}), \ldots, \mathbf{u_k}(S), \mathbf{v_k}(\bar{S})\big).$$

If we had the list of all such vectors, we could find $\sum_{i=1}^k \sigma_i\mathbf{u}_i(S)\mathbf{v}_i(\bar{S})$ for each of them and take the maximum. There are 2^n subsets S, but several S could have the same $\mathbf{w}(S)$, and in that case it suffices to list just one of them. Round each coordinate of each $\mathbf{u_i}$ to the nearest integer multiple of $\frac{1}{nk^2}$. Call the rounded vector $\tilde{\mathbf{u}}_i$. Similarly obtain $\tilde{\mathbf{v}}_i$. Let $\tilde{\mathbf{w}}(S)$ denote the vector $(\tilde{\mathbf{u}}_1(S), \tilde{\mathbf{v}}_1(\bar{S}), \tilde{\mathbf{u}}_2(S), \tilde{\mathbf{v}}_2(\bar{S}), \ldots, \tilde{\mathbf{u}}_k(S), \tilde{\mathbf{v}}_k(\bar{S}))$. We will construct a list of all possible values of the vector $\tilde{\mathbf{w}}(S)$. Again, if several different S's lead to the same vector $\tilde{\mathbf{w}}(S)$, we will keep only one copy on the list. The list will be constructed by dynamic programming. For the recursive step, assume we already have a list of all such vectors for $S \subseteq \{1, 2, \ldots, i\}$ and wish to construct the list for $S \subseteq \{1, 2, \ldots, i + 1\}$. Each $S \subseteq \{1, 2, \ldots, i\}$ leads to two possible $S' \subseteq \{1, 2, \ldots, i + 1\}$, namely S and $S \cup \{i + 1\}$. In the first case, the vector $\tilde{\mathbf{w}}(S') = (\tilde{\mathbf{u}}_1(S), \tilde{\mathbf{v}}_1(\bar{S}) + \tilde{v}_{1,i+1}, \tilde{\mathbf{u}}_2(S), \tilde{\mathbf{v}}_2(\bar{S}) + \tilde{v}_{2,i+1}, \ldots, \ldots)$. In the second case, it is $\tilde{\mathbf{w}}(S') = (\tilde{\mathbf{u}}_1(S) + \tilde{u}_{1,i+1}, \tilde{\mathbf{v}}_1(\bar{S}), \tilde{\mathbf{u}}_2(S) + \tilde{u}_{2,i+1}, \tilde{\mathbf{v}}_2(\bar{S}), \ldots, \ldots)$. We put in these two vectors for each vector in the previous list. Then, crucially, we prune – i.e., eliminate duplicates.

Assume that k is constant. Now, we show that the error is at most $\frac{n^2}{\sqrt{k+1}}$ as claimed. Since $\mathbf{u}_i$ and $\mathbf{v}_i$ are unit length vectors, $|\mathbf{u}_i(S)|, |\mathbf{v}_i(\bar{S})| \leq \sqrt{n}$. Also $|\tilde{\mathbf{u}}_i(S) - \mathbf{u}_i(S)| \leq \frac{n}{nk^2} = \frac{1}{k^2}$ and similarly for $\mathbf{v}_i$. To bound the error, we use an elementary fact: if a and b are reals with $|a|, |b| \leq M$ and we estimate a by a' and b by b' so that $|a-a'|, |b-b'| \leq \delta \leq M$, then $a'b'$ is an estimate of ab in the sense

$$|ab - a'b'| = |a(b - b') + b'(a - a')| \leq |a||b - b'| + (|b| + |b - b'|)|a - a'| \leq 3M\delta.$$

Using this,

$$\left| \sum_{i=1}^{k} \sigma_i \tilde{\mathbf{u}}_i(S) \tilde{\mathbf{v}}_i(\bar{S}) \quad - \quad \sum_{i=1}^{k} \sigma_i \mathbf{u}_i(S) \mathbf{v}_i(S) \right| \leq 3k\sigma_1 \sqrt{n}/k^2 \leq 3n^{3/2}/k \leq n^2/k,$$

and this meets the claimed error bound.

Next, we show that the running time is polynomially bounded. First, $|\tilde{\mathbf{u}}_i(S)|$, $|\tilde{\mathbf{v}}_i(S)| \leq 2\sqrt{n}$. Since $\tilde{\mathbf{u}}_i(S)$ and $\tilde{\mathbf{v}}_i(S)$ are all integer multiples of $1/(nk^2)$, there are at most $2n^{3/2}k^2$ possible values of $\tilde{\mathbf{u}}_i(S)$ and $\tilde{\mathbf{v}}_i(S)$ from which it follows that the list of $\tilde{\mathbf{w}}(S)$ never gets larger than $(2n^{3/2}k^2)^{2k}$, which for fixed k is polynomially bounded.

We summarize what we have accomplished.

Theorem 3.19 *Given a directed graph $G(V, E)$, a cut of size at least the maximum cut minus $O\left(\frac{n^2}{\sqrt{k}}\right)$ can be computed in time polynomial in n for any fixed k.*

Note that achieving the same accuracy in time polynomial in n and k would give an exact max cut in polynomial time.

3.10. Bibliographic Notes

Singular value decomposition is fundamental to numerical analysis and linear algebra. There are many texts on these subjects, and the interested reader may want to study these. A good reference is [GvL96]. The material on clustering a mixture of Gaussians in Section 3.9.3 is from [VW02]. Modeling data with a mixture of Gaussians is a standard tool in statistics. Several well-known heuristics like the expectation-minimization algorithm are used to learn (fit) the mixture model to data. Recently, in theoretical computer science, there has been modest progress on provable polynomial-time algorithms for learning mixtures. Some references are [DS07], [AK05], [AM05], and [MV10]. The application to the discrete optimization problem is from [FK99]. The section on ranking documents/web pages is from two influential papers, one on hubs and authorities by Jon Kleinberg [Kle99] and the other on pagerank by Page, Brin, Motwani, and Winograd [BMPW98]. Exercise 3.17 is from [EVL10].

3.11. Exercises

Exercise 3.1 (Least squares vertical error) In many experiments one collects the value of a parameter at various instances of time. Let y_i be the value of the parameter y at time x_i. Suppose we wish to construct the best linear approximation to the data in the sense that we wish to minimize the mean square error. Here error is measured vertically rather than perpendicular to the line. Develop formulas for m and b to minimize the mean square error of the points $\{(x_i, y_i) \mid 1 \le i \le n\}$ to the line $y = mx + b$.

Exercise 3.2 Given five observed variables – height, weight, age, income, and blood pressure of n people – how would one find the best least squares fit affine subspace of the form

$$a_1 \text{ (height)} + a_2 \text{ (weight)} + a_3 \text{ (age)} + a_4 \text{ (income)} + a_5 \text{ (blood pressure)} = a_6?$$

Here $a_1, a_2, \ldots, a_6$ are the unknown parameters. If there is a good best-fit four-dimensional affine subspace, then one can think of the points as lying close to a four-dimensional sheet rather than points lying in five dimensions. Why might it be better to use the perpendicular distance to the affine subspace rather than vertical distance where vertical distance is measured along the coordinate axis corresponding to one of the variables?

Exercise 3.3 Manually find the best-fit lines (not subspaces, which must contain the origin) through the points in the sets below. Best fit means minimize the perpendicular distance. Subtract the center of gravity of the points in the set from each of the points in the set and find the best-fit line for the resulting points. Does the best-fit line for the original data go through the origin?

1. (4,4) (6,2)
2. (4,2) (4,4) (6,2) (6,4)
3. (3,2.5) (3,5) (5,1) (5,3.5)

Exercise 3.4 Manually determine the best-fit line through the origin for each of the following sets of points. Is the best-fit line unique? Justify your answer for each of the subproblems.

1. $\{(0, 1), (1, 0)\}$
2. $\{(0, 1), (2, 0)\}$

Exercise 3.5 Manually find the left-singular and right-singular vectors, the singular values, and the SVD decomposition of the matrices in Figure 3.6.

Exercise 3.6 Let A be a square $n \times n$ matrix whose rows are orthonormal. Prove that the columns of A are orthonormal.

Exercise 3.7 Suppose A is a $n \times n$ matrix with block diagonal structure with k equal size blocks where all entries of the ith block are a_i with $a_1 > a_2 > \cdots > a_k > 0$. Show that A has exactly k non-zero singular vectors $v_1, v_2, \ldots, v_k$ where v_i has the value $(\frac{k}{n})^{1/2}$ in the coordinates corresponding to the ith block and 0 elsewhere. In other words, the singular vectors exactly identify the blocks of the diagonal. What happens if $a_1 = a_2 = \cdots = a_k$? In the case where the a_i are equal, what is the structure of the set of all possible singular vectors?

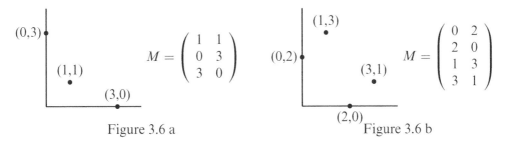

Figure 3.6 a   Figure 3.6 b

Figure 3.6: SVD problem

Hint. By symmetry, the top singular vector's components must be constant in each block.

Exercise 3.8 Interpret the first right and left-singular vectors for the document term matrix.

Exercise 3.9 Verify that the sum of r-rank one matrices $\sum_{i=1}^{r} c_i \mathbf{x_i y_i}^T$ can be written as XCY^T, where the $\mathbf{x_i}$ are the columns of X, the $\mathbf{y_i}$ are the columns of Y, and C is a diagonal matrix with the constants c_i on the diagonal.

Exercise 3.10 Let $\sum_{i=1}^{r} \sigma_i \mathbf{u_i v_i}^T$ be the SVD of A. Show that $\left| \mathbf{u_1}^T A \right| = \sigma_1$ and that $\left| \mathbf{u_1}^T A \right| = \max_{|\mathbf{u}|=1} \left| \mathbf{u}^T A \right|$.

Exercise 3.11 If $\sigma_1, \sigma_2, \ldots, \sigma_r$ are the singular values of A and $\mathbf{v}_1, \mathbf{v}_2, \ldots, \mathbf{v}_r$ are the corresponding right-singular vectors, show that

1. $A^T A = \sum_{i=1}^{r} \sigma_i^2 \mathbf{v_i v_i}^T$
2. $\mathbf{v}_1, \mathbf{v}_2, \ldots \mathbf{v}_r$ are eigenvectors of $A^T A$.
3. Assuming that the eigenvectors of $A^T A$ are unique up to multiplicative constants, conclude that the singular vectors of A (which by definition must be unit length) are unique up to sign.

Exercise 3.12 Let $\sum_i \sigma_i u_i v_i^T$ be the singular value decomposition of a rank r matrix A. Let $A_k = \sum_{i=1}^{k} \sigma_i u_i v_i^T$ be a rank k approximation to A for some $k < r$. Express the following quantities in terms of the singular values $\{\sigma_i, 1 \leq i \leq r\}$.

1. $\|A_k\|_F^2$
2. $\|A_k\|_2^2$
3. $\|A - A_k\|_F^2$
4. $\|A - A_k\|_2^2$

Exercise 3.13 If A is a symmetric matrix with distinct singular values, show that the left and right singular vectors are the same and that $A = VDV^T$.

Exercise 3.14 Use the power method to compute the singular value decomposition of the matrix

$$A = \begin{pmatrix} 1 & 2 \\ 3 & 4 \end{pmatrix}$$

Exercise 3.15 Consider the matrix

$$
A = \begin{pmatrix} 1 & 2 \\ -1 & 2 \\ 1 & -2 \\ -1 & -2 \end{pmatrix}
$$

1. Run the power method starting from $x = \binom{1}{1}$ for $k = 3$ steps. What does this give as an estimate of v_1?
2. What actually are the v_i's, σ_i's, and u_i's? It may be easiest to do this by computing the eigenvectors of $B = A^T A$.
3. Suppose matrix A is a database of restaurant ratings: each row is a person, each column is a restaurant, and a_{ij} represents how much person i likes restaurant j. What might v_1 represent? What about u_1? How about the gap $\sigma_1 - \sigma_2$?

Exercise 3.16

1. Write a program to implement the power method for computing the first singular vector of a matrix. Apply your program to the matrix

$$
A = \begin{pmatrix} 1 & 2 & 3 & \cdots & 9 & 10 \\ 2 & 3 & 4 & \cdots & 10 & 0 \\ \vdots & \vdots & \vdots & & & \vdots \\ 9 & 10 & 0 & \cdots & 0 & 0 \\ 10 & 0 & 0 & \cdots & 0 & 0 \end{pmatrix}.
$$

2. Modify the power method to find the first four singular vectors of a matrix A as follows. Randomly select four vectors and find an orthonormal basis for the space spanned by the four vectors. Then multiply each of the basis vectors times A and find a new orthonormal basis for the space spanned by the resulting four vectors. Apply your method to find the first four singular vectors of matrix A from part 1. In Matlab the command orth finds an orthonormal basis for the space spanned by a set of vectors.

Exercise 3.17

1. For $n = 5, 10, \ldots, 25$ create random graphs by generating random vectors $x = (x_1, x_2, \ldots, x_n)$ and $y = (y_1, y_2, \ldots, y_n)$. Create edges $(x_i, y_i) - (x_{i+1}, y_{i+1})$ for $i = 1 : n$ and an edge $(x_n, y_n) - (x_1, y_1)$.
2. For each graph create a new graph by selecting the midpoint of each edge for the coordinates of the vertices and add edges between vertices corresponding to the midpoints of two adjacent edges of the original graph. What happens when you iterate this process? It is best to draw the graphs.
3. Repeat the above step but normalize the vectors x and y to have unit length after each iteration. What happens?
4. One could implement the process by matrix multiplication where $x(t)$ and $y(t)$ are the vectors at the t iteration. What is the matrix A such that $x(t + 1) = Ax(t)$?
5. What is the first singular vector of A and the first two singular values of A? Does this explain what happens and how long the process takes to converge?
6. If A is invertible, what happens when you run the process backwards?

Exercise 3.18 A matrix A is positive semi-definite if for all $\mathbf{x}, \mathbf{x}^T A \mathbf{x} \geq 0$.

1. Let A be a real valued matrix. Prove that $B = AA^T$ is positive semi-definite.
2. Let A be the adjacency matrix of a graph. The Laplacian of A is $L = D - A$ where D is a diagonal matrix whose diagonal entries are the row sums of A. Prove that L is positive semi-definite by showing that $L = B^T B$ where B is an m-by-n matrix with a row for each edge in the graph, a column for each vertex, and we define

$$b_{ei} = \begin{cases} -1 & \text{if } i \text{ is the endpoint of } e \text{ with lesser index} \\ 1 & \text{if } i \text{ is the endpoint of } e \text{ with greater index} \\ 0 & \text{if } i \text{ is not an endpoint of } e \end{cases}$$

Exercise 3.19 Prove that the eigenvalues of a symmetric real valued matrix are real.

Exercise 3.20 Suppose A is a square invertible matrix and the SVD of A is $A = \sum_i \sigma_i u_i v_i^T$. Prove that the inverse of A is $\sum_i \frac{1}{\sigma_i} v_i u_i^T$.

Exercise 3.21 Suppose A is square but not necessarily invertible and has SVD $A = \sum_{i=1}^r \sigma_i u_i v_i^T$. Let $B = \sum_{i=1}^r \frac{1}{\sigma_i} v_i u_i^T$. Show that $BA\mathbf{x} = \mathbf{x}$ for all $\mathbf{x}$ in the span of the right-singular vectors of A. For this reason B is sometimes called the pseudo-inverse of A and can play the role of A^{-1} in many applications.

Exercise 3.22

1. For any matrix A, show that $\sigma_k \leq \frac{||A||_F}{\sqrt{k}}$.
2. Prove that there exists a matrix B of rank at most k such that $||A - B||_2 \leq \frac{||A||_F}{\sqrt{k}}$.
3. Can the 2-norm on the left-hand side in (2) be replaced by Frobenius norm?

Exercise 3.23 Suppose an $n \times d$ matrix A is given and you are allowed to preprocess A. Then you are given a number of d-dimensional vectors $\mathbf{x_1}, \mathbf{x_2}, \ldots, \mathbf{x_m}$ and for each of these vectors you must find the vector $A\mathbf{x_j}$ approximately, in the sense that you must find a vector $\mathbf{y_j}$ satisfying $|\mathbf{y_j} - A\mathbf{x_j}| \leq \varepsilon ||A||_F |\mathbf{x_j}|$. Here $\varepsilon > 0$ is a given error bound. Describe an algorithm that accomplishes this in time $O\left(\frac{d+n}{\varepsilon^2}\right)$ per $\mathbf{x_j}$ not counting the preprocessing time. Hint: use Exercise 3.22.

Exercise 3.24 Find the values of c_i to maximize $\sum_{i=1}^r c_i^2 \sigma_i^2$ where $\sigma_1^2 \geq \sigma_2^2 \geq \ldots$ and $\sum_{i=1}^r c_i^2 = 1$.

Exercise 3.25 (Document-Term Matrices) Suppose we have an $m \times n$ document-term matrix A where each row corresponds to a document and has been normalized to length 1. Define the "similarity" between two such documents by their dot product.

1. Consider a "synthetic" document whose sum of squared similarities with all documents in the matrix is as high as possible. What is this synthetic document and how would you find it?
2. How does the synthetic document in (1) differ from the center of gravity?
3. Building on (1), given a positive integer k, find a set of k synthetic documents such that the sum of squares of the mk similarities between each document in the matrix and each synthetic document is maximized. To avoid the trivial solution of selecting k copies of the document in (1), require the k synthetic

documents to be orthogonal to each other. Relate these synthetic documents to singular vectors.

4. Suppose that the documents can be partitioned into k subsets (often called clusters), where documents in the same cluster are similar and documents in different clusters are not very similar. Consider the computational problem of isolating the clusters. This is a hard problem in general. But assume that the terms can also be partitioned into k clusters so that for $i \neq j$, no term in the ith cluster occurs in a document in the jth cluster. If we knew the clusters and arranged the rows and columns in them to be contiguous, then the matrix would be a block-diagonal matrix. Of course the clusters are not known. By a "block" of the document-term matrix we mean a submatrix with rows corresponding to the ith cluster of documents and columns corresponding to the ith cluster of terms. We can also partition any n vector into blocks. Show that any right-singular vector of the matrix must have the property that each of its blocks is a right-singular vector of the corresponding block of the document-term matrix.

5. Suppose now that the k singular values are all distinct. Show how to solve the clustering problem.

Hint. (4) Use the fact that the right-singular vectors must be eigenvectors of $A^T A$. Show that $A^T A$ is also block-diagonal and use properties of eigenvectors.

Exercise 3.26 Let $\mathbf{u}$ be a fixed vector. Show that maximizing $\mathbf{x}^T \mathbf{u} \mathbf{u}^T (\mathbf{1} - \mathbf{x})$ subject to $x_i \in \{0, 1\}$ is equivalent to partitioning the coordinates of $\mathbf{u}$ into two subsets where the sum of the elements in both subsets are as equal as possible.

Exercise 3.27 Read in a photo and convert to a matrix. Perform a singular value decomposition of the matrix. Reconstruct the photo using only 1,2,4, and 16 singular values.

1. Print the reconstructed photo. How good is the quality of the reconstructed photo?
2. What percent of the Frobenius norm is captured in each case?

Hint. If you use MATLAB, the command to read a photo is imread. The types of files that can be read are given by imformats. To print the file use imwrite. Print using jpeg format. To access the file afterwards you may need to add the file extension .jpg. The command imread will read the file in uint8 and you will need to convert to double for the SVD code. Afterwards you will need to convert back to uint8 to write the file. If the photo is a color photo, you will get three matrices for the three colors used.

Exercise 3.28

1. Create a 100×100 matrix of random numbers between 0 and 1 such that each entry is highly correlated with the adjacent entries. Find the SVD of A. What fraction of the Frobenius norm of A is captured by the top 10 singular vectors? How many singular vectors are required to capture 95% of the Frobenius norm?
2. Repeat (1) with a 100×100 matrix of statistically independent random numbers between 0 and 1.

Exercise 3.29 Show that the running time for the maximum cut algorithm in Section 3.9.6 can be carried out in time $O(n^3 + \text{poly}(n)k^k)$, where poly is some polynomial.

Exercise 3.30 Let $x_1, x_2, \ldots, x_n$ be n points in d-dimensional space and let X be the $n \times d$ matrix whose rows are the n points. Suppose we know only the matrix D of pairwise distances between points and not the coordinates of the points themselves. The set of points $x_1, x_2, \ldots, x_n$ giving rise to the distance matrix D is not unique, since any translation, rotation, or reflection of the coordinate system leaves the distances invariant. Fix the origin of the coordinate system so that the centroid of the set of points is at the origin. That is, $\sum_{i=1}^{n} x_i = 0$.

1. Show that the elements of XX^T are given by

$$
x_i x_j^T = -\frac{1}{2}\left[d_{ij}^2 - \frac{1}{n}\sum_{k=1}^{n} d_{ik}^2 - \frac{1}{n}\sum_{k=1}^{n} d_{kj}^2 + \frac{1}{n^2}\sum_{k=1}^{n}\sum_{l=1}^{n} d_{kl}^2 \right].
$$

2. Describe an algorithm for determining the matrix X whose rows are the x_i.

Exercise 3.31

1. Consider the pairwise distance matrix for 20 US cities given below. Use the algorithm of Exercise 3.30 to place the cities on a map of the United States. The algorithm is called classical multidimensional scaling, cmdscale, in MATLAB. Alternatively use the pairwise distance matrix of 12 Chinese cities to place the cities on a map of China.

    Note: Any rotation or a mirror image of the map will have the same pairwise distances.

2. Suppose you had airline distances for 50 cities around the world. Could you use these distances to construct a three-dimensional world model?

	B O S	B U F	C H I	D A L	D E N	H O U	L A	M E M	M A	M I M
Boston	-	400	851	1551	1769	1605	2596	1137	1255	1123
Buffalo	400	-	454	1198	1370	1286	2198	803	1181	731
Chicago	851	454	-	803	920	940	1745	482	1188	355
Dallas	1551	1198	803	-	663	225	1240	420	1111	862
Denver	1769	1370	920	663	-	879	831	879	1726	700
Houston	1605	1286	940	225	879	-	1374	484	968	1056
Los Angeles	2596	2198	1745	1240	831	1374	-	1603	2339	1524
Memphis	1137	803	482	420	879	484	1603	-	872	699
Miami	1255	1181	1188	1111	1726	968	2339	872	-	1511
Minneapolis	1123	731	355	862	700	1056	1524	699	1511	-
New York	188	292	713	1374	1631	1420	2451	957	1092	1018
Omaha	1282	883	432	586	488	794	1315	529	1397	290
Philadelphia	271	279	666	1299	1579	1341	2394	881	1019	985
Phoenix	2300	1906	1453	887	586	1017	357	1263	1982	1280
Pittsburgh	483	178	410	1070	1320	1137	2136	660	1010	743
Saint Louis	1038	662	262	547	796	679	1589	240	1061	466
Salt Lake City	2099	1699	1260	999	371	1200	579	1250	2089	987
San Francisco	2699	2300	1858	1483	949	1645	347	1802	2594	1584
Seattle	2493	2117	1737	1681	1021	1891	959	1867	2734	1395
Washington DC	393	292	597	1185	1494	1220	2300	765	923	934

	N Y A	O M I	P H O	P H T	P I L	S t C	S L	S F A	S E	D C
Boston	188	1282	271	2300	483	1038	2099	2699	2493	393
Buffalo	292	883	279	1906	178	662	1699	2300	2117	292
Chicago	713	432	666	1453	410	262	1260	1858	1737	597
Dallas	1374	586	1299	887	1070	547	999	1483	1681	1185
Denver	1631	488	1579	586	1320	796	371	949	1021	1494
Houston	1420	794	1341	1017	1137	679	1200	1645	1891	1220
Los Angeles	2451	1315	2394	357	2136	1589	579	347	959	2300
Memphis	957	529	881	1263	660	240	1250	1802	1867	765
Miami	1092	1397	1019	1982	1010	1061	2089	2594	2734	923
Minneapolis	1018	290	985	1280	743	466	987	1584	1395	934
New York	-	1144	83	2145	317	875	1972	2571	2408	230
Omaha	1144	-	1094	1036	836	354	833	1429	1369	1014
Philadelphia	83	1094	-	2083	259	811	1925	2523	2380	123
Phoenix	2145	1036	2083	-	1828	1272	504	653	1114	1973
Pittsburgh	317	836	259	1828	-	559	1668	2264	2138	192
Saint Louis	875	354	811	1272	559	-	1162	1744	1724	712
Salt Lake City	1972	833	1925	504	1668	1162	-	600	701	1848
San Francisco	2571	1429	2523	653	2264	1744	600	-	678	2442
Seattle	2408	1369	2380	1114	2138	1724	701	678	-	2329
Washington DC	230	1014	123	1973	192	712	1848	2442	2329	-

Exercise 3.32 One's data in a high-dimensional space may lie on a lower-dimensional sheath. To test for this, one might for each data point find the set of closest data points and calculate the vector distance from the data point to each of the close points. If the set of these distance vectors is a lower-dimensional space than the number of distance points, then it is likely that the data is on a low-dimensional sheath. To test the dimension of the space of the distance vectors, one might use the singular value decomposition to find the singular values. The dimension of the space is the number of large singular values. The low singular values correspond to noise or slight curvature of the sheath. To test this concept, generate a data set of points that lie on a one-dimensional curve in three-dimensional space. For each point find maybe 10 nearest points, form the matrix of distance, and do a singular value decomposition on the matrix. Report what happens.

City	Bei-jing	Tian-jin	Shang-hai	Chong-qing	Hoh-hot	Urum-qi	Lha-sa	Yin-chuan	Nan-ning	Har-bin	Chang-chun	Shen-yang
Beijing	0	125	1239	3026	480	3300	3736	1192	2373	1230	979	684
Tianjin	125	0	1150	1954	604	3330	3740	1316	2389	1207	955	661
Shanghai	1239	1150	0	1945	1717	3929	4157	2092	1892	2342	2090	1796
Chongqing	3026	1954	1945	0	1847	3202	2457	1570	993	3156	2905	2610
Hohhot	480	604	1717	1847	0	2825	3260	716	2657	1710	1458	1164
Urumqi	3300	3330	3929	3202	2825	0	2668	2111	4279	4531	4279	3985
Lhasa	3736	3740	4157	2457	3260	2668	0	2547	3431	4967	4715	4421
Yinchuan	1192	1316	2092	1570	716	2111	2547	0	2673	2422	2170	1876
Nanning	2373	2389	1892	993	2657	4279	3431	2673	0	3592	3340	3046
Harbin	1230	1207	2342	3156	1710	4531	4967	2422	3592	0	256	546
Changchun	979	955	2090	2905	1458	4279	4715	2170	3340	256	0	294
Shenyang	684	661	1796	2610	1164	3985	4421	1876	3046	546	294	0

Use code such as the following to create the data.

```
function [ data, distance ] = create_sheath( n )
%creates n data points on a one dimensional sheath in
    three dimensional
%space
%
if nargin==0
    n=100;
end
```

```
data=zeros(3,n);
for i=1:n
    x=sin((pi/100)*i);
    y=sqrt(1-x^2);
    z=0.003*i;
    data(:,i)=[x;y;z];
end
%subtract adjacent vertices
distance=zeros(3,10);
for i=1:5
    distance(:,i)=data(:,i)-data(:,6);
    distance(:,i+5)=data(:,i+6)-data(:,6);
end
end
```

CHAPTER FOUR

Random Walks and Markov Chains

A random walk on a directed graph consists of a sequence of vertices generated from a start vertex by randomly selecting an incident edge, traversing the edge to a new vertex, and repeating the process.

We generally assume the graph is *strongly connected*, meaning that for any pair of vertices x and y, the graph contains a path of directed edges starting at x and ending at y. If the graph is strongly connected, then no matter where the walk begins, the fraction of time the walk spends at the different vertices of the graph converges to a stationary probability distribution.

Start a random walk at a vertex x and think of the starting probability distribution as putting a mass of one on x and zero on every other vertex. More generally, one could start with any probability distribution $\mathbf{p}$, where $\mathbf{p}$ is a row vector with nonnegative components summing to 1, with p_x being the probability of starting at vertex x. The probability of being at vertex x at time $t + 1$ is the sum over each adjacent vertex y of being at y at time t and taking the transition from y to x. Let $\mathbf{p(t)}$ be a row vector with a component for each vertex specifying the probability mass of the vertex at time t, and let $\mathbf{p(t + 1)}$ be the row vector of probabilities at time $t + 1$. In matrix notation,[1]

$$\mathbf{p(t)}P = \mathbf{p(t + 1)},$$

where the ij^{th} entry of the matrix P is the probability of the walk at vertex i selecting the edge to vertex j.

A fundamental property of a random walk is that in the limit, the long-term average probability of being at a particular vertex is independent of the start vertex, or an initial probability distribution over vertices, provided only that the underlying graph is strongly connected. The limiting probabilities are called the *stationary probabilities*. This fundamental theorem is proved in the next section.

A special case of random walks, namely random walks on undirected graphs, has important connections to electrical networks. Here, each edge has a parameter called *conductance*, like electrical conductance. If the walk is at vertex x, it chooses an edge to traverse next from among all edges incident to x with probability proportional to its conductance. Certain basic quantities associated with random walks are hitting time, which is the expected time to reach vertex y starting at vertex x, and cover time, which is the expected time to visit every vertex. Qualitatively, for undirected graphs

---

[1]Probability vectors are represented by row vectors to simplify notation in equations like the one here.

Table 4.1: Correspondence between terminology of random walks and Markov chains

Random walk	Markov chain
graph	stochastic process
vertex	state
strongly connected	persistent
aperiodic	aperiodic
strongly connected and aperiodic	ergodic
edge weighted undirected graph	time reversible

these quantities are all bounded above by polynomials in the number of vertices. The proofs of these facts will rely on the analogy between random walks and electrical networks.

Aspects of the theory of random walks were developed in computer science with a number of applications including defining the pagerank of pages on the World Wide Web by their stationary probability. An equivalent concept called a *Markov chain* had previously been developed in the statistical literature. A Markov chain has a finite set of *states*. For each pair of states x and y, there is a *transition probability* p_{xy} of going from state x to state y where for each x, $\sum_y p_{xy} = 1$. A random walk in the Markov chain starts at some state. At a given time step, if it is in state x, the next state y is selected randomly with probability p_{xy}. A Markov chain can be represented by a directed graph with a vertex representing each state and a directed edge with weight p_{xy} from vertex x to vertex y. We say that the Markov chain is *connected* if the underlying directed graph is strongly connected: that is, if there is a directed path from every vertex to every other vertex. The matrix P consisting of the p_{xy} is called the *transition probability matrix* of the chain. The terms *random walk* and *Markov chain* are used interchangeably. The correspondence between the terminologies of random walks and Markov chains is given in Table 4.1.

A state of a Markov chain is *persistent* if it has the property that should the state ever be reached, the random process will return to it with probability one. This is equivalent to the property that the state is in a strongly connected component with no out edges. For most of the chapter, we assume that the underlying directed graph is strongly connected. We discuss here briefly what might happen if we do not have strong connectivity. Consider the directed graph in Figure 4.1b with three strongly connected components, A, B, and C. Starting from any vertex in A, there is a non-zero probability of eventually reaching any vertex in A. However, the probability of returning to a vertex in A is less than one, and thus vertices in A, and similarly vertices in B, are not persistent. From any vertex in C, the walk eventually will return with probability 1 to the vertex, since there is no way of leaving component C. Thus, vertices in C are persistent.

A connected Markov Chain is said to be *aperiodic* if the greatest common divisor of the lengths of directed cycles is one. It is known that for connected aperiodic chains, the probability distribution of the random walk converges to a unique stationary distribution. Aperiodicity is a technical condition needed in this proof. Here, we do not prove this theorem and do not worry about aperiodicity at all. It turns out that if we take the average probability distribution of the random walk over the first

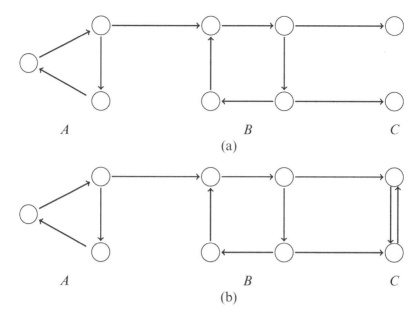

A B C

(a)

A B C

(b)

Figure 4.1: (a) A directed graph with some vertices having no out edges and a strongly connected component A with no in edges. (b) A directed graph with three strongly connected components.

t steps, then this average converges to a limiting distribution for connected chains (without assuming aperiodicity), and this average is what one uses in practice. We prove this limit theorem and explain its uses in what is called the Markov Chain Monte Carlo (MCMC) method.

Markov chains are used to model situations where all the information of the system necessary to predict the future can be encoded in the current state. A typical example is speech, where for a small k the current state encodes the last k syllables uttered by the speaker. Given the current state, there is a certain probability of each syllable being uttered next, and these can be used to calculate the transition probabilities. Another example is a gambler's assets, which can be modeled as a Markov chain where the current state is the amount of money the gambler has on hand. The model would only be valid if the gambler's bets depend only on current assets, not the past history.

Later in the chapter, we study the widely used Markov Chain Monte Carlo method (MCMC). Here, the objective is to sample a large space according to some probability distribution p. The number of elements in the space may be very large, say 10^{100}. One designs a Markov chain where states correspond to the elements of the space. The transition probabilities of the chain are designed so that the stationary probability of the chain is the probability distribution p with which we want to sample. One chooses samples by taking a random walk until the probability distribution is close to the stationary distribution of the chain and then selects the current state of the walk. Then the walk continues a number of steps until the probability distribution is nearly independent of where the walk was when the first element was selected. A second point is then selected, and so on. Although it is impossible to store the graph in a computer, since it has 10^{100} vertices, to do the walk, one needs only store the current vertex of the walk and be able to generate the adjacent vertices by some algorithm. What is critical is that the probability distribution of the walk converges to the stationary distribution in time logarithmic in the number of states.

We mention two motivating examples. The first is to select a point at random in d-space according to a probability density such as a Gaussian. Put down a grid and let each grid point be a state of the Markov chain. Given a probability density p, design transition probabilities of a Markov chain so that the stationary distribution is p. In general, the number of states grows exponentially in the dimension d, but if the time to converge to the stationary distribution grows polynomially in d, then one can do a random walk on the graph until convergence to the stationary probability. Once the stationary probability has been reached, one selects a point. To select a set of points, one must walk a number of steps between each selection so that the probability of the current point is independent of the previous point. By selecting a number of points one can estimate the probability of a region by observing the number of selected points in the region.

A second example is from physics. Consider an $n \times n$ grid in the plane with a particle at each grid point. Each particle has a spin of ± 1. A configuration is a n^2-dimensional vector $\mathbf{v} = (v_1, v_2, \ldots, v_{n^2})$, where v_i is the spin of the ith particle. There are 2^{n^2} spin configurations. The energy of a configuration is a function $f(\mathbf{v})$ of the configuration, not of any single spin. A central problem in statistical mechanics is to sample spin configurations according to their probability. It is easy to design a Markov chain with one state per spin configuration so that the stationary probability of a state is proportional to the state's energy. If a random walk gets close to the stationary probability in time polynomial in n rather than 2^{n^2}, then one can sample spin configurations according to their probability.

The Markov Chain has 2^{n^2} states, one per configuration. Two states in the Markov chain are adjacent if and only if the corresponding configurations $\mathbf{v}$ and $\mathbf{u}$ differ in just one coordinate ($u_i = v_i$ for all but one i). The Metropolis–Hastings random walk, described in more detail in Section 4.2, has a transition probability from a configuration $\mathbf{v}$ to an adjacent configuration $\mathbf{u}$ of

$$\frac{1}{n^2} \min\left(1, \frac{f(\mathbf{u})}{f(\mathbf{v})}\right).$$

As we will see, the Markov Chain has a stationary probability proportional to the energy. There are two more crucial facts about this chain. The first is that to execute a step in the chain, we do not need the whole chain, just the ratio $\frac{f(\mathbf{u})}{f(\mathbf{v})}$. The second is that under suitable assumptions, the chain approaches stationarity in time polynomial in n.

A quantity called the *mixing time*, loosely defined as the time needed to get close to the stationary distribution, is often much smaller than the number of states. In Section 4.4, we relate the mixing time to a combinatorial notion called *normalized conductance* and derive upper bounds on the mixing time in several cases.

4.1. Stationary Distribution

Let $\mathbf{p}(t)$ be the probability distribution after t steps of a random walk. Define the *long-term average probability distribution* $\mathbf{a}(t)$ by

$$\mathbf{a}(t) = \frac{1}{t}\big(\mathbf{p}(0) + \mathbf{p}(1) + \cdots + \mathbf{p}(t-1)\big).$$

The fundamental theorem of Markov chains asserts that for a connected Markov chain, $\mathbf{a(t)}$ converges to a limit probability vector $\mathbf{x}$ that satisfies the equations $\mathbf{x}P = \mathbf{x}$. Before proving the fundamental theorem of Markov chains, we first prove a technical lemma.

Lemma 4.1 *Let P be the transition probability matrix for a connected Markov chain. The $n \times (n+1)$ matrix $A = [P - I, \mathbf{1}]$ obtained by augmenting the matrix $P - I$ with an additional column of ones has rank n.*

Proof If the rank of $A = [P - I, \mathbf{1}]$ was less than n, there would be a subspace of solutions to $A\mathbf{x} = \mathbf{0}$ of at least two dimensions. Each row in P sums to one, so each row in $P - I$ sums to zero. Thus $\mathbf{x} = (\mathbf{1}, 0)$, where all but the last coordinate of $\mathbf{x}$ is 1, is one solution to $A\mathbf{x} = \mathbf{0}$. Assume there was a second solution $(\mathbf{x}, \alpha)$ perpendicular to $(\mathbf{1}, 0)$. Then $(P - I)\mathbf{x} + \alpha\mathbf{1} = \mathbf{0}$, and for each $i, x_i = \sum_j p_{ij}x_j + \alpha$. Each x_i is a convex combination of some x_j plus α. Let S be the set of i for which x_i attains its maximum value. Since $\mathbf{x}$ is perpendicular to $\mathbf{1}$, some x_i is negative, and thus $\bar{S}$ is not empty. Connectedness implies that some x_k of maximum value is adjacent to some x_l of lower value. Thus, $x_k > \sum_j p_{kj}x_j$. Therefore, α must be greater than 0 in $x_k = \sum_j p_{kj}x_j + \alpha$.

Using the same argument with T the set of i for which x_i takes its minimum value implies $\alpha < 0$. This contradiction falsifies the assumption of a second solution, thereby proving the lemma. ∎

Theorem 4.2 (Fundamental Theorem of Markov Chains) *For a connected Markov chain, there is a unique probability vector $\boldsymbol{\pi}$ satisfying $\boldsymbol{\pi}P = \boldsymbol{\pi}$. Moreover, for any starting distribution, $\lim_{t \to \infty} \mathbf{a(t)}$ exists and equals $\boldsymbol{\pi}$.*

Proof Note that $\mathbf{a(t)}$ is itself a probability vector, since its components are nonnegative and sum to 1. Run one step of the Markov chain starting with distribution $\mathbf{a(t)}$; the distribution after the step is $\mathbf{a(t)}P$. Calculate the change in probabilities due to this step.

$$
\begin{aligned}
\mathbf{a(t)}P - \mathbf{a(t)} &= \frac{1}{t}\Big[\mathbf{p}(0)P + \mathbf{p}(1)P + \cdots + \mathbf{p}(t-1)P\Big] \\
&\quad - \frac{1}{t}\Big[\mathbf{p}(0) + \mathbf{p}(1) + \cdots + \mathbf{p}(t-1)\Big] \\
&= \frac{1}{t}\Big[\mathbf{p}(1) + \mathbf{p}(2) + \cdots + \mathbf{p}(t)\Big] - \frac{1}{t}\Big[\mathbf{p}(0) + \mathbf{p}(1) + \cdots + \mathbf{p}(t-1)\Big] \\
&= \frac{1}{t}\left(\mathbf{p}(t) - \mathbf{p}(0)\right).
\end{aligned}
$$

Thus, $\mathbf{b(t)} = \mathbf{a(t)}P - \mathbf{a(t)}$ satisfies $|\mathbf{b(t)}| \leq \frac{2}{t} \to 0$, as $t \to \infty$.

By Lemma 4.1 above, $A = [P - I, \mathbf{1}]$ has rank n. The $n \times n$ submatrix B of A consisting of all its columns except the first is invertible. Let $\mathbf{c(t)}$ be obtained from $\mathbf{b(t)}$ by removing the first entry. Since $\mathbf{a(t)}P - \mathbf{a(t)} = \mathbf{b(t)}$ and B is obtained by deleting the first column of $P - I$ and adding a column of 1's, $\mathbf{a(t)}B = [\mathbf{c(t)}, 1]$. Then $\mathbf{a(t)} = [\mathbf{c(t)}, 1]B^{-1} \to [\mathbf{0}, 1]B^{-1}$ establishing the theorem with $\boldsymbol{\pi} = [\mathbf{0}, 1]B^{-1}$. ∎

We finish this section with the following lemma useful in establishing that a probability distribution is the stationary probability distribution for a random walk on a connected graph with edge probabilities.

Lemma 4.3 *For a random walk on a strongly connected graph with probabilities on the edges, if the vector π satisfies $\pi_x p_{xy} = \pi_y p_{yx}$ for all x and y and $\sum_x \pi_x = 1$, then π is the stationary distribution of the walk.*

Proof Since π satisfies $\pi_x p_{xy} = \pi_y p_{yx}$, summing both sides, $\pi_x = \sum_y \pi_y p_{yx}$, and hence π satisfies $\pi = \pi P$. By Theorem 4.2, π is the unique stationary probability. ∎

4.2. Markov Chain Monte Carlo

The Markov Chain Monte Carlo (MCMC) method is a technique for sampling a multivariate probability distribution $p(\mathbf{x})$, where $\mathbf{x} = (x_1, x_2, \ldots, x_d)$. The MCMC method is used to estimate the expected value of a function $f(\mathbf{x})$:

$$E(f) = \sum_{\mathbf{x}} f(\mathbf{x}) p(\mathbf{x}).$$

If each x_i can take on two or more values, then there are at least 2^d values for $\mathbf{x}$, so an explicit summation requires exponential time. Instead, one could draw a set of samples, where each sample $\mathbf{x}$ is selected with probability $p(\mathbf{x})$. Averaging f over these samples provides an estimate of the sum.

To sample according to $p(\mathbf{x})$, design a Markov Chain whose states correspond to the possible values of $\mathbf{x}$ and whose stationary probability distribution is $p(\mathbf{x})$. There are two general techniques to design such a Markov Chain: the Metropolis-Hastings algorithm and Gibbs sampling, which we will describe in the next two subsections. The Fundamental Theorem of Markov Chains, Theorem 4.2, states that the average of the function f over states seen in a sufficiently long run is a good estimate of $E(f)$. The harder task is to show that the number of steps needed before the long-run average probabilities are close to the stationary distribution grows polynomially in d, though the total number of states may grow exponentially in d. This phenomenon, known as *rapid mixing*, happens for a number of interesting examples. Section 4.4 presents a crucial tool used to show rapid mixing.

We used $\mathbf{x} \in \mathbf{R}^d$ to emphasize that distributions are multivariate. From a Markov chain perspective, each value $\mathbf{x}$ can take on is a state, i.e., a vertex of the graph on which the random walk takes place. Henceforth, we will use the subscripts $i, j, k, \ldots$ to denote states and will use p_i instead of $p(x_1, x_2, \ldots, x_d)$ to denote the probability of the state corresponding to a given set of values for the variables. Recall that in the Markov chain terminology, vertices of the graph are called states.

Recall the notation that $\mathbf{p(t)}$ is the row vector of probabilities of the random walk being at each state (vertex of the graph) at time t. So, $\mathbf{p(t)}$ has as many components as there are states, and its ith component is the probability of being in state i at time t. Recall the long-term t-step average is

$$\mathbf{a(t)} = \frac{1}{t} \left[\mathbf{p(0)} + \mathbf{p(1)} + \cdots + \mathbf{p(t-1)} \right]. \tag{4.1}$$

The expected value of the function f under the probability distribution $\mathbf{p}$ is $E(f) = \sum_i f_i p_i$ where f_i is the value of f at state i. Our estimate of this quantity will be the average value of f at the states seen in a t step walk. Call this estimate γ. Clearly, the expected value of γ is

$$E(\gamma) = \sum_i f_i \left(\frac{1}{t} \sum_{j=1}^{t} \text{Prob}(\text{walk is in state } i \text{ at time } j) \right) = \sum_i f_i a_i(t).$$

The expectation here is with respect to the "coin tosses" of the algorithm, not with respect to the underlying distribution $\mathbf{p}$. Let $f_{\max}$ denote the maximum absolute value of f. It is easy to see that

$$\left| \sum_i f_i p_i - E(\gamma) \right| \leq f_{\max} \sum_i |p_i - a_i(t)| = f_{\max} ||\mathbf{p} - \mathbf{a(t)}||_1 \qquad (4.2)$$

where the quantity $||\mathbf{p} - \mathbf{a(t)}||_1$ is the l_1 distance between the probability distributions $\mathbf{p}$ and $\mathbf{a(t)}$, often called the *total variation distance* between the distributions. We will build tools to upper bound $||\mathbf{p} - \mathbf{a(t)}||_1$. Since $\mathbf{p}$ is the stationary distribution, the t for which $||\mathbf{p} - \mathbf{a(t)}||_1$ becomes small is determined by the rate of convergence of the Markov chain to its steady state.

The following proposition is often useful.

Proposition 4.4 *For two probability distributions* $\mathbf{p}$ *and* $\mathbf{q}$,

$$||\mathbf{p} - \mathbf{q}||_1 = 2 \sum_i (p_i - q_i)^+ = 2 \sum_i (q_i - p_i)^+$$

where $x^+ = x$ *if* $x \geq 0$ *and* $x^+ = 0$ *if* $x < 0$.

The proof is left as an exercise.

4.2.1. Metropolis-Hasting Algorithm

The Metropolis-Hasting algorithm is a general method to design a Markov chain whose stationary distribution is a given target distribution $\mathbf{p}$. Start with a connected undirected graph G on the set of states. If the states are the lattice points $(x_1, x_2, \ldots, x_d)$ in $\mathbf{R}^d$ with $x_i \in \{0, 1, 2, \ldots, n\}$, then G could be the lattice graph with $2d$ coordinate edges at each interior vertex. In general, let r be the maximum degree of any vertex of G. The transitions of the Markov chain are defined as follows. At state i select neighbor j with probability $\frac{1}{r}$. Since the degree of i may be less than r, with some probability no edge is selected and the walk remains at i. If a neighbor j is selected and $p_j \geq p_i$, go to j. If $p_j < p_i$, go to j with probability p_j/p_i and stay at i with probability $1 - \frac{p_j}{p_i}$. Intuitively, this favors "heavier" states with higher p_i values. For i adjacent to j in G,

$$p_{ij} = \frac{1}{r} \min\left(1, \frac{p_j}{p_i}\right)$$

and

$$p_{ii} = 1 - \sum_{j \neq i} p_{ij}.$$

Thus,

$$p_i p_{ij} = \frac{p_i}{r} \min\left(1, \frac{p_j}{p_i}\right) = \frac{1}{r} \min(p_i, p_j) = \frac{p_j}{r} \min\left(1, \frac{p_i}{p_j}\right) = p_j p_{ji}.$$

By Lemma 4.3, the stationary probabilities are indeed p_i as desired.

Example Consider the graph in Figure 4.2. Using the Metropolis-Hasting algorithm, assign transition probabilities so that the stationary probability of a random walk is $p(a) = \frac{1}{2}, p(b) = \frac{1}{4}, p(c) = \frac{1}{8}$, and $p(d) = \frac{1}{8}$. The maximum degree of any vertex is 3, so at a, the probability of taking the edge (a, b) is $\frac{1}{3}\frac{1}{4}\frac{2}{1}$ or $\frac{1}{6}$. The probability of taking the edge (a, c) is $\frac{1}{3}\frac{1}{8}\frac{2}{1}$ or $\frac{1}{12}$ and of taking the edge (a, d) is $\frac{1}{3}\frac{1}{8}\frac{2}{1}$ or $\frac{1}{12}$. Thus, the probability of staying at a is $\frac{2}{3}$. The probability of taking the edge from b to a is $\frac{1}{3}$. The probability of taking the edge from c to a is $\frac{1}{3}$, and the probability of taking the edge from d to a is $\frac{1}{3}$. Thus, the stationary probability of a is $\frac{1}{4}\frac{1}{3} + \frac{1}{8}\frac{1}{3} + \frac{1}{8}\frac{1}{3} + \frac{1}{2}\frac{2}{3} = \frac{1}{2}$, which is the desired probability. ∎

$$p(a) = p(a)p(a \to a) + p(b)p(b \to a) + p(c)p(c \to a) + p(d)p(d \to a)$$
$$= \frac{1}{2}\frac{2}{3} + \frac{1}{4}\frac{1}{3} + \frac{1}{8}\frac{1}{3} + \frac{1}{8}\frac{1}{3} = \frac{1}{2}$$

$$p(b) = p(a)p(a \to b) + p(b)p(b \to b) + p(c)p(c \to b)$$
$$= \frac{1}{2}\frac{1}{6} + \frac{1}{4}\frac{1}{2} + \frac{1}{8}\frac{1}{3} = \frac{1}{4}$$

$$p(c) = p(a)p(a \to c) + p(b)p(b \to c) + p(c)p(c \to c) + p(d)p(d \to c)$$
$$= \frac{1}{2}\frac{1}{12} + \frac{1}{4}\frac{1}{6} + \frac{1}{8}0 + \frac{1}{8}\frac{1}{3} = \frac{1}{8}$$

$$p(d) = p(a)p(a \to d) + p(c)p(c \to d) + p(d)p(d \to d)$$
$$= \frac{1}{2}\frac{1}{12} + \frac{1}{8}\frac{1}{3} + \frac{1}{8}\frac{1}{3} = \frac{1}{8}$$

Alternative check of stationary probability

$p_a p_{ab} = p_b p_{ba}$	$\frac{1}{2}\frac{1}{6} = \frac{1}{4}\frac{1}{3}$		$p_a p_{ac} = p_c p_{ca}$	$\frac{1}{2}\frac{1}{12} = \frac{1}{8}\frac{1}{3}$	
$p_a p_{ad} = p_d p_{da}$	$\frac{1}{2}\frac{1}{12} = \frac{1}{8}\frac{1}{3}$				
$p_b p_{bc} = p_c p_{cb}$	$\frac{1}{4}\frac{1}{6} = \frac{1}{8}\frac{1}{3}$		$p_c p_{cd} = p_d p_{dc}$	$\frac{1}{8}\frac{1}{3} = \frac{1}{8}\frac{1}{3}$	

Figure 4.2: Using the Metropolis-Hasting algorithm to set probabilities for a random walk so that the stationary probability will be the desired probability.

4.2.2. Gibbs Sampling

Gibbs sampling is another Markov Chain Monte Carlo method to sample from a multivariate probability distribution. Let $p(\mathbf{x})$ be the target distribution where $\mathbf{x} = (x_1, \ldots, x_d)$. Gibbs sampling consists of a random walk on an undirected graph whose vertices correspond to the values of $\mathbf{x} = (x_1, \ldots, x_d)$ and in which there is an edge from $\mathbf{x}$ to $\mathbf{y}$ if $\mathbf{x}$ and $\mathbf{y}$ differ in only one coordinate. Thus, the underlying graph is like a d-dimensional lattice except that the vertices in the same coordinate line form a clique.

To generate samples of $\mathbf{x} = (x_1, \ldots, x_d)$ with a target distribution $p(\mathbf{x})$, the Gibbs sampling algorithm repeats the following steps. One of the variables x_i is chosen to be updated. Its new value is chosen based on the marginal probability of x_i with the other variables fixed. There are two commonly used schemes to determine which x_i to update. One scheme is to choose x_i randomly, the other is to choose x_i by sequentially scanning from x_1 to x_d.

Suppose that $\mathbf{x}$ and $\mathbf{y}$ are two states that differ in only one coordinate. Without loss of generality, let that coordinate be the first. Then, in the scheme where a coordinate is randomly chosen to modify, the probability $p_{\mathbf{xy}}$ of going from $\mathbf{x}$ to $\mathbf{y}$ is

$$p_{\mathbf{xy}} = \frac{1}{d} p(y_1 | x_2, x_3, \ldots, x_d).$$

Similarly,

$$p_{\mathbf{yx}} = \frac{1}{d} p(x_1 | y_2, y_3, \ldots, y_d)$$

$$= \frac{1}{d} p(x_1 | x_2, x_3, \ldots, x_d).$$

Here use was made of the fact that for $j \neq 1, x_j = y_j$.

It is simple to see that this chain has stationary probability proportional to $p(\mathbf{x})$. Rewrite $p_{\mathbf{xy}}$ as

$$p_{\mathbf{xy}} = \frac{1}{d} \frac{p(y_1 | x_2, x_3, \ldots, x_d) p(x_2, x_3, \ldots, x_d)}{p(x_2, x_3, \ldots, x_d)}$$

$$= \frac{1}{d} \frac{p(y_1, x_2, x_3, \ldots, x_d)}{p(x_2, x_3, \ldots, x_d)}$$

$$= \frac{1}{d} \frac{p(\mathbf{y})}{p(x_2, x_3, \ldots, x_d)}$$

again using $x_j = y_j$ for $j \neq 1$. Similarly write

$$p_{\mathbf{yx}} = \frac{1}{d} \frac{p(\mathbf{x})}{p(x_2, x_3, \ldots, x_d)}$$

from which it follows that $p(\mathbf{x}) p_{\mathbf{xy}} = p(\mathbf{y}) p_{\mathbf{yx}}$. By Lemma 4.3, the stationary probability of the random walk is $p(\mathbf{x})$. An example illustrating the Gibbs algorithm is given in Figure 4.3.

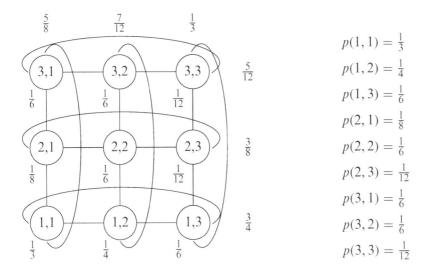

$$p(1,1) = \tfrac{1}{3}$$
$$p(1,2) = \tfrac{1}{4}$$
$$p(1,3) = \tfrac{1}{6}$$
$$p(2,1) = \tfrac{1}{8}$$
$$p(2,2) = \tfrac{1}{6}$$
$$p(2,3) = \tfrac{1}{12}$$
$$p(3,1) = \tfrac{1}{6}$$
$$p(3,2) = \tfrac{1}{6}$$
$$p(3,3) = \tfrac{1}{12}$$

Calculation of edge probability $p_{(11)(12)}$

$$p_{(11)(12)} = \tfrac{1}{d}p_{12}/(p_{11} + p_{12} + p_{13}) = \tfrac{1}{2} \, (\tfrac{1}{4})/(\tfrac{1}{3} \, \tfrac{1}{4} \, \tfrac{1}{6}) = \tfrac{1}{8}/\tfrac{9}{12} = \tfrac{1}{8} \, \tfrac{4}{3} = \tfrac{1}{6}$$

Edge probabilities.

$$p_{(11)(12)} = \tfrac{1}{2} \, \tfrac{1}{4} \, \tfrac{4}{3} = \tfrac{1}{6} \quad p_{(12)(11)} = \tfrac{1}{2} \, \tfrac{1}{3} \, \tfrac{4}{3} = \tfrac{2}{9} \quad p_{(13)(11)} = \tfrac{1}{2} \, \tfrac{1}{3} \, \tfrac{4}{3} = \tfrac{2}{9} \quad p_{(21)(22)} = \tfrac{1}{2} \, \tfrac{1}{6} \, \tfrac{8}{3} = \tfrac{2}{9}$$

$$p_{(11)(13)} = \tfrac{1}{2} \, \tfrac{1}{6} \, \tfrac{4}{3} = \tfrac{1}{9} \quad p_{(12)(13)} = \tfrac{1}{2} \, \tfrac{1}{6} \, \tfrac{4}{3} = \tfrac{1}{9} \quad p_{(13)(12)} = \tfrac{1}{2} \, \tfrac{1}{4} \, \tfrac{4}{3} = \tfrac{1}{6} \quad p_{(21)(23)} = \tfrac{1}{2} \, \tfrac{1}{12} \, \tfrac{8}{3} = \tfrac{1}{9}$$

$$p_{(11)(21)} = \tfrac{1}{2} \, \tfrac{1}{8} \, \tfrac{8}{5} = \tfrac{1}{10} \quad p_{(12)(22)} = \tfrac{1}{2} \, \tfrac{1}{6} \, \tfrac{12}{7} = \tfrac{1}{7} \quad p_{(13)(23)} = \tfrac{1}{2} \, \tfrac{1}{12} \, \tfrac{3}{1} = \tfrac{1}{8} \quad p_{(21)(11)} = \tfrac{1}{2} \, \tfrac{1}{3} \, \tfrac{8}{5} = \tfrac{4}{15}$$

$$p_{(11)(31)} = \tfrac{1}{2} \, \tfrac{1}{6} \, \tfrac{8}{5} = \tfrac{2}{15} \quad p_{(12)(32)} = \tfrac{1}{2} \, \tfrac{1}{6} \, \tfrac{12}{7} = \tfrac{1}{7} \quad p_{(13)(33)} = \tfrac{1}{2} \, \tfrac{1}{12} \, \tfrac{3}{1} = \tfrac{1}{8} \quad p_{(21)(31)} = \tfrac{1}{2} \, \tfrac{1}{6} \, \tfrac{8}{5} = \tfrac{2}{15}$$

Verification of a few edges, $p_i p_{ij} = p_j p_{ji}$.

$$p_{11}p_{(11)(12)} = \tfrac{1}{3} \, \tfrac{1}{6} = \tfrac{1}{4} \, \tfrac{2}{9} = p_{12}p_{(12)(11)}$$

$$p_{11}p_{(11)(13)} = \tfrac{1}{3} \, \tfrac{1}{9} = \tfrac{1}{6} \, \tfrac{2}{9} = p_{13}p_{(13)(11)}$$

$$p_{11}p_{(11)(21)} = \tfrac{1}{3} \, \tfrac{1}{10} = \tfrac{1}{8} \, \tfrac{4}{15} = p_{21}p_{(21)(11)}$$

Note that the edge probabilities out of a state such as (1,1) do not add up to 1. That is, with some probability, the walk stays at the state that it is in. For example,

$$p_{(11)(11)} = 1 - (p_{(11)(12)} + p_{(11)(13)} + p_{(11)(21)} + p_{(11)(31)}) = 1 - \tfrac{1}{6} - \tfrac{1}{24} - \tfrac{1}{32} - \tfrac{1}{24} = \tfrac{9}{32}.$$

Figure 4.3: Using the Gibbs algorithm to set probabilities for a random walk so that the stationary probability will be a desired probability.

4.3. Areas and Volumes

Computing areas and volumes is a classical problem. For many regular figures in two and three dimensions there are closed-form formulae. In Chapter 2, we saw how to compute volume of a high-dimensional sphere by integration. For general convex sets in d-space, there are no closed-form formulae. Can we estimate volumes of d-dimensional convex sets in time that grows as a polynomial function of d? The MCMC method answers this question in the affirmative.

One way to estimate the area of the region is to enclose it in a rectangle and estimate the ratio of the area of the region to the area of the rectangle by picking random points in the rectangle and seeing what proportion land in the region. Such methods fail in high dimensions. Even for a sphere in high dimension, a cube enclosing the sphere has exponentially larger area, so exponentially many samples are required to estimate the volume of the sphere.

It turns out, however, that the problem of estimating volumes of sets can be reduced to the problem of drawing uniform random samples from sets. Suppose one wants to estimate the volume of a convex set R. Create a concentric series of larger and larger spheres[2] $S_1, S_2, \ldots, S_k$ such that S_1 is contained in R and S_k contains R. Then

$$\text{Vol}(R) = \text{Vol}(S_k \cap R) = \frac{\text{Vol}(S_k \cap R)}{\text{Vol}(S_{k-1} \cap R)} \frac{\text{Vol}(S_{k-1} \cap R)}{\text{Vol}(S_{k-2} \cap R)} \cdots \frac{\text{Vol}(S_2 \cap R)}{\text{Vol}(S_1 \cap R)} \text{Vol}(S_1).$$

If the radius of the sphere S_i is $1 + \frac{1}{d}$ times the radius of the sphere S_{i-1}, then we have:

$$1 \leq \frac{\text{Vol}(S_i \cap R)}{\text{Vol}(S_{i-1} \cap R)} < e$$

because $\text{Vol}(S_i)/\text{Vol}(S_{i-1}) = \left(1 + \frac{1}{d}\right)^d < e$, and the fraction of S_i occupied by R is less than or equal to the fraction of S_{i-1} occupied by R (due to the convexity of R and the fact that the center of the spheres lies in R). This implies that the ratio $\frac{Vol(S_i \cap R)}{Vol(S_{i-1} \cap R)}$ can be estimated by rejection sampling, i.e., selecting points in $S_i \cap R$ uniformly at random and computing the fraction in $S_{i-1} \cap R$, provided one can select points at random from a d-dimensional convex region. This is illustrated in Figure 4.4.

Solving $(1 + \frac{1}{d})^k = r$ for k where r is the ratio of the radius of S_k to the radius of S_1 bounds the number of spheres.

$$k = O(\log_{1+(1/d)} r) = O(d \ln r).[3]$$

This means that it suffices to estimate each ratio to a factor of $(1 \pm \frac{\epsilon}{ed \ln r})$ in order to estimate the overall volume to error $1 \pm \epsilon$.

It remains to show how to draw a uniform random sample from a d-dimensional convex set. Here we will use the convexity of the set R and thus the sets $S_i \cap R$ so that the Markov chain technique will converge quickly to its stationary probability. To select a random sample from a d-dimensional convex set, impose a grid on the region and do a random walk on the grid points. At each time, pick one of the $2d$ coordinate neighbors of the current grid point, each with probability $1/(2d)$ and go to the neighbor if it is still in the set; otherwise, stay put and repeat. If the grid length in each of the d coordinate directions is at most some a, the total number of grid points in the set is at most a^d. Although this is exponential in d, the Markov chain turns out to be rapidly mixing (the proof is beyond our scope here) and leads to polynomial time bounded algorithm to estimate the volume of any convex set in $\mathbf{R}^d$.

---

[2]One could also use rectangles instead of spheres.
[3]Using $log_a r = \frac{log_b r}{log_b a}$ and $\ln(1 + x) \leq x$.

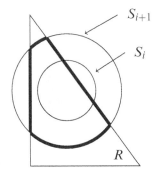
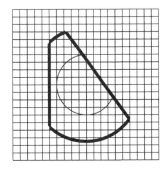

Figure 4.4: By sampling the area inside the dark line and determining the fraction of points in the shaded region we compute $\frac{Vol(S_{i+1} \cap R)}{Vol(S_i \cap R)}$.

To sample, we create a grid and assign a probability of one to each grid point inside the dark lines and zero outside. Using Metropolis-Hasting edge probabilities, the stationary probability will be uniform for each point inside the the region, and we can sample points uniformly and determine the fraction within the shaded region.

4.4. Convergence of Random Walks on Undirected Graphs

In an undirected graph where $\pi_x p_{xy} = \pi_y p_{yx}$, edges can be assigned weights such that $P_{xy} = \frac{w_{xy}}{\sum_y w_{xy}}$. See Exercise 4.19. Thus the Metropolis-Hasting algorithm and Gibbs sampling both involve random walks on edge-weighted undirected graphs. Given an edge-weighted undirected graph, let w_{xy} denote the weight of the edge between nodes x and y, with $w_{xy} = 0$ if no such edge exists. Let $w_x = \sum_y w_{xy}$. The Markov chain has transition probabilities $p_{xy} = w_{xy}/w_x$. We assume the chain is connected.

We now claim that the stationary distribution π of this walk has π_x proportional to w_x, i.e., $\pi_x = w_x/w_{total}$ for $w_{total} = \sum_{x'} w_{x'}$. Specifically, notice that

$$w_x p_{xy} = w_x \frac{w_{xy}}{w_x} = w_{xy} = w_{yx} = w_y \frac{w_{yx}}{w_y} = w_y p_{yx}.$$

Therefore, $(w_x/w_{total})p_{xy} = (w_y/w_{total})p_{yx}$, and Lemma 4.3 implies that the values $\pi_x = w_x/w_{total}$ are the stationary probabilities.

An important question is how fast the walk starts to reflect the stationary probability of the Markov process. If the convergence time was proportional to the number of states, algorithms such as Metropolis-Hasting and Gibbs sampling would not be very useful, since the number of states can be exponentially large.

There are clear examples of connected chains that take a long time to converge. A chain with a constriction (see Figure 4.5) takes a long time to converge, since the walk is unlikely to cross the narrow passage between the two halves, both of which are reasonably big. We will show in Theorem 4.5 that the time to converge is quantitatively related to the tightest constriction.

We define below a combinatorial measure of constriction for a Markov chain, called the *normalized conductance*. We will relate normalized conductance to the time by which the average probability distribution of the chain is guaranteed to be close to the stationary probability distribution. We call this ε-mixing time:

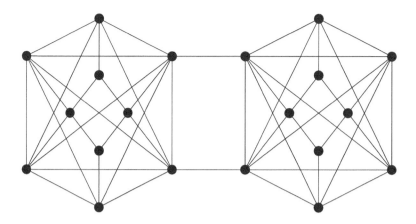

Figure 4.5: A network with a constriction. All edges have weight 1.

Definition 4.1 *Fix $\varepsilon > 0$. The ε-mixing time of a Markov chain is the minimum integer t such that for any starting distribution* **p**, *the 1-norm difference between the t-step running average probability distribution[4] and the stationary distribution is at most ε.*

Definition 4.2 *For a subset S of vertices, let $\pi(S)$ denote $\sum_{x \in S} \pi_x$. The normalized conductance $\Phi(S)$ of S is*

$$\Phi(S) = \frac{\displaystyle\sum_{(x,y) \in (S,\bar{S})} \pi_x p_{xy}}{\min\left(\pi(S), \pi(\bar{S})\right)}.$$

There is a simple interpretation of $\Phi(S)$. Suppose without loss of generality that $\pi(S) \leq \pi(\bar{S})$. Then, we may write $\Phi(S)$ as

$$\Phi(S) = \sum_{x \in S} \underbrace{\frac{\pi_x}{\pi(S)}}_{a} \underbrace{\sum_{y \in \bar{S}} p_{xy}}_{b}.$$

Here, a is the probability of being in x if we were in the stationary distribution restricted to S and b is the probability of stepping from x to $\bar{S}$ in a single step. Thus, $\Phi(S)$ is the probability of moving from S to $\bar{S}$ in one step if we are in the stationary distribution restricted to S.

Definition 4.3 *The normalized conductance of the Markov chain, denoted Φ, is defined by*

$$\Phi = \min_{S \subset V, S \neq \{\}} \Phi(S).$$

As we just argued, normalized conductance being high is a necessary condition for rapid mixing. The theorem below proves the converse that normalized conductance being high is sufficient for mixing. Intuitively, if Φ is large, the walk rapidly leaves

---

[4]Recall that $\mathbf{a(t)} = \frac{1}{t}(\mathbf{p(0)} + \mathbf{p(1)} + \cdots + \mathbf{p(t-1)})$ is called the running average distribution.

any subset of states. But the proof of the theorem is quite difficult. After we prove it, we will see examples where the mixing time is much smaller than the cover time. That is, the number of steps before a random walk reaches a random state independent of its starting state is much smaller than the average number of steps needed to reach every state. In fact, for graphs whose conductance is bounded below by a constant, called expanders, the mixing time is logarithmic in the number of states.

Theorem 4.5 *The ε-mixing time of a random walk on an undirected graph is*

$$O\left(\frac{\ln(1/\pi_{min})}{\Phi^2 \varepsilon^3}\right)$$

where π_{min} is the minimum stationary probability of any state.

Proof Let $t = \frac{c \ln(1/\pi_{min})}{\Phi^2 \varepsilon^3}$ for a suitable constant c. Let

$$\mathbf{a} = \mathbf{a(t)} = \frac{1}{t}\left(\mathbf{p(0)} + \mathbf{p(1)} + \cdots + \mathbf{p(t-1)}\right)$$

be the running average distribution. We need to show that $||\mathbf{a} - \boldsymbol{\pi}||_1 \leq \varepsilon$. Let

$$v_i = \frac{a_i}{\pi_i},$$

and renumber states so that $v_1 \geq v_2 \geq v_3 \geq \cdots$. Thus, early indices i for which $v_i > 1$ are states that currently have too much probability, and late indices i for which $v_i < 1$ are states that currently have too little probability.

Intuitively, to show that $||\mathbf{a} - \boldsymbol{\pi}||_1 \leq \varepsilon$ it is enough to show that the values v_i are relatively flat and do not drop too fast as we increase i. We begin by reducing our goal to a formal statement of that form. Then, in the second part of the proof, we prove that v_i do not fall fast using the concept of "probability flows."

We call a state i for which $v_i > 1$ "heavy," since it has more probability according to $\mathbf{a}$ than its stationary probability. Let i_0 be the maximum i such that $v_i > 1$; it is the last heavy state. By Proposition (4.4):

$$||\mathbf{a} - \boldsymbol{\pi}||_1 = 2\sum_{i=1}^{i_0}(v_i - 1)\pi_i = 2\sum_{i \geq i_0+1}(1 - v_i)\pi_i. \tag{4.3}$$

Let

$$\gamma_i = \pi_1 + \pi_2 + \cdots + \pi_i.$$

Define a function $f : [0, \gamma_{i_0}] \to \Re$ by $f(x) = v_i - 1$ for $x \in [\gamma_{i-1}, \gamma_i)$. See Figure 4.6. Now,

$$\sum_{i=1}^{i_0}(v_i - 1)\pi_i = \int_0^{\gamma_{i_0}} f(x)\, dx. \tag{4.4}$$

We make one more technical modification. We divide $\{1, 2, \ldots, i_0\}$ into groups $G_1, G_2, G_3, \ldots, G_r$, of contiguous subsets. We specify the groups later. Let $u_s = \text{Max}_{i \in G_s} v_i$ be the maximum value of v_i within G_s. Define a new function $g(x)$ by $g(x) = u_s - 1$ for $x \in \cup_{i \in G_s}[\gamma_{i-1}, \gamma_i)$; see Figure 4.6. Since $g(x) \geq f(x)$,

$$\int_0^{\gamma_{i_0}} f(x)\, dx \leq \int_0^{\gamma_{i_0}} g(x)\, dx. \tag{4.5}$$

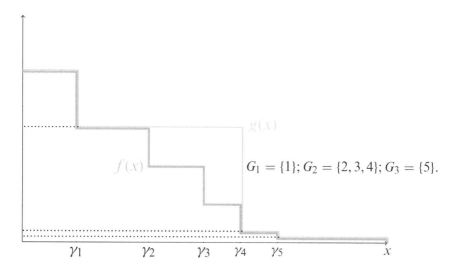

Figure 4.6: Bounding l_1 distance.

We now assert (with $u_{r+1} = 1$):

$$\int_0^{\gamma_{i_0}} g(x)\, dx = \sum_{t=1}^{r} \pi(G_1 \cup G_2 \cup \ldots \cup G_t)(u_t - u_{t+1}). \qquad (4.6)$$

This is just the statement that the area under $g(x)$ in the figure is exactly covered by the rectangles whose bottom sides are the dotted lines. We leave the formal proof of this to the reader. We now focus on proving that

$$\sum_{s=1}^{r} \pi(G_1 \cup G_2 \cup \ldots \cup G_s)(u_s - u_{s+1}) \leq \varepsilon/2, \qquad (4.7)$$

for a subdivision into groups we specify, which suffices by 4.3, 4.4, 4.5, and 4.6. While we start the proof of (4.7) with a technical observation (4.8), its proof will involve two nice ideas: the notion of probability flow and reckoning probability flow in two different ways. First, the technical observation: if $2 \sum_{i \geq i_0+1} (1 - v_i)\pi_i \leq \varepsilon$, then we would be done by (4.3). So assume now that $\sum_{i \geq i_0+1} (1 - v_i)\pi_i > \varepsilon/2$ from which it follows that $\sum_{i \geq i_0+1} \pi_i \geq \varepsilon/2$, and so, for any subset A of heavy nodes,

$$\mathrm{Min}(\pi(A), \pi(\bar{A})) \geq \frac{\varepsilon}{2}\pi(A). \qquad (4.8)$$

We now define the subsets. G_1 will be just $\{1\}$. In general, suppose $G_1, G_2, \ldots, G_{s-1}$ have already been defined. We start G_s at $i_s = 1+$ (end of G_{s-1}). Let $i_s = k$. We will define l, the last element of G_s, to be the largest integer greater than or equal to k and at most i_0 so that

$$\sum_{j=k+1}^{l} \pi_j \leq \frac{\varepsilon \Phi \gamma_k}{4}.$$

In Lemma 4.6, which follows this theorem, prove that for groups $G_1, G_2, \ldots, G_r$, $u_1.u_2, \ldots, u_r, u_{r+1}$ as above,

$$\pi(G_1 \cup G_2 \cup \ldots G_s)(u_s - u_{s+1}) \leq \frac{8}{t\Phi\varepsilon}.$$

Now to prove (4.7), we only need an upper bound on r, the number of groups. If $G_s = \{k, k+1, \ldots, l\}$, with $l < i_0$, then by definition of l, we have $\gamma_{l+1} \geq (1 + \frac{\varepsilon\Phi}{2})\gamma_k$. So, $r \leq \ln_{1+(\varepsilon\Phi/2)}(1/\pi_1) + 2 \leq \ln(1/\pi_1)/(\varepsilon\Phi/2) + 2$. This completes the proof of (4.7) and the theorem. ∎

We complete the proof of Theorem 4.5 with the proof of Lemma 4.6. The notation in the lemma is that from the theorem.

Lemma 4.6 *Suppose groups* $G_1, G_2, \ldots, G_r, u_1.u_2, \ldots, u_r, u_{r+1}$ *are as above. Then,*

$$\pi(G_1 \cup G_2 \cup \ldots G_s)(u_s - u_{s+1}) \leq \frac{8}{t\Phi\varepsilon}.$$

Proof This is the main lemma. The proof of the lemma uses a crucial idea of probability flows. We will use two ways of calculating the probability flow from heavy states to light states when we execute one step of the Markov chain starting at probabilities **a**. The probability vector after that step is **a**P. Now, **a** $-$ **a**P is the net loss of probability for each state due to the step.

Consider a particular group $G_s = \{k, k+1, \ldots, l\}$, say. First consider the case when $k < i_0$. Let $A = \{1, 2, \ldots, k\}$. The net loss of probability for each state from the set A in one step is $\sum_{i=1}^{k}(a_i - (\mathbf{a}P)_i)$, which is at most $\frac{2}{t}$ by the proof of Theorem 4.2.

Another way to reckon the net loss of probability from A is to take the difference of the probability flow from A to $\bar{A}$ and the flow from $\bar{A}$ to A. For any $i < j$,

$$\text{net-flow}(i, j) = \text{flow}(i, j) - \text{flow}(j, i) = \pi_i p_{ij} v_i - \pi_j p_{ji} v_j = \pi_j p_{ji}(v_i - v_j) \geq 0.$$

Thus, for any two states i and j, with i heavier than j, i.e., $i < j$, there is a nonnegative net flow from i to j. (This is intuitively reasonable, since it says that probability is flowing from heavy to light states.) Since $l \geq k$, the flow from A to $\{k+1, k+2, \ldots, l\}$ minus the flow from $\{k+1, k+2, \ldots, l\}$ to A is nonnegative. Since for $i \leq k$ and $j > l$, we have $v_i \geq v_k$ and $v_j \leq v_{l+1}$, the net loss from A is at least

$$\sum_{\substack{i \leq k \\ j > l}} \pi_j p_{ji}(v_i - v_j) \geq (v_k - v_{l+1}) \sum_{\substack{i \leq k \\ j > l}} \pi_j p_{ji}.$$

Thus,

$$(v_k - v_{l+1}) \sum_{\substack{i \leq k \\ j > l}} \pi_j p_{ji} \leq \frac{2}{t}. \tag{4.9}$$

Since

$$\sum_{i=1}^{k} \sum_{j=k+1}^{l} \pi_j p_{ji} \leq \sum_{j=k+1}^{l} \pi_j \leq \varepsilon\Phi\pi(A)/4$$

and by the definition of Φ, using (4.8),

$$\sum_{i \leq k < j} \pi_j p_{ji} \geq \Phi \mathrm{Min}(\pi(A), \pi(\bar{A})) \geq \varepsilon \Phi \gamma_k / 2,$$

we have, $\sum_{\substack{i \leq k \\ j > l}} \pi_j p_{ji} = \sum_{i \leq k < j} \pi_j p_{ji} - \sum_{i \leq k; j \leq l} \pi_j p_{ji} \geq \varepsilon \Phi \gamma_k / 4$. Substituting this into the inequality (4.9) gives

$$v_k - v_{l+1} \leq \frac{8}{t \varepsilon \Phi \gamma_k}, \tag{4.10}$$

proving the lemma provided $k < i_0$. If $k = i_0$, the proof is similar but simpler. ∎

Theorem 4.5 gives an upper bound on the mixing time in terms of the conductance. Conversely, $\Omega(1/\Phi)$ is a known lower bound. We do not prove this here.

4.4.1. Using Normalized Conductance to Prove Convergence

We now apply Theorem 4.5 to some examples to illustrate how the normalized conductance bounds the rate of convergence. In each case we compute the mixing time for the uniform probability function on the vertices. Our first examples will be simple graphs. The graphs do not have rapid converge, but their simplicity helps illustrate how to bound the normalized conductance and hence the rate of convergence.

A One-Dimensional Lattice

Consider a random walk on an undirected graph consisting of an n-vertex path with self-loops at the both ends. With the self loops, we have $p_{xy} = 1/2$ on all edges (x, y), and so the stationary distribution is a uniform $\frac{1}{n}$ over all vertices by Lemma 4.3. The set with minimum normalized conductance is the set S with probability $\pi(S) \leq \frac{1}{2}$ having the smallest ratio of probability mass exiting it, $\sum_{(x,y) \in (S, \bar{S})} \pi_x p_{xy}$, to probability mass inside it, $\pi(S)$. This set consists of the first $n/2$ vertices, for which the numerator is $\frac{1}{2n}$ and denominator is $\frac{1}{2}$. Thus,

$$\Phi(S) = \frac{1}{n}.$$

By Theorem 4.5, for ε a constant such as $1/100$, after $O((n^2 \log n)/\epsilon^3)$ steps, $||a_t - \pi||_1 \leq 1/100$. This graph does not have rapid convergence. The hitting time and the cover time are $O(n^2)$. In many interesting cases, the mixing time may be much smaller than the cover time. We will see such an example later.

A Two-Dimensional Lattice

Consider the $n \times n$ lattice in the plane where from each point there is a transition to each of the coordinate neighbors with probability $1/4$. At the boundary there are self-loops with probability 1-(number of neighbors)/4. It is easy to see that the chain is connected. Since $p_{ij} = p_{ji}$, the function $f_i = 1/n^2$ satisfies $f_i p_{ij} = f_j p_{ji}$ and, by Lemma 4.3, $\mathbf{f}$ is the stationary distribution. Consider any subset S consisting of at most half the states. If $|S| \geq \frac{n^2}{4}$, then the subset with the fewest edges leaving it consists of some number of columns plus perhaps one additional partial column. The number of edges leaving S is at least n. Thus,

$$\sum_{i \in S} \sum_{j \in \bar{S}} \pi_i p_{ij} \geq \Omega\left(n \frac{1}{n^2}\right) = \Omega\left(\frac{1}{n}\right).$$

Since $|S| \geq \frac{n^2}{4}$, in this case,

$$\Phi(S) \geq \Omega\left(\frac{1/n}{\min\left(\frac{S}{n^2}, \frac{\bar{S}}{n^2}\right)}\right) = \Omega\left(\frac{1}{n}\right).$$

If $|S| < \frac{n^2}{4}$, the subset S of a given size that has the minimum number of edges leaving consists of a square located at the lower left-hand corner of the grid (Exercise 4.24). If $|S|$ is not a perfect square, then the right-most column of S is short. Thus at least $2\sqrt{|S|}$ points in S are adjacent to points in $\bar{S}$. Each of these points contributes $\pi_i p_{ij} = \Omega(\frac{1}{n^2})$ to the flow$(S, \bar{S})$. Thus,

$$\sum_{i \in S} \sum_{j \in \bar{S}} \pi_i p_{ij} \geq \frac{c\sqrt{|S|}}{n^2}$$

and

$$\Phi(S) = \frac{\sum_{i \in S} \sum_{j \in \bar{S}} \pi_i p_{ij}}{\min\left(\pi(S), \pi(\bar{S})\right)} \geq \frac{c\sqrt{|S|}/n^2}{|S|/n^2} = \frac{c}{\sqrt{|S|}} = \Omega\left(\frac{1}{n}\right).$$

Thus, in either case, after $O(n^2 \ln n/\epsilon^3)$ steps, $|\mathbf{a(t)} - \boldsymbol{\pi}|_1 \leq \epsilon$.

A Lattice in d Dimensions

Next consider the $n \times n \times \cdots \times n$ lattice in d dimensions with a self-loop at each boundary point with probability $1 - $ (number of neighbors)$/2d$. The self loops make all π_i equal to n^{-d}. View the lattice as an undirected graph and consider the random walk on this undirected graph. Since there are n^d states, the cover time is at least n^d and thus exponentially dependent on d. It is possible to show (Exercise 4.25) that Φ is $\Omega(\frac{1}{dn})$. Since all π_i are equal to n^{-d}, the mixing time is $O(d^3 n^2 \ln n/\varepsilon^3)$, which is polynomially bounded in n and d.

The d-dimensional lattice is related to the Metropolis-Hastings algorithm and Gibbs sampling, although in those constructions there is a nonuniform probability distribution at the vertices. However, the d-dimension lattice case suggests why the Metropolis-Hastings and Gibbs sampling constructions might converge fast.

A Clique

Consider an n vertex clique with a self loop at each vertex. For each edge, $p_{xy} = \frac{1}{n}$, and thus for each vertex, $\pi_x = \frac{1}{n}$. Let S be a subset of the vertices. Then

$$\sum_{x \in S} \pi_x = \frac{|S|}{n}.$$

$$\sum_{(x,y) \in (S,\bar{S})} \pi_x p_{xy} = \pi_x p_{xy} |S||\bar{S}| = \frac{1}{n^2}|S||\bar{S}|$$

and

$$\Phi(S) = \frac{\sum_{(x,y)\in(S,\bar{S})} \pi_x p_{xy}}{\min\left(\pi(S), \pi(\bar{S})\right)} = \frac{\frac{1}{n^2}|S||\bar{S}|}{\frac{1}{n}\min(|S|,|\bar{S}|)} = \frac{1}{n}\max(|S|,|\bar{S}|) = \frac{1}{2}.$$

This gives a bound on the ε-mixing time of

$$O\left(\frac{\ln\frac{1}{\pi_{\min}}}{\Phi^2 \varepsilon^3}\right) = O\left(\frac{\ln n}{\varepsilon^3}\right).$$

However, a walker on the clique starting from any probability distribution will in one step be exactly at the stationary probability distribution.

A Connected Undirected Graph

Next consider a random walk on a connected n vertex undirected graph where at each vertex all edges are equally likely. The stationary probability of a vertex equals the degree of the vertex divided by the sum of degrees. That is, if the degree of vertex x is d_x and the number of edges in the graph is m, then $\pi_x = \frac{d_x}{2m}$. Notice that for any edge (x, y) we have

$$\pi_x p_{xy} = \left(\frac{d_x}{2m}\right)\left(\frac{1}{d_x}\right) = \frac{1}{2m}.$$

Therefore, for any S, the total conductance of edges out of S is at least $\frac{1}{2m}$, and so Φ is at least $\frac{1}{m}$. Since $\pi_{\min} \geq \frac{1}{2m} \geq \frac{1}{n^2}$, $\ln\frac{1}{\pi_{\min}} = O(\ln n)$. Thus, the mixing time is $O(m^2 \ln n/\varepsilon^3) = O(n^4 \ln n/\varepsilon^3)$.

The Gaussian Distribution on the Interval $[-1,1]$

Consider the interval $[-1, 1]$. Let δ be a "grid size" specified later and let G be the graph consisting of a path on the $\frac{2}{\delta} + 1$ vertices $\{-1, -1 + \delta, -1 + 2\delta, \ldots, 1 - \delta, 1\}$ having self loops at the two ends. Let $\pi_x = ce^{-\alpha x^2}$ for $x \in \{-1, -1+\delta, -1+2\delta, \ldots, 1-\delta, 1\}$ where $\alpha > 1$ and c has been adjusted so that $\sum_x \pi_x = 1$.

We now describe a simple Markov chain with the π_x as its stationary probability and argue its fast convergence. With the Metropolis-Hastings' construction, the transition probabilities are

$$p_{x,x+\delta} = \frac{1}{2}\min\left(1, \frac{e^{-\alpha(x+\delta)^2}}{e^{-\alpha x^2}}\right) \text{ and } p_{x,x-\delta} = \frac{1}{2}\min\left(1, \frac{e^{-\alpha(x-\delta)^2}}{e^{-\alpha x^2}}\right).$$

Let S be any subset of states with $\pi(S) \leq \frac{1}{2}$. First consider the case when S is an interval $[k\delta, 1]$ for $k \geq 2$. It is easy to see that

$$\pi(S) \leq \int_{x=(k-1)\delta}^{\infty} ce^{-\alpha x^2}\, dx$$

$$\leq \int_{(k-1)\delta}^{\infty} \frac{x}{(k-1)\delta} ce^{-\alpha x^2}\, dx$$

$$= O\left(\frac{ce^{-\alpha((k-1)\delta)^2}}{\alpha(k-1)\delta}\right).$$

Now there is only one edge from S to $\bar{S}$, and total conductance of edges out of S is

$$\sum_{i \in S} \sum_{j \notin S} \pi_i p_{ij} = \pi_{k\delta} p_{k\delta,(k-1)\delta} = \min(ce^{-\alpha k^2 \delta^2}, ce^{-\alpha(k-1)^2 \delta^2}) = ce^{-\alpha k^2 \delta^2}.$$

Using $2 \leq k \leq 1/\delta, \alpha \geq 1$, and $\pi(\bar{S}) \leq 1$,

$$\Phi(S) = \frac{\text{flow}(S, \bar{S})}{\min(\pi(S), \pi(\bar{S}))} \geq ce^{-\alpha k^2 \delta^2} \frac{\alpha(k-1)\delta}{ce^{-\alpha((k-1)\delta)^2}}$$

$$\geq \Omega(\alpha(k-1)\delta e^{-\alpha \delta^2 (2k-1)}) \geq \Omega(\alpha \delta e^{-O(\alpha \delta)}).$$

For the grid size less than the variance of the Gaussian distribution, $\delta < \frac{1}{\alpha}$, we have $\alpha\delta < 1$, so $e^{-O(\alpha\delta)} = \Omega(1)$, thus, $\Phi(S) \geq \Omega(\alpha\delta)$. Now, $\pi_{\min} \geq ce^{-\alpha} \geq e^{-1/\delta}$, so $\ln(1/\pi_{\min}) \leq 1/\delta$.

If S is not an interval of the form $[k, 1]$ or $[-1, k]$, then the situation is only better, since there is more than one "boundary" point, which contributes to flow$(S, \bar{S})$. We do not present this argument here. By Theorem 4.5 in $\Omega(1/\alpha^2 \delta^3 \varepsilon^3)$ steps, a walk gets within ε of the steady state distribution.

In the uniform probability case, the ϵ-mixing time is bounded by $n^2 \log n$. For comparison, in the Gaussian case set $\delta = 1/n$ and $\alpha = 1/3$. This gives an ϵ-mixing time bound of n^3. In the Gaussian case with the entire initial probability on the first vertex, the chain begins to converge faster to the stationary probability than the uniform distribution case, since the chain favors higher-degree vertices. However, ultimately the distribution must reach the lower-probability vertices on the other side of the Gaussian's maximum, and here the chain is slower, since it favors not leaving the higher-probability vertices.

In these examples, we have chosen simple probability distributions. The methods extend to more complex situations.

4.5. Electrical Networks and Random Walks

In the next few sections, we study the relationship between electrical networks and random walks on undirected graphs. The graphs have nonnegative weights on each edge. A step is executed by picking a random edge from the current vertex with probability proportional to the edge's weight and traversing the edge.

An electrical network is a connected, undirected graph in which each edge (x, y) has a resistance $r_{xy} > 0$. In what follows, it is easier to deal with conductance defined as the reciprocal of resistance, $c_{xy} = \frac{1}{r_{xy}}$, rather than resistance. Associated with an electrical network is a random walk on the underlying graph defined by assigning a probability $p_{xy} = c_{xy}/c_x$ to the edge (x, y) incident to the vertex x, where the normalizing constant c_x equals $\sum_y c_{xy}$. Note that although c_{xy} equals c_{yx}, the probabilities p_{xy} and p_{yx} may not be equal due to the normalization required to make the probabilities at each vertex sum to 1. We shall soon see that there is a relationship between current flowing in an electrical network and a random walk on the underlying graph.

Since we assume that the undirected graph is connected, by Theorem 4.2 there is a unique stationary probability distribution. The stationary probability distribution is π where $\pi_x = \frac{c_x}{c_0}$ with $c_0 = \sum_x c_x$. To see this, for all x and y,

$$\pi_x p_{xy} = \frac{c_x}{c_0}\frac{c_{xy}}{c_x} = \frac{c_y}{c_0}\frac{c_{yx}}{c_y} = \pi_y p_{yx},$$

and hence by Lemma 4.3, π is the unique stationary probability.

Harmonic Functions

Harmonic functions are useful in developing the relationship between electrical networks and random walks on undirected graphs. Given an undirected graph, designate a non-empty set of vertices as boundary vertices and the remaining vertices as interior vertices. A harmonic function g on the vertices is a function whose value at the boundary vertices is fixed to some boundary condition, and whose value at any interior vertex x is a weighted average of its values at all the adjacent vertices y, with weights p_{xy} satisfying $\sum_y p_{xy} = 1$ for each x. Thus, if at every interior vertex x for some set of weights p_{xy} satisfying $\sum_y p_{xy} = 1, g_x = \sum_y g_y p_{xy}$, then g is an harmonic function. An illustration of a harmonic function is given in Figure 4.7.

Example Convert an electrical network with conductances c_{xy} to a weighted, undirected graph with probabilities p_{xy}. Let $\mathbf{f}$ be a function satisfying $\mathbf{f}P = \mathbf{f}$ where P is the matrix of probabilities. It follows that the function $g_x = \frac{f_x}{c_x}$ is harmonic.

$$g_x = \frac{f_x}{c_x} = \frac{1}{c_x}\sum_y f_y p_{yx} = \frac{1}{c_x}\sum_y f_y \frac{c_{yx}}{c_y}$$

$$= \frac{1}{c_x}\sum_y f_y \frac{c_{xy}}{c_y} = \sum_y \frac{f_y}{c_y}\frac{c_{xy}}{c_x} = \sum_y g_y p_{xy} \qquad \blacksquare$$

A harmonic function on a connected graph takes on its maximum and minimum on the boundary. This is easy to see for the following reason. Suppose the maximum does not occur on the boundary. Let S be the set of vertices at which the

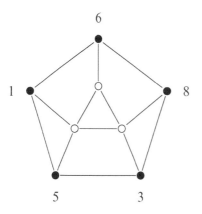

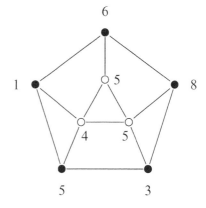

Graph with boundary vertices dark and boundary conditions specified.

Values of harmonic function satisfying boundary conditions where the edge weights at each vertex are equal

Figure 4.7: Graph illustrating a harmonic function.

maximum value is attained. Since S contains no boundary vertices, $\bar{S}$ is non-empty. Connectedness implies that there is at least one edge (x, y) with $x \in S$ and $y \in \bar{S}$. The value of the function at x is the weighted average of the value at its neighbors, all of which are less than or equal to the value at x and the value at y is strictly less, a contradiction. The proof for the minimum value is identical.

There is at most one harmonic function satisfying a given set of equations and boundary conditions. For suppose there were two solutions, $f(x)$ and $g(x)$. The difference of two solutions is itself harmonic. Since $h(x) = f(x) - g(x)$ is harmonic and has value zero on the boundary, by the min and max principles it has value zero everywhere. Thus $f(x) = g(x)$.

The Analogy between Electrical Networks and Random Walks

There are important connections between electrical networks and random walks on undirected graphs. Choose two vertices a and b. Attach a voltage source between a and b so that the voltage v_a equals 1 volt and the voltage v_b equals zero. Fixing the voltages at v_a and v_b induces voltages at all other vertices, along with a current flow through the edges of the network. What we will show below is the following. Having fixed the voltages at the vertices a and b, the voltage at an arbitrary vertex x equals the probability that a random walk that starts at x will reach a before it reaches b. We will also show there is a related probabilistic interpretation of current as well.

Probabilistic Interpretation of Voltages

Before relating voltages and probabilities, we first show that the voltages form a harmonic function. Let x and y be adjacent vertices and let i_{xy} be the current flowing through the edge from x to y. By Ohm's law,

$$i_{xy} = \frac{v_x - v_y}{r_{xy}} = (v_x - v_y)c_{xy}.$$

By Kirchhoff's law, the currents flowing out of each vertex sum to zero:

$$\sum_y i_{xy} = 0.$$

Replacing currents in the above sum by the voltage difference times the conductance yields

$$\sum_y (v_x - v_y)c_{xy} = 0$$

or

$$v_x \sum_y c_{xy} = \sum_y v_y c_{xy}.$$

Observing that $\sum_y c_{xy} = c_x$ and that $p_{xy} = \frac{c_{xy}}{c_x}$ yields $v_x c_x = \sum_y v_y p_{xy} c_x$. Hence, $v_x = \sum_y v_y p_{xy}$. Thus, the voltage at each vertex x is a weighted average of the voltages at the adjacent vertices. Hence the voltages form a harmonic function with $\{a, b\}$ as the boundary.

Let p_x be the probability that a random walk starting at vertex x reaches a before b. Clearly $p_a = 1$ and $p_b = 0$. Since $v_a = 1$ and $v_b = 0$, it follows that $p_a = v_a$ and $p_b = v_b$. Furthermore, the probability of the walk reaching a from x before reaching

b is the sum over all y adjacent to x of the probability of the walk going from x to y in the first step and then reaching a from y before reaching b. That is,

$$p_x = \sum_y p_{xy} p_y.$$

Hence, p_x is the same harmonic function as the voltage function v_x, and $\mathbf{v}$ and $\mathbf{p}$ satisfy the same boundary conditions at a and b. Thus, they are identical functions. The probability of a walk starting at x reaching a before reaching b is the voltage v_x.

Probabilistic Interpretation of Current

In a moment, we will set the current into the network at a to have a value that we will equate with one random walk. We will then show that the current i_{xy} is the net frequency with which a random walk from a to b goes through the edge xy before reaching b. Let u_x be the expected number of visits to vertex x on a walk from a to b before reaching b. Clearly $u_b = 0$. Consider a node x not equal to a or b. Every time the walk visits x, it must have come from some neighbor y. Thus, the expected number of visits to x before reaching b is the sum over all neighbors y of the expected number of visits u_y to y before reaching b times the probability p_{yx} of going from y to x. That is,

$$u_x = \sum_y u_y p_{yx}.$$

Since $c_x p_{xy} = c_y p_{yx}$,

$$u_x = \sum_y u_y \frac{c_x p_{xy}}{c_y}$$

and hence $\frac{u_x}{c_x} = \sum_y \frac{u_y}{c_y} p_{xy}$. It follows that $\frac{u_x}{c_x}$ is harmonic with a and b as the boundary where the boundary conditions are $u_b = 0$ and u_a equals some fixed value. Now, $\frac{u_b}{c_b} = 0$. Setting the current into a to 1, fixes the value of v_a. Adjust the current into a so that v_a equals $\frac{u_a}{c_a}$. Now $\frac{u_x}{c_x}$ and v_x satisfy the same boundary conditions and thus are the same harmonic function. Let the current into a correspond to one walk. Note that if the walk starts at a and ends at b, the expected value of the difference between the number of times the walk leaves a and enters a must be one. This implies that the amount of current into a corresponds to one walk.

Next we need to show that the current i_{xy} is the net frequency with which a random walk traverses edge xy:

$$i_{xy} = (v_x - v_y)c_{xy} = \left(\frac{u_x}{c_x} - \frac{u_y}{c_y}\right)c_{xy} = u_x \frac{c_{xy}}{c_x} - u_y \frac{c_{xy}}{c_y} = u_x p_{xy} - u_y p_{yx}.$$

The quantity $u_x p_{xy}$ is the expected number of times the edge xy is traversed from x to y, and the quantity $u_y p_{yx}$ is the expected number of times the edge xy is traversed from y to x. Thus, the current i_{xy} is the expected net number of traversals of the edge xy from x to y.

Effective Resistance and Escape Probability

Set $v_a = 1$ and $v_b = 0$. Let i_a be the current flowing into the network at vertex a and out at vertex b. Define the *effective resistance* r_{eff} between a and b to be $r_{eff} = \frac{v_a}{i_a}$ and the *effective conductance* c_{eff} to be $c_{eff} = \frac{1}{r_{eff}}$. Define the *escape probability*, p_{escape}, to be the probability that a random walk starting at a reaches b before returning to a. We now show that the escape probability is $\frac{c_{eff}}{c_a}$. For convenience, assume that a and b are not adjacent. A slight modification of the argument suffices for the case when a and b are adjacent:

$$i_a = \sum_y (v_a - v_y)c_{ay}.$$

Since $v_a = 1$,

$$i_a = \sum_y c_{ay} - c_a \sum_y v_y \frac{c_{ay}}{c_a}$$

$$= c_a \left[1 - \sum_y p_{ay} v_y \right].$$

For each y adjacent to the vertex a, p_{ay} is the probability of the walk going from vertex a to vertex y. Earlier we showed that v_y is the probability of a walk starting at y going to a before reaching b. Thus, $\sum_y p_{ay} v_y$ is the probability of a walk starting at a returning to a before reaching b and $1 - \sum_y p_{ay} v_y$ is the probability of a walk starting at a reaching b before returning to a. Thus, $i_a = c_a p_{escape}$. Since $v_a = 1$ and $c_{eff} = \frac{i_a}{v_a}$, it follows that $c_{eff} = i_a$. Thus, $c_{eff} = c_a p_{escape}$ and hence $p_{escape} = \frac{c_{eff}}{c_a}$.

For a finite connected graph, the escape probability will always be non-zero. Consider an infinite graph such as a lattice and a random walk starting at some vertex a. Form a series of finite graphs by merging all vertices at distance d or greater from a into a single vertex b for larger and larger values of d. The limit of p_{escape} as d goes to infinity is the probability that the random walk will never return to a. If $p_{escape} \to 0$, then eventually any random walk will return to a. If $p_{escape} \to q$ where $q > 0$, then a fraction of the walks never return. This is the reason for the escape probability terminology.

4.6. Random Walks on Undirected Graphs with Unit Edge Weights

We now focus our discussion on random walks on undirected graphs with uniform edge weights. At each vertex, the random walk is equally likely to take any edge. This corresponds to an electrical network in which all edge resistances are one. Assume the graph is connected. We consider questions such as what is the expected time for a random walk starting at a vertex x to reach a target vertex y, what is the expected time until the random walk returns to the vertex it started at, and what is the expected time to reach every vertex.

4.6.1. Hitting Time

The *hitting time* h_{xy}, sometimes called *discovery time*, is the expected time of a random walk starting at vertex x to reach vertex y. Sometimes a more general definition is given where the hitting time is the expected time to reach a vertex y from a given starting probability distribution.

One interesting fact is that adding edges to a graph may either increase or decrease h_{xy} depending on a particular situation. Adding an edge can shorten the distance from x to y thereby decreasing h_{xy}, or the edge could increase the probability of a random walk going to some far-off portion of the graph thereby increasing h_{xy}. Another interesting fact is that hitting time is not symmetric. The expected time to reach a vertex y from a vertex x in an undirected graph may be radically different from the time to reach x from y.

We start with two technical lemmas. The first lemma states that the expected time to traverse a path of n vertices is $\Theta(n^2)$.

Lemma 4.7 *The expected time for a random walk starting at one end of a path of n vertices to reach the other end is $\Theta(n^2)$.*

Proof Consider walking from vertex 1 to vertex n in a graph consisting of a single path of n vertices. Let $h_{ij}, i < j$, be the hitting time of reaching j starting from i. Now $h_{12} = 1$ and

$$h_{i,i+1} = \frac{1}{2} + \frac{1}{2}(1 + h_{i-1,i+1}) = 1 + \frac{1}{2}\left(h_{i-1,i} + h_{i,i+1}\right) \quad 2 \le i \le n - 1.$$

Solving for $h_{i,i+1}$ yields the recurrence

$$h_{i,i+1} = 2 + h_{i-1,i}.$$

Solving the recurrence yields

$$h_{i,i+1} = 2i - 1.$$

To get from 1 to n, you need to first reach 2, then from 2 (eventually) reach 3, then from 3 (eventually) reach 4, and so on. Thus, by linearity of expectation,

$$h_{1,n} = \sum_{i=1}^{n-1} h_{i,i+1} = \sum_{i=1}^{n-1} (2i - 1)$$

$$= 2\sum_{i=1}^{n-1} i - \sum_{i=1}^{n-1} 1$$

$$= 2\frac{n(n-1)}{2} - (n-1)$$

$$= (n-1)^2.$$

■

The next lemma shows that the expected time spent at vertex i by a random walk from vertex 1 to vertex n in a chain of n vertices is $2(i - 1)$ for $2 \le i \le n - 1$.

Lemma 4.8 *Consider a random walk from vertex 1 to vertex n in a chain of n vertices. Let $t(i)$ be the expected time spent at vertex i. Then*

$$t(i) = \begin{cases} n - 1 & i = 1 \\ 2(n - i) & 2 \le i \le n - 1 \\ 1 & i = n. \end{cases}$$

Proof Now $t(n) = 1$, since the walk stops when it reaches vertex n. Half of the time when the walk is at vertex $n - 1$ it goes to vertex n. Thus, $t(n - 1) = 2$. For

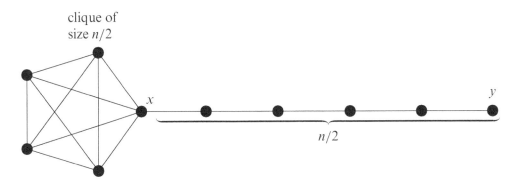

Figure 4.8: Illustration that adding edges to a graph can either increase or decrease hitting time.

$3 \leq i < n - 1$, $t(i) = \frac{1}{2}[t(i-1) + t(i+1)]$ and $t(1)$ and $t(2)$ satisfy $t(1) = \frac{1}{2}t(2) + 1$ and $t(2) = t(1) + \frac{1}{2}t(3)$. Solving for $t(i+1)$ for $3 \leq i < n - 1$ yields

$$t(i+1) = 2t(i) - t(i-1),$$

which has solution $t(i) = 2(n - i)$ for $3 \leq i < n - 1$. Then solving for $t(2)$ and $t(1)$ yields $t(2) = 2(n-2)$ and $t(1) = n - 1$. Thus, the total time spent at vertices is

$$n - 1 + 2(1 + 2 + \cdots + n - 2) + 1 = (n-1) + 2\frac{(n-1)(n-2)}{2} + 1$$

$$= (n-1)^2 + 1,$$

which is one more than h_{1n} and thus is correct. ∎

Adding edges to a graph might either increase or decrease the hitting time h_{xy}. Consider the graph consisting of a single path of n vertices. Add edges to this graph to get the graph in Figure 4.8 consisting of a clique of size $n/2$ connected to a path of $n/2$ vertices. Then add still more edges to get a clique of size n. Let x be the vertex at the midpoint of the original path and let y be the other endpoint of the path consisting of $n/2$ vertices as shown in the figure. In the first graph consisting of a single path of length n, $h_{xy} = \Theta(n^2)$. In the second graph consisting of a clique of size $n/2$ along with a path of length $n/2$, $h_{xy} = \Theta(n^3)$. To see this latter statement, note that starting at x, the walk will go down the path toward y and return to x for $n/2 - 1$ times on average before reaching y for the first time, by Lemma 4.8. Each time the walk in the path returns to x, with probability $(n/2 - 1)/(n/2)$ it enters the clique and thus on average enters the clique $\Theta(n)$ times before starting down the path again. Each time it enters the clique, it spends $\Theta(n)$ time in the clique before returning to x. It then reenters the clique $\Theta(n)$ times before starting down the path to y. Thus, each time the walk returns to x from the path, it spends $\Theta(n^2)$ time in the clique before starting down the path toward y for a total expected time that is $\Theta(n^3)$ before reaching y. In the third graph, which is the clique of size n, $h_{xy} = \Theta(n)$. Thus, adding edges first increased h_{xy} from n^2 to n^3 and then decreased it to n.

Hitting time is not symmetric, even in the case of undirected graphs. In the graph of Figure 4.8, the expected time, h_{xy}, of a random walk from x to y, where x is the vertex of attachment and y is the other end vertex of the chain, is $\Theta(n^3)$. However, h_{yx} is $\Theta(n^2)$.

4.6.2. Commute Time

The *commute time*, commute(x, y), is the expected time of a random walk starting at x reaching y and then returning to x. So commute$(x, y) = h_{xy} + h_{yx}$. Think of going from home to office and returning home. Note that commute time is symmetric. We now relate the commute time to an electrical quantity, the effective resistance. The *effective resistance* between two vertices x and y in an electrical network is the voltage difference between x and y when one unit of current is inserted at vertex x and withdrawn from vertex y.

Theorem 4.9 *Given a connected, undirected graph, consider the electrical network where each edge of the graph is replaced by a 1-ohm resistor. Given vertices x and y, the commute time, commute(x, y), equals $2mr_{xy}$ where r_{xy} is the effective resistance from x to y and m is the number of edges in the graph.*

Proof Insert at each vertex i a current equal to the degree d_i of vertex i. The total current inserted is $2m$ where m is the number of edges. Extract from a specific vertex j all of this $2m$ current (note: for this to be legal, the graph must be connected). Let v_{ij} be the voltage difference from i to j. The current into i divides into the d_i resistors at vertex i. The current in each resistor is proportional to the voltage across it. Let k be a vertex adjacent to i. Then the current through the resistor between i and k is $v_{ij} - v_{kj}$, the voltage drop across the resistor. The sum of the currents out of i through the resistors must equal d_i, the current injected into i.

$$d_i = \sum_{\substack{k \text{ adj} \\ \text{to } i}} (v_{ij} - v_{kj}) = d_i v_{ij} - \sum_{\substack{k \text{ adj} \\ \text{to } i}} v_{kj}.$$

Solving for v_{ij},

$$v_{ij} = 1 + \sum_{\substack{k \text{ adj} \\ \text{to } i}} \frac{1}{d_i} v_{kj} = \sum_{\substack{k \text{ adj} \\ \text{to } i}} \frac{1}{d_i}(1 + v_{kj}). \tag{4.11}$$

Now the hitting time from i to j is the average time over all paths from i to k adjacent to i and then on from k to j. This is given by

$$h_{ij} = \sum_{\substack{k \text{ adj} \\ \text{to } i}} \frac{1}{d_i}(1 + h_{kj}). \tag{4.12}$$

Subtracting (4.12) from (4.11) gives $v_{ij} - h_{ij} = \sum_{\substack{k \text{ adj} \\ \text{to } i}} \frac{1}{d_i}(v_{kj} - h_{kj})$. Thus, the function of i, $v_{ij} - h_{ij}$, is harmonic. Designate vertex j as the only boundary vertex. The value of $v_{ij} - h_{ij}$ at $i = j$, namely $v_{jj} - h_{jj}$, is zero, since both v_{jj} and h_{jj} are zero. So the function $v_{ij} - h_{ij}$ must be zero everywhere. Thus, the voltage v_{ij} equals the expected time h_{ij} from i to j.

To complete the proof of Theorem 4.9, note that $h_{ij} = v_{ij}$ is the voltage from i to j when currents are inserted at all vertices in the graph and extracted at vertex j. If the current is extracted from i instead of j, then the voltages change and $v_{ji} = h_{ji}$ in the new setup. Finally, reverse all currents in this latter step. The voltages change again and for the new voltages $-v_{ji} = h_{ji}$. Since $-v_{ji} = v_{ij}$, we get $h_{ji} = v_{ij}$.

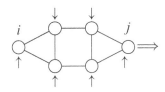

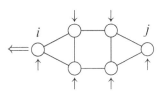

Insert current at each vertex
equal to degree of the vertex.
Extract $2m$ at vertex j, $v_{ij} = h_{ij}$.

(a)

Extract current from i instead of j.
For new voltages $v_{ji} = h_{ji}$.

(b)

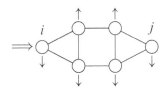

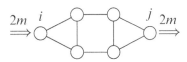

Reverse currents in (b).
For new voltages $-v_{ji} = h_{ji}$.
Since $-v_{ji} = v_{ij}$, $h_{ji} = v_{ij}$.

(c)

Superpose currents in (a) and (c).
$2mr_{ij} = v_{ij} = h_{ij} + h_{ji} = commute(i,j)$.

(d)

Figure 4.9: Illustration of proof that commute$(x, y) = 2mr_{xy}$ where m is the number of edges in the undirected graph and r_{xy} is the effective resistance between x and y.

Thus, when a current is inserted at each vertex equal to the degree of the vertex and the current is extracted from j, the voltage v_{ij} in this setup equals h_{ij}. When we extract the current from i instead of j and then reverse all currents, the voltage v_{ij} in this new setup equals h_{ji}. Now, superpose both situations, i.e., add all the currents and voltages. By linearity, for the resulting v_{ij}, which is the sum of the other two v_{ij}'s, is $v_{ij} = h_{ij} + h_{ji}$. All currents into or out of the network cancel except the $2m$ amps injected at i and withdrawn at j. Thus, $2mr_{ij} = v_{ij} = h_{ij} + h_{ji} = commute(i,j)$ or $commute(i,j) = 2mr_{ij}$ where r_{ij} is the effective resistance from i to j. The overall argument is illustrated in Figure 4.9. ∎

The following corollary follows from Theorem 4.9, since the effective resistance r_{uv} is less than or equal to 1 when u and v are connected by an edge.

Corollary 4.10 *If vertices x and y are connected by an edge, then $h_{xy} + h_{yx} \leq 2m$ where m is the number of edges in the graph.*

Proof If x and y are connected by an edge, then the effective resistance r_{xy} is less than or equal to 1. ∎

Corollary 4.11 *For vertices x and y in an n vertex graph, the commute time, commute(x, y), is less than or equal to n^3.*

Proof By Theorem 4.9, the commute time is given by the formula commute $(x, y) = 2mr_{xy}$ where m is the number of edges. In an n vertex graph there exists a path from x to y of length at most n. Since the resistance cannot be greater than that of any path from x to y, $r_{xy} \leq n$. Since the number of edges is at most $\binom{n}{2}$,

$$\text{commute}(x, y) = 2mr_{xy} \leq 2\binom{n}{2}n \cong n^3.$$

∎

While adding edges into a graph can never increase the effective resistance between two given nodes x and y, it may increase or decrease the commute time. To see this, consider three graphs: the graph consisting of a chain of n vertices, the graph of Figure 4.8, and the clique on n vertices.

4.6.3. Cover Time

The *cover time*, $\text{cover}(x, G)$, is the expected time of a random walk starting at vertex x in the graph G to reach each vertex at least once. We write $\text{cover}(x)$ when G is understood. The cover time of an undirected graph G, denoted $\text{cover}(G)$, is

$$\text{cover}(G) = \max_x \text{cover}(x, G).$$

For cover time of an undirected graph, increasing the number of edges in the graph may increase or decrease the cover time depending on the situation. Again consider three graphs: a chain of length n that has cover time $\Theta(n^2)$, the graph in Figure 4.8 that has cover time $\Theta(n^3)$, and the complete graph on n vertices that has cover time $\Theta(n \log n)$. Adding edges to the chain of length n to create the graph in Figure 4.8 increases the cover time from n^2 to n^3, and then adding even more edges to obtain the complete graph reduces the cover time to $n \log n$.

Note The cover time of a clique is $\Theta(n \log n)$, since this is the time to select every integer out of n integers with high probability, drawing integers at random. This is called the *coupon collector problem*. The cover time for a straight line is $\Theta(n^2)$, since it is the same as the hitting time. For the graph in Figure 4.8, the cover time is $\Theta(n^3)$, since one takes the maximum over all start states and $\text{cover}(x, G) = \Theta(n^3)$ where x is the vertex of attachment.

Theorem 4.12 *Let G be a connected graph with n vertices and m edges. The time for a random walk to cover all vertices of the graph G is bounded above by $4m(n-1)$.*

Proof Consider a depth first search of the graph G starting from some vertex z and let T be the resulting depth first search spanning tree of G. The depth first search covers every vertex. Consider the expected time to cover every vertex in the order visited by the depth first search. Clearly this bounds the cover time of G starting from vertex z. Note that each edge in T is traversed twice, once in each direction:

$$\text{cover}(z, G) \leq \sum_{\substack{(x,y)\in T \\ (y,x)\in T}} h_{xy}.$$

If (x, y) is an edge in T, then x and y are adjacent, and thus Corollary 4.10 implies $h_{xy} \leq 2m$. Since there are $n - 1$ edges in the dfs tree and each edge is traversed twice, once in each direction, cover$(z) \leq 4m(n - 1)$. This holds for all starting vertices z. Thus, cover$(G) \leq 4m(n - 1)$. ∎

The theorem gives the correct answer of n^3 for the $n/2$ clique with the $n/2$ tail. It gives an upper bound of n^3 for the n-clique where the actual cover time is $n \log n$.

Let r_{xy} be the effective resistance from x to y. Define the resistance $r_{eff}(G)$ of a graph G by $r_{eff}(G) = \max_{x,y}(r_{xy})$.

Theorem 4.13 *Let G be an undirected graph with m edges. Then the cover time for G is bounded by the following inequality*

$$m\, r_{eff}(G) \leq cover(G) \leq 6e\, m\, r_{eff}(G) \ln n + n$$

where $e \approx 2.718$ is Euler's constant and $r_{eff}(G)$ is the resistance of G.

Proof By definition, $r_{eff}(G) = \max_{x,y}(r_{xy})$. Let u and v be the vertices of G for which r_{xy} is maximum. Then $r_{eff}(G) = r_{uv}$. By Theorem 4.9, commute$(u, v) = 2mr_{uv}$. Hence $mr_{uv} = \frac{1}{2}$commute(u, v). Note that $\frac{1}{2}$commute(u, v) is the average of h_{uv} and h_{vu}, which is clearly less than or equal to $\max(h_{uv}, h_{vu})$. Finally, $\max(h_{uv}, h_{vu})$ is less than or equal to $\max($cover$(u, G),$ cover$(v, G))$, which is clearly less than the cover time of G. Putting these facts together gives the first inequality in the theorem:

$$m\, r_{eff}(G) = mr_{uv} = \frac{1}{2}\text{commute}(u, v) \leq \max(h_{uv}, h_{vu}) \leq cover(G).$$

For the second inequality in the theorem, by Theorem 4.9, for any x and y, commute(x, y) equals $2mr_{xy}$ which is less than or equal to $2m\, r_{eff}(G)$, implying $h_{xy} \leq 2m\, r_{eff}(G)$. By the Markov inequality, since the expected time to reach y starting at any x is less than $2m\, r_{eff}(G)$, the probability that y is not reached from x in $2m\, r_{eff}(G)e$ steps is at most $\frac{1}{e}$. Thus, the probability that a vertex y has not been reached in $6e\, m\, r_{eff}(G) \log n$ steps is at most $\frac{1}{e}^{3 \ln n} = \frac{1}{n^3}$ because a random walk of length $6e\, mr_{eff}(G) \log n$ is a sequence of $3 \log n$ random walks, each of length $2emr_{eff}(G)$ and each possibly starting from different vertices. Suppose after a walk of $6em\, r_{eff}(G) \log n$ steps, vertices $v_1, v_2, \ldots, v_l$ had not been reached. Walk until v_1 is reached, then v_2, etc. By Corollary 4.11, the expected time for each of these is n^3, but since each happens only with probability $1/n^3$, we effectively take $O(1)$ time per v_i, for a total time at most n. More precisely,

$$cover(G) \leq 6em\, r_{eff}(G) \log n$$
$$+ \sum_v \text{Prob}\left(v \text{ was not visited in the first } 6em\, r_{eff}(G) \text{ steps}\right) n^3$$
$$\leq 6em\, r_{eff}(G) \log n + \sum_v \frac{1}{n^3}n^3 \leq 6em\, r_{eff}(G) + n.$$

∎

4.7. Random Walks in Euclidean Space

Many physical processes such as Brownian motion are modeled by random walks.

Random walks in Euclidean d-space consisting of fixed-length steps parallel to the coordinate axes are really random walks on a d-dimensional lattice and are a special case of random walks on graphs. In a random walk on a graph, at each time unit an edge from the current vertex is selected at random and the walk proceeds to the adjacent vertex.

4.7.1. Random Walks on Lattices

We now apply the analogy between random walks and current to lattices. Consider a random walk on a finite segment $-n, \ldots, -1, 0, 1, 2, \ldots, n$ of a one dimensional lattice starting from the origin. Is the walk certain to return to the origin or is there some probability that it will escape, i.e., reach the boundary before returning? The probability of reaching the boundary before returning to the origin is called the escape probability. We shall be interested in this quantity as n goes to infinity.

Convert the lattice to an electrical network by replacing each edge with a 1-ohm resistor. Then the probability of a walk starting at the origin reaching n or $-n$ before returning to the origin is the escape probability given by

$$p_{escape} = \frac{c_{eff}}{c_a}$$

where c_{eff} is the effective conductance between the origin and the boundary points and c_a is the sum of the conductances at the origin. In a d-dimensional lattice, $c_a = 2d$ assuming that the resistors have value 1. For the d-dimensional lattice,

$$p_{escape} = \frac{1}{2d\, r_{eff}}.$$

In one dimension, the electrical network is just two series connections of n 1-ohm resistors connected in parallel. So as n goes to infinity, r_{eff} goes to infinity, and the escape probability goes to zero as n goes to infinity. Thus, the walk in the unbounded one-dimensional lattice will return to the origin with probability 1. Note, however, that the expected time to return to the origin having taken one step away, which is equal to commute$(1, 0)$, is infinite (Theorem 4.9).

4.7.2. Two Dimensions

For the two-dimensional lattice, consider a larger and larger square about the origin for the boundary as shown in Figure 4.10a and consider the limit of r_{eff} as the squares get larger. Shorting the resistors on each square can only reduce r_{eff}. Shorting the resistors results in the linear network shown in Figure 4.10b. As the paths get longer, the number of resistors in parallel also increases. The resistance between vertex i and $i + 1$ is really $4(2i + 1)$ unit resistors in parallel. The effective resistance of $4(2i + 1)$ resistors in parallel is $1/4(2i + 1)$. Thus,

$$r_{eff} \geq \frac{1}{4} + \frac{1}{12} + \frac{1}{20} + \cdots = \frac{1}{4}\left(1 + \frac{1}{3} + \frac{1}{5} + \cdots\right) = \Theta(\ln n).$$

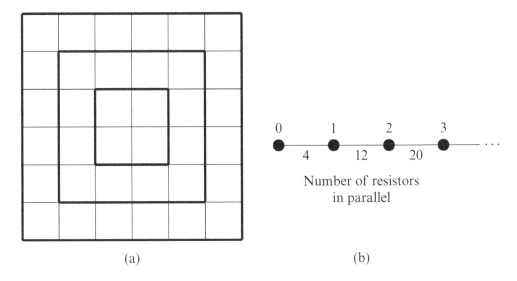

(a)   (b)

Figure 4.10: Two-dimensional lattice along with the linear network resulting from shorting resistors on the concentric squares about the origin.

Since the lower bound on the effective resistance and hence the effective resistance goes to infinity, the escape probability goes to zero for the two-dimensional lattice.

4.7.3. Three Dimensions

In three dimensions, the resistance along any path to infinity grows to infinity, but the number of paths in parallel also grows to infinity. It turns out there are a sufficient number of paths that r_{eff} remains finite, and thus there is a non-zero escape probability. We will prove this now. First note that shorting any edge decreases the resistance, so we do not use shorting in this proof, since we seek to prove an upper bound on the resistance. Instead we remove some edges, which increases their resistance to infinity and hence increases the effective resistance, giving an upper bound. To simplify things, we consider walks on a quadrant rather than the full grid. The resistance to infinity derived from only the quadrant is an upper bound on the resistance of the full grid.

The construction used in three dimensions is easier to explain first in two dimensions (see Figure 4.11). Draw dotted diagonal lines at $x + y = 2^n - 1$. Consider two paths that start at the origin. One goes up and the other goes to the right. Each time a path encounters a dotted diagonal line, split the path into two, one which goes right and the other up. Where two paths cross, split the vertex into two, keeping the paths separate. By a symmetry argument, splitting the vertex does not change the resistance of the network. Remove all resistors except those on these paths. The resistance of the original network is less than that of the tree produced by this process, since removing a resistor is equivalent to increasing its resistance to infinity.

The distances between splits increase and are 1, 2, 4, etc. At each split the number of paths in parallel doubles. See Figure 4.12. Thus, the resistance to infinity in this two-dimensional example is

$$\frac{1}{2} + \frac{1}{4}2 + \frac{1}{8}4 + \cdots = \frac{1}{2} + \frac{1}{2} + \frac{1}{2} + \cdots = \infty.$$

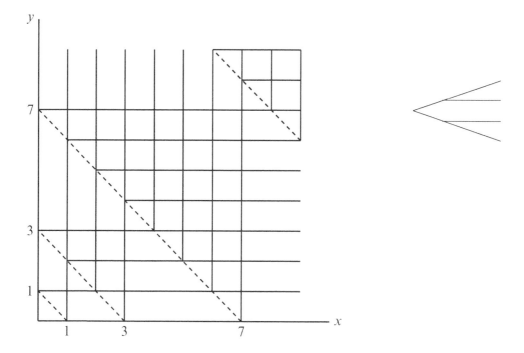

Figure 4.11: Paths in a two-dimensional lattice obtained from the three-dimensional construction applied in two-dimensions.

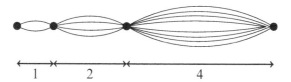

Figure 4.12: Paths obtained from a two-dimensional lattice. Distances between splits double, as do the number of parallel paths.

In the analogous three-dimensional construction, paths go up, to the right, and out of the plane of the paper. The paths split three ways at planes given by $x + y + z = 2^n - 1$. Each time the paths split, the number of parallel segments triple. Segments of the paths between splits are of length 1, 2, 4, etc., and the resistance of the segments is equal to the lengths. The resistance out to infinity for the tree is

$$\frac{1}{3} + \frac{1}{9}2 + \frac{1}{27}4 + \cdots = \frac{1}{3}\left(1 + \frac{2}{3} + \frac{4}{9} + \cdots\right) = \frac{1}{3}\frac{1}{1 - \frac{2}{3}} = 1.$$

The resistance of the three-dimensional lattice is less. It is important to check that the paths are edge-disjoint and so the tree is a subgraph of the lattice. Going to a subgraph is equivalent to deleting edges, which increases the resistance. That is why the resistance of the lattice is less than that of the tree. Thus, in three dimensions, the escape probability is non-zero. The upper bound on r_{eff} gives the lower bound:

$$p_{escape} = \frac{1}{2d}\frac{1}{r_{eff}} \geq \frac{1}{6}.$$

A lower bound on r_{eff} gives an upper bound on p_{escape}. To get the upper bound on p_{escape}, short all resistors on surfaces of boxes at distances 1, 2, 3, etc. Then

$$r_{eff} \geq \frac{1}{6}\left[1 + \frac{1}{9} + \frac{1}{25} + \cdots\right] \geq \frac{1.23}{6} \geq 0.2$$

This gives

$$p_{escape} = \frac{1}{2d}\frac{1}{r_{eff}} \leq \frac{5}{6}.$$

4.8. The Web as a Markov Chain

A modern application of random walks on directed graphs comes from trying to establish the importance of pages on the World Wide Web. Search engines output an ordered list of webpages in response to each search query. To do this, they have to solve two problems at query time: (1) find the set of all webpages containing the query term(s) and (2) rank the webpages and display them (or the top subset of them) in ranked order. (1) is done by maintaining a "reverse index" that we do not discuss here. (2) cannot be done at query time, since this would make the response too slow. So search engines rank the entire set of webpages (in the billions) "offline" and use that single ranking for all queries. At query time, the webpages containing the query terms(s) are displayed in this ranked order.

One way to do this ranking would be to take a random walk on the web viewed as a directed graph (which we call the web graph) with an edge corresponding to each hypertext link and rank pages according to their stationary probability. Hypertext links are one-way and the web graph may not be strongly connected. Indeed, for a node at the "bottom" level there may be no out-edges. When the walk encounters this vertex, the walk disappears. Another difficulty is that a vertex or a strongly connected component with no in edges is never reached. One way to resolve these difficulties is to introduce a random restart condition. At each step, with some probability r, jump to a vertex selected uniformly at random in the entire graph; with probability $1 - r$, select an out-edge at random from the current node and follow it. If a vertex has no out-edges, the value of r for that vertex is set to one. This makes the graph strongly connected so that the stationary probabilities exist.

4.8.1. Pagerank

The pagerank of a vertex in a directed graph is the stationary probability of the vertex, where we assume a positive restart probability of, say, $r = 0.15$. The restart ensures that the graph is strongly connected. The pagerank of a page is the frequency with which the page will be visited over a long period of time. If the pagerank is p, then the expected time between visits or return time is $1/p$. Notice that one can increase the pagerank of a page by reducing the return time, and this can be done by creating short cycles.

Consider a vertex i with a single edge in from vertex j and a single edge out. The stationary probability π satisfies $\pi P = \pi$, and thus

$$\pi_i = \pi_j p_{ji}.$$

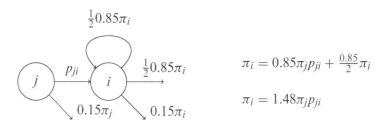

$$\pi_i = 0.85\pi_j p_{ji} + \frac{0.85}{2}\pi_i$$

$$\pi_i = 1.48\pi_j p_{ji}$$

Figure 4.13: Impact on pagerank of adding a self loop

Adding a self-loop at i, as illustrated in Figure 4.13, results in a new equation,

$$\pi_i = \pi_j p_{ji} + \frac{1}{2}\pi_i$$

or

$$\pi_i = 2\,\pi_j p_{ji}.$$

Of course, π_j would have changed too, but ignoring this for now, pagerank is doubled by the addition of a self loop. Adding k self loops, results in the equation

$$\pi_i = \pi_j p_{ji} + \frac{k}{k+1}\pi_i,$$

and again ignoring the change in π_j, we now have $\pi_i = (k+1)\pi_j p_{ji}$. What prevents one from increasing the pagerank of a page arbitrarily? The answer is the restart. We neglected the 0.15 probability that is taken off for the random restart. With the restart taken into account, the equation for π_i when there is no self-loop is

$$\pi_i = 0.85\pi_j p_{ji}$$

whereas, with k self loops, the equation is

$$\pi_i = 0.85\pi_j p_{ji} + 0.85\frac{k}{k+1}\pi_i.$$

Solving for π_i yields

$$\pi_i = \frac{0.85k + 0.85}{0.15k + 1}\pi_j p_{ji}$$

which for $k = 1$ is $\pi_i = 1.48\pi_j p_{ji}$ and in the limit as $k \to \infty$ is $\pi_i = 5.67\pi_j p_{ji}$. Adding a single loop only increases pagerank by a factor of 1.74.

4.8.2. Relation to Hitting Time

Recall the definition of hitting time h_{xy}, which for two states x and y is the expected time to reach y starting from x. Here, we deal with h_y, the average time to hit y, starting at a random node. Namely, $h_y = \frac{1}{n}\sum_x h_{xy}$, where the sum is taken over all n nodes x. Hitting time h_y is closely related to return time and thus to the reciprocal of page rank. Return time is clearly less than the expected time until a restart plus hitting time. With r as the restart value, this gives:

$$\text{Return time to } y \leq \frac{1}{r} + h_y.$$

In the other direction, the fastest one could return would be if there were only paths of length 2 (assume we remove all self loops). A path of length 2 would be traversed with at most probability $(1 - r)^2$. With probability $r + (1 - r)r = (2 - r)r$, one restarts and then hits v. Thus, the return time is at least $2(1 - r)^2 + (2 - r)r \times$ (hitting time). Combining these two bounds yields

$$2(1 - r)^2 + (2 - r)r(\text{hitting time}) \leq (\text{return time}) \leq \frac{1}{r} + (\text{hitting time}) .$$

The relationship between return time and hitting time can be used to see if a vertex has unusually high probability of short loops. However, there is no efficient way to compute hitting time for all vertices as there is for return time. For a single vertex v, one can compute hitting time by removing the edges out of the vertex v for which one is computing hitting time and then run the pagerank algorithm for the new graph. The hitting time for v is the reciprocal of the pagerank in the graph with the edges out of v removed. Since computing hitting time for each vertex requires removal of a different set of edges, the algorithm only gives the hitting time for one vertex at a time. Since one is probably only interested in the hitting time of vertices with low hitting time, an alternative would be to use a random walk to estimate the hitting time of low hitting time vertices.

4.8.3. Spam

Suppose one has a web page and would like to increase its pagerank by creating other web pages with pointers to the original page. The abstract problem is the following. We are given a directed graph G and a vertex v whose pagerank we want to increase. We may add new vertices to the graph and edges from them to any vertices we want. We can also add or delete edges from v. However, we cannot add or delete edges out of other vertices.

The pagerank of v is the stationary probability for vertex v with random restarts. If we delete all existing edges out of v, creating a new vertex u and edges (v, u) and (u, v), then the pagerank will be increased, since any time the random walk reaches v it will be captured in the loop $v \rightarrow u \rightarrow v$. A search engine can counter this strategy by more frequent random restarts.

A second method to increase pagerank would be to create a star consisting of the vertex v at its center along with a large set of new vertices each with a directed edge to v. These new vertices will sometimes be chosen as the target of the random restart, and hence the vertices increase the probability of the random walk reaching v. This second method is countered by reducing the frequency of random restarts.

Notice that the first technique of capturing the random walk increases pagerank but does not affect hitting time. One can negate the impact on pagerank of someone capturing the random walk by increasing the frequency of random restarts. The second technique of creating a star increases pagerank due to random restarts and decreases hitting time. One can check if the pagerank is high and hitting time is low, in which case the pagerank is likely to have been artificially inflated by the page capturing the walk with short cycles.

4.8.4. Personalized Pagerank

In computing pagerank, one uses a restart probability, typically 0.15, in which at each step, instead of taking a step in the graph, the walk goes to a vertex selected uniformly at random. In personalized pagerank, instead of selecting a vertex uniformly at random, one selects a vertex according to a personalized probability distribution. Often the distribution has probability 1 for a single vertex, and whenever the walk restarts, it restarts at that vertex. Note that this may make the graph disconnected.

4.8.5. Algorithm for *Computing Personalized Pagerank*

First, consider the normal pagerank. Let α be the restart probability with which the random walk jumps to an arbitrary vertex. With probability $1 - \alpha$, the random walk selects a vertex uniformly at random from the set of adjacent vertices. Let $\mathbf{p}$ be a row vector denoting the pagerank and let A be the adjacency matrix with rows normalized to sum to one. Then

$$\mathbf{p} = \frac{\alpha}{n}(1, 1, \ldots, 1) + (1 - \alpha)\,\mathbf{p}A$$

$$\mathbf{p}[I - (1 - \alpha)A] = \frac{\alpha}{n}(1, 1, \ldots, 1)$$

or

$$\mathbf{p} = \frac{\alpha}{n}(1, 1, \ldots, 1)\,[I - (1 - \alpha)\,A]^{-1}.$$

Thus, in principle, $\mathbf{p}$ can be found by computing the inverse of $[I - (1 - \alpha)A]^{-1}$. But this is far from practical, since for the whole web, one would be dealing with matrices with billions of rows and columns. A more practical procedure is to run the random walk and observe using the basics of the power method in Chapter 3 that the process converges to the solution $\mathbf{p}$.

For the personalized pagerank, instead of restarting at an arbitrary vertex, the walk restarts at a designated vertex. More generally, it may restart in some specified neighborhood. Suppose the restart selects a vertex using the probability distribution s. Then, in the above calculation, replace the vector $\frac{1}{n}(1, 1, \ldots, 1)$ by the vector $\mathbf{s}$. Again, the computation could be done by a random walk. However, we wish to do the random walk calculation for personalized pagerank quickly, since it is to be performed repeatedly. With more care, this can be done, though we do not describe it here.

4.9. Bibliographic Notes

The material on the analogy between random walks on undirected graphs and electrical networks is from [DS84], as is the material on random walks in Euclidean space. Additional material on Markov chains can be found in [MR95b], [MU05], and [per10]. For material on Markov Chain Monte Carlo methods, see [Jer98] and [Liu01].

The use of normalized conductance to prove convergence of Markov Chains is by Sinclair and Jerrum [SJ89] and Alon [Alo86]. A polynomial time-bounded Markov chain – based method for estimating the volume of convex sets was developed by Dyer, Frieze, and Kannan [DFK91].

4.10. Exercises

Exercise 4.1 The Fundamental Theorem of Markov chains says that for a connected Markov chain, the long-term average distribution $\mathbf{a(t)}$ converges to a stationary distribution. Does the t step distribution $\mathbf{p(t)}$ also converge for every connected Markov Chain? Consider the following examples: (i) A two-state chain with $p_{12} = p_{21} = 1$. (ii) A three-state chain with $p_{12} = p_{23} = p_{31} = 1$ and the other $p_{ij} = 0$. Generalize these examples to produce Markov Chains with many states.

Exercise 4.2 Does $\lim_{t\to\infty} a(t) - a(t+1) = 0$ imply that $a(t)$ converges to some value? Hint: consider the average cumulative sum of the digits in the sequence $10^2 1^4 0^8 1^{16} \cdots$.

Exercise 4.3 What is the stationary probability for the following networks?

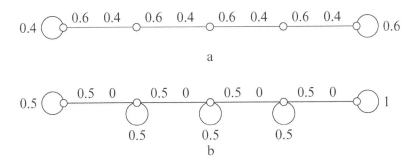

a

b

Exercise 4.4 A Markov chain is said to be symmetric if for all i and j, $p_{ij} = p_{ji}$. What is the stationary distribution of a connected symmetric chain? Prove your answer.

Exercise 4.5 Prove $|\mathbf{p} - \mathbf{q}|_1 = 2\sum_i (p_i - q_i)^+$ for probability distributions $\mathbf{p}$ and $\mathbf{q}$, (Proposition 4.4).

Exercise 4.6 Let $p(\mathbf{x})$, where $\mathbf{x} = (x_1, x_2, \ldots, x_d)$ $x_i \in \{0, 1\}$, be a multivariate probability distribution. For $d = 100$, how would you estimate the marginal distribution

$$p(x_1) = \sum_{x_2, \ldots, x_d} p(x_1, x_2, \ldots, x_d)?$$

Exercise 4.7 Using the Metropolis-Hasting Algorithm, create a Markov chain whose stationary probability is that given in the following table. Use the 3×3 lattice for the underlying graph.

$x_1 x_2$	00	01	02	10	11	12	20	21	22
Prob	1/16	1/8	1/16	1/8	1/4	1/8	1/16	1/8	1/16

Exercise 4.8 Using Gibbs sampling, create a 4×4 lattice where vertices in rows and columns are cliques whose stationary probability is that given in the following table.

x/y	1	2	3	4
1	$\frac{1}{16}$	$\frac{1}{32}$	$\frac{1}{32}$	$\frac{1}{16}$
2	$\frac{1}{32}$	$\frac{1}{8}$	$\frac{1}{8}$	$\frac{1}{32}$
3	$\frac{1}{32}$	$\frac{1}{8}$	$\frac{1}{8}$	$\frac{1}{32}$
4	$\frac{1}{16}$	$\frac{1}{32}$	$\frac{1}{32}$	$\frac{1}{16}$

Note by symmetry there are only three types of vertices and only two types of rows or columns.

Exercise 4.9 How would you integrate a high-dimensional multivariate polynomial distribution over some convex region?

Exercise 4.10 Given a time-reversible Markov chain, modify the chain as follows. At the current state, stay put (no move) with probability 1/2. With the other 1/2 probability, move as in the old chain. Show that the new chain has the same stationary distribution. What happens to the convergence time in this modification?

Exercise 4.11 Let $\mathbf{p}$ be a probability vector (nonnegative components adding up to 1) on the vertices of a connected graph that is sufficiently large that it cannot be stored in a computer. Set p_{ij} (the transition probability from i to j) to p_j for all adjacent $j \neq i$ in the graph and with the remaining probability stay at the current node. Show that the stationary probability vector is $\mathbf{p}$. Is a random walk an efficient way to sample according to a probability distribution that is close to $\mathbf{p}$? Think, for example, of the graph G being the n-dimensional hypercube with 2^n vertices, and $\mathbf{p}$ as the uniform distribution over those vertices.

Exercise 4.12 Construct the edge probability for a three-state Markov chain where each pair of states is connected by an undirected edge so that the stationary probability is $\left(\frac{1}{2}, \frac{1}{3}, \frac{1}{6}\right)$. Repeat adding a self loop with probability $\frac{1}{2}$ to the vertex with probability $\frac{1}{2}$.

Exercise 4.13 Consider a three-state Markov chain with stationary probability $\left(\frac{1}{2}, \frac{1}{3}, \frac{1}{6}\right)$. Consider the Metropolis-Hastings algorithm with G the complete graph on these three vertices. For each edge and each direction, what is the expected probability that we would actually make a move along the edge?

Exercise 4.14 Consider a distribution $\mathbf{p}$ over $\{0, 1\}^2$ with $p(00) = p(11) = \frac{1}{2}$ and $p(01) = p(10) = 0$. Give a connected graph on $\{0, 1\}^2$ that would be bad for running Metropolis-Hastings and a graph that would be good for running Metropolis-Hastings. What would be the problem with Gibbs sampling?

Exercise 4.15 Consider $p(\mathbf{x})$ where $\mathbf{x} \in \{0, 1\}^{100}$ such that $p(\mathbf{0}) = \frac{1}{2}$ and $p(\mathbf{x}) = \frac{1/2}{(2^{100}-1)}$ for $\mathbf{x} \neq \mathbf{0}$. How does Gibbs sampling behave?

Exercise 4.16 Given a connected graph G and an integer k, how would you generate connected subgraphs of G with k vertices with probability proportional to the number of edges in the subgraph? A subgraph of G does not need to have all edges of G that join vertices of the subgraph. The probabilities need not be exactly proportional to the number of edges, and you are not expected to prove your algorithm for this problem.

——— **100** ———

Exercise 4.17 Suppose one wishes to generate uniformly at random a regular, degree three, undirected, not necessarily connected multi-graph with 1,000 vertices. A multi-graph may have multiple edges between a pair of vertices and self loops. One decides to do this by a Markov Chain Monte Carlo technique. In particular, consider a (very large) network where each vertex corresponds to a regular degree three, 1,000-vertex multi-graph. For edges, say that the vertices corresponding to two graphs are connected by an edge if one graph can be obtained from the other by a flip of a pair of edges. In a flip, a pair of edges (a, b) and (c, d) are replaced by (a, c) and (b, d).

1. Prove that the network whose vertices correspond to the desired graphs is connected. That is, for any two 1000-vertex degree-three multi-graphs, it is possible to walk from one to the other in this network.
2. Prove that the stationary probability of the random walk is uniform over all vertices.
3. Give an upper bound on the diameter of the network.
4. How would you modify the process if you wanted to uniformly generate connected degree three multi-graphs?

In order to use a random walk to generate the graphs in a reasonable amount of time, the random walk must rapidly converge to the stationary probability. Proving this is beyond the material in this book.

Exercise 4.18 Construct, program, and execute an algorithm to estimate the volume of a unit radius sphere in 20-dimensions by carrying out a random walk on a 20-dimensional grid with 0.1 spacing.

Exercise 4.19 For an undirected graph G with edge weights $w_{x,y} = w_{y,x}$, set $p_{x,y} = \frac{w_{x,y}}{\sum_y w_{x,y}}$.

1. Given an undirected graph with edge probabilities, can you always select edge weights that will give rise to the desired probabilities?
2. Lemma 4.1 states that if for all x and y, $\pi_x p_{xy} = \pi_y p_{yx}$, then π is the stationary probability. However is the converse true? If π is the stationary probability, must $\pi_x p_{xy} = \pi_y p_{yx}$ for all x and y?
3. Give a necessary and sufficient condition that π is the stationary probability.
4. In an undirected graph where for some x and y $\pi_x p_{xy} \neq \pi_y p_{yx}$ there is a flow through the edges. How can the probability be stationary?
5. In an undirected graph where $\pi_x p_{xy} = \pi_y p_{yx}$ prove that you can always assign weights to edges so that $p_{x,y} = \frac{w_{x,y}}{\sum_y w_{x,y}}$.

Exercise 4.20 In the graph below, what is the probability flow in each edge?

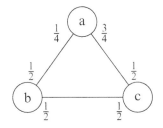

Exercise 4.21 In computing the ϵ-mixing time, we defined the normalized conductance of a subset of vertices S as

$$\Phi(S) = \sum_{x \in S} \frac{\pi_x}{\pi(S)} \sum_{y \in \bar{S}} p_{xy}.$$

$\Phi(S)$ is the probability of leaving S if we are at vertices in S according to the marginalized stationary probability. Does the following formula give the expected time to leave S?

$$1\Phi(S) + 2(1 - \Phi(S))\Phi(S) + 3(1 - \Phi(S))^2\Phi(S) + \cdots = \frac{1}{\Phi(S)}$$

Prove your answer.

Exercise 4.22 What is the mixing time for the undirected graphs:

1. Two cliques connected by a single edge? To simplify the problem assume vertices have self loops except for the two vertices with the edge connecting the two cliques. Thus all vertices have the same degree.
2. A graph consisting of an n vertex clique plus one additional vertex connected to one vertex in the clique? To simplify the problem add self loops to all vertices in the clique except for the vertex connected to the additional vertex.

Exercise 4.23 What is the mixing time for

1. $G(n, p)$ with $p = \frac{\log n}{n}$?
2. A circle with n vertices where at each vertex an edge has been added to another vertex chosen at random? On average, each vertex will have degree four, two circle edges, and an edge from that vertex to a vertex chosen at random, and possibly some edges that are the ends of the random edges from other vertices.

Exercise 4.24 Find the ϵ-mixing time for a two-dimensional lattice with n vertices in each coordinate direction with a uniform probability distribution. To do this, solve the following problems assuming that the set S has $|S| \leq n^2/2$.

1. The minimum number of edges leaving a set S of size greater than or equal to $n^2/4$ is n.
2. The minimum number of edges leaving a set S of size less than or equal to $n^2/4$ is $2\lfloor \sqrt{S} \rfloor$.
3. Compute $\Phi(S)$.
4. Compute Φ.
5. Compute the ϵ-mixing time.

Exercise 4.25 Find the ϵ-mixing time for a d-dimensional lattice with n vertices in each coordinate direction with a uniform probability distribution. To do this, solve the following problems.

1. Select a direction, say x_1, and push all elements of S in each column perpendicular to $x_1 = 0$ as close to $x_1 = 0$ as possible. Prove that the number of edges leaving S is at least as large as the number leaving the modified version of S.
2. Repeat step one for each direction. Argue that for a direction, say x_1, as x_1 gets larger, a set in the perpendicular plane is contained in the previous set.

3. Optimize the arrangements of elements in the plane $x_1 = 0$ and move elements from farthest out plane in to make all planes the same shape as $x_1 = 0$ except for some leftover elements of S in the last plane. Argue that this does not increase the number of edges out.

4. What configurations might we end up with?

5. Argue that for a given size, S has at least as many edges as the modified version of S.

6. What is $\Phi(S)$ for a modified form S?

7. What is Φ for a d-dimensional lattice?

8. What is the ϵ-mixing time?

Exercise 4.26

1. What is the set of possible harmonic functions on a connected graph if there are only interior vertices and no boundary vertices that supply the boundary condition?

2. Let q_x be the stationary probability of vertex x in a random walk on an undirected graph where all edges at a vertex are equally likely and let d_x be the degree of vertex x. Show that $\frac{q_x}{d_x}$ is a harmonic function.

3. If there are multiple harmonic functions when there are no boundary conditions, why is the stationary probability of a random walk on an undirected graph unique?

4. What is the stationary probability of a random walk on an undirected graph?

Exercise 4.27 In Section 4.5, given an electrical network, we define an associated Markov chain such that voltages and currents in the electrical network corresponded to properties of the Markov chain. Can we go in reverse order and for any Markov chain construct the equivalent electrical network?

Exercise 4.28 What is the probability of reaching vertex 1 before vertex 5 when starting a random walk at vertex 4 in each of the following graphs?

1.

2.

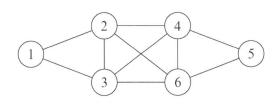

Exercise 4.29 Consider the electrical resistive network in Figure 4.14 consisting of vertices connected by resistors. Kirchoff's law states that the currents at each vertex sum to zero. Ohm's law states that the voltage across a resistor equals the product of the resistance times the current through it. Using these laws, calculate the effective resistance of the network.

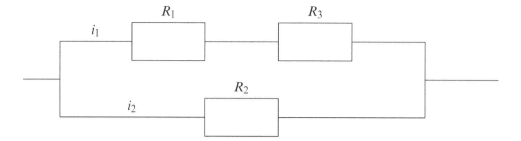

Figure 4.14: An electrical network of resistors.

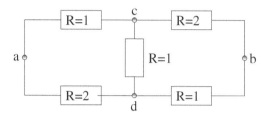

Figure 4.15: An electrical network of resistors.

Exercise 4.30 Consider the electrical network of Figure 4.15.

1. Set the voltage at a to one and at b to zero. What are the voltages at c and d?
2. What is the current in the edges a to c, a to d, c to d, c to b, and d to b?
3. What is the effective resistance between a and b?
4. Convert the electrical network to a graph. What are the edge probabilities at each vertex so that the probability of a walk starting at c (d) reaches a before b equals the voltage at c (the voltage at d)?
5. What is the probability of a walk starting at c reaching a before b? A walk starting at d reaching a before b?
6. What is the net frequency that a walk from a to b goes through the edge from c to d?
7. What is the probability that a random walk starting at a will return to a before reaching b?

Exercise 4.31 Consider a graph corresponding to an electrical network with vertices a and b. Prove directly that $\frac{c_{eff}}{c_a}$ must be less than or equal to 1. We know that this is the escape probability and must be at most 1. But for this exercise, do not use that fact.

Exercise 4.32 (**Thomson's Principle**) The energy dissipated by the resistance of edge xy in an electrical network is given by $i_{xy}^2 r_{xy}$. The total energy dissipation in the network is $E = \frac{1}{2} \sum_{x,y} i_{xy}^2 r_{xy}$ where the $\frac{1}{2}$ accounts for the fact that the dissipation in each edge is counted twice in the summation. Show that the current distribution that minimizes energy dissipation satisfies Ohm's law.

Exercise 4.33 (**Rayleigh's law**) Prove that reducing the value of a resistor in a network cannot increase the effective resistance. Prove that increasing the value of a resistor cannot decrease the effective resistance. You may use Thomson's principle Exercise 4.32.

Exercise 4.34 What is the hitting time h_{uv} for two adjacent vertices on a cycle of length n? What is the hitting time if the edge (u, v) is removed?

Exercise 4.35 What is the hitting time h_{uv} for the three graphs in Figure 4.16?

Exercise 4.36 Show that adding an edge can either increase or decrease hitting time by calculating h_{24} for the three graphs in Figure 4.17.

Exercise 4.37 Consider the n vertex connected graph shown in Figure 4.18 consisting of an edge (u, v) plus a connected graph on $n - 1$ vertices with m edges. Prove that $h_{uv} = 2m + 1$ where m is the number of edges in the $n - 1$ vertex subgraph.

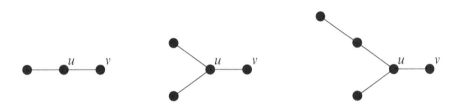

Figure 4.16: Three graphs

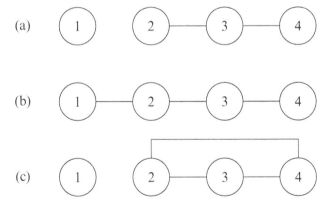

Figure 4.17: Three graphs

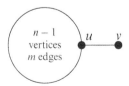

Figure 4.18: A connected graph consisting of $n - 1$ vertices and m edges along with a single edge (u, v).

Exercise 4.38 Consider a random walk on a clique of size n. What is the expected number of steps before a given vertex is reached?

Exercise 4.39 What is the most general solution to the difference equation $t(i + 2) - 5t(i + 1) + 6t(i) = 0$? How many boundary conditions do you need to make the solution unique?

Exercise 4.40 Given the difference equation $a_k t(i + k) + a_{k-1} t(i + k - 1) + \cdots + a_1 t(i + 1) + a_0 t(i) = 0$, the polynomial $a_k t^k + a_{k-i} t^{k-1} + \cdots + a_1 t + a_0 = 0$ is called the characteristic polynomial.

1. If the equation has a set of r distinct roots, what is the most general form of the solution?
2. If the roots of the characteristic polynomial are not distinct, what is the most general form of the solution?
3. What is the dimension of the solution space?
4. If the difference equation is not homogeneous (i.e., the right hand side is not 0) and f(i) is a specific solution to the nonhomogeneous difference equation, what is the full set of solutions to the nonhomogeneous difference equation?

Exercise 4.41 Show that adding an edge to a graph can either increase or decrease commute time.

Exercise 4.42 Consider the set of integers $\{1, 2, \ldots, n\}$.

1. What is the expected number of draws with replacement until the integer 1 is drawn?
2. What is the expected number of draws with replacement so that every integer is drawn?

Exercise 4.43 For each of the three graphs below, what is the return time starting at vertex A? Express your answer as a function of the number of vertices, n, and then express it as a function of the number of edges m.

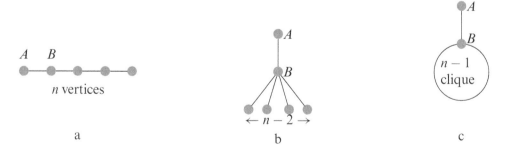

a

b

c

Exercise 4.44 Suppose that the clique in Exercise 4.43 was replaced by an arbitrary graph with $m - 1$ edges. What would be the return time to A in terms of m, the total number of edges?

Exercise 4.45 Suppose that the clique in Exercise 4.43 was replaced by an arbitrary graph with $m - d$ edges and there were d edges from A to the graph. What would be the expected length of a random path starting at A and ending at A after returning to A exactly d times?

Exercise 4.46 Given an undirected graph with a component consisting of a single edge, find two eigenvalues of the Laplacian $L = D - A$ where D is a diagonal matrix with vertex degrees on the diagonal and A is the adjacency matrix of the graph.

Exercise 4.47 A researcher was interested in determining the importance of various edges in an undirected graph. He computed the stationary probability for a random walk on the graph and let p_i be the probability of being at vertex i. If vertex i was of degree d_i, the frequency that edge (i, j) was traversed from i to j would be $\frac{1}{d_i}p_i$ and the frequency that the edge was traversed in the opposite direction would be $\frac{1}{d_j}p_j$. Thus, he assigned an importance of $\left|\frac{1}{d_i}p_i - \frac{1}{d_j}p_j\right|$ to the edge. What is wrong with his idea?

Exercise 4.48 Prove that two independent random walks starting at the origin on a two-dimensional lattice will eventually meet with probability 1.

Exercise 4.49 Suppose two individuals are flipping balanced coins and each is keeping track of the number of heads minus the number of tails. Is it the case that with probability 1, at some time the counts of the two individuals will be the same?

Exercise 4.50 Consider the lattice in two-dimensions. In each square add the two diagonal edges. What is the escape probability for the resulting graph?

Exercise 4.51 Determine by simulation the escape probability for the three-dimensional lattice.

Exercise 4.52 What is the escape probability for a random walk starting at the root of an infinite binary tree?

Exercise 4.53 Consider a random walk on the positive half line, that is the integers $0, 1, 2, \ldots$. At the origin, always move right one step. At all other integers move right with probability 2/3 and left with probability 1/3. What is the escape probability?

Exercise 4.54 Consider the graphs in Figure 4.19. Calculate the stationary distribution for a random walk on each graph and the flow through each edge. What condition holds on the flow through edges in the undirected graph? In the directed graph?

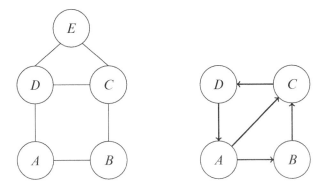

Figure 4.19: An undirected and a directed graph.

Exercise 4.55 Create a random directed graph with 200 vertices and roughly eight edges per vertex. Add k new vertices and calculate the pagerank with and without directed edges from the k added vertices to vertex 1. How much does adding the k edges change the pagerank of vertices for various values of k and restart frequency? How much does adding a loop at vertex 1 change the pagerank? To do the experiment carefully one needs to consider the pagerank of a vertex to which the star is attached. If it has low pagerank its page rank is likely to increase a lot.

Exercise 4.56 Repeat the experiment in Exercise 4.55 for hitting time.

Exercise 4.57 Search engines ignore self loops in calculating pagerank. Thus, to increase pagerank, one needs to resort to loops of length 2. By how much can you increase the pagerank of a page by adding a number of loops of length 2?

Exercise 4.58 Number the vertices of a graph $\{1, 2, \ldots, n\}$. Define hitting time to be the expected time from vertex 1. In (2) assume that the vertices in the cycle are sequentially numbered.

1. What is the hitting time for a vertex in a complete directed graph with self loops?
2. What is the hitting time for a vertex in a directed cycle with n vertices?

Exercise 4.59 Using a web browser, bring up a webpage and look at the source html. How would you extract the urls of all hyperlinks on the page if you were doing a crawl of the web? With Internet Explorer, click on "source" under "view" to access the html representation of the web page. With Firefox, click on "page source" under "view".

Exercise 4.60 Sketch an algorithm to crawl the World Wide Web. There is a time delay between the time you seek a page and the time you get it. Thus, you cannot wait until the page arrives before starting another fetch. There are conventions that must be obeyed if one were to actually do a search. Sites specify information as to how long or which files can be searched. Do not attempt an actual search without guidance from a knowledgeable person.

CHAPTER FIVE

Machine Learning

5.1. Introduction

Machine learning algorithms are general-purpose tools for generalizing from data. They are able to solve problems from many disciplines without detailed domain-specific knowledge. To date they have been highly successful for a wide range of tasks including computer vision, speech recognition, document classification, automated driving, computational science, and decision support.

5.1.1. The Core Problem

The core problem underlying many machine learning applications is learning a good classification rule from labeled data. This problem consists of a domain of interest, called the *instance space*, such as e-mail messages or patient records, and a classification task, such as classifying e-mail messages into spam versus non-spam or determining which patients will respond well to a given medical treatment. We will typically assume our instance space is $\{0, 1\}^d$ or $\mathbb{R}^d$, corresponding to data described by d Boolean or real-valued features. Features for e-mail messages could be the presence or absence of various types of words, and features for patient records could be the results of various medical tests. Our learning algorithm is given a set of labeled *training examples*, which are points in our instance space along with their correct classification. This training data could be a collection of e-mail messages, each labeled as spam or not spam, or a collection of patients, each labeled by whether or not they responded well to a given medical treatment. Our algorithm aims to use the training examples to produce a classification rule that will perform well on new data. A key feature of machine learning, which distinguishes it from other algorithmic tasks, is that our goal is *generalization*: to use one set of data in order to perform well on new data not seen yet. We focus on *binary classification* where items in the domain of interest are classified into two categories (called the positive class and the negative class), as in the medical and spam detection examples above, but nearly all the techniques described here also apply to multi-way classification.

5.1.2. How to Learn

A high-level approach is to find a "simple" rule with good performance on the training data. In the case of classifying e-mail messages, we might find a set of highly indicative words such that every spam e-mail in the training data has at least one of these words and none of the non-spam e-mails has any of them. In this case, the rule "if the message has any of these words, then it is spam else it is not" would be a simple rule that performs well on the training data. We might weight words with positive and negative weights such that the total weighted sum of words in the e-mail message is positive on the spam e-mails in the training data and negative on the non-spam e-mails. This would produce a classification rule called a *linear separator*. We will then argue that so long as the training data are representative of what future data will look like, we can be confident that any sufficiently "simple" rule that performs well on the training data will also perform well on future data. To make this into a formal mathematical statement, we need to be precise about the meaning of "simple" as well as what it means for training data to be "representative" of future data. We will see several notions of complexity, including bit-counting and VC-dimension, that will allow us to make mathematical statements of this form.

5.2. The Perceptron Algorithm

A simple rule in d-dimensional space is a linear separator or half-space. Does a weighted sum of feature values exceed a threshold? Such a rule may be thought of as being implemented by a threshold gate that takes the feature values as inputs, computes their weighted sum, and outputs "yes" or "no" depending on whether or not the sum is greater than the threshold. One could also look at a network of interconnected threshold gates called a neural net. Threshold gates are sometimes called perceptrons, since one model of human perception is that it is done by a neural net in the brain.

The problem of fitting a half-space or a linear separator consists of n labeled examples $x_1, x_2, \ldots, x_n$ in d-dimensional space. Each example has label $+1$ or -1. The task is to find a d-dimensional vector $\mathbf{w}$, if one exists, and a threshold t such that

$$\mathbf{w} \cdot \mathbf{x_i} > t \text{ for each } \mathbf{x_i} \text{ labeled } +1$$
$$\mathbf{w} \cdot \mathbf{x_i} < t \text{ for each } \mathbf{x_i} \text{ labeled } -1. \tag{5.1}$$

A vector-threshold pair, $(\mathbf{w}, t)$, satisfying the inequalities is called a *linear separator*.

The above formulation is a linear program in the unknowns $\mathbf{w}$ and t that can be solved by a general-purpose linear programming algorithm. A simpler algorithm called the *Perceptron Algorithm* can be much faster when there is a feasible solution $\mathbf{w}$ with a lot of "wiggle room" or margin.

We begin with a technical modification, adding an extra coordinate to each x_i and $\mathbf{w}$, writing $\hat{x}_i = (x_i, 1)$ and $\hat{\mathbf{w}} = (\mathbf{w}, -t)$. Suppose l_i is the ± 1 label on x_i. Then, the inequalities in (5.1) can be rewritten as

$$(\hat{\mathbf{w}} \cdot \hat{x}_i) l_i > 0 \quad 1 \le i \le n.$$

Adding the extra coordinate increased the dimension by 1, but now the separator contains the origin. In particular, for examples of label $+1$, $\hat{\mathbf{w}} \cdot \hat{x}_i > 0$ and for examples of label -1, $\hat{\mathbf{w}} \cdot \hat{x}_i < 0$. For simplicity of notation, in the rest of this section, we drop the hats and let x_i and $\mathbf{w}$ stand for the corresponding $\hat{x}_i$ and $\hat{\mathbf{w}}$.

The Perceptron Algorithm is very simple and follows below. It is important to note that the weight vector $\mathbf{w}$ will be a linear combination of the x_i.

The Perceptron Algorithm:

$\mathbf{w} \leftarrow 0$

while there exists $\mathbf{x_i}$ with $\mathbf{x_i} l_i \cdot \mathbf{w} \leq 0$, update $\mathbf{w} \leftarrow \mathbf{w} + \mathbf{x_i} l_i$

The intuition is that correcting $\mathbf{w}$ by adding $\mathbf{x_i} l_i$ causes the new $(\mathbf{w} \cdot \mathbf{x_i}) l_i$ to be higher by $\mathbf{x_i} \cdot \mathbf{x_i} l_i^2 = |\mathbf{x_i}|^2$. This is good for this $\mathbf{x_i}$, but the change may be bad for the other $\mathbf{x_j}$. The proof below shows that this very simple process yields a solution $\mathbf{w}$ with a number of steps that depends on the *margin of separation* of the data. If a weight vector $\mathbf{w}^*$ satisfies $(\mathbf{w} \cdot \mathbf{x_i}) l_i > 0$ for $1 \leq i \leq n$, the minimum distance of any example $\mathbf{x_i}$ to the linear separator $\mathbf{w}^* \cdot \mathbf{x} = 0$ is called the *margin* of the separator. Scale $\mathbf{w}^*$ so that $(\mathbf{w}^* \cdot \mathbf{x_i}) l_i \geq 1$ for all i. Then the margin of the separator is at least $1/|\mathbf{w}^*|$. If all points lie inside a ball of radius r, then $r|\mathbf{w}^*|$ is the ratio of the radius of the ball to the margin. Theorem 5.1 below shows that the number of update steps of the Perceptron Algorithm is at most the square of this quantity. Thus, the number of update steps will be small when data are separated by a large margin relative to the radius of the smallest enclosing ball of the data.

Theorem 5.1 *If there is a $\mathbf{w}^*$ satisfying $(\mathbf{w}^* \cdot \mathbf{x_i}) l_i \geq 1$ for all i, then the Perceptron Algorithm finds a solution $\mathbf{w}$ with $(\mathbf{w} \cdot \mathbf{x_i}) l_i > 0$ for all i in at most $r^2 |\mathbf{w}^*|^2$ updates where $r = \max\limits_{i} |\mathbf{x_i}|$.*

Proof Let $\mathbf{w}^*$ satisfy the "if" condition of the theorem. We will keep track of two quantities, $\mathbf{w}^T \mathbf{w}^*$ and $|\mathbf{w}|^2$. Each update increases $\mathbf{w}^T \mathbf{w}^*$ by at least 1.

$$(\mathbf{w} + \mathbf{x_i} l_i)^T \mathbf{w}^* = \mathbf{w}^T \mathbf{w}^* + \mathbf{x_i}^T l_i \mathbf{w}^* \geq \mathbf{w}^T \mathbf{w}^* + 1$$

On each update, $|\mathbf{w}|^2$ increases by at most r^2:

$$(\mathbf{w} + \mathbf{x_i} l_i)^T (\mathbf{w} + \mathbf{x_i} l_i) = |\mathbf{w}|^2 + 2\mathbf{x_i}^T l_i \mathbf{w} + |\mathbf{x_i} l_i|^2 \leq |\mathbf{w}|^2 + |\mathbf{x_i}|^2 \leq |\mathbf{w}|^2 + r^2,$$

where the middle inequality comes from the fact that an update is only performed on an $\mathbf{x_i}$ when $\mathbf{x_i}^T l_i \mathbf{w} \leq 0$.

If the Perceptron Algorithm makes m updates, then $\mathbf{w}^T \mathbf{w}^* \geq m$, and $|\mathbf{w}|^2 \leq mr^2$, or equivalently $|\mathbf{w}||\mathbf{w}^*| \geq m$ and $|\mathbf{w}| \leq r\sqrt{m}$. Then

$$m \leq |\mathbf{w}||\mathbf{w}^*|$$
$$m/|\mathbf{w}^*| \leq |\mathbf{w}|$$
$$m/|\mathbf{w}^*| \leq r\sqrt{m}$$
$$\sqrt{m} \leq r|\mathbf{w}^*|$$
$$m \leq r^2 |\mathbf{w}^*|^2$$

as desired. ∎

5.3. Kernel Functions and Nonlinearly Separable Data

If the data is linearly separable, then the Perceptron Algorithm finds a solution. If the data is not linearly separable, then perhaps one can map the data to a higher-dimensional space where it is linearly separable. Consider two-dimensional data consisting of two circular rings of radius 1 and 2. Clearly the data is not linearly separable. The mapping

$$(x, y) \overset{\varphi}{\to} (x, y, x^2 + y^2)$$

would move the ring of radius 2 farther from the plane than the ring of radius 1, making the mapped data linearly separable.

If a function φ maps the data to another space, one can run the Perceptron Algorithm in the new space. The weight vector will be a linear function $\sum_{i=1}^{n} c_i \varphi(\mathbf{x_i})$ of the new input data. To determine if a pattern $\mathbf{x_j}$ is correctly classified, compute

$$\mathbf{w}^T \varphi(\mathbf{x_j}) = \sum_{i=1}^{n} c_i \varphi(\mathbf{x_i})^T \varphi(\mathbf{x_j}).$$

Since only products of the $\varphi(\mathbf{x_i})$ appear, we do not need to explicitly compute, or even to know, the mapping φ if we have a function

$$k(\mathbf{x_i}, \mathbf{x_j}) = \varphi(\mathbf{x_i})^T \varphi(\mathbf{x_j})$$

called a *kernel function*. To add $\varphi(\mathbf{x_j})$ to the weight vector, instead of computing the mapping φ, just add 1 to the coefficient c_j.

Given a collection of examples $\mathbf{x_1}, \mathbf{x_2}, \ldots, \mathbf{x_n}$ and a kernel function k, the associated *kernel matrix K* is defined as $k_{ij} = \varphi(\mathbf{x_i})^T \varphi(\mathbf{x_j})$. A natural question here is for a given matrix K, how can one tell if there exists a function φ such that $k_{ij} = \varphi(\mathbf{x_i})^T \varphi(\mathbf{x_j})$. The following lemma resolves this issue.

Lemma 5.2 *A matrix K is a kernel matrix, i.e., there is a function φ such that $k_{ij} = \varphi(\mathbf{x_i})^T \varphi(\mathbf{x_j})$, if and only if K is positive semi-definite.*

Proof If K is positive semi-definite, then it can be expressed as $K = BB^T$. Define $\varphi(\mathbf{x_i})^T$ to be the ith row of B. Then $k_{ij} = \varphi(\mathbf{x_i})^T \varphi(\mathbf{x_j})$. Conversely, if there is an embedding φ such that $k_{ij} = \varphi(\mathbf{x_i})^T \varphi(\mathbf{x_j})$, then using the $\varphi(\mathbf{x_i})^T$ for the rows of a matrix B, $K = BB^T$, and so K is positive semi-definite. ∎

Many different pairwise functions are legal kernel functions. One easy way to create a kernel function is by combining other kernel functions together, via the following theorem.

Theorem 5.3 *Suppose k_1 and k_2 are kernel functions. Then*

1. *For any constant $c \geq 0$, ck_1 is a legal kernel. In fact, for any scalar function f, the function $k_3(\mathbf{x}, \mathbf{y}) = f(\mathbf{x})f(\mathbf{y})k_1(\mathbf{x}, \mathbf{y})$ is a legal kernel.*
2. *The sum $k_1 + k_2$, is a legal kernel.*
3. *The product, $k_1 k_2$, is a legal kernel.*

The proof of Theorem 5.3 is relegated to Exercise 5.6. Notice that Theorem 5.3 immediately implies that the function $k(\mathbf{x}, \mathbf{y}) = (1 + \mathbf{x}^T \mathbf{y})^k$ is a legal kernel by using the fact that $k_1(\mathbf{x}, \mathbf{y}) = 1$ is a legal kernel, $k_2(\mathbf{x}, \mathbf{y}) = \mathbf{x}^T \mathbf{y}$ is a legal kernel, then adding them, and multiplying the sum by itself k times. This kernel is illustrated in Figure 5.1.

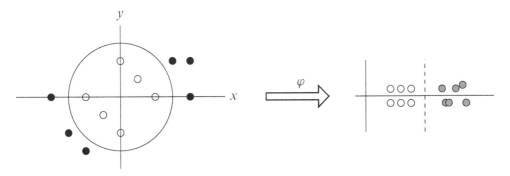

Figure 5.1: Data that are not linearly separable in the input space $\mathbb{R}^2$ but that is linearly separable in the "φ-space," $\varphi(\mathbf{x}) = (1, \sqrt{2}x_1, \sqrt{2}x_2, x_1^2, \sqrt{2}x_1 x_2, x_2^2)$, corresponding to the kernel function $k(\mathbf{x}, \mathbf{y}) = (1 + x_1 y_1 + x_2 y_2)^2$.

Another popular kernel is the Gaussian kernel, defined as:

$$k(\mathbf{x}, \mathbf{y}) = e^{-c|\mathbf{x}-\mathbf{y}|^2}.$$

If we think of a kernel as a measure of similarity, then this kernel defines the similarity between two data objects as a quantity that decreases exponentially with the squared distance between them. The Gaussian kernel can be shown to be a true kernel function by first writing it as

$$e^{-c|\mathbf{x}-\mathbf{y}|^2} = f(\mathbf{x})f(\mathbf{y})e^{2c\mathbf{x}^T\mathbf{y}}$$

for $f(\mathbf{x}) = e^{-c|\mathbf{x}|^2}$ and then taking the Taylor expansion of $e^{2c\mathbf{x}^T\mathbf{y}}$ and applying the rules in Theorem 5.3. Technically, this last step requires considering countably infinitely many applications of the rules and allowing for infinite-dimensional vector spaces.

5.4. Generalizing to New Data

So far, we have focused on finding an algorithm that performs well on a given set S of training data. But what we really want is an algorithm that performs well on new data not seen yet. To make guarantees of this form, we need some assumption that our training data are representative of what new data will look like. Formally, we assume that the training data and the new data are drawn from the same probability distribution. Additionally, we want our algorithm's classification rule to be simple. These two conditions allow us to guarantee the ability of our trained algorithm to perform well on new unseen data.

Formalizing the Problem
To formalize the learning problem, assume there is some probability distribution D over the instance space X, such that

1. our training set S consists of points drawn independently at random from D, and
2. our objective is to predict well on new points that are also drawn from D.

This is the sense in which we assume that our training data are representative of future data. Let c^*, called the *target concept*, denote the subset of X corresponding to the positive class for a desired binary classification. For example, c^* would correspond to the set of all patients who would respond well to a given treatment in a medical scenario, or it could correspond to the set of all possible spam e-mails in a spam detection scenario. Each point in our training set S is labeled according to whether or not it belongs to c^*. Our goal is to produce a set $h \subseteq X$, called our *hypothesis*, that is close to c^* with respect to the distribution D. The *true error* of h is $err_D(h) = \text{Prob}(h \triangle c^*)$ where $\triangle$ denotes symmetric difference, and the probability mass is according to D. In other words, the true error of h is the probability it incorrectly classifies a data point drawn at random from D. Our goal is to produce an h of low true error. The *training error* of h, denoted $err_S(h)$, is the fraction of points in S on which h and c^* disagree. That is, $err_S(h) = |S \cap (h \triangle c^*)|/|S|$. Note that even though S is assumed to consist of points randomly drawn from D, it is possible for an hypothesis h to have low training error or even to completely agree with c^* over the training sample, and yet have high true error. This is called *overfitting* the training data. For instance, a hypothesis h that simply consists of listing the positive examples in S, which is equivalent to an algorithm that memorizes the training sample and predicts positive on an example if and only if it already appeared positively in the training sample, would have zero training error. However, this hypothesis likely would have high true error and therefore would be highly overfitting the training data. More generally, overfitting is a concern because algorithms will typically be optimizing over the training sample. To design and analyze algorithms for learning, we need to address the issue of overfitting.

To analyze overfitting, we introduce the notion of a hypothesis class, also called a concept class or set system. A hypothesis class $\mathcal{H}$ over X is a collection of subsets of X, called hypotheses or concepts. For instance, the class of *intervals* over $X = \mathbb{R}$ is the collection $\{[a,b]|a \leq b\}$. The class of *linear separators* over $\mathbb{R}^d$ is the collection

$$\{\{\mathbf{x} \in \mathbb{R}^d | \mathbf{w} \cdot \mathbf{x} \geq t\} | \mathbf{w} \in \mathbb{R}^d, t \in \mathbb{R}\}.$$

It is the collection of all sets in $\mathbb{R}^d$ that are linearly separable from their complement. In the case that X is the set of four points in the plane $\{(-1,-1), (-1,1), (1,-1), (1,1)\}$, the class of linear separators contains 14 of the $2^4 = 16$ possible subsets of X.[1] Given a hypothesis class $\mathcal{H}$ and training set S, we aim to find a hypothesis in $\mathcal{H}$ that closely agrees with c^* over S. For example, the Perceptron Algorithm will find a linear separator that agrees with the target concept over S so long as S is linearly separable. To address overfitting, we argue that if the training set S is large enough compared to some property of $\mathcal{H}$, then with high probability, all $h \in \mathcal{H}$ have their training error close to their true error, so that if we find a hypothesis whose training error is low, we can be confident its true error will be low as well.

5.4.1. Overfitting and Uniform Convergence

We now present two generalization guarantees that explain how one can guard against overfitting. To keep things simple, assume our hypothesis class $\mathcal{H}$ is finite.

---

[1] The only two subsets that are not in the class are the sets $\{(-1,-1), (1,1)\}$ and $\{(-1,1), (1,-1)\}$.

In the Perceptron Algorithm with d-dimensional data, if we quantize the weights to be 32-bit integers, then there are only 2^{32d} possible hypotheses. Later, we will see how to extend these results to infinite classes as well. Given a class of hypotheses $\mathcal{H}$, the first result states that for ϵ greater than zero, so long as the training data set is large compared to $\frac{1}{\epsilon} \ln(|\mathcal{H}|)$, it is unlikely any hypothesis h in $\mathcal{H}$ with true error greater than ϵ will have zero training error. This means that with high probability, any hypothesis that our algorithm finds that agrees with the target hypothesis on the training data will have low true error. The second result states that if the training data set is large compared to $\frac{1}{\epsilon^2} \ln(|\mathcal{H}|)$, then it is unlikely that the training error and true error will differ by more than ϵ for any hypothesis in $\mathcal{H}$.

The basic idea is the following. For h with large true error and an element $x \in X$ selected at random, there is a reasonable chance that x will belong to the symmetric difference $h \triangle c^*$. If the training sample S is large enough with each point drawn independently from X, the chance that S is completely disjoint from $h \triangle c^*$ is incredibly small. This is for a single hypothesis, h. When $\mathcal{H}$ is finite, we can apply the union bound over all $h \in \mathcal{H}$ of large true error. We formalize this below.

Theorem 5.4 *Let $\mathcal{H}$ be an hypothesis class and let ϵ and δ be greater than zero. If a training set S of size*

$$n \geq \frac{1}{\epsilon}\Big(\ln |\mathcal{H}| + \ln(1/\delta)\Big)$$

is drawn from distribution D, then with probability greater than or equal to $1 - \delta$ every h in $\mathcal{H}$ with true error $err_D(h) \geq \epsilon$ has training error $err_S(h) > 0$. Equivalently, with probability greater than or equal to $1 - \delta$, every $h \in \mathcal{H}$ with training error zero has true error less than ϵ.

Proof Let $h_1, h_2, \ldots$ be the hypotheses in $\mathcal{H}$ with true error greater than or equal to ϵ. These are the hypotheses that we don't want to output. Consider drawing the sample S of size n and let A_i be the event that h_i has zero training error. Since every h_i has true error greater than or equal to ϵ,

$$\text{Prob}(A_i) \leq (1 - \epsilon)^n.$$

This is illustrated in Figure 5.2. By the union bound over all i, the probability that any of these h_i is consistent with S is given by

$$\text{Prob}(\cup_i A_i) \leq |\mathcal{H}|(1 - \epsilon)^n.$$

				Not spam								Spam				
x_1	x_2	x_3	x_4	x_5	x_6	x_7	x_8	x_9	x_{10}	x_{11}	x_{12}	x_{13}	x_{14}	x_{15}	x_{16}	e-mails
					↓				↓		↓					
0	0	0	0	0	0	0	0	1	1	1	1	1	1	1	1	target concept
					↕				↕		↕					
0	1	0	0	0	0	1	0	1	1	1	0	1	0	1	1	hypothesis h_i
					↑				↑		↑					

Figure 5.2: The hypothesis h_i disagrees with the truth in one-quarter of the e-mails. Thus with a training set S, the probability that the hypothesis will survive is $(1 - 0.25)^{|S|}$. The arrows represent three elements in S, one of which contributes to the training error.

Using the fact that $(1 - \epsilon) \leq e^{-\epsilon}$, the probability that any hypothesis in $\mathcal{H}$ with true error greater than or equal to ϵ has training error zero is at most $|\mathcal{H}|e^{-\epsilon n}$. Replacing n by the sample size bound from the theorem statement, this is at most $|\mathcal{H}|e^{-\ln|\mathcal{H}|-\ln(1/\delta)} = \delta$ as desired. $\blacksquare$

The conclusion of Theorem 5.4 is sometimes called a *PAC-learning guarantee*, since it states that an $h \in \mathcal{H}$ consistent with the sample is *Probably Approximately Correct*.

Theorem 5.4 addressed the case where there exists a hypothesis in $\mathcal{H}$ with zero training error. What if the best h in $\mathcal{H}$ has 5% error on S? Can we still be confident that its true error is low, say at most 10%? For this, we want an analog of Theorem 5.4 that says for a sufficiently large training set S, every $h \in \mathcal{H}$ with high probability has training error within $\pm\epsilon$ of the true error. Such a statement is called *uniform convergence* because we are asking that the training set errors converge to their true errors uniformly over all sets in $\mathcal{H}$. To see why such a statement should be true for sufficiently large S and a single hypothesis h, consider two strings that differ in 10% of the positions and randomly select a large sample of positions. The number of positions that differ in the sample will be close to 10%.

To prove uniform convergence bounds, we use a tail inequality for sums of independent Bernoulli random variables (i.e., coin tosses). The following is particularly convenient and is a variation on the Chernoff bounds in Section 12.5.1 in Chapter 12.

Theorem 5.5 (Hoeffding bounds) *Let $x_1, x_2, \ldots, x_n$ be independent $\{0, 1\}$-valued random variables with $Prob(x_i = 1) = p$. Let $s = \sum_i x_i$ (equivalently, flip n coins of bias p and let s be the total number of heads). For any $0 \leq \alpha \leq 1$,*

$$Prob(s/n > p + \alpha) \leq e^{-2n\alpha^2}$$
$$Prob(s/n < p - \alpha) \leq e^{-2n\alpha^2}.$$

Theorem 5.5 implies the following uniform convergence analog of Theorem 5.4.

Theorem 5.6 (Uniform convergence) *Let $\mathcal{H}$ be a hypothesis class and let ϵ and δ be greater than zero. If a training set S of size*

$$n \geq \frac{1}{2\epsilon^2}\left(\ln|\mathcal{H}| + \ln(2/\delta)\right),$$

is drawn from distribution D, then with probability greater than or equal to $1 - \delta$, every h in $\mathcal{H}$ satisfies $|err_S(h) - err_D(h)| \leq \epsilon$.

Proof Fix some $h \in \mathcal{H}$ and let x_j be the indicator random variable for the event that h makes a mistake on the jth example in S. The x_j are independent $\{0, 1\}$ random variables and the probability that x_j equals 1 is the true error of h, and the fraction of the x_j's equal to 1 is exactly the training error of h. Therefore, Hoeffding bounds guarantee that the probability of the event A_h that $|err_D(h) - err_S(h)| > \epsilon$ is less than or equal to $2e^{-2n\epsilon^2}$. Applying the union bound to the events A_h over all $h \in \mathcal{H}$, the probability that there exists an $h \in \mathcal{H}$ with the difference between true error and empirical error greater than ϵ is less than or equal to $2|\mathcal{H}|e^{-2n\epsilon^2}$. Using the value of n from the theorem statement, the right-hand side of the above inequality is at most δ as desired. $\blacksquare$

Theorem 5.6 justifies the approach of optimizing over our training sample S even if we are not able to find a rule of zero training error. If our training set S is sufficiently large, with high probability, good performance on S will translate to good performance on D.

Note that Theorems 5.4 and 5.6 require $|\mathcal{H}|$ to be finite in order to be meaningful. The notion of growth functions and VC-dimension in Section 5.5 extend Theorem 5.6 to certain infinite hypothesis classes.

5.4.2. Occam's Razor

Occam's razor is the notion, stated by William of Occam around AD 1320, that in general one should prefer simpler explanations over more complicated ones.[2] Why should one do this, and can we make a formal claim about why this is a good idea? What if each of us disagrees about precisely which explanations are simpler than others? It turns out we can use Theorem 5.4 to make a mathematical statement of Occam's razor that addresses these issues.

What do we mean by a rule being "simple"? Assume that each of us has some way of describing rules, using bits. The methods, also called *description languages*, used by each of us may be different, but one fact is that in any given description language, there are at most 2^b rules that can be described using fewer than b bits (because $1 + 2 + 4 + \cdots + 2^{b-1} < 2^b$). Therefore, by setting $\mathcal{H}$ to be the set of all rules that can be described in fewer than b bits and plugging into Theorem 5.4, we have the following:

Theorem 5.7 (Occam's razor) *Fix any description language and consider a training sample S drawn from distribution $\mathcal{D}$. With probability at least $1 - \delta$, any rule h with $err_S(h) = 0$ that can be described using fewer than b bits will have $err_D(h) \leq \epsilon$ for $|S| = \frac{1}{\epsilon}[b \ln(2) + \ln(1/\delta)]$. Equivalently, with probability at least $1 - \delta$, all rules with $err_S(h) = 0$ that can be described in fewer than b bits will have $err_D(h) \leq \frac{b \ln(2) + \ln(1/\delta)}{|S|}$.*

Using the fact that $\ln(2) < 1$ and ignoring the low-order $\ln(1/\delta)$ term, this means that if the number of bits it takes to write down a rule consistent with the training data is at most 10% of the number of data points in our sample, then we can be confident it will have error at most 10% with respect to $\mathcal{D}$. What is perhaps surprising about this theorem is that it means that we can each have different ways of describing rules and yet all use Occam's razor. Note that the theorem does not say that complicated rules are necessarily bad, or even that given two rules consistent with the data that the complicated rule is necessarily worse. What it does say is that Occam's razor is a good policy in that simple rules are unlikely to fool us since there are just not that many simple rules.

5.4.3. Regularization: Penalizing Complexity

Theorems 5.6 and 5.7 suggest the following idea. Suppose that there is no simple rule that is perfectly consistent with the training data, but there are very simple rules

---

[2]The statement more explicitly was that "Entities should not be multiplied unnecessarily."

with training error 20%, and some more complex rules with training error 10%, and so on. In this case, perhaps we should optimize some combination of training error and simplicity. This is the notion of *regularization*, also called *complexity penalization*.

Specifically, a *regularizer* is a penalty term that penalizes more complex hypotheses. So far, a natural measure of complexity of a hypothesis is the number of bits needed to write it down.[3] Consider fixing some description language, and let $\mathcal{H}_i$ denote those hypotheses that can be described in i bits in this language, so $|\mathcal{H}_i| \leq 2^i$. Let $\delta_i = \delta/2^i$. Rearranging the bound of Theorem 5.6, with probability at least $1 - \delta_i$, all h in $\mathcal{H}_i$ satisfy $err_D(h) \leq err_S(h) + \sqrt{\frac{\ln(|\mathcal{H}_i|) + \ln(2/\delta_i)}{2|S|}}$. Applying the union bound over all i, using the fact that $\delta = \delta_1 + \delta_2 + \delta_3 + \cdots$, and also the fact that $\ln(|\mathcal{H}_i|) + \ln(2/\delta_i) \leq i \ln(4) + \ln(2/\delta)$, gives the following corollary.

Corollary 5.8 *Fix any description language and a training sample S. With probability greater than or equal to $1 - \delta$, all hypotheses h satisfy*

$$err_D(h) \leq err_S(h) + \sqrt{\frac{\text{size}(h) \ln(4) + \ln(2/\delta)}{2|S|}}$$

where size(h) *denotes the number of bits needed to describe h in the given language.*

Corollary 5.8 tells us that rather than searching for a rule of low training error, we may want to search for a rule with a low right-hand side in the displayed formula. If we can find an hypothesis for which this quantity is small, we can be confident true error will be low as well.

To see how this works, consider a complex network made up of many threshold logic units. It turns out one can give a description language such that networks with many weights set to zero a have smaller size than networks with fewer weights set to zero. Thus, if we use a regularizer that penalizes weights that are non-zero in the training, the training will change the size of the network by setting some weights to zero. Given a very simple network with training error 20% and possibly true error 21% or 22% and a complex network with training error 10% but true error 21% or 22%, we can train with the regularizer and maybe get training error 15% and true error 18%.

5.5. VC-Dimension

In Section 5.4.1 we showed that if the training set S is large compared to $\frac{1}{\epsilon} \log(|\mathcal{H}|)$, we can be confident that every h in $\mathcal{H}$ with true error greater than or equal to ϵ will have training error greater than zero. If S is large compared to $\frac{1}{\epsilon^2} \log(|\mathcal{H}|)$, then we can be confident that every h in $\mathcal{H}$ will have $|err_D(h) - err_S(h)| \leq \epsilon$. These results used $\log(|\mathcal{H}|)$ as a measure of complexity of the concept class $\mathcal{H}$, which required that $\mathcal{H}$ be a finite set. VC-dimension is a tighter measure of complexity for a concept class

---

[3]Later we will see support vector machines that use a regularizer for linear separators based on the margin of separation of data.

and also yields confidence bounds. For any class $\mathcal{H}$, VC-dim$(\mathcal{H}) \leq \log_2(|\mathcal{H}|)$,[4] but it can also be quite a bit smaller and is finite in some cases where $\mathcal{H}$ is infinite.

This issue of how big a sample is required comes up in many application besides learning theory. One such application is how large a sample of a data set do we need to insure that using the sample to answer questions gives a reliable answer with high probability. The answer relies on the complexity of the class of questions, which in some sense corresponds to how sophisticated the learning algorithm is. To introduces the concept of VC-dimension, we will consider sampling a database instead of training a network.

Consider a database consisting of the salary and age for a random sample of the adult population in the United States. Suppose we are interested in using the database to answer questions of the form: What fraction of the adult population in the United States has age between 35 and 45 and salary between \$50,000 and \$70,000? If the data are plotted in two dimensions, we are interested in queries that ask about the fraction of the adult population within some axis-parallel rectangle. To answer a query, calculate the fraction of the database satisfying the query. This brings up the question: How large does our database need to be so that with probability greater than or equal to $1 - \delta$, our answer will be within $\pm\epsilon$ of the truth for every possible rectangle query of this form?

If we assume our values are discretized such as 100 possible ages and 1,000 possible salaries, then there are at most $(100 \times 1,000)^2 = 10^{10}$ possible rectangles. This means we can apply Theorem 5.6 with $|\mathcal{H}| \leq 10^{10}$, and a sample size of $\frac{1}{2\epsilon^2}(10\ln 10 + \ln(2/\delta))$ would be sufficient.

If there are only n adults in the United States, there are at most n^4 rectangles that are truly different, and so we could use $|\mathcal{H}| \leq n^4$. Still, this suggests that S needs to grow with n, albeit logarithmically, and one might wonder if that is really necessary. VC-dimension, and the notion of the *growth function* of concept class $\mathcal{H}$, will give us a way to avoid such discretization and avoid any dependence on the size of the support of the underlying distribution D.

5.5.1. Definitions and Key Theorems

Definition 5.1 *A set system $(X, \mathcal{H})$ consists of a set X and a class $\mathcal{H}$ of subsets of X.*

In learning theory, the set X is the instance space, such as all possible e-mails, and $\mathcal{H}$ is the class of potential hypotheses, where a hypothesis h is a subset of X, such as the e-mails that our algorithm chooses to classify as spam.

An important concept in set systems is shattering.

Definition 5.2 *A set system $(X, \mathcal{H})$ shatters a set A if each subset of A can be expressed as $A \cap h$ for some h in $\mathcal{H}$.*

---

[4]The definition of VC-dimension is that if VCdim$(H) = d$, then there exist d points $x_1, \ldots, x_d$ such that all ways of labeling them are achievable using hypotheses in H. For each way of labeling them, choose some hypothesis h_i in H that agrees with that labeling. Notice that the hypotheses $h_1, h_2, \ldots, h_{2^d}$ must all be distinct, because they disagree on their labeling of $x_1, \ldots, x_d$. Therefore, $|H| \geq 2^d$. This means that $\log_2(|H|) \geq d$.

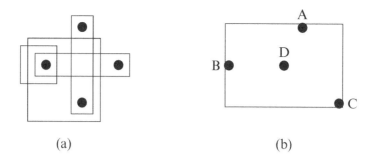

(a) (b)

Figure 5.3: (a) shows a set of four points that can be shattered by rectangles along with some of the rectangles that shatter the set. Not every set of four points can be shattered as seen in (b). Any rectangle containing points A, B, and C must contain D. No set of five points can be shattered by rectangles with axis-parallel edges. No set of three collinear points can be shattered, since any rectangle that contains the two end points must also contain the middle point. More generally, since rectangles are convex, a set with one point inside the convex hull of the others cannot be shattered.

Definition 5.3 *The* **VC-dimension** *of $\mathcal{H}$ is the size of the largest set shattered by $\mathcal{H}$.*

For instance, there exist sets of four points in the plane that can be shattered by rectangles with axis-parallel edges, e.g., four points at the vertices of a diamond (see Figure 5.3). For each of the 16 subsets of the four points, there exists a rectangle with the points of the subset inside the rectangle and the remaining points outside the rectangle. However, rectangles with axis-parallel edges cannot shatter any set of five points. Assume for contradiction that there is a set of five points shattered by the family of axis-parallel rectangles. Start with an enclosing rectangle for the five points. Move parallel edges toward each other without crossing any point until each edge is stopped by at least one point. Identify one such point for each edge. The same point may be identified as stopping two edges if it is at a corner of the minimum enclosing rectangle. If two or more points have stopped an edge, designate only one as having stopped the edge. Now, at most four points have been designated. Any rectangle enclosing the designated points must include the undesignated points. Thus, the subset of designated points cannot be expressed as the intersection of a rectangle with the five points. Therefore, the VC-dimension of axis-parallel rectangles is four.

5.5.2. VC-Dimension of Some Set Systems

Rectangles with Axis-Parallel Edges

We saw above, the class of axis-parallel rectangles in the plane has VC-dimension four.

Intervals of the Reals

Intervals on the real line can shatter any set of two points but no set of three points, since the subset of the first and last points cannot be isolated. Thus, the VC-dimension of intervals is two.

Pairs of Intervals of the Reals

Consider the family of pairs of intervals, where a pair of intervals is viewed as the set of points that are in at least one of the intervals. There exists a set of size four that can be shattered but no set of size five, since the subset of first, third, and last point cannot be isolated. Thus, the VC-dimension of pairs of intervals is four.

Finite Sets

The system of finite sets of real numbers can shatter any finite set of real numbers, and thus the VC-dimension of finite sets is infinite.

Convex Polygons

For any positive integer n, place n points on the unit circle. Any subset of the points are the vertices of a convex polygon. Clearly that polygon does not contain any of the points not in the subset. This shows that convex polygons can shatter arbitrarily large sets, so the VC-dimension is infinite.

Halfspaces in d-dimensions

Define a halfspace to be the set of all points on one side of a linear separator, i.e., a set of the form $\{x|w^T x \geq t\}$. The VC-dimension of halfspaces in d-dimensions is $d + 1$.

There exists a set of size $d+1$ that can be shattered by halfspaces. Select the d unit-coordinate vectors plus the origin to be the $d + 1$ points. Suppose A is any subset of these $d + 1$ points. Without loss of generality assume that the origin is in A. Take a 0-1 vector w, which has 1's precisely in the coordinates corresponding to vectors not in A. Clearly A lies in the halfspace $w^T x \leq 0$ and the complement of A lies in the complementary halfspace.

We now show that no set of $d + 2$ points in d-dimensions can be shattered by halfspaces. This is done by proving that any set of $d + 2$ points can be partitioned into two disjoint subsets A and B whose convex hulls intersect. This establishes the claim, since any linear separator with A on one side must have its entire convex hull on that side,[5] so it is not possible to have a linear separator with A on one side and B on the other.

Let $convex(S)$ denote the convex hull of the point set S.

Theorem 5.9 (Radon) *Any set $S \subseteq R^d$ with $|S| \geq d + 2$, can be partitioned into two disjoint subsets A and B such that $convex(A) \cap convex(B) \neq \phi$.*

Proof Without loss of generality, assume $|S| = d+2$. Form a $d \times (d+2)$ matrix with one column for each point of S. Call the matrix A. Add an extra row of all 1's to construct a $(d + 1) \times (d + 2)$ matrix B. Clearly the rank of this matrix is at most $d+1$ and the columns are linearly dependent. Say $x = (x_1, x_2, \ldots, x_{d+2})$ is a non-zero vector with $Bx = 0$. Reorder the columns so that $x_1, x_2, \ldots, x_s \geq 0$ and $x_{s+1}, x_{s+2}, \ldots, x_{d+2} < 0$. Normalize x so $\sum_{i=1}^{s} |x_i| = 1$. Let b_i (respectively a_i) be the ith column of B (respectively A). Then, $\sum_{i=1}^{s} |x_i| b_i = \sum_{i=s+1}^{d+2} |x_i| b_i$,

---

[5]If any two points x_1 and x_2 lie on the same side of a linear separator, so must any convex combination. If $w \cdot x_1 \geq b$ and $w \cdot x_2 \geq b$ then $w \cdot (ax_1 + (1 - a)x_2) \geq b$.

from which it follows that $\sum_{i=1}^{s} |x_i| \mathbf{a_i} = \sum_{i=s+1}^{d+2} |x_i| \mathbf{a_i}$ and $\sum_{i=1}^{s} |x_i| = \sum_{i=s+1}^{d+2} |x_i|$. Since $\sum_{i=1}^{s} |x_i| = 1$ and $\sum_{i=s+1}^{d+2} |x_i| = 1$, each side of $\sum_{i=1}^{s} |x_i| \mathbf{a_i} = \sum_{i=s+1}^{d+2} |x_i| \mathbf{a_i}$ is a convex combination of columns of A, which proves the theorem. Thus, S can be partitioned into two sets, the first consisting of the first s points after the rearrangement and the second consisting of points $s + 1$ through $d + 2$. Their convex hulls intersect as required. ∎

Radon's theorem immediately implies that halfspaces in d-dimensions do not shatter any set of $d + 2$ points.

Spheres in d-dimensions

A *sphere* in d-dimensions is a set of points of the form $\{\mathbf{x}| \ |\mathbf{x} - \mathbf{x_0}| \leq r\}$. The VC-dimension of spheres is $d + 1$. It is the same as that of halfspaces. First, we prove that no set of $d + 2$ points can be shattered by spheres. Suppose some set S with $d + 2$ points can be shattered. Then for any partition A_1 and A_2 of S, there are spheres B_1 and B_2 such that $B_1 \cap S = A_1$ and $B_2 \cap S = A_2$. Now B_1 and B_2 may intersect, but there is no point of S in their intersection. It is easy to see that there is a hyperplane perpendicular to the line joining the centers of the two spheres with all of A_1 on one side and all of A_2 on the other, and this implies that halfspaces shatter S, a contradiction. Therefore, no $d + 2$ points can be shattered by spheres.

It is also not difficult to see that the set of $d + 1$ points consisting of the unit-coordinate vectors and the origin can be shattered by spheres. Suppose A is a subset of the $d + 1$ points. Let a be the number of unit vectors in A. The center $\mathbf{a_0}$ of our sphere will be the sum of the vectors in A. For every unit vector in A, its distance to this center will be $\sqrt{a - 1}$, and for every unit vector outside A, its distance to this center will be $\sqrt{a + 1}$. The distance of the origin to the center is $\sqrt{a}$. Thus, we can choose the radius so that precisely the points in A are in the hypersphere.

5.5.3. Shatter Function for Set Systems of Bounded VC-Dimension

For a set system $(X, \mathcal{H})$, the shatter function $\pi_{\mathcal{H}}(n)$ is the maximum number of subsets of any set A of size n that can be expressed as $A \cap h$ for h in $\mathcal{H}$. The function $\pi_{\mathcal{H}}(n)$ equals 2^n for n less than or equal to the VC-dimension of $\mathcal{H}$. We will soon see that for n greater than the VC-dimension of $\mathcal{H}$, $\pi_{\mathcal{H}}(n)$ grows polynomially with n, with the polynomial degree equal to the VC-dimension. Define

$$\binom{n}{\leq d} = \binom{n}{0} + \binom{n}{1} + \cdots + \binom{n}{d}$$

to be the number of ways of choosing d or fewer elements out of n. Note that $\binom{n}{\leq d} \leq n^d + 1$.[6] We will show that for any set system $(X, \mathcal{H})$ of VC-dimension d, that $\pi_{\mathcal{H}}(n) \leq \binom{n}{\leq d}$. That is, $\binom{n}{\leq d}$ bounds the number of subsets of any n point set A that can be expressed as the intersection of A with a set of $\mathcal{H}$. Thus, the shatter function $\pi_{\mathcal{H}}(n)$ is either 2^n if d is infinite or it is bounded by a polynomial of degree d.

---

[6]To choose between 1 and d elements out of n, for each element there are n possible items if we allow duplicates. Thus, $\binom{n}{1} + \binom{n}{2} + \cdots + \binom{n}{d} \leq n^d$. The +1 is for $\binom{n}{0}$.

Lemma 5.10 **(Sauer)** *For any set system* $(X, \mathcal{H})$ *of VC-dimension at most* $d, \pi_{\mathcal{H}}(n) \leq \binom{n}{\leq d}$ *for all* n.

Proof First, note the following identity. For $n \geq 1$ and $d \geq 1$,

$$\binom{n}{\leq d} = \binom{n-1}{\leq d-1} + \binom{n-1}{\leq d}.$$

This is because to choose d or fewer elements out of n, we can either choose the first element and then choose $d-1$ or fewer out of the remaining $n-1$, or not choose the first element and then choose d or fewer out of the remaining $n-1$. The proof of the lemma is by induction on n and d. In particular, the base case will handle all pairs (n, d) with either $n \leq d$ or $d = 0$, and the general case (n, d) will use the inductive assumption on the cases $(n-1, d-1)$ and $(n-1, d)$.

For the base case $n \leq d$, $\binom{n}{\leq d} = 2^n$ and $\pi_{\mathcal{H}}(n) = 2^n$. For the base case VC-dimension $d = 0$, a set system $(X, \mathcal{H})$ can have at most one set in $\mathcal{H}$, since if there were two sets in $\mathcal{H}$, there would exist a set A consisting of a single element that was contained in one of the sets but not in the other and thus could be shattered. Therefore, for $d = 0$, we have $\pi_{\mathcal{H}}(n) = 1 = \binom{n}{\leq 0}$.

Consider the case for general d and n. Select a subset A of X of size n such that $\pi_{\mathcal{H}}(n)$ subsets of A can be expressed as $A \cap h$ for h in H. Without loss of generality, assume that $X = A$ and replace each set $h \in \mathcal{H}$ by $h \cap A$ removing duplicate sets; i.e., if $h_1 \cap A = h_2 \cap A$ for h_1 and h_2 in $\mathcal{H}$, keep only one of them. Now each set in $\mathcal{H}$ corresponds to a subset of A and $\pi_{\mathcal{H}}(n) = |\mathcal{H}|$. To show $\pi_{\mathcal{H}}(n) \leq \binom{n}{\leq d}$, we only need to show $|\mathcal{H}| \leq \binom{n}{\leq d}$.

Remove some element u from the set A and from each set in $\mathcal{H}$. Consider the set system $\mathcal{H}_1 = (A - \{u\}, \{h - \{u\} | h \in \mathcal{H}\})$. For $h \subseteq A - \{u\}$, if exactly one of h and $h \cup \{u\}$ is in $\mathcal{H}$, then the set h contributes one set to both $\mathcal{H}$ and $\mathcal{H}_1$, whereas if both h and $h \cup \{u\}$ are in $\mathcal{H}$, then they together contribute two sets to $\mathcal{H}$ but only one to $\mathcal{H}_1$. Thus $|\mathcal{H}_1|$ is less than $|\mathcal{H}|$ by the number of pairs of sets in $\mathcal{H}$ that differ only in the element u. To account for this difference, define another set system,

$$\mathcal{H}_2 = (A - \{u\}, \{h | u \notin h \text{ and both } h \text{ and } h \cup \{u\} \text{ are in } \mathcal{H}\}).$$

Then

$$|\mathcal{H}| = |\mathcal{H}_1| + |\mathcal{H}_2| = \pi_{\mathcal{H}_1}(n-1) + \pi_{\mathcal{H}_2}(n-1)$$

or

$$\pi_{\mathcal{H}}(n) = \pi_{\mathcal{H}_1}(n-1) + \pi_{\mathcal{H}_2}(n-1).$$

We make use of two facts

(1) $\mathcal{H}_1$ has dimension at most d, and
(2) $\mathcal{H}_2$ has dimension at most $d - 1$.

(1) follows because if $\mathcal{H}_1$ shatters a set of cardinality $d + 1$, then $\mathcal{H}$ also would shatter that set producing a contradiction. (2) follows because if $\mathcal{H}_2$ shattered a set $B \subseteq A - \{u\}$ with $|B| \geq d$, then $B \cup \{u\}$ would be shattered by $\mathcal{H}$ where $|B \cup \{u\}| \geq d + 1$, again producing a contradiction.

—— **123** ——

By the induction hypothesis applied to $\mathcal{H}_1$, $|\mathcal{H}_1| = \pi_{\mathcal{H}_1}(n-1) \le \binom{n-1}{\le d}$. By the induction hypotheses applied to $\mathcal{H}_2$, $|\mathcal{H}_2| = \pi_{\mathcal{H}_2}(n-1) \le \binom{n-1}{\le d-1}$. Finally, by the identity at the beginning of the proof, we have

$$\pi_{\mathcal{H}}(n) = \pi_{\mathcal{H}_1}(n-1) + \pi_{\mathcal{H}_2}(n-1) \le \binom{n-1}{\le d} + \binom{n-1}{\le d-1} \le \binom{n}{\le d}$$

as desired. ∎

5.5.4. VC-Dimension of Combinations of Concepts

Often one wants to create concepts out of other concepts. For example, given several linear separators, one could take their intersection to create a convex polytope. Or given several disjunctions, one might want to take their majority vote. We can use Sauer's lemma (Lemma 5.10) to show that such combinations do not increase the VC-dimension of the class by too much.

Let $(X, \mathcal{H}_1)$ and $(X, \mathcal{H}_2)$ be two set systems on the same underlying set X. Define another set system, called the intersection system, $(X, \mathcal{H}_1 \cap \mathcal{H}_2)$, where $\mathcal{H}_1 \cap \mathcal{H}_2 = \{h_1 \cap h_2 | h_1 \in \mathcal{H}_1 ; h_2 \in \mathcal{H}_2\}$. In other words, take the intersections of every set in $\mathcal{H}_1$ with every set in $\mathcal{H}_2$. A simple example is $U = R^d$ and $\mathcal{H}_1$ and $\mathcal{H}_2$ are both the set of all half-spaces. Then $\mathcal{H}_1 \cap \mathcal{H}_2$ consists of all sets defined by the intersection of two halfspaces. This corresponds to taking the Boolean AND of the output of two threshold gates and is the most basic neural net besides a single gate. We can repeat this process and take the intersection of k half spaces. The following simple lemma bounds the growth of the shatter function as we do this.

Lemma 5.11 *Suppose $(X, \mathcal{H}_1)$ and $(X, \mathcal{H}_2)$ are two set systems on the same set X. Then*

$$\pi_{\mathcal{H}_1 \cap \mathcal{H}_2}(n) \le \pi_{\mathcal{H}_1}(n)\pi_{\mathcal{H}_2}(n).$$

Proof Let $A \subseteq X$ be a set of size n. We are interested in the size of $\mathcal{S} = \{A \cap h \mid h \in \mathcal{H}_1 \cap \mathcal{H}_2\}$. By definition of $\mathcal{H}_1 \cap \mathcal{H}_2$, we have $\mathcal{S} = \{A \cap (h_1 \cap h_2) \mid h_1 \in \mathcal{H}_1, h_2 \in \mathcal{H}_2\}$, which we can rewrite as $\mathcal{S} = \{(A \cap h_1) \cap (A \cap h_2) \mid h_1 \in \mathcal{H}_1, h_2 \in \mathcal{H}_2\}$. Therefore, $|\mathcal{S}| \le |\{A \cap h_1 \mid h_1 \in \mathcal{H}_1\}| \times |\{A \cap h_2 \mid h_2 \in \mathcal{H}_2\}|$, as desired. ∎

We can generalize the idea of an intersection system to other ways of combining concepts. This will be useful later for our discussion of Boosting in Section 5.11 where we will be combining hypotheses via majority vote.

Specifically, given k concepts $h_1, h_2, \ldots, h_k$ and a Boolean function f, define the set $comb_f(h_1, \ldots, h_k) = \{x \in X | f(h_1(x), \ldots, h_k(x)) = 1\}$, where here we are using $h_i(x)$ to denote the indicator for whether or not $x \in h_i$. For example, if f is the AND function, then $comb_f(h_1, \ldots, h_k)$ is the intersection of the h_i, or if f is the majority-vote function, then $comb_f(h_1, \ldots, h_k)$ is the set of points that lie in more than half of the sets h_i. The concept $comb_f(h_1, \ldots, h_k)$ can also be viewed as a depth-two neural network. Given a concept class $\mathcal{H}$, a Boolean function f, and an integer k, define the new concept class $COMB_{f,k}(\mathcal{H}) = \{comb_f(h_1, \ldots, h_k) | h_i \in \mathcal{H}\}$. The same reasoning used to prove Lemma 5.11 also gives us the following lemma.

Lemma 5.12 *For any Boolean function f, hypothesis class $\mathcal{H}$, and integer k,*

$$\pi_{COMB_{f,k}(\mathcal{H})}(n) \leq \pi_{\mathcal{H}}(n)^k.$$

We can now use Lemma 5.12 to prove the following theorem about the VC-dimension of hypothesis classes defined by combining other hypothesis classes.

Theorem 5.13 *If concept class $\mathcal{H}$ has VC-dimension V, then for any Boolean function f and integer k, the class $COMB_{f,k}(\mathcal{H})$ has VC-dimension $O(kV \log(kV))$.*

Proof Let n be the VC-dimension of $COMB_{f,k}(\mathcal{H})$, so by definition, there must exist a set S of n points shattered by $COMB_{f,k}(\mathcal{H})$. We know by Sauer's lemma that there are at most n^V ways of partitioning the points in S using sets in $\mathcal{H}$. Since each set in $COMB_{f,k}(\mathcal{H})$ is determined by k sets in $\mathcal{H}$, and there are at most $(n^V)^k = n^{kV}$ different k-tuples of such sets, this means there are at most n^{kV} ways of partitioning the points using sets in $COMB_{f,k}(\mathcal{H})$. Since S is shattered, we must have $2^n \leq n^{kV}$, or equivalently $n \leq kV \log_2(n)$. We solve this as follows. First, assuming $n \geq 16$, we have $\log_2(n) \leq \sqrt{n}$ so $kV \log_2(n) \leq kV\sqrt{n}$, which implies that $n \leq (kV)^2$. To get the better bound, plug back into the original inequality. Since $n \leq (kV)^2$, it must be that $\log_2(n) \leq 2\log_2(kV)$. Substituting $\log n \leq 2\log_2(kV)$ into $n \leq kV \log_2 n$ gives $n \leq 2kV \log_2(kV)$. ∎

5.5.5. The Key Theorem

Theorem 5.14 *Let $(X, \mathcal{H})$ be a set system, D a probability distribution over X, and let n be an integer satisfying $n \geq \frac{8}{\epsilon}$ and*

$$n \geq \frac{2}{\epsilon}\left[\log_2 2\pi_{\mathcal{H}}(2n) + \log_2 \frac{1}{\delta}\right].$$

Let S_1 consists of n points drawn from D. With probability greater than or equal to $1 - \delta$, every set in $\mathcal{H}$ of probability mass greater than ϵ intersects S_1.

Note n occurs on both sides of the inequality above. If $\mathcal{H}$ has finite VC-dimension d, this does not lead to circularity, since, by Lemma 5.10, $\log(\pi_{\mathcal{H}}(2n)) = O(d \log n)$, and an inequality of the form $n \geq a \log n$ (for a positive integer $a \geq 4$) is implied by $n \geq ca \ln a$ for some constant c, thus eliminating n from the right hand side.

Proof Let A be the event that there exists a set h in $\mathcal{H}$ of probability mass greater than or equal to ϵ that is disjoint from S_1. Draw a second set S_2 of n points from D. Let B be the event that there exists h in $\mathcal{H}$ that is disjoint from S_1 but that contains at least $\frac{\epsilon}{2}n$ points in S_2. That is,

B: there exists a set $h \in \mathcal{H}$ with $|S_1 \cap h| = 0$ but $|S_2 \cap h| \geq \frac{\epsilon}{2}n$.

By Chebyshev,[7] if $n \geq \frac{8}{\epsilon}$, then $\text{Prob}(B|A) \geq \frac{1}{2}$. In particular, if h is disjoint from S_1 and has probability mass greater than or equal to ϵ, there is at least a $\frac{1}{2}$

---

[7]If $x = (x_1, x_2, \ldots, x_n)$ and $E(x_i) = \epsilon$, then $E(x) = n\epsilon$, $Var(x) = n\epsilon$, and $\text{Prob}(|x - E(x)| \leq \frac{n\epsilon}{2}) \leq Var(x)\left(\frac{2}{n\epsilon}\right)^2 = \frac{4}{n\epsilon}$. If $n \geq 8/\epsilon$, then $\text{Prob}(|x - E(x)| \leq \frac{n\epsilon}{2}) \leq \frac{1}{2}$.

chance that h will contain at least an $\frac{\epsilon}{2}$ fraction of the points in a new random set S_2. This means that

$$\text{Prob}(B) \geq \text{Prob}(A, B) = \text{Prob}(B|A)\text{Prob}(A) \geq \frac{1}{2}\text{Prob}(A).$$

Therefore, to prove that $\text{Prob}(A) \leq \delta$, it suffices to prove that $\text{Prob}(B) \leq \frac{\delta}{2}$. For this, we consider a second way of picking S_1 and S_2. Draw a random set S_3, i.e., of $2n$ points from D, and then randomly partition S_3 into two equal pieces; let S_1 be the first piece and S_2 the second. It is obvious that this yields the same probability distribution for S_1 and S_2 as picking each independently.

Now, consider the point in time after S_3 has been drawn but before it has been randomly partitioned into S_1 and S_2. Even though $\mathcal{H}$ may contain infinitely many sets, we know it has at most $\pi_{\mathcal{H}}(2n)$ distinct intersections with S_3. That is, $|\{S_3 \cap h | h \in \mathcal{H}\}| \leq \pi_{\mathcal{H}}(2n)$. Thus, to prove that $\text{Prob}(B) \leq \frac{\delta}{2}$, it is sufficient to prove that for any given subset h' of S_3, the probability over the random partition of S_3 into S_1 and S_2 that $|S_1 \cap h'| = 0$ but $|S_2 \cap h'| \geq \frac{\epsilon}{2}n$ is at most $\frac{\delta}{2\pi_{\mathcal{H}}(2n)}$.

To analyze this, first note that if h' contains fewer than $\frac{\epsilon}{2}n$ points, it is impossible to have $|S_2 \cap h'| \geq \frac{\epsilon}{2}n$. For h' larger than $\frac{\epsilon}{2}n$, the probability over the random partition of S_3 that none of the points in h' fall into S_1 is at most $(\frac{1}{2})^{\epsilon n/2}$. Plugging in our bound on n in the theorem statement we get

$$2^{-\epsilon n/2} \leq 2^{-\log 2\pi_{\mathcal{H}}(2n) + \log \delta} = \frac{\delta}{2\pi_{\mathcal{H}}(2n)}$$

as desired. Thus, $\text{Prob}(B) \leq \frac{\delta}{2}$ and $\text{Prob}(A) \leq \delta$. This type of argument where we used two ways of picking S_1 and S_2 is called "double sampling" or the "ghost sample" method. The key idea is that we postpone certain random choices to the future until after we have converted our problem into one of finite size. Double sampling is useful in other contexts as well. ∎

5.6. VC-Dimension and Machine Learning

We now apply the concept of VC-dimension to machine learning. In machine learning we have a target concept c^* such as spam e-mails and a set of hypotheses $\mathcal{H}$, which are sets of e-mails we claim are spam. Let $\mathcal{H}' = \{h \triangle c^* | h \in \mathcal{H}\}$ be the collection of error regions of hypotheses in $\mathcal{H}$. Note that $\mathcal{H}'$ and $\mathcal{H}$ have the same VC-dimension and shatter function. We now draw a training sample S of e-mails, and apply Theorem 5.14 to $\mathcal{H}'$ to argue that with high probability, every h with $\text{Prob}(h \triangle c^*) \geq \epsilon$ has $|S \cap (h \triangle c^*)| > 0$. In other words, with high probability, only hypotheses of low true error are fully consistent with the training sample. This is formalized in the theorem statement below.

Theorem 5.15 (sample bound) *For any class $\mathcal{H}$ and distribution D, if a training sample S is drawn from D of size*

$$n \geq \frac{2}{\epsilon}\left[\log(2\pi_{\mathcal{H}}(2n)) + \log \frac{1}{\delta}\right],$$

then with probability greater than or equal to $1 - \delta$, *every* $h \in \mathcal{H}$ *with true error* $err_{\mathcal{D}}(h) \geq \epsilon$ *has* $err_S(h) > 0$. *Equivalently, every* $h \in \mathcal{H}$ *with training error* $err_S(h) = 0$ *has* $err_{\mathcal{D}}(h) < \epsilon$.

Proof The proof follows from Theorem 5.14 applied to $\mathcal{H}' = \{h \triangle c^* | h \in \mathcal{H}\}$. ∎

Theorem 5.16 (Growth function uniform convergence) *For any class* $\mathcal{H}$ *and distribution* $\mathcal{D}$, *if a training sample* S *is drawn from* $\mathcal{D}$ *of size*

$$n \geq \frac{8}{\epsilon^2} \left[\ln(2\pi_{\mathcal{H}}(2n)) + \ln \frac{1}{\delta} \right],$$

then with probability greater than or equal to $1 - \delta$, *every* $h \in \mathcal{H}$ *will have* $|err_S(h) - err_{\mathcal{D}}(h)| \leq \epsilon$.

Proof This proof is similar to the proof of Theorem 5.15 and 5.14. The main changes are that B is defined to be the event that some h has intersections with S_1 and S_2 that differ in size by $\frac{\epsilon}{2}n$, and then Hoeffding bounds are used to analyze the probability of this occurring for a fixed h. ∎

Finally, we can apply Lemma 5.10 to write the above theorems in terms of VC-dimension rather than the shatter function. We do this for the case of Theorem 5.15; the case of Theorem 5.16 is similar.

Corollary 5.17 *For any class* $\mathcal{H}$ *and distribution* D, *a training sample* S *of size*

$$O\left(\frac{1}{\epsilon} \left[VCdim(\mathcal{H}) \log \frac{1}{\epsilon} + \log \frac{1}{\delta} \right] \right)$$

is sufficient to ensure that with probability greater than or equal to $1 - \delta$, *every* $h \in \mathcal{H}$ *with true error* $err_D(h) \geq \epsilon$ *has training error* $err_S(h) > 0$. *Equivalently, every* $h \in \mathcal{H}$ *with* $err_S(h) = 0$ *has* $err_D(h) < \epsilon$.

5.7. Other Measures of Complexity

VC-dimension and number of bits needed to describe a set are not the only measures of complexity one can use to derive generalization guarantees. There has been significant work on a variety of measures. One measure, called Rademacher complexity, measures the extent to which a given concept class $\mathcal{H}$ can fit random noise. Given a set of n examples $S = \{x_1, \ldots, x_n\}$, the *empirical Rademacher complexity* of $\mathcal{H}$ is defined as

$$R_S(\mathcal{H}) = \mathbf{E}_{\sigma_1,\ldots,\sigma_n} \max_{h \in \mathcal{H}} \frac{1}{n} \sum_{i=1}^{n} \sigma_i h(x_i),$$

where $\sigma_i \in \{-1, 1\}$ are independent random labels with $\text{Prob}[\sigma_i = 1] = \frac{1}{2}$. For example, if you assign random ± 1 labels to the points in S and the best classifier in $\mathcal{H}$ on average gets error 0.45, then $R_S(\mathcal{H}) = 0.55 - 0.45 = 0.1$. One can prove that with probability greater than or equal to $1 - \delta$, every $h \in \mathcal{H}$ satisfies true error less than or equal to training error plus $R_S(\mathcal{H}) + 3\sqrt{\frac{\ln(2/\delta)}{2n}}$. For more on results such as this, see [BM02].

5.8. Deep Learning

Deep learning, or a *deep neural network*, refers to training a many-layered network of nonlinear computational units. Each computational unit or gate works as follows: there are a set of "wires" bringing inputs to the gate. Each wire has a "weight," and the gate's output is a real number obtained by applying a nonlinear "activation function" to the the weighted sum of the input values. The activation function is generally the same for all gates in the network, though the number of inputs to individual gates may differ.

The input to the network is an example $\mathbf{x} \in R^d$. The first layer of the network transforms the example into a new vector $f_1(\mathbf{x})$. Then the second layer transforms $f_1(\mathbf{x})$ into a new vector $f_2(f_1(\mathbf{x}))$, and so on. Finally, the kth layer outputs the final prediction $f(\mathbf{x}) = f_k(f_{k-1}(\dots(f_1(\mathbf{x}))))$.

In supervised learning, we are given training examples $\mathbf{x_1}, \mathbf{x_2}, \dots$, and corresponding labels $c^*(\mathbf{x_1}), c^*(\mathbf{x_2}), \dots$. The training process finds a set of weights of all wires so as to minimize the error: $(f_0(\mathbf{x_1}) - c^*(\mathbf{x_1}))^2 + (f_0(\mathbf{x_2}) - c^*(\mathbf{x_2}))^2 + \cdots$. One could alternatively aim to minimize other quantities besides the sum of squared errors of training examples. Often training is carried out by running stochastic gradient descent in the weights space.

The motivation for deep learning is that often we are interested in data, such as images, that are given to us in terms of very low-level features, such as pixel intensity values. Our goal is to achieve some higher-level understanding of each image, such as what objects are in the image and what they are doing. To do so, it is natural to first convert the given low-level representation into one of higher-level features. That is what the layers of the network aim to do. Deep learning is also motivated by multitask learning, with the idea that a good higher-level representation of data should be useful for a wide range of tasks. Indeed, a common use of deep learning for multitask learning is to share initial levels of the network across tasks.

A typical architecture of a deep neural network consists of layers of logic units. In a fully connected layer, the output of each gate in the layer is connected to the input of every gate in the next layer. However, if the input is an image, one might like to recognize features independent of where they are located in the image. To achieve this, one often uses a number of convolution layers. In a convolution layer, illustrated in Figure 5.4, each gate gets inputs from a small $k \times k$ grid where k may be 5 to 10. There is a gate for each $k \times k$ square array of the image. The weights on each gate are tied together so that each gate recognizes the same feature. There will be several such collections of gates, so several different features can be learned. Such a level is called a convolution level, and the fully connected layers are called autoencoder levels. A technique called *pooling* is used to keep the number of gates reasonable. A small $k \times k$ grid with k typically set to two is used to scan a layer. The stride is set so the grid will provide a non-overlapping cover of the layer. Each $k \times k$ input grid will be reduced to a single cell by selecting the maximum input value or the average of the inputs. For $k = 2$ this reduces the number of cells by a factor of 4. A typical architecture is shown in Figure 5.5, and a fully connected network is illustrated in Figure 5.6.

Deep learning networks are trained by stochastic gradient descent (Section 5.9.1), sometimes called back propagation in the network context. An error function is constructed and the weights are adjusted using the derivative of the error function.

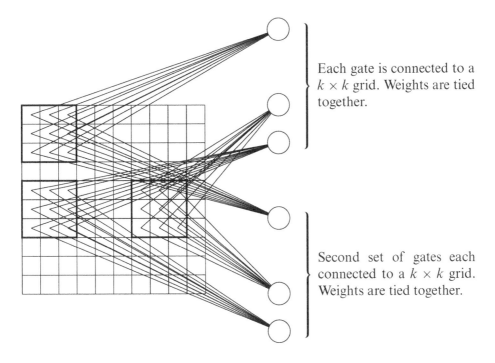

Each gate is connected to a $k \times k$ grid. Weights are tied together.

Second set of gates each connected to a $k \times k$ grid. Weights are tied together.

Figure 5.4: Convolution layers

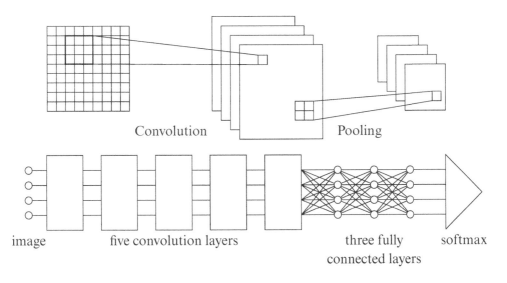

Convolution   Pooling

image   five convolution layers   three fully   softmax
                                                     connected layers

Figure 5.5: A convolution level, top, and AlexNet consisting of five convolution levels, followed by three fully connected levels, and then Softmax.

This requires that the error function be differentiable. A smooth threshold is used such as

$$\tanh(x) = \frac{e^x - e^{-x}}{e^x + e^{-x}} \quad \text{where} \quad \frac{\partial}{\partial x} \frac{e^e - e^{-e}}{e^x + e^{-x}} = 1 - \left(\frac{e^x - e^{-x}}{e^x + e^{-x}}\right)^2$$

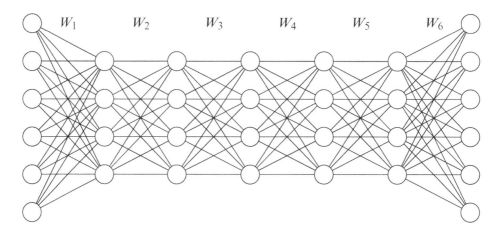

Figure 5.6: A deep learning fully connected network.

or $\text{sigmod}(x) = \frac{1}{1+e^{-x}}$ where

$$\frac{\partial\,\text{sigmod}(x)}{\partial x} = \frac{e^{-x}}{(1+e^{-x})^2} = \text{sigmod}(x)\frac{e^{-x}}{1+e^{-x}} = \text{sigmoid}(x)\big(1 - \text{sigmoid}(x)\big).$$

In fact, the function

$$ReLU(x) = max(0, x)$$
$$= \begin{cases} x & x \geq 0 \\ 0 & \text{otherwise} \end{cases}$$

where $\frac{\partial ReLU(x)}{\partial x} = \begin{cases} 1 & x \geq 0 \\ 0 & x < 0 \end{cases}$ seems to work well even though its derivative at $x = 0$ is undefined. An advantage of ReLU over sigmoid is that ReLU does not saturate far from the origin.

The output of the hidden gates is an encoding of the input. An image might be a 10^8-dimensional input and there may only be 10^5 hidden gates. However, the number of images might be 10^7, so even though the dimension of the hidden layer is smaller than the dimension of the input, the number of possible codes far exceeds the number of inputs and thus the hidden layer is a compressed representation of the input. If the hidden layer were the same dimension as the input layer one might get the identity mapping. This does not happen for gradient descent starting with random weights.

The output layer of a deep network typically uses a softmax procedure. Softmax is a generalization of logistic regression. Given a set of vectors $\{x_1, x_2, \ldots x_n\}$ with labels $l_1, l_2, \ldots l_n, l_i \in \{0, 1\}$, a weight vector $\mathbf{w}$ defines the probability that the label l given x equals 0 or 1 by

$$\text{Prob}(l = 1|\mathbf{x}) = \frac{1}{1 + e^{-\mathbf{w}^\mathsf{T}\mathbf{x}}} = \sigma(\mathbf{w}^\mathsf{T}\mathbf{x})$$

and

$$\text{Prob}(l = 0|\mathbf{x}) = 1 - \text{Prob}(l = 1/\mathbf{x})$$

where σ is the sigmoid function.

Define a cost function

$$J(\mathbf{w}) = \sum_i \Big(l_i \log(\text{Prob}(l = 1|\mathbf{x_i})) + (1 - l_i) \log(1 - \text{Prob}(l = 1|\mathbf{x_i})) \Big)$$

$$= \sum_i \Big(l_i \log(\sigma(\mathbf{w}^\mathrm{T}\mathbf{x_i})) + (1 - l_i) \log(1 - \sigma(\mathbf{w}^\mathrm{T}\mathbf{x_i})) \Big)$$

and compute $\mathbf{w}$ to minimize $J(\mathbf{x})$. Since $\frac{\partial \sigma(\mathbf{w}^\mathrm{T}\mathbf{x})}{\partial w_j} = \sigma(\mathbf{w}^\mathrm{T}\mathbf{x})(1 - \sigma(\mathbf{w}^\mathrm{T}\mathbf{x}))x_j$, it follows that $\frac{\partial \log(\sigma(\mathbf{w}^\mathrm{T}\mathbf{x}))}{\partial w_j} = \frac{\sigma(\mathbf{w}^\mathrm{T}\mathbf{x})(1 - \sigma(\mathbf{w}^\mathrm{T}\mathbf{x}))x_j}{\sigma(\mathbf{w}^\mathrm{T}\mathbf{x})}$, thus

$$\frac{\partial J}{\partial w_j} = \sum_i \left(l_i \frac{\sigma(\mathbf{w}^\mathrm{T}\mathbf{x})(1 - \sigma(\mathbf{w}^\mathrm{T}\mathbf{x}))}{\sigma(\mathbf{w}^\mathrm{T}\mathbf{x})} x_j - (1 - l_i) \frac{(1 - \sigma(\mathbf{w}^\mathrm{T}\mathbf{x}))\sigma(\mathbf{w}^\mathrm{T}\mathbf{x})}{1 - \sigma(\mathbf{w}^\mathrm{T}\mathbf{x})} x_j \right)$$

$$= \sum_i \Big(l_i(1 - \sigma(\mathbf{w}^\mathrm{T}\mathbf{x}))x_j - (1 - l_i)\sigma(\mathbf{w}^\mathrm{T}\mathbf{x})x_j \Big)$$

$$= \sum_i \Big((l_i x_j - l_i\sigma(\mathbf{w}^\mathrm{T}\mathbf{x})x_j - \sigma(\mathbf{w}^\mathrm{T}\mathbf{x})x_j + l_i\sigma(\mathbf{w}^\mathrm{T}\mathbf{x})x_j \Big)$$

$$= \sum_i \Big(l_i - \sigma(\mathbf{w}^\mathrm{T}\mathbf{x}) \Big) x_j.$$

Softmax is a generalization of logistic regression to multiple classes. Thus, the labels l_i take on values $\{1, 2, \ldots, k\}$. For an input $\mathbf{x}$, softmax estimates the probability of each label. The hypothesis is of the form

$$h_w(x) = \begin{bmatrix} \text{Prob}(l = 1|\mathbf{x}, \mathbf{w_1}) \\ \text{Prob}(l = 2|\mathbf{x}, \mathbf{w_2}) \\ \vdots \\ \text{Prob}(l = k|\mathbf{x}, \mathbf{w_k}) \end{bmatrix} = \frac{1}{\sum_{i=1}^{k} e^{\mathbf{w_i}^\mathrm{T}\mathbf{x}}} \begin{bmatrix} e^{\mathbf{w_1}^\mathrm{T}\mathbf{x}} \\ e^{\mathbf{w_2}^\mathrm{T}\mathbf{x}} \\ \vdots \\ e^{\mathbf{w_k}^\mathrm{T}\mathbf{x}} \end{bmatrix}$$

where the matrix formed by the weight vectors is

$$W = (\mathbf{w_1}, \mathbf{w_2}, \ldots, \mathbf{w_k})^T.$$

W is a matrix since for each label l_i, there is a vector $\mathbf{w_i}$ of weights.

Consider a set of n inputs $\{\mathbf{x_1}, \mathbf{x_2}, \ldots, \mathbf{x_n}\}$. Define

$$\delta(l = k) = \begin{cases} 1 & \text{if } l = k \\ 0 & \text{otherwise} \end{cases}$$

and

$$J(W) = \sum_{i=1}^{n} \sum_{j=1}^{k} \delta(l_i = j) \log \frac{e^{\mathbf{w_j}^\mathrm{T}x_i}}{\sum_{h=1}^{k} e^{\mathbf{w_h}^\mathrm{T}x_i}}.$$

The derivative of the cost function with respect to the weights is

$$\nabla_{\mathbf{w_i}} J(W) = -\sum_{j=1}^{n} \mathbf{x_j}\big(\delta(l_j = k) - \text{Prob}(l_j = k)|\mathbf{x_j}, W\big).$$

Note $\nabla_{\mathbf{w_i}} J(W)$ is a vector. Since $\mathbf{w_i}$ is a vector, each component of $\nabla_{\mathbf{w_i}} J(W)$ is the derivative with respect to one component of the vector $\mathbf{w_i}$.

Overfitting is a major concern in deep learning, since large networks can have hundreds of millions of weights. In image recognition, the number of training images can be significantly increased by random jittering of the images. Another technique, called *dropout*, randomly deletes a fraction of the weights at each training iteration. Regularization is used to assign a cost to the size of weights, and many other ideas are being explored.

Deep learning is an active research area. We explore a few of the directions here. For a given gate one can construct an activation vector where each coordinate corresponds to an image and the coordinate value is the gate's output for the corresponding image. Alternatively one could define an image activation vector whose coordinates correspond to gate values for the image. Basically these activation vectors correspond to rows and columns of a matrix whose ij^{th} element is the output of gate i for image j.

A gate activation vector indicates which images an individual gate responds to. The coordinates can be permuted so that the activation increases. This then gives the set of images with high activation. To determine whether two gates learn the same feature, one computes the covariance of the two gate activation vectors:

$$\text{covariance}(a_i, a_j) = \frac{E\Big(\big(a_i - E(a_i)\big)\big(a_j - E(a_j)\big)\Big)}{\sigma(a_i)\sigma(a_j)}.$$

A value close to ±1 indicates a strong relationship between what gates i and j learned. Another interesting question is: If a network is trained twice starting from different sets of random weights, do the gates learn the same features or do they carry out the classification in totally different ways? To match gates that learn the same features, one constructs a matrix where the ij^{th} entry is the covariance of the gate i activation vector in one training and gate j activation vector in the other training.

Recreating Image from Activation Vector

Given an image, one can easily get the corresponding gate activation vector. However, given a gate activation vector, how does one get the corresponding image? There are many ways to do this. One way would be to find the gate activation vector for a random image and then by gradient descent on the pixels of the image reduce the L2 norm between the gate activation vector of the random image and the gate activation vector for which you want the image that produced it.

Style Transfer

Given that one can produce the image that produced a given activation vector, one can reproduce an image from its content using the style of a different image. To do this, define the content of an image to be the gate activation vector corresponding to the first level of gates in the network [GEB15]. The reason for selecting the first level of gates is that a network discards information in subsequent levels that is not relevant for classification; to define the style of an image, form a matrix with the inner product of the last activation vector with itself. Now one can create an image using the content of one image and the style of another. For example, you could create the image of a student using the style of a much older individual [GKL+15].

Random Weights

An interesting observation is that one can do style transfer without training a network. One uses random weights instead. This raises the issue of which tasks require training and which tasks require only the structure of the network.

Structure of Activation Space

Understanding the structure of activation space is an important area of research. One can examine the region of space that corresponds to images of cats, or one can examine the the region of space that gets classified as cat. Every input, even if it is random noise, will get classified. It appears that every image in one classification is close to an image in each of the other classifications.

Fooling

One can make small changes to an image that will change the image's classification without changing the image enough for a human to recognize that the image had been modified. There are many ways to do this. To change the classification of an image of a cat to automobile, simply test each pixel value and see which way it increases the probability of the image being classified as an automobile. Create a $0,1,-1$ matrix where 1 means increasing the pixel value increases the likelihood of an automobile classification and a -1 means decreasing the pixel value increases the likelihood of an automobile classification. Then

$$image + \alpha(0,1,\text{-}1 \text{ matrix})$$

will cause the modified image to be classified as an automobile for a small value of α. The reason for this is that the change of each pixel value makes a small change in the probability of the classification, but a large number of small changes can be big. For more information about deep learning, see [Ben09].[8]

5.8.1. Generative Adversarial Networks (GANs)

Image generation has become an important area where one enters a word or phrase into an image generation program that produces the desired image. One might ask: Why not search the web instead? If one wanted an image of a cat, searching the web would be fine. However, if one wants a more complex image of a cat watching someone fishing while the sun was setting, it might not be possible to find such an image.

A method that is promising in trying to generate images that look real is to create code that tries to discern between real images and synthetic images.
One first trains the synthetic image discriminator to distinguish between real images and synthetic ones. Then one trains the image generator to generate images that the discriminator believes are real images. Alternating the training between the two units ends up forcing the image generator to produce real-looking images. This is the idea of Generative Adversarial Networks. See Figure 5.7.

---

[8]See also the tutorials: http://deeplearning.net/tutorial/deeplearning.pdf and http://deeplearning.stanford .edu/tutorial/.

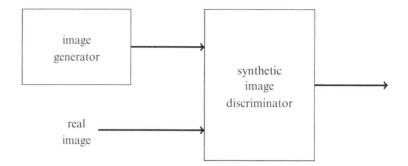

Figure 5.7: Components of a Generative Adversarial Network.

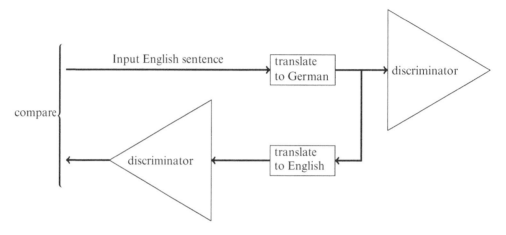

Figure 5.8: Schematic for use of a Generative Adversarial Network for translation between English and German.

There are many possible applications for this technique. Suppose you wanted to train a network to translate from English to German. First train a discriminator to determine if a sentence is a real sentence as opposed to a synthetic sentence. Then train a translator for English to German, which translates the English words to German words in such a way that the output will convince the discriminator that it is a German sentence. Next take the German sentence and translate it to English words in such as way that the output will convince the discriminator that it is an English sentence. Finally train the entire system so the generated English sentence agrees with the original English sentence. At this point the German sentence is likely to be a good translation. See Figure 5.8.

5.9. Gradient Descent

The gradient of a function $f(\mathbf{x})$ of d variables, $\mathbf{x} = (x_1, x_2, \ldots, x_d)$, at a point $\mathbf{x_0}$ is denoted $\nabla f(\mathbf{x_0})$. It is a d-dimensional vector with components $\left(\frac{\partial f(\mathbf{x_0})}{\partial x_1}, \frac{\partial f(\mathbf{x_0})}{\partial x_2}, \ldots, \frac{\partial f(\mathbf{x_0})}{\partial x_d} \right)$, where $\frac{\partial f}{\partial x_i}$ are partial derivatives. Without explicitly stating, we assume that the derivatives referred to exist. The rate of increase of the function f as we move from $\mathbf{x_0}$ in a direction $\mathbf{u}$ is $\triangledown f(\mathbf{x_0}) \cdot \mathbf{u}$. So the direction of steepest descent is $-\triangledown f(\mathbf{x_0})$. This is a natural direction to move to minimize f.

By how much should we move? This is primarily an experimental area and how much we should move depends on the specific problem. In general one starts with a large move and when a point is reached where the function no longer decreases, since one is possibly overshooting the minimum, the move size is reduced. Another option is to use a quadratic approximation and use both the first and second derivatives to determine how far to move.

There are significantly improved versions of gradient descent involving momentum and various versions of it such as Nesterov's Accelerated Gradient. If the minimum is in a long narrow ravine, this may result in an oscillation across the ravine slowing convergence rather than travel along the ravine. Momentum is one method of forcing the move along the ravine. The formula is

$$\mathbf{v} = \gamma \mathbf{v} + \alpha \triangledown f$$
$$\mathbf{x} = \mathbf{x} - \mathbf{v}.$$

Here $\mathbf{v}$ is a velocity vector, α is the learning rate, and γ is a constant that is usually set to 0.5 until the initial learning stabilizes and then increased to 0.9. The velocity vector averages out the oscillation across the ravine and helps steer the descent in high-dimensional problems. However, one may not wish to move down the bottom of the narrow ravine if the slope is shallow. Although one can improve the training error slightly, one really wants to improve the true error and avoid over fitting by a regularizer that reduces some measure of complexity.

The step size and how it is changed are important. For educational purposes, we now focus on infinitesimal gradient descent where the algorithm makes infinitesimal moves in the $-\triangledown f(\mathbf{x_0})$ direction. Whenever $\triangledown \mathbf{f}$ is not the zero vector, we strictly decrease the function in the direction $-\triangledown \mathbf{f}$, so the current point is not a minimum of the function. Conversely, a point $\mathbf{x}$ where $\triangledown \mathbf{f} = \mathbf{0}$ is called a *first-order local optimum* of f. A first-order local optimum may be a local minimum, local maximum, or a saddle point. We ignore saddle points, since numerical error is likely to prevent gradient descent from stopping at a saddle point at least in low dimensions. In a million dimensions, if there is a decrease in only one dimension and in a million dimensions there is an increase, gradient descent is not likely to find the decrease and stop at the saddle point thinking it is a local minima.

In general, local minima do not have to be global minima, and gradient descent may converge to a local minimum that is not a global minimum. When the function f is convex, this is not the case. A function f of a single variable x is said to be convex if for any two points a and b, the line joining $f(a)$ and $f(b)$ is above the curve $f(\cdot)$. A function of many variables is convex if on any line segment in its domain, it acts as a convex function of one variable on the line segment.

Definition 5.4 *A function f over a convex domain is a convex function if for any two points $\mathbf{x}$ and $\mathbf{y}$ in the domain, and any λ in $[0, 1]$*

$$f(\lambda \mathbf{x} + (1 - \lambda)\mathbf{y}) \leq \lambda f(\mathbf{x}) + (1 - \lambda)f(\mathbf{y}).$$

The function is concave if the inequality is satisfied with $\geq$ instead of $\leq$.

Theorem 5.18 *Suppose f is a convex, differentiable function defined on a closed bounded convex domain. Then any first-order local minimum is also a global minimum. Infinitesimal gradient descent always reaches the global minimum.*

Proof We will prove that if $\mathbf{x}$ is a local minimum, then it must be a global minimum. If not, consider a global minimum point $\mathbf{y} \neq \mathbf{x}$. On the line joining $\mathbf{x}$ and $\mathbf{y}$, the function must not go above the line joining $f(\mathbf{x})$ and $f(\mathbf{y})$. This means for an infinitesimal $\varepsilon > 0$, moving distance ε from $\mathbf{x}$ toward $\mathbf{y}$, the function must decrease, so $\bigtriangledown \mathbf{f}(\mathbf{x})$ is not $\mathbf{0}$, contradicting the assumption that $\mathbf{x}$ is a local minimum. ∎

The second derivatives $\frac{\partial^2}{\partial x_i \partial x_j}$ form a matrix, called the Hessian, denoted $H(f(\mathbf{x}))$. The Hessian of f at $\mathbf{x}$ is a symmetric $d \times d$ matrix with ij^{th} entry $\frac{\partial^2 f}{\partial x_i \partial x_j}(\mathbf{x})$. The second derivative of f at $\mathbf{x}$ in the direction $\mathbf{u}$ is the rate of change of the first derivative in the direction $\mathbf{u}$ from $\mathbf{x}$. It is easy to see that it equals

$$\mathbf{u}^T H(f(\mathbf{x}))\mathbf{u}.$$

To see this, note that the second derivative of f along the unit vector $\mathbf{u}$ is

$$\sum_j u_j \frac{\partial}{\partial x_j}\left(\bigtriangledown f(\mathbf{x}) \cdot \mathbf{u}\right) = \sum_j u_j \sum_i \frac{\partial}{\partial x_j}\left(u_i \frac{\partial f(\mathbf{x})}{\partial x_i}\right)$$

$$= \sum_{j,i} u_j u_i \frac{\partial^2 f(\mathbf{x})}{\partial x_j \partial x_i}.$$

Theorem 5.19 *Suppose f is a function from a closed convex domain in $\mathbf{R}^d$ to the reals and the Hessian of f exists everywhere in the domain. Then f is convex (concave) on the domain if and only if the Hessian of f is positive (negative) semi-definite everywhere on the domain.*

Gradient descent requires the gradient to exist. But even if the gradient is not always defined, one can minimize a convex function over a convex domain efficiently, i.e., in polynomial time. Technically, one can only find an approximate minimum with the time depending on the error parameter as well as the presentation of the convex set. We do not go into these details. But in principle, we can minimize a convex function over a convex domain. We can also maximize a concave function over a concave domain. However, in general, we do not have efficient procedures to maximize a convex function over a convex domain. It is easy to see that at a first-order local minimum of a possibly non-convex function, the gradient vanishes. But a second-order local decrease of the function may be possible. The steepest second-order decrease is in the direction of $\pm\mathbf{v}$, where $\mathbf{v}$ is the eigenvector of the Hessian corresponding to the largest absolute valued eigenvalue.

5.9.1. Stochastic Gradient Descent

We now describe a widely used algorithm in machine learning, called *stochastic gradient descent* . Often the function $f(x)$ that we are trying to minimize is actually the sum of many simple functions. We may have 100,000 images that we are trying to

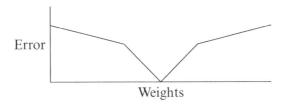

Figure 5.9: Error function for a single image

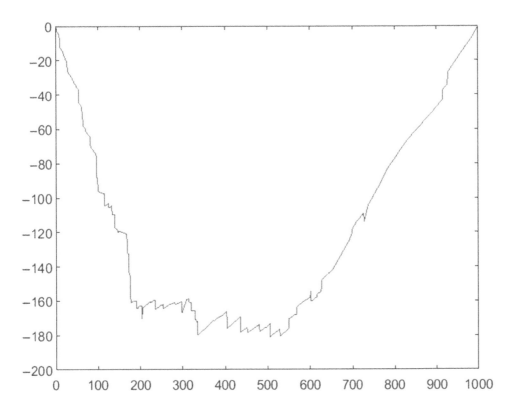

Figure 5.10: Full error function for 1,000 images.

classify and $f(x) = \sum_{i=1}^{n} f(x_i)$ where $f(x_i)$ is the error for the ith image. The function f may have a million weights and gradient descent would take the derivation of the 100,000 terms in f with respect to each of the million weights. A better method might be at each iteration to randomly select one of the images and take the derivatives with respect to just a single term in the summation. This should speed the convergence up significantly. In practice, initially one randomly selects one term each iteration, after a number of iterations 50 terms are selected, then maybe 200, and finally full gradient descent. This usually get one to a better minimum then the full gradient descent. So not only is it faster but it gets a better solution.

To understand why stochastic gradient descent sometimes gets a better minimum than gradient descent, consider Figures 5.9 and 5.10 Here the true error function is the sum of 1,000 simpler error functions. If in Figure 5.10 one starts gradient descent at 1,000, they probably would get stuck at the local minimum around 750. However, stochastic gradient descent would alternate in minimizing different simple error functions and would move into the region 180 to 600 if the batch size was 1. If one then switched the batch size to 50, the variance would decrease and one might range around 450 to 600. Finally with gradient descent, they would converge to a much better minimum.

We have been talking about a local minimum being good in terms of the training error. What we also want are good generalization. If the training data are a good sample of the full data, then intuitively a broad local minimum should be better than a sharp local minimum, since a small shift in the error function for a broad minimum will not result in a large increase in error where as a small shift will cause a large increase in error for a sharp local minimum.

5.9.2. Regularizer

Often one modifies the error function by adding a regularizer term to achieve some property. If the amount of data is not sufficient to prevent overfitting, one might, in training a deep network, add a term that would penalize the number of non-zero weight vectors. A complex network might have 10% training error with 20% real error, whereas a simple network might have 15% training error with 20% real error. With a regularizer, one might balance the size of the network with training error and get a training error of 12% and real error 18%.

5.10. Online Learning

So far we have been considering batch learning. You are given a "batch" of data, a training sample S, and your goal is to use the training example to produce a hypothesis h that will have low error on new data. We now switch to the more challenging *online learning* scenario where we remove the assumption that data are sampled from a fixed probability distribution, or from any probabilistic process at all.

The online learning scenario proceeds as follows. At each time $t = 1, 2, \ldots$, two events occur:

1. The algorithm is presented with an arbitrary example $x_t \in \mathcal{X}$ and is asked to make a prediction ℓ_t of its label.
2. Then, the algorithm is told the true label of the example $c^*(x_t)$ and is charged for a mistake if $c^*(x_t) \neq \ell_t$.

The goal of the learning algorithm is to make as few mistakes as possible. For example, consider an e-mail classifier that, when a new e-mail message arrives, must classify it as "important" or "it can wait." The user then looks at the e-mail and informs the algorithm if it was incorrect. We might not want to model e-mail messages as independent random objects from a fixed probability distribution because they often are replies to previous e-mails and build on each other. Thus, the online learning model would be more appropriate than the batch model for this setting.

Intuitively, the online learning model is harder than the batch model because we have removed the requirement that our data consist of independent draws from a fixed probability distribution. Indeed, we will see shortly that any algorithm with good performance in the online model can be converted to an algorithm with good performance in the batch model. Nonetheless, the online model can sometimes be a cleaner model for design and analysis of algorithms.

5.10.1. An Example: Learning Disjunctions

A *disjunction* is an OR of features. For example, an e-mail may be important if it comes from one of your instructors, or comes from a family member, or is a reply to an e-mail you sent earlier. Consider the problem of learning disjunctions over the instance space $\mathcal{X} = \{0, 1\}^d$, that is, disjunctions over d Boolean features. There are 2^d possible disjunctions over this instance space, ranging from the disjunction of nothing, which is always negative, to the disjunction $h(x) = x_1 \vee x_2 \vee \cdots \vee x_d$ that is positive on any example with at least one feature set to 1. In general, a typical disjunction such as $h(x) = x_1 \vee x_4 \vee x_8$ will have some *relevant* variables (in this case, $x_1, x_4,$ and x_8) and some *irrelevant* variables (in this case, everything else), and outputs positive on any input that has one or more relevant variables set to 1.

We can solve the problem of learning disjunctions in the online model by starting with the disjunction of all of the variables $h(x) = x_1 \vee x_2 \vee \cdots \vee x_d$. Our algorithm will maintain the invariant that every relevant variable for the target function is present in the hypothesis h, along with perhaps some irrelevant variables. This is certainly true at the start. Given this invariant, the only mistakes possible are on inputs x for which $h(x)$ is positive but the true label $c^*(x)$ is negative. When such a mistake occurs, we just remove from h any variable set to 1 in x, since it cannot possibly be a relevant variable for the target function. This shrinks the size of the hypothesis h by at least 1, and maintains the invariant. This implies that the algorithm makes at most d mistakes total on any series of examples consistent with a target disjunction c^*. In fact, one can show this bound is tight by showing that no deterministic algorithm can guarantee to make fewer than d mistakes.

Theorem 5.20 *For any deterministic online learning algorithm A, there exists a sequence σ of examples over $\{0, 1\}^d$ and a target disjunction c^* such that A makes at least d mistakes on the sequence of examples σ labeled by c^*.*

Proof Let σ be the sequence $e_1, e_2, \ldots, e_d$ where e_j is the example that sets every variable to zero except $x_j = 1$. Imagine running A on sequence σ and telling A it made a mistake on every example; that is, if A predicts positive on e_j, we set $c^*(e_j) = -1$, and if A predicts negative on e_j, we set $c^*(e_j) = +1$. This target corresponds to the disjunction of all x_j such that A predicted negative on e_j, so it is a legal disjunction. Since A is deterministic, the fact that we constructed c^* by running A is not a problem: it would make the same mistakes if rerun from scratch on the same sequence and same target. Therefore, A makes d mistakes on this σ and c^*. ■

5.10.2. The Halving Algorithm

If we are not concerned with running time, a simple online algorithm that guarantees to make at most $\log_2(|\mathcal{H}|)$ mistakes for a target belonging to any given class

$\mathcal{H}$ is called the *halving algorithm*. This algorithm simply maintains the *version space* $\mathcal{V} \subseteq \mathcal{H}$ consisting of all $h \in \mathcal{H}$ consistent with the labels on every example seen so far, and predicts based on majority vote over these functions. Each mistake is guaranteed to reduce the size of the version space $\mathcal{V}$ by at least half (hence the name), thus the total number of mistakes is at most $\log_2(|\mathcal{H}|)$. Note that this can be viewed as the number of bits needed to write a function in $\mathcal{H}$ down.

5.10.3. The Perceptron Algorithm

Earlier we described the Perceptron Algorithm as a method for finding a linear separator consistent with a given training set S. However, the Perceptron Algorithm also operates naturally in the online setting.

Recall that the basic assumption of the Perceptron Algorithm is that the target function can be described by a vector $\mathbf{w}^*$ such that for each positive example $\mathbf{x}$ we have $\mathbf{x}^T \mathbf{w}^* \geq 1$ and for each negative example $\mathbf{x}$ we have $\mathbf{x}^T \mathbf{w}^* \leq -1$. Recall also that we can interpret $\mathbf{x}^T \mathbf{w}^* / |\mathbf{w}^*|$ as the distance of $\mathbf{x}$ to the hyperplane $\mathbf{x}^T \mathbf{w}^* = 0$. Thus, our assumption states that there exists a linear separator through the origin with all positive examples on one side, all negative examples on the other side, and all examples at distance at least $\gamma = 1/|\mathbf{w}^*|$ from the separator, where γ is called the margin of separation.

The guarantee of the Perceptron Algorithm will be that the total number of mistakes is at most $(r/\gamma)^2$ where $r = \max_t |\mathbf{x}_t|$ over all examples $\mathbf{x}_t$ seen so far. Thus, if there exists a hyperplane through the origin that correctly separates the positive examples from the negative examples by a large margin relative to the radius of the smallest ball enclosing the data, then the total number of mistakes will be small. The algorithm, restated in the online setting, is as follows.

The Perceptron Algorithm:
Start with the all-zeroes weight vector $\mathbf{w} = \mathbf{0}$. Then, for $t = 1, 2, \ldots$ do:

1. Given example $\mathbf{x}_t$, predict $\text{sgn}(\mathbf{x}_t^T \mathbf{w})$.
2. If the prediction was a mistake, then update $\mathbf{w} \leftarrow \mathbf{w} + \mathbf{x}_t l_t$.

The Perceptron Algorithm enjoys the following guarantee on its total number of mistakes.

Theorem 5.21 *On any sequence of examples* $\mathbf{x}_1, \mathbf{x}_2, \ldots$, *if there exists a vector* $\mathbf{w}^*$ *such that* $\mathbf{x}_t^T \mathbf{w}^* l_t \geq 1$ *for all t, i.e., a linear separator of margin* $\gamma = 1/|\mathbf{w}^*|$, *then the Perceptron Algorithm makes at most* $r^2 |\mathbf{w}^*|^2$ *mistakes, where* $r = \max_t |\mathbf{x}_t|$.

Proof Fix some consistent $\mathbf{w}^*$. Keep track of two quantities, $\mathbf{w}^T \mathbf{w}^*$ and $|\mathbf{w}|^2$. Each mistake increases $\mathbf{w}^T \mathbf{w}^*$ by at least 1, since

$$(\mathbf{w} + \mathbf{x}_t l_t)^T \mathbf{w}^* = \mathbf{w}^T \mathbf{w}^* + \mathbf{x}_t^T l_t \mathbf{w}^* \geq \mathbf{w}^T \mathbf{w}^* + 1.$$

Next, each mistake increases $|\mathbf{w}|^2$ by at most r^2. For each mistake,

$$(\mathbf{w} + \mathbf{x}_t l_t)^T (\mathbf{w} + \mathbf{x}_t l_t) = |\mathbf{w}|^2 + 2\mathbf{x}_t^T l_t \mathbf{w} + |\mathbf{x}_t|^2 \leq |\mathbf{w}|^2 + |\mathbf{x}_t|^2 \leq |\mathbf{w}|^2 + r^2,$$

where the middle inequality comes from the fact that $\mathbf{x}_t^T l_t \mathbf{w} \leq 0$. Note that it is important here that we only update on a mistake.

So, if we make m mistakes, then $\mathbf{w}^T \mathbf{w}^* \geq m$, and $|\mathbf{w}|^2 \leq mr^2$, or equivalently, $|\mathbf{w}| \leq r\sqrt{m}$. Finally, we use the fact that $\mathbf{w}^T \mathbf{w}^* / |\mathbf{w}^*| \leq |\mathbf{w}|$, which is just saying that the projection of $\mathbf{w}$ in the direction of $\mathbf{w}^*$ cannot be larger than the length of $\mathbf{w}$. This gives us:

$$m \leq \mathbf{w}^T \mathbf{w}^*$$
$$m/|\mathbf{w}^*| \leq |\mathbf{w}|$$
$$m/|\mathbf{w}^*| \leq r\sqrt{m}$$
$$\sqrt{m} \leq r|\mathbf{w}^*|$$
$$m \leq r^2|\mathbf{w}^*|^2$$

as desired. ∎

5.10.4. Inseparable Data and Hinge Loss

We assumed above that there exists a perfect $\mathbf{w}^*$ that correctly classifies all the examples, e.g., correctly classifies all the e-mails into important versus non-important. This is rarely the case in real-life data. What if even the best $\mathbf{w}^*$ isn't perfect? We can see what this does to the above proof (Theorem 5.21). If there is an example that $\mathbf{w}^*$ doesn't correctly classify, then while the second part of the proof still holds, the first part (the dot product of $\mathbf{w}$ with $\mathbf{w}^*$ increasing) breaks down. However, if this doesn't happen too often, and also $\mathbf{x}_t^T \mathbf{w}^*$ is just a "little bit wrong," then we will only make a few more mistakes.

Define the *hinge-loss* of $\mathbf{w}^*$ for a positive example $\mathbf{x}_i$ as the amount $\mathbf{x}_i^T \mathbf{w}^*$ is less than 1 and for a negative example $\mathbf{x}_i$ as the amount $\mathbf{x}_i^T \mathbf{w}^*$ is greater than -1. That is, $L_{hinge}(\mathbf{w}^*, x_i) = \max(0, 1 - \mathbf{x}_i^T \mathbf{w}^* l_i)$. The total hinge-loss, $L_{hinge}(\mathbf{w}^*, S)$ for a set of examples S, is the sum of the hinge-loss of each example in S.

Theorem 5.22 *On any sequence of examples* $S = \mathbf{x}_1, \mathbf{x}_2, \ldots,$ *the Perceptron Algorithm makes at most*

$$\min_{\mathbf{w}^*} \left(r^2|\mathbf{w}^*|^2 + 2L_{hinge}(\mathbf{w}^*, S) \right)$$

mistakes, where $r = \max_t |\mathbf{x}_t|$.

Proof As before, each update of the Perceptron Algorithm increases $|\mathbf{w}|^2$ by at most r^2, so if the algorithm makes m mistakes, we have $|\mathbf{w}|^2 \leq mr^2$. What we can no longer say is that each update of the algorithm increases $\mathbf{w}^T \mathbf{w}^*$ by at least 1. Instead, on a positive example, we are "increasing" $\mathbf{w}^T \mathbf{w}^*$ by $\mathbf{x}_t^T \mathbf{w}^*$ (it could be negative), which is at least $1 - L_{hinge}(\mathbf{w}^*, \mathbf{x}_t)$. Similarly, on a negative example, we "increase" $\mathbf{w}^T \mathbf{w}^*$ by $-\mathbf{x}_t^T \mathbf{w}^*$, which is also at least $1 - L_{hinge}(\mathbf{w}^*, \mathbf{x}_t)$. Summing this up over all mistakes yields $\mathbf{w}^T \mathbf{w}^* \geq m - L_{hinge}(\mathbf{w}^*, S)$, where we are using the fact that hinge-loss is never negative so summing over all of S is only larger than summing over the mistakes that $\mathbf{w}$ made.

Let $l = L_{hinge}(\mathbf{w}^*, S)$. Then

$$\mathbf{w}^T \mathbf{w}^* \leq |\mathbf{w}||\mathbf{w}^*|$$
$$(m - l)^2 \leq |\mathbf{w}|^2 |\mathbf{w}^*|^2$$
$$m^2 - 2ml + l^2 \leq mr^2 |\mathbf{w}^*|^2$$
$$m - 2l + l^2/m \leq r^2 |\mathbf{w}^*|^2$$
$$m \leq r^2 |\mathbf{w}^*|^2 + 2l - l^2/m$$
$$m \leq r^2 |\mathbf{w}^*|^2 + 2l$$

as desired. ∎

5.10.5. Online to Batch Conversion

Suppose we have an online algorithm with a good mistake bound, such as the Perceptron Algorithm. Can we use it to get a guarantee in the distributional (batch) learning setting? Intuitively, the answer should be yes, since the online setting is only harder. Indeed, this intuition is correct. We present here two natural approaches for such online to batch conversion.

Conversion Procedure 1: Random Stopping
Suppose we have an online algorithm $\mathcal{A}$ with mistake-bound m. Run the algorithm in a single pass on a sample S of size m/ϵ. Let i_t be the indicator random variable for the event that $\mathcal{A}$ makes a mistake on example $\mathbf{x}_t$. Since $\sum_{t=1}^{|S|} i_t \leq m$ for any set S, $\mathbf{E}[\sum_{t=1}^{|S|} i_t] \leq m$ where the expectation is taken over the random draw of S from $\mathcal{D}^{|S|}$. By linearity of expectation, and dividing both sides by $|S|$,

$$\frac{1}{|S|} \sum_{t=1}^{|S|} \mathbf{E}[i_t] \leq m/|S| = \epsilon. \tag{5.2}$$

Let h_t denote the hypothesis used by algorithm $\mathcal{A}$ to predict on the tth example. Since the tth example was randomly drawn from $\mathcal{D}$, $\mathbf{E}[err_{\mathcal{D}}(h_t)] = \mathbf{E}[i_t]$. This means that if we choose t at random from 1 to $|S|$, that is, stopping the algorithm at a random time, the expected error of the resulting prediction rule, taken over the randomness in the draw of S and the choice of t, is at most ϵ as given by Equation (5.2). Thus we have the following theorem.

Theorem 5.23 (Online to Batch via Random Stopping) *If an online algorithm $\mathcal{A}$ with mistake-bound m is run on a sample S of size m/ϵ and stopped at a random time between 1 and $|S|$, the expected error of the hypothesis h produced satisfies $\mathbf{E}[err_{\mathcal{D}}(h)] \leq \epsilon$.*

Conversion Procedure 2: Controlled Testing
A second approach to using an online learning algorithm $\mathcal{A}$ for learning in the distributional setting is as follows. At each step of algorithm $\mathcal{A}$, we test its current hypothesis h on a large enough sample to determine if with high probability, the true error of h is less than ϵ. If h correctly classifies all the examples in the set, then

we stop and output the hypothesis h. Otherwise, we select an example x, which was misclassified by h, and submit it to the online algorithm $\mathcal{A}$ and get a new hypothesis. We repeat the process until we find an h that correctly classifies a large enough sample to ensure with probability greater than or equal to $1 - \delta$, h's true error will be less than ϵ. The technical details follow.

Specifically, suppose that the initial hypothesis produced by algorithm $\mathcal{A}$ is h_1. Define $\delta_i = \delta/(i + 2)^2$ so $\sum_{i=0}^{\infty} \delta_i = (\frac{\pi^2}{6} - 1)\delta \leq \delta$. Draw a set of $n_1 = \frac{1}{\epsilon} \log(\frac{1}{\delta_1})$ random examples and test to see whether h_1 gets all of them correct. Note that if $err_D(h_1) \geq \epsilon$, then the chance h_1 would get them all correct is at most $(1 - \epsilon)^{n_1} \leq \delta_1$. So, if h_1 indeed gets them all correct, we output h_1 as our hypothesis and halt. If not, we choose some example x_1 in the sample on which h_1 made a mistake and give it to algorithm $\mathcal{A}$. Algorithm $\mathcal{A}$ then produces some new hypothesis h_2 and we again repeat, testing h_2 on a fresh set of $n_2 = \frac{1}{\epsilon} \log(\frac{1}{\delta_2})$ random examples, and so on.

In general, given h_t, we draw a fresh set of $n_t = \frac{1}{\epsilon} \log(\frac{1}{\delta_t})$ random examples and test to see whether h_t gets all of them correct. If so, we output h_t and halt; if not, we choose some x_t on which $h_t(x_t)$ was incorrect and give it to algorithm $\mathcal{A}$. By choice of n_t, if h_t had error rate ϵ or larger, the chance we would mistakenly output it is at most δ_t. By choice of the values δ_t, the chance we ever halt with a hypothesis of error ϵ or larger is at most $\delta_1 + \delta_2 + \cdots \leq \delta$. Thus, we have the following theorem.

Theorem 5.24 (**Online to Batch via Controlled Testing**) *Let $\mathcal{A}$ be an online learning algorithm with mistake-bound m. Then this procedure will halt after $O(\frac{m}{\epsilon} \log(\frac{m}{\delta}))$ examples and with probability at least $1 - \delta$ will produce a hypothesis of error at most ϵ.*

Note that in this conversion we cannot reuse our samples. Since the hypothesis h_t depends on the previous data, we need to draw a fresh set of n_t examples to use for testing it.

5.10.6. Combining (Sleeping) Expert Advice

Imagine you have access to a large collection of rules-of-thumb that specify what to predict in different situations. For example, in classifying news articles, you might have a rule that says, "if the article has the word 'football,' then classify it as sports" and another that says, "if the article contains a dollar figure, then classify it as business." In predicting the stock market, there could be different economic indicators. These predictors might at times contradict each other, e.g., a news article that has both the word "football" and a dollar figure, or a day in which two economic indicators are pointing in different directions. It also may be that no predictor is perfectly accurate with some predictors much better than others. We present here an algorithm for combining a large number of such predictors with the guarantee that if any of them are good, the algorithm will perform nearly as well as each good predictor on the examples on which that predictor fires.

Formally, define a "sleeping expert" to be a predictor h that on any given example x either makes a prediction on its label or chooses to stay silent (asleep). Now, suppose we have access to n such sleeping experts $h_1, \ldots, h_n$, and let S_i denote the subset of examples on which h_i makes a prediction (e.g., this could be articles with the word "football" in them). We consider the online learning model and let $mistakes(A, S)$ denote the number of mistakes of an algorithm A on a sequence of examples S. Then the guarantee of our algorithm A will be that for all i

$$E\big(mistakes(A, S_i)\big) \leq (1 + \epsilon)mistakes(h_i, S_i) + O\left(\frac{\log n}{\epsilon}\right)$$

where ϵ is a parameter of the algorithm and the expectation is over internal randomness in the randomized algorithm A.

As a special case, if $h_1, \ldots, h_n$ are concepts from a concept class $\mathcal{H}$, so they all make predictions on every example, then A performs nearly as well as the best concept in $\mathcal{H}$. This can be viewed as a noise-tolerant version of the Halving Algorithm of Section 5.10.2 for the case that no concept in $\mathcal{H}$ is perfect. The case of predictors that make predictions on every example is called the problem of *combining expert advice*, and the more general case of predictors that sometimes fire and sometimes are silent is called the *sleeping experts* problem.

Combining Sleeping Experts Algorithm:
Initialize each expert h_i with a weight $w_i = 1$. Let $\epsilon \in (0, 1)$. For each example x, do the following:

1. [Make prediction] Let H_x denote the set of experts h_i that make a prediction on x, and let $w_x = \sum_{h_j \in H_x} w_j$. Choose $h_i \in H_x$ with probability $p_{ix} = w_i/w_x$ and predict $h_i(x)$.
2. [Receive feedback] Given the correct label, for each $h_i \in H_x$ let $m_{ix} = 1$ if $h_i(x)$ was incorrect, else let $m_{ix} = 0$.
3. [Update weights] For each $h_i \in H_x$, update its weight as follows:
   - Let $r_{ix} = \left(\sum_{h_j \in H_x} p_{jx} m_{jx}\right)/(1 + \epsilon) - m_{ix}$.
   - Update $w_i \leftarrow w_i(1 + \epsilon)^{r_{ix}}$.
   Note that $\sum_{h_j \in H_x} p_{jx} m_{jx}$ represents the algorithm's probability of making a mistake on example x. So, h_i is rewarded for predicting correctly ($m_{ix} = 0$) when the algorithm had a high probability of making a mistake, and h_i is penalized for predicting incorrectly ($m_{ix} = 1$) when the algorithm had a low probability of making a mistake.

For each $h_i \notin H_x$, leave w_i alone.

Theorem 5.25 *For any set of n sleeping experts $h_1, \ldots, h_n$, and for any sequence of examples S, the Combining Sleeping Experts Algorithm A satisfies for all i*

$$E\big(mistakes(A, S_i)\big) \leq (1 + \epsilon)mistakes(h_i, S_i) + O\left(\frac{\log n}{\epsilon}\right)$$

where $S_i = \{x \in S | h_i \in H_x\}$.

Proof Consider sleeping expert h_i. The weight of h_i after the sequence of examples S is exactly

$$w_i = (1 + \epsilon)^{\sum_{x \in S_i}\left[\left(\sum_{h_j \in H_x} p_{jx} m_{jx}\right)/(1+\epsilon) - m_{ix}\right]}$$
$$= (1 + \epsilon)^{E[mistakes(A, S_i)]/(1+\epsilon) - mistakes(h_i, S_i)}.$$

Let $w = \sum_j w_j$. Clearly $w_i \leq w$. Therefore, taking logs:

$$E\big(mistakes(A, S_i)\big)/(1 + \epsilon) - mistakes(h_i, S_i) \leq \log_{1+\epsilon} w.$$

So, using the fact that $\log_{1+\epsilon} w = O\big(\frac{\log W}{\epsilon}\big)$,

$$E\big(mistakes(A, S_i)\big) \leq (1 + \epsilon)mistakes(h_i, S_i) + O\left(\frac{\log w}{\epsilon}\right).$$

Initially, $w = n$. To prove the theorem, it is sufficient to prove that w never increases. To do so, we need to show that for each x, $\sum_{h_i \in H_x} w_i(1 + \epsilon)^{r_{ix}} \leq \sum_{h_i \in H_x} w_i$, or equivalently dividing both sides by $\sum_{h_j \in H_x} w_j$ that $\sum_i p_{ix}(1 + \epsilon)^{r_{ix}} \leq 1$, where for convenience we define $p_{ix} = 0$ for $h_i \notin H_x$.

For this we will use the inequalities that for $\beta, z \in [0, 1]$, $\beta^z \leq 1 - (1 - \beta)z$ and $\beta^{-z} \leq 1 + (1 - \beta)z/\beta$. Specifically, we will use $\beta = (1+\epsilon)^{-1}$. We now have:

$$\sum_i p_{ix}(1 + \epsilon)^{r_{ix}} = \sum_i p_{ix}\beta^{m_{ix} - (\sum_j p_{jx}m_{jx})\beta}$$

$$\leq \sum_i p_{ix}\Big(1 - (1 - \beta)m_{ix}\Big)\left(1 + (1 - \beta)\left(\sum_j p_{jx}m_{jx}\right)\right)$$

$$\leq \left(\sum_i p_{ix}\right) - (1 - \beta)\sum_i p_{ix}m_{ix} + (1 - \beta)\sum_i p_{ix}\sum_j p_{jx}m_{jx}$$

$$= 1 - (1 - \beta)\sum_i p_{ix}m_{ix} + (1 - \beta)\sum_j p_{jx}m_{jx}$$

$$= 1,$$

where the second-to-last line follows from using $\sum_i p_{ix} = 1$ in two places. So w never increases and the bound follows as desired. ∎

5.11. Boosting

We now describe *boosting*, which is important both as a theoretical result and as a practical and easy-to-use learning method. A *strong learner* for a problem is an algorithm that with high probability is able to achieve any desired error rate ϵ using a sufficient number of samples that may depend polynomially on $1/\epsilon$. A *weak learner* for a problem is an algorithm that does just a little bit better than random guessing. It is only required to get with high probability an error rate less than or equal to $\frac{1}{2} - \gamma$ for some $0 < \gamma \leq \frac{1}{2}$. We show here that a weak learner for a problem that achieves the weak-learning guarantee for any distribution of data can be boosted to a strong learner, using the technique of boosting. At the high level, the idea will be to take our training sample S, and run the weak learner on different data distributions produced by weighting the points in the training sample in different ways. Running the weak learner on these different weightings of the training sample will produce a series of hypotheses $h_1, h_2, \ldots$. The idea of the reweighting procedure will be to focus attention on the parts of the sample that previous hypotheses have performed poorly on. At the end the hypotheses are combined together by a majority vote.

Boosting Algorithm

Given a sample S of n labeled examples $\mathbf{x}_1, \ldots, \mathbf{x}_n$, initialize each example $\mathbf{x}_i$ to have a weight $w_i = 1$. Let $\mathbf{w} = (w_1, \ldots, w_n)$.

For $t = 1, 2, \ldots, t_0$ do

Call the weak learner on the weighted sample $(S, \mathbf{w})$, receiving hypothesis h_t.

Multiply the weight of each example that was misclassified by h_t by $\alpha = \frac{\frac{1}{2} + \gamma}{\frac{1}{2} - \gamma}$. Leave the other weights as they are.

End

Output the classifier $\text{MAJ}(h_1, \ldots, h_{t_0})$, which takes the majority vote of the hypotheses returned by the weak learner. Assume t_0 is odd so there is no tie.

Figure 5.11: The boosting algorithm.

Assume the weak learning algorithm A outputs hypotheses from some class $\mathcal{H}$. Our boosting algorithm will produce hypotheses that will be majority votes over t_0 hypotheses from $\mathcal{H}$, for t_0 defined below. By Theorem 5.13, the class of functions that can be produced by the booster running for t_0 rounds has VC-dimension $O(t_0 \text{VCdim}(\mathcal{H}) \log(t_0 \text{VCdim}(\mathcal{H})))$. This gives a bound on the number of samples needed, via Corollary 5.17, to ensure that high accuracy on the sample will translate to high accuracy on new data.

To make the discussion simpler, assume that the weak learning algorithm A, when presented with a weighting of the points in our training sample, always (rather than with high probability) produces a hypothesis that performs slightly better than random guessing with respect to the distribution induced by weighting. Specifically:

Definition 5.5 (γ-**Weak learner on sample**) *A γ-weak learner is an algorithm that given examples, their labels, and a nonnegative real weight w_i on each example $\mathbf{x}_i$, produces a classifier that correctly labels a subset of the examples with total weight at least $(\frac{1}{2} + \gamma) \sum_{i=1}^{n} w_i$.*

At the high level, boosting makes use of the intuitive notion that if an example was misclassified, one needs to pay more attention to it. More specifically, boosting multiplies the weight of the misclassified examples by a value $\alpha > 1$ designed to raise their total weight to equal the total weight of the correctly-classified examples. The boosting procedure is in Figure 5.11.

Theorem 5.26 *Let A be a γ-weak learner for sample S of n samples. Then $t_0 = O(\frac{1}{\gamma^2} \log n)$ is sufficient so that the classifier $MAJ(h_1, \ldots, h_{t_0})$ produced by the boosting procedure has training error zero.*

Proof Suppose m is the number of examples the final classifier gets wrong. Each of these m examples was misclassified at least $t_0/2$ times so each has weight at least $\alpha^{t_0/2}$. Thus the total weight is at least $m\alpha^{t_0/2}$. On the other hand, at time $t + 1$, only the weights of examples misclassified at time t were increased. By the property of weak learning, the total weight of misclassified examples is at most $\left(\frac{1}{2} - \gamma\right)$ of the total weight at time t. Let weight(t) be the total weight at time t. Then

$$\text{weight}(t + 1) \leq \left(\alpha \left(\tfrac{1}{2} - \gamma\right) + \left(\tfrac{1}{2} + \gamma\right)\right) \times \text{weight}(t) = (1 + 2\gamma) \times \text{weight}(t),$$

where $\alpha = \frac{\frac{1}{2}+\gamma}{\frac{1}{2}-\gamma}$ is the constant that the weights of misclassified examples are multiplied by. Since weight$(0) = n$, the total weight at the end is at most $n(1 + 2\gamma)^{t_0}$. Thus,

$$m\alpha^{t_0/2} \leq \text{total weight at end} \leq n(1 + 2\gamma)^{t_0}.$$

Substituting $\alpha = \frac{1/2+\gamma}{1/2-\gamma} = \frac{1+2\gamma}{1-2\gamma}$ and solving for m,

$$m \leq n(1 - 2\gamma)^{t_0/2}(1 + 2\gamma)^{t_0/2} = n[1 - 4\gamma^2]^{t_0/2}.$$

Using $1 - x \leq e^{-x}, m \leq ne^{-2t_0\gamma^2}$. For $t_0 > \frac{\ln n}{2\gamma^2}, m < 1$, so the number of misclassified items must be zero. ∎

Having completed the proof of the boosting result, here are two interesting observations:

Connection to Hoeffding bounds: The boosting result applies even if our weak learning algorithm is "adversarial," giving us the least helpful classifier possible subject to Definition 5.5. This is why we don't want the α in the boosting algorithm to be larger than $\frac{0.5+\gamma}{0.5-\gamma}$, since in that case the misclassified examples would get higher total weight than the correctly classified examples, and the weak learner could then choose to just return the negation of the classifier it gave the last time. Suppose that the weak learning algorithm gave a classifier each time that for each example flipped a coin and produced the correct answer with probability $\frac{1}{2} + \gamma$ and the wrong answer with probability $\frac{1}{2} - \gamma$, so it is a γ-weak learner in expectation. In that case, if we called the weak learner t_0 times, for any fixed $\mathbf{x}_i$, Hoeffding bounds imply the chance the majority vote of those classifiers is incorrect on $\mathbf{x}_i$ is at most $e^{-2t_0\gamma^2}$. So, the expected total number of mistakes m is at most $ne^{-2t_0\gamma^2}$. What is interesting is that this is the exact bound we get from boosting without the expectation for an adversarial weak learner.

A minimax view: Consider a two-player zero-sum game[9] with one row for each example $\mathbf{x}_i$ and one column for each hypothesis h_j that the weak-learning algorithm might output. If the row player chooses row i and the column player chooses column j, then the column player gets a payoff of one if $h_j(\mathbf{x}_i)$ is correct and gets a payoff of zero if $h_j(\mathbf{x}_i)$ is incorrect. The γ-weak learning assumption

---

[9]A two-player zero-sum game consists of a matrix whose columns correspond to moves for Player 1 and whose rows correspond to moves for Player 2. The ij^{th} entry of the matrix is the payoff for Player 1 if Player 1 choose the jth column and Player 2 choose the ith row. Player 2's payoff is the negative of Player 1's.

implies that for any randomized strategy for the row player (any "mixed strategy" in the language of game theory), there exists a response h_j that gives the column player an expected payoff of at least $\frac{1}{2} + \gamma$. The von Neumann minimax theorem[10] states that this implies there exists a probability distribution on the columns (a mixed strategy for the column player) such that for any $\mathbf{x}_i$, at least a $\frac{1}{2} + \gamma$ probability mass of the columns under this distribution is correct on $\mathbf{x}_i$. We can think of boosting as a fast way of finding a very simple probability distribution on the columns (just an average over $O(\log n)$ columns, possibly with repetitions) that is nearly as good (for any $\mathbf{x}_i$, more than half are correct) that moreover works even if our only access to the columns is by running the weak learner and observing its outputs.

We argued above that $t_0 = O(\frac{1}{\gamma^2} \log n)$ rounds of boosting are sufficient to produce a majority-vote rule h that will classify all of S correctly. Using our VC-dimension bounds, this implies that if the weak learner is choosing its hypotheses from concept class $\mathcal{H}$, then a sample size

$$n = \tilde{O}\left(\frac{1}{\epsilon}\left(\frac{\text{VCdim}(\mathcal{H})}{\gamma^2}\right)\right)$$

is sufficient to conclude that with probability $1 - \delta$ the error is less than or equal to ϵ, where we are using the $\tilde{O}$ notation to hide logarithmic factors. It turns out that running the boosting procedure for larger values of t_0, i.e., continuing past the point where S is classified correctly by the final majority vote, does not actually lead to greater overfitting. The reason is that using the same type of analysis used to prove Theorem 5.26, one can show that as t_0 increases, not only will the majority vote be correct on each $\mathbf{x} \in S$, but in fact each example will be correctly classified by a $\frac{1}{2} + \gamma'$ fraction of the classifiers, where $\gamma' \to \gamma$ as $t_0 \to \infty$. That is, the vote is approaching the minimax optimal strategy for the column player in the minimax view given above. This in turn implies that h can be well approximated over S by a vote of a random sample of $O(1/\gamma^2)$ of its component weak hypotheses h_j. Since these small random majority votes are not overfitting by much, our generalization theorems imply that h cannot be overfitting by much either.

5.12. Further Current Directions

We now briefly discuss a few additional current directions in machine learning, focusing on *semi-supervised* learning, *active* learning, and *multitask* learning.

5.12.1. Semi-Supervised Learning

Semi-supervised learning uses a large unlabeled data set U to augment a given labeled data set L to produce more accurate rules than would have been achieved using just L alone. In many settings (e.g., document classification, image classification,

---

[10]The von Neumann minimax theorem states that for some value v (the value of the game), there exists a mixed strategy for Player 1 such that no matter what Player 2 chooses, Player 1's expected gain is at least v, and there exists a mixed strategy for Player 2 such that no matter what Player 1 chooses, Player 1's expected gain is at most v. A mixed strategy is a randomized strategy over rows (for Player 1) or columns (for Player 2).

speech recognition), unlabeled data are much more plentiful than labeled data, so one would like to make use of it. Unlabeled data are missing the labels but often contain information that an algorithm can take advantage of.

Suppose one believes the target function is a linear separator that separates most of the data by a large margin. By observing enough unlabeled data to estimate the probability mass near to any given linear separator, one could in principle discard separators in advance that slice through dense regions and instead focus attention on those that separate most of the distribution by a large margin. This is the high-level idea behind a technique known as *semi-supervised SVMs*. Alternatively, suppose data objects can be described by two different kinds of features (e.g., a webpage could be described using words on the page itself or using words on links pointing to the page), and one believes that each kind should be sufficient to produce an accurate classifier. Then one might want to train a pair of classifiers, one on each type of feature, and use unlabeled data for which one classifier is confident but the other is not to bootstrap, labeling such examples with the confident classifier and then feeding them as training data to the less confident one. This is the high-level idea behind a technique known as *Co-Training*. Or, if one believes "similar examples should generally have the same label," one might construct a graph with an edge between examples that are sufficiently similar, and aim for a classifier that is correct on the labeled data and has a small cut value on the unlabeled data; this is the high-level idea behind graph-based methods.

A formal model: The batch learning model introduced in Section 5.4 in essence assumes that one's prior beliefs about the target function be described in terms of a class of functions $\mathcal{H}$. In order to capture the reasoning used in semi-supervised learning, we need to also describe beliefs about the *relation* between the target function and the data distribution. One way to do this is via a *notion of compatibility* χ between a hypothesis h and a distribution $\mathcal{D}$. Formally, χ maps pairs $(h, \mathcal{D})$ to $[0, 1]$ with $\chi(h, \mathcal{D}) = 1$ meaning that h is highly compatible with $\mathcal{D}$ and $\chi(h, \mathcal{D}) = 0$ meaning that h is highly *in*compatible with $\mathcal{D}$. For example, if you believe that nearby points should generally have the same label, then if h slices through the middle of a high-density region of $\mathcal{D}$ (a cluster), you might call h incompatible with $\mathcal{D}$, whereas if no high-density region is split by h, then you might call it compatible with $\mathcal{D}$. The quantity $1 - \chi(h, \mathcal{D})$ is called the *unlabeled error rate* of h, and denoted $err_{unl}(h)$. Note that for χ to be useful, it must be estimatable from a finite sample; to this end, let us further require that χ is an expectation over individual examples. That is, overloading notation for convenience, we require $\chi(h, \mathcal{D}) = \mathbf{E}_{x \sim \mathcal{D}}[\chi(h, x)]$, where $\chi : \mathcal{H} \times X \rightarrow [0, 1]$.

For instance, suppose we believe the target should separate most data by margin γ. We can represent this belief by defining $\chi(h, x) = 0$ if x is within distance γ of the decision boundary of h, and $\chi(h, x) = 1$ otherwise. In this case, $err_{unl}(h)$ will denote the probability mass of $\mathcal{D}$ within distance γ of h's decision boundary. As a different example, in co-training, we assume each example x can be described using two "views" x_1 and x_2 such that each is sufficient for classification. That is, we assume there exist c_1^* and c_2^* such that for each example $x = \langle x_1, x_2 \rangle$ we have $c_1^*(x_1) = c_2^*(x_2)$. We can represent this belief by defining a hypothesis $h = \langle h_1, h_2 \rangle$ to be compatible with an example $\langle x_1, x_2 \rangle$ if $h_1(x_1) = h_2(x_2)$ and incompatible otherwise; $err_{unl}(h)$ is then the probability mass of examples on which h_1 and h_2 disagree.

As with the class $\mathcal{H}$, one can either assume that the target is fully compatible, i.e., $err_{unl}(c^*) = 0$, or instead aim to do well as a function of how compatible the target is. The case that we assume $c^* \in \mathcal{H}$ and $err_{unl}(c^*) = 0$ is termed the "doubly realizable case." The concept class $\mathcal{H}$ and compatibility notion χ are both viewed as known. Suppose one is given a concept class $\mathcal{H}$ (such as linear separators) and a compatibility notion χ (such as penalizing h for points within distance γ of the decision boundary). Suppose also that one believes $c^* \in \mathcal{H}$ (or at least is close) and that $err_{unl}(c^*) = 0$ (or at least is small). Then, unlabeled data can help by allowing one to estimate the *unlabeled error rate* of all $h \in \mathcal{H}$, thereby in principle reducing the search space from $\mathcal{H}$ (all linear separators) down to just the subset of $\mathcal{H}$ that is highly compatible with $\mathcal{D}$. The key challenge is how this can be done efficiently (in theory, in practice, or both) for natural notions of compatibility, as well as identifying types of compatibility that data in important problems can be expected to satisfy.

The following is a semi-supervised analog of our basic sample complexity theorem, Theorem 5.4. First, fix some set of functions $\mathcal{H}$ and compatibility notion χ. Given a labeled sample L, define $\widehat{err}(h)$ to be the fraction of mistakes of h on L. Given an unlabeled sample U, define $\chi(h, U) = \mathbf{E}_{x \sim U}[\chi(h, x)]$ and define $\widehat{err}_{unl}(h) = 1 - \chi(h, U)$. That is, $\widehat{err}(h)$ and $\widehat{err}_{unl}(h)$ are the empirical error rate and unlabeled error rate of h, respectively. Finally, given $\alpha > 0$, define $\mathcal{H}_{\mathcal{D},\chi}(\alpha)$ to be the set of functions $f \in \mathcal{H}$ such that $err_{unl}(f) \leq \alpha$.

Theorem 5.27 *If $c^* \in \mathcal{H}$, then with probability at least $1 - \delta$, for labeled set L and unlabeled set U drawn from $\mathcal{D}$, the $h \in \mathcal{H}$ that optimizes $\widehat{err}_{unl}(h)$ subject to $\widehat{err}(h) = 0$ will have $err_{\mathcal{D}}(h) \leq \epsilon$ for*

$$|U| \geq \frac{2}{\epsilon^2}\left[\ln|\mathcal{H}| + \ln\frac{4}{\delta}\right], \text{ and } |L| \geq \frac{1}{\epsilon}\left[\ln|\mathcal{H}_{\mathcal{D},\chi}(err_{unl}(c^*) + 2\epsilon)| + \ln\frac{2}{\delta}\right].$$

Equivalently, for $|U|$ satisfying this bound, for any $|L|$, whp the $h \in \mathcal{H}$ that minimizes $\widehat{err}_{unl}(h)$ subject to $\widehat{err}(h) = 0$ has

$$err_{\mathcal{D}}(h) \leq \frac{1}{|L|}\left[\ln|\mathcal{H}_{\mathcal{D},\chi}(err_{unl}(c^*) + 2\epsilon)| + \ln\frac{2}{\delta}\right].$$

Proof By Hoeffding bounds, $|U|$ is sufficiently large so that with probability at least $1 - \delta/2$, all $h \in \mathcal{H}$ have $|\widehat{err}_{unl}(h) - err_{unl}(h)| \leq \epsilon$. Thus we have:

$$\{f \in \mathcal{H} | \widehat{err}_{unl}(f) \leq err_{unl}(c^*) + \epsilon\} \subseteq \mathcal{H}_{\mathcal{D},\chi}(err_{unl}(c^*) + 2\epsilon).$$

The given bound on $|L|$ is sufficient so that with probability at least $1 - \delta$, all $h \in \mathcal{H}$ with $\widehat{err}(h) = 0$ and $\widehat{err}_{unl}(h) \leq err_{unl}(c^*) + \epsilon$ have $err_{\mathcal{D}}(h) \leq \epsilon$; furthermore, $\widehat{err}_{unl}(c^*) \leq err_{unl}(c^*) + \epsilon$, so such a function h exists. Therefore, with probability at least $1 - \delta$, the $h \in \mathcal{H}$ that optimizes $\widehat{err}_{unl}(h)$ subject to $\widehat{err}(h) = 0$ has $err_{\mathcal{D}}(h) \leq \epsilon$, as desired. ∎

One can view Theorem 5.27 as bounding the number of labeled examples needed to learn well as a function of the "helpfulness" of the distribution $\mathcal{D}$ with respect to χ. Namely, a helpful distribution is one in which $\mathcal{H}_{\mathcal{D},\chi}(\alpha)$ is small for α slightly larger than the compatibility of the true target function, so we do not need much labeled data to identify a good function among those in $\mathcal{H}_{\mathcal{D},\chi}(\alpha)$. For more information on semi-supervised learning, see [BB10, BM98, CSZ06, Joa99, Zhu06, ZGL03].

5.12.2. Active Learning

Active learning refers to algorithms that take an active role in the selection of which examples are labeled. The algorithm is given an initial unlabeled set U of data points drawn from distribution $\mathcal{D}$ and then interactively requests for the labels of a small number of these examples. The aim is to reach a desired error rate ϵ using many fewer labels than would be needed by labeling random examples, i.e., passive learning.

Suppose that data consist of points on the real line and $\mathcal{H} = \{f_a | f_a(x) = 1$ iff $x \geq a\}$ for $a \in R$. That is, $\mathcal{H}$ is the set of all threshold functions on the line. It is not hard to show (see Exercise 5.12) that a random labeled sample of size $O(\frac{1}{\epsilon} \log(\frac{1}{\delta}))$ is sufficient to ensure that with probability greater than or equal to $1 - \delta$, any consistent threshold a' has error at most ϵ. Moreover, it is not hard to show that $\Omega(\frac{1}{\epsilon})$ random examples are necessary for passive learning. Suppose that the data consist of points in the interval $[0, 1]$ where the points in the interval $[0, a)$ are negative and the points in the interval $[a, 1]$ are positive. Given a hypothesis set $\{[b, 1] | 0 \leq b \leq 1\}$, a random labeled sample of size $O\left(\frac{1}{\epsilon} \log \frac{1}{\delta}\right)$ is sufficient to ensure that with probability greater than or equal to $1 - \delta$ any hypothesis with zero training error has true error at most ϵ. However, with active learning we can achieve error ϵ using only $O\left(\log(\frac{1}{\epsilon}) + \log \log(\frac{1}{\delta})\right)$ labels. The idea is as follows. Assume we are given an unlabeled sample U of size $O(\frac{1}{\epsilon} \log(\frac{1}{\delta}))$. Now, query the leftmost and rightmost points. If both are negative, output $b = 1$. If both are positive, output $b = 0$. Otherwise (the leftmost is negative and the rightmost is positive), use binary search to find two adjacent examples x, x' of U such that x is negative and x' is positive, and output $b = (x + x')/2$. This threshold b is consistent with the labels on the entire set U, and so, by the above argument, has error less than or equal to ϵ with probability greater than or equal to $1 - \delta$.

The agnostic case, where the target need not belong in the given class $\mathcal{H}$, is quite a bit more subtle, and addressed in a quite general way in the "A^2" Agnostic Active learning algorithm [BBL09]. For more information on active learning, see [Das11, BU14].

5.12.3. Multitask Learning

In this chapter we have focused on scenarios where our goal is to learn a single target function c^*. However, there are also scenarios where one would like to learn *multiple* target functions $c_1^*, c_2^*, \ldots, c_n^*$. If these functions are related in some way, then one could hope to do so with less data per function than one would need to learn each function separately. This is the idea of *multitask learning*.

One natural example is object recognition. Given an image $\mathbf{x}$, $c_1^*(\mathbf{x})$ might be 1 if $\mathbf{x}$ is a coffee cup and 0 otherwise; $c_2^*(\mathbf{x})$ might be 1 if $\mathbf{x}$ is a pencil and 0 otherwise; $c_3^*(\mathbf{x})$ might be 1 if $\mathbf{x}$ is a laptop and 0 otherwise. These recognition tasks are related in that image features that are good for one task are likely to be helpful for the others as well. Thus, one approach to multitask learning is to try to learn a common representation under which each of the target functions can be described as a simple function. Another natural example is personalization. Consider a speech recognition system with n different users. In this case there are n target tasks (recognizing the speech of each user) that are clearly related to each other. Some good references for multitask learning are [TM95, Thr96].

5.13. Bibliographic Notes

The basic theory underlying learning in the distributional setting was developed by Vapnik [Vap82], Vapnik and Chervonenkis [VC71], and Valiant [Val84]. The connection of this to the notion of Occam's razor is due to [BEHW87]. For more information on uniform convergence, regularization, and complexity penalization, see [Vap98]. The Perceptron Algorithm for online learning of linear separators was first analyzed by Block [Blo62] and Novikoff [Nov62]; the proof given here is from [MP69]. A formal description of the online learning model and its connections to learning in the distributional setting is given in [Lit87]. Support Vector Machines and their connections to kernel functions were first introduced by [BGV92], and extended by [CV95], with analysis in terms of margins given by [STBWA98]. For further reading on SVMs, learning with kernel functions, and regularization, see [SS01]. VC dimension is due to Vapnik and Chervonenkis [VC71] with the results presented here given in Blumer, Ehrenfeucht, Haussler, and Warmuth [BEHW89]. Boosting was first introduced by Schapire [Sch90], and Adaboost and its guarantees are due to Freund and Schapire [FS97]. Analysis of the problem of combining expert advice was given by Littlestone and Warmuth [LW94] and Cesa-Bianchi et al. [CBFH+97]; the analysis of the sleeping experts problem given here is from [BM07].

5.14. Exercises

Exercise 5.1 Each of the following data sets consists of a subset of the d-dimensional 0/1 vectors labeled $+1$. The remaining 0/1 vectors are labeled -1. Which sets are linearly separable?

1. $\{010, 011, 100, 111\}$
2. $\{011, 100, 110, 111\}$
3. $\{0100, 0101, 0110, 1000, 1100, 1101, 1110, 1111\}$

Exercise 5.2 Run the Perceptron Algorithm on each of the examples in Exercise 5.1. What happens?

Exercise 5.3 (representation and linear separators) A logical disjunction is the OR of a set of Boolean variables such as $x_1 \vee x_2 \vee x_4$. Show that any disjunction over $\{0, 1\}^d$ can be represented as a linear separator. Show that, moreover, the margin of separation is $\Omega(1/\sqrt{d})$.

Exercise 5.4 (representation and linear separators) Show that the parity function on $d \geq 2$ Boolean variables cannot be represented by a linear threshold function. The parity function is 1 if and only if an odd number of inputs is 1.

Exercise 5.5 Given two sets of d dimensional vectors S_1 and S_2, how would you determine if the convex hulls of the two sets intersect? Assume that either they intersect, or else if they do not, then there is at least a γ gap of separation between them.

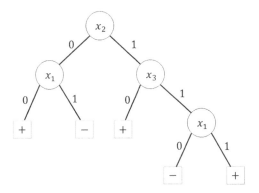

Figure 5.12: A decision tree with three internal nodes and four leaves. This tree corresponds to the Boolean function $\bar{x}_1\bar{x}_2 \vee x_1 x_2 x_3 \vee x_2 \bar{x}_3$.

Exercise 5.6 (kernels) Prove Theorem 5.3.

Exercise 5.7 Find the mapping $\varphi(\mathbf{x})$ that gives rise to the kernel

$$K(\mathbf{x}, \mathbf{y}) = (x_1 y_1 + x_2 y_2)^2.$$

Exercise 5.8 Give an example of overfitting, that is, where training error is much less than true error.

Exercise 5.9 One popular practical method for machine learning is to learn a decision tree (Figure 5.12). While finding the smallest decision tree that fits a given training sample S is NP-hard, there are a number of heuristics that are used in practice. Suppose we run such a heuristic on a training set S and it outputs a tree with k nodes. Show that such a tree can be described using $O(k \log d)$ bits, where d is the number of features. Assume all features are binary valued (as in Figure 5.12). By Theorem 5.7, we can be confident the true error is low if we can produce a consistent tree with fewer than $\epsilon|S|/\log(d)$ nodes.

Exercise 5.10 Consider the class of OR-functions (disjunctions) over d binary (0/1-valued) features. For instance, one such OR-function is $x_1 \vee x_2 \vee x_4$. Using Theorem 5.4, how many examples are sufficient so that with probability at least $1 - \delta$, only OR-functions of true error less than ϵ will have zero training error?

Exercise 5.11 Consider the instance space $\mathcal{X} = \{0, 1\}^d$ and let $\mathcal{H}$ be the class of 3-CNF formulas. That is, $\mathcal{H}$ is the set of concepts that can be described as a conjunction of clauses where each clause is an OR of up to 3 literals. (These are also called 3-SAT formulas.) For example, c^* might be $(x_1 \vee \bar{x}_2 \vee x_3)(x_2 \vee x_4)(\bar{x}_1 \vee x_3)(x_2 \vee x_3 \vee x_4)$. Assume we are in the PAC learning setting, so examples are drawn from some underlying distribution D and labeled by some 3-CNF formula c^*.

1. Give a number of examples m that would be sufficient to ensure that with probability greater than or equal to $1 - \delta$, all 3-CNF formulas consistent with the data have error at most ϵ with respect to D.
2. Give a polynomial-time algorithm that finds a 3-CNF formula consistent with the sample if one exists.

Exercise 5.12 Consider an instance space X consisting of integers 1 to 1,000,000 and a target concept c^* where $c^*(i) = 1$ for $500,001 \leq i \leq 1,000,000$. If your hypothesis class $\mathcal{H}$ is $\{h_j | h_j(i) = 1$ for $i \geq j$ and $h_j(i) = 0$ for $i < j\}$, how large a training set S do you need to ensure that with probability 99%, any consistent hypothesis in $\mathcal{H}$ will have true error less than 10%?

Exercise 5.13 Consider a deep network with 100,000 parameters each given by a 32-bit floating point number. Suppose the network is trained on 100,000,000 training examples. Corollary 5.8 says that with probability 99.9%, the true error will differ from the empirical error by some ϵ. What is the value of ϵ?

Exercise 5.14 (**Regularization**) Pruning a decision tree: Let S be a labeled sample drawn iid from some distribution $\mathcal{D}$ over $\{0, 1\}^n$, and suppose S was used to create some decision tree T. However, the tree T is large, and we might be overfitting. Give a polynomial-time algorithm for pruning T that finds the pruning h of T that optimizes the right-hand side of Corollary 5.8, i.e., that for a given $\delta > 0$ minimizes:

$$err_S(h) + \sqrt{\frac{size(h)\ln(4) + \ln(2/\delta)}{2|S|}}.$$

To discuss this, we define the meaning of "pruning" of T and the meaning of "size" of h. A pruning h of T is a tree in which some internal nodes of T have been turned into leaves, labeled "+" or "−" depending on whether the majority of examples in S that reach that node are positive or negative. Let $size(h) = L(h)\log(n)$ where $L(h)$ is the number of leaves in h.

    Hint. #1: it is sufficient, for each integer $L = 1, 2, \ldots, L(T)$, to find the pruning of T with L leaves of lowest empirical error on S, that is, $h_L = \text{argmin}_{h:L(h)=L} err_S(h)$. Then plug them all into the displayed formula above and pick the best formula.
    Hint #2: use dynamic programming.

Exercise 5.15 Consider the instance space $X = R^2$. What is the VC-dimension of right corners with axis-aligned edges that are oriented with one edge going to the right and the other edge going up?

Exercise 5.16 (**VC-dimension; Section 5.5**) What is the VC-dimension of the class $\mathcal{H}$ of axis-parallel boxes in R^d? That is, $\mathcal{H} = \{h_{a,b} | a, b \in R^d\}$ where $h_{a,b}(x) = 1$ if $a_i \leq x_i \leq b_i$ for all $i = 1, \ldots, d$ and $h_{a,b}(x) = -1$ otherwise. Select a set of points V that is shattered by the class and

1. prove that the VC-dimension is at least $|V|$ by proving V shattered, and
2. prove that the VC-dimension is at most $|V|$ by proving that no set of $|V| + 1$ points can be shattered.

Exercise 5.17 (**VC-dimension**) Prove that the VC-dimension of circles in the plane is three.

Exercise 5.18 (**VC-dimension, Perceptron, and Margins**) A set of points S is "shattered by linear separators of margin γ" if every labeling of the points in S is achievable by a linear separator of margin at least γ. Prove that no set of $1/\gamma^2 + 1$ points in the unit ball is shattered by linear separators of margin γ.

    Hint. think about the Perceptron Algorithm and try a proof by contradiction.

Exercise 5.19 (Squares) Show that there is a set of three points that can be shattered by axis-parallel squares. Show that the system of axis-parallel squares cannot shatter any set of four points.

Exercise 5.20 Show that the VC-dimension of axis-aligned right triangles with the right angle in the lower left corner is 4.

Exercise 5.21 Prove that the VC-dimension of $45°, 45°, 90°$ triangles with right angle in the lower left is 4.

Exercise 5.22 If a class contains only convex sets, prove that it cannot shatter any set in which some point is in the convex hull of other points in the set.

Exercise 5.23 What is the VC-dimension of the family of quadrants? A quadrant Q is a set of points of one of the four types below:

1. $Q = \{(x, y) : (x - x_0, y - y_0) \geq (0, 0)\}$,
2. $Q = \{(x, y) : (x_0 - x, y - y_0) \geq (0, 0)\}$,
3. $Q = \{(x, y) : (x_0 - x, y_0 - y) \geq (0, 0)\}$, or
4. $Q = \{(x, y) : (x - x_0, y_0 - y) \geq (0, 0)\}$.

Exercise 5.24 For large n, how should you place n points on the plane so that the maximum number of subsets of the n points are defined by rectangles? Can you achieve 4n subsets of size 2? Can you do better? What about size 3? What about size 10?

Exercise 5.25 For large n, how should you place n points on the plane so that the maximum number of subsets of the n points are defined by

1. half spaces?
2. circles?
3. axis-parallel rectangles?
4. some other simple shape of your choosing?

For each of the shapes, how many subsets of size 2, 3, etc. can you achieve?

Exercise 5.26 What is the shatter function for two-dimensional halfspaces? That is, given n points in the plane, how many subsets can be defined by halfspaces?

Exercise 5.27 What does it mean to shatter the empty set? How many subsets does one get?

Exercise 5.28 Intuitively define the most general form of a set system of VC-dimension one. Give an example of such a set system that can generate n subsets of an n element set. What is the form of the most general set system of dimension 2.

Exercise 5.29 Given two fully connected levels without a nonlinear element, one can combine the two levels into one level. Can this be done for two convolution levels without pooling and without a nonlinear element?

Exercise 5.30 At present there are many interesting research directions in deep learning that are being explored. This exercise focuses on whether gates in networks learn the same thing independent of the architecture or how the network is trained. On the web there are several copies of Alexnet that have been trained starting from different random initial weights. Select two copies and form a matrix where the columns of the matrix correspond to gates in the first copy of Alexnet and the rows of the matrix correspond to gates of the same level in the second copy. The ij^{th} entry of the matrix is the covariance of the activation of the jth gate in the first copy of Alexnet with the ith gate in the second copy. The covariance is the expected value over all images in the data set.

1. Match the gates in the two copies of the network using a bipartite graph matching algorithm. What is the fraction of matches that have a high covariance?
2. It is possible that there is no good one-to-one matching of gates but that some small set of gates in the first copy of the network learn what some small set of gates in the second copy learn. Explore a clustering technique to match sets of gates and carry out an experiment to do this.

Exercise 5.31

1. Input an image to a deep learning network. Reproduce the image from the activation vector, a_{image}, it produced by inputting a random image and producing an activation vector a_{random}. Then by gradient descent modify the pixels in the random image to minimize the error function $|a_{image} - a_{random}|^2$.
2. Train a deep learning network to produce an image from an activation network.

Exercise 5.32

1. Create and train a simple deep learning network consisting of a convolution level with pooling, a fully connected level, and then softmax. Keep the network small. For input data, use the MNIST data set http://yann.lecun.com/exdb/mnist/ with 28×28 images of digits. Use maybe 20 channels for the convolution level and 100 gates for the fully connected level.
2. Create and train a second network with two fully connected levels, the first level with 200 gates and the second level with 100 gates. How does the accuracy of the second network compare to the first?
3. Train the second network again but this time use the activation vector of the 100 gate level of the first network and train the second network to produce that activation vector and only then train the softmax. How does the accuracy compare to direct training of the second network and the first network?

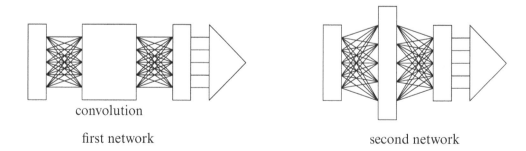

convolution

first network   second network

Exercise 5.33 (Perceptron and Stochastic Gradient Descent) We know the Perceptron Algorithm makes at most $1/\gamma^2$ updates on any sequence of examples that is separable by margin γ (assume all examples have length at most 1). However, it need not find a separator of large margin. If we also want to find a separator of large margin, a natural alternative is to update on any example $\mathbf{x}_i$ such that $l_i(\mathbf{w} \cdot \mathbf{x}_i) < 1$; this is called the *margin perceptron* algorithm.

1. Argue why margin perceptron is equivalent to running stochastic gradient descent with learning rate 1 (on each example, add the negative gradient of the loss function to the current weight vector) on the class of linear predictors with hinge-loss as the loss function.
2. Prove that on any sequence of examples that are separable by margin γ, this algorithm will make at most $3/\gamma^2$ updates.
3. In Part 2 you probably proved that each update increases $|\mathbf{w}|^2$ by at most 3. Use this and your result from Part 2 to conclude that if you have a data set S that is separable by margin γ, and cycle through the data until the margin perceptron algorithm makes no more updates, that it will find a separator of margin at least $\gamma/3$.

Exercise 5.34 Consider running the Perceptron Algorithm in the online model on some sequence of examples S. Let S' be the same set of examples as S but presented in a different order. Does the Perceptron Algorithm necessarily make the same number of mistakes on S as it does on S'? If so, why? If not, show such an S and S' consisting of the same set of examples in a different order where the Perceptron Algorithm makes a different number of mistakes on S' than it does on S.

Exercise 5.35 (**Sleeping Experts and Decision trees**) "Pruning" a Decision Tree Online via Sleeping Experts: Suppose that, as in Exercise 5.14, we are given a decision tree T, but now we are faced with a sequence of examples that arrive online. One interesting way we can make predictions is as follows. For each node v of T (internal node or leaf) create two sleeping experts: one that predicts positive on any example that reaches v and one that predicts negative on any example that reaches v. So, the total number of sleeping experts is equal to the number of nodes of T which is proportional to the number of leaves $L(T)$ of T.

1. Say why any pruning h of T, and any assignment of $\{+, -\}$ labels to the leaves of h, corresponds to a subset of sleeping experts with the property that exactly one sleeping expert in the subset makes a prediction on any given example.
2. Prove that for any sequence S of examples, and any given number of leaves L, if we run the sleeping-experts algorithm using $\epsilon = \sqrt{\frac{L \log(L(T))}{|S|}}$, then the expected error rate of the algorithm on S (the total number of mistakes of the algorithm divided by $|S|$) will be at most $err_S(h_L) + O(\sqrt{\frac{L \log(L(T))}{|S|}})$, where $h_L = \text{argmin}_{h:L(h)=L} \, err_S(h)$ is the pruning of T with L leaves of lowest error on S.
3. In the above question, we assumed L was given. Explain how we can remove this assumption and achieve a bound of $\min_L \left[err_S(h_L) + O(\sqrt{\frac{L \log(L(T))}{|S|}}) \right]$ by instantiating $L(T)$ copies of the above algorithm (one for each value of L) and then combining *these* algorithms using the experts algorithm (in this case, none of them will be sleeping).

Exercise 5.36 (**Boosting**) Consider the boosting algorithm given in Figure 5.11. Suppose hypothesis h_t has error rate β_t on the weighted sample $(S, \mathbf{w})$ for β_t much less than $\frac{1}{2} - \gamma$. Then, after the booster multiples the weight of misclassified examples by α, hypothesis h_t will *still* have error less than $\frac{1}{2} - \gamma$ under the new weights. This means that h_t could be given again to the booster (perhaps for several times in a row). Calculate, as a function of α and β_t, approximately how many times in a row h_t could be given to the booster before its error rate rises to above $\frac{1}{2} - \gamma$. You may assume β_t is much less than $\frac{1}{2} - \gamma$.

Note The AdaBoost boosting algorithm [FS97] can be viewed as performing this experiment internally, multiplying the weight of misclassified examples by $\alpha_t = \frac{1-\beta_t}{\beta_t}$, and then giving h_t a weight proportional to the quantity you computed in its final majority-vote function.

CHAPTER SIX

Algorithms for Massive Data Problems

Streaming, Sketching, and Sampling

6.1. Introduction

This chapter deals with massive data problems where the input data is too large to be stored in random access memory. One model for such problems is the streaming model, where n data items $a_1, a_2, \ldots, a_n$ arrive one at a time. For example, the a_i might be IP addresses being observed by a router on the internet. The goal is to compute some statistics, property, or summary of these data items without using too much memory, much less than n. More specifically, we assume each a_i itself is a b-bit quantity where b is not too large. For example, each a_i might be an integer, $1 \le a_i \le m$, where $m = 2^b$. The goal is to produce some desired output using space polynomial in b and $\log n$; see Figure 6.1.

For example, a very easy problem to solve in the streaming model is to compute the sum of the a_i. If each a_i is an integer between 1 and $m = 2^b$, then the sum of all the a_i is an integer between 1 and mn, and so the number of bits of memory needed to maintain the sum is $O(b + \log n)$. A harder problem, discussed shortly, is computing the number of distinct numbers in the input sequence.

One natural approach for tackling a range of problems in the streaming model is to perform random sampling of the input "on the fly." To introduce the basic flavor of sampling on the fly, consider a stream $a_1, a_2, \ldots, a_n$ from which we are to select an index i with probability proportional to the value of a_i. When we see an element, we do not know the probability with which to select it since the normalizing constant depends on all of the elements including those we have not yet seen. However, the following method works. Let s be the sum of the a_i's seen so far. Maintain s and an index i selected with probability $\frac{a_i}{s}$. Initially $i = 1$ and $s = a_1$. Having seen symbols $a_1, a_2, \ldots, a_j$, s will equal $a_1 + a_2 + \cdots + a_j$ and for i in $\{1, \ldots, j\}$, the selected index will be i with probability $\frac{a_i}{s}$. On seeing a_{j+1}, change the selected index to $j + 1$ with probability $\frac{a_{j+1}}{s + a_{j+1}}$ and otherwise keep the same index as before with probability $1 - \frac{a_{j+1}}{s + a_{j+1}}$. If we change the index to $j + 1$, clearly it was selected with the correct probability. If we keep i as our selection, then it will have been selected with probability

$$\left(1 - \frac{a_{j+1}}{s + a_{j+1}}\right) \frac{a_i}{s} = \frac{s}{s + a_{j+1}} \frac{a_i}{s} = \frac{a_i}{s + a_{j+1}},$$

which is the correct probability for selecting index i. Finally s is updated by adding a_{j+1} to s. This problem comes up in many areas such as sleeping experts where there

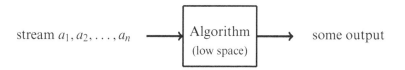

stream $a_1, a_2, \ldots, a_n$ ⟶ Algorithm (low space) ⟶ some output

Figure 6.1: High-level representation of the streaming model.

is a sequence of weights and we want to pick an expert with probability proportional to its weight. The a_i's are the weights and the subscript i denotes the expert.

6.2. Frequency Moments of Data Streams

An important class of problems concerns the frequency moments of data streams. As mentioned above, a data stream $a_1, a_2, \ldots, a_n$ of length n consists of symbols a_i from an alphabet of m possible symbols, which for convenience we denote as $\{1, 2, \ldots, m\}$. Throughout this section, n, m, and a_i will have these meanings and s (for symbol) will denote a generic element of $\{1, 2, \ldots, m\}$. The frequency f_s of the symbol s is the number of occurrences of s in the stream. For a nonnegative integer p, the pth frequency moment of the stream is

$$\sum_{s=1}^{m} f_s^p.$$

Note that the $p = 0$ frequency moment corresponds to the number of distinct symbols occurring in the stream using the convention $0^0 = 0$. The first frequency moment is just n, the length of the string. The second frequency moment, $\sum_s f_s^2$, is useful in computing the variance of the stream, i.e., the average squared difference from the average frequency.

$$\frac{1}{m}\sum_{s=1}^{m}\left(f_s - \frac{n}{m}\right)^2 = \frac{1}{m}\sum_{s=1}^{m}\left(f_s^2 - 2\frac{n}{m}f_s + \left(\frac{n}{m}\right)^2\right) = \left(\frac{1}{m}\sum_{s=1}^{m}f_s^2\right) - \frac{n^2}{m^2}.$$

In the limit as p becomes large, $\left(\sum_{s=1}^{m} f_s^p\right)^{1/p}$ is the frequency of the most frequent element(s).

We will describe sampling-based algorithms to compute these quantities for streaming data shortly. First, a note on the motivation for these problems. The identity and frequency of the most frequent item, or more generally items whose frequency exceeds a given fraction of n, are clearly important in many applications. If the items are packets on a network with source and/or destination addresses, the high-frequency items identify the heavy bandwidth users. If the data consists of purchase records in a supermarket, the high-frequency items are the best-selling items. Determining the number of distinct symbols is the abstract version of determining such things as the number of accounts, web users, or credit card holders. The second moment and variance are useful in networking as well as in database and other applications. Large amounts of network log data are generated by routers that can record the source address, destination address, and the number of packets for all the messages passing through them. This massive data cannot be easily sorted or aggregated into totals for each source/destination. But it is important to know if some popular source–destination pairs have a lot of traffic for which the variance is one natural measure.

6.2.1. Number of Distinct Elements in a Data Stream

Consider a sequence $a_1, a_2, \ldots, a_n$ of n elements, each a_i an integer in the range 1 to m where n and m are very large. Suppose we wish to determine the number of distinct a_i in the sequence. Each a_i might represent a credit card number extracted from a sequence of credit card transactions and we wish to determine how many distinct credit card accounts there are. Note that this is easy to do in $O(m)$ space by just storing a bit-vector that records which elements have been seen so far and which have not. It is also easy to do in $O(n \log m)$ space by storing a list of all distinct elements that have been seen. However, our goal is to use space logarithmic in m and n. We first show that this is impossible using an exact deterministic algorithm. Any deterministic algorithm that determines the number of distinct elements exactly must use at least m bits of memory on some input sequence of length $O(m)$. We then will show how to get around this problem using randomization and approximation.

Lower bound on memory for exact deterministic algorithm. We show that any exact deterministic algorithm must use at least m bits of memory on some sequence of length $m+1$. Suppose we have seen $a_1, \ldots, a_m$, and our algorithm uses less than m bits of memory on all such sequences. There are $2^m - 1$ possible subsets of $\{1, 2, \ldots, m\}$ that the sequence could contain and yet only 2^{m-1} possible states of our algorithm's memory. Therefore, there must be two different subsets S_1 and S_2 that lead to the same memory state. If S_1 and S_2 are of different sizes, then clearly this implies an error for one of the input sequences. On the other hand, if they are the same size and the next element is in S_1 but not S_2, the algorithm will give the same answer in both cases and therefore must give an incorrect answer on at least one of them.

Algorithm for the number of distinct elements. To beat the above lower bound, consider approximating the number of distinct elements. Our algorithm will produce a number that is within a constant factor of the correct answer using randomization and thus a small probability of failure. Suppose the set S of distinct elements was chosen uniformly at random from $\{1, \ldots, m\}$. Let min denote the minimum element in S. What is the expected value of min? If there was one distinct element, then its expected value would be roughly $\frac{m}{2}$. If there were two distinct elements, their expected value would be roughly $\frac{m}{3}$. More generally, for a random set S, the expected value of the minimum is approximately $\frac{m}{|S|+1}$. See Figure 6.2. Solving $min = \frac{m}{|S|+1}$ yields $|S| = \frac{m}{min} - 1$. This suggests keeping track of the minimum element in $O(\log m)$ space and using this equation to give an estimate of $|S|$.

Converting the intuition into an algorithm via hashing. In general, the set S might not have been chosen uniformly at random. If the elements of S were obtained by selecting the $|S|$ smallest elements of $\{1, 2, \ldots, m\}$, the above technique would give a very bad answer. However, we can convert our intuition into an algorithm that works well with high probability on every sequence via hashing. Specifically, we will use a hash function h where

$$h : \{1, 2, \ldots, m\} \rightarrow \{0, 1, 2, \ldots, M - 1\},$$

$|S| + 1$ subsets

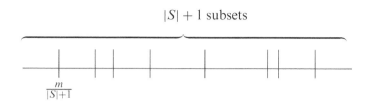

$\dfrac{m}{|S|+1}$

Figure 6.2: Estimating the size of S from the minimum element in S which has value approximately $\frac{m}{|S|+1}$. The elements of S partition the set $\{1, 2, \ldots, m\}$ into $|S| + 1$ subsets each of size approximately $\frac{m}{|S|+1}$.

and then instead of keeping track of the minimum element $a_i \in S$, we will keep track of the minimum *hash value*. The question now is: What properties of a hash function do we need? Since we need to store h, we cannot use a totally random mapping, since that would take too many bits. Luckily, a pairwise independent hash function, which can be stored compactly is sufficient.

We recall the formal definition of pairwise independence below. But first recall that a hash function is always chosen at random from a family of hash functions and phrases like "probability of collision" refer to the probability in the choice of hash function.

2-universal (pairwise independent) hash functions. Various applications use different amounts of randomness. Full randomness for a vector $\mathbf{x} = (x_1, x_2, \ldots x_d)$ where each $x_i \in \{0, 1\}$ would require selecting $\mathbf{x}$ uniformly at random from the set of all 2^d 0,1 vectors. However, if we only need that each x_i be equally likely to be 0 or 1, we can select $\mathbf{x}$ from the set of two vectors $\{(0, 0, \ldots, 0), (1, 1, \ldots, 1)\}$. If in addition, we want each pair of coordinates x_i and x_j to be statistically independent, we need a larger set to chose from which has the property that for each pair i and j, (x_i, x_j) is equally likely to be (0,0), (0,1), (1,0) or (1,1).

A set of hash functions

$$H = \left\{ h \mid h : \{1, 2, \ldots, m\} \to \{0, 1, 2, \ldots, M - 1\} \right\}$$

is *2-universal* or *pairwise independent* if for all x and y in $\{1, 2, \ldots, m\}$ with $x \neq y, h(x)$ and $h(y)$ are each equally likely to be any element of $\{0, 1, 2, \ldots, M - 1\}$ and are statistically independent. It follows that a set of hash functions H is 2-universal if and only if for all x and y in $\{1, 2, \ldots, m\}, x \neq y, h(x)$ and $h(y)$ are each equally likely to be any element of $\{0, 1, 2, \ldots, M - 1\}$, and for all w and z

$$\Prob_{h \sim H}\big(h(x) = w \text{ and } h(y) = z\big) = \frac{1}{M^2}.$$

We now give an example of a 2-universal family of hash functions. Let M be a prime greater than m. For each pair of integers a and b in the range $[0, M - 1]$, define a hash function

$$h_{ab}(x) = ax + b \pmod{M}.$$

To store the hash function h_{ab}, store the two integers a and b. This requires only $O(\log M)$ space. To see that the family is 2-universal note that $h(x) = w$ and $h(y) = z$ if and only if

$$\begin{pmatrix} x & 1 \\ y & 1 \end{pmatrix} \begin{pmatrix} a \\ b \end{pmatrix} = \begin{pmatrix} w \\ z \end{pmatrix} \quad (\text{mod } M).$$

If $x \neq y$, the matrix $\begin{pmatrix} x & 1 \\ y & 1 \end{pmatrix}$ is invertible modulo M.[1] Thus,

$$\begin{pmatrix} a \\ b \end{pmatrix} = \begin{pmatrix} x & 1 \\ y & 1 \end{pmatrix}^{-1} \begin{pmatrix} w \\ z \end{pmatrix} \quad (\text{mod } M)$$

and for each $\binom{w}{z}$ there is a unique $\binom{a}{b}$. Hence,

$$\text{Prob}\big(h(x) = w \text{ and } h(y) = z\big) = \frac{1}{M^2}$$

and H is 2-universal.

Analysis of distinct element counting algorithm. Let $b_1, b_2, \ldots, b_d$ be the distinct values that appear in the input. Select h from the 2-universal family of hash functions H. Then the set $S = \{h(b_1), h(b_2), \ldots, h(b_d)\}$ is a set of d random and pairwise independent values from the set $\{0, 1, 2, \ldots, M - 1\}$. We now show that $\frac{M}{min}$ is a good estimate for d, the number of distinct elements in the input, where $min = min(S)$.

Lemma 6.1 *With probability at least $\frac{2}{3} - \frac{d}{M}$, the estimate of the number of distinct elements satisfies, $\frac{d}{6} \leq \frac{M}{min} \leq 6d$, where min is the smallest element of S. That is, $\frac{M}{6d} \leq min \leq \frac{6M}{d}$.*

Proof The two inequalities we need to show are illustrated in Figure 6.3. First, we show that $\text{Prob}\left(min \leq \frac{M}{6d}\right) \leq \frac{1}{6} + \frac{d}{M}$. This part does not require pairwise independence.

$$\text{Prob}\left(min \leq \frac{M}{6d}\right) = \text{Prob}\left(\exists k, \ h(b_k) \leq \frac{M}{6d}\right)$$

$$\leq \sum_{i=1}^{d} \text{Prob}\left(h(b_i) \leq \frac{M}{6d}\right) \leq d\left(\frac{\lceil \frac{M}{6d} \rceil}{M}\right)$$

$$\leq d\left(\frac{1}{6d} + \frac{1}{M}\right) \leq \frac{1}{6} + \frac{d}{M}.$$

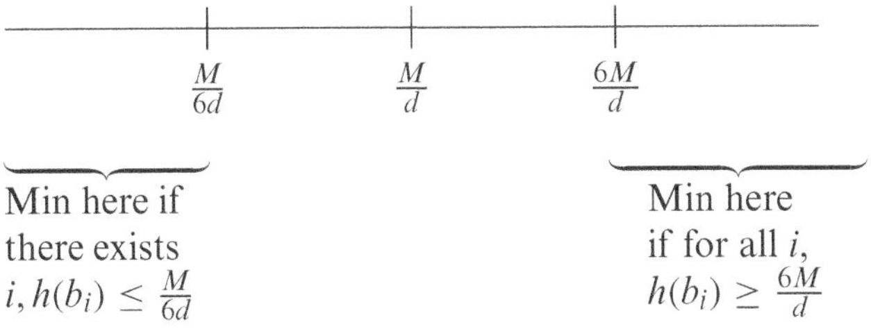

Figure 6.3: Location of the minimum in the distinct counting algorithm.

[1] The primality of M ensures that inverses of elements exist in Z_M^* and $M > m$ ensures that if $x \neq y$, then x and y are not equal mod M.

Next, we show that $\text{Prob}\left(\min \geq \frac{6M}{d}\right) \leq \frac{1}{6}$. This part will use pairwise independence. First,

$$\text{Prob}\left(\min \geq \frac{6M}{d}\right) = \text{Prob}\left(\forall k,\ h\left(b_k\right) \geq \frac{6M}{d}\right).$$

For $i = 1, 2, \ldots, d$, define the indicator variable

$$y_i = \begin{cases} 0 & \text{if } h\left(b_i\right) \geq \frac{6M}{d} \\ 1 & \text{otherwise} \end{cases}$$

and let

$$y = \sum_{i=1}^{d} y_i.$$

We want to show that $\text{Prob}(y = 0)$ is small. Now $\text{Prob}\left(y_i = 1\right) \geq \frac{6}{d}, E\left(y_i\right) \geq \frac{6}{d}$, and $E\left(y\right) \geq 6$. For two-way independent random variables, the variance of their sum is the sum of their variances. So $\text{Var}\left(y\right) = d\text{Var}\left(y_1\right)$. Further, since y_1 is 0 or 1, $\text{Var}(y_1) = E\left[\left(y_1 - E(y_1)\right)^2\right] = E(y_1^2) - E^2(y_1) = E(y_1) - E^2(y_1) \leq E\left(y_1\right)$. Thus $\text{Var}(y) \leq E\left(y\right)$. By the Chebyshev inequality,

$$\text{Prob}\left(\min \geq \frac{6M}{d}\right) = \text{Prob}\left(\forall k\ h\left(b_k\right) \geq \frac{6M}{d}\right)$$
$$= \text{Prob}\left(y = 0\right)$$
$$\leq \text{Prob}\left(|y - E\left(y\right)| \geq E\left(y\right)\right)$$
$$\leq \frac{\text{Var}(y)}{E^2\left(y\right)} \leq \frac{1}{E\left(y\right)} \leq \frac{1}{6}.$$

Since $\frac{M}{\min} \geq 6d$ with probability at most $\frac{1}{6} + \frac{d}{M}$ and $\frac{M}{\min} \leq \frac{d}{6}$ with probability at most $\frac{1}{6}, \frac{d}{6} \leq \frac{M}{\min} \leq 6d$ with probability at least $\frac{2}{3} - \frac{d}{M}$. ∎

6.2.2. Number of Occurrences of a Given Element

To count the number of occurrences of a given element in a stream requires at most $\log n$ space where n is the length of the stream. Clearly, for any length stream that occurs in practice, one can afford $\log n$ space. For this reason, the following material may never be used in practice, but the technique is interesting and may give insight into how to solve some other problem.

Consider a string of 0's and 1's of length n in which we wish to count the number of occurrences of 1's. Clearly with $\log n$ bits of memory we could keep track of the exact number of 1's. However, the number can be approximated with only $\log \log n$ bits.

Let m be the number of 1's that occur in the sequence. Keep a value k such that 2^k is approximately the number m of occurrences. Storing k requires only $\log \log n$ bits of memory. The algorithm works as follows. Start with $k = 0$. For each occurrence of a 1, add one to k with probability $1/2^k$. At the end of the string, the quantity $2^k - 1$ is the estimate of m. To obtain a coin that comes down heads with probability $1/2^k$, flip a fair coin, one that comes down heads with probability $1/2, k$ times and report heads if the fair coin comes down heads in all k flips.

Given k, on average it will take 2^k ones before k is incremented. Thus, the expected number of 1's to produce the current value of k is $1 + 2 + 4 + \cdots + 2^{k-1} = 2^k - 1$.

6.2.3. Frequent Elements

The majority and frequent algorithms. First consider the very simple problem of n people voting. There are m candidates, $\{1, 2, \ldots, m\}$. We want to determine if one candidate gets a majority vote and if so who. Formally, we are given a stream of integers $a_1, a_2, \ldots, a_n$, each a_i belonging to $\{1, 2, \ldots, m\}$, and want to determine whether there is some $s \in \{1, 2, \ldots, m\}$ that occurs more than $n/2$ times and, if so, which s. It is easy to see that to solve the problem exactly on read-once streaming data with a deterministic algorithm requires $\Omega(\min(n, m))$ space. Suppose n is even and the last $n/2$ items are identical. Suppose also that after reading the first $n/2$ items, there are two different sets of elements that result in the same content of our memory. In that case, a mistake would occur if the second half of the stream consists solely of an element that is in one set but not in the other. If $n/2 \geq m$ then there are at least $2^m - 1$ possible subsets of the first $n/2$ elements. If $n/2 \leq m$ then there are $\sum_{i=1}^{n/2} \binom{m}{i}$ subsets. By the above argument, the number of bits of memory must be at least the base 2 logarithm of the number of subsets, which is $\Omega(\min(m, n))$.

Surprisingly, we can bypass the above lower bound by slightly weakening our goal. Again let's require that if some element appears more than $n/2$ times, then we must output it. But now, let us say that if no element appears more than $n/2$ times, then our algorithm may output whatever it wants, rather than requiring that it output "no." That is, there may be "false positives", but no "false negatives."

Majority Algorithm

Store a_1 and initialize a counter to one. For each subsequent a_i, if a_i is the same as the currently stored item, increment the counter by one. If it differs, decrement the counter by one provided the counter is non-zero. If the counter is zero, then store a_i and set the counter to one.

To analyze the algorithm, it is convenient to view the decrement counter step as "eliminating" two items, the new one and the one that caused the last increment in the counter. It is easy to see that if there is a majority element s, it must be stored at the end. If not, each occurrence of s was eliminated; but each such elimination also causes another item to be eliminated. Thus, for a majority item not to be stored at the end, more than n items must have eliminated, a contradiction.

Next we modify the above algorithm so that not just the majority, but also items with frequency above some threshold are detected. More specifically, the algorithm below finds the frequency (number of occurrences) of each element of $\{1, 2, \ldots, m\}$ to within an additive term of $\frac{n}{k+1}$. That is, for each symbol s, the algorithm produces a value $\tilde{f}_s$ in $[f_s - \frac{n}{k+1}, f_s]$, where f_s is the true number of occurrences of symbol s in the sequence. It will do so using $O(k \log n + k \log m)$ space by keeping k counters instead of just one counter.

Algorithm Frequent

Maintain a list of items being counted. Initially the list is empty. For each item, if it is the same as some item on the list, increment its counter by one. If it differs from all the items on the list, then if there are less than k items on the list, add the item to the list with its counter set to one. If there are already k items on the list, decrement each of the current counters by one. Delete an element from the list if its count becomes zero.

Theorem 6.2 *At the end of Algorithm Frequent, for each $s \in \{1, 2, \ldots, m\}$, if it is on the list, then its counter $\tilde{f}_s$ satisfies $\tilde{f}_s \in [f_s - \frac{n}{k+1}, f_s]$. If some s does not occur on the list, its counter is zero and the theorem asserts that $f_s \leq \frac{n}{k+1}$.*

Proof The fact that $\tilde{f}_s \leq f_s$ is immediate. To show $\tilde{f}_s \geq f_s - \frac{n}{k+1}$, view each decrement counter step as eliminating some items. An item is eliminated if the current a_i being read is not on the list and there are already k symbols different from it on the list; in this case, a_i and k other distinct symbols are simultaneously eliminated. Thus, the elimination of each occurrence of an $s \in \{1, 2, \ldots, m\}$ is really the elimination of $k + 1$ items corresponding to distinct symbols. Thus, no more than $n/(k+1)$ occurrences of any symbol can be eliminated. It is clear that if an item is not eliminated, then it must still be on the list at the end. This proves the theorem. ■

Theorem 6.2 implies that we can compute the true frequency of every $s \in \{1, 2, \ldots, m\}$ to within an additive term of $\frac{n}{k+1}$.

6.2.4. The Second Moment

This section focuses on computing the second moment of a stream with symbols from $\{1, 2, \ldots, m\}$. Let f_s denote the number of occurrences of the symbol s in the stream, and recall that the second moment of the stream is given by $\sum_{s=1}^{m} f_s^2$. To calculate the second moment, for each symbol s, $1 \leq s \leq m$, independently set a random variable x_s to ± 1 with probability $1/2$. In particular, think of x_s as the output of a random hash function $h(s)$ whose range is just the two buckets $\{-1, 1\}$. For now, think of h as a fully independent hash function. Maintain a sum by adding x_s to the sum each time the symbol s occurs in the stream. At the end of the stream, the sum will equal $\sum_{s=1}^{m} x_s f_s$. The expected value of the sum will be zero where the expectation is over the choice of the ± 1 value for the x_s.

$$E\left(\sum_{s=1}^{m} x_s f_s\right) = 0$$

Although the expected value of the sum is zero, its actual value is a random variable and the expected value of the square of the sum is given by

$$E\left(\sum_{s=1}^{m} x_s f_s\right)^2 = E\left(\sum_{s=1}^{m} x_s^2 f_s^2\right) + 2E\left(\sum_{s \neq t} x_s x_t f_s f_t\right) = \sum_{s=1}^{m} f_s^2.$$

The last equality follows since $E(x_s x_t) = E(x_s)E(x_t) = 0$ for $s \neq t$, using pairwise independence of the random variables. Thus,

$$a = \left(\sum_{s=1}^{m} x_s f_s\right)^2$$

is an unbiased estimator of $\sum_{s=1}^{m} f_s^2$ in that it has the correct expectation. Note that at this point we could use Markov's inequality to state that $\text{Prob}(a \geq 3\sum_{s=1}^{m} f_s^2) \leq 1/3$, but we want to get a tighter guarantee. To do so, consider the second moment of a:

$$E(a^2) = E\left(\sum_{s=1}^{m} x_s f_s\right)^4 = E\left(\sum_{1 \le s,t,u,v \le m} x_s x_t x_u x_v f_s f_t f_u f_v\right).$$

The last equality is by expansion. Assume that the random variables x_s are 4-wise independent, or equivalently that they are produced by a 4-wise independent hash function. Then, since the x_s are independent in the last sum, if any one of s, u, t, or v is distinct from the others, then the expectation of the term is zero. Thus, we need to deal only with terms of the form $x_s^2 x_t^2$ for $t \ne s$ and terms of the form x_s^4.

Each term in the above sum has four indices, s, t, u, v, and there are $\binom{4}{2}$ ways of choosing two indices that have the same x value. Thus,

$$E(a^2) \le \binom{4}{2} E\left(\sum_{s=1}^{m}\sum_{t=s+1}^{m} x_s^2 x_t^2 f_s^2 f_t^2\right) + E\left(\sum_{s=1}^{m} x_s^4 f_s^4\right)$$

$$= 6 \sum_{s=1}^{m}\sum_{t=s+1}^{m} f_s^2 f_t^2 + \sum_{s=1}^{m} f_s^4$$

$$\le 3 \left(\sum_{s=1}^{m} f_s^2\right)^2 = 3E^2(a).$$

Therefore, $Var(a) = E(a^2) - E^2(a) \le 2E^2(a)$.

Since the variance is comparable to the square of the expectation, repeating the process several times and taking the average, gives high accuracy with high probability.

Theorem 6.3 *The average x of $r = \frac{2}{\varepsilon^2 \delta}$ estimates $a_1, \ldots, a_r$ using independent sets of 4-way independent random variables is*

$$Prob\left(|x - E(x)| > \varepsilon E(x)\right) < \frac{Var(x)}{\epsilon^2 E^2(x)} \le \delta.$$

Proof The proof follows from the fact that taking the average of r independent repetitions reduces variance by a factor of r, so that $Var(x) \le \delta \varepsilon^2 E^2(x)$, and then applying Chebyshev's inequality. ∎

It remains to show that we can implement the desired 4-way independent random variables using $O(\log m)$ space. We earlier gave a construction for a pairwise-independent set of hash functions; now we need 4-wise independence, though only into a range of $\{-1, 1\}$. Below we present one such construction.

Error-correcting codes, polynomial interpolation and limited-way independence. Consider the problem of generating a random m-dimensional vector $\mathbf{x}$ of ± 1's so that any four coordinates are mutually independent. Such an m-dimensional vector may be generated from a truly random "seed" of only $O(\log m)$ mutually independent bits. Thus, we need only store the $O(\log m)$ bits and can generate any of the m coordinates when needed. For any k, there is a finite field F with exactly 2^k elements, each of which can be represented with k bits and arithmetic operations in the field can be carried out in $O(k^2)$ time. Here, k is the ceiling of $\log_2 m$. A basic fact about polynomial interpolation is that a polynomial of degree at most three is uniquely determined by its value over any field F at four points. More precisely, for any four distinct points a_1, a_2, a_3, a_4 in F and any four possibly not distinct values b_1, b_2, b_3, b_4 in F, there is a unique polynomial $f(x) = f_0 + f_1 x + f_2 x^2 + f_3 x^3$ of degree at most three, so that with computations done over F, $f(a_i) = b_i$ $1 \leq i \leq 4$.

The definition of the pseudo-random ± 1 vector $\mathbf{x}$ with 4-way independence is simple. Choose four elements f_0, f_1, f_2, f_3 at random from F and form the polynomial $f(s) = f_0 + f_1 s + f_2 s^2 + f_3 s^3$. This polynomial represents $\mathbf{x}$ as follows. For $s = 1$, $2, \ldots, m$, x_s is the leading bit of the k-bit representation of $f(s)$.[2] Thus, the m-dimensional vector $\mathbf{x}$ requires only $O(k)$ bits where $k = \lceil \log m \rceil$.

Lemma 6.4 *The $\mathbf{x}$ defined above has 4-way independence.*

Proof Assume that the elements of F are represented in binary using ± 1 instead of the traditional 0 and 1. Let s, t, u, and v be any four coordinates of $\mathbf{x}$ and let α, β, γ, and δ have values in ± 1. There are exactly 2^{k-1} elements of F whose leading bit is α and similarly for β, γ, and δ. So, there are exactly $2^{4(k-1)}$ 4-tuples of elements b_1, b_2, b_3, and b_4 in F so that the leading bit of b_1 is α, the leading bit of b_2 is β, the leading bit of b_3 is γ, and the leading bit of b_4 is δ. For each such b_1, b_2, b_3, and b_4, there is precisely one polynomial f so that $f(s) = b_1, f(t) = b_2, f(u) = b_3$, and $f(v) = b_4$. The probability that $x_s = \alpha, x_t = \beta, x_u = \gamma$, and $x_v = \delta$ is precisely

$$\frac{2^{4(k-1)}}{\text{total number of } f} = \frac{2^{4(k-1)}}{2^{4k}} = \frac{1}{16}.$$

Four-way independence follows since $\text{Prob}(x_s = \alpha) = \text{Prob}(x_t = \beta) = \text{Prob}(x_u = \gamma) = \text{Prob}(x_v = \delta) = 1/2$, and thus

$$\text{Prob}(x_s = \alpha)\text{Prob}(x_t = \beta)\text{Prob}(x_u = \gamma)\text{Prob}(x_v = \delta)$$
$$= \text{Prob}(x_s = \alpha, x_t = \beta, x_u = \gamma \text{ and } x_s = \delta) \quad \blacksquare$$

Lemma 6.4 describes how to get one vector $\mathbf{x}$ with 4-way independence. However, we need $r = O(1/\varepsilon^2)$ mutually independent vectors. Choose r independent polynomials at the outset.

To implement the algorithm with low space, store only the polynomials in memory. This requires $4k = O(\log m)$ bits per polynomial for a total of $O(\frac{\log m}{\varepsilon^2})$ bits. When a symbol s in the stream is read, compute each polynomial at s to obtain the value for the corresponding value of the x_s and update the running sums. x_s is just the leading bit of the value of the polynomial evaluated at s. This calculation requires $O(\log m)$ time. Thus, we repeatedly compute the x_s from the "seeds," namely the coefficients of the polynomials.

This idea of polynomial interpolation is also used in other contexts. Error-correcting codes are an important example. To transmit n bits over a channel which may introduce noise, one can introduce redundancy into the transmission so that some channel errors can be corrected. A simple way to do this is to view the n bits to be transmitted as coefficients of a polynomial $f(x)$ of degree $n - 1$. Now transmit f evaluated at points $1, 2, 3, \ldots, n + m$. At the receiving end, any n correct values will

---

[2] Here we have numbered the elements of the field F $s = 1, 2, \ldots, m$.

suffice to reconstruct the polynomial and the true message. So up to m errors can be tolerated. But even if the number of errors is at most m, it is not a simple matter to know which values are corrupted. We do not elaborate on this here.

6.3. Matrix Algorithms Using Sampling

We now move from the streaming model to a model where the input is stored in memory, but because the input is so large, one would like to produce a much smaller approximation to it, or perform an approximate computation on it in low space. For instance, the input might be stored in a large slow memory and we would like a small "sketch" that can be stored in smaller fast memory and yet retain the important properties of the original input. In fact, one can view a number of results from the chapter on machine learning in this way: we have a large population, and we want to take a small sample, perform some optimization on the sample, and then argue that the optimum solution on the sample will be approximately optimal over the whole population. In the chapter on machine learning, our sample consisted of independent random draws from the overall population or data distribution. Here we will be looking at matrix algorithms, and to achieve errors that are small compared to the Frobenius norm of the matrix rather than compared to the total number of entries, we will perform non-uniform sampling.

Algorithms for matrix problems like matrix multiplication, low-rank approximations, singular value decomposition, compressed representations of matrices, linear regression, etc. are widely used, but some require $O(n^3)$ time for $n \times n$ matrices.

The natural alternative to working on the whole input matrix is to pick a random sub-matrix and compute with that. Here, we will pick a subset of columns or rows of the input matrix. If the sample size s is the number of columns we are willing to work with, we will do s independent identical trials. In each trial, we select a column of the matrix. All that we have to decide is what the probability of picking each column is. Sampling uniformly at random is one option, but it is not always good if we want our error to be a small fraction of the Frobenius norm of the matrix. For example, suppose the input matrix has all entries in the range $[-1, 1]$ but most columns are close to the zero vector with only a few significant columns. Then, uniformly sampling a small number of columns is unlikely to pick up any of the significant columns and essentially will approximate the original matrix with the all-zeroes matrix.[3]

We will see that the "optimal" probabilities are proportional to the squared length of columns. This is referred to as length squared sampling, and since its first discovery in the mid-1990s, it has been proved to have several desirable properties that we will explore. Note that all sampling we will discuss here is done with replacement.

Two general notes on this approach:

(i) We will prove error bounds that hold for all input matrices. Our algorithms are randomized, i.e., use a random number generator, so the error bounds are

---

[3]There are, on the other hand, many positive statements one *can* make about uniform sampling. For example, suppose the columns of A are data points in an m-dimensional space (one dimension per row). Fix any k-dimensional subspace, such as the subspace spanned by the k top singular vectors. If we randomly sample $\tilde{O}(k/\epsilon^2)$ columns uniformly, by the VC-dimension bounds given in Chapter 6, with high probability for every vector $\mathbf{v}$ in the k-dimensional space and every threshold τ, the fraction of the sampled columns $\mathbf{a}$ that satisfy $\mathbf{v}^T \mathbf{a} \geq \tau$ will be within $\pm\epsilon$ of the fraction of the columns $\mathbf{a}$ in the overall matrix A satisfying $\mathbf{v}^T \mathbf{a} \geq \tau$.

random variables. The bounds are on the expected error or tail probability bounds on large errors and apply to any matrix. Note that this contrasts with the situation where we have a stochastic model of the input matrix and only assert error bounds for "most" matrices drawn from the probability distribution of the stochastic model. A mnemonic is: our algorithms can toss coins, but our data does not toss coins. A reason for proving error bounds for any matrix is that in real problems, like the analysis of the web hypertext link matrix or the patient-genome expression matrix, it is the one matrix the user is interested in, not a random matrix. In general, we focus on general algorithms and theorems, not specific applications.

(ii) There is "no free lunch." Since we only work on a small random sample and not on the whole input matrix, our error bounds will not be good for certain matrices. For example, if the input matrix is the identity, it is intuitively clear that picking a few random columns will miss the other directions.

To the Reader: Why aren't (i) and (ii) mutually contradictory?

6.3.1. Matrix Multiplication Using Sampling

Suppose A is an $m \times n$ matrix and B is an $n \times p$ matrix and the product AB is desired. We show how to use sampling to get an approximate product faster than the traditional multiplication. Let $A(:, k)$ denote the kth column of A. $A(:, k)$ is a $m \times 1$ matrix. Let $B(k, :)$ be the kth row of B. $B(k, :)$ is a $1 \times n$ matrix. It is easy to see that

$$AB = \sum_{k=1}^{n} A(:, k) B(k, :).$$

Note that for each value of k, $A(:, k)B(k, :)$ is an $m \times p$ matrix each element of which is a single product of elements of A and B. An obvious use of sampling suggests itself. Sample some values for k and compute $A(:, k) B(k, :)$ for the sampled k's and use their suitably scaled sum as the estimate of AB. It turns out that nonuniform sampling probabilities are useful. Define a random variable z that takes on values in $\{1, 2, \ldots, n\}$. Let p_k denote the probability that z assumes the value k. We will solve for a good choice of probabilities later, but for now just consider the p_k as nonnegative numbers that sum to one. Define an associated random matrix variable that has value

$$X = \frac{1}{p_k} A(:, k) B(k, :) \tag{6.1}$$

with probability p_k. Let $E(X)$ denote the entry-wise expectation:

$$E(X) = \sum_{k=1}^{n} \text{Prob}(z = k) \frac{1}{p_k} A(:, k) B(k, :) = \sum_{k=1}^{n} A(:, k) B(k, :) = AB.$$

This explains the scaling by $\frac{1}{p_k}$ in X. In particular, X is a matrix-valued random variable each of whose components is correct in expectation. We will be interested in

$$E\left(||AB - X||_F^2\right).$$

This can be viewed as the variance of X, defined as the sum of the variances of all its entries:

$$\text{Var}(X) = \sum_{i=1}^{m}\sum_{j=1}^{p}\text{Var}\left(x_{ij}\right) = \sum_{ij}E\left(x_{ij}^2\right) - E\left(x_{ij}\right)^2 = \left(\sum_{ij}\sum_{k}p_k\frac{1}{p_k^2}a_{ik}^2 b_{kj}^2\right) - \|AB\|_F^2.$$

We want to choose p_k to minimize this quantity, and notice that we can ignore the $\|AB\|_F^2$ term, since it doesn't depend on the p_k's at all. We can now simplify by exchanging the order of summations to get

$$\sum_{ij}\sum_{k}p_k\frac{1}{p_k^2}a_{ik}^2 b_{kj}^2 = \sum_{k}\frac{1}{p_k}\left(\sum_{i}a_{ik}^2\right)\left(\sum_{j}b_{kj}^2\right) = \sum_{k}\frac{1}{p_k}\left|A\left(:,k\right)\right|^2\left|B\left(k,:\right)\right|^2.$$

What is the best choice of p_k to minimize this sum? It can be seen by calculus[4] that the minimizing p_k are proportional to $|A(:,k)||B(k,:)|$. In the important special case when $B = A^T$, pick columns of A with probabilities proportional to the squared length of the columns. Even in the general case when B is not A^T, doing so simplifies the bounds. This sampling is called *length squared sampling*. If p_k is proportional to $|A\left(:,k\right)|^2$, i.e, $p_k = \frac{|A(:,k)|^2}{\|A\|_F^2}$, then

$$E\left(\|AB - X\|_F^2\right) = \text{Var}(X) \leq \|A\|_F^2 \sum_{k}|B\left(k,:\right)|^2 = \|A\|_F^2\|B\|_F^2.$$

To reduce the variance, we can do s independent trials. Each trial $i, i = 1, 2, \ldots, s$ yields a matrix X_i as in (6.1). We take $\frac{1}{s}\sum_{i=1}^{s}X_i$ as our estimate of AB. Since the variance of a sum of independent random variables is the sum of variances, the variance of $\frac{1}{s}\sum_{i=1}^{s}X_i$ is $\frac{1}{s}\text{Var}(X)$ and so is at most $\frac{1}{s}\|A\|_F^2\|B\|_F^2$. Let $k_1, \ldots, k_s$ be the k's chosen in each trial. Expanding this, gives:

$$\frac{1}{s}\sum_{i=1}^{s}X_i = \frac{1}{s}\left(\frac{A\left(:,k_1\right)B\left(k_1,:\right)}{p_{k_1}} + \frac{A\left(:,k_2\right)B\left(k_2,:\right)}{p_{k_2}} + \cdots + \frac{A\left(:,k_s\right)B\left(k_s,:\right)}{p_{k_s}}\right).$$

$$(6.2)$$

We will find it convieneint to write this as the product of an $m \times s$ matrix with a $s \times p$ matrix as follows: Let C be the $m \times s$ matrix consisting of the following columns that are scaled versions of the chosen columns of A:

$$\frac{A(:,k_1)}{\sqrt{sp_{k_1}}}, \frac{A(:,k_2)}{\sqrt{sp_{k_2}}}, \ldots \frac{A(:,k_s)}{\sqrt{sp_{k_s}}}.$$

Note that the scaling has a nice property, which the reader can verify:

$$E\left(CC^T\right) = AA^T.$$

$$(6.3)$$

Define R to be the $s \times p$ matrix with the corresponding rows of B similarly scaled, namely R has rows

$$\frac{B(k_1,:)}{\sqrt{sp_{k_1}}}, \frac{B(k_2,:)}{\sqrt{sp_{k_2}}}, \ldots \frac{B(k_s,:)}{\sqrt{sp_{k_s}}}.$$

---

[4]By taking derivatives, for any set of nonnegative numbers c_k, $\sum_k \frac{c_k}{p_k}$ is minimized with p_k proportional to $\sqrt{c_k}$.

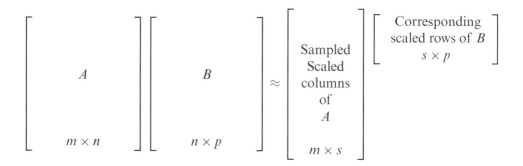

Figure 6.4: Approximate Matrix Multiplication using sampling.

The reader may verify that

$$E\left(R^T R\right) = B^T B. \tag{6.4}$$

From (6.2), we see that $\frac{1}{s}\sum_{i=1}^{s} X_i = CR$. This is represented in Figure 6.4. We summarize our discussion in Theorem 6.5.

Theorem 6.5 *Suppose A is an $m \times n$ matrix and B is an $n \times p$ matrix. The product AB can be estimated by CR, where C is an $m \times s$ matrix consisting of s columns of A picked according to length-squared distribution and scaled to satisfy (6.3) and R is the $s \times p$ matrix consisting of the corresponding rows of B scaled to satisfy (6.4). The error is bounded by:*

$$E\left(||AB - CR||_F^2\right) \le \frac{||A||_F^2 \, ||B||_F^2}{s}.$$

Thus, to ensure $E\left(||AB - CR||_F^2\right) \le \varepsilon^2 ||A||_F^2 ||B||_F^2$, it suffices to make s greater than or equal to $1/\varepsilon^2$. If ε is $\Omega(1)$, so $s \in O(1)$, then the multiplication CR can be carried out in time $O(mp)$.

When is this error bound good and when is it not? Let's focus on the case that $B = A^T$ so we have just one matrix to consider. If A is the identity matrix, then the guarantee is not very good. In this case, $||AA^T||_F^2 = n$, but the right-hand side of the inequality is $\frac{n^2}{s}$. So we would need $s > n$ for the bound to be any better than approximating the product with the zero matrix.

More generally, the trivial estimate of the all-zero matrix for AA^T makes an error in Frobenius norm of $||AA^T||_F$. What s do we need to ensure that the error is at most this? If $\sigma_1, \sigma_2, \dots$ are the singular values of A, then the singular values of AA^T are $\sigma_1^2, \sigma_2^2, \dots$ and

$$||AA^T||_F^2 = \sum_t \sigma_t^4 \quad \text{and} \quad ||A||_F^2 = \sum_t \sigma_t^2.$$

So from Theorem 6.5, $E(||AA^T - CR||_F^2) \le ||AA^T||_F^2$ provided

$$s \ge \frac{(\sigma_1^2 + \sigma_2^2 + \cdots)^2}{\sigma_1^4 + \sigma_2^4 + \cdots}.$$

If rank$(A) = r$, then there are r non-zero σ_t and the best general upper bound on the ratio $\frac{(\sigma_1^2 + \sigma_2^2 + \cdots)^2}{\sigma_1^4 + \sigma_2^4 + \cdots}$ is r, so in general, s needs to be at least r. If A is full rank, this means sampling will not gain us anything over taking the whole matrix!

However, if there is a constant c and a small integer p such that

$$\sigma_1^2 + \sigma_2^2 + \cdots + \sigma_p^2 \geq c(\sigma_1^2 + \sigma_2^2 + \cdots + \sigma_r^2), \tag{6.5}$$

then,

$$\frac{(\sigma_1^2 + \sigma_2^2 + \cdots)^2}{\sigma_1^4 + \sigma_2^4 + \cdots} \leq c^2 \frac{(\sigma_1^2 + \sigma_2^2 + \cdots + \sigma_p^2)^2}{\sigma_1^4 + \sigma_2^4 + \cdots + \sigma_p^2} \leq c^2 p,$$

and so $s \geq c^2 p$ gives us a better estimate than the zero matrix. Increasing s by a factor decreases the error by the same factor. Condition 6.5 is indeed the hypothesis of the subject of Principal Component Analysis (PCA), and there are many situations when the data matrix does satisfy the condition and sampling algorithms are useful.

6.3.2. Implementing Length Squared Sampling in Two Passes

Traditional matrix algorithms often assume that the input matrix is in random access memory (RAM) and so any particular entry of the matrix can be accessed in unit time. For massive matrices, RAM may be too small to hold the entire matrix, but may be able to hold and compute with the sampled columns and rows.

Consider a high-level model where the input matrix or matrices have to be read from external memory using one pass in which one can read sequentially all entries of the matrix and sample.

It is easy to see that two passes suffice to draw a sample of columns of A according to length squared probabilities, even if the matrix is not in row-order or column-order and entries are presented as a linked list. In the first pass, compute the length squared of each column and store this information in RAM. The lengths squared can be computed as running sums. Then, use a random number generator in RAM to determine according to length squared probability the columns to be sampled. Then, make a second pass picking the columns to be sampled.

If the matrix is already presented in external memory in column-order, then one pass will do. The idea is to use the primitive in Section 6.1: given a read-once stream of positive numbers $a_1, a_2, \ldots, a_n$, at the end have an $i \in \{1, 2, \ldots, n\}$ such that the probability that i was chosen is $\frac{a_i}{\sum_{j=1}^n a_j}$. Filling in the specifics is left as an exercise for the reader.

6.3.3. Sketch of a Large Matrix

The main result of this section is that for any matrix, a sample of columns and rows, each picked according to length squared distribution provides a good sketch of the matrix. Let A be an $m \times n$ matrix. Pick s columns of A according to length squared distribution. Let C be the $m \times s$ matrix containing the picked columns scaled so as to satisy (6.3), i.e., if $A(:, k)$ is picked, it is scaled by $1/\sqrt{sp_k}$. Similarly, pick r rows of A according to length squared distribution on the rows of A. Let R be the $r \times n$ matrix of the picked rows, scaled as follows: If row k of A is picked, it is scaled by

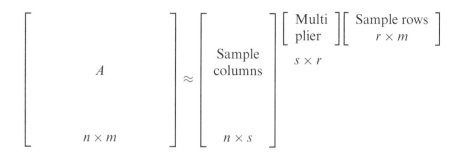

Figure 6.5: Schematic diagram of the approximation of A by a sample of s columns and r rows.

$1/\sqrt{rp_k}$. We then have $E(R^T R) = A^T A$. From C and R, one can find a matrix U so that $A \approx CUR$. The schematic diagram is given in Figure 6.5.

One may recall that the top k singular vectors of the SVD of A give a similar picture; however, the SVD takes more time to compute, requires all of A to be stored in RAM, and does not have the property that the rows and columns are directly from A. The last property, that the approximation involves actual rows/columns of the matrix rather than linear combinations, is called an *interpolative approximation* and is useful in many contexts. On the other hand, the SVD yields the best 2-norm approximation. Error bounds for the approximation CUR are weaker.

We briefly touch on two motivations for such a sketch. Suppose A is the document-term matrix of a large collection of documents. We are to "read" the collection at the outset and store a sketch so that later, when a query represented by a vector with one entry per term arrives, we can find its similarity to each document in the collection. Similarity is defined by the dot product. In Figure 6.5 it is clear that the matrix-vector product of a query with the right-hand side can be done in time $O(ns+sr+rm)$, which would be linear in n and m if s and r are $O(1)$. To bound errors for this process, we need to show that the difference between A and the sketch of A has small 2-norm. Recall that the 2-norm $||A||_2$ of a matrix A is $\max_{|\mathbf{x}|=1} |A\mathbf{x}|$. The fact that the sketch is an interpolative approximation means that our approximation essentially consists a subset of documents and a subset of terms, which may be thought of as a representative set of documents and terms. Additionally, if A is sparse in its rows and columns, each document contains only a small fraction of the terms and each term is in only a small fraction of the documents, then this sparsity property will be preserved in C and R, unlike with SVD.

A second motivation comes from analyzing gene microarray data. Here, A is a matrix in which each row is a gene and each column is a condition. Entry (i,j) indicates the extent to which gene i is expressed in condition j. In this context, a CUR decomposition provides a sketch of the matrix A in which rows and columns correspond to actual genes and conditions, respectively. This can often be easier for biologists to interpret than a singular value decomposition in which rows and columns would be linear combinations of the genes and conditions.

It remains now to describe how to find U from C and R. There is a $n \times n$ matrix P of the form $P = QR$ that acts as the identity on the space spanned by the rows of R and zeros out all vectors orthogonal to this space. We state this now and postpone the proof.

Lemma 6.6 *If RR^T is invertible, then $P = R^T(RR^T)^{-1}R$ has the following properties:*

(i) *It acts as the identity matrix on the row space of R. I.e., $P\mathbf{x} = \mathbf{x}$ for every vector $\mathbf{x}$ of the form $\mathbf{x} = R^T\mathbf{y}$ (this defines the row space of R). Furthermore,*

(ii) *if $\mathbf{x}$ is orthogonal to the row space of R, then $P\mathbf{x} = \mathbf{0}$.*

If RR^T is not invertible, let rank $(RR^T) = r$ and $RR^T = \sum_{t=1}^{r} \sigma_t \mathbf{u_t}\mathbf{v_t}^T$ be the SVD of RR^T. Then,

$$P = R^T \left(\sum_{t=1}^{r} \frac{1}{\sigma_t^2} \mathbf{u_t}\mathbf{v_t}^T \right) R$$

satisfies (i) and (ii).

We begin with some intuition. In particular, we first present a simpler idea that does not work, but that motivates an idea that does. Write A as AI, where I is the $n \times n$ identity matrix. Approximate the product AI using the algorithm of Theorem 6.5, i.e., by sampling s columns of A according to a length squared distribution. Then, as in the last section, write $AI \approx CW$, where W consists of a scaled version of the s rows of I corresponding to the s columns of A that were picked. Theorem 6.5 bounds the error $||A - CW||_F^2$ by $||A||_F^2||I||_F^2/s = \frac{n}{s}||A||_F^2$. But we would like the error to be a small fraction of $||A||_F^2$, which would require $s \geq n$, which clearly is of no use, since this would pick as many or more columns than the whole of A.

Let's use the identity-like matrix P instead of I in the above discussion. Using the fact that R is picked according to length squared sampling, we will show the following proposition later.

Proposition 6.7 *$A \approx AP$ and the error $E(||A - AP||_2^2)$ is at most $\frac{1}{\sqrt{r}}||A||_F^2$.*

We then use Theorem 6.5 to argue that instead of doing the multiplication AP, we can use the sampled columns of A and the corresponding rows of P. The s sampled columns of A form C. We have to take the corresponding s rows of $P = R^T(RR^T)^{-1}R$, which is the same as taking the corresponding s rows of R^T, and multiplying this by $(RR^T)^{-1}R$. It is easy to check that this leads to an expression of the form CUR. Further, by Theorem 6.5, the error is bounded by

$$E\left(||AP - CUR||_2^2\right) \leq E\left(||AP - CUR||_F^2\right) \leq \frac{||A||_F^2||P||_F^2}{s} \leq \frac{r}{s}||A||_F^2, \qquad (6.6)$$

since we will show later that:

Proposition 6.8 *$||P||_F^2 \leq r$.*

Putting (6.6) and Proposition 6.7 together, and using the fact that by triangle inequality $||A - CUR||_2 \leq ||A - AP||_2 + ||AP - CUR||_2$, which in turn implies that $||A - CUR||_2^2 \leq 2||A - AP||_2^2 + 2||AP - CUR||_2^2$, the main result below follows.

Theorem 6.9 *Let A be an $m \times n$ matrix and r and s be positive integers. Let C be an $m \times s$ matrix of s columns of A picked according to length squared sampling* *and let R be a matrix of r rows of A picked according to length squared sampling. Then, we can find from C and R an s × r matrix U so that*

$$E\left(||A - CUR||_2^2\right) \le ||A||_F^2 \left(\frac{2}{\sqrt{r}} + \frac{2r}{s}\right).$$

If s is fixed, the error is minimized when $r = s^{2/3}$. Choosing $s = 1/\varepsilon^3$ and $r = 1/\varepsilon^2$, the bound becomes $O(\varepsilon)||A||_F^2$. When is this bound meaningful? We discuss this further after first proving all the claims used in the discussion above.

Proof of Lemma 6.6 First consider the case that RR^T is invertible. For $\mathbf{x} = R^T\mathbf{y}$, $R^T(RR^T)^{-1}R\mathbf{x} = R^T(RR^T)^{-1}RR^T\mathbf{y} = R^T\mathbf{y} = \mathbf{x}$. If $\mathbf{x}$ is orthogonal to every row of R, then $R\mathbf{x} = \mathbf{0}$, so $P\mathbf{x} = \mathbf{0}$. More generally, if $RR^T = \sum_t \sigma_t \mathbf{u}_t \mathbf{v}_t{}^T$, then $R^T \sum_t \frac{1}{\sigma_t^2} R = \sum_t \mathbf{v}_t \mathbf{v}_t{}^T$ and clearly satisfies (i) and (ii). ∎

Next we prove Proposition 6.7. First, recall that

$$||A - AP||_2^2 = \max_{\{\mathbf{x}:|\mathbf{x}|=1\}} |(A - AP)\mathbf{x}|^2.$$

Now suppose $\mathbf{x}$ is in the row space V of R. From Lemma 6.6, $P\mathbf{x} = \mathbf{x}$, so for $\mathbf{x} \in V$, $(A - AP)\mathbf{x} = \mathbf{0}$. Since every vector can be written as a sum of a vector in V plus a vector orthogonal to V, this implies that the maximum must therefore occur at some $\mathbf{x} \in V^{\perp}$. For such $\mathbf{x}$, by Lemma 6.6, $(A - AP)\mathbf{x} = A\mathbf{x}$. Thus, the question becomes: for unit-length $\mathbf{x} \in V^{\perp}$, how large can $|A\mathbf{x}|^2$ be? To analyze this, write:

$$|A\mathbf{x}|^2 = \mathbf{x}^T A^T A \mathbf{x} = \mathbf{x}^T (A^T A - R^T R)\mathbf{x} \le ||A^T A - R^T R||_2 |\mathbf{x}|^2 \le ||A^T A - R^T R||_2.$$

This implies that $||A - AP||_2^2 \le ||A^T A - R^T R||_2$. So, it suffices to prove that $||A^T A - R^T R||_2^2 \le ||A||_F^4/r$ which follows directly from Theorem 6.5, since we can think of $R^T R$ as a way of estimating $A^T A$ by picking according to length squared distribution columns of A^T, i.e., rows of A. This proves Proposition 6.7.

Proposition 6.8 is easy to see. By Lemma 6.6, P is the identity on the space V spanned by the rows of R, and $P\mathbf{x} = 0$ for $\mathbf{x}$ perpendicular to the rows of R. Thus $||P||_F^2$ is the sum of its singular values squared which is at most r as claimed.

We now briefly look at the time needed to compute U. The only involved step in computing U is to find $(RR^T)^{-1}$ or do the SVD of RR^T. But note that RR^T is an $r \times r$ matrix, and since r is much smaller than n and m, this is fast.

Understanding the Bound in Theorem 6.9

To better understand the bound in Theorem 6.9, consider when it is meaningful and when it is not. First, choose parameters $s = \Theta(1/\varepsilon^3)$ and $r = \Theta(1/\varepsilon^2)$ so that the bound becomes $E(||A - CUR||_2^2) \le \varepsilon ||A||_F^2$. Recall that $||A||_F^2 = \sum_i \sigma_i^2(A)$, i.e., the sum of squares of all the singular values of A. Also, for convenience, scale A so that $\sigma_1^2(A) = 1$. Then

$$\sigma_1^2(A) = ||A||_2^2 = 1 \quad \text{and} \quad E(||A - CUR||_2^2) \le \varepsilon \sum_i \sigma_i^2(A).$$

This gives an intuitive sense of when the guarantee is good and when it is not. If the top k singular values of A are all $\Omega(1)$ for $k \gg m^{1/3}$, so that $\sum_i \sigma_i^2(A) \gg m^{1/3}$, then the guarantee is only meaningful when $\varepsilon = o(m^{-1/3})$, which is not interesting because it requires $s > m$. On the other hand, if just the first few singular values of A are large and the rest are quite small, e.g., A represents a collection of points that lie very close to a low-dimensional subspace, and in particular if $\sum_i \sigma_i^2(A)$ is a constant, then to be meaningful the bound requires ε to be a small constant. In this case, the guarantee is indeed meaningful because it implies that a constant number of rows and columns provides a good 2-norm approximation to A.

6.4. Sketches of Documents

Suppose one wished to store all the webpages from the World Wide Web. Since there are billions of webpages, one might want to store just a sketch of each page where a sketch is some type of compact description that captures sufficient information to do whatever task one has in mind. For the current discussion, we will think of a webpage as a string of characters, and the task at hand will be one of estimating similarities between pairs of webpages.

We begin this section by showing how to estimate similarities between sets via sampling, and then how to convert the problem of estimating similarities between strings into a problem of estimating similarities between sets.

Consider subsets of size 1,000 of the integers from 1 to 10^6. Suppose one wished to compute the resemblance of two subsets A and B by the formula

$$\text{resemblance } (A, B) = \frac{|A \cap B|}{|A \cup B|}.$$

Suppose that instead of using the sets A and B, one sampled the sets and compared random subsets of size ten. How accurate would the estimate be? One way to sample would be to select 10 elements uniformly at random from A and B. Suppose A and B were each of size 1,000, overlapped by 500, and both were represented by six samples. Even though half of the six samples of A were in B, they would not likely be among the samples representing B. See Figure 6.6. This method is unlikely to produce overlapping samples. Another way would be to select the 10 smallest elements from each of A and B. If the sets A and B overlapped significantly, one might expect the sets of 10 smallest elements from each of A and B to also overlap. One difficulty that might arise is that the small integers might be used for some special purpose and appear in essentially all sets and thus distort the results. To overcome this potential problem, rename all elements using a random permutation.

Suppose two subsets of size 1,000 overlapped by 900 elements. What might one expect the overlap of the 10 smallest elements from each subset to be? One would expect the 9 smallest elements from the 900 common elements to be in each of the two sampled subsets for an overlap of 90%. The expected resemblance (A, B) for the size 10 sample would be $9/11 = 0.81$.

Another method would be to select the elements equal to zero mod m for some integer m. If one samples mod m, the size of the sample becomes a function of n. Sampling mod m allows one to handle containment.

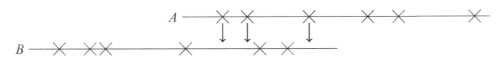

Figure 6.6: Samples of overlapping sets A and B.

In another version of the problem one has a string of characters rather than a set. Here one converts the string into a set by replacing it by the set of all of its substrings of some small length k. Corresponding to each string is a set of length k substrings. If k is modestly large, then two strings are highly unlikely to give rise to the same set of substrings. Thus, we have converted the problem of sampling a string to that of sampling a set. Instead of storing all the substrings of length k, we need only store a small subset of the length k substrings.

Suppose you wish to be able to determine if two webpages are minor modifications of one another or to determine if one is a fragment of the other. Extract the sequence of words occurring on the page, viewing each word as a character. Then define the set of substrings of k consecutive words from the sequence. Let $S(D)$ be the set of all substrings of k consecutive words occurring in document D. Define resemblance of A and B by

$$\text{resemblance}\,(A, B) = \frac{|S(A) \cap S(B)|}{|S(A) \cup S(B)|}$$

and define containment as

$$\text{containment}\,(A, B) = \frac{|S(A) \cap S(B)|}{|S(A)|}$$

Let π be a random permutation of all length k substrings. Define $F(A)$ to be the s smallest elements of A and $V(A)$ to be the set mod m in the ordering defined by the permutation.

Then

$$\frac{F(A) \cap F(B)}{F(A) \cup F(B)}$$

and

$$\frac{|V(A) \cap V(B)|}{|V(A) \cup V(B)|}$$

are unbiased estimates of the resemblance of A and B. The value

$$\frac{|V(A) \cap V(B)|}{|V(A)|}$$

is an unbiased estimate of the containment of A in B.

6.5. Bibliographic Notes

The hashing-based algorithm for counting the number of distinct elements in a data stream described in Section 6.2.1 is due to Flajolet and Martin [FM85]. Algorithm Frequent for identifying the most frequent elements is due to Misra and Gries [MG82]. The algorithm for estimating the second moment of a data stream described in Section 6.2.4 is due to Alon, Matias, and Szegedy [AMS96], who also gave algorithms and lower bounds for other k^{th} moments. These early algorithms for streaming data significantly influenced further research in the area. Improvements and generalizations of Algorithm Frequent were made in [MM02].

Length-squared sampling was introduced by Frieze, Kannan, and Vempala [FKV04]; the algorithms of Section 6.3 are from [DKM06a, DKM06b]. The material in Section 6.4 on sketches of documents is from Broder et al. [BGMZ97].

6.6. Exercises

Exercise 6.1 Let $a_1, a_2, \ldots, a_n$, be a stream of symbols each an integer in $\{1, \ldots, m\}$.

1. Give an algorithm that will select a symbol uniformly at random from the stream. How much memory does your algorithm require?
2. Give an algorithm that will select a symbol with probability proportional to a_i^2.

Exercise 6.2 How would one pick a random word from a very large book where the probability of picking a word is proportional to the number of occurrences of the word in the book?

Exercise 6.3 Consider a matrix where each element has a probability of being selected. Can you select a row according to the sum of probabilities of elements in that row by just selecting an element according to its probability and selecting the row that the element is in?

Exercise 6.4 For the streaming model give an algorithm to draw t independent samples of indices i, each with probability proportional to the value of a_i. Some indices may be drawn multiple times. What is its memory usage?

Exercise 6.5 Randomly generate 1,000 integers in the range $[1, 10^6]$ and calculate $10^6/\min$ 100 times. What is the probability that the estimate for the number of distinct elements in the range $[167. 6,000]$? How would you improve the probability?

Exercise 6.6 For some constant $c > 0$, it is possible to create 2^{cm} subsets of $\{1, \ldots, m\}$, each with $m/2$ elements, such that no two of the subsets share more than $3m/8$ elements in common.[5] Use this fact to argue that any deterministic algorithm that even guarantees to *approximate* the number of distinct elements in a data stream with error less than $\frac{m}{16}$ must use $\Omega(m)$ bits of memory on some input sequence of length $n \leq 2m$.

Exercise 6.7 Consider an algorithm that uses a random hash function and gives an estimate $\hat{x}$ of the true value x of some variable. Suppose that $\frac{x}{4} \leq \hat{x} \leq 4x$ with probability at least 0.6. The probability of the estimate is with respect to choice of the hash function. How would you improve the probability that $\frac{x}{4} \leq \hat{x} \leq 4x$ to 0.8? Hint: Since we do not know the variance, taking average may not help and we need to use some other function of multiple runs.

Exercise 6.8 Give an example of a set H of hash functions such that $h(x)$ is equally likely to be any element of $\{0, \ldots, M-1\}$ (H is 1-universal) but H is not 2-universal.

Exercise 6.9 Let p be a prime. A set of hash functions

$$H = \{h \mid \{0, 1, \ldots, p-1\} \to \{0, 1, \ldots, p-1\}\}$$

is 3-universal if for all x, y, z, u, v, w in $\{0, 1, \ldots, p-1\}$, where x, y, z are distinct we have

$$\text{Prob}\big(h(x) = u, \ h(y) = v, \ h(z) = w\big) = \frac{1}{p^3}.$$

---

[5]For example, choosing them randomly will work with high probability. You expect two subsets of size $m/2$ to share $m/4$ elements in common, and with high probability they will share no more than $3m/8$.

(a) Is the set $\{h_{ab}(x) = ax + b \mod p \mid 0 \le a, b < p\}$ of hash functions 3-universal?

(b) Give a 3-universal set of hash functions.

Exercise 6.10 Select a value for k and create a set

$$H = \{\mathbf{x} | \mathbf{x} = (x_1, x_2, \ldots, x_k), x_i \in \{0, 1, \ldots, k-1\}\}$$

where the set of vectors H is pairwise independent and $|H| < k^k$. We say that a set of vectors is pairwise independent if for any subset of two of the coordinates, all of the k^2 possible pairs of values that could appear in those coordinates such as $(0, 0), (0, 1), \ldots, (1, 0), (1, 1), \ldots$ occur the exact same number of times.

Exercise 6.11 Consider a coin that comes down heads with probability p. Prove that the expected number of flips needed to see a heads is $1/p$.

Exercise 6.12 Randomly generate a string $x_1 x_2 \cdots x_n$ of 10^6 0's and 1's with probability $1/2$ of x_i being a 1. Count the number of 1's in the string and also estimate the number of 1's by the coin-flip approximate counting algorithm, in Section 6.2.2. Repeat the process for $p = 1/4$, 1/8, and 1/16. How close is the approximation?

Exercise 6.13

1. Construct an example in which the majority algorithm gives a false positive, i.e., stores a non-majority element at the end.
2. Construct an example in which the frequent algorithm in fact does as badly as in the theorem, i.e., it under counts some item by $n/(k+1)$.

Exercise 6.14 Let p be a prime and $n \ge 2$ be an integer. What representation do you use to do arithmetic in the finite field with p^n elements? How do you do addition? How do you do multiplication?

Exercise 6.15 Let F be a field. Prove that for any four distinct points a_1, a_2, a_3, and a_4 in F and any four possibly not distinct values b_1, b_2, b_3, and b_4 in F, there is a unique polynomial $f(x) = f_0 + f_1 x + f_2 x^2 + f_3 x^3$ of degree at most three so that $f(a_i) = b_i, 1 \le i \le 4$ with all computations done over F. If you use the Vandermonde matrix you can use the fact that the matrix is non-singular.

Exercise 6.16 Suppose we want to pick a row of a matrix at random where the probability of picking row i is proportional to the sum of squares of the entries of that row. How would we do this in the streaming model?

(a) Do the problem when the matrix is given in column order.

(b) Do the problem when the matrix is represented in sparse notation: it is just presented as a list of triples (i, j, a_{ij}), in arbitrary order.

Exercise 6.17 Suppose A and B are two matrices. Prove that $AB = \sum_{k=1}^{n} A(:, k) B(k, :)$.

Exercise 6.18 Generate two 100-by-100 matrices A and B with integer values between 1 and 100. Compute the product AB both directly and by sampling. Plot the difference in L_2 norm between the results as a function of the number of samples. In generating the matrices make sure that they are skewed. One method would be the following. First generate two 100 dimensional vectors a and b with integer values between 1 and 100. Next generate the ith row of A with integer values between 1 and a_i and the ith column of B with integer values between 1 and b_i.

Exercise 6.19 Suppose $a_1, a_2, \ldots, a_m$ are nonnegative reals. Show that the minimum of $\sum_{k=1}^{m} \frac{a_k}{x_k}$ subject to the constraints $x_k \geq 0$ and $\sum_k x_k = 1$ is attained when the x_k are proportional to $\sqrt{a_k}$.

Exercise 6.20 Construct two different strings of 0's and 1's having the same set of substrings of length $k = 3$.

Exercise 6.21 (Random strings, empirical analysis) Consider random strings of length n composed of the integers 0 through 9, where we represent a string $\mathbf{x}$ by its set $S_k(\mathbf{x})$ of length k-substrings. Perform the following experiment: choose two random strings $\mathbf{x}$ and $\mathbf{y}$ of length $n = 10,000$ and compute their resemblance $\frac{|S_k(\mathbf{x}) \cap S_k(\mathbf{y})|}{|S_k(\mathbf{x}) \cup S_k(\mathbf{y})|}$ for $k = 1, 2, 3 \ldots$. What does the graph of resemblance as a function of k look like?

Exercise 6.22 (Random strings, theoretical analysis) Consider random strings of length n composed of the integers 0 through 9, where we represent a string $\mathbf{x}$ by its set $S_k(\mathbf{x})$ of length k-substrings. Consider now drawing two random strings $\mathbf{x}$ and $\mathbf{y}$ of length n and computing their resemblance $\frac{|S_k(\mathbf{x}) \cap S_k(\mathbf{y})|}{|S_k(\mathbf{x}) \cup S_k(\mathbf{y})|}$.

1. Prove that for $k \leq \frac{1}{2} \log_{10}(n)$, with high probability as n goes to infinity the two strings have resemblance equal to 1.
2. Prove that for $k \geq 3 \log_{10}(n)$, with high probability as n goes to infinity the two strings have resemblance equal to 0.

Exercise 6.23 Discuss how you might go about detecting plagiarism in term papers.

Exercise 6.24 Suppose you had one billion webpages and you wished to remove duplicates. How might you do this?

Exercise 6.25 Consider the following lyrics:

When you walk through the storm hold your head up high and don't be afraid of the dark. At the end of the storm there's a golden sky and the sweet silver song of the lark.

Walk on, through the wind, walk on through the rain though your dreams be tossed and blown. Walk on, walk on, with hope in your heart and you'll never walk alone, you'll never walk alone.

How large must k be to uniquely recover the lyric from the set of all length-k subsequences of symbols? Treat the blank as a symbol.

Exercise 6.26 **Blast**: Given a long string A, say of length 10^9, and a shorter string B, say 10^5, how do we find a position in A which is the start of a substring B' that is close to B? This problem can be solved by dynamic programming in polynomial time, but find a faster algorithm to solve this problem.

> **Hint. (Shingling approach)** One possible approach would be to fix a small length, say seven, and consider the shingles of A and B of length seven. If a close approximation to B is a substring of A, then a number of shingles of B must be shingles of A. This should allows us to find the approximate location in A of the approximation of B. Some final algorithm should then be able to find the best match.

—— **181** ——

CHAPTER SEVEN

Clustering

7.1. Introduction

Clustering refers to partitioning a set of objects into subsets according to some desired criterion. Often it is an important step in making sense of large amounts of data. Clustering comes up in many contexts. One might want to partition a set of news articles into clusters based on the topics of the articles. Given a set of pictures of people, one might want to group them into clusters based on who is in the image. Or one might want to cluster a set of protein sequences according to the protein function. A related problem is not finding a full partitioning but rather just identifying natural clusters that exist. For example, given a collection of friendship relations among people, one might want to identify any tight-knit groups that exist. In some cases we have a well-defined correct answer, e.g., in clustering photographs of individuals by who is in them, but in other cases the notion of a good clustering may be more subjective.

Before running a clustering algorithm, one first needs to choose an appropriate representation for the data. One common representation is as vectors in R^d. This corresponds to identifying d real-valued features that are then computed for each data object. For example, to represent documents one might use a "bag of words" representation, where each feature corresponds to a word in the English language and the value of the feature is how many times that word appears in the document. Another common representation is as vertices in a graph, with edges weighted by some measure of how similar or dissimilar the two endpoints are. For example, given a set of protein sequences, one might weight edges based on an edit-distance measure that essentially computes the cost of transforming one sequence into the other. This measure is typically symmetric and satisfies the triangle inequality, and so can be thought of as a finite metric. A point worth noting up front is that often the "correct" clustering of a given set of data depends on your goals. For instance, given a set of photographs of individuals, we might want to cluster the images by who is in them, or we might want to cluster them by facial expression. When representing the images as points in space or as nodes in a weighted graph, it is important that the features we use be relevant to the criterion we care about. In any event, the issue of how best to represent data to highlight the relevant information for a given task is generally addressed using knowledge of the specific domain. From our perspective, the job of the clustering algorithm begins after the data has been represented in some appropriate way.

In this chapter, our goals are to discuss (a) some commonly used clustering algorithms and what one can prove about them, and (b) models and assumptions on data under which we can find a clustering close to the correct clustering.

7.1.1. Preliminaries

We will follow the standard notation of using n to denote the number of data points and k to denote the number of desired clusters. We will primarily focus on the case that k is known up front, but will also discuss algorithms that produce a sequence of solutions, one for each value of k, as well as algorithms that produce a cluster tree that can encode multiple clusterings at each value of k. We will generally use $A = \{a_1, \ldots, a_n\}$ to denote the n data points. We also think of A as a matrix with rows $a_1, \ldots, a_n$.

7.1.2. Two General Assumptions on the Form of Clusters

Before choosing a clustering algorithm, it is useful to have some general idea of what a good clustering should look like. In general, there are two types of assumptions often made that in turn lead to different classes of clustering algorithms.

Center-based clusters: One assumption commonly made is that clusters are *center-based*. This means that the clustering can be defined by k centers $c_1, \ldots, c_k$, with each data point assigned to whichever center is closest to it. Note that this assumption does not yet tell whether one choice of centers is better than another. For this, one needs an objective, or optimization criterion. Three standard criteria often used are k-center, k-median, and k-means clustering, defined as follows.

k-center clustering: Find a partition $\mathcal{C} = \{C_1, \ldots, C_k\}$ of A into k clusters, with corresponding centers $c_1, \ldots, c_k$, to minimize the *maximum* distance between any data point and the center of its cluster. That is, we want to minimize

$$\Phi_{kcenter}(\mathcal{C}) = \max_{j=1}^{k} \max_{a_i \in C_j} d(a_i, c_j).$$

k-center clustering makes sense when we believe clusters should be local regions in space. It is also often thought of as the "firehouse location problem," since one can think of it as the problem of locating k fire-stations in a city so as to minimize the maximum distance a fire-truck might need to travel to put out a fire.

k-median clustering: Find a partition $\mathcal{C} = \{C_1, \ldots, C_k\}$ of A into k clusters, with corresponding centers $c_1, \ldots, c_k$, to minimize the *sum* of distances between data points and the centers of their clusters. That is, we want to minimize

$$\Phi_{kmedian}(\mathcal{C}) = \sum_{j=1}^{k} \sum_{a_i \in C_j} d(a_i, c_j).$$

k-median clustering is more noise-tolerant than k-center clustering because we are taking a sum rather than a max. A small number of outliers will typically not change the optimal solution by much, unless they are very far away or there are several quite different near-optimal solutions.

183

k-means clustering: Find a partition $\mathcal{C} = \{C_1, \ldots, C_k\}$ of A into k clusters, with corresponding centers $\mathbf{c}_1, \ldots, \mathbf{c}_k$, to minimize the *sum of squares* of distances between data points and the centers of their clusters. That is, we want to minimize

$$\Phi_{kmeans}(\mathcal{C}) = \sum_{j=1}^{k} \sum_{\mathbf{a}_i \in C_j} d^2(\mathbf{a}_i, \mathbf{c}_j).$$

k-means clustering puts more weight on outliers than k-median clustering, because we are squaring the distances, which magnifies large values. This puts it somewhat in between k-median and k-center clustering in that regard. Using distance squared has some mathematical advantages over using pure distances when data are points in R^d. For example, Corollary 7.2 that asserts that with the distance squared criterion, the optimal center for a given group of data points is its centroid.

The k-means criterion is more often used when data consists of points in R^d, whereas k-median is more commonly used when we have a finite metric, that is, data are nodes in a graph with distances on edges.

When data are points in R^d, there are in general two variations of the clustering problem for each of the criteria. We could require that each cluster center be a data point or allow a cluster center to be any point in space. If we require each center to be a data point, the optimal clustering of n data points into k clusters can be solved in time $\binom{n}{k}$ times a polynomial in the length of the data. First, exhaustively enumerate all sets of k data points as the possible sets of k cluster centers, then associate each point to its nearest center and select the best clustering. No such naive enumeration procedure is available when cluster centers can be any point in space. But, for the k-means problem, Corollary 7.2 shows that once we have identified the data points that belong to a cluster, the best choice of cluster center is the centroid of that cluster, which might not be a data point.

When k is part of the input or may be a function of n, the above optimization problems are all NP-hard.[1] So, guarantees on algorithms will typically involve either some form of approximation or some additional assumptions, or both.

High-density clusters: If we do not believe our desired clusters will be center-based, an alternative assumption often made is that clusters consist of high-density regions surrounded by low-density "moats" between them. For example, in the clustering of Figure 7.1 we have one natural cluster A that looks center-based but the other cluster B consists of a ring around cluster A. As seen in the figure, this assumption does not require clusters to correspond to convex regions and it can allow them to be long and stringy. We describe a non-center-based clustering method in Section 7.7. In Section 7.9 we prove the effectiveness of an algorithm which finds a "moat", cuts up data "inside" the moat and 'outside" into two pieces and recursively applies the same procedure to each piece.

---

[1] If k is a constant, then as noted above, the version where the centers must be data points can be solved in polynomial time.

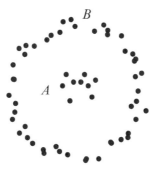

Figure 7.1: Example where the natural clustering is not center-based.

7.1.3. Spectral Clustering

An important part of a clustering toolkit when data lies in R^d is Singular Value Decomposition. Spectral Clustering refers to the following algorithm: Find the space V spanned by the top k right singular vectors of the matrix A whose rows are the data points. Project data points to V and cluster in the projection.

An obvious reason to do this is dimension reduction, clustering in the d dimensional space where data lies is reduced to clustering in a k dimensional space (usually, $k << d$). A more important point is that under certain assumptions one can prove that spectral clustering gives a clustering close to the true clustering. We already saw this in the case when data is from a mixture of spherical Gaussians, Section 3.9.3. The assumption used is "the means separated by a constant number of Standard Deviations". In Section 7.5, we will see that in a much more general setting, which includes common stochastic models, the same assumption, in spirit, yields similar conclusions. Section 7.4, has another setting with a similar result.

7.2. *k*-Means Clustering

We assume in this section that data points lie in R^d and focus on the k-means criterion.

7.2.1. A Maximum-Likelihood Motivation

We now consider a maximum-likelihood motivation for using the k-means criterion. Suppose that the data was generated according to an equal weight mixture of k spherical well-separated Gaussian densities centered at $\mu_1, \mu_2, \ldots, \mu_k$, each with variance one in every direction. Then the density of the mixture is

$$\text{Prob}(\mathbf{x}) = \frac{1}{(2\pi)^{d/2}} \frac{1}{k} \sum_{i=1}^{k} e^{-|\mathbf{x}-\mu_i|^2}.$$

Denote by $\mu(\mathbf{x})$ the center nearest to $\mathbf{x}$. Since the exponential function falls off fast, assuming x is noticeably closer to its nearest center than to any other center, we can approximate $\sum_{i=1}^{k} e^{-|\mathbf{x}-\mu_i|^2}$ by $e^{-|\mathbf{x}-\mu(\mathbf{x})|^2}$ since the sum is dominated by its largest term. Thus

$$\text{Prob}(\mathbf{x}) \approx \frac{1}{(2\pi)^{d/2}k}e^{-|\mathbf{x}-\mu(\mathbf{x})|^2}.$$

The likelihood of drawing the sample of points $\mathbf{x}_1, \mathbf{x}_2, \ldots, \mathbf{x}_n$ from the mixture, if the centers were $\mu_1, \mu_2, \ldots, \mu_k$, is approximately

$$\frac{1}{k^n}\frac{1}{(2\pi)^{nd/2}}\prod_{i=1}^{n}e^{-|\mathbf{x}^{(i)}-\mu(\mathbf{x}^{(i)})|^2} = ce^{-\sum_{i=1}^{n}|\mathbf{x}^{(i)}-\mu(\mathbf{x}^{(i)})|^2}.$$

Minimizing the sum of squared distances to cluster centers finds the maximum likelihood $\mu_1, \mu_2, \ldots, \mu_k$. This motivates using the sum of distance squared to the cluster centers.

7.2.2. Structural Properties of the k-Means Objective

Suppose we have already determined the clustering or the partitioning into $C_1, C_2, \ldots, C_k$. What are the best centers for the clusters? The following lemma shows that the answer is the centroids, the coordinate means, of the clusters.

Lemma 7.1 *Let $\{\mathbf{a}_1, \mathbf{a}_2, \ldots, \mathbf{a}_n\}$ be a set of points. The sum of the squared distances of the $\mathbf{a}_i$ to any point $\mathbf{x}$ equals the sum of the squared distances to the centroid of the $\mathbf{a}_i$ plus n times the squared distance from $\mathbf{x}$ to the centroid. That is,*

$$\sum_i |\mathbf{a}_i - \mathbf{x}|^2 = \sum_i |\mathbf{a}_i - \mathbf{c}|^2 + n\,|\mathbf{c} - \mathbf{x}|^2$$

where $\mathbf{c} = \frac{1}{n}\sum_{i=1}^{n}\mathbf{a}_i$ is the centroid of the set of points.

Proof

$$\sum_i |\mathbf{a}_i - \mathbf{x}|^2 = \sum_i |\mathbf{a}_i - \mathbf{c} + \mathbf{c} - \mathbf{x}|^2$$

$$= \sum_i |\mathbf{a}_i - \mathbf{c}|^2 + 2(\mathbf{c} - \mathbf{x})\cdot\sum_i(\mathbf{a}_i - \mathbf{c}) + n\,|\mathbf{c} - \mathbf{x}|^2$$

Since $\mathbf{c}$ is the centroid, $\sum_i(\mathbf{a}_i - \mathbf{c}) = 0$. Thus, $\sum_i |\mathbf{a}_i - \mathbf{x}|^2 = \sum_i |\mathbf{a}_i - \mathbf{c}|^2 + n\,|\mathbf{c} - \mathbf{x}|^2$ ∎

A corollary of Lemma 7.1 is that the centroid minimizes the sum of squared distances since the first term, $\sum_i |\mathbf{a}_i - \mathbf{c}|^2$, is a constant independent of $\mathbf{x}$ and setting $\mathbf{x} = \mathbf{c}$ sets the second term, $n\,\|\mathbf{c} - \mathbf{x}\|^2$, to zero.

Corollary 7.2 *Let $\{\mathbf{a}_1, \mathbf{a}_2, \ldots, \mathbf{a}_n\}$ be a set of points. The sum of squared distances of the $\mathbf{a}_i$ to a point $\mathbf{x}$ is minimized when $\mathbf{x}$ is the centroid, namely $\mathbf{x} = \frac{1}{n}\sum_i \mathbf{a}_i$.*

7.2.3. Lloyd's Algorithm

Corollary 7.2 suggests the following natural strategy for k-means clustering, known as Lloyd's algorithm. Lloyd's algorithm does not necessarily find a globally optimal solution but will find a locally-optimal one. An important but unspecified step in the algorithm is its initialization: how the starting k centers are chosen. We discuss this after discussing the main algorithm.

Lloyd's algorithm:

Start with k centers.

Cluster each point with the center nearest to it.

Find the centroid of each cluster and replace the set of old centers with the centroids.

Repeat the above two steps until the centers converge according to some criterion, such as the k-means score no longer improving.

This algorithm always converges to a local minimum of the objective. To show convergence, we argue that the sum of the squares of the distances of each point to its cluster center always improves. Each iteration consists of two steps. First, consider the step that finds the centroid of each cluster and replaces the old centers with the new centers. By Corollary 7.2, this step improves the sum of internal cluster distances squared. The second step reclusters by assigning each point to its nearest cluster center, which also improves the internal cluster distances.

A problem that arises with some implementations of the k-means clustering algorithm is that one or more of the clusters becomes empty and there is no center from which to measure distance. A simple case where this occurs is illustrated in the following example. You might think how you would modify the code to resolve this issue.

Example Consider running the k-means clustering algorithm to find three clusters on the following 1-dimension data set: {2,3,7,8} starting with centers {0,5,10}.

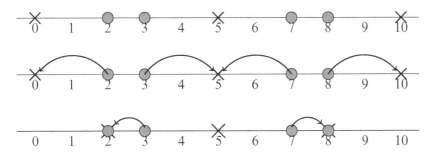

The center at 5 ends up with no items and there are only two clusters instead of the desired three. ∎

As noted above, Lloyd's algorithm only finds a local optimum to the k-means objective that might not be globally optimal. Consider, for example, Figure 7.2. Here data lies in three dense clusters in R^2: one centered at $(0, 1)$, one centered at $(0, -1)$ and one centered at $(3, 0)$. If we initialize with one center at $(0, 1)$ and two centers near $(3, 0)$, then the center at $(0, 1)$ will move to near $(0, 0)$ and capture the points near $(0, 1)$ and $(0, -1)$, whereas the centers near $(3, 0)$ will just stay there, splitting that cluster.

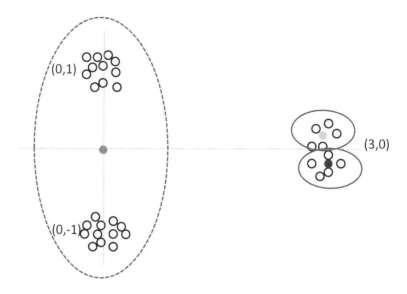

Figure 7.2: A locally-optimal but globally-suboptimal k-means clustering.

Because the initial centers can substantially influence the quality of the result, there has been significant work on initialization strategies for Lloyd's algorithm. One popular strategy is called "farthest traversal". Here, we begin by choosing one data point as initial center c_1 (say, randomly), then pick the farthest data point from c_1 to use as c_2, then pick the farthest data point from $\{c_1, c_2\}$ to use as c_3, and so on. These are then used as the initial centers. Notice that this will produce the correct solution in the example in Figure 7.2.

Farthest traversal can unfortunately get fooled by a small number of outliers. To address this, a smoother, probabilistic variation known as k-means++ instead weights data points based on their distance squared from the previously chosen centers. Then it selects the next center probabilistically according to these weights. This approach has the nice property that a small number of outliers will not overly influence the algorithm so long as they are not too far away, in which case perhaps they should be their own clusters anyway.

Another approach is to run some other approximation algorithm for the k-means problem, and then use its output as the starting point for Lloyd's algorithm. Note that applying Lloyd's algorithm to the output of any other algorithm can only improve its score. An alternative SVD-based method for initialization is described and analyzed in Section 7.5.

7.2.4. Ward's Algorithm

Another popular heuristic for k-means clustering is Ward's algorithm. Ward's algorithm begins with each data point in its own cluster, and then repeatedly merges pairs of clusters until only k clusters remain. Specifically, Ward's algorithm merges the two clusters that minimize the immediate increase in k-means cost. That is, for a cluster C, define $cost(C) = \sum_{a_i \in C} d^2(a_i, c)$, where c is the centroid of C. Then Ward's algorithm merges the pair (C, C') minimizing $cost(C \cup C') - cost(C) - cost(C')$. Thus, Ward's algorithm can be viewed as a greedy k-means algorithm.

7.2.5. k-Means Clustering on the Line

One case where the optimal k-means clustering can be found in polynomial time is when points lie in R^1, i.e., on the line. This can be done using dynamic programming, as follows.

First, assume without loss of generality that the data points $a_1, \ldots, a_n$ have been sorted, so $a_1 \leq a_2 \leq \ldots \leq a_n$. Now, suppose that for some $i \geq 1$ we have already computed the optimal k'-means clustering for points $a_1, \ldots, a_i$ for all $k' \leq k$; note that this is trivial to do for the base case of $i = 1$. Our goal is to extend this solution to points $a_1, \ldots, a_{i+1}$. To do so, observe that each cluster will contain a consecutive sequence of data points. So, given k', for each $j \leq i + 1$, compute the cost of using a single center for points $a_j, \ldots, a_{i+1}$, which is the sum of distances of each of these points to their mean value. Then add to that the cost of the optimal $k' - 1$ clustering of points $a_1, \ldots, a_{j-1}$ which we computed earlier. Store the minimum of these sums, over choices of j, as our optimal k'-means clustering of points $a_1, \ldots, a_{i+1}$. This has running time of $O(kn)$ for a given value of i. So overall our running time is $O(kn^2)$.

7.3. k-Center Clustering

In this section, instead of using the k-means clustering criterion, we use the k-center criterion. Recall that the k-center criterion partitions the points into k clusters so as to minimize the maximum distance of any point to its cluster center. Call the maximum distance of any point to its cluster center the *radius* of the clustering. There is a k-clustering of radius r if and only if there are k spheres, each of radius r, which together cover all the points. Below, we give a simple algorithm to find k spheres covering a set of points. The following lemma shows that this algorithm only needs to use a radius that is at most twice that of the optimal k-center solution. Note that this algorithm is equivalent to the farthest traversal strategy for initializing Lloyd's algorithm.

The Farthest Traversal k-clustering Algorithm

> Pick any data point to be the first cluster center. At time t, for $t = 2, 3, \ldots, k$, pick the farthest data point from any existing cluster center; make it the tth cluster center.

Theorem 7.3 *If there is a k-clustering of radius $\frac{r}{2}$, then the above algorithm finds a k-clustering with radius at most r.*

Proof Suppose for contradiction that there is some data point x that is distance greater than r from all centers chosen. This means that each new center chosen was distance greater than r from all previous centers, because we could always have chosen x. This implies that we have $k + 1$ data points, namely the centers chosen plus x, that are pairwise more than distance r apart. Clearly, no two such points can belong to the same cluster in any k-clustering of radius $\frac{r}{2}$, contradicting the hypothesis. ∎

7.4. Finding Low-Error Clusterings

In the previous sections we saw algorithms for finding a local optimum to the k-means clustering objective, for finding a global optimum to the k-means objective on the line, and for finding a factor 2 approximation to the k-center objective. But what about finding a clustering that is close to the correct answer, such as the true clustering of proteins by function or a correct clustering of news articles by topic? For this we need some assumption about the data and what the correct answer looks like. The next few sections consider algorithms based on different such assumptions.

7.5. Spectral Clustering

Let A be a $n \times d$ data matrix with each row a data point and suppose we want to partition the data points into k clusters. *Spectral Clustering* refers to a class of clustering algorithms which share the following outline:

- Find the space V spanned by the top k (right) singular vectors of A.
- Project data points into V.
- Cluster the projected points.

7.5.1. Why Project?

The reader may want to read Section 3.9.3, which shows the efficacy of spectral clustering for data stochastically generated from a mixture of spherical Gaussians. Here, we look at general data which may not have a stochastic generation model.

We will later describe the last step in more detail. First, lets understand the central advantage of doing the projection to V. It is simply that for any reasonable (unknown) clustering of data points, the projection brings data points closer to their cluster centers. This statement sounds mysterious and likely false, since the assertion is for ANY reasonable unknown clustering. We quantify it in Theorem 7.4. First some notation: We represent a k-clustering by a $n \times d$ matrix C (same dimensions as A), where row i of C is the center of the cluster to which data point i belongs. So, there are only k distinct rows of C and each other row is a copy of one of these rows. The k-means objective function, namely the sum of squares of the distances of data points to their cluster centers, is

$$\sum_{i=1}^{n} |\mathbf{a_i} - \mathbf{c_i}|^2 = ||A - C||_F^2.$$

The projection reduces the sum of distance squares to cluster centers from $||A - C||_F^2$ to at most $8k||A - C||_2^2$ in the projection. Recall that $||A - C||_2$ is the spectral norm, which is the top singular value of $A - C$. Now, $||A - C||_F^2 = \sum_t \sigma_t^2(A)$, and often $||A - C||_F >> \sqrt{k}||A - C||_2$, and so the projection substantially reduces the sum of squared distances to cluster centers.

We will see later that in many clustering problems, including models like mixtures of Gaussians and Stochastic Block Models of communities, there is a desired clustering C where the regions overlap in the whole space but are separated in the projection. Figure 7.3 is a schematic illustration. Now we state the theorem and give its surprisingly simple proof.

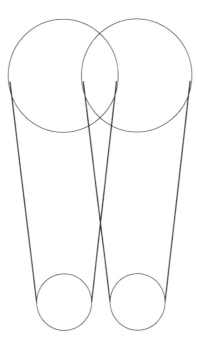

Figure 7.3: Clusters in the full space and their projections

Theorem 7.4 *Let A be an $n \times d$ matrix with A_k the projection of the rows of A to the subspace of the first k right singular vectors of A. For any matrix C of rank less than or equal to k*

$$||A_k - C||_F^2 \leq 8k||A - C||_2^2.$$

A_k is a matrix that is close to every C, in the sense that $||A_k - C||_F^2 \leq 8k||A - C||_2^2$. While this seems contradictory, another way to state this is that for C far away from A_k in Frobenius norm, $||A - C||_2$ will also be high.

Proof Since the rank of $(A_k - C)$ is less than or equal to $2k$,

$$||A_k - C||_F^2 \leq 2k||A_k - C||_2^2 \quad \text{and}$$
$$||A_k - C||_2 \leq ||A_k - A||_2 + ||A - C||_2 \leq 2||A - C||_2.$$

The last inequality follows since A_k is the best rank k approximation in spectral norm (Theorem 3.9) and C has rank at most k. The theorem follows. ∎

Suppose now in the clustering C we would like to find, the cluster centers that are pairwise at least $\Omega(\sqrt{k}||A - C||_2)$ apart. This holds for many clustering problems including data generated by stochastic models. Then, it will be easy to see that in the projection, most data points are a constant factor farther from centers of other clusters than their own cluster center, and this makes it very easy for the following algorithm to find the clustering C modulo a small fraction of errors.

7.5.2. The Algorithm

Denote $||A - C||_2/\sqrt{n}$ by $\sigma(C)$. In the next section, we give an interpretation of $||A - C||_2$ indicating that $\sigma(C)$ is akin to the standard deviation of clustering C and hence the notation $\sigma(C)$. We assume for now that $\sigma(C)$ is known to us for the desired clustering C. This assumption can be removed by essentially doing a binary search.

Spectral Clustering – The Algorithm

1. Find the top k right singular vectors of data matrix A and project rows of A to the space spanned by them to get A_k.(cf. Section 3.5).
2. Select a random row from A_k and form a cluster with all rows of A_k at distance less than $6k\sigma(C)/\varepsilon$ from it.
3. Repeat Step 2 k times.

Theorem 7.5 *If in a k-clustering C, every pair of centers is separated by at least $15k\sigma(C)/\varepsilon$ and every cluster has at least εn points in it, then with probability at least $1 - \varepsilon$, spectral clustering finds a clustering C' that differs from C on at most $\varepsilon^2 n$ points.*

Proof Let $\mathbf{v_i}$ denote row i of A_k. We first show that for most data points, the projection of the data point is within distance $3k\sigma(C)/\varepsilon$ of its cluster center. That is, we show that $|M|$ is small, where,

$$M = \{i : |\mathbf{v_i} - \mathbf{c_i}| \geq 3k\sigma(C)/\varepsilon\}.$$

Now, $||A_k - C||_F^2 = \sum_i |\mathbf{v_i} - \mathbf{c_i}|^2 \geq \sum_{i \in M} |\mathbf{v_i} - \mathbf{c_i}|^2 \geq |M|\frac{9k^2\sigma^2(C)}{\varepsilon^2}$. So, using Theorem 7.4, we get:

$$|M|\frac{9k^2\sigma^2(C)}{\varepsilon^2} \leq ||A_k - C||_F^2 \leq 8kn\sigma^2(C) \implies |M| \leq \frac{8\varepsilon^2 n}{9k}. \qquad (7.1)$$

Call a data point i "good" if $i \notin M$. For any two good data points i and j belonging to the same cluster, since their projections are within $3k\sigma(C)/\varepsilon$ of the center of the cluster, projections of the two data points are within $6k\sigma(C)/\varepsilon$ of each other. On the other hand, if two good data points i and k are in different clusters, since the centers of the two clusters are at least $15k\sigma(C)/\varepsilon$ apart, their projections must be greater than $15k\sigma(C)/\varepsilon - 6k\sigma(C)/\varepsilon = 9k\sigma(C)/\varepsilon$ apart. So, if we picked a good data point (say, point i) in Step 2, the set of good points we put in its cluster is exactly the set of good points in the same cluster as i. Thus, if in each of the k executions of Step 2 we picked a good point, all good points are correctly clustered, and since $|M| \leq \varepsilon^2 n$, the theorem would hold.

To complete the proof, we must argue that the probability of any pick in Step 2 being bad is small. The probability that the first pick in Step 2 is bad is at most $|M|/n \leq \varepsilon^2/k$. For each subsequent execution of Step 2, all the good points in at least one cluster are remaining candidates. So there are at least $(\varepsilon - \varepsilon^2)n$ good points left, and so the probability that we pick a bad point is at most $|M|/(\varepsilon-\varepsilon^2)n$, which is at most ε/k. The union bound over the k executions yields the desired result. ∎

7.5.3. Means Separated by $\Omega(1)$ Standard Deviations

For probability distribution on the real line, generally "means separated by six standard deviations" suffices to distinguish different components. Spectral clustering enables us to do the same thing in higher dimensions provided $k \in O(1)$ and six is replaced by some constant. First we define standard deviation for general, not necessarily stochastically generated data: it is just the maximum over all unit vectors $\mathbf{v}$ of the square root of the mean squared distance of data points from their cluster centers in the direction $\mathbf{v}$; namely, the standard deviation $\sigma(C)$ of clustering C is defined as:

$$\sigma(C)^2 = \frac{1}{n}\text{Max}_{\mathbf{v}:|\mathbf{v}|=1} \sum_{i=1}^{n} [(\mathbf{a_i} - \mathbf{c_i}) \cdot \mathbf{v}]^2 = \frac{1}{n}\text{Max}_{\mathbf{v}:|\mathbf{v}|=1}|(A - C)\mathbf{v}|^2 = \frac{1}{n}||A - C||_2^2.$$

This coincides with the definition of $\sigma(C)$ we made earlier. Assuming $k \in O(1)$, it is easy to see that the Theorem 7.5 can be restated as:

> If cluster centers in C are separated by $\Omega(\sigma(C))$, then the spectral clustering algorithm finds C' that differs from C only in a small fraction of data points.

It can be seen that the "means separated by $\Omega(1)$ standard deviations" condition holds for many stochastic models. We illustrate with two examples here. First, suppose we have a mixture of $k \in O(1)$ spherical Gaussians, each with standard deviation one. The data is generated according to this mixture. If the means of the Gaussians are $\Omega(1)$ apart, then the condition – means separated by $\Omega(1)$ standard deviations – is satisfied, and so if we project to the SVD subspace and cluster, we will get (nearly) the correct clustering. This was already discussed in detail in Chapter 3.

We discuss a second example. *Stochastic block models* are models of communities. Suppose there are k communities $C_1, C_2, \ldots, C_k$ among a population of n people. Suppose the probability of two people in the same community knowing each other is p and if they are in different communities, the probability is q, where, $q < p$.[2] We assume the events that person i knows person j are *independent* across all i and j.

Specifically, we are given an $n \times n$ data matrix A, where $a_{ij} = 1$ if and only if i and j know each other. We assume the a_{ij} are independent random variables, and use $\mathbf{a_i}$ to denote the ith row of A. It is useful to think of A as the adjacency matrix of a graph, such as the friendship network in Facebook. We will also think of the rows $\mathbf{a_i}$ as data points. The clustering problem is to classify the data points into the communities they belong to. In practice, the graph is fairly sparse, i.e., p and q are small, namely $O(1/n)$ or $O(\ln n/n)$.

Consider the simple case of two communities with $n/2$ people in each and with

$$p = \frac{\alpha}{n} \qquad q = \frac{\beta}{n} \qquad \text{where } \alpha, \beta \in O(\ln n).$$

Let $\mathbf{u}$ and $\mathbf{v}$ be the centroids of the data points in community one and community two, respectively; so $u_i \approx p$ for $i \in C_1$ and $u_j \approx q$ for $j \in C_2$ and $v_i \approx q$ for $i \in C_1$ and $v_j \approx p$ for $j \in C_2$. We have

---

[2]More generally, for each pair of communities a and b, there could be a probability p_{ab} that a person from community a knows a person from community b. But for the discussion here, we take $p_{aa} = p$ for all a and $p_{ab} = q$, for all $a \neq b$.

$$|\mathbf{u} - \mathbf{v}|^2 = \sum_{j=1}^{n}(u_j - v_j)^2 \approx \frac{(\alpha - \beta)^2}{n^2}n = \frac{(\alpha - \beta)^2}{n}.$$

$$\text{Inter-centroid distance} \approx \frac{\alpha - \beta}{\sqrt{n}}.$$

We need to upper bound $||A - C||_2$. This is nontrivial, since we have to prove a uniform upper bound on $|(A - C)\mathbf{v}|$ for all unit vectors $\mathbf{v}$. Fortunately, the subject to Random Matrix Theory (RMT) already does this for us. RMT tells that

$$||A - C||_2 \le \tilde{O}(\sqrt{np}) = \tilde{O}(\sqrt{\alpha}),$$

where $\tilde{O}$ hides logarithmic factors. So as long as $\alpha - \beta \in \tilde{\Omega}(\sqrt{\alpha})$, we have the means separated by $\Omega(1)$ standard deviations and spectral clustering works.

One important observation is that in these examples as well as many others, the k-means objective function in the whole space is too high, and so the projection is essential before we can cluster.

7.5.4. Laplacians

An important special case of spectral clustering is when $k = 2$ and a spectral algorithm is applied to the Laplacian matrix L of a graph, which is defined as

$$L = D - A$$

where A is the adjacency matrix and D is a diagonal matrix of degrees. Since A has a negative sign, we look at the lowest two singular values and corresponding vectors rather than the highest.

L is a symmetric matrix and is easily seen to be posiitve semi-definite: for any vector $\mathbf{x}$, we have

$$\mathbf{x}^T L \mathbf{x} = \sum_{i} d_{ii}x_i^2 - \sum_{(i,j)\in E} x_i x_j = \frac{1}{2}\sum_{(i,j)\in E}(x_i - x_j)^2.$$

Also since all row sums of L (and L is symmetric) are zero, its lowest eigenvalue is 0 with the eigenvector $\mathbf{1}$ of all 1's. This is also the lowest singular vector of L. The projection of all data points (rows) to this vector is just the origin and so gives no information. If we take the second lowest singular vector and project to it which is essentially projecting to the space of the bottom two singular vectors, we get the very simple problem of n real numbers that we need to cluster into two clusters.

7.5.5. Local Spectral Clustering

So far our emphasis has been on partitioning the data into disjoint clusters. However, the structure of many data sets consists of overlapping communities. In this case using k-means with spectral clustering, the overlap of two communities shows up as a community. This is illustrated in Figure 7.4.

An alternative to using k-means with spectral clustering is to find the minimum 1-norm vector in the space spanned by the top singular vectors. Let A be the matrix

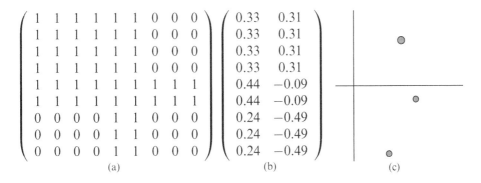

Figure 7.4: (a) illustrates the adjacency matrix of a graph with a six-vertex clique that overlaps a five-vertex clique in two vertices, (b) illustrates the matrix where columns consist of the top two singular vectors, and (c) illustrates the mapping of rows in the singular vector matrix to three points in two-dimensional space. Instead of two cliques we get the non-overlapping portion of each of the two cliques plus their intersection as communities instead of the two cliques as communities.

whose columns are the singular vectors. To find a vector y in the space spanned by the columns of A, solve the linear system $Ax = y$. This is a slightly different-looking problem then $Ax = c$ where c is a constant vector. To convert $Ax = y$ to the more usual form, write it as $[A, -I] \begin{pmatrix} x \\ y \end{pmatrix} = 0$. However, if we want to minimize $||y||_1$, the solution is $x = y = 0$. Thus we add the row $1, 1, \dots 1, 0, 0, \dots 0$ to $[A, -I]$ and a 1 to the top of the vector $[x, y]$ to force the coordinates of x to add up to 1. Minimizing $||y||_1$ does not appear to be a linear program, but we can write $y = y_a - y_b$ and require $y_a \geq 0$ and $y_b \geq 0$. Now finding the minimum 1-norm vector in the span of the columns of A is the linear program

$$\min \left(\sum_i y_{ai} + \sum_i y_{bi} \right) \text{ subject to } (A, -I, I) \begin{pmatrix} x \\ y_a \\ y_b \end{pmatrix} = 0 \quad y_a \geq 0 \quad y_b \geq 0.$$

Local Communities
In large social networks with a billion vertices, global clustering is likely to result in communities of several hundred million vertices. What you may actually want is a local community containing several individuals with only 50 vertices. To do this, if one starts a random walk at a vertex v and computes the frequency of visiting vertices, it will converge to the first singular vector. However, the distribution after a small number of steps will be primarily in the small community containing v and will be proportional to the first singular vector distribution restricted to the vertices in the small community containing v, only will be higher by some constant value. If one wants to determine the local communities containing vertices v_1, v_2, and v_3, start with three probability distributions, one with probability 1 at v_1, one with probability 1 at v_2, and one with probability 1 at v_3 and find early approximation to the first three singular vectors. Then find the minimum 1-norm vector in the space spanned by the early approximations.

Hidden Structure

In the previous section we discussed overlapping communities. Another issue is hidden structure. Suppose the vertices of a social network could be partitioned into a number of strongly connected communities. By strongly connected we mean the probability of an edge between two vertices in a community is much higher than the probability of an edge between two vertices in different communities. Suppose the vertices of the graph could also be partitioned in a different way that perhaps groups together communities from the first partitioning, where the probability of an edge between two vertices inside one of these new communities is still higher than the probability of an edge between two of them. If the probability of an edge between two vertices in a community of this second partitioning is less than that in the first, then a clustering algorithm is likely to find the first partitioning rather than the second. However, the second partitioning, which we refer to as hidden structure, may be the structure that we want to find. The way to do this is to use your favorite clustering algorithm to produce the dominant structure and then stochastically weaken the dominant structure by removing some community edges in the graph. Now if you apply the clustering algorithm to the modified graph, it can find the hidden community structure. Having done this, go back to the original graph, weaken the hidden structure, and reapply the clustering algorithm. It will now find a better approximation to the dominant structure. This technology can be used to find a number of hidden levels in several types of social networks.

Block Model

One technique for generating graphs with communities is to use the block model where the vertices are partitioned into blocks and each block is a GNP graph generated with some edge probability. The edges in off diagonal blocks are generated with a lower probability. One can also generate graphs with hidden structure. For example, the vertices in an n vertex graph might be partitioned into two communities, the first community having vertices 1 to $n/2$ and the second community having vertices $n/2+1$ to n. The dominant structure is generated with probability p_1 for edges within communities and probability q_1 for edges between communities. The vertices are randomly permuted and the hidden structure is generated using the first $n/2$ vertices in the permuted order for one community and the remaining vertices for the second community with probabilities p_2 and q_2 that are lower than p_1 and q_1.

An interesting question is how to determine the quality of a community found. Many researchers use an existing standard of what the communities are. However, if you want to use clustering techniques to find communities, there probably is no external standard, or you would just use that instead of clustering. A way to determine if you have found a real community structure is to ask if the graph is more likely generated by a model of the structure found than by a completely random model. Suppose you found a partition of two communities each with $n/2$ vertices. Using the number of edges in each community and the number of inter-community edges, ask what is the probability of the graph being generated by a bloc model where p and q are the probabilities determined by the edge density within communities and the edge density between communities. One can compare this probability with the probability that the graph was generated by a GNP model with probability $(p+q)/2$.

7.6. Approximation Stability

7.6.1. The Conceptual Idea

We now consider another condition that will allow us to produce accurate clusters from data. To think about this condition, imagine that we are given a few thousand news articles that we want to cluster by topic. These articles could be represented as points in a high-dimensional space (e.g., axes could correspond to different meaningful words, with coordinate i indicating the frequency of that word in a given article). Or, alternatively, it could be that we have developed some text-processing program that, given two articles x and y, computes some measure of distance $d(x, y)$ between them. We assume there exists some correct clustering C_T of our news articles into k topics; of course, we do not know what C_T is; that is what we want our algorithm to find.

If we are clustering with an algorithm that aims to minimize the k-means score of its solution, then implicitly this means we believe that the clustering C_{kmeans}^{OPT} of minimum k-means score is either equal or very similar to the clustering C_T. Unfortunately, finding the clustering of minimum k-means score is NP-hard. So, let us broaden our belief a bit and assume that any clustering C whose k-means score is within 10% of the minimum is also very similar to C_T. This should give us a little bit more slack. Unfortunately, finding a clustering of score within 10% of the minimum is also an NP-hard problem. Nonetheless, *we will be able to use this assumption to efficiently find a clustering that is close to C_T*. The trick is that NP-hardness is a worst-case notion, whereas in contrast, this assumption implies structure on our data. In particular, by the triangle inequality, it implies that all clusterings that have score within 10% of the minimum have to be similar to each other. We will then be able to utilize this structure in a natural "ball-growing" clustering algorithm.

7.6.2. Making This Formal

To make this discussion formal, we first specify what we mean when we say that two different ways of clustering some data are "similar" to each other. Let $C = \{C_1, \ldots, C_k\}$ and $C' = \{C'_1, \ldots, C'_k\}$ be two different k-clusterings of some data set A. For example, C could be the correct clustering that our algorithm produces, and C' could be the correct clustering C_T. Let us define the distance between these two clusterings to be the fraction of points that would have to be re-clustered in C to make C match C', where by "match" we mean that there should be a bijection between the clusters of C and the clusters of C'. We can write this distance mathematically as:

$$dist(C, C') = \min_\sigma \frac{1}{n} \sum_{i=1}^{k} |C_i \setminus C'_{\sigma(i)}|,$$

where the minimum is over all permutations σ of $\{1, \ldots, k\}$.

For $c > 1$ and $\epsilon > 0$ we say that a data set satisfies (c, ϵ)-*approximation-stability* with respect to a given objective (such as k-means or k-median) if every clustering C whose cost is within a factor c of the minimum-cost clustering for that objective satisfies $dist(C, C_T) < \epsilon$. That is, it is sufficient to be within a factor c of optimal to our objective in order for the fraction of points clustered incorrectly to be less than ϵ.

We will specifically focus in this discussion on the *k-median* objective rather than the *k*-means objective, since it is a bit easier to work with.

What we will now show is that under this condition, even though it may be NP-hard in general to find a clustering that is within a factor c of optimal, we can nonetheless efficiently find a clustering C' such that $dist(C', C_T) \leq \epsilon$, so long as all clusters in C_T are reasonably large. To simplify notation, let C^* denote the clustering of minimum k-median cost, and to keep the discussion simpler, let us also assume that $C_T = C^*$; that is, the target clustering is also the clustering with the minimum k-median score.

7.6.3. Algorithm and Analysis

Before presenting an algorithm, we begin with a helpful lemma that will guide our design. For a given data point $\mathbf{a}_i$, define its *weight* $w(\mathbf{a}_i)$ to be its distance to the center of its cluster in C^*. Notice that the k-median cost of C^* is $OPT = \sum_{i=1}^{n} w(\mathbf{a}_i)$. Define $w_{avg} = OPT/n$ to be the average weight of the points in A. Finally, define $w_2(\mathbf{a}_i)$ to be the distance of $\mathbf{a}_i$ to its second-closest center in C^*.

> **Lemma 7.6** *Assume data set A satisfies (c, ϵ) approximation-stability with respect to the k-median objective, each cluster in C_T has size at least $2\epsilon n$, and $C_T = C^*$. Then,*
>
> 1. *Fewer than ϵn points $\mathbf{a}_i$ have $w_2(\mathbf{a}_i) - w(\mathbf{a}_i) \leq (c-1)w_{avg}/\epsilon$.*
> 2. *At most $5\epsilon n/(c-1)$ points $\mathbf{a}_i$ have $w(\mathbf{a}_i) \geq (c-1)w_{avg}/(5\epsilon)$.*

> ***Proof*** For part (1), suppose that ϵn points $\mathbf{a}_i$ have $w_2(\mathbf{a}_i) - w(\mathbf{a}_i) \leq (c-1)$ w_{avg}/ϵ. Consider modifying C_T to a new clustering C' by moving each of these points $\mathbf{a}_i$ into the cluster containing its second-closest center. By assumption, the k-means cost of the clustering has increased by at most $\epsilon n(c-1)w_{avg}/\epsilon = (c-1) \cdot OPT$. This means that the cost of the new clustering is at most $cOPT$. However, $dist(C', C_T) = \epsilon$ because (a) we moved ϵn points to different clusters, and (b) each cluster in C_T has size at least $2\epsilon n$ so the optimal permutation σ in the definition of *dist* remains the identity. So, this contradicts approximation stability. Part (2) follows from the definition of "average"; if it did not hold, then $\sum_{i=1}^{n} w(\mathbf{a}_i) > nw_{avg}$, a contradiction. ∎

A datapoint $\mathbf{a}_i$ is *bad* if it satisfies either item (1) or (2) of Lemma 7.6 and *good* if it satisfies neither one. So, there are at most $b = \epsilon n + \frac{5\epsilon n}{c-1}$ bad points and the rest are good. Define "critical distance" $d_{crit} = \frac{(c-1)w_{avg}}{5\epsilon}$. Lemma 7.6 implies that the good points have distance at most d_{crit} to the center of their own cluster in C^* and distance at least $5d_{crit}$ to the center of any other cluster in C^*.

This suggests the following algorithm. Suppose we create a graph G with the points $\mathbf{a}_i$ as vertices, and edges between any two points $\mathbf{a}_i$ and $\mathbf{a}_j$ with $d(\mathbf{a}_i, \mathbf{a}_j) < 2d_{crit}$. Notice that by triangle inequality, the good points within the same cluster in C^* have distance less than $2d_{crit}$ from each other so they will be fully connected and form a clique. Also, again by triangle inequality, any edge that goes between different clusters must be between two bad points. In particular, if $\mathbf{a}_i$ is a good point in one cluster, and it has an edge to some other point $\mathbf{a}_j$, then $\mathbf{a}_j$ must have distance less than $3d_{crit}$ to the center of a_i's cluster. This means that if a_j had a different closest center, which obviously would also be at distance less than $3d_{crit}$, then a_i would have distance less than $2d_{crit} + 3d_{crit} = 5d_{crit}$ to that center, violating its goodness. So, bridges in G between different clusters can only occur between bad points.

Assume now that each cluster in C_T has size at least $2b + 1$; this is the sense in which we are requiring that ϵn be small compared to the smallest cluster in C_T. In this case, create a new graph H by connecting any two points a_i and a_j that share at least $b + 1$ neighbors in common in G, themselves included. Since every cluster has at least $2b + 1 - b = b + 1$ good points, and these points are fully connected in G, this means that H will contain an edge between every pair of good points in the same cluster. On the other hand, since the only edges in G between different clusters are between bad points, and there are at most b bad points, this means that H will not have any edges between different clusters in C_T. Thus, if we take the k largest connected components in H, these will all correspond to subsets of different clusters in C_T, with at most b points remaining.

At this point we have a correct clustering of all but at most b points in A. Call these clusters $C_1, \ldots, C_k$, where $C_j \subseteq C_j^*$. To cluster the remaining points a_i, we assign them to the cluster C_j that minimizes the median distance between a_i and points in C_j. Since each C_j has more good points than bad points, and each good point in C_j has distance at most d_{crit} to center c_j^*, by triangle inequality the median of these distances must lie in the range $[d(a_i, c_i^*) - d_{crit}, d(a_i, c_i^*) + d_{crit}]$. This means that this second step will correctly cluster all points a_i for which $w_2(a_i) - w(a_i) > 2d_{crit}$. In particular, we correctly cluster all points except possibly for at most ϵn satisfying item (1) of Lemma 7.6.

The above discussion assumes the value d_{crit} is known to our algorithm; we leave it as an exercise to the reader to modify the algorithm to remove this assumption. Summarizing, we have the following algorithm and theorem.

Algorithm k-Median Stability (given c, ϵ, d_{crit})

1. Create a graph G with a vertex for each datapoint in A, and an edge between vertices i and j if $d(a_i, a_j) \leq 2d_{crit}$.
2. Create a graph H with a vertex for each vertex in G and an edge between vertices i and j if i and j share at least $b + 1$ neighbors in common, themselves included, for $b = \epsilon n + \frac{5\epsilon n}{c-1}$. Let $C_1, \ldots, C_k$ denote the k largest connected components in H.
3. Assign each point not in $C_1 \cup \ldots \cup C_k$ to the cluster C_j of smallest median distance.

Theorem 7.7 *Assume A satisfies (c, ϵ) approximation-stability with respect to the k-median objective, that each cluster in C_T has size at least $\frac{10\epsilon}{c-1}n + 2\epsilon n + 1$, and that $C_T = C^*$. Then Algorithm k-Median Stability will find a clustering C such that $dist(C, C_T) \leq \epsilon$.*

7.7. High-Density Clusters

We now turn from the assumption that clusters are center-based to the assumption that clusters consist of high-density regions, separated by low-density moats such as in Figure 7.1.

7.7.1. Single Linkage

One natural algorithm for clustering under the high-density assumption is called *single linkage*. This algorithm begins with each point in its own cluster and then repeatedly merges the two "closest" clusters into one, where the distance between two clusters is defined as the *minimum* distance between points in each cluster. That is, $d_{min}(C, C') = \min_{x \in C, y \in C'} d(x, y)$, and the algorithm merges the two clusters C and C' whose d_{min} value is smallest over all pairs of clusters breaking ties arbitrarily. It then continues until there are only k clusters. This is called an *agglomerative* clustering algorithm because it begins with many clusters and then starts merging, or agglomerating them together.[3] Single-linkage is equivalent to running Kruskal's minimum-spanning-tree algorithm but halting when there are k trees remaining. The following theorem is fairly immediate.

Theorem 7.8 *Suppose the desired clustering $C_1^*, \ldots, C_k^*$ satisfies the property that there exists some distance σ such that*

1. *any two data points in different clusters have distance at least σ, and*
2. *for any cluster C_i^* and any partition of C_i^* into two non-empty sets A and $C_i^* \backslash A$, there exist points on each side of the partition of distance less than σ.*

Then, single-linkage will correctly recover the clustering $C_1^*, \ldots, C_k^*$.

Proof Consider running the algorithm until all pairs of clusters C and C' have $d_{min}(C, C') \geq \sigma$. At that point, by (2), each target cluster C_i^* will be fully contained within some cluster of the single-linkage algorithm. On the other hand, by (1) and by induction, each cluster C of the single-linkage algorithm will be fully contained within some C_i^* of the target clustering, since any merger of subsets of distinct target clusters would require $d_{min} \geq \sigma$. Therefore, the single-linkage clusters are indeed the target clusters. ∎

7.7.2. Robust Linkage

The single-linkage algorithm is fairly brittle. A few points bridging the gap between two different clusters can cause it to do the wrong thing. As a result, there has been significant work developing more robust versions of the algorithm.

One commonly used robust version of single linkage is Wishart's algorithm. A ball of radius r is created for each point with the point as center. The radius r is gradually increased starting from $r = 0$. The algorithm has a parameter t. When a ball has t or more points, the center point becomes active. When two balls with active centers intersect, the two center points are connected by an edge. The parameter t prevents a thin string of points between two clusters from causing a spurious merger. Note that Wishart's algorithm with $t = 1$ is the same as single linkage.

In fact, if one slightly modifies the algorithm to define a point to be live if its ball of radius $r/2$ contains at least t points, then it is known [CD10] that a value of

---

[3] Other agglomerative algorithms include *complete linkage* that merges the two clusters whose *maximum* distance between points is smallest, and Ward's algorithm described earlier that merges the two clusters that cause the k-means cost to increase by the least.

$t = O(d \log n)$ is sufficient to recover a nearly correct solution under a natural distributional formulation of the clustering problem. Specifically, suppose data points are drawn from some probability distribution D over R^d, and that the clusters correspond to high-density regions surrounded by lower-density moats. More specifically, the assumption is that

1. for some distance $\sigma > 0$, the σ-interior of each target cluster C_i^* has density at least some quantity λ (the σ-interior is the set of all points at distance at least σ from the boundary of the cluster),
2. the region between target clusters has density less than $\lambda(1 - \epsilon)$ for some $\epsilon > 0$,
3. the clusters should be separated by distance greater than 2σ, and
4. the σ-interior of the clusters contains most of their probability mass.

Then, for sufficiently large n, the algorithm will with high probability find nearly correct clusters. In this formulation, we allow points in low-density regions that are not in any target clusters at all. For details, see [CD10].

Robust Median Neighborhood Linkage robustifies single linkage in a different way. This algorithm guarantees that if it is possible to delete a small fraction of the data such that for all remaining points x, most of their $|C^*(x)|$ nearest neighbors indeed belong to their own cluster $C^*(x)$, then the hierarchy on clusters produced by the algorithm will include a close approximation to the true clustering. We refer the reader to [BLG14] for the algorithm and proof.

7.8. Kernel Methods

Kernel methods combine aspects of both center-based and density-based clustering. In center-based approaches like k-means or k-center, once the cluster centers are fixed, the Voronoi diagram of the cluster centers determines which cluster each data point belongs to. This implies that clusters are pairwise linearly separable.

If we believe that the true desired clusters may not be linearly separable, and yet we wish to use a center-based method, then one approach, as in the chapter on learning, is to use a kernel. Recall that a kernel function $K(\mathbf{x}, \mathbf{y})$ can be viewed as performing an implicit mapping ϕ of the data into a possibly much higher-dimensional space, and then taking a dot product in that space. That is, $K(\mathbf{x}, \mathbf{y}) = \phi(\mathbf{x}) \cdot \phi(\mathbf{y})$. This is then viewed as the affinity between points $\mathbf{x}$ and $\mathbf{y}$. We can extract distances in this new space using the equation $|\mathbf{z}_1 - \mathbf{z}_2|^2 = \mathbf{z}_1 \cdot \mathbf{z}_1 + \mathbf{z}_2 \cdot \mathbf{z}_2 - 2\mathbf{z}_1 \cdot \mathbf{z}_2$, so in particular we have $|\phi(\mathbf{x}) - \phi(\mathbf{y})|^2 = K(\mathbf{x}, \mathbf{x}) + K(\mathbf{y}, \mathbf{y}) - 2K(\mathbf{x}, \mathbf{y})$. We can then run a center-based clustering algorithm on these new distances.

One popular kernel function to use is the Gaussian kernel. The Gaussian kernel uses an affinity measure that emphasizes closeness of points and drops off exponentially as the points get farther apart. Specifically, we define the affinity between points $\mathbf{x}$ and $\mathbf{y}$ by

$$K(\mathbf{x}, \mathbf{y}) = e^{-\frac{1}{2\sigma^2}\|\mathbf{x} - \mathbf{y}\|^2}.$$

Another way to use affinities is to put them in an affinity matrix, or weighted graph. This graph can then be separated into clusters using a graph partitioning procedure such as the one in following section.

7.9. Recursive Clustering Based on Sparse Cuts

We now consider the case that data are nodes in an undirected connected graph $G(V, E)$ where an edge indicates that the end point vertices are similar. Recursive clustering starts with all vertices in one cluster and recursively splits a cluster into two parts whenever there is a small number of edges from one part to the other part of the cluster. Formally, for two disjoint sets S and T of vertices, define

$$\Phi(S, T) = \frac{\text{Number of edges from } S \text{ to } T}{\text{Total number of edges incident to } S \text{ in } G}.$$

$\Phi(S, T)$ measures the relative strength of similarities between S and T. Let $d(i)$ be the degree of vertex i, and for a subset S of vertices, let $d(S) = \sum_{i \in S} d(i)$. Let m be the total number of edges in the graph. The following algorithm aims to cut only a small fraction of the edges and to produce clusters that are internally consistent in that no subset of the cluster has low similarity to the rest of the cluster.

> **Recursive Clustering:** Select an appropriate value for ϵ. If a current cluster W has a subset S with $d(S) \leq \frac{1}{2}d(W)$ and $\Phi(S, S \subseteq W) \leq \varepsilon$, then split W into two clusters S and $W \setminus S$. Repeat until no such split is possible.

Theorem 7.9 *At termination of Recursive Clustering, the total number of edges between vertices in different clusters is at most $O(\varepsilon m \ln n)$.*

Proof Each edge between two different clusters at the end was deleted at some stage by the algorithm. We will "charge" edge deletes to vertices and bound the total charge. When the algorithm partitions a cluster W into S and $W \setminus S$ with $d(S) \leq (1/2)d(W)$, each $k \in S$ is charged $\frac{d(k)}{d(W)}$ times the number of edges being deleted. Since $\Phi(S, W \setminus S) \leq \varepsilon$, the charge added to each $k \in W$ is at most $\varepsilon d(k)$. A vertex is charged only when it is in the smaller part, $d(S) \leq d(W)/2$, of the cut. So between any two times it is charged, $d(W)$ is reduced by a factor of at least two, and so a vertex can be charged at most $\log_2 m \leq O(\ln n)$ times, proving the theorem. ∎

Implementing the algorithm requires computing $\text{Min}_{S \subseteq W} \Phi(S, W \setminus S)$, which is an NP-hard problem. So the theorem cannot be implemented right away. Luckily, eigenvalues and eigenvectors, which can be computed fast, give an approximate answer. The connection between eigenvalues and sparsity, known as Cheeger's inequality, is deep with applications to Markov chains among others. We do not discuss this here.

7.10. Dense Submatrices and Communities

Represent n data points in d-space by the rows of an $n \times d$ matrix A. Assume that A has all nonnegative entries. Examples to keep in mind for this section are the document-term matrix and the customer-product matrix. We address the question of how to define and find efficiently a coherent large subset of rows. To this end, the matrix A can be represented by a bipartite graph Figure 7.5. One side has a vertex for each row and the other side a vertex for each column. Between the vertex for row i and the vertex for column j, there is an edge with weight a_{ij}.

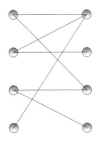

Figure 7.5: Example of a bipartite graph.

We want a subset S of row vertices and a subset T of column vertices so that

$$A(S, T) = \sum_{i \in S, j \in T} a_{ij}$$

is high. This simple definition is not good, since $A(S, T)$ will be maximized by taking all rows and columns. We need a balancing criterion that ensures that $A(S, T)$ is high relative to the sizes of S and T. One possibility is to maximize $\frac{A(S,T)}{|S||T|}$. This is not a good measure either, since it is maximized by the single edge of highest weight. The definition we use is the following. Let A be a matrix with nonnegative entries. For a subset S of rows and a subset T of columns, the *density* $d(S, T)$ of S and T is $d(S, T) = \frac{A(S,T)}{\sqrt{|S||T|}}$. The *density* $d(A)$ of A is defined as the maximum value of $d(S, T)$ over all subsets of rows and columns. This definition applies to bipartite as well as non-bipartite graphs.

One important case is when A's rows and columns both represent the same set and a_{ij} is the similarity between object i and object j. Here $d(S, S) = \frac{A(S,S)}{|S|}$. If A is an $n \times n$ 0-1 matrix, it can be thought of as the adjacency matrix of an undirected graph, and $d(S, S)$ is the average degree of a vertex in S. The subgraph of maximum average degree in a graph can be found exactly by network flow techniques, as we will show in the next section. We do not know an efficient (polynomial-time) algorithm for finding $d(A)$ exactly in general. However, we show that $d(A)$ is within a $O(\log^2 n)$ factor of the top singular value of A assuming $|a_{ij}| \leq 1$ for all i and j. This is a theoretical result. The gap may be much less than $O(\log^2 n)$ for many problems, making singular values and singular vectors quite useful. Also, S and T with $d(S, T) \geq \Omega(d(A) / \log^2 n)$ can be found algorithmically.

Theorem 7.10 *Let A be an $n \times d$ matrix with entries between 0 and 1. Then*

$$\sigma_1(A) \geq d(A) \geq \frac{\sigma_1(A)}{4 \log n \log d}.$$

Furthermore, subsets S and T satisfying $d(S, T) \geq \frac{\sigma_1(A)}{4 \log n \log d}$ may be found from the top singular vector of A.

Proof Let S and T be the subsets of rows and columns that achieve $d(A) = d(S, T)$. Consider an n-vector $\mathbf{u}$ that is $\frac{1}{\sqrt{|S|}}$ on S and 0 elsewhere and a d-vector $\mathbf{v}$ that is $\frac{1}{\sqrt{|T|}}$ on T and 0 elsewhere. Then,

$$\sigma_1(A) \ge \mathbf{u}^T A \mathbf{v} = \sum_{ij} u_i v_j a_{ij} = d(S, T) = d(A)$$

establishing the first inequality.

To prove the second inequality, express $\sigma_1(A)$ in terms of the first left and right singular vectors $\mathbf{x}$ and $\mathbf{y}$.

$$\sigma_1(A) = \mathbf{x}^T A \mathbf{y} = \sum_{i,j} x_i a_{ij} y_j, \qquad |\mathbf{x}| = |\mathbf{y}| = 1.$$

Since the entries of A are nonnegative, the components of the first left and right singular vectors must all be nonnegative, that is, $x_i \ge 0$ and $y_j \ge 0$ for all i and j. To bound $\sum_{i,j} x_i a_{ij} y_j$, break the summation into $O(\log n \log d)$ parts. Each part corresponds to a given α and β and consists of all i such that $\alpha \le x_i < 2\alpha$ and all j such that $\beta \le y_j < 2\beta$. The $\log n \log d$ parts are defined by breaking the rows into $\log n$ blocks with α equal to $\frac{1}{2}\frac{1}{\sqrt{n}}, \frac{1}{\sqrt{n}}, 2\frac{1}{\sqrt{n}}, 4\frac{1}{\sqrt{n}}, \ldots, 1$ and by breaking the columns into $\log d$ blocks with β equal to $\frac{1}{2}\frac{1}{\sqrt{d}}, \frac{1}{\sqrt{d}}, \frac{2}{\sqrt{d}}, \frac{4}{\sqrt{d}}, \ldots, 1$. The i such that $x_i < \frac{1}{2\sqrt{n}}$ and the j such that $y_j < \frac{1}{2\sqrt{d}}$ will be ignored at a loss of at most $\frac{1}{4}\sigma_1(A)$. Exercise 7.27 proves the loss is at most this amount.

Since $\sum_i x_i^2 = 1$, the set $S = \{i | \alpha \le x_i < 2\alpha\}$ has $|S| \le \frac{1}{\alpha^2}$ and similarly, $T = \{j | \beta \le y_j \le 2\beta\}$ has $|T| \le \frac{1}{\beta^2}$. Thus,

$$\sum_{\substack{i \\ \alpha \le x_i \le 2\alpha}} \sum_{\substack{j \\ \beta \le y_j \le 2\beta}} x_i y_j a_{ij} \le 4\alpha\beta A(S, T)$$

$$\le 4\alpha\beta d(S, T)\sqrt{|S||T|}$$
$$\le 4d(S, T)$$
$$\le 4d(A).$$

From this it follows that

$$\sigma_1(A) \le 4d(A) \log n \log d$$

or

$$d(A) \ge \frac{\sigma_1(A)}{4 \log n \log d}$$

proving the second inequality.

It is clear that for each of the values of (α, β), we can compute $A(S, T)$ and $d(S, T)$ as above and taking the best of these $d(S, T)$, gives us an algorithm as claimed in the theorem. ∎

Note that in many cases, the non-zero values of x_i and y_j after zeroing out the low entries will only go from $\frac{1}{2}\frac{1}{\sqrt{n}}$ to $\frac{c}{\sqrt{n}}$ for x_i and $\frac{1}{2}\frac{1}{\sqrt{d}}$ to $\frac{c}{\sqrt{d}}$ for y_j, since the singular vectors are likely to be balanced given that a_{ij} are all between 0 and 1. In this case, there will be $O(1)$ groups only and the log factors disappear.

Another measure of density is based on similarities. Recall that the similarity between objects represented by vectors (rows of A) is defined by their dot products. Thus, similarities are entries of the matrix AA^T. Define the average cohesion $f(S)$ of a set S of rows of A to be the sum of all pairwise dot products of rows in S divided by $|S|$. The average cohesion of A is the maximum over all subsets of rows of the average cohesion of the subset.

Since the singular values of AA^T are squares of singular values of A, we expect $f(A)$ to be related to $\sigma_1(A)^2$ and $d(A)^2$. Indeed it is. We state the following without proof.

Lemma 7.11 $d(A)^2 \leq f(A) \leq d(A) \log n$. *Also,* $\sigma_1(A)^2 \geq f(A) \geq \frac{c\sigma_1(A)^2}{\log n}$.

$f(A)$ can be found exactly using flow techniques as we will see later.

7.11. Community Finding and Graph Partitioning

Assume that data are nodes in a possibly weighted graph where edges represent some notion of affinity between their endpoints. In particular, let $G = (V, E)$ be a weighted graph. Given two sets of nodes S and T, define

$$E(S, T) = \sum_{\substack{i \in S \\ j \in T}} e_{ij}.$$

We then define the *density* of a set S to be

$$d(S, S) = \frac{E(S, S)}{|S|}.$$

If G is an undirected graph, then $d(S, S)$ can be viewed as the average degree in the vertex-induced subgraph over S. The set S of maximum density is therefore the subgraph of maximum average degree. Finding such a set can be viewed as finding a tight-knit community inside some network. In the next section, we describe an algorithm for finding such a set using network flow techniques.

Flow Methods

Here we consider dense induced subgraphs of a graph. An induced subgraph of a graph consists of a subset of the vertices of the graph along with all edges of the graph that connect pairs of vertices in the subset of vertices. We show that finding an induced subgraph with maximum average degree can be done by network flow techniques. This is simply maximizing the density $d(S, S)$ over all subsets S of the graph. First consider the problem of finding a subset of vertices such that the induced subgraph has average degree at least λ for some parameter λ. Then do a binary search on the value of λ until the maximum λ for which there exists a subgraph with average degree at least λ is found.

Given a graph G in which one wants to find a dense subgraph, construct a directed graph H from the given graph and then carry out a flow computation on H. H has a node for each edge of the original graph, a node for each vertex of the original graph, plus two additional nodes s and t. There is a directed edge with capacity 1 from s to each node corresponding to an edge of the original graph and a directed edge with infinite capacity from each node corresponding to an edge of the original graph to the two nodes corresponding to the vertices the edge connects. Finally, there is a directed edge with capacity λ from each node corresponding to a vertex of the original graph to t.

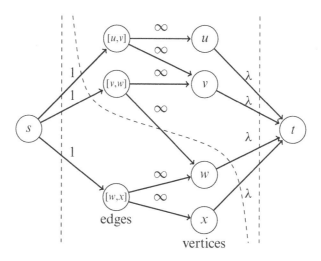

Figure 7.6: The directed graph H used by the flow technique to find a dense subgraph.

Notice there are three types of cut sets of the directed graph that have finite capacity, Figure 7.6. The first cuts all arcs from the source. It has capacity e, the number of edges of the original graph. The second cuts all edges into the sink. It has capacity λv, where v is the number of vertices of the original graph. The third cuts some arcs from s and some arcs into t. It partitions the set of vertices and the set of edges of the original graph into two blocks. The first block contains the source node s, a subset of the edges e_s, and a subset of the vertices v_s defined by the subset of edges. The first block must contain both end points of each edge in e_s; otherwise an infinite arc will be in the cut. The second block contains t and the remaining edges and vertices. The edges in this second block either connect vertices in the second block or have one endpoint in each block. The cut set will cut some infinite arcs from edges not in e_s coming into vertices in v_s. However, these arcs are directed from nodes in the block containing t to nodes in the block containing s. Note that any finite capacity cut that leaves an edge node connected to s must cut the two related vertex nodes from t (see Figures 7.6 and 7.7). Thus, there is a cut of capacity $e - e_s + \lambda v_s$ where v_s and e_s are the vertices and edges of a subgraph. For this cut to be the minimal cut, the quantity $e - e_s + \lambda v_s$ must be minimal over all subsets of vertices of the original graph and the capacity must be less than e and also less than λv.

If there is a subgraph with v_s vertices and e_s edges where the ratio $\frac{e_s}{v_s}$ is sufficiently large so that $\frac{e_s}{v_s} > \frac{e}{v}$, then for λ such that $\frac{e_s}{v_s} > \lambda > \frac{e}{v}$, we have $e_s - \lambda v_s > 0$ and $e - e_s + \lambda v_s < e$. Similarly $e < \lambda v$ and thus $e - e_s + \lambda v_s < \lambda v$. This implies that the cut $e - e_s + \lambda v_s$ is less than either e or λv and the flow algorithm will find a nontrivial cut and hence a proper subset. For different values of λ in the above range there may be different nontrivial cuts.

Note that for a given density of edges, the number of edges grows as the square of the number of vertices and $\frac{e_s}{v_s}$ is less likely to exceed $\frac{e}{v}$ if v_S is small. Thus, the flow method works well in finding large subsets, since it works with $\frac{e_s}{v_s}$. To find small communities, one would need to use a method that worked with $\frac{e_s}{v_S^2}$ as the following example illustrates.

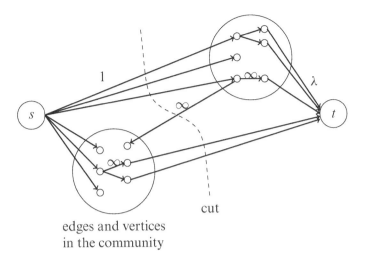

edges and vertices
in the community

Figure 7.7: Cut in flow graph

Example Consider finding a dense subgraph of 1,000 vertices and 2,000 internal edges in a graph of 10^6 vertices and 6×10^6 edges. For concreteness, assume the graph was generated by the following process. First, a 1,000-vertex graph with 2,000 edges was generated as a random regular degree 4 graph. The 1,000-vertex graph was then augmented to have 10^6 vertices and edges were added at random until all vertices were of degree 12. Note that each vertex among the first 1,000 has four edges to other vertices among the first 1,000 and eight edges to other vertices. The graph on the 1,000 vertices is much denser than the whole graph in some sense. Although the subgraph induced by the 1,000 vertices has four edges per vertex and the full graph has twelve edges per vertex, the probability of two vertices of the 1,000 being connected by an edge is much higher than for the graph as a whole. The probability is given by the ratio of the actual number of edges connecting vertices among the 1,000 to the number of possible edges if the vertices formed a complete graph:

$$p = \frac{e}{\left(\binom{v}{2}\right)} = \frac{2e}{v(v-1)}.$$

For the 1,000 vertices, this number is $p = \frac{2 \times 2,000}{1,000 \times 999} \cong 4 \times 10^{-3}$. For the entire graph, this number is $p = \frac{2 \times 6 \times 10^6}{10^6 \times 10^6} = 12 \times 10^{-6}$. This difference in probability of two vertices being connected should allow us to find the dense subgraph. ∎

In our example, the cut of all arcs out of s is of capacity 6×10^6, the total number of edges in the graph, and the cut of all arcs into t is of capacity λ times the number of vertices or $\lambda \times 10^6$. A cut separating the 1,000 vertices and 2,000 edges would have capacity $6 \times 10^6 - 2,000 + \lambda \times 1,000$. This cut cannot be the minimum cut for any value of λ, since $\frac{e_s}{v_s} = 2$ and $\frac{e}{v} = 6$, hence $\frac{e_s}{v_s} < \frac{e}{v}$. The point is that to find the 1,000 vertices, we have to maximize $A(S, S)/|S|^2$ rather than $A(S, S)/|S|$. Note that $A(S, S)/|S|^2$ penalizes large $|S|$ much more and therefore can find the 1,000 node "dense" subgraph.

7.12. Spectral Clustering Applied to Social Networks

Finding communities in social networks is different from other clustering for several reasons. First, we often want to find communities of size say 20 to 50 in networks with 100 million vertices. Second, a person is in a number of overlapping communities and thus we are not finding disjoint clusters. Third, there often are a number of levels of structure, and a set of dominant communities may be hiding a set of weaker communities that are of interest. Spectral clustering is one approach to these issues.

In spectral clustering of the vertices of a graph, one creates a matrix V whose columns correspond to the first k singular vectors of the adjacency matrix. Each row of V is the projection of a row of the adjacency matrix to the space spanned by the k singular vectors. In the example below, the graph has five vertices divided into two cliques, one consisting of the first three vertices and the other the last two vertices. The top two right singular vectors of the adjacency matrix, not normalized to length one, are $(1, 1, 1, 0, 0)^T$ and $(0, 0, 0, 1, 1)^T$. The five rows of the adjacency matrix projected to these vectors form the 5×2 matrix in Figure 7.8. Here, there are two ideal clusters with all edges inside a cluster being present including self-loops and all edges between clusters being absent. The five rows project to just two points, depending on which cluster the rows are in. If the clusters were not so ideal and, instead of the graph consisting of two disconnected cliques, the graph consisted of two dense subsets of vertices where the two sets were connected by only a few edges, then the singular vectors would not be indicator vectors for the clusters but close to indicator vectors. The rows would be mapped to two clusters of points instead of two points. A k-means clustering algorithm would find the clusters.

If the clusters were overlapping, then instead of two clusters of points, there would be three clusters of points where the third cluster corresponds to the overlapping vertices of the two clusters. Instead of using k-means clustering, we might instead find the minimum 1-norm vector in the space spanned by the two singular vectors. The minimum 1-norm vector will not be an indicator vector, so we would threshold its values to create an indicator vector for a cluster. Instead of finding the minimum 1-norm vector in the space spanned by the singular vectors in V, we might look for a small 1-norm vector close to the subspace:

$$\min_{\mathbf{x}}(1 - |\mathbf{x}|_1 + \alpha \cos(\theta)).$$

Here θ is the cosine of the angle between $\mathbf{x}$ and the space spanned by the two singular vectors. α is a control parameter that determines how close we want the vector to be to the subspace. When α is large, $\mathbf{x}$ must be close to the subspace. When α is zero, $\mathbf{x}$ can be anywhere.

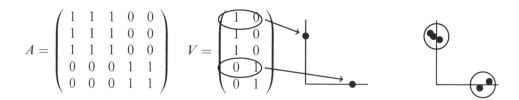

$$A = \begin{pmatrix} 1 & 1 & 1 & 0 & 0 \\ 1 & 1 & 1 & 0 & 0 \\ 1 & 1 & 1 & 0 & 0 \\ 0 & 0 & 0 & 1 & 1 \\ 0 & 0 & 0 & 1 & 1 \end{pmatrix} \qquad V = \begin{pmatrix} 1 & 0 \\ 1 & 0 \\ 1 & 0 \\ 0 & 1 \\ 0 & 1 \end{pmatrix}$$

Figure 7.8: Illustration of spectral clustering.

Finding the minimum 1-norm vector in the space spanned by a set of vectors can be formulated as a linear programming problem. To find the minimum 1-norm vector in V, write $V\mathbf{x} = \mathbf{y}$ where we want to solve for both $\mathbf{x}$ and $\mathbf{y}$. Note that the format is different from the usual format for a set of linear equations $A\mathbf{x} = \mathbf{b}$ where $\mathbf{b}$ is a known vector.

Finding the minimum 1-norm vector looks like a nonlinear problem:

$$\min |\mathbf{y}|_1 \text{ subject to } V\mathbf{x} = \mathbf{y}.$$

To remove the absolute value sign, write $\mathbf{y} = \mathbf{y}_1 - \mathbf{y}_2$ with $\mathbf{y}_1 \geq 0$ and $\mathbf{y}_2 \geq 0$. Then solve

$$\min \left(\sum_{i=1}^{n} y_{1i} + \sum_{i=1}^{n} y_{2i} \right) \text{ subject to } V\mathbf{x} = \mathbf{y}, \ \mathbf{y}_1 \geq 0, \text{ and } \mathbf{y}_2 \geq 0.$$

Write $V\mathbf{x} = \mathbf{y}_1 - \mathbf{y}_2$ as $V\mathbf{x} - \mathbf{y}_1 + \mathbf{y}_2 = 0$. Then we have the linear equations in a format we are accustomed to:

$$[V, -I, I] \begin{pmatrix} \mathbf{x} \\ \mathbf{y}_1 \\ \mathbf{y}_2 \end{pmatrix} = \begin{pmatrix} 0 \\ 0 \\ \vdots \\ 0 \end{pmatrix}.$$

This is a linear programming problem. The solution, however, happens to be $\mathbf{x} = 0$, $\mathbf{y}_1 = 0$, and $\mathbf{y}_2 = 0$. To resolve this, add the equation $y_{1i} = 1$ to get a community containing the vertex i.

Often we are looking for communities of 50 or 100 vertices in graphs with hundreds of million of vertices. We want a method to find such communities in time proportional to the size of the community and not the size of the entire graph. Here spectral clustering can be used, but instead of calculating singular vectors of the entire graph, we do something else. Consider a random walk on a graph. If we walk long enough, the probability distribution converges to the first eigenvector. However, if we take only a few steps from a start vertex or small group of vertices that we believe define a cluster, the probability will distribute over the cluster with some of the probability leaking out to the remainder of the graph. To get the early convergence of several vectors that ultimately converge to the first few singular vectors, take a subspace $[\mathbf{x}, A\mathbf{x}, A^2\mathbf{x}, A^3\mathbf{x}]$ and propagate the subspace. At each iteration find an orthonormal basis and then multiply each basis vector by A. Then take the resulting basis vectors after a few steps, say five, and find a minimum 1-norm vector in the subspace.

A third issue that arises is when a dominant structure hides an important weaker structure. One can run their algorithm to find the dominant structure and then weaken the dominant structure by randomly removing edges in the clusters so that the edge density is similar to the remainder of the network. Then reapplying the algorithm often will uncover the weaker structure. Real networks often have several levels of structure. The technique can also be used to improve state-of-the-art clustering algorithms. After weakening the dominant structure to find the weaker hidden structure, one can go back to the original data and weaken the hidden structure and reapply the algorithm to again find the dominant structure. This improves most state-of-the-art clustering algorithms.

7.13. Bibliographic Notes

Clustering has a long history. For a good general survey, see [Jai10]. For a collection of surveys giving an in-depth treatment of many different approaches to, applications of, and perspectives on clustering, see [HMMR15]; e.g., see [AB15] for a good discussion of center-based clustering. Lloyd's algorithm for k-means clustering is from [Llo82], and the k-means++ initialization method is due to Arthur and Vassilvitskii [AV07]. Ward's algorithm, from 1963, appears in [War63]. Analysis of the farthest-traversal algorithm for the k-center problem is due to Gonzalez [Gon85].

Theorem 7.4 is from [KV09]. Analysis of spectral clustering in stochastic models is given in [McS01], and the analysis of spectral clustering without a stochastic model and 7.5.2 is due to [KK10].

The definition of approximation-stability is from [BBG13] and [BBV08], and the analysis given in Section 7.6 is due to [BBG13].

Single-linkage clustering goes back at least to Florek et al. [FŁP+51], and Wishart's robust version is from [Wis69]. Extensions of Theorem 7.8 are given in [BBV08], and theoretical guarantees for different forms of robust linkage are given in [CD10] and [BLG14]. A good survey of kernel methods in clustering appears in [FCMR08].

Section 7.9 is a simplified version of [KVV04]. Section 7.10 is from [RV99].

For details on local spectral method, see [HSB+15] and [LHBH15], and for hidden structure, see [HSC+15] and [HLSH18]. A different approach to defining and identifying overlapping communities appears in [BBB+13].

7.14. Exercises

Exercise 7.1 Construct examples where using distances instead of distance squared gives bad results for Gaussian densities. For example, pick samples from two one-dimensional unit variance Gaussians, with their centers 10 units apart. Cluster these samples by trial and error into two clusters, first according to k-means and then according to the k-median criteria. The k-means clustering should essentially yield the centers of the Gaussians as cluster centers. What cluster centers do you get when you use the k-median criterion?

Exercise 7.2 Let $v = (1, 3)$. What is the L_1 norm of v? The L_2 norm? The square of the L_1 norm?

Exercise 7.3 Show that in one dimension, the center of a cluster that minimizes the sum of distances of data points to the center is in general not unique. Suppose we now require the center also to be a data point; then show that it is the median element (not the mean). Further in one dimension, show that if the center minimizes the sum of squared distances to the data points, then it is unique.

Exercise 7.4 Construct a block diagonal matrix A with three blocks of size 50. Each matrix element in a block has value $p = 0.7$ and each matrix element not in a block has value $q = 0.3$. Generate a 150×150 matrix B of random numbers in the range $[0,1]$. If $b_{ij} \geq a_{ij}$ replace a_{ij} with the value 1. Otherwise replace a_{ij} with value zero. The rows of A have three natural clusters. Generate a random permutation and use it to permute the rows and columns of the matrix A so that the rows and columns of each cluster are randomly distributed.

1. Apply Lloyd's algorithm with random initialization to A with $k = 3$. Do you find the correct clusters?
2. Apply Lloyd's algorithm with random initialization to A for $1 \le k \le 10$. Plot the value of the sum of squares to the cluster centers versus k. Was three the correct value for k?

Exercise 7.5 Let M be a $k \times k$ matrix whose elements are numbers in the range [0,1]. A matrix entry close to 1 indicates that the row and column of the entry correspond to closely related items, and an entry close to zero indicates unrelated entities. Develop an algorithm to match each row with a closely related column where a column can be matched with only one row.

Exercise 7.6 The simple greedy algorithm of Section 7.3 assumes that we know the clustering radius r. Suppose we do not. Describe how we might arrive at the correct r?

Exercise 7.7 For the k-median problem, show that there is at most a factor of two ratio between the optimal value when we either require all cluster centers to be data points or allow arbitrary points to be centers.

Exercise 7.8 For the k-means problem, show that there is at most a factor of four ratio between the optimal value when we either require all cluster centers to be data points or allow arbitrary points to be centers.

Exercise 7.9 Consider clustering points in the plane according to the k-median criterion, where cluster centers are required to be data points. Enumerate all possible clustering's and select the one with the minimum cost. The number of possible ways of labeling n points, each with a label from $\{1, 2, \ldots, k\}$, is k^n, which is prohibitive. Show that we can find the optimal clustering in time at most a constant times $\binom{n}{k} + k^2$. Note that $\binom{n}{k} \le n^k$, which is much smaller than k^n when $k << n$.

Exercise 7.10 Suppose in the previous exercise, we allow any point in space (not necessarily data points) to be cluster centers. Show that the optimal clustering may be found in time at most a constant times n^{2k^2}.

Exercise 7.11 Corollary 7.2 shows that for a set of points $\{a_1, a_2, \ldots, a_n\}$, there is a unique point x, namely their centroid, which minimizes $\sum_{i=1}^{n} |a_i - x|^2$. Show examples where the x minimizing $\sum_{i=1}^{n} |a_i - x|$ is not unique. (Consider just points on the real line.) Show examples where the x defined as above are far apart from each other.

Exercise 7.12 Let $\{a_1, a_2, \ldots, a_n\}$ be a set of unit vectors in a cluster. Let $c = \frac{1}{n} \sum_{i=1}^{n} a_i$ be the cluster centroid. The centroid c is not in general a unit vector. Define the similarity between two points a_i and a_j as their dot product. Show that the average cluster similarity $\frac{1}{n^2} \sum_{i,j} a_i a_j^T$ is the same whether it is computed by averaging all pairs or by computing the average similarity of each point with the centroid of the cluster.

Exercise 7.13 For some synthetic data estimate the number of local minima for k-means by using the birthday estimate. Is your estimate an unbaised estimate of the number? An upper bound? A lower bound? Why?

Exercise 7.14 Give an example of a set of data points where optimizing the k-center objective produces a clustering that is different from the most natural k-clustering of that data. Do the same for the k-median objective. You may wish to use k = 2.

Exercise 7.15 Prove that for any two vectors $\mathbf{a}$ and $\mathbf{b}$, $|\mathbf{a} - \mathbf{b}|^2 \geq \frac{1}{2}|\mathbf{a}|^2 - |\mathbf{b}|^2$.

Exercise 7.16 Let A be an $n \times d$ data matrix, B its best rank k approximation, and C the optimal centers for k-means clustering of rows of A. How is it possible that $\|A - B\|_F^2 < \|A - C\|_F^2$?

Exercise 7.17 Suppose S is a finite set of points in space with centroid $\mu(S)$. If a set T of points is added to S, show that the centroid $\mu(S \cup T)$ of $S \cup T$ is at distance at most $\frac{|T|}{|S|+|T|}|\mu(T) - \mu(S)|$ from $\mu(S)$.

Exercise 7.18 What happens if we relax this restriction – for example, if we allow for S, the entire set?

Exercise 7.19 Given the graph $G = (V, E)$ of a social network where vertices represent individuals and edges represent relationships of some kind, one would like to define the concept of a community. A number of different definitions are possible.

1. A subgraph $S = (V_S, E_S)$ whose density $\frac{E_S}{V_S^2}$ is greater than that of the graph $\frac{E}{V^2}$.
2. A subgraph S with a low conductance like property such as the number of graph edges leaving the subgraph normalized by the minimum size of S or $V-S$ where size is measured by the sum of degrees of vertices in S or in $V - S$.
3. A subgraph that has more internal edges than in a random graph with the same degree distribution.

Which would you use and why?

Exercise 7.20 A stochastic matrix is a matrix with nonnegative entries in which each row sums to one. Show that for a stochastic matrix, the largest eigenvalue is 1. Show that the eigenvalue has multiplicity 1 if and only if the corresponding Markov Chain is connected.

Exercise 7.21 Show that if P is a stochastic matrix and π satisfies $\pi_i p_{ij} = \pi_j p_{ji}$, then for any left eigenvector $\mathbf{v}$ of P, the vector $\mathbf{u}$ with components $u_i = \frac{v_i}{\pi_i}$ is a right eigenvector with the same eigenvalue.

Exercise 7.22 Give an example of a clustering problem where the clusters are not linearly separable in the original space, but are separable in a higher dimensional space.

Hint. Look at the example for Gaussian kernels in the chapter on learning.

Exercise 7.23 The Gaussian kernel maps points to a higher dimensional space. What is this mapping?

Exercise 7.24 Agglomerative clustering requires that one calculate the distances between all pairs of points. If the number of points is a million or more, then this is impractical. One might try speeding up the agglomerative clustering algorithm by maintaining 100 clusters at each unit of time. Start by randomly selecting

100 points and place each point in a cluster by itself. Each time a pair of clusters is merged randomly, select one of the remaining data points and create a new cluster containing that point. Suggest some other alternatives.

Exercise 7.25 Let A be the adjacency matrix of an undirected graph. Let $d(S, S) = \frac{A(S,S)}{|S|}$ be the density of the subgraph induced by the set of vertices S. Prove that $d(S, S)$ is the average degree of a vertex in S. Recall that $A(S, T) = \sum_{i \in S, j \in T} a_{ij}$.

Exercise 7.26 Suppose A is a matrix with nonnegative entries. Show that $A(S, T)/(|S||T|)$ is maximized by the single edge with highest a_{ij}. Recall that $A(S, T) = \sum_{i \in S, j \in T} a_{ij}$.

Exercise 7.27 Suppose A is a matrix with nonnegative entries and

$$\sigma_1(A) = \mathbf{x}^T A \mathbf{y} = \sum_{i,j} x_i a_{ij} y_j, \qquad |\mathbf{x}| = |\mathbf{y}| = 1.$$

Zero out all x_i less than $1/2\sqrt{n}$ and all y_j less than $1/2\sqrt{d}$. Show that the loss is no more than one-fourth of $\sigma_1(A)$.

Exercise 7.28 Consider other measures of density such as $\frac{A(S,T)}{|S|^\rho |T|^\rho}$ for different values of ρ. Discuss the significance of the densest subgraph according to these measures.

Exercise 7.29 Let A be the adjacency matrix of an undirected graph. Let M be the matrix whose ij^{th} element is $a_{ij} - \frac{d_i d_j}{2m}$. Partition the vertices into two groups, S and $\bar{S}$. Let s be the indicator vector for the set S and let $\bar{s}$ be the indicator variable for $\bar{S}$. Then $s^T M s$ is the number of edges in S above the expected number given the degree distribution and $s^T M \bar{s}$ is the number of edges from S to $\bar{S}$ above the expected number given the degree distribution. Prove that if $s^T M s$ is positive $s^T M \bar{s}$ must be negative.

Exercise 7.30 An algorithm is said to satisfy scale invariance if multiplying all distances by a constant factor does not change the clustering it produces. It is said to satisfy k-richness if, for any partition of n points into k groups, there exist distances between points such that given these distances, the algorithm will produce this partition. Finally, the algorithm is said to satisfy consistency if reducing distances between points inside the same cluster (even non-uniformly) will never cause the algorithm to output a different clustering. Which of these properties is satisfied by the following clustering algorithms?

1. Single linkage
2. Spectral clustering.

Exercise 7.31 (**Research Problem**) What are good measures of density that are also effectively computable? Is there empirical/theoretical evidence that some are better than others?

Exercise 7.32 Create a graph with a small community and start a random walk in the community. Calculate the frequency distribution over the vertices of the graph and normalize the frequency distribution by the stationary probability. Plot the ratio of the normalized frequency for the vertices of the graph. What is the shape of the plot for vertices in the small community?

Exercise 7.33

1. Create a random graph with the following two structures imbedded in it. The first structure has three equal size communities with no edges between communities, and the second structure has five equal size communities with no edges between communities.
2. Apply a clustering algorithm to find the dominate structure. Which structure did you get?
3. Weaken the dominant structure by removing a fraction of its edges and see if you can find the hidden structure.

Exercise 7.34 Experiment with finding hidden communities.

Exercise 7.35 Generate a bloc model with two equal-size communities where p and q are the probabilities for the edge density within communities and the edge density between communities. Then generated a GNP model with probability $(p + q)/2$. Which of two models most likely generates a community with half of the vertices?

CHAPTER EIGHT

Random Graphs

Large graphs appear in many contexts such as the World Wide Web, the internet, social networks, journal citations, and other places. What is different about the modern study of large graphs from traditional graph theory and graph algorithms is that here one seeks statistical properties of these very large graphs rather than an exact answer to questions on specific graphs. This is akin to the switch physics had made in the late nineteenth century in going from mechanics to statistical mechanics. Just as the physicists did, one formulates abstract models of graphs that are not completely realistic in every situation, but that admit a nice mathematical development that can guide what happens in practical situations. Perhaps the most basic model is the $G(n, p)$ model of a random graph. In this chapter, we study properties of the $G(n, p)$ model as well as other models.

8.1. The $G(n, p)$ Model

The $G(n, p)$ model, due to Erdös and Rényi, has two parameters, n and p. Here n is the number of vertices of the graph and p is the edge probability. For each pair of distinct vertices, v and w, p is the probability that the edge (v, w) is present. The presence of each edge is statistically independent of all other edges. The graph-valued random variable with these parameters is denoted by $G(n, p)$. When we refer to the graph $G(n, p)$, we mean one realization of the random variable. In many cases, p will be a function of n such as $p = d/n$ for some constant d. For example, if $p = d/n$, then the expected degree of a vertex of the graph is $(n - 1)\frac{d}{n} \approx d$. In order to simplify calculations in this chapter, we will often use the approximation that $\frac{n-1}{n} \approx 1$. In fact, conceptually it is helpful to think of n as both the total number of vertices and as the number of potential neighbors of any given node, even though the latter is really $n - 1$; for all our calculations, when n is large, the correction is just a low-order term.

The interesting thing about the $G(n, p)$ model is that even though edges are chosen independently with no "collusion," certain global properties of the graph emerge from the independent choices. For small p, with $p = d/n, d < 1$, each connected component in the graph is small. For $d > 1$, there is a giant component consisting of a constant fraction of the vertices. In addition, there is a rapid transition at the threshold $d = 1$. Below the threshold, the probability of a giant component is very small, and above the threshold, the probability is almost 1.

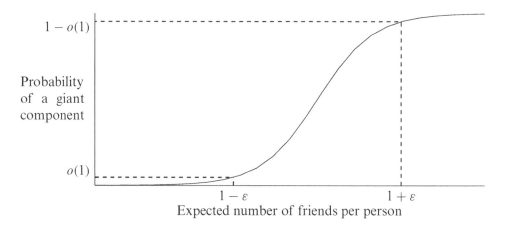

Figure 8.1: Probability of a giant component as a function of the expected number of people each person knows directly.

The phase transition at the threshold $d = 1$ from very small $o(n)$-size components to a giant $\Omega(n)$-sized component is illustrated by the following example. Suppose the vertices represent people, and an edge means the two people it connects know each other. Given a chain of connections, such as A knows B, B knows C, C knows D, ..., and Y knows Z, we say that A indirectly knows Z. Thus, all people belonging to a connected component of the graph indirectly know each other. Suppose each pair of people, independent of other pairs, tosses a coin that comes up heads with probability $p = d/n$. If it is heads, they know each other; if it comes up tails, they don't. The value of d can be interpreted as the expected number of people a single person directly knows. The question arises as to how large are sets of people who indirectly know each other.

If the expected number of people each person knows is more than one, then a giant component of people, all of whom indirectly know each other, will be present, consisting of a constant fraction of all the people. On the other hand, if in expectation, each person knows less than one person, the largest set of people who know each other indirectly is a vanishingly small fraction of the whole. Furthermore, the transition from the vanishing fraction to a constant fraction of the whole happens abruptly between d slightly less than 1 to d slightly more than 1. See Figure 8.1. Note that there is no global coordination of who knows whom. Each pair of individuals decides independently. Indeed, many large real-world graphs, with constant average degree, have a giant component. This is perhaps the most important global property of the $G(n, p)$ model. See Figure 8.2 for examples of typical and atypical graphs in this model.

8.1.1. Degree Distribution

One of the simplest quantities to observe in a real graph is the number of vertices of given degree, called the vertex degree distribution. It is also very simple to study these distributions in $G(n, p)$, since the degree of each vertex is the sum of n independent random variables, which results in a binomial distribution.

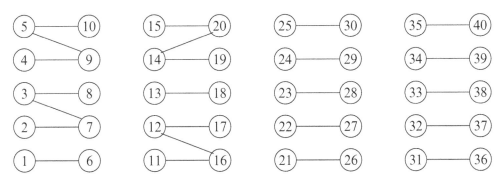

A graph with 40 vertices and 24 edges

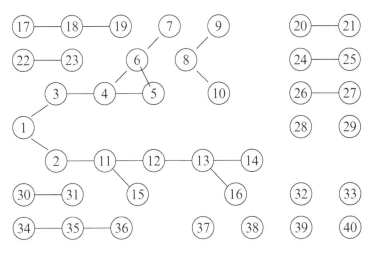

A randomly generated $G(n, p)$ graph with 40 vertices and 24 edges

Figure 8.2: Two graphs, each with 40 vertices and 24 edges. The second graph was randomly generated using the $G(n, p)$ model with $p = 1.2/n$. A graph similar to the top graph is almost surely not going to be randomly generated in the $G(n, p)$ model, whereas a graph similar to the lower graph will almost surely occur. Note that the lower graph consists of a giant component along with a number of small components that are trees.

Example In $G(n, \frac{1}{2})$, each vertex is of degree close to $n/2$. In fact, for any $\varepsilon > 0$, the degree of each vertex almost surely is within $1 \pm \varepsilon$ times $n/2$. To see this, note that the degree of a vertex is the sum of $n - 1 \approx n$ indicator variables that take on value 1 or zero depending on whether the edge is present or not, each of mean $\frac{1}{2}$ and variance $\frac{1}{4}$. The expected value of the sum is the sum of the expected values and the variance of the sum is the sum of the variances, and hence the degree has mean $\approx \frac{n}{2}$ and variance $\approx \frac{n}{4}$. Thus, the probability mass is within an additive term of $\pm c\sqrt{n}$ of the mean for some constant c and thus within a multiplicative factor of $1 \pm \epsilon$ of $\frac{n}{2}$ for sufficiently large n. ■

The degree distribution of $G(n, p)$ for general p is also binomial. Since p is the probability of an edge being present, the expected degree of a vertex is $p(n-1) \approx pn$. The degree distribution is given by

$$\text{Prob(vertex has degree } k) = \binom{n-1}{k} p^k (1-p)^{n-k-1} \approx \binom{n}{k} p^k (1-p)^{n-k}.$$

The quantity $\binom{n}{k}$ is the number of ways of choosing k edges, out of the possible n edges, and $p^k(1-p)^{n-k}$ is the probability that the k selected edges are present and the remaining $n - k$ are not.

The binomial distribution falls off exponentially fast as one moves away from the mean. However, the degree distributions of graphs that appear in many applications do not exhibit such sharp drops. Rather, the degree distributions are much broader. This is often referred to as having a "heavy tail." The term *tail* refers to values of a random variable far away from its mean, usually measured in a number of standard deviations. Thus, although the $G(n, p)$ model is important mathematically, more complex models are needed to represent real-world graphs.

Consider an airline route graph. The graph has a wide range of degrees from degree 1 or 2 for a small city to degree 100 or more, for a major hub. The degree distribution is not binomial. Many large graphs that arise in various applications appear to have power law degree distributions. A power law degree distribution is one in which the number of vertices having a given degree decreases as a power of the degree, as in

$$\text{Number(degree } k \text{ vertices)} = c\frac{n}{k^r},$$

for some small positive real r, often just slightly less than 3. Later, we will consider a random graph model giving rise to such degree distributions. Binomial and power law distributions are illustrated in Figure 8.3.

The following theorem states that the degree distribution of the random graph $G(n, p)$ is tightly concentrated about its expected value. That is, the probability that

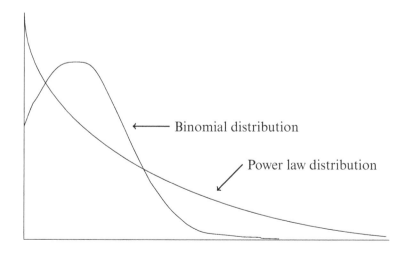

Figure 8.3: Illustration of the binomial and the power law distributions.

the degree of a vertex differs from its expected degree by more than $\lambda\sqrt{np}$ drops off exponentially fast with λ.

Theorem 8.1 *Let v be a vertex of the random graph $G(n, p)$. Let α be a real number in $(0, \sqrt{np})$.*

$$Prob(|np - deg(v)| \geq \alpha\sqrt{np}) \leq 3e^{-\alpha^2/8}.$$

Proof The degree $deg(v)$ is the sum of $n - 1$ independent Bernoulli random variables, $x_1, x_2, \ldots, x_{n-1}$, where x_i is the indicator variable that the ith edge from v is present. So, approximating $n - 1$ with n, the theorem follows from Theorem 12.6 in Chapter 12. ∎

Although the probability that the degree of a single vertex differs significantly from its expected value drops exponentially, the statement that the degree of every vertex is close to its expected value requires that p is $\Omega(\frac{\log n}{n})$. That is, the expected degree grows at least logarithmically with the number of vertices.

Corollary 8.2 *Suppose ε is a positive constant. If $p \geq \frac{9\ln n}{n\varepsilon^2}$, then almost surely every vertex has degree in the range $(1 - \varepsilon)np$ to $(1 + \varepsilon)np$.*

Proof Apply Theorem 8.1 with $\alpha = \varepsilon\sqrt{np}$ to get that the probability that an individual vertex has degree outside the range $[(1 - \varepsilon)np, (1 + \varepsilon)np]$ is at most $3e^{-\varepsilon^2 np/8}$. By the union bound, the probability that some vertex has degree outside this range is at most $3ne^{-\varepsilon^2 np/8}$. For this to be $o(1)$, it suffices for $p \geq \frac{9\ln n}{n\varepsilon^2}$. ∎

Note that the assumption p is $\Omega(\frac{\log n}{n})$ is necessary. If $p = d/n$ for d a constant, then some vertices may well have degrees outside the range $[(1 - \varepsilon)d, (1 + \varepsilon)d]$. Indeed, shortly we will see that it is highly likely that for $p = \frac{1}{n}$ there is a vertex of degree $\Omega(\log n/\log\log n)$. Moreover, for $p = \frac{1}{n}$ it is easy to see that with high probability there will be at least one vertex of degree zero.

When p is a constant, the expected degree of vertices in $G(n, p)$ increases with n. In $G(n, \frac{1}{2})$ the expected degree of a vertex is approximately $n/2$. In many real applications, we will be concerned with $G(n, p)$ where $p = d/n$, for d a constant, i.e., graphs whose expected degree is a constant d independent of n. As n goes to infinity, the binomial distribution with $p = \frac{d}{n}$

$$Prob(k) = \binom{n}{k}\left(\frac{d}{n}\right)^k\left(1 - \frac{d}{n}\right)^{n-k}$$

approaches the Poisson distribution

$$Prob(k) = \frac{d^k}{k!}e^{-d}.$$

To see this, assume $k = o(n)$ and use the approximations $\binom{n}{k} \approx \frac{n^k}{k!}, n - k \approx n$, and $\left(1 - \frac{d}{n}\right)^{n-k} \approx \left(1 - \frac{d}{n}\right)^n \approx e^{-d}$. Then

$$\lim_{n \to \infty} \binom{n}{k}\left(\frac{d}{n}\right)^k\left(1 - \frac{d}{n}\right)^{n-k} = \frac{n^k}{k!}\frac{d^k}{n^k}e^{-d} = \frac{d^k}{k!}e^{-d}.$$

Note that for $p = \frac{d}{n}$, where d is a constant independent of n, the probability of the binomial distribution falls off rapidly for $k > d$, and is essentially zero once $k!$ dominates d^k. This justifies the $k = o(n)$ assumption. Thus, the Poisson distribution is a good approximation.

Example In $G(n, \frac{1}{n})$ many vertices are of degree 1, but not all. Some are of degree zero and some are of degree greater than 1. In fact, it is highly likely that there is a vertex of degree $\Omega(\log n / \log \log n)$. The probability that a given vertex is of degree k is

$$\text{Prob}(k) = \binom{n-1}{k} \left(\frac{1}{n}\right)^k \left(1 - \frac{1}{n}\right)^{n-1-k} \approx \binom{n}{k} \left(\frac{1}{n}\right)^k \left(1 - \frac{1}{n}\right)^{n-k} \approx \frac{e^{-1}}{k!}.$$

If $k = \log n / \log \log n$,

$$\log k^k = k \log k = \frac{\log n}{\log \log n} (\log \log n - \log \log \log n) \leq \log n$$

and thus $k^k \leq n$. Since $k! \leq k^k \leq n$, the probability that a vertex has degree $k = \log n / \log \log n$ is at least $\frac{1}{k!} e^{-1} \geq \frac{1}{en}$. If the degrees of vertices were independent random variables, then this would be enough to argue that there would be a vertex of degree $\log n / \log \log n$ with probability at least $1 - \left(1 - \frac{1}{en}\right)^n = 1 - e^{-\frac{1}{e}} \cong 0.31$. But the degrees are not quite independent, since when an edge is added to the graph it affects the degree of two vertices. This is a minor technical point, which one can get around. ∎

8.1.2. Existence of Triangles in $G(n, d/n)$

What is the expected number of triangles in $G(n, \frac{d}{n})$ when d is a constant? As the number of vertices increases, one might expect the number of triangles to increase, but this is not the case. Although the number of triples of vertices grows as n^3, the probability of an edge between two specific vertices decreases linearly with n. Thus, the probability of all three edges between the pairs of vertices in a triple of vertices being present goes down as n^{-3}, exactly canceling the rate of growth of triples.

A random graph with n vertices and edge probability d/n has an expected number of triangles that is independent of n, namely $d^3/6$. There are $\binom{n}{3}$ triples of vertices. Each triple has probability $\left(\frac{d}{n}\right)^3$ of being a triangle. Let Δ_{ijk} be the indicator variable for the triangle with vertices i, j, and k being present. That is, all three edges (i,j), (j,k), and (i,k) being present. Then the number of triangles is $x = \sum_{ijk} \Delta_{ijk}$. Even though the existence of the triangles are not statistically independent events, by linearity of expectation, which does not assume independence of the variables, the expected value of a sum of random variables is the sum of the expected values. Thus, the expected number of triangles is

$$E(x) = E\left(\sum_{ijk} \Delta_{ijk}\right) = \sum_{ijk} E(\Delta_{ijk}) = \binom{n}{3}\left(\frac{d}{n}\right)^3 \approx \frac{d^3}{6}.$$

Even though on average there are $\frac{d^3}{6}$ triangles per graph, this does not mean that with high probability a graph has a triangle. Maybe half of the graphs have

$\frac{d^3}{3}$ triangles and the other half have none for an average of $\frac{d^3}{6}$ triangles. Then, with probability $1/2$, a graph selected at random would have no triangle. If $1/n$ of the graphs had $\frac{d^3}{6}n$ triangles and the remaining graphs had no triangles, then as n goes to infinity, the probability that a graph selected at random would have a triangle would go to zero.

We wish to assert that with some non-zero probability there is at least one triangle in $G(n, p)$ when $p = \frac{d}{n}$. If all the triangles were on a small number of graphs, then the number of triangles in those graphs would far exceed the expected value, and hence the variance would be high. A second moment argument rules out this scenario where a small fraction of graphs have a large number of triangles and the remaining graphs have none.

Let's calculate $E(x^2)$ where x is the number of triangles. Write x as $x = \sum_{ijk} \Delta_{ijk}$, where Δ_{ijk} is the indicator variable of the triangle with vertices i, j, and k being present. Expanding the squared term,

$$E(x^2) = E\left(\sum_{i,j,k} \Delta_{ijk}\right)^2 = E\left(\sum_{\substack{i,j,k \\ i',j',k'}} \Delta_{ijk}\Delta_{i'j'k'}\right).$$

Split the above sum into three parts. In Part 1, let S_1 be the set of i, j, k and i', j', k' that share at most one vertex and hence the two triangles share no edge. In this case, Δ_{ijk} and $\Delta_{i'j'k'}$ are independent and

$$E\left(\sum_{S_1} \Delta_{ijk}\Delta_{i'j'k'}\right) = \sum_{S_1} E(\Delta_{ijk})E(\Delta_{i'j'k'}) \leq \left(\sum_{\substack{\text{all} \\ ijk}} E(\Delta_{ijk})\right)\left(\sum_{\substack{\text{all} \\ i'j'k'}} E(\Delta_{i'j'k'})\right) = E^2(x).$$

In Part 2, i, j, k and i', j', k' share two vertices and hence one edge. See Figure 8.4. Four vertices and five edges are involved overall. There are at most $\binom{n}{4} \in O(n^4)$, four-vertex subsets and $\binom{4}{2}$ ways to partition the four vertices into two triangles with a common edge. The probability of all five edges in the two triangles being present is p^5, so this part sums to $O(n^4 p^5) = O(d^5/n)$ and is $o(1)$. There are so few triangles in the graph, the probability of two triangles sharing an edge is extremely unlikely.

In Part 3, i, j, k and i', j', k' are the same sets. The contribution of this part of the summation to $E(x^2)$ is $E(x)$. Thus, putting all three parts together,

$$E(x^2) \leq E^2(x) + E(x) + o(1),$$

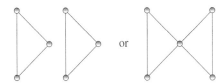

The two triangles of Part 1 are either disjoint or share at most one vertex

The two triangles of Part 2 share an edge

The two triangles in Part 3 are the same triangle

Figure 8.4: The triangles in Part 1, Part 2, and Part 3 of the second moment argument for the existence of triangles in $G(n, \frac{d}{n})$.

which implies

$$\text{Var}(x) = E(x^2) - E^2(x) \le E(x) + o(1).$$

For x to be equal to zero, it must differ from its expected value by at least its expected value. Thus,

$$\text{Prob}(x = 0) \le \text{Prob}\left(|x - E(x)| \ge E(x)\right).$$

By Chebychev inequality,

$$\text{Prob}(x = 0) \le \frac{\text{Var}(x)}{E^2(x)} \le \frac{E(x) + o(1)}{E^2(x)} \le \frac{6}{d^3} + o(1). \tag{8.1}$$

Thus, for $d > \sqrt[3]{6} \cong 1.8, \text{Prob}(x = 0) < 1$ and $G(n, p)$ has a triangle with non-zero probability. For $d < \sqrt[3]{6}, E(x) = \frac{d^3}{6} < 1$ and there simply are not enough edges in the graph for there to be a triangle.

8.2. Phase Transitions

Many properties of random graphs undergo structural changes as the edge probability passes some threshold value. This phenomenon is similar to the abrupt phase transitions in physics as the temperature or pressure increases. Some examples of this are the abrupt appearance of cycles in $G(n, p)$ when p reaches $1/n$ and the disappearance of isolated vertices when p reaches $\frac{\ln n}{n}$. The most important of these transitions is the emergence of a giant component, a connected component of size $\Theta(n)$, which happens at $d = 1$. Recall Figure 8.1.

For these and many other properties of random graphs, a threshold exists where an abrupt transition from not having the property to having the property occurs. If there exists a function $p(n)$ such that when $\lim_{n \to \infty} \frac{p_1(n)}{p(n)} = 0, G(n, p_1(n))$ almost surely does not have the property, and when $\lim_{n \to \infty} \frac{p_2(n)}{p(n)} = \infty, G(n, p_2(n))$ almost surely has the property, then we say that a *phase transition* occurs, and $p(n)$ is the *threshold*. Recall

Table 8.1: Phase transitions.

Probability	Transition
$p = o\left(\frac{1}{n}\right)$	Forest of trees, no component of size greater than $O(\log n)$
$p = \frac{d}{n}, d < 1$	Cycles appear, no component of size greater than $O(\log n)$
$p = \frac{d}{n}, d = 1$	Components of size $O\left(n^{\frac{2}{3}}\right)$
$p = \frac{d}{n}, d > 1$	Giant component plus $O(\log n)$ components
$p = \frac{1}{2} \frac{\ln n}{n}$	Giant component plus isolated vertices
$p = \frac{\ln n}{n}$	Disappearance of isolated vertices Appearance of Hamilton circuit Diameter $O(\log n)$
$p = \sqrt{\frac{2 \ln n}{n}}$	Diameter two
$p = \frac{1}{2}$	Clique of size $(2 - \epsilon) \ln n$

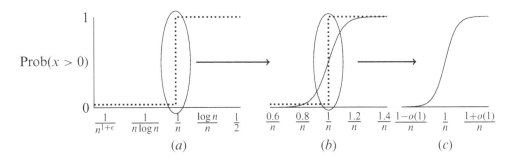

Figure 8.5: (a) shows a phase transition at $p = \frac{1}{n}$. The dotted line shows an abrupt transition in Prob(x) from 0 to 1. For any function asymptotically less than $\frac{1}{n}$, Prob(x)>0 is zero, and for any function asymptotically greater than $\frac{1}{n}$, Prob(x)>0 is one. (b) expands the scale and shows a less abrupt change in probability unless the phase transition is sharp, as illustrated by the dotted line. (c) is a further expansion, and the sharp transition is now more smooth.

that $G(n, p)$ "almost surely does not have the property" means that the probability that it has the property goes to zero in the limit as n goes to infinity. We shall soon see that every increasing property has a threshold. This is true not only for increasing properties of $G(n, p)$ but for increasing properties of any combinatorial structure. If for $cp(n), c < 1$, the graph almost surely does not have the property and for $cp(n), c > 1$, the graph almost surely has the property, then $p(n)$ is a *sharp threshold*. The existence of a giant component has a sharp threshold at $1/n$. We will prove this later. Figure 8.5 provides a pictorial illustration of a phase transition.

In establishing phase transitions, we often use a variable $x(n)$ to denote the number of occurrences of an item in a random graph. If the expected value of $x(n)$ goes to zero as n goes to infinity, then a graph picked at random almost surely has no occurrence of the item. This follows from Markov's inequality. Since x is a nonnegative random variable, Prob$(x \geq a) \leq \frac{1}{a}E(x)$, which implies that the probability of $x(n) \geq 1$ is at most $E(x(n))$. That is, if the expected number of occurrences of an item in a graph goes to zero, the probability that there are one or more occurrences of the item in a randomly selected graph goes to zero. This is called the *first moment method*, and it is illustrated in Figure 8.6.

The previous section showed that the property of having a triangle has a threshold at $p(n) = 1/n$. If the edge probability $p_1(n)$ is $o(1/n)$, then the expected number of triangles goes to zero and by the first moment method, the graph almost surely has no triangle. However, if the edge probability $p_2(n)$ satisfies $\frac{p_2(n)}{1/n} \to \infty$, then from (8.1), the probability of having no triangle is at most $6/d^3 + o(1) = 6/(np_2(n))^3 + o(1)$, which goes to zero. This latter case uses what we call the second moment method. The first and second moment methods are broadly used. We describe the second moment method in some generality now.

When the expected value of $x(n)$, the number of occurrences of an item, goes to infinity, we cannot conclude that a graph picked at random will likely have a copy, since the items may all appear on a vanishingly small fraction of the graphs. We resort to a technique called the *second moment method*. It is a simple idea based on Chebyshev's inequality.

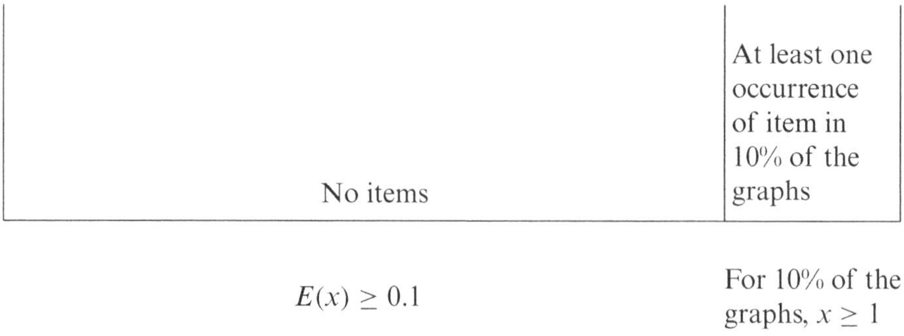

	At least one occurrence of item in 10% of the graphs
No items	

$E(x) \geq 0.1$	For 10% of the graphs, $x \geq 1$

Figure 8.6: If the expected fraction of the number of graphs in which an item occurs did not go to zero, then $E(x)$, the expected number of items per graph, could not be zero. Suppose 10% of the graphs had at least one occurrence of the item. Then the expected number of occurrences per graph must be at least 0.1. Thus, $E(x) \to 0$ implies the probability that a graph has an occurrence of the item goes to zero. However, the other direction needs more work. If $E(x)$ is large, a second moment argument is needed to conclude that the probability that a graph picked at random has an occurrence of the item is non-negligible, since there could be a large number of occurrences concentrated on a vanishingly small fraction of all graphs. The second moment argument claims that for a nonnegative random variable x with $E(x) > 0$, if $Var(x)$ is $o(E^2(x))$ or alternatively if $E(x^2) \leq E^2(x)(1 + o(1))$, then almost surely $x > 0$.

Theorem 8.3 (Second Moment method) *Let $x(n)$ be a random variable with $E(x) > 0$. If*

$$Var(x) = o\big(E^2(x)\big),$$

then x is almost surely greater than zero.

Proof If $E(x) > 0$, then for x to be less than or equal to zero, it must differ from its expected value by at least its expected value. Thus,

$$\text{Prob}(x \leq 0) \leq \text{Prob}\left(|x - E(x)| \geq E(x)\right).$$

By Chebyshev inequality,

$$\text{Prob}\left(|x - E(x)| \geq E(x)\right) \leq \frac{Var(x)}{E^2(x)} \to 0.$$

Thus, $\text{Prob}(x \leq 0)$ goes to zero if $Var(x)$ is $o\left(E^2(x)\right)$. ∎

Corollary 8.4 *Let x be a random variable with $E(x) > 0$. If*

$$E(x^2) \leq E^2(x)\big(1 + o(1)\big),$$

then x is almost surely greater than zero.

Proof If $E(x^2) \leq E^2(x)(1 + o(1))$, then

$$Var(x) = E(x^2) - E^2(x) \leq E^2(x)o(1) = o\big(E^2(x)\big).$$

∎

224

Second moment arguments are more difficult than first moment arguments, since they deal with variance and without independence we do not have $E(xy) = E(x)E(y)$. In the triangle example, dependence occurs when two triangles share a common edge. However, if $p = \frac{d}{n}$, there are so few triangles that almost surely no two triangles share a common edge and the lack of statistical independence does not affect the answer. In looking for a phase transition, almost always the transition in probability of an item being present occurs when the expected number of items transitions.

Threshold for Graph Diameter 2 (two degrees of separation)

We now present the first example of a sharp phase transition for a property. This means that slightly increasing the edge probability p near the threshold takes us from almost surely not having the property to almost surely having it. The property is that of a random graph having diameter less than or equal to 2. The diameter of a graph is the maximum length of the shortest path between a pair of nodes. In other words, the property is that every pair of nodes has "at most two degrees of separation."

The following technique for deriving the threshold for a graph having diameter 2 is a standard method often used to determine the threshold for many other objects. Let x be a random variable for the number of objects such as triangles, isolated vertices, or Hamiltonian circuits, for which we wish to determine a threshold. Then we determine the value of p, say p_0, where the expected value of x goes from vanishingly small to unboundedly large. For $p < p_0$ almost surely a graph selected at random will not have a copy of the item. For $p > p_0$, a second moment argument is needed to establish that the items are not concentrated on a vanishingly small fraction of the graphs and that a graph picked at random will almost surely have a copy.

Our first task is to figure out what to count to determine the threshold for a graph having diameter 2. A graph has diameter 2 if and only if for each pair of vertices i and j, either there is an edge between them or there is another vertex k to which both i and j have an edge. So, what we will count is the number of pairs i and j that fail, i.e., the number of pairs i and j that have more than two degrees of separation. The set of neighbors of i and the set of neighbors of j are random subsets of expected cardinality np. For these two sets to intersect requires $np \approx \sqrt{n}$ or $p \approx \frac{1}{\sqrt{n}}$. Such statements often go under the general name of "birthday paradox" though it is not a paradox. In what follows, we will prove a threshold of $O(\sqrt{\ln n}/\sqrt{n})$ for a graph to have diameter 2. The extra factor of $\sqrt{\ln n}$ ensures that every one of the $\binom{n}{2}$ pairs of i and j has a common neighbor. When $p = c\sqrt{\frac{\ln n}{n}}$, for $c < \sqrt{2}$, the graph almost surely has diameter greater than 2 and for $c > \sqrt{2}$, the graph almost surely has diameter less than or equal to 2.

Theorem 8.5 *The property that $G(n, p)$ has diameter two has a sharp threshold at $p = \sqrt{2}\sqrt{\frac{\ln n}{n}}$.*

Proof If G has diameter greater than 2, then there exists a pair of non-adjacent vertices i and j such that no other vertex of G is adjacent to both i and j. This motivates calling such a pair *bad*.

---
225 ———

Introduce a set of indicator variables I_{ij}, one for each pair of vertices (i,j) with $i < j$, where I_{ij} is 1 if and only if the pair (i,j) is bad. Let

$$x = \sum_{i<j} I_{ij}$$

be the number of bad pairs of vertices. Putting $i < j$ in the sum ensures each pair (i,j) is counted only once. A graph has diameter at most 2 if and only if it has no bad pair, i.e., $x = 0$. Thus, if $\lim_{n\to\infty} E(x) = 0$, then for large n, almost surely, a graph has no bad pair and hence has diameter at most 2.

The probability that a given vertex is adjacent to both vertices in a pair of vertices (i,j) is p^2. Hence, the probability that the vertex is not adjacent to both vertices is $1 - p^2$. The probability that no vertex is adjacent to the pair (i,j) is $\left(1 - p^2\right)^{n-2}$ and the probability that i and j are not adjacent is $1 - p$. Since there are $\binom{n}{2}$ pairs of vertices, the expected number of bad pairs is

$$E(x) = \binom{n}{2} (1 - p) \left(1 - p^2\right)^{n-2}.$$

Setting $p = c\sqrt{\frac{\ln n}{n}}$,

$$E(x) \cong \frac{n^2}{2} \left(1 - c\sqrt{\frac{\ln n}{n}}\right) \left(1 - c^2\frac{\ln n}{n}\right)^n$$

$$\cong \frac{n^2}{2} e^{-c^2 \ln n}$$

$$\cong \frac{1}{2} n^{2-c^2}.$$

For $c > \sqrt{2}$, $\lim_{n\to\infty} E(x) = 0$. By the first moment method, for $p = c\sqrt{\frac{\ln n}{n}}$ with $c > \sqrt{2}$, $G(n,p)$ almost surely has no bad pair and hence has diameter at most 2.

Next, consider the case $c < \sqrt{2}$ where $\lim_{n\to\infty} E(x) = \infty$. We appeal to a second moment argument to claim that almost surely a graph has a bad pair and thus has diameter greater than 2.

$$E(x^2) = E\left(\sum_{i<j} I_{ij}\right)^2 = E\left(\sum_{i<j} I_{ij} \sum_{k<l} I_{kl}\right) = E\left(\sum_{\substack{i<j \\ k<l}} I_{ij}I_{kl}\right) = \sum_{\substack{i<j \\ k<l}} E\left(I_{ij}I_{kl}\right).$$

The summation can be partitioned into three summations depending on the number of distinct indices among $i, j, k,$ and l. Call this number a.

$$E\left(x^2\right) = \sum_{\substack{i<j \\ k<l}} E\left(I_{ij}I_{kl}\right) + \sum_{\substack{\{i,j,k\} \\ i<j}} E\left(I_{ij}I_{ik}\right) + \sum_{i<j} E\left(I_{ij}^2\right). \tag{8.2}$$

$$a = 4 \qquad\qquad a = 3 \qquad\qquad a = 2$$

Consider the case $a = 4$ where $i, j, k,$ and l are all distinct. If $I_{ij}I_{kl} = 1$, then both pairs (i,j) and (k,l) are bad and so for each u not in $\{i, j, k, l\}$, at least one of the edges (i, u) or (j, u) is absent and, in addition, at least one of the edges (k, u) or (l, u) is absent. The probability of this for one u not in $\{i, j, k, l\}$ is $(1 - p^2)^2$. As u ranges over all the $n - 4$ vertices not in $\{i, j, k, l\}$, these events are all independent. Thus,

$$E(I_{ij}I_{kl}) \le \left(1 - p^2\right)^{2(n-4)} \le \left(1 - c^2 \frac{\ln n}{n}\right)^{2n} (1 + o(1)) \le n^{-2c^2}(1 + o(1))$$

and the first sum is

$$\sum_{\substack{i < j \\ k < l}} E(I_{ij}I_{kl}) \le \frac{1}{4} n^{4 - 2c^2}(1 + o(1)),$$

where, the $\frac{1}{4}$ is because only a fourth of the 4-tupples (i, j, k, l) have $i < j$ and $k < l$.

For the second summation, observe that if $I_{ij}I_{ik} = 1$, then for every vertex u not equal to i, j, or k, either there is no edge between i and u or there is an edge (i, u) and both edges (j, u) and (k, u) are absent. The probability of this event for one u is

$$1 - p + p(1 - p)^2 = 1 - 2p^2 + p^3 \approx 1 - 2p^2.$$

Thus, the probability for all such u is $\left(1 - 2p^2\right)^{n-3}$. Substituting $c\sqrt{\frac{\ln n}{n}}$ for p yields

$$\left(1 - \frac{2c^2 \ln n}{n}\right)^{n-3} \cong e^{-2c^2 \ln n} = n^{-2c^2},$$

which is an upper bound on $E(I_{ij}I_{kl})$ for one i, j, k, and l with $a = 3$. Summing over all distinct triples yields $n^{3 - 2c^2}$ for the second summation in (8.2).

For the third summation, since the value of I_{ij} is zero or one, $E(I_{ij}^2) = E(I_{ij})$. Thus,

$$\sum_{ij} E(I_{ij}^2) = E(x).$$

Hence, $E(x^2) \le \frac{1}{4} n^{4 - 2c^2} + n^{3 - 2c^2} + n^{2 - c^2}$ and $E(x) \cong \frac{1}{2} n^{2 - c^2}$, from which it follows that for $c < \sqrt{2}$, $E(x^2) \le E^2(x)(1 + o(1))$. By a second moment argument, Corollary 8.4, a graph almost surely has at least one bad pair of vertices and thus has diameter greater than two. Therefore, the property that the diameter of $G(n, p)$ is less than or equal to 2 has a sharp threshold at $p = \sqrt{2}\sqrt{\frac{\ln n}{n}}$. ∎

Disappearance of Isolated Vertices

The disappearance of isolated vertices in $G(n, p)$ has a sharp threshold at $\frac{\ln n}{n}$. At this point the giant component has absorbed all the small components and with the disappearance of isolated vertices, the graph becomes connected.

Theorem 8.6 *The disappearance of isolated vertices in $G(n, p)$ has a sharp threshold of $\frac{\ln n}{n}$.*

Proof Let x be the number of isolated vertices in $G(n, p)$. Then,

$$E(x) = n(1 - p)^{n-1}.$$

Since we believe the threshold to be $\frac{\ln n}{n}$, consider $p = c\frac{\ln n}{n}$. Then,

$$\lim_{n\to\infty} E(x) = \lim_{n\to\infty} n\left(1 - \frac{c\ln n}{n}\right)^n = \lim_{n\to\infty} ne^{-c\ln n} = \lim_{n\to\infty} n^{1-c}.$$

If $c > 1$, the expected number of isolated vertices goes to zero. If $c < 1$, the expected number of isolated vertices goes to infinity. If the expected number of isolated vertices goes to zero, it follows that almost all graphs have no isolated vertices. On the other hand, if the expected number of isolated vertices goes to infinity, a second moment argument is needed to show that almost all graphs have an isolated vertex and that the isolated vertices are not concentrated on some vanishingly small set of graphs with almost all graphs not having isolated vertices.

Assume $c < 1$. Write $x = I_1 + I_2 + \cdots + I_n$ where I_i is the indicator variable indicating whether vertex i is an isolated vertex. Then $E(x^2) = \sum_{i=1}^{n} E(I_i^2) + 2\sum_{i<j} E(I_i I_j)$. Since I_i equals 0 or 1, $I_i^2 = I_i$ and the first sum has value $E(x)$. Since all elements in the second sum are equal

$$E(x^2) = E(x) + n(n - 1) E(I_1 I_2)$$
$$= E(x) + n(n - 1)(1 - p)^{2(n-1)-1}.$$

The minus one in the exponent $2(n-1) - 1$ avoids counting the edge from vertex 1 to vertex 2 twice. Now,

$$\frac{E(x^2)}{E^2(x)} = \frac{n(1 - p)^{n-1} + n(n - 1)(1 - p)^{2(n-1)-1}}{n^2(1 - p)^{2(n-1)}}$$

$$= \frac{1}{n(1 - p)^{n-1}} + \left(1 - \frac{1}{n}\right)\frac{1}{1 - p}.$$

For $p = c\frac{\ln n}{n}$ with $c < 1$, $\lim_{n\to\infty} E(x) = \infty$ and

$$\lim_{n\to\infty} \frac{E(x^2)}{E^2(x)} = \lim_{n\to\infty} \left[\frac{1}{n^{1-c}} + \left(1 - \frac{1}{n}\right)\frac{1}{1 - c\frac{\ln n}{n}}\right]$$

$$= \lim_{n\to\infty} \left(1 + c\frac{\ln n}{n}\right) = o(1) + 1.$$

By the second moment argument, Corollary 8.4, the probability that $x = 0$ goes to zero, implying that almost all graphs have an isolated vertex. Thus, $\frac{\ln n}{n}$ is a sharp threshold for the disappearance of isolated vertices. For $p = c\frac{\ln n}{n}$, when $c > 1$, there almost surely are no isolated vertices, and when $c < 1$, there almost surely are isolated vertices. ∎

Hamilton Circuits

So far in establishing phase transitions in the $G(n, p)$ model for an item such as the disappearance of isolated vertices, we introduced a random variable x that was the number of occurrences of the item. We then determined the probability p for which the expected value of x went from zero to infinity. For values of p for which $E(x) \to 0$, we argued that with high probability, a graph generated at random had no occurrences of x. For values of x for which $E(x) \to \infty$, we used the second moment argument to conclude that with high probability, a graph generated at random had occurrences of x. That is, the occurrences that forced $E(x)$ to infinity were not all concentrated on a vanishingly small fraction of the graphs. One might raise the question for the $G(n, p)$ graph model: Do there exist items that are so concentrated on a small fraction of the graphs that the value of p where $E(x)$ goes from zero to infinity is not the threshold? An example where this happens is Hamilton circuits.

A Hamilton circuit is a simple cycle that includes all the vertices. For example, in a graph of four vertices, there are three possible Hamilton circuits: $(1, 2, 3, 4)$, $(1, 2, 4, 3)$, and $(1, 3, 2, 4)$. Note that our graphs are undirected, so the circuit $(1, 2, 3, 4)$ is the same as the circuit $(1, 4, 3, 2)$.

Let x be the number of Hamilton circuits in $G(n, p)$ and let $p = \frac{d}{n}$ for some constant d. There are $\frac{1}{2}(n - 1)!$ potential Hamilton circuits in a graph and each has probability $(\frac{d}{n})^n$ of actually being a Hamilton circuit. Thus,

$$E(x) = \frac{1}{2}(n - 1)! \left(\frac{d}{n}\right)^n$$

$$\simeq \left(\frac{n}{e}\right)^n \left(\frac{d}{n}\right)^n$$

$$\to \begin{cases} 0 & d < e \\ \infty & d > e \end{cases}.$$

This suggests that the threshold for Hamilton circuits occurs when d equals Euler's constant e. This is not possible, since the graph still has isolated vertices and is not even connected for $p = \frac{e}{n}$. Thus, the second moment argument is indeed necessary.

The actual threshold for Hamilton circuits is $\frac{1}{n} \log n$. For any $p(n)$ asymptotically greater, $G(n, p)$ will have a Hamilton circuit with probability 1. This is the same threshold as for the disappearance of degree 1 vertices. Clearly a graph with a degree 1 vertex cannot have a Hamilton circuit. But it may seem surprising that Hamilton circuits appear as soon as degree 1 vertices disappear. You may ask why at the moment degree 1 vertices disappear there cannot be a subgraph consisting of a degree 3 vertex adjacent to three degree 2 vertices as shown in Figure 8.7. The reason is that the frequency of degree 2 and 3 vertices in the graph is very small and the probability

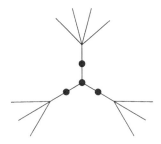

Figure 8.7: A degree 3 vertex with three adjacent degree 2 vertices. Graph cannot have a Hamilton circuit.

that four such vertices would occur together in such a subgraph is too small for it to happen with non-negligible probability.

Explanation of Component Sizes

In $G(n, \frac{d}{n})$ with $d < 1$, there are only small components of size at most $\ln n$. With $d > 1$, there is a giant component and small components of size at most $\ln n$ until the graph becomes fully connected at $p = \frac{\ln n}{n}$. There never are components of size between $\ln n$ and $\Omega(n)$ except during the phase transition at $p = \frac{1}{n}$. To understand why there are no intermediate-size components in $G(n, \frac{d}{n})$ with $d > 1$, consider a breadth first search (bfs). Discovered but unexplored vertices are called the frontier. When the frontier becomes empty, the component has been found. The expected size of the frontier initially grows as $d - 1$, then slows down and eventually decreases until it becomes zero where the number of discovered vertices is a constant fraction of n. The actual size of the frontier is a random variable. Initially when the expected size of the frontier is small, the actual size can differ substantially from the expectation, and reach zero, resulting in a small $O(\ln n)$ component. After $\ln n$ steps, the expected size of the frontier is sufficiently large that the actual size cannot differ sufficiently to be zero, and thus no component can be found until the expected size of the frontier is again close to zero, which occurs when the number of discovered vertices is a constant fraction of n. At this point the actual size of the frontier can differ enough from its expectation so it can be zero, resulting in a giant component.

Expected size of frontier

To compute the size of a connected component of $G(n, \frac{d}{n})$, do a breadth first search of a component starting from an arbitrary vertex and generate an edge only when the search process needs to know if the edge exists. Let us define a step in this process as the full exploration of one vertex. To aid in our analysis, let us imagine that whenever the bfs finishes, we create a brand-new $(n+1)$st vertex (call it a *red vertex*) that is connected to each real vertex with probability $\frac{d}{n}$, and we then continue the bfs from there. The red vertex becomes "explored" but it was never "discovered." This modified process has the useful property that for each real (non-red) vertex u other than the start vertex, the probability that u is undiscovered after the first i steps is exactly $(1 - \frac{d}{n})^i$. Define the size of the frontier to be the number of discovered vertices minus the number of explored vertices; this equals the number of vertices in the bfs frontier in the true bfs process, but it can now go negative once the true bfs completes and we start creating red vertices. The key point to keep in mind is that the true bfs must have completed by the time the size of the frontier reaches zero. For large n,

$$1 - \left(1 - \frac{d}{n}\right)^i \cong 1 - e^{-\frac{d}{n}i}$$

and the expected size of the frontier after i steps is $n(1 - e^{-\frac{d}{n}i}) - i$. Normalize the size of the frontier by dividing by n to get $1 - e^{-\frac{d}{n}i} - \frac{i}{n}$. Let $x = \frac{i}{n}$ be the normalized number of steps and let $f(x) = 1 - e^{-dx} - x$ be the normalized expected size of the frontier. When $d > 1, f(0) = 0$ and $f'(0) = d - 1 > 0$, so f is increasing at 0. But $f(1) = -e^{-d} < 0$. So, for some value $\theta, 0 < \theta < 1, f(\theta) = 0$ (see Figure 8.8). When $d = 2, \theta = 0.7968$.

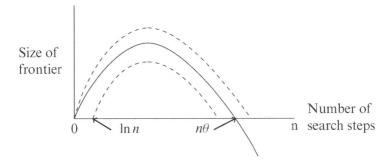

Figure 8.8: The solid curve is the expected size of the frontier. The two dashed curves indicate the high-probability range of possible values for the actual size of the frontier.

Difference of Actual Size of Frontier from Expected Size

For $d > 1$, the expected size of the frontier grows as $(d - 1)i$ for small i. The actual size of the frontier is a random variable. What is the probability that the actual size of the frontier will differ from the expected size of the frontier by a sufficient amount so that the actual size of the frontier is zero? To answer this, we need to understand the distribution of the number of discovered vertices after i steps. For small i, the probability that a vertex has been discovered is $1 - (1 - d/n)^i \approx id/n$ and the binomial distribution for the number of discovered vertices, binomial$(n, \frac{id}{n})$, is well approximated by the Poisson distribution with the same mean id. The probability that a total of k vertices have been discovered in i steps is approximately $e^{-di}\frac{(di)^k}{k!}$. For a connected component to have exactly i vertices, the frontier must drop to zero for the first time at step i. A necessary condition is that exactly i vertices must have been discovered in the first i steps. The probability of this is approximately

$$e^{-di}\frac{(di)^i}{i!} = e^{-di}\frac{d^i i^i}{i^i}e^i = e^{-(d-1)i}d^i = e^{-(d-1-\ln d)i}.$$

For $d \neq 1, d - 1 - \ln d > 0.$[1] Thus, the probability $e^{-(d-1-\ln d)i}$ drops off exponentially with i. For $i > c \ln n$ and sufficiently large c, the probability that the breadth first search starting from a particular vertex terminates with a component of size i is $o(1/n)$ as long as the Poisson approximation is valid. In the range of this approximation, the probability that a breadth first search started from any vertex terminates with $i > c \ln n$ vertices is $o(1)$. Intuitively, if the component has not stopped growing within $\Omega(\ln n)$ steps, it is likely to continue to grow until it becomes much larger and the expected value of the size of the frontier again becomes small. While the expected value of the frontier is large, the probability that the actual size will differ from the expected size sufficiently for the actual size of the frontier to be zero is vanishingly small.

For i near $n\theta$ the absolute value of the expected size of the frontier increases linearly with $|i - n\theta|$. Thus for the actual size of the frontier to be zero, the frontier size must deviate from its expected value by an amount proportional to $|i - n\theta|$.

---

[1] Let $f(d) = d - 1 - \ln d$. Then $\frac{\partial f}{\partial d} = 1 - \frac{1}{d}$ and $\frac{\partial f}{\partial d} < 0$ for $d < 1$ and $\frac{\partial f}{\partial d} > 0$ for $d > 1$. Now $f(d) = 0$ at $d = 1$ and is positive for all other $d > 1$.

For values of i near $n\theta$, the binomial distribution can be approximated by a Gaussian distribution. The Gaussian falls off exponentially fast with the square of the distance from its mean. The distribution falls off proportional to $e^{-\frac{k^2}{\sigma^2}}$ where σ^2 is the variance and is proportional to n. Thus to have a non-vanishing probability, k must be at most $\sqrt{n}$. This implies that the giant component is in the range $[n\theta - \sqrt{n}, n\theta + \sqrt{n}]$. Thus a component is either small or in the range $[n\theta - \sqrt{n}, n\theta + \sqrt{n}]$.

8.3. Giant Component

Consider $G(n, p)$ for $p = \frac{1+\epsilon}{n}$ where ϵ is a constant greater than zero. We now show that with high probability, such a graph contains a *giant component*, namely a component of size $\Omega(n)$. Moreover, with high probability, the graph contains only one such component, and all other components are much smaller, of size only $O(\log n)$. We begin by arguing the existence of a giant component.

8.3.1. Existence of a Giant Component

To see that with high probability the graph has a giant component, do a depth first search (dfs) on $G(n, p)$ where $p = (1 + \epsilon)/n$ with $0 < \epsilon < 1/8$. Note that it suffices to consider this range of ϵ, since increasing the value of p only increases the probability that the graph has a giant component.

To perform the dfs, generate $\binom{n}{2}$ Bernoulli(p) independent random bits and answer the tth edge query according to the tth bit. As the dfs proceeds, let

$E =$ set of fully explored vertices whose exploration is complete

$U =$ set of unvisited vertices

$F =$ frontier of visited and still being explored vertices.

Initially the set of fully explored vertices E and the frontier F are empty and the set of unvisited vertices U equals $\{1, 2, \ldots, n\}$. If the frontier is not empty and u is the active vertex of the dfs, the dfs queries each unvisited vertex in U until it finds a vertex v for which there is an edge (u, v) and moves v from U to the frontier and v becomes the active vertex. If no edge is found from u to an unvisited vertex in U, then u is moved from the frontier to the set of fully explored vertices E. If frontier is empty, the dfs moves an unvisited vertex from U to the frontier and starts a new component. If both the frontier and U are empty, all connected components of G have been found. At any time all edges between the current fully explored vertices, E, and the current unvisited vertices, U, have been queried, since a vertex is moved from the frontier to E only when there is no edge from the vertex to an unexplored vertex in U.

Intuitively, after $\epsilon n^2/2$ edge queries, a large number of edges must have been found, since $p = \frac{1+\epsilon}{n}$. None of these can connect components already found with the set of unvisited vertices, and we will use this to show that with high probability the frontier must be large. Since the frontier will be in a connected component, a giant component exists with high probability (see Figure 8.9). We first prove that after $\epsilon n^2/2$ edge queries the set of fully explored vertices is of size less than $n/3$.

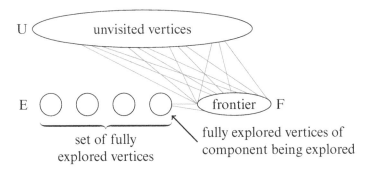

Figure 8.9: Picture after $\epsilon n^2/2$ edge queries. The potential edges from the small connected components to unvisited vertices have all been explored and do not exist in the graph. However, since many edges must have been found, the frontier must be big, and hence there is a giant component.

Lemma 8.7 *After $\epsilon n^2/2$ edge queries, with high probability $|E| < n/3$.*

Proof If not, at some $t \le \varepsilon n^2/2, |E| = n/3$. A vertex is added to the frontier only when an edge query is answered yes. So at time $t, |F|$ is less than or equal to the sum of $\varepsilon n^2/2$ Bernoulli(p) random variables, which with high probability is at most $\varepsilon n^2 p \le n/3$. So, at $t, |U| = n - |E| - |F| \ge n/3$. Since there are no edges between fully explored vertices and unvisited vertices, $|E| \, |U| \ge n^2/9$ edge queries must have already been answered in the negative. But $t > n^2/9$ contradicts $t \le \epsilon n^2/2 \le n^2/16$. Thus, $|E| \le n/3$. ∎

The frontier vertices in the search of a connected component are all in the component being searched. Thus, if at any time the frontier set has $\Omega(n)$ vertices, there is a giant component.

Lemma 8.8 *After $\epsilon n^2/2$ edge queries, with high probability the frontier F consists of at least $\epsilon^2 n/30$ vertices.*

Proof After $\varepsilon n^2/2$ queries, say, $|F| < \varepsilon^2 n/30$. Then

$$|U| = n - |E| - |F| \ge n - \frac{n}{3} - \frac{\epsilon^2 n}{30} \ge 1$$

and so the dfs is still active. Each positive answer to an edge query so far resulted in some vertex moving from U to F, which possibly later moved to E. The expected number of yes answers so far is $p\varepsilon n^2/2 = (1+\varepsilon)\varepsilon n/2$, and with high probability the number of yes answers is at least $(\varepsilon n/2) + (\varepsilon^2 n/3)$. So,

$$|E| + |F| \ge \frac{\varepsilon n}{2} + \frac{\varepsilon^2 n}{3} \implies |E| \ge \frac{\varepsilon n}{2} + \frac{3\varepsilon^2 n}{10}.$$

We must have $|E| \, |U| \le \varepsilon n^2/2$. Now, $|E||U| = |E|(n - |E| - |F|)$ increases as $|E|$ increases from $\frac{\varepsilon n}{2} + \frac{3\varepsilon^2 n}{10}$ to $n/3$, so we have

$$|E||U| \ge \left(\frac{\varepsilon n}{2} + \frac{3\varepsilon^2 n}{10}\right)\left(n - \frac{\varepsilon n}{2} - \frac{3\varepsilon^2 n}{10} - \frac{\varepsilon^2 n}{30}\right) > \frac{\varepsilon n^2}{2},$$

a contradiction. ∎

8.3.2. No Other Large Components

We now argue that for $p = (1 + \epsilon)/n$ for constant $\epsilon > 0$, with high probability there is only one giant component, and in fact all other components have size $O(\log n)$.

We begin with a preliminary observation. Suppose that a $G(n, p)$ graph had at least a δ probability of having two (or more) components of size $\omega(\log n)$, i.e., asymptotically greater than $\log n$. Then, there would be at least a $\delta/2$ probability of the graph having two (or more) components with $\omega(\log n)$ vertices *inside the subset* $A = \{1, 2, \ldots, \epsilon n/2\}$. The reason is that an equivalent way to construct a graph $G(n, p)$ is to first create it in the usual way and then to randomly permute the vertices. Any component of size $\omega(\log n)$ will with high probability after permutation have at least an $\epsilon/4$ fraction of its vertices within the first $\epsilon n/2$. Thus, it suffices to prove that with high probability at most one component has $\omega(\log n)$ vertices within the set A to conclude that with high probability the graph has only one component with $\omega(\log n)$ vertices overall.

We now prove that with high probability a $G(n, p)$ graph for $p = (1 + \epsilon)/n$ has at most one component with $\omega(\log n)$ vertices inside the set A. To do so, let B be the set of $(1 - \epsilon/2)n$ vertices not in A. Now, construct the graph as follows. First, randomly flip coins of bias p to generate the edges within set A and the edges within set B. At this point, with high probability, B has at least one giant component, by the argument from Section 8.3.1, since $p = (1 + \epsilon)/n \geq (1 + \epsilon/4)/|B|$ for $0 < \epsilon \leq 1/2$. Let C^* be a giant component inside B. Now, flip coins of bias p to generate the edges between A and B *except* for those incident to C^*. At this point, let us name all components with $\omega(\log n)$ vertices inside A as $C_1, C_2, C_3, \ldots$. Finally, flip coins of bias p to generate the edges between A and C^*.

In the final step above, notice that with high probability each C_i is connected to C^*. In particular, there are $\omega(n \log n)$ possible edges between any given C_i and C^*, each one of which is present with probability p. Thus the probability that this particular C_i is *not* connected to C^* is at most $(1 - p)^{\omega(n \log n)} = 1/n^{\omega(1)}$. Thus, by the union bound, with high probability all such C_i are connected to C^*, and there is only one component with $\omega(\log n)$ vertices within A as desired.

8.3.3. The Case of $p < 1/n$

When $p < 1/n$, then with high probability all components in $G(n, p)$ are of size $O(\log n)$. This is easiest to see by considering a variation on the above dfs that (a) begins with F containing a specific start vertex u_{start}, and then (b) when a vertex u is taken from F to explore, it pops u off of F, explores u fully by querying to find *all* edges between u and U, and then pushes the end points v of those edges onto F. Thus, this is like an explicit-stack version of dfs, compared to the previous recursive-call version of dfs. Let us call the exploration of such a vertex u a *step*. To make this process easier to analyze, let us say that if F ever becomes empty, we create a brand-new, fake "red vertex," connect it to each vertex in U with probability p, place the new red vertex into F, and then continue the dfs from there.

Let z_k denote the number of real (non-red) vertices discovered after k steps, not including u_{start}. For any given real vertex $u \neq u_{start}$, the probability that u is not discovered in k steps is $(1 - p)^k$, and notice that these events are independent over the different vertices $u \neq u_{start}$. Therefore, the distribution of z_k is

Binomial$(n - 1, 1 - (1 - p)^k)$. Note that if $z_k < k$, then the process must have required creating a fake red vertex by step k, meaning that u_{start} is in a component of size at most k. Thus, it suffices to prove that Prob$(z_k \geq k) < 1/n^2$, for $k = c \ln n$ for a suitably large constant c, to then conclude by union bound over choices of u_{start} that with high probability *all* vertices are in components of size at most $c \ln n$.

To prove that Prob$(z_k \geq k) < 1/n^2$ for $k = c \ln n$, we use the fact that $(1 - p)^k \geq 1 - pk$ so $1 - (1 - p)^k \leq pk$. So, the probability that z_k is greater than or equal to k is at most the probability that a coin of bias pk flipped $n - 1$ times will have at least k heads. But since $pk(n - 1) \leq (1 - \epsilon)k$ for some constant $\epsilon > 0$, by Chernoff bounds this probability is at most $e^{-c_0 k}$ for some constant $c_0 > 0$. When $k = c \ln n$ for a suitably large constant c, this probability is at most $1/n^2$, as desired.

8.4. Cycles and Full Connectivity

This section considers when cycles form and when the graph becomes fully connected. For both of these problems, we look at each subset of k vertices and see when they form either a cycle or when they form a connected component.

8.4.1. Emergence of Cycles

The emergence of cycles in $G(n, p)$ has a threshold when p equals to $1/n$. However, the threshold is not sharp.

Theorem 8.9 *The threshold for the existence of cycles in $G(n, p)$ is $p = 1/n$.*

Proof Let x be the number of cycles in $G(n, p)$. To form a cycle of length k, the vertices can be selected in $\binom{n}{k}$ ways. Given the k vertices of the cycle, they can be ordered by arbitrarily selecting a first vertex, then a second vertex in one of k-1 ways, a third in one of $k - 2$ ways, etc. Since a cycle and its reversal are the same cycle, divide by 2. Thus, there are $\binom{n}{k} \frac{(k-1)!}{2}$ possible cycles of length k and

$$E(x) = \sum_{k=3}^{n} \binom{n}{k} \frac{(k-1)!}{2} p^k \leq \sum_{k=3}^{n} \frac{n^k}{2k} p^k \leq \sum_{k=3}^{n} (np)^k = (np)^3 \frac{1-(np)^{n-2}}{1-np} \leq 2(np)^3,$$

provided that $np < 1/2$. When p is asymptotically less than $1/n$, then $\lim_{n \to \infty} np = 0$ and $\lim_{n \to \infty} \sum_{k=3}^{n} (np)^k = 0$. So, as n goes to infinity, $E(x)$ goes to zero. Thus, the graph almost surely has no cycles by the first moment method. A second moment argument can be used to show that for $p = d/n, d > 1$, a graph will have a cycle with probability tending to one. ∎

The argument above does not yield a sharp threshold, since we argued that $E(x) \to 0$ only under the assumption that p is asymptotically less than $\frac{1}{n}$. A sharp threshold requires $E(x) \to 0$ for $p = d/n, d < 1$.

Consider what happens in more detail when $p = d/n$, d a constant.

$$E(x) = \sum_{k=3}^{n} \binom{n}{k} \frac{(k-1)!}{2} p^k$$

$$= \frac{1}{2} \sum_{k=3}^{n} \frac{n(n-1)\cdots(n-k+1)}{k!} (k-1)! \, p^k$$

$$= \frac{1}{2} \sum_{k=3}^{n} \frac{n(n-1)\cdots(n-k+1)}{n^k} \frac{d^k}{k}.$$

$E(x)$ converges if $d < 1$ and diverges if $d \geq 1$. If $d < 1$, $E(x) \leq \frac{1}{2}\sum_{k=3}^{n} \frac{d^k}{k}$ and $\lim_{n\to\infty}$ $E(x)$ equals a constant greater than zero. If $d = 1$, $E(x) = \frac{1}{2}\sum_{k=3}^{n} \frac{n(n-1)\cdots(n-k+1)}{n^k} \frac{1}{k}$. Consider only the first $\log n$ terms of the sum. Since $\frac{n}{n-i} = 1 + \frac{i}{n-i} \leq e^{i/n-i}$, it follows that $\frac{n(n-1)\cdots(n-k+1)}{n^k} \geq 1/2$. Thus,

$$E(x) \geq \frac{1}{2} \sum_{k=3}^{\log n} \frac{n(n-1)\cdots(n-k+1)}{n^k} \frac{1}{k} \geq \frac{1}{4} \sum_{k=3}^{\log n} \frac{1}{k}.$$

Then, in the limit as n goes to infinity

$$\lim_{n\to\infty} E(x) \geq \lim_{n\to\infty} \frac{1}{4} \sum_{k=3}^{\log n} \frac{1}{k} \geq \lim_{n\to\infty} (\log\log n) = \infty.$$

For $p = d/n$, $d < 1$, $E(x)$ converges to a non-zero constant. For $d > 1$, $E(x)$ converges to infinity and a second moment argument shows that graphs will have an unbounded number of cycles increasing with n.

8.4.2. Full Connectivity

As p increases from $p = 0$, small components form. At $p = 1/n$ a giant component emerges and swallows up smaller components, starting with the larger components and ending up swallowing isolated vertices forming a single connected component at $p = \frac{\ln n}{n}$, at which point the graph becomes connected. We begin our development with a technical lemma.

Table 8.2: Thresholds for various properties

Property	Threshold
cycles	$1/n$
giant component	$1/n$
giant component + isolated vertices	$\frac{1}{2}\frac{\ln n}{n}$
connectivity, disappearance of isolated vertices	$\frac{\ln n}{n}$
diameter two	$\sqrt{\frac{2\ln n}{n}}$

Lemma 8.10 *The expected number of connected components of size k in $G(n,p)$ is at most*

$$\binom{n}{k}k^{k-2}p^{k-1}(1-p)^{kn-k^2}.$$

Proof The probability that k vertices form a connected component consists of the product of two probabilities. The first is the probability that the k vertices are connected, and the second is the probability that there are no edges out of the component to the remainder of the graph. The first probability is at most the sum over all spanning trees of the k vertices, that the edges of the spanning tree are present. The "at most" in the lemma statement is because $G(n,p)$ may contain more than one spanning tree on these nodes and, in this case, the union bound is higher than the actual probability. There are k^{k-2} spanning trees on k nodes. The probability of all the $k-1$ edges of one spanning tree being present is p^{k-1} and the probability that there are no edges connecting the k vertices to the remainder of the graph is $(1-p)^{k(n-k)}$. Thus, the probability of one particular set of k vertices forming a connected component is at most $k^{k-2}p^{k-1}(1-p)^{kn-k^2}$. Thus, the expected number of connected components of size k is at most $\binom{n}{k}k^{k-2}p^{k-1}(1-p)^{kn-k^2}$. ∎

We now prove that for $p = \frac{1}{2}\frac{\ln n}{n}$, the giant component has absorbed all small components except for isolated vertices.

Theorem 8.11 *For $p = c\frac{\ln n}{n}$ with $c > 1/2$, almost surely there are only isolated vertices and a giant component. For $c > 1$, almost surely the graph is connected.*

Proof We prove that almost surely for $c > 1/2$, there is no connected component with k vertices for any $k, 2 \le k \le n/2$. This proves the first statement of the theorem since, if there were two or more components that are not isolated vertices, both of them could not be of size greater than $n/2$. The second statement that for $c > 1$ the graph is connected then follows from Theorem 8.6 which states that isolated vertices disappear at $c = 1$.

We now show that for $p = c\frac{\ln n}{n}$, the expected number of components of size k, $2 \le k \le n/2$, is less than n^{1-2c}, and thus for $c > 1/2$ there are no components, except for isolated vertices and the giant component. Let x_k be the number of connected components of size k. Substitute $p = c\frac{\ln n}{n}$ into $\binom{n}{k}k^{k-2}p^{k-1}(1-p)^{kn-k^2}$ and simplify using $\binom{n}{k} \le (en/k)^k$, $1 - p \le e^{-p}$, $k - 1 < k$, and $x = e^{\ln x}$ to get

$$E(x_k) \le \exp\left(\ln n + k + k\ln\ln n - 2\ln k + k\ln c - ck\ln n + ck^2\frac{\ln n}{n}\right).$$

Keep in mind that the leading terms here for large k are the last two and, in fact, at $k = n$, they cancel each other so that our argument does not prove the fallacious statement for $c \ge 1$ that there is no connected component of size n, since there is. Let

$$f(k) = \ln n + k + k\ln\ln n - 2\ln k + k\ln c - ck\ln n + ck^2\frac{\ln n}{n}.$$

Differentiating with respect to k,

$$f'(k) = 1 + \ln \ln n - \frac{2}{k} + \ln c - c \ln n + \frac{2ck \ln n}{n}$$

and

$$f''(k) = \frac{2}{k^2} + \frac{2c \ln n}{n} > 0.$$

Thus, the function $f(k)$ attains its maximum over the range $[2, n/2]$ at one of the extreme points 2 or $n/2$. At $k = 2, f(2) \approx (1 - 2c) \ln n$ and at $k = n/2, f(n/2) \approx -c\frac{n}{4} \ln n$. So $f(k)$ is maximum at $k = 2$. For $k = 2$, $E(x_k) = e^{f(k)}$ is approximately $e^{(1-2c)\ln n} = n^{1-2c}$ and is geometrically falling as k increases from 2. At some point $E(x_k)$ starts to increase but never gets above $n^{-\frac{c}{4}n}$. Thus, the expected sum of the number of components of size k, for $2 \leq k \leq n/2$ is

$$E\left(\sum_{k=2}^{n/2} x_k\right) = O(n^{1-2c}).$$

This expected number goes to zero for $c > 1/2$ and the first moment method implies that, almost surely, there are no components of size between 2 and $n/2$. This completes the proof of Theorem 8.11. ∎

8.4.3. Threshold for $O(\ln n)$ Diameter

We now show that within a constant factor of the threshold for graph connectivity, not only is the graph connected, but its diameter is $O(\ln n)$. That is, if $p > c\frac{\ln n}{n}$ for sufficiently large constant c, the diameter of $G(n, p)$ is $O(\ln n)$ with high probability.

Consider a particular vertex v. Let S_i be the set of vertices at distance i from v. We argue that as i increases, with high probability $|S_1| + |S_2| + \cdots + |S_i|$ grows by at least a factor of two, up to a size of $n/1000$. This implies that in $O(\ln n)$ steps, at least $n/1000$ vertices are connected to v. Then, there is a simple argument at the end of the proof of Theorem 8.13 that a pair of $n/1000$ sized subsets, connected to two different vertices v and w, have an edge between them with high probability.

Lemma 8.12 *Consider $G(n, p)$ for sufficiently large n with $p = c\frac{\ln n}{n}$ for any $c > 0$. Let S_i be the set of vertices at distance i from some fixed vertex v. If $|S_1| + |S_2| + \cdots + |S_i| \leq n/1000$, then*

$$Prob\left(|S_{i+1}| < 2(|S_1| + |S_2| + \cdots + |S_i|)\right) \leq e^{-10|S_i|}.$$

Proof Let $|S_i| = k$. For each vertex u not in $S_1 \cup S_2 \cup \cdots \cup S_i$, the probability that u is not in S_{i+1} is $(1 - p)^k$, and these events are independent. So, $|S_{i+1}|$ is the sum of $n - (|S_1| + |S_2| + \cdots + |S_i|)$ independent Bernoulli random variables, each with probability of

$$1 - (1 - p)^k \geq 1 - e^{-ck \ln n/n}$$

of being 1. Note that $n - (|S_1| + |S_2| + \cdots + |S_i|) \geq 999n/1000$. So,

$$E(|S_{i+1}|) \geq \frac{999n}{1000}(1 - e^{-ck\frac{\ln n}{n}}).$$

Subtracting $200k$ from each side,

$$E(|S_{i+1}|) - 200k \geq \frac{n}{2}\left(1 - e^{-ck\frac{\ln n}{n}} - 400\frac{k}{n}\right).$$

Let $\alpha = \frac{k}{n}$ and $f(\alpha) = 1 - e^{-c\alpha \ln n} - 400\alpha$. By differentiation, $f''(\alpha) \leq 0$, so f is concave and the minimum value of f over the interval $[0, 1/1000]$ is attained at one of the end points. It is easy to check that both $f(0)$ and $f(1/1000)$ are greater than or equal to zero for sufficiently large n. Thus, f is nonnegative throughout the interval, proving that $E(|S_{i+1}|) \geq 200|S_i|$. The lemma follows from Chernoff bounds. ∎

Theorem 8.13 *For $p \geq c\ln n/n$, where c is a sufficiently large constant, almost surely, $G(n, p)$ has diameter $O(\ln n)$.*

Proof By Corollary 8.2, almost surely, the degree of every vertex is $\Omega(np) = \Omega(\ln n)$, which is at least $20\ln n$ for c sufficiently large. Assume that this holds. So, for a fixed vertex v, S_1 as defined in Lemma 8.12 satisfies $|S_1| \geq 20\ln n$.

Let i_0 be the least i such that $|S_1| + |S_2| + \cdots + |S_i| > n/1000$. From Lemma 8.12 and the union bound, the probability that for some $i, 1 \leq i \leq i_0 - 1, |S_{i+1}| < 2(|S_1| + |S_2| + \cdots + |S_i|)$ is at most $\sum_{k=20\ln n}^{n/1000} e^{-10k} \leq 1/n^4$. So, with probability at least $1 - (1/n^4)$, each S_{i+1} is at least double the sum of the previous S_j's, which implies that in $O(\ln n)$ steps, $i_0 + 1$ is reached.

Consider any other vertex w. We wish to find a short $O(\ln n)$ length path between v and w. By the same argument as above, the number of vertices at distance $O(\ln n)$ from w is at least $n/1000$. To complete the argument, either these two sets intersect, in which case we have found a path from v to w of length $O(\ln n)$, or they do not intersect. In the latter case, with high probability there is some edge between them. For a pair of disjoint sets of size at least $n/1000$, the probability that none of the possible $n^2/10^6$ or more edges between them is present is at most $(1 - p)^{n^2/10^6} = e^{-\Omega(n\ln n)}$. There are at most 2^{2n} pairs of such sets, and so the probability that there is some such pair with no edges is $e^{-\Omega(n\ln n)+O(n)} \to 0$. Note that there is no conditioning problem, since we are arguing this for every pair of such sets. Think of whether such an argument made for just the n subsets of vertices, which are vertices at distance at most $O(\ln n)$ from a specific vertex, would work. ∎

8.5. Phase Transitions for Increasing Properties

For many graph properties such as connectivity, having no isolated vertices, having a cycle, etc., the probability of a graph having the property increases as edges are added to the graph. Such a property is called an increasing property. Q is an *increasing property* of graphs if, when a graph G has the property, any graph obtained by adding edges to G must also have the property. In this section we show that any increasing property has a threshold, although not necessarily a sharp one.

The notion of increasing property is defined in terms of adding edges. The following intuitive lemma proves that if Q is an increasing property, then increasing p in $G(n, p)$ increases the probability of the property Q.

239

Lemma 8.14 *If Q is an increasing property of graphs and $0 \leq p \leq q \leq 1$, then the probability that $G(n, q)$ has property Q is greater than or equal to the probability that $G(n, p)$ has property Q.*

Proof This proof uses an interesting relationship between $G(n, p)$ and $G(n, q)$. Generate $G(n, q)$ as follows. First generate $G(n, p)$. This means generating a graph on n vertices with edge probabilities p. Then, independently generate another graph $G\left(n, \frac{q-p}{1-p}\right)$ and take the union by including an edge if either of the two graphs has the edge. Call the resulting graph H. The graph H has the same distribution as $G(n, q)$. This follows since the probability that an edge is in H is $p + (1 - p)\frac{q-p}{1-p} = q$, and, clearly, the edges of H are independent. The lemma follows since whenever $G(n, p)$ has the property Q, H also has the property Q. ∎

We now introduce a notion called *replication*. An m-fold replication of $G(n, p)$ is a random graph obtained as follows. Generate m independent copies of $G(n, p)$ on the same set of vertices. Include an edge in the m-fold replication if the edge is in any one of the m copies of $G(n, p)$. The resulting random graph has the same distribution as $G(n, q)$ where $q = 1 - (1 - p)^m$, since the probability that a particular edge is not in the m-fold replication is the product of probabilities that it is not in any of the m copies of $G(n, p)$. If the m-fold replication of $G(n, p)$ does not have an increasing property Q, then none of the m copies of $G(n, p)$ has the property. The converse is not true. If no copy has the property, their union may have it (see Figure 8.10). Since Q is an increasing property and $q = 1 - (1 - p)^m \leq 1 - (1 - mp) = mp$,

$$\text{Prob}\left(G(n, mp) \text{ has } Q\right) \geq \text{Prob}\left(G(n, q) \text{ has } Q\right). \tag{8.3}$$

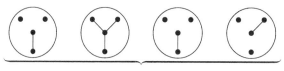

copies of G | The m-fold replication H

If any graph has three or more edges, then the m-fold replication has three or more edges.

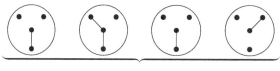

copies of G | The m-fold replication H

Even if no graph has three or more edges, the m-fold replication might have three or more edges.

Figure 8.10: The property that G has three or more edges is an increasing property. Let H be the m-fold replication of G. If any copy of G has three or more edges, H has three or more edges. However, H can have three or more edges even if no copy of G has three or more edges.

We now show that every increasing property Q has a phase transition. The transition occurs at the point $p(n)$ at which the probability that $G(n, p(n))$ has property Q is $\frac{1}{2}$. We will prove that for any function asymptotically less then $p(n)$ the probability of having property Q goes to zero as n goes to infinity.

Theorem 8.15 *Each increasing property Q of $G(n, p)$ has a phase transition at $p(n)$, where for each n, $p(n)$ is the minimum real number a_n for which the probability that $G(n, a_n)$ has property Q is $1/2$.*

Proof Let $p_0(n)$ be any function such that

$$\lim_{n \to \infty} \frac{p_0(n)}{p(n)} = 0.$$

We assert that almost surely $G(n, p_0)$ does not have the property Q. Suppose, for contradiction, that this is not true. That is, the probability that $G(n, p_0)$ has the property Q does not converge to zero. By the definition of a limit, there exists $\varepsilon > 0$ for which the probability that $G(n, p_0)$ has property Q is at least ε on an infinite set I of n. Let $m = \lceil (1/\varepsilon) \rceil$. Let $G(n, q)$ be the m-fold replication of $G(n, p_0)$. The probability that $G(n, q)$ does not have Q is at most $(1 - \varepsilon)^m \le e^{-1} \le 1/2$ for all $n \in I$. For these n, by (8.3),

$$\text{Prob}(G(n, mp_0) \text{ has } Q) \ge \text{Prob}(G(n, q) \text{ has } Q) \ge 1/2.$$

Since $p(n)$ is the minimum real number a_n for which the probability that $G(n, a_n)$ has property Q is $1/2$, it must be that $mp_0(n) \ge p(n)$. This implies that $\frac{p_0(n)}{p(n)}$ is at least $1/m$ infinitely often, contradicting the hypothesis that $\lim_{n \to \infty} \frac{p_0(n)}{p(n)} = 0$.

A symmetric argument shows that for any $p_1(n)$ such that $\lim_{n \to \infty} \frac{p(n)}{p_1(n)} = 0$, $G(n, p_1)$ almost surely has property Q. ∎

8.6. Branching Processes

A *branching process* is a method for creating a random tree. Starting with the root node, each node has a probability distribution for the number of its children. The root of the tree is a parent and its descendants are the children with their descendants being the grandchildren. The children of the root are the first generation, their children the second generation, and so on. Branching processes have obvious applications in population studies.

We analyze a simple case of a branching process where the distribution of the number of children at each node in the tree is the same. The basic question asked is: What is the probability that the tree is finite, i.e., the probability that the branching process dies out? This is called the *extinction probability*.

Our analysis of the branching process will give the probability of extinction, as well as the expected size of the components conditioned on extinction.

An important tool in our analysis of branching processes is the generating function. The generating function for a nonnegative integer valued random variable y is $f(x) = \sum_{i=0}^{\infty} p_i x^i$ where p_i is the probability that y equals i. The reader not familiar with generating functions should consult Section 12.8 in Chapter 12.

Let the random variable z_j be the number of children in the jth generation and let $f_j(x)$ be the generating function for z_j. Then $f_1(x) = f(x)$ is the generating function for the first generation where $f(x)$ is the generating function for the number of children at a node in the tree. The generating function for the second generation is $f_2(x) = f(f(x))$. In general, the generating function for the $j + 1^{st}$ generation is given by $f_{j+1}(x) = f_j(f(x))$. To see this, observe two things.

First, the generating function for the sum of two identically distributed integer valued random variables x_1 and x_2 is the square of their generating function,

$$f^2(x) = p_0^2 + (p_0 p_1 + p_1 p_0) x + (p_0 p_2 + p_1 p_1 + p_2 p_0) x^2 + \cdots .$$

For $x_1 + x_2$ to have value zero, both x_1 and x_2 must have value zero, for $x_1 + x_2$ to have value 1, exactly one of x_1 or x_2 must have value zero and the other must have value 1, and so on. In general, the generating function for the sum of i independent random variables, each with generating function $f(x)$, is $f^i(x)$.

The second observation is that the coefficient of x^i in $f_j(x)$ is the probability of there being i children in the jth generation. If there are i children in the jth generation, the number of children in the $j + 1^{st}$ generation is the sum of i independent random variables each with generating function $f(x)$. Thus, the generating function for the $j + 1^{st}$ generation, given i children in the jth generation, is $f^i(x)$. The generating function for the $j + 1^{st}$ generation is given by

$$f_{j+1}(x) = \sum_{i=0}^{\infty} \text{Prob}(z_j = i) f^i(x).$$

If $f_j(x) = \sum_{i=0}^{\infty} a_i x^i$, then f_{j+1} is obtained by substituting $f(x)$ for x in $f_j(x)$.

Since $f(x)$ and its iterates, $f_2, f_3, \ldots$, are all polynomials in x with nonnegative coefficients, $f(x)$ and its iterates are all monotonically increasing and convex on the unit interval. Since the probabilities of the number of children of a node sum to 1, if $p_0 < 1$, some coefficient of x to a power other than zero in $f(x)$ is non-zero and $f(x)$ is strictly increasing.

Let q be the probability that the branching process dies out. If there are i children in the first generation, then each of the i subtrees must die out, and this occurs with probability q^i. Thus, q equals the summation over all values of i of the product of the probability of i children times the probability that i subtrees will die out. This gives $q = \sum_{i=0}^{\infty} p_i q^i$. Thus, q is the root of $x = \sum_{i=0}^{\infty} p_i x^i$, that is, the root of $x = f(x)$.

This suggests focusing on roots of the equation $f(x) = x$ in the interval $[0,1]$. The value $x = 1$ is always a root of the equation $f(x) = x$, since $f(1) = \sum_{i=0}^{\infty} p_i = 1$. When is there a smaller nonnegative root? The derivative of $f(x)$ at $x = 1$ is $f'(1) = p_1 + 2p_2 + 3p_3 + \cdots$. Let $m = f'(1)$. Thus, m is the expected number of children of a node. If $m > 1$, one might expect the tree to grow forever, since each node at time j is expected to have more than one child. But this does not imply that the probability of extinction is zero. In fact, if $p_0 > 0$, then with positive probability the root will have no children and the process will become extinct right away. Recall that for $G(n, \frac{d}{n})$, the expected number of children is d, so the parameter m plays the role of d.

If $m < 1$, then the slope of $f(x)$ at $x = 1$ is less than 1. This fact along with convexity of $f(x)$ implies that $f(x) > x$ for x in $[0, 1)$ and there is no root of $f(x) = x$ in the interval $[0, 1)$ (see Figure 8.11).

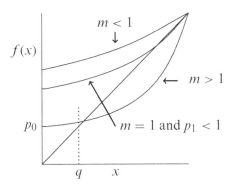

Figure 8.11: Illustration of the root of equation $f(x) = x$ in the interval $[0,1)$.

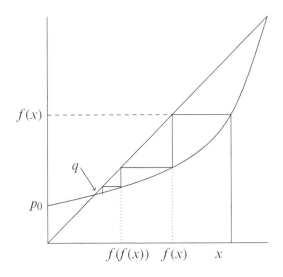

Figure 8.12: Illustration of convergence of the sequence of iterations $f_1(x), f_2(x), \ldots$ to q.

If $m = 1$ and $p_1 < 1$, then once again convexity implies that $f(x) > x$ for $x \in [0, 1)$ and there is no root of $f(x) = x$ in the interval $[0, 1)$. If $m = 1$ and $p_1 = 1$, then $f(x)$ is the straight line $f(x) = x$.

If $m > 1$, then the slope of $f(x)$ is greater than the slope of x at $x = 1$. This fact, along with convexity of $f(x)$, implies $f(x) = x$ has a unique root in $[0,1)$. When $p_0 = 0$, the root is at $x = 0$.

Let q be the smallest non-negative root of the equation $f(x) = x$. For $m < 1$ and for $m=1$ and $p_0 < 1$, q equals one and for $m > 1$, q is strictly less than one. We shall see that the value of q is the *extinction probability* of the branching process and that $1 - q$ is the *immortality probability*. That is, q is the probability that for some j, the number of children in the jth generation is zero. To see this, note that for $m > 1$, $\lim_{j \to \infty} f_j(x) = q$ for $0 \le x < 1$. Figure 8.12 illustrates the proof given in Lemma 8.16. Similarly note that when $m < 1$ or $m = 1$ with $p_0 < 1$, $f_j(x)$ approaches 1 as j approaches infinity.

Lemma 8.16 *Assume m > 1. Let q be the unique root of f(x)=x in [0,1). In the limit as j goes to infinity, $f_j(x) = q$ for x in [0, 1).*

Proof If $0 \le x \le q$, then $x < f(x) \le f(q)$ and iterating this inequality

$$x < f_1(x) < f_2(x) < \cdots < f_j(x) < f(q) = q.$$

Clearly, the sequence converges and it must converge to a fixed point where $f(x) = x$. Similarly, if $q \le x < 1$, then $f(q) \le f(x) < x$ and iterating this inequality

$$x > f_1(x) > f_2(x) > \cdots > f_j(x) > f(q) = q.$$

In the limit as j goes to infinity $f_j(x) = q$ for all $x, 0 \le x < 1$. That is,

$$\lim_{j \to \infty} f_j(x) = q + 0x + 0x^2 + \cdots$$

and there are no children with probability q and no finite number of children with probability zero. ∎

Recall that $f_j(x)$ is the generating function $\sum_{i=0}^{\infty} \text{Prob}\left(z_j = i\right) x^i$. The fact that in the limit the generating function equals the constant q, and is not a function of x, says that $\text{Prob}\left(z_j = 0\right) = q$ and $\text{Prob}\left(z_j = i\right) = 0$ for all finite non-zero values of i. The remaining probability is the probability of a non-finite component. Thus, when $m > 1$, q is the extinction probability and $1-q$ is the probability that z_j grows without bound.

Theorem 8.17 *Consider a tree generated by a branching process. Let $f(x)$ be the generating function for the number of children at each node.*

1. *If the expected number of children at each node is less than or equal to 1, then the probability of extinction is 1 unless the probability of exactly one child is 1.*
2. *If the expected number of children of each node is greater than 1, then the probability of extinction is the unique solution to $f(x) = x$ in [0, 1).*

Proof Let p_i be the probability of i children at each node. Then $f(x) = p_0 + p_1 x + p_2 x^2 + \cdots$ is the generating function for the number of children at each node and $f'(1) = p_1 + 2p_2 + 3p_3 + \cdots$ is the slope of $f(x)$ at $x = 1$. Observe that $f'(1)$ is the expected number of children at each node.

Since the expected number of children at each node is the slope of $f(x)$ at $x = 1$, if the expected number of children is less than or equal to 1, the slope of $f(x)$ at $x = 1$ is less than or equal to 1 and the unique root of $f(x) = x$ in $(0, 1]$ is at $x = 1$ and the probability of extinction is 1 unless $f'(1) = 1$ and $p_1 = 1$. If $f'(1) = 1$ and $p_1 = 1, f(x) = x$ and the tree is an infinite degree 1 chain. If the slope of $f(x)$ at $x = 1$ is greater than 1, then the probability of extinction is the unique solution to $f(x) = x$ in [0, 1). ∎

A branching process can be viewed as the process of creating a component in an infinite graph. In a finite graph, the probability distribution of descendants is not a constant as more and more vertices of the graph get discovered.

The simple branching process defined here either dies out or goes to infinity. In biological systems there are other factors, since processes often go to stable populations. One possibility is that the probability distribution for the number of descendants of a child depends on the total population of the current generation.

Expected Size of Extinct Families

We now show that the expected size of an extinct family is finite, provided that $m \neq 1$. Note that at extinction, the size must be finite. However, the expected size at extinction could conceivably be infinite, if the probability of dying out did not decay fast enough. For example, suppose that with probability $\frac{1}{2}$ it became extinct with size 3, with probability $\frac{1}{4}$ it became extinct with size 9, with probability $\frac{1}{8}$ it became extinct with size 27, etc. In such a case the expected size at extinction would be infinite even though the process dies out with probability 1. We now show this does not happen.

Lemma 8.18 *If the slope $m = f'(1)$ does not equal 1, then the expected size of an extinct family is finite. If the slope m equals 1 and $p_1 = 1$, then the tree is an infinite degree 1 chain and there are no extinct families. If $m=1$ and $p_1 < 1$, then the expected size of the extinct family is infinite.*

Proof Let z_i be the random variable denoting the size of the ith generation and let q be the probability of extinction. The probability of extinction for a tree with k children in the first generation is q^k, since each of the k children has an extinction probability of q. Note that the expected size of z_1, the first generation, over extinct trees will be smaller than the expected size of z_1 over all trees, since when the root node has a larger number of children than average, the tree is more likely to be infinite.

By Bayes rule,

$$\text{Prob}(z_1 = k | \text{extinction}) = \text{Prob}(z_1 = k) \frac{\text{Prob}(\text{extinction}|z_1 = k)}{\text{Prob}(\text{extinction})}$$

$$= p_k \frac{q^k}{q} = p_k q^{k-1}.$$

Knowing the probability distribution of z_1 given extinction, allows us to calculate the expected size of z_1 given extinction:

$$E(z_1 | \text{extinction}) = \sum_{k=0}^{\infty} k p_k q^{k-1} = f'(q).$$

We now prove, using independence, that the expected size of the ith generation given extinction is

$$E(z_i | \text{extinction}) = \left(f'(q) \right)^i.$$

For $i = 2$, z_2 is the sum of z_1 independent random variables, each independent of the random variable z_1. So, $E(z_2 | z_1 = j \text{ and extinction}) = E(\text{sum of } j \text{ copies of } z_1 | \text{extinction}) = j E(z_1 | \text{extinction})$. Summing over all values of j,

$$E(z_2|\text{extinction}) = \sum_{j=1}^{\infty} E(z_2|z_1 = j \text{ and extinction})\text{Prob}(z_1 = j|\text{extinction})$$

$$= \sum_{j=1}^{\infty} jE(z_1|\text{extinction})\text{Prob}(z_1 = j|\text{extinction})$$

$$= E(z_1|\text{extinction}) \sum_{j=1}^{\infty} j\,\text{Prob}(z_1 = j|\text{extinction})$$

$$= E^2(z_1|\text{extinction}).$$

Since $E(z_1|\text{extinction}) = f'(q)$, $E(z_2|\text{extinction}) = (f'(q))^2$. Similarly, $E(z_i|\text{extinction}) = (f'(q))^i$. The expected size of the tree is the sum of the expected sizes of each generation. That is,

$$\text{Expected size of tree given extinction} = \sum_{i=0}^{\infty} E(z_i|\text{extinction}) = \sum_{i=0}^{\infty} (f'(q))^i = \frac{1}{1 - f'(q)}.$$

Thus, the expected size of an extinct family is finite, since $f'(q) < 1$ provided $m \neq 1$.

The fact that $f'(q) < 1$ is illustrated in Figure 8.11. If $m < 1$, then $q = 1$ and $f'(q) = m$ is less than 1. If $m > 1$, then $q \in [0, 1)$ and again $f'(q) < 1$ since q is the solution to $f(x) = x$ and $f'(q)$ must be less than 1 for the curve $f(x)$ to cross the line x. Thus, for $m < 1$ or $m > 1$, $f'(q) < 1$ and the expected tree size of $\frac{1}{1-f'(q)}$ is finite. For $m = 1$ and $p_1 < 1$, one has $q = 1$, and thus $f'(q) = 1$ and the formula for the expected size of the tree diverges. ■

8.7. CNF-SAT

Phase transitions occur not only in random graphs but in other random structures as well. An important example is that of satisfiability of Boolean formulas in conjunctive normal form. A conjunctive normal form (CNF) formula over n variables $x_1, \ldots, x_n$ is an AND of ORs of *literals*, where a literal is a variable or its negation. For example, the following is a CNF formula over the variables $\{x_1, x_2, x_3, x_4\}$:

$$(x_1 \vee \bar{x}_2 \vee x_3)(x_2 \vee \bar{x}_4)(x_1 \vee x_4)(x_3 \vee x_4)(x_2 \vee \bar{x}_3 \vee x_4).$$

Each OR of literals is called a *clause*; for example, the above formula has five clauses. A *k-CNF* formula is a CNF formula in which each clause has size at most k, so the above formula is a 3-CNF formula. An assignment of true/false values to variables is said to *satisfy* a CNF formula if it satisfies every clause in it. Setting all variables to true satisfies the above CNF formula, and in fact this formula has multiple satisfying assignments. A formula is said to be *satisfiable* it there exists at least one assignment of truth values to variables that satisfies it.

Many important problems can be converted into questions of finding satisfying assignments of CNF formulas. Indeed, the CNF-SAT problem of whether a given CNF formula is satisfiable is *NP-Complete*, meaning that any problem in the class NP, which consists of all problems for which a positive solution can be verified in polynomial time, can be converted into it. As a result, it is believed to be highly unlikely that there will ever exist an efficient algorithm for worst-case instances. However, there are solvers that turn out to work very well in practice on instances arising from a wide range of applications. There is also substantial structure and understanding of the satisfiability of *random* CNF formulas. The next two sections discuss each in turn.

8.7.1. SAT-Solvers in Practice

While the SAT problem is NP-complete, a number of algorithms have been developed that perform extremely well in practice on SAT formulas arising in a range of applications. Such applications include hardware and software verification, creating action plans for robots and robot teams, solving combinatorial puzzles, and even proving mathematical theorems.

Broadly, there are two classes of solvers: *complete* solvers and *incomplete* solvers. Complete solvers are guaranteed to find a satisfying assignment whenever one exists; if they do not return a solution, then you know the formula is not satisfiable. Complete solvers are often based on some form of recursive tree search. Incomplete solvers instead make a "best effort"; they are typically based on some local-search heuristic, and they may fail to output a solution even when a formula is satisfiable. However, they are typically much faster than complete solvers.

An example of a complete solver is the following DPLL (Davis-Putnam-Logemann-Loveland) style procedure. First, if there are any variables x_i that never appear in negated form in any clause, then set those variables to true and delete clauses where the literal x_i appears. Similarly, if there are any x_i that *only* appear in negated form, then set those variables to false and delete clauses where the literal $\bar{x}_i$ appears. Second, if there are any clauses that have only one literal in them (such clauses are called unit clauses), then set that literal as needed to satisfy the clause. E.g., if the clause was "$(\bar{x}_3)$," then one would set x_3 to false. Then remove that clause along with any other clause containing that literal, and shrink any clause containing the negation of that literal (e.g., a clause such as $(x_3 \vee x_4)$ would now become just (x_4), and one would then run this rule again on this clause). Finally, if neither of the above two cases applies, then one chooses some literal and recursively tries both settings for it. Specifically, choose some literal ℓ and recursively check if the formula is satisfiable conditioned on setting ℓ to true; if the answer is "yes," then we are done, but if the answer is "no," then recursively check if the formula is satisfiable conditioned on setting ℓ to false. Notice that this procedure is guaranteed to find a satisfying assignment whenever one exists.

An example of an incomplete solver is the following local-search procedure called *Walksat*. Walksat begins with a random assignment of truth-values to variables. If this happens to satisfy the formula, then it outputs success. If not, then it chooses some unsatisfied clause C at random. If C contains some variable x_i whose truth-value can be flipped (causing C to be satisfied) without causing any *other* clause to be unsatisfied, then x_i's truth-value is flipped. Otherwise, Walksat either (a) flips the truth-value of the variable in C that causes the *fewest* other clauses to become unsatisfied, or else (b) flips the truth-value of a *random* x_i in C; the choice of whether to perform (a) or (b) is determined by flipping a coin of bias p. Thus, Walksat is performing a kind of random walk in the space of truth-assignments, hence the name. Walksat also has two time-thresholds, T_{flips} and $T_{restarts}$. If the above procedure has not found a satisfying assignment after T_{flips} flips, it then restarts with a fresh initial random assignment and tries again; if that entire process has not found a satisfying assignment after $T_{restarts}$ restarts, then it outputs "no assignment found."

The above solvers are just two simple examples. Due to the importance of the CNF-SAT problem, development of faster SAT-solvers is an active area of computer science research. SAT-solving competitions are held each year, and solvers are routinely being used to solve challenging verification, planning, and scheduling problems.

8.7.2. Phase Transitions for CNF-SAT

We now consider the question of phase transitions in the satisfiability of *random k*-CNF formulas.

Generate a random CNF formula f with n variables, m clauses, and k literals per clause. Specifically, each clause in f is selected independently at random from the set of all $\binom{n}{k}2^k$ possible clauses of size k. Equivalently, to generate a clause, choose a random set of k distinct variables, and then for each of those variables choose to either negate it or not with equal probability. Here, the number of variables n is going to infinity, m is a function of n, and k is a fixed constant. A reasonable value to think of for k is $k = 3$. Unsatisfiability is an increasing property, since adding more clauses preserves unsatisfiability. By arguments similar to Section 8.5, there is a phase transition, i.e., a function $m(n)$ such that if $m_1(n)$ is $o(m(n))$, a random formula with $m_1(n)$ clauses is, almost surely, satisfiable and for $m_2(n)$ with $m_2(n)/m(n) \to \infty$, a random formula with $m_2(n)$ clauses is, almost surely, unsatisfiable. It has been conjectured that there is a constant r_k independent of n such that $r_k n$ is a sharp threshold.

Here we derive upper and lower bounds on r_k. It is relatively easy to get an upper bound on r_k. A fixed truth assignment satisfies a random k clause with probability $1 - \frac{1}{2^k}$ because of the 2^k truth assignments to the k variables in the clause, only one fails to satisfy the clause. Thus, with probability $\frac{1}{2^k}$, the clause is not satisfied, and with probability $1 - \frac{1}{2^k}$, the clause is satisfied. Let $m = cn$. Now, cn independent clauses are all satisfied by the fixed assignment with probability $\left(1 - \frac{1}{2^k}\right)^{cn}$. Since there are 2^n truth assignments, the expected number of satisfying assignments for a formula with cn clauses is $2^n\left(1 - \frac{1}{2^k}\right)^{cn}$. If $c = 2^k \ln 2$, the expected number of satisfying assignments is

$$2^n \left(1 - \frac{1}{2^k}\right)^{n2^k \ln 2}.$$

$\left(1 - \frac{1}{2^k}\right)^{2^k}$ is at most $1/e$ and approaches $1/e$ in the limit. Thus,

$$2^n \left(1 - \frac{1}{2^k}\right)^{n2^k \ln 2} \leq 2^n e^{-n \ln 2} = 2^n 2^{-n} = 1.$$

For $c > 2^k \ln 2$, the expected number of satisfying assignments goes to zero as $n \to \infty$. Here the expectation is over the choice of clauses that is random, not the choice of a truth assignment. From the first moment method, it follows that a random formula with cn clauses is almost surely not satisfiable. Thus, $r_k \leq 2^k \ln 2$.

The other direction, showing a lower bound for r_k, is not that easy. From now on, we focus only on the case $k = 3$. The statements and algorithms given here can be extended to $k \geq 4$, but with different constants. It turns out that the second moment method cannot be directly applied to get a lower bound on r_3 because the variance is too high. A simple algorithm, called the Smallest Clause Heuristic (abbreviated SC), yields a satisfying assignment with probability tending to one if $c < \frac{2}{3}$, proving that $r_3 \geq \frac{2}{3}$. Other, more difficult-to-analyze algorithms push the lower bound on r_3 higher.

The Smallest Clause Heuristic repeatedly executes the following. Assign true to a random literal in a random shortest clause and delete the clause, since it is now satisfied. In more detail, pick at random a 1-literal clause, if one exists, and set that literal to true. If there is no 1-literal clause, pick a 2-literal clause, select one of its two literals, and set the literal to true. Otherwise, pick a 3-literal clause and a literal in it and set the literal to true. If we encounter a 0-length clause, then we have failed to find a satisfying assignment; otherwise, once we eliminate all clauses, we have found a satisfying assignment.

A related heuristic, called the Unit Clause Heuristic, selects a random clause with one literal, if there is one, and sets the literal in it to true. Otherwise, it picks a random as yet unset literal and sets it to true. Another variation is the "pure literal" heuristic. It sets a random "pure literal," a literal whose negation does not occur in any clause, to true, if there are any pure literals; otherwise, it sets a random literal to true.

When a literal w is set to true, all clauses containing w are deleted, since they are satisfied, and $\bar{w}$ is deleted from any clause containing $\bar{w}$. If a clause is reduced to length zero (no literals), then the algorithm has failed to find a satisfying assignment to the formula. The formula may, in fact, be satisfiable, but the algorithm has failed.

Example Consider a 3-CNF formula with n variables and cn clauses. With n variables there are $2n$ literals, since a variable and its complement are distinct literals. The expected number of times a literal occurs is calculated as follows. Each clause has three literals. Thus, each of the $2n$ different literals occurs $\frac{(3cn)}{2n} = \frac{3}{2}c$ times on average. Suppose $c = 5$. Then each literal appears 7.5 times on average. If one sets a literal to true, one would expect to satisfy 7.5 clauses. However, this process is not repeatable, since after setting a literal to true there is conditioning so that the formula is no longer random. ∎

Theorem 8.19 *If the number of clauses in a random 3-CNF formula grows as cn where c is a constant less than $2/3$, then with probability $1 - o(1)$, the Shortest Clause (SC) Heuristic finds a satisfying assignment.*

The proof of this theorem will take the rest of the section. A general impediment to proving that simple algorithms work for random instances of many problems is conditioning. At the start, the input is random and has properties enjoyed by random instances. But, as the algorithm is executed, the data is no longer random; it is conditioned on the steps of the algorithm so far. In the case of SC and other heuristics for finding a satisfying assignment for a Boolean formula, the argument to deal with conditioning is relatively simple.

We supply some intuition before giving the proof. Imagine maintaining a queue of 1 and 2-clauses. A 3-clause enters the queue when one of its literals is set to false and it becomes a 2-clause. SC always picks a 1 or 2-clause if there is one and sets one of its literals to true. At any step when the total number of 1 and 2-clauses is positive, one of the clauses is removed from the queue. Consider the arrival rate, that is, the expected number of arrivals into the queue at a given time t. For a particular clause to arrive into the queue at time t to become a 2-clause, it must contain the negation of the literal being set to true at time t. It can contain any two other literals not yet set. The number of such clauses is $\binom{n-t}{2}2^2$. So, the probability that a particular clause arrives in the queue at time t is at most

$$\frac{\binom{n-t}{2}2^2}{\binom{n}{3}2^3} \leq \frac{3}{2(n-2)}.$$

Since there are cn clauses in total, the arrival rate is $\frac{3c}{2}$, which for $c < 2/3$ is a constant strictly less than 1. The arrivals into the queue of different clauses occur independently (Lemma 8.20), the queue has arrival rate strictly less than 1, and the queue loses one or more clauses whenever it is non-empty. This implies that the queue never has too many clauses in it. A slightly more complicated argument will show that no clause remains as a 1 or 2-clause for $\omega(\ln n)$ steps (Lemma 8.21). This implies that the probability of two contradictory 1-length clauses, which is a precursor to a 0-length clause, is very small.

Lemma 8.20 *Let T_i be the first time that clause i turns into a 2-clause. T_i is ∞ if clause i gets satisfied before turning into a 2-clause. The T_i are mutually independent over the randomness in constructing the formula and the randomness in SC, and for any t,*

$$Prob(T_i = t) \leq \frac{3}{2(n-2)}.$$

Proof For the proof, generate the clauses in a different way. The important thing is that the new method of generation, called the method of *deferred decisions*, results in the same distribution of input formulae as the original. The method of deferred decisions is tied in with the SC algorithm and works as follows. At any time, the length of each clause (number of literals) is all that we know; we have not yet picked which literals are in each clause. At the start, every clause has length three and SC picks one of the clauses uniformly at random. Now, SC wants to pick one of the three literals in that clause to set to true, but we do not know which literals are in the clause. At this point, we pick uniformly at random one of the $2n$ possible literals. Say, for illustration, we picked $\bar{x}_{102}$. The literal $\bar{x}_{102}$ is placed in the clause and set to true. The literal x_{102} is set to false. We must also deal with occurrences of the literal or its negation in all other clauses, but again, we do not know which clauses have such an occurrence. We decide that now. For each clause, independently, with probability $3/n$ include either the literal $\bar{x}_{102}$ or its negation x_{102}, each with probability $1/2$. In the case that we included $\bar{x}_{102}$ (the literal we had set to true), the clause is now deleted, and if we included x_{102} (the literal we had set to false), we decrease the residual length of the clause by one.

At a general stage, suppose the fates of i variables have already been decided and $n-i$ remain. The residual length of each clause is known. Among the clauses that are not yet satisfied, choose a random shortest length clause. Among the $n - i$ variables remaining, pick one uniformly at random, then pick it or its negation as the new literal. Include this literal in the clause, thereby satisfying it. Since the clause is satisfied, the algorithm deletes it. For each other clause, do the following. If its residual length is l, decide with probability $l/(n - i)$ to include the new variable in the clause and if so with probability 1/2 each, include it or its negation. If the literal that was set to true is included in a clause, delete the clause as it is now satisfied. If its negation is included in a clause, then just delete the literal and decrease the residual length of the clause by one.

Why does this yield the same distribution as the original one? First, observe that the order in which the variables are picked by the method of deferred decisions is independent of the clauses; it is just a random permutation of the n variables. Look at any one clause. For a clause, we decide in order whether each variable or its negation is in the clause. So for a particular clause and a particular triple i, j, and k with $i < j < k$, the probability that the clause contains the ith, the jth, and k^{th} literal (or their negations) in the order determined by deferred decisions is:

$$\left(1 - \tfrac{3}{n}\right)\left(1 - \tfrac{3}{n-1}\right)\cdots\left(1 - \tfrac{3}{n-i+2}\right)\tfrac{3}{n-i+1}$$

$$\left(1 - \tfrac{2}{n-i}\right)\left(1 - \tfrac{2}{n-i-1}\right)\cdots\left(1 - \tfrac{2}{n-j+2}\right)\tfrac{2}{n-j+1}$$

$$\left(1 - \tfrac{1}{n-j}\right)\left(1 - \tfrac{1}{n-j-1}\right)\cdots\left(1 - \tfrac{1}{n-k+2}\right)\tfrac{1}{n-k+1} = \tfrac{3}{n(n-1)(n-2)},$$

where the $(1 - \cdots)$ factors are for not picking the current variable or negation to be included and the others are for including the current variable or its negation. Independence among clauses follows from the fact that we have never let the occurrence or non-occurrence of any variable in any clause influence our decisions on other clauses.

Now, we prove the lemma by appealing to the method of deferred decisions to generate the formula. $T_i = t$ if and only if the method of deferred decisions does not put the current literal at steps $1, 2, \ldots, t - 1$ into the ith clause, but puts the negation of the literal at step t into it. Thus, the probability is precisely

$$\tfrac{1}{2}\left(1 - \tfrac{3}{n}\right)\left(1 - \tfrac{3}{n-1}\right)\cdots\left(1 - \tfrac{3}{n-t+2}\right)\tfrac{3}{n-t+1} \leq \tfrac{3}{2(n-2)},$$

as claimed. Clearly the T_i are independent, since again deferred decisions deal with different clauses independently. ∎

Lemma 8.21 *There exists a constant c_2 such that with probability $1 - o(1)$, no clause remains a 2 or 1-clause for more than $c_2 \ln n$ steps. I.e., once a 3-clause becomes a 2-clause, it is either satisfied or reduced to a 0-clause in $O(\ln n)$ steps.*

Proof Say that t is a "busy time" if there exists at least one 2-clause or 1-clause at time t, and define a time-window $[r + 1, s]$ to be a "busy window" if time r is not busy but then each $t \in [r + 1, s]$ is a busy time. We will prove that for some constant c_2, with probability $1 - o(1)$, all busy windows have length at most $c_2 \ln n$.

Fix some r and s and consider the event that $[r+1, s]$ is a busy window. Since SC always decreases the total number of 1 and 2-clauses by one whenever it is positive, we must have generated at least $s - r$ new 2-clauses between r and s. Now, define an indicator variable for each 3-clause that has value 1 if the clause turns into a 2-clause between r and s. By Lemma 8.20, these variables are independent and the probability that a particular 3-clause turns into a 2-clause at a time t is at most $3/(2(n-2))$. Summing over t between r and s,

$$\text{Prob (a 3-clause turns into a 2-clause during } [r, s]) \leq \frac{3(s-r)}{2(n-2)}.$$

Since there are cn clauses in all, the expected sum of the indicator variables is $cn\frac{3(s-r)}{2(n-2)} \approx \frac{3c(s-r)}{2}$. Note that $3c/2 < 1$, which implies the arrival rate into the queue of 2 and 1-clauses is a constant strictly less than 1. Using Chernoff bounds, if $s - r \geq c_2 \ln n$ for appropriate constant c_2, the probability that more than $s - r$ clauses turn into 2-clauses between r and s is at most $1/n^3$. Applying the union bound over all $O(n^2)$ possible choices of r and s, we get that the probability that any clause remains a 2 or 1-clause for more than $c_2 \ln n$ steps is $o(1)$. ∎

Now, assume the $1 - o(1)$ probability event of Lemma 8.21 that no clause remains a 2 or 1-clause for more than $c_2 \ln n$ steps. We will show that this implies it is unlikely the SC algorithm terminates in failure.

Suppose SC terminates in failure. This means that at some time t, the algorithm generates a 0-clause. At time $t - 1$, this clause must have been a 1-clause. Suppose the clause consists of the literal w. Since at time $t - 1$, there is at least one 1-clause, the shortest clause rule of SC selects a 1-clause and sets the literal in that clause to true. This other clause must have been $\bar{w}$. Let t_1 be the first time either of these two clauses, w or $\bar{w}$, became a 2-clause. We have $t - t_1 \leq c_2 \ln n$. Clearly, until time t, neither of these two clauses is picked by SC. So, the literals that are set to true during this period are chosen independent of these clauses. Say the two clauses were $w + x + y$ and $\bar{w} + u + v$ at the start. x, y, u, and v must all be negations of literals set to true during steps t_1 to t. So, there are only $O\left((\ln n)^4\right)$ choices for x, y, u, and v for a given value of t. There are $O(n)$ choices of w, $O(n^2)$ choices of which two clauses i and j of the input become these w and $\bar{w}$, and n choices for t. Thus, there are $O\left(n^4(\ln n)^4\right)$ choices for what these clauses contain and which clauses they are in the input. On the other hand, for any given i and j, the probability that clauses i and j both match a given set of literals is $O(1/n^6)$. Thus the probability that these choices are actually realized is therefore $O\left(n^4(\ln n)^4/n^6\right) = o(1)$, as required.

8.8. Nonuniform Models of Random Graphs

So far we have considered the $G(n, p)$ random graph model in which all vertices have the same expected degree, and moreover degrees are concentrated close to their expectation. However, large graphs occurring in the real world tend to have *power law* degree distributions. For a power law degree distribution, the number $f(d)$ of vertices of degree d scales as $1/d^\alpha$ for some constant $\alpha > 0$.

One way to generate such graphs is to stipulate that there are $f(d)$ vertices of degree d and choose uniformly at random from the set of graphs with this degree distribution. Clearly, in this model the graph edges are not independent, and this makes these random graphs harder to analyze. But the question of when phase transitions occur in random graphs with arbitrary degree distributions is still of interest. In this section, we consider when a random graph with a nonuniform degree distribution has a giant component. Our treatment in this section, and subsequent ones, will be more intuitive without providing rigorous proofs.

8.8.1. Giant Component in Graphs with Given Degree Distribution

Molloy and Reed address the issue of when a random graph with a nonuniform degree distribution has a giant component. Let λ_i be the fraction of vertices of degree i. There will be a giant component if and only if $\sum_{i=0}^{\infty} i(i-2)\lambda_i > 0$.

To see intuitively that this is the correct formula, consider exploring a component of a graph starting from a given seed vertex. Degree zero vertices do not occur except in the case where the vertex is the seed. If a degree 1 vertex is encountered, then that terminates the expansion along the edge into the vertex. Thus, we do not want to encounter too many degree 1 vertices. A degree 2 vertex is neutral in that the vertex is entered by one edge and left by the other. There is no net increase in the size of the frontier. Vertices of degree i greater than 2 increase the frontier by $i - 2$ vertices. The vertex is entered by one of its edges, and thus there are $i - 1$ edges to new vertices in the frontier for a net gain of $i - 2$. The $i\lambda_i$ in $(i-2)i\lambda_i$ is proportional to the probability of reaching a degree i vertex (see Figure 8.13), and the $i - 2$ accounts for the increase or decrease in size of the frontier when a degree i vertex is reached.

Example Consider applying the Molloy Reed conditions to the $G(n, p)$ model, and use p_i to denote the probability that a vertex has degree i, i.e., in analog to λ_i. It turns out that the summation $\sum_{i=0}^{n} i(i-2)p_i$ gives value zero precisely when $p = 1/n$, the point at which the phase transition occurs. At $p = 1/n$, the average degree of each vertex is one and there are $n/2$ edges. However, the actual degree distribution of the vertices is binomial, where the probability that a vertex is of degree i is given by $p_i = \binom{n}{i}p^i(1-p)^{n-i}$. We now show that $\lim_{n \to \infty} \sum_{i=0}^{n} i(i-2)p_i = 0$ for $p_i = \binom{n}{i}p^i(1-p)^{n-i}$ when $p = 1/n$.

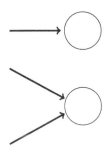

Consider a graph in which half of the vertices are degree 1 and half are degree 2. If a vertex is selected at random, it is equally likely to be degree 1 or degree 2. However, if we select an edge at random and walk to a random end point, the vertex is twice as likely to be degree 2 as degree 1. In many graph algorithms, a vertex is reached by randomly selecting an edge and traversing the edge to reach an end point. In this case, the probability of reaching a degree i vertex is proportional to $i\lambda_i$ where λ_i is the fraction of vertices that are degree i.

Figure 8.13: Probability of encountering a degree d vertex when following a path in a graph.

$$\lim_{n \to \infty} \sum_{i=0}^{n} i(i-2) \binom{n}{i} \left(\frac{1}{n}\right)^i \left(1 - \frac{1}{n}\right)^{n-i}$$

$$= \lim_{n \to \infty} \sum_{i=0}^{n} i(i-2) \frac{n(n-1)\cdots(n-i+1)}{i! \; n^i} \left(1 - \frac{1}{n}\right)^n \left(1 - \frac{1}{n}\right)^{-i}$$

$$= \frac{1}{e} \lim_{n \to \infty} \sum_{i=0}^{n} i(i-2) \frac{n(n-1)\cdots(n-i+1)}{i! \; n^i} \left(\frac{n}{n-1}\right)^i$$

$$\leq \sum_{i=0}^{\infty} \frac{i(i-2)}{i!}.$$

To see that $\sum_{i=0}^{\infty} \frac{i(i-2)}{i!} = 0$, note that

$$\sum_{i=0}^{\infty} \frac{i}{i!} = \sum_{i=1}^{\infty} \frac{i}{i!} = \sum_{i=1}^{\infty} \frac{1}{(i-1)!} = \sum_{i=0}^{\infty} \frac{1}{i!}$$

and

$$\sum_{i=0}^{\infty} \frac{i^2}{i!} = \sum_{i=1}^{\infty} \frac{i}{(i-1)!} = \sum_{i=0}^{\infty} \frac{i+1}{i!} = \sum_{i=0}^{\infty} \frac{i}{i!} + \sum_{i=0}^{\infty} \frac{1}{i!} = 2 \sum_{i=0}^{\infty} \frac{1}{i!}.$$

Thus,

$$\sum_{i=0}^{\infty} \frac{i(i-2)}{i!} = \sum_{i=0}^{\infty} \frac{i^2}{i!} - 2 \sum_{i=0}^{\infty} \frac{i}{i!} = 0. \qquad \blacksquare$$

8.9. Growth Models

Many graphs that arise in the outside world started as small graphs that grew over time. In a model for such graphs, vertices and edges are added to the graph over time. In such a model there are many ways in which to select the vertices for attaching a new edge. One is to select two vertices uniformly at random from the set of existing vertices. Another is to select two vertices with probability proportional to their degree. This latter method is referred to as preferential attachment. A variant of this method would be to add a new vertex at each unit of time and with probability δ add an edge where one end of the edge is the new vertex and the other end is a vertex selected with probability proportional to its degree. The graph generated by this latter method is a tree with a power law degree distribution.

8.9.1. Growth Model without Preferential Attachment

Consider a growth model for a random graph without preferential attachment. Start with zero vertices. At each unit of time a new vertex is created and with probability δ two vertices chosen at random are joined by an edge. The two vertices may already have an edge between them. In this case, we add another edge. So, the resulting structure is a multi-graph rather then a graph. Since at time t there are t vertices and in expectation only $O(\delta t)$ edges where there are t^2 pairs of vertices, it is very unlikely that there will be many multiple edges.

The degree distribution for this growth model is calculated as follows. The number of vertices of degree k at time t is a random variable. Let $d_k(t)$ be the expectation of the number of vertices of degree k at time t. The number of isolated vertices increases by one at each unit of time and decreases by the number of isolated vertices, $b(t)$, that are picked to be end points of the new edge. $b(t)$ can take on values $0, 1$, or 2. Taking expectations,

$$d_0(t+1) = d_0(t) + 1 - E(b(t)).$$

Now $b(t)$ is the sum of two 0-1 valued random variables whose values are the number of degree zero vertices picked for each end point of the new edge. Even though the two random variables are not independent, the expectation of $b(t)$ is the sum of the expectations of the two variables and is $2\delta \frac{d_0(t)}{t}$. Thus,

$$d_0(t+1) = d_0(t) + 1 - 2\delta \frac{d_0(t)}{t}.$$

The number of degree k vertices increases whenever a new edge is added to a degree $k-1$ vertex and decreases when a new edge is added to a degree k vertex. Reasoning as above,

$$d_k(t+1) = d_k(t) + 2\delta \frac{d_{k-1}(t)}{t} - 2\delta \frac{d_k(t)}{t}. \tag{8.4}$$

Note that this formula, as others in this section, is not quite precise. For example, the same vertex may be picked twice, so that the new edge is a self-loop. For $k << t$, this problem contributes a minuscule error. Restricting k to be a fixed constant and letting $t \to \infty$ in this section avoids these problems.

Assume that the above equations are exactly valid. Clearly, $d_0(1) = 1$ and $d_1(1) = d_2(1) = \cdots = 0$. By induction on t, there is a unique solution to (8.4), since given $d_k(t)$ for all k, the equation determines $d_k(t+1)$ for all k. There is a solution of the form $d_k(t) = p_k t$, where p_k depends only on k and not on t, provided k is fixed and $t \to \infty$. Again, this is not precisely true since $d_1(1) = 0$ and $d_1(2) > 0$ clearly contradict the existence of a solution of the form $d_1(t) = p_1 t$.

Set $d_k(t) = p_k t$. Then,

$$(t+1)p_0 = p_0 t + 1 - 2\delta \frac{p_0 t}{t}$$

$$p_0 = 1 - 2\delta p_0$$

$$p_0 = \frac{1}{1+2\delta}$$

and

$$(t+1)p_k = p_k t + 2\delta \frac{p_{k-1} t}{t} - 2\delta \frac{p_k t}{t}$$

$$p_k = 2\delta p_{k-1} - 2\delta p_k$$

$$p_k = \frac{2\delta}{1+2\delta} p_{k-1}$$

$$= \left(\frac{2\delta}{1+2\delta}\right)^k p_0$$

$$= \frac{1}{1+2\delta} \left(\frac{2\delta}{1+2\delta}\right)^k. \tag{8.5}$$

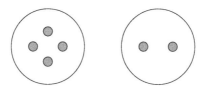

Figure 8.14: In selecting a component at random, each of the two components is equally likely to be selected. In selecting the component containing a random vertex, the larger component is twice as likely to be selected.

Thus, the model gives rise to a graph with a degree distribution that falls off exponentially fast with the degree.

The Generating Function for Component Size

Let $n_k(t)$ be the expected number of components of size k at time t. Then $n_k(t)$ is proportional to the probability that a randomly picked component is of size k. This is not the same as picking the component containing a randomly selected vertex (see Figure 8.14). Indeed, the probability that the size of the component containing a randomly selected vertex is k is proportional to $kn_k(t)$. We will show that there is a solution for $n_k(t)$ of the form $a_k t$ where a_k is a constant independent of t. After showing this, we focus on the generating function $g(x)$ for the numbers $ka_k(t)$ and use $g(x)$ to find the threshold for giant components.

Consider $n_1(t)$, the expected number of isolated vertices at time t. At each unit of time, an isolated vertex is added to the graph and an expected $\frac{2\delta n_1(t)}{t}$ many isolated vertices are chosen for attachment and thereby leave the set of isolated vertices. Thus,

$$n_1(t+1) = n_1(t) + 1 - 2\delta \frac{n_1(t)}{t}.$$

For $k > 1$, $n_k(t)$ increases when two smaller components whose sizes sum to k are joined by an edge and decreases when a vertex in a component of size k is chosen for attachment. The probability that a vertex selected at random will be in a size k component is $\frac{kn_k(t)}{t}$. Thus,

$$n_k(t+1) = n_k(t) + \delta \sum_{j=1}^{k-1} \frac{jn_j(t)}{t} \frac{(k-j)n_{k-j}(t)}{t} - 2\delta \frac{kn_k(t)}{t}.$$

To be precise, one needs to consider the actual number of components of various sizes, rather than the expected numbers. Also, if both vertices at the end of the edge are in the same k-vertex component, then $n_k(t)$ does not go down as claimed. These small inaccuracies can be ignored.

Consider solutions of the form $n_k(t) = a_k t$. Note that $n_k(t) = a_k t$ implies the number of vertices in a connected component of size k is $ka_k t$. Since the total number of vertices at time t is t, ka_k is the probability that a random vertex is in a connected component of size k. The recurrences here are valid only for k fixed as $t \to \infty$. So $\sum_{k=0}^{\infty} ka_k$ may be less than 1, in which case, there are non-finite size components whose sizes are growing with t. Solving for a_k yields $a_1 = \frac{1}{1+2\delta}$ and $a_k = \frac{\delta}{1+2k\delta} \sum_{j=1}^{k-1} j(k-j)a_j a_{k-j}$.

Consider the generating function $g(x)$ for the distribution of component sizes where the coefficient of x^k is the probability that a vertex chosen at random is in a component of size k.

$$g(x) = \sum_{k=1}^{\infty} k a_k x^k.$$

Now, $g(1) = \sum_{k=0}^{\infty} k a_k$ is the probability that a randomly chosen vertex is in a finite-sized component. For $\delta = 0$, this is clearly 1, since all vertices are in components of size 1. On the other hand, for $\delta = 1$, the vertex created at time 1 has expected degree $\log n$ (since its expected degree increases by $2/t$ and $\sum_{t=1}^{n}(2/t) = \Theta(\log n)$); so, it is in a non-finite-sized component. This implies that for $\delta = 1$, $g(1) < 1$ and there is a non-finite-sized component. Assuming continuity, there is a $\delta_{critical}$ above which $g(1) < 1$. From the formula for the $a_i's$, we will derive the differential equation

$$g = -2\delta x g' + 2\delta x g g' + x$$

and then use the equation for g to determine the value of δ at which the phase transition for the appearance of a non-finite-sized component occurs.

Derivation of $g(x)$

From

$$a_1 = \frac{1}{1 + 2\delta}$$

and

$$a_k = \frac{\delta}{1 + 2k\delta} \sum_{j=1}^{k-1} j(k - j) a_j a_{k-j}$$

derive the equations

$$a_1 (1 + 2\delta) - 1 = 0$$

and

$$a_k (1 + 2k\delta) = \delta \sum_{j=1}^{k-1} j(k - j) a_j a_{k-j}$$

for $k \geq 2$. The generating function is formed by multiplying the kth equation by $k x^k$ and summing over all k. This gives

$$-x + \sum_{k=1}^{\infty} k a_k x^k + 2\delta x \sum_{k=1}^{\infty} a_k k^2 x^{k-1} = \delta \sum_{k=1}^{\infty} k x^k \sum_{j=1}^{k-1} j(k - j) a_j a_{k-j}.$$

Note that

$$g(x) = \sum_{k=1}^{\infty} k a_k x^k \text{ and } g'(x) = \sum_{k=1}^{\infty} a_k k^2 x^{k-1}.$$

Thus,

$$-x + g(x) + 2\delta x g'(x) = \delta \sum_{k=1}^{\infty} k x^k \sum_{j=1}^{k-1} j(k - j) a_j a_{k-j}.$$

Working with the right-hand side,

$$\delta \sum_{k=1}^{\infty} kx^k \sum_{j=1}^{k-1} j(k-j)a_j a_{k-j} = \delta x \sum_{k=1}^{\infty} \sum_{j=1}^{k-1} j(k-j)(j+k-j)x^{k-1} a_j a_{k-j}.$$

Now breaking the $j + k - j$ into two sums gives

$$\delta x \sum_{k=1}^{\infty} \sum_{j=1}^{k-1} j^2 a_j x^{j-1} (k-j) a_{k-j} x^{k-j} + \delta x \sum_{k=1}^{\infty} \sum_{j=1}^{k-1} j a_j x^j (k-j)^2 a_{k-j} x^{k-j-1}.$$

Notice that the second sum is obtained from the first by substituting $k - j$ for j and that both terms are $\delta x g' g$. Thus,

$$-x + g(x) + 2\delta x g'(x) = 2\delta x g'(x)g(x).$$

Hence,

$$g' = \frac{1}{2\delta} \frac{1 - \frac{g}{x}}{1 - g}.$$

Phase Transition for Non-Finite Components

The generating function $g(x)$ contains information about the finite components of the graph. A finite component is a component of size $1, 2, \ldots$, which does not depend on t. Observe that $g(1) = \sum_{k=0}^{\infty} ka_k$, and hence $g(1)$ is the probability that a randomly chosen vertex will belong to a component of finite size. If $g(1) = 1$, there are no infinite components. When $g(1) \neq 1$, then $1 - g(1)$ is the expected fraction of the vertices that are in non-finite components. Potentially, there could be many such non-finite components. But an argument similar to that given in Section 8.3.2 concludes that two fairly large components would merge into one. Suppose there are two connected components at time t, each of size at least $t^{4/5}$. Consider the earliest created $\frac{1}{2}t^{4/5}$ vertices in each part. These vertices must have lived for at least $\frac{1}{2}t^{4/5}$ time after creation. At each time, the probability of an edge forming between two such vertices, one in each component, is at least $\delta\Omega(t^{-2/5})$, and so the probability that no such edge formed is at most $(1 - \delta t^{-2/5})^{t^{4/5}/2} \le e^{-\Omega(\delta t^{2/5})} \to 0$. So with high probability such components would have merged into one. But this still leaves open the possibility of many components of size t^{ε}, $(\ln t)^2$, or some other slowly growing function of t.

We now calculate the value of δ at which the phase transition for a non-finite component occurs. Recall that the generating function for $g(x)$ satisfies

$$g'(x) = \frac{1}{2\delta} \frac{1 - \frac{g(x)}{x}}{1 - g(x)}.$$

If δ is greater than some $\delta_{critical}$, then $g(1) \neq 1$. In this case the above formula at $x = 1$ simplifies with $1 - g(1)$ canceling from the numerator and denominator, leaving just $\frac{1}{2\delta}$. Since ka_k is the probability that a randomly chosen vertex is in a component of size k, the average size of the finite components is $g'(1) = \sum_{k=1}^{\infty} k^2 a_k$. Now, $g'(1)$ is given by

$$g'(1) = \frac{1}{2\delta} \tag{8.6}$$

for all δ greater than $\delta_{critical}$. If δ is less than $\delta_{critical}$, then all vertices are in finite components. In this case $g(1) = 1$ and both the numerator and the denominator approach zero. Appling L'Hopital's rule,

$$\lim_{x \to 1} g'(x) = \frac{1}{2\delta} \left. \frac{\frac{xg'(x)-g(x)}{x^2}}{g'(x)} \right|_{x=1}$$

or

$$(g'(1))^2 = \frac{1}{2\delta}\big(g'(1) - g(1)\big).$$

The quadratic $(g'(1))^2 - \frac{1}{2\delta}g'(1) + \frac{1}{2\delta}g(1) = 0$ has solutions

$$g'(1) = \frac{\frac{1}{2\delta} \pm \sqrt{\frac{1}{4\delta^2} - \frac{4}{2\delta}}}{2} = \frac{1 \pm \sqrt{1 - 8\delta}}{4\delta}. \tag{8.7}$$

The two solutions given by (8.7) become complex for $\delta > 1/8$ and thus can be valid only for $0 \le \delta \le 1/8$. For $\delta > 1/8$, the only solution is $g'(1) = \frac{1}{2\delta}$ and an infinite component exists. As δ is decreased, at $\delta = 1/8$ there is a singular point where for $\delta < 1/8$ there are three possible solutions, one from (8.6) that implies a giant component and two from (8.7) that imply no giant component. To determine which one of the three solutions is valid, consider the limit as $\delta \to 0$. In the limit all components are of size 1, since there are no edges. Only (8.7) with the minus sign gives the correct solution,

$$g'(1) = \frac{1 - \sqrt{1 - 8\delta}}{4\delta} = \frac{1 - \left(1 - \frac{1}{2}8\delta - \frac{1}{4}64\delta^2 + \cdots\right)}{4\delta} = 1 + 4\delta + \cdots = 1.$$

In the absence of any non-analytic behavior in the equation for $g'(x)$ in the region $0 \le \delta < 1/8$, we conclude that (8.7) with the minus sign is the correct solution for $0 \le \delta < 1/8$, and hence the critical value of δ for the phase transition is $1/8$. As we shall see, this is different from the static case.

As the value of δ is increased, the average size of the finite components increase from 1 to

$$\left. \frac{1 - \sqrt{1 - 8\delta}}{4\delta} \right|_{\delta=1/8} = 2$$

when δ reaches the critical value of $1/8$. At $\delta = 1/8$, the average size of the finite components jumps to $\frac{1}{2\delta}\big|_{\delta=1/8} = 4$ and then decreases as $\frac{1}{2\delta}$ as the giant component swallows up the finite components starting with the larger components.

Comparison to Static Random Graph

Consider a static random graph with the same degree distribution as the graph in the growth model. Again let p_k be the probability of a vertex being of degree k. From (8.5),

$$p_k = \frac{(2\delta)^k}{(1 + 2\delta)^{k+1}}.$$

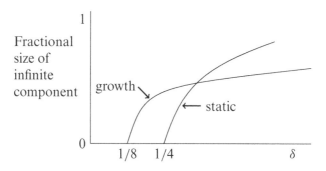

Figure 8.15: Comparison of the static random graph model and the growth model. The curve for the growth model is obtained by integrating g'.

Recall the Molloy Reed analysis of random graphs with given degree distributions, which asserts that there is a phase transition at $\sum_{i=0}^{\infty} i(i-2)p_i = 0$. Using this, it is easy to see that a phase transition occurs for $\delta = 1/4$. For $\delta = 1/4$,

$$p_k = \frac{(2\delta)^k}{(1+2\delta)^{k+1}} = \frac{\left(\frac{1}{2}\right)^k}{\left(1+\frac{1}{2}\right)^{k+1}} = \frac{\left(\frac{1}{2}\right)^k}{\frac{3}{2}\left(\frac{3}{2}\right)^k} = \frac{2}{3}\left(\frac{1}{3}\right)^k$$

and

$$\sum_{i=0}^{\infty} i(i-2)\frac{2}{3}\left(\frac{1}{3}\right)^i = \frac{2}{3}\sum_{i=0}^{\infty} i^2\left(\frac{1}{3}\right)^i - \frac{4}{3}\sum_{i=0}^{\infty} i\left(\frac{1}{3}\right)^i = \frac{2}{3}\times\frac{3}{2} - \frac{4}{3}\times\frac{3}{4} = 0.$$

Recall that $1+a+a^2+\cdots = \frac{1}{1-a}$, $a+2a^2+3a^3\cdots = \frac{a}{(1-a)^2}$, and $a+4a^2+9a^3\cdots = \frac{a(1+a)}{(1-a)^3}$.

See references at end of the chapter for calculating the fractional size S_{static} of the giant component in the static graph. The result (see Figure 8.15) is

$$S_{static} = \begin{cases} 0 & \delta \leq \frac{1}{4} \\ 1 - \frac{1}{\delta+\sqrt{\delta^2+2\delta}} & \delta > \frac{1}{4} \end{cases}$$

8.9.2. Growth Model with Preferential Attachment

Consider a growth model with preferential attachment. At each time unit, a vertex is added to the graph. Then with probability δ, an edge is attached to the new vertex and to a vertex selected at random with probability proportional to its degree. This model generates a tree with a power law distribution.

Let $d_i(t)$ be the expected degree of the ith vertex at time t. The sum of the expected degrees of all vertices at time t is $2\delta t$, and thus the probability that an edge is connected to vertex i at time t is $\frac{d_i(t)}{2\delta t}$. The degree of vertex i is governed by the equation

$$\frac{\partial}{\partial t}d_i(t) = \delta\frac{d_i(t)}{2\delta t} = \frac{d_i(t)}{2t}$$

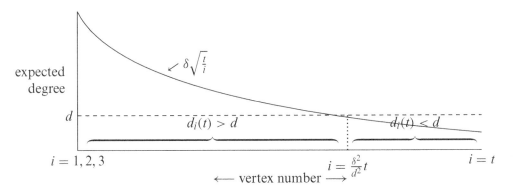

Figure 8.16: Illustration of degree of ith vertex at time t. At time t, vertices numbered 1 to $\frac{\delta^2}{d^2}t$ have degrees greater than d.

where δ is the probability that an edge is added at time t and $\frac{d_i(t)}{2\delta t}$ is the probability that the vertex i is selected for the end point of the edge.

The two in the denominator governs the solution, which is of the form $at^{\frac{1}{2}}$. The value of a is determined by the initial condition $d_i(t) = \delta$ at $t = i$. Thus, $\delta = ai^{\frac{1}{2}}$ or $a = \delta i^{-\frac{1}{2}}$. Hence, $d_i(t) = \delta\sqrt{\frac{t}{i}}$.

Next, we determine the probability distribution of vertex degrees. (See Figure 8.16 for an illustration.) Now, $d_i(t)$ is less than d provided $i > \frac{\delta^2}{d^2}t$. The fraction of the t vertices at time t for which $i > \frac{\delta^2}{d^2}t$ and thus that the degree is less than d is $1 - \frac{\delta^2}{d^2}$. Hence, the probability that a vertex has degree less than d is $1 - \frac{\delta^2}{d^2}$. The probability density $p(d)$ satisfies

$$\int_0^d p(d)\partial d = \text{Prob}(\text{degree} < d) = 1 - \frac{\delta^2}{d^2}$$

and can be obtained from the derivative of $\text{Prob}(\text{degree} < d)$:

$$p(d) = \frac{\partial}{\partial d}\left(1 - \frac{\delta^2}{d^2}\right) = 2\frac{\delta^2}{d^3},$$

a power law distribution.

8.10. Small-World Graphs

In the 1960s, Stanley Milgram carried out an experiment that indicated that most pairs of individuals in the United States were connected by a short sequence of acquaintances. Milgram would ask a source individual, say in Nebraska, to start a letter on its journey to a target individual in Massachusetts. The Nebraska individual would be given basic information about the target including his address and occupation and asked to send the letter to someone he knew on a first-name basis, who was closer to the target individual, in order to transmit the letter to the target in as few steps as possible. Each person receiving the letter would be given the same instructions. In successful experiments, it would take on average five to six steps for a letter to reach its target. This research generated the phrase "six degrees of separation" along with substantial research in social science on the interconnections between people. Surprisingly, there was no work on how to find the short paths using only local information.

In many situations, phenomena are modeled by graphs whose edges can be partitioned into local and long-distance. We adopt a simple model of a directed graph due to Kleinberg, having local and long-distance edges. Consider a two-dimensional $n \times n$ grid where each vertex is connected to its four adjacent vertices via bidirectional local edges. In addition to these local edges, there is one long-distance edge out of each vertex. The probability that the long-distance edge from vertex u terminates at v, $v \neq u$, is a function of the distance $d(u, v)$ from u to v. Here distance is measured by the shortest path consisting only of local grid edges. The probability is proportional to $1/d^r(u, v)$ for some constant r. This gives a one-parameter family of random graphs. For r equal zero, $1/d^0(u, v) = 1$ for all u and v, and thus the end of the long-distance edge at u is uniformly distributed over all vertices independent of distance. As r increases, the expected length of the long-distance edge decreases. As r approaches infinity, there are no long-distance edges and thus no paths shorter than that of the lattice path. What is interesting is that for r less than 2, there are always short paths but no local algorithm to find them. A local algorithm is an algorithm that is only allowed to remember the source, the destination, and its current location and can query the graph to find the long-distance edge at the current location. Based on this information, it decides the next vertex on the path.

The difficulty is that for $r < 2$, the end points of the long-distance edges are toouniformly distributed over the vertices of the grid. Although short paths exist, it is unlikely on a short path to encounter a long-distance edge whose end point is close to the destination (see Figure 8.17). When r equals 2, there are short paths, and the simple algorithm that always selects the edge that ends closest to the destination will find a short path. For r greater than 2, again there is no local algorithm to find a short path. Indeed, with high probability, there are no short paths at all. Specifically,

$r > 2$ The lengths of long distance edges tend to be short so the probability of encountering a sufficiently long, long-distance edge is too low.

$r = 2$ Selecting the edge with end point closest to the destination finds a short path.

$r < 2$ The ends of long distance edges tend to be uniformly distributed. Short paths exist but a polylog length path is unlikely to encounter a long distance edge whose end point is close to the destination.

The probability that the long-distance edge from u goes to v is proportional to $d^{-r}(u, v)$. Note that the constant of proportionality will vary with the vertex u depending on where u is relative to the border of the $n \times n$ grid. However, the number of vertices at distance exactly k from u is at most $4k$ and for $k \leq n/2$ is at least k. Let $c_r(u) = \sum_v d^{-r}(u, v)$ be the normalizing constant. It is the inverse of the constant of proportionality.

For $r > 2$, $c_r(u)$ is lower bounded by

$$c_r(u) = \sum_v d^{-r}(u, v) \geq \sum_{k=1}^{n/2} (k)k^{-r} = \sum_{k=1}^{n/2} k^{1-r} \geq 1.$$

No matter how large r is, the first term of $\sum_{k=1}^{n/2} k^{1-r}$ is at least 1.

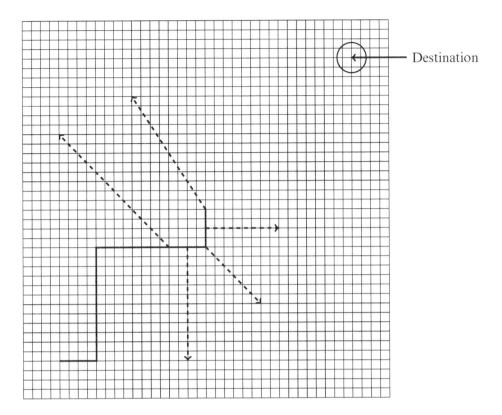

Figure 8.17: For $r < 2$, on a short path you are unlikely to encounter a long-distance edge that takes you close to the destination.

For $r = 2$, the normalizing constant $c_r(u)$ is upper bounded by

$$c_r(u) = \sum_v d^{-r}(u, v) \leq \sum_{k=1}^{2n} (4k)k^{-2} \leq 4 \sum_{k=1}^{2n} \frac{1}{k} = \theta(\ln n).$$

For $r < 2$, the normalizing constant $c_r(u)$ is lower bounded by

$$c_r(u) = \sum_v d^{-r}(u, v) \geq \sum_{k=1}^{n/2} (k)k^{-r} \geq \sum_{k=n/4}^{n/2} k^{1-r}.$$

The summation $\sum_{k=n/4}^{n/2} k^{1-r}$ has $\frac{n}{4}$ terms, the smallest of which is $\left(\frac{n}{4}\right)^{1-r}$ or $\left(\frac{n}{2}\right)^{1-r}$ depending on whether r is greater or less than 1. This gives the following lower bound on $c_r(u)$.

$$c_r(u) \geq \frac{n}{4}\omega(n^{1-r}) = \omega(n^{2-r}).$$

No Short Paths Exist for the $r > 2$ Case

For $r > 2$, we first show that for at least half of the pairs of vertices, there is no short path between them. We begin by showing that the expected number of edges of length greater than $n^{\frac{r+2}{2r}}$ goes to zero. The probability of an edge from u to v is

$d^{-r}(u, v)/c_r(u)$ where $c_r(u)$ is lower bounded by a constant. The probability that a particular edge of length greater than or equal to $n^{\frac{r+2}{2r}}$ is chosen is upper bounded by $cn^{-\left(\frac{r+2}{2}\right)}$ for some constant c. Since there are n^2 long edges, the expected number of edges of length at least $n^{\frac{r+2}{2r}}$ is at most $cn^2 n^{-\frac{(r+2)}{2}}$ or $cn^{\frac{2-r}{2}}$, which for $r > 2$ goes to zero. Thus, by the first moment method, almost surely there are no such edges.

For at least half of the pairs of vertices, the grid distance, measured by grid edges between the vertices, is greater than or equal to $n/4$. Any path between them must have at least $\frac{1}{4}n/n^{\frac{r+2}{2r}} = \frac{1}{4}n^{\frac{r-2}{2r}}$ edges, since there are no edges longer than $n^{\frac{r+2}{2r}}$ and so there is no polylog length path.

An Algorithm for the $r = 2$ Case

For $r = 2$, the local algorithm that selects the edge that ends closest to the destination t finds a path of expected length $O(\ln n)^3$. Suppose the algorithm is at a vertex u, which is at distance k from t. Then within an expected $O(\ln n)^2$ steps, the algorithm reaches a point at distance at most $k/2$. The reason is that there are $\Omega(k^2)$ vertices at distance at most $k/2$ from t. Each of these vertices is at distance at most $k + k/2 = O(k)$ from u. See Figure 8.18. Recall that the normalizing constant c_r is upper bounded by $O(\ln n)$, and hence, the constant of proportionality is lower bounded by some constant times $1/\ln n$. The probability that the long-distance edge from u goes to one of these vertices is at least

$$\Omega(k^2 k^{-2}/\ln n) = \Omega(1/\ln n).$$

Consider $\Omega(\ln n)^2$ steps of the path from u. The long-distance edges from the points visited at these steps are chosen independently and each has probability $\Omega(1/\ln n)$ of reaching within $k/2$ of t. The probability that none of them does is

$$\left(1 - \Omega(1/\ln n)\right)^{c(\ln n)^2} = c_1 e^{-\ln n} = \frac{c_1}{n}$$

for a suitable choice of constants. Thus, the distance to t is halved every $O(\ln n)^2$ steps and the algorithm reaches t in an expected $O(\ln n)^3$ steps.

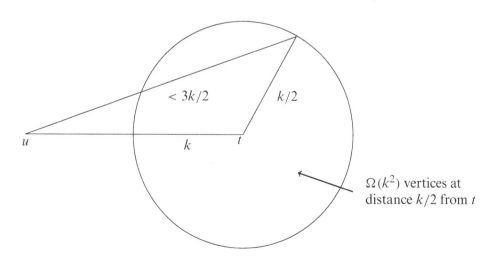

Figure 8.18: Small worlds.

A Local Algorithm Cannot Find Short Paths for the $r < 2$ Case

For $r < 2$, no local polylog time algorithm exists for finding a short path. To illustrate the proof, we first give the proof for the special case $r = 0$ and then give the proof for $r < 2$.

When $r = 0$, all vertices are equally likely to be the end point of a long-distance edge. Thus, the probability of a long-distance edge hitting one of the n vertices that are within distance $\sqrt{n}$ of the destination is $1/n$. Along a path of length $\sqrt{n}$, the probability that the path does not encounter such an edge is $(1 - 1/n)^{\sqrt{n}}$. Now,

$$\lim_{n \to \infty} \left(1 - \frac{1}{n}\right)^{\sqrt{n}} = \lim_{n \to \infty} \left(1 - \frac{1}{n}\right)^{n\frac{1}{\sqrt{n}}} = \lim_{n \to \infty} e^{-\frac{1}{\sqrt{n}}} = 1.$$

Since with probability $1/2$ the starting point is at distance at least $n/4$ from the destination and in $\sqrt{n}$ steps, the path will not encounter a long-distance edge ending within distance $\sqrt{n}$ of the destination, for at least half of the starting points the path length will be at least $\sqrt{n}$. Thus, the expected time is at least $\frac{1}{2}\sqrt{n}$ and hence not in polylog time.

For the general $r < 2$ case, we show that a local algorithm cannot find paths of length $O(n^{(2-r)/4})$. Let $\delta = (2 - r)/4$ and suppose the algorithm finds a path with at most n^{δ} edges. There must be a long-distance edge on the path that terminates within distance n^{δ} of t; otherwise, the path would end in n^{δ} grid edges and would be too long. There are $O(n^{2\delta})$ vertices within distance n^{δ} of t and the probability that the long-distance edge from one vertex of the path ends at one of these vertices is at most $n^{2\delta}\left(\frac{1}{n^{2-r}}\right) = n^{(r-2)/2}$. To see this, recall that the lower bound on the normalizing constant is $\theta(n^{2-r})$ and hence an upper bound on the probability of a long-distance edge hitting v is $\theta\left(\frac{1}{n^{2-r}}\right)$ independent of where v is. Thus, the probability that the long-distance edge from one of the n^{δ} vertices on the path hits any one of the $n^{2\delta}$ vertices within distance n^{δ} of t is $n^{2\delta}\frac{1}{n^{2-r}} = n^{\frac{r-2}{2}}$. The probability that this happens for any one of the n^{δ} vertices on the path is at most $n^{\frac{r-2}{2}}n^{\delta} = n^{\frac{r-2}{2}}n^{\frac{2-r}{4}} = n^{(r-2)/4} = o(1)$ as claimed.

Short Paths Exist for $r < 2$

Finally we show for $r < 2$ that there are $O(\ln n)$ length paths between s and t. The proof is similar to the proof of Theorem 8.13 showing $O(\ln n)$ diameter for $G(n, p)$ when p is $\Omega(\ln n/n)$, so we do not give all the details here. We give the proof only for the case when $r = 0$.

For a particular vertex v, let S_i denote the set of vertices at distance i from v. Using only local edges, if i is $O(\sqrt{\ln n})$, then $|S_i|$ is $\Omega(\ln n)$. For later i, we argue a constant factor growth in the size of S_i as in Theorem 8.13. As long as $|S_1| + |S_2| + \cdots + |S_i| \leq n^2/2$, for each of the $n^2/2$ or more vertices outside, the probability that the vertex is not in S_{i+1} is $(1 - \frac{1}{n^2})^{|S_i|} \leq 1 - \frac{|S_i|}{2n^2}$, since the long-distance edge from each vertex of S_i chooses a long-distance neighbor at random. So, the expected size of S_{i+1} is at least $|S_i|/4$, and using Chernoff, we get constant factor growth up to $n^2/2$. Thus, for any two vertices v and w, the number of vertices at distance $O(\ln n)$ from each is at least $n^2/2$. Any two sets of cardinality at least $n^2/2$ must intersect giving us a $O(\ln n)$ length path from v to w.

8.11. Bibliographic Notes

The $G(n,p)$ random graph model is from Erdös Rényi [ER60]. Among the books written on properties of random graphs a reader may wish to consult Frieze and Karonski [FK15], Jansen, Luczak, and Ruciński [JLR00], or Bollobás [Bol01]. Material on phase transitions can be found in [BT87]. The argument for existence of a giant component is from Krivelevich and Sudakov [KS13]. For additional material on the giant component, consult [Kar90] or [JKLP93].

For further description of ideas used in practical CNF-SAT solvers, see [GKSS08]. A discussion of solvers used in the 2015 SAT Race appears in [BBIS16]. The work on phase transitions for CNF was started by Chao and Franco [CF86]. Further work was done in [FS96], [AP03], [Fri99], and others. The proof here that the SC algorithm produces a solution when the number of clauses is cn for $c < \frac{2}{3}$ is from [Chv92].

Material on branching process can be found in [AN72]. The phase transition for giant components in random graphs with given degree distributions is from Molloy and Reed [MR95a].

There are numerous papers on growth models. The material in this chapter was based primarily on [CHK$^+$01] and [BA]. The material on small world is based on Kleinberg [Kle00], which follows earlier work by Watts and Strogatz [WS98].

8.12. Exercises

Exercise 8.1 Search the World Wide Web to find some real-world graphs in machine-readable form or databases that could automatically be converted to graphs.

1. Plot the degree distribution of each graph.
2. Count the number of connected components of each size in each graph.
3. Count the number of cycles in each graph.
4. Describe what you find.
5. What is the average vertex degree in each graph? If the graph were a $G(n,p)$ graph, what would the value of p be?
6. Spot differences between your graphs and $G(n,p)$ for p from Item 5. Look at sizes of connected components, cycles, size of giant component.

Exercise 8.2 In $G(n,p)$ the probability of a vertex having degree k is $\binom{n}{k}p^k(1-p)^{n-k}$.

1. Show by direct calculation that the expected degree is np.
2. Compute directly the variance of the degree distribution.
3. Where is the mode of the binomial distribution for a given value of p? The mode is the point at which the probability is maximum.

Exercise 8.3

1. Plot the degree distribution for $G(1000, 0.003)$.
2. Plot the degree distribution for $G(1000, 0.030)$.

Exercise 8.4 To better understand the binomial distribution, plot $\binom{n}{k}p^k(1-p)^{n-k}$ as a function of k for $n = 50$ and $k = 0.05, 0.5, 0.95$. For each value of p check the sum over all k to ensure that the sum is 1.

Exercise 8.5 In $G(n, \frac{1}{n})$, argue that with high probability there is no vertex of degree greater than $\frac{6 \log n}{\log \log n}$ (i.e., the probability that such a vertex exists goes to zero as n goes to infinity). You may use the Poisson approximation and may wish to use the fact that $k! \geq (\frac{k}{e})^k$.

Exercise 8.6 The example of Section 8.1.1 showed that if the degrees in $G(n, \frac{1}{n})$ were independent, there would almost surely be a vertex of degree $\Omega(\log n / \log \log n)$. However, the degrees are not independent. Show how to overcome this difficulty.

Exercise 8.7 Let $f(n)$ be a function that is asymptotically less than n. Some such functions are $1/n$, a constant d, $\log n$ or $n^{\frac{1}{3}}$. Show that

$$\left(1 + \frac{f(n)}{n}\right)^n \simeq e^{f(n)(1 \pm o(1))}.$$

for large n. That is

$$\lim_{n \to \infty} \frac{\ln\left[\left(1 + \frac{f(n)}{n}\right)^n\right]}{f(n)} = 1.$$

Exercise 8.8

1. In the limit as n goes to infinity, how does $\left(1 - \frac{1}{n}\right)^{n \ln n}$ behave?

2. What is $\lim_{n \to \infty} \left(\frac{n+1}{n}\right)^n$?

Exercise 8.9 Consider a random permutation of the integers 1 to n. The integer i is said to be a fixed point of the permutation if i is the integer in the ith position of the permutation. Use indicator variables to determine the expected number of fixed points in a random permutation.

Exercise 8.10 Generate a graph $G(n, \frac{d}{n})$ with $n = 1000$ and $d = 2, 3$, and 6. Count the number of triangles in each graph. Try the experiment with $n = 100$.

Exercise 8.11 What is the expected number of squares (4-cycles) in $G(n, \frac{d}{n})$? What is the expected number of 4-cliques in $G(n, \frac{d}{n})$? A 4-clique consists of four vertices with all $\binom{4}{2}$ edges present.

Exercise 8.12 Carry out an argument, similar to the one used for triangles, to show that $p = \frac{1}{n^{2/3}}$ is a threshold for the existence of a 4-clique. A 4-clique consists of four vertices with all $\binom{4}{2}$ edges present.

Exercise 8.13 What is the expected number of simple paths of length 3, $\log n$, $\sqrt{n}$, and $n - 1$ in $G(n, \frac{d}{n})$? A simple path is a path where no vertex appears twice as in a cycle. The expected number of simple paths of a given length being infinite does not imply that a graph selected at random has such a path.

Exercise 8.14 Let x be an integer chosen uniformly at random from $\{1, 2, \ldots, n\}$. Count the number of distinct prime factors of n. The exercise is to show that the number of prime factors almost surely is $\Theta(\ln \ln n)$. Let p stand for a prime number between 2 and n.

1. For each fixed prime p, let I_p be the indicator function of the event that p divides x. Show that $E(I_p) = \frac{1}{p} + O\left(\frac{1}{n}\right)$.

2. The random variable of interest, $y = \sum_p I_p$, is the number of prime divisors of x picked at random. Show that the variance of y is $O(\ln \ln n)$. For this, assume the known result that the number of primes p between 2 and n is $O(n/\ln n)$ and that $\sum_p \frac{1}{p} = \ln \ln n$. To bound the variance of y, think of what $E(I_p I_q)$ is for $p \neq q$, both primes.

3. Use (1) and (2) to prove that the number of prime factors is almost surely $\theta(\ln \ln n)$.

Exercise 8.15 Suppose one hides a clique of size k in a random graph $G(n, \frac{1}{2})$. I.e., in the random graph, choose some subset S of k vertices and put in the missing edges to make S a clique. Presented with the modified graph, the goal is to find S. The larger S is, the easier it should be to find. In fact, if k is more than $c\sqrt{n \ln n}$, then with high probability the clique leaves a telltale sign identifying S as the k vertices of largest degree. Prove this statement by appealing to Theorem 8.1. It remains a puzzling open problem to find such hidden cliques when k is smaller, say, $O(n^{1/3})$.

Exercise 8.16 The clique problem in a graph is to find the maximal-size clique. This problem is known to be NP-hard, and so a polynomial time algorithm is thought unlikely. We can ask the corresponding question about random graphs. For example, in $G(n, \frac{1}{2})$ there almost surely is a clique of size $(2 - \varepsilon) \log n$ for any $\varepsilon > 0$. But it is not known how to find one in polynomial time.

1. Show that in $G(n, \frac{1}{2})$ there almost surely are no cliques of size greater than or equal to $2 \log_2 n$.

2. Use the second moment method to show that in $G(n, \frac{1}{2})$, almost surely there are cliques of size $(2 - \varepsilon) \log_2 n$.

3. Show that for any $\varepsilon > 0$, a clique of size $(2 - \varepsilon) \log n$ can be found in $G(n, \frac{1}{2})$ in time $n^{O(\ln n)}$ if one exists.

4. Give an $O(n^2)$ algorithm that finds a clique of size $\Omega(\log n)$ in $G(n, \frac{1}{2})$ with high probability. Hint: use a greedy algorithm. Apply your algorithm to $G(1000, \frac{1}{2})$. What size clique do you find?

5. An independent set in a graph is a set of vertices such that no two of them are connected by an edge. Give a polynomial time algorithm for finding an independent set in $G(n, \frac{1}{2})$ of size $\Omega(\log n)$ with high probability.

Exercise 8.17 Suppose H is a fixed graph on cn vertices with $\frac{1}{4}c^2(\log n)^2$ edges. Show that if $c \geq 2$, with high probability, H does not occur as a vertex-induced subgraph of $G(n, 1/4)$. In other words, there is no subset of cn vertices of G such that the graph G restricted to these vertices is isomorphic to H. Or, equivalently, for any subset S of cn vertices of G and any 1-1 mapping f between these vertices and the vertices of H, there is either an edge (i, j) within S such that the edge $(f(i), f(j))$ does not exist in H or there is a non-edge i, j in S such that $(f(i), f(j))$ does exist in H.

Exercise 8.18 Given two instances, G_1 and G_2 of $G(n, \frac{1}{2})$, consider the size of the largest vertex-induced subgraph common to both G_1 and G_2. In other words, consider the largest k such that for some subset S_1 of k vertices of G_1 and some subset S_2 of k vertices of G_2, the graph G_1 restricted to S_1 is isomorphic to the graph G_2 restricted to S_2. Prove that with high probability $k < 4 \log_2 n$.

Exercise 8.19 (Birthday problem) What is the number of integers that must be drawn with replacement from a set of n integers so that some integer almost surely will be selected twice?

Exercise 8.20 Suppose you have an algorithm for finding communities in a social network. Assume that the way the algorithm works is that given the graph G for the social network, it finds a subset of vertices satisfying a desired property P. The specifics of property P are unimportant for this question. If there are multiple subsets S of vertices that satisfy property P, assume that the algorithm finds one such set S at random.

In running the algorithm you find thousands of communities and wonder how many communities there are in the graph. Finally, when you find the $10,000^{th}$ community, it is a duplicate. It is the same community as the one found earlier. Use the birthday problem to derive an estimate of the total number of communities in G.

Exercise 8.21 Do a breadth first search in $G(n, \frac{d}{n})$ with $d > 1$ starting from some vertex. The number of discovered vertices, z_i, after i steps has distribution Binomial(n, p_i) where $p_i = 1 - (1 - \frac{d}{n})^i$. If the connected component containing the start vertex has i vertices, then $z_i = i$. Show that as $n \to \infty$ (and d is a fixed constant), Prob$(z_i = i)$ is $o(1/n)$ unless $i \le c_1 \ln n$ or $i \ge c_2 n$ for some constants c_1, c_2.

Exercise 8.22 For $f(x) = 1 - e^{-dx} - x$, what is the value of $x_{max} = \arg\max f(x)$? What is the value of $f(x_{max})$? Recall from the text that in a breadth first search of $G(n, \frac{d}{n})$, $f(x)$ is the expected normalized size of the frontier (size of frontier divided by n) at normalized time x ($x = t/n$). Where does the maximum expected value of the frontier of a breadth search in $G(n, \frac{d}{n})$ occur as a function of n?

Exercise 8.23 Generate a random graph on 50 vertices by starting with the empty graph and then adding random edges one at a time. How many edges do you need to add until cycles first appear (repeat the experiment a few times and take the average)? How many edges do you need to add until the graph becomes connected (repeat the experiment a few times and take the average)?

Exercise 8.24 Consider $G(n, p)$ with $p = \frac{1}{3n}$.

1. Use the second moment method to show that with high probability there exists a simple path of length 10. In a simple path no vertex appears twice.
2. Argue that on the other hand, it is unlikely there exists any cycle of length 10.

Exercise 8.25 Complete the second moment argument of Theorem 8.9 to show that for $p = \frac{d}{n}, d > 1$, $G(n, p)$ almost surely has a cycle. Hint: If two cycles share one or more edges, then the union of the two cycles greater by at least 1 than the union of the vertices.

Exercise 8.26 What is the expected number of isolated vertices in $G(n, p)$ for $p = \frac{1}{2}\frac{\ln n}{n}$ as a function of n?

Exercise 8.27 Theorem 8.13 shows that for some $c > 0$ and $p = c \ln n/n$, $G(n, p)$ has diameter $O(\ln n)$. Tighten the argument to pin down as low a value as possible for c.

Exercise 8.28 What is diameter of G(n,p) for various values of p? Remember that the graph becomes fully connected at $\frac{\ln n}{n}$ and has diameter two at $\sqrt{2}\frac{\sqrt{\ln n}}{n}$.

Exercise 8.29

1. List five increasing properties of $G(n,p)$.
2. List five non-increasing properties.

Exercise 8.30 If y and z are independent, nonnegative, integer-valued random variables, then the generating function of the sum $y+z$ is the product of the generating function of y and z. Show that this follows from $E(x^{y+z}) = E(x^y x^z) = E(x^y)E(x^z)$.

Exercise 8.31 Let $f_j(x)$ be the jth iterate of the generating function $f(x)$ of a branching process. When $m > 1$, $lim_{j \to \infty} f_j(x) = q$ for $0 \le x < 1$. In the limit this implies $\text{Prob}(z_j = 0) = q$ and $\text{Prob}(z_j = i) = 0$ for all non-zero finite values of i. Shouldn't the probabilities add up to 1? Why is this not a contradiction?

Exercise 8.32 Try to create a probability distribution for a branching process that varies with the current population in which future generations neither die out nor grow to infinity.

Exercise 8.33 Consider generating the edges of a random graph by flipping two coins, one with probability p_1 of heads and the other with probability p_2 of heads. Add the edge to the graph if either coin comes down heads. What is the value of p for the generated $G(n, p)$ graph?

Exercise 8.34 In the proof of Theorem 8.15 that every increasing property has a threshold, we proved for $p_0(n)$ such that $\lim_{n \to \infty} \frac{p_0(n)}{p(n)} = 0$ that $G(n, p_0)$ almost surely did not have property Q. Give the symmetric argument that for any $p_1(n)$ such that $\lim_{n \to \infty} \frac{p(n)}{p_1(n)} = 0$, $G(n, p_1)$ almost surely has property Q.

Exercise 8.35 Consider a model of a random subset $N(n,p)$ of integers $\{1, 2, \ldots n\}$ defined by independently at random including each of $\{1, 2, \ldots n\}$ into the set with probability p. Define what an "increasing property" of $N(n,p)$ means. Prove that every increasing property of $N(n,p)$ has a threshold.

Exercise 8.36 $N(n,p)$ is a model of a random subset of integers $\{1, 2, \ldots n\}$ defined by independently at random including each of $\{1, 2, \ldots n\}$ into the set with probability p. What is the threshold for $N(n,p)$ to contain

1. a perfect square?
2. a perfect cube?
3. an even number?
4. three numbers such that $x + y = z$?

Exercise 8.37 Explain why the property that $N(n,p)$ contains the integer 1 has a threshold. What is the threshold?

Exercise 8.38 The Sudoku game consists of a 9×9 array of squares. The array is partitioned into nine 3×3 squares. Each small square should be filled with an integer between 1 and 9 so that each row, each column, and each 3×3 square contains exactly one copy of each integer. Initially the board has some of the small squares filled in in such a way that there is exactly one way to complete the assignments of integers to squares. Some simple rules can be developed to fill in the remaining squares such as if a row does not contain a given integer and if every column except one in which the square in the row is blank contains the integer, then place the integer in the remaining blank square in the row. Explore phase transitions for the Sudoku game. Some possibilities are:

1. Start with a 9×9 array of squares with each square containing a number between 1 and 9 such that no row, column, or 3×3 square has two copies of any integer. Develop a set of simple rules for filling in squares such as if a row does not contain a given integer and if every column except one in which the square in the row is blank contains the integer, then place the integer in the remaining blank entry in the row. How many integers can you randomly erase and your rules will still completely fill in the board?
2. Generalize the Sudoku game for arrays of size $n^2 \times n^2$. Develop a simple set of rules for completing the game. Start with a legitimate completed array and erase k entries at random. Experimentally determine the threshold for the integer k such that if only k entries of the array are erased, your set of rules will find a solution.

Exercise 8.39 In a square $n \times n$ grid, each of the $O(n^2)$ edges is randomly chosen to be present with probability p and absent with probability $1 - p$. Consider the increasing property that there is a path from the bottom left corner to the top right corner which always goes to the right or up. Show that $p = 1/2$ is a threshold for the property. Is it a sharp threshold?

Exercise 8.40 The threshold property seems to be related to uniform distributions. What if we considered other distributions? Consider a model where i is selected from the set $\{1, 2, \ldots, n\}$ with probability proportional to $\frac{1}{i}$. Is there a threshold for perfect squares? Is there a threshold for arithmetic progressions?

Exercise 8.41 Modify the proof that every increasing property of $G(n, p)$ has a threshold to apply to the 3-CNF satisfiability problem.

Exercise 8.42 Evaluate $\left(1 - \frac{1}{2^k}\right)^{2^k}$ for $k = 3, 5$, and 7. How close is it to $1/e$?

Exercise 8.43 For a random 3-CNF formula with n variables and cn clauses for some constant c, what is the expected number of satisfying assignments?

Exercise 8.44 Which of the following variants of the SC algorithm admit a theorem like Theorem 8.20?

1. Among all clauses of least length, pick the first one in the order in which they appear in the formula.
2. Set the literal appearing in most clauses independent of length to 1.

Exercise 8.45 Suppose we have a queue of jobs serviced by one server. There is a total of n jobs in the system. At time t, each remaining job independently decides to join the queue to be serviced with probability $p = d/n$, where $d < 1$ is a constant. Each job has a processing time of 1 and at each time the server services one job, if the queue is non-empty. Show that with high probability, no job waits more than $\Omega(\ln n)$ time to be serviced once it joins the queue.

Exercise 8.46 Consider $G(n, p)$. Show that there is a threshold (not necessarily sharp) for 2-colorability at $p = 1/n$. In particular, first show that for $p = d/n$ with $d < 1$, with high probability $G(n,p)$ is acyclic, so it is bipartite and hence 2-colorable. Next, when $pn \to \infty$, the expected number of triangles goes to infinity. Show that in that case, there is a triangle almost surely and therefore almost surely the graph is not 2-colorable.

Exercise 8.47 A vertex cover of size k for a graph is a set of k vertices such that one end of each edge is in the set. Experimentally play with the following problem. For $G(20, \frac{1}{2})$, for what value of k is there a vertex cover of size k?

Exercise 8.48 Construct an example of a formula which is satisfiable, but the SC heuristic fails to find a satisfying assignment.

Exercise 8.49 In $G(n,p)$, let x_k be the number of connected components of size k. Using x_k, write down the probability that a randomly chosen vertex is in a connected component of size k. Also write down the expected size of the connected component containing a randomly chosen vertex.

Exercise 8.50 Describe several methods of generating a random graph with a given degree distribution. Describe differences in the graphs generated by the different methods.

Exercise 8.51 Consider generating a random graph adding one edge at a time. Let n(i,t) be the number of components of size i at time t.

$$n(1,1) = n$$
$$n(1,t) = 0 \quad t > 1$$
$$n(i,t) = n(i, t-1) + \sum \frac{j(i-j)}{n^2} n(j, t-1) n(i-j, t-1) - \frac{2i}{n} n(i)$$

Compute n(i,t) for a number of values of i and t. What is the behavior? What is the sum of n(i,t) for fixed t and all i? Can you write a generating function for n(i,t)?

Exercise 8.52 In the growth model with preferential attachment where at time t a single edge is added from the new vertex to an existing vertex with probability δ, the resulting graph consists of a set of trees. To generate a more complex graph, at each unit of time add d edges each with probability δ. Derive the degree distribution of the generated graph.

Exercise 8.53 The global clustering coefficient of a graph is defined as follows. Let d_v be the degree of vertex v and let e_v be the number of edges connecting pairs of vertices that are adjacent to vertex v. The global clustering coefficient c is given by

$$c = \sum_v \frac{2e_v}{d_v(d_v-1)}.$$

In a social network, for example, it measures what fraction of pairs of friends of each person are themselves friends. If many are, the clustering coefficient is high. What is c for a random graph with $p = \frac{d}{n}$ in the limit as n goes to infinity? For a denser graph? Compare this value to that for some social network.

Exercise 8.54 Consider a structured graph, such as a grid or cycle, and gradually add edges or reroute edges at random. Let L be the average distance between all pairs of vertices in a graph and let C be the ratio of triangles to connected sets of three vertices. Plot L and C as a function of the randomness introduced.

Exercise 8.55 Consider an $n \times n$ grid in the plane.

1. Prove that for any vertex u, there are at least k vertices at distance k for $1 \le k \le n/2$.
2. Prove that for any vertex u, there are at most $4k$ vertices at distance k.
3. Prove that for one half of the pairs of points, the distance between them is at least $n/4$.

Exercise 8.56 Recall the definition of a small-world graph in Section 8.10. Show that in a small-world graph with $r \le 2$, that there exist short paths with high probability. The proof for $r = 0$ is in the text.

Exercise 8.57 Change the small-world graph as follows. Start with a $n \times n$ grid where each vertex has one long-distance edge to a vertex chosen uniformly at random. These are exactly like the long-distance edges for $r = 0$. Instead of having grid edges, we have some other graph with the property that for each vertex there are $\Theta(t^2)$ vertices at distance t from the vertex for $t \le n$. Show that, almost surely, the diameter is $O(\ln n)$.

Exercise 8.58 Consider an n-node directed graph with two random out-edges from each node. For two vertices s and t chosen at random, prove that with high probability there exists a path of length at most $O(\ln n)$ from s to t.

Exercise 8.59 Explore the concept of small world by experimentally determining the answers to the following questions:

1. How many edges are needed to disconnect a small-world graph? By disconnect we mean at least two pieces each of reasonable size. Is this connected to the emergence of a giant component?
2. How does the diameter of a graph consisting of a cycle change as one adds a few random long-distance edges?

Exercise 8.60 In the small-world model with $r < 2$, would it help if the algorithm could look at edges at any node at a cost of one for each node looked at?

Exercise 8.61 Make a list of the ten most interesting things you learned about random graphs.

CHAPTER NINE

Topic Models, Nonnegative Matrix Factorization, Hidden Markov Models, and Graphical Models

In the chapter on machine learning, we saw many algorithms for fitting functions to data. For example, suppose we want to learn a rule to distinguish spam from non-spam e-mail and we were able to represent e-mail messages as points in R^d such that the two categories are linearly separable. Then, we could run the Perceptron algorithm to find a linear separator that correctly partitions our training data. Furthermore, we could argue that if our training sample was large enough, then with high probability this translates to high accuracy on future data coming from the same probability distribution. An interesting point to note here is that these algorithms did not aim to explicitly learn a model of the distribution D^+ of spam e-mails or the distribution D^- of non-spam e-mails. Instead, they aimed to learn a separator to distinguish spam from non-spam. In this chapter, we look at algorithms that, in contrast, aim to explicitly learn a probabilistic model of the process used to generate the observed data. This is a more challenging problem, and typically requires making additional assumptions about the generative process. For example, in the chapter on high-dimensional space, we assumed data came from a Gaussian distribution and we learned the parameters of the distribution. In the chapter on SVD, we considered the more challenging case that data comes from a mixture of k Gaussian distributions. For $k = 2$, this is similar to the spam detection problem, but harder in that we are not told which training e-mails are spam and which are non-spam, but easier in that we assume D^+ and D^- are Gaussian distributions. In this chapter, we examine other important model-fitting problems, where we assume a specific type of process is used to generate data, and then aim to learn the parameters of this process from observations.

9.1. Topic Models

Topic Modeling is the problem of fitting a certain type of stochastic model to a given collection of documents. The model assumes there exist r "topics," that each document is a mixture of these topics, and that the topic mixture of a given document determines the probabilities of different words appearing in the document. For a collection of news articles, the topics may be politics, sports, science, etc. A topic is a set of word frequencies. For the topic of politics, words like "president" and "election" may have high frequencies, whereas for the topic of sports, words like "pitcher" and "goal" may have high frequencies. A document (news item) may be

60% politics and 40% sports. In that case, the word frequencies in the document are assumed to be convex combinations of word frequencies for each of these topics with weights 0.6 and 0.4, respectively.

Each document is viewed as a "bag of words" or *terms*.[1] Namely, we disregard the order and context in which each word occurs in the document and instead only list the frequency of occurrences of each word. Frequency is the number of occurrences of the word divided by the total count of all words in the document. Throwing away context information may seem wasteful, but this approach works fairly well in practice. Each document is a vector with d components where d is the total number of different terms that exist; each component of the vector is the frequency of a particular term in the document.

We can represent a collection of n documents by a $d \times n$ matrix A called the *term-document* matrix, with one column per document and one row per term. The topic model hypothesizes that there exist r topics (r is typically small) such that each document is a mixture of these topics. In particular, each document has an associated vector with r nonnegative components summing to one, telling us the fraction of the document that is on each of the topics. In the example above, this vector would have 0.6 in the component for politics and 0.4 in the component for sports. These vectors can be arranged as the columns of a $r \times n$ matrix C, called the *topic-document* matrix. Finally, there is a third $d \times r$ matrix B for the topics. Each column of B is a vector corresponding to one topic; it is the vector of expected frequencies of terms in that topic. The vector of expected frequencies for a document is a convex combination of the expected frequencies for topics, with the topic weights given by the vector in C for that document. In matrix notation, let P be a $n \times d$ matrix with column $P(:, j)$ denoting the expected frequencies of terms in document j. Then,

$$P = BC. \tag{9.1}$$

Pictorially, we can represent this as:

Topic Models are stochastic models that generate documents according to the frequency matrix P above. p_{ij} is viewed as the probability that a random term of document j is the ith term in the dictionary. We make the assumption that terms in a document are drawn independently. In general, B is assumed to be a fixed matrix, whereas C is random. So, the process to generate n documents, each containing m terms, is the following:

---

[1]In practice, terms are typically words or phrases, and not all words are chosen as terms. For example, articles and simple verbs, pronouns, etc. may not be considered terms.

Definition 9.1 (Document Generation Process) *Let $\mathcal{D}$ be a distribution over a mixture of topics. Let B be the term-topic matrix. Create a $d \times n$ term-document matrix A as follows:*

- *Intialize $a_{ij} = 0$ for $i = 1, 2, \ldots, d; j = 1, 2, \ldots, n$.[2]*
- *For $j = 1, 2, \ldots, n$*

  - *Pick column j of C from distribution $\mathcal{D}$. This will be the topic mixture for document j, and induces $P(:, j) = BC(:, j)$.*
  - *For $t = 1, 2, \ldots, m$, do:*

    * *Generate the tth term x_t of document j from the multinomial distribution over $\{1, 2, \ldots, d\}$ with probability vector $P(:, j)$ i.e., $Prob(x_t = i) = p_{ij}$.*
    * *Add $1/m$ to $a_{x_t, j}$.*

The topic modeling problem is to infer B and C from A. The probability distribution $\mathcal{D}$ of the columns of C is not yet specified. The most commonly used distribution is the Dirichlet distribution that we study in detail in Section 9.6.

Often we are given fewer terms of each document than the number of terms or the number of documents. Even though

$$E(a_{ij}|P) = p_{ij}, \tag{9.2}$$

and in expectation A equals P, the variance is high. For example, for the case when $p_{ij} = 1/d$ for all i with m much less than $\sqrt{d}$, $A(:, j)$ is likely to have $1/m$ in a random subset of m coordinates, since no term is likely to be picked more than once. Thus,

$$||A(:, j) - P(:, j)||_1 = m\left(\frac{1}{m} - \frac{1}{d}\right) + (d - m)\left(\frac{1}{d}\right) \approx 2,$$

the maximum possible. This says that in l_1 norm, which is the right norm when dealing with probability vectors, the "noise" $\mathbf{a}_{.,j} - \mathbf{p}_{.,j}$ is likely to be larger than $\mathbf{p}_{.,j}$. This is one of the reasons why the model inference problem is hard. Write

$$A = BC + N, \tag{9.3}$$

where A is the $d \times n$ term-document matrix, B is a $d \times r$ term-topic matrix, and C is a $r \times n$ topic-document matrix. N stands for noise, which can have high norm. The l_1 norm of each column of N could be as high as that of BC.

There are two main ways of tackling the computational difficulty of finding B and C from A. One is to make assumptions on the matrices B and C that are both realistic and also admit efficient computation of B and C. The trade-off between these two desirable properties is not easy to strike, and we will see several approaches, beginning with the strongest assumptions on B and C, in Section 9.2. The other way is to restrict N. Here again, an idealized way would be to assume $N = 0$, which leads to what is called the Nonnegative Matrix Factorization (NMF) (Section 9.3) problem of factoring the given matrix A into the product of two nonnegative matrices B and C. With a further restriction on B, called Anchor terms, (Section 9.4), there is a polynomial time algorithm to do NMF. The strong restriction of $N = 0$ can be relaxed, but at the cost of computational efficiency.

---

[2]We will use i to index into the set of all terms, j to index documents and l to index topics.

The most common approach to topic modeling makes an assumption on the probability distribution of C, namely that the columns of C are independent Dirichlet distributed random vectors. This is called the Latent Dirichlet Allocation model (Section 9.6), which does not admit an efficient computational procedure. We show that the Dirichlet distribution leads to many documents having a "primary topic," whose weight is much larger than average in the document. This motivates a model called the Dominant Admixture model (Section 9.7), which admits an efficient algorithm.

On top of whatever other assumptions are made, we assume that in each document, the m terms in it are drawn independently as in Definition 9.1. This is perhaps the biggest assumption of all.

9.2. An Idealized Model

The Topic Model inference problem is in general computationally hard. But under certain reasonable assumptions, it can be solved in polynomial time as we will see in this chapter. We start here with a highly idealized model that was historically the first for which a polynomial time algorithm was devised. In this model, we make two assumptions:

The Pure Topic Assumption Each document is purely on a single topic. That is, each column j of C has a single entry equal to 1, and the rest of the entries are 0.

Separability Assumption The sets of terms occurring in different topics are disjoint. That is, for each row i of B, there is a unique column l with $b_{il} \neq 0$.

Under these assumptions, the data matrix A has a block structure. Let T_l denote the set of documents on topic l and S_l the set of terms occurring in topic l. After rearranging columns and rows so that the rows in each S_l occur consecutively and the columns of each T_l occur consecutively, the matrix A looks like:

$$
\begin{array}{c}
\text{T} \quad \text{O} \quad \text{P} \quad \text{I} \quad \text{C} \\
\end{array}
$$

$$
A =
\begin{array}{c}
S_1 \\
\\
\\
S_2 \\
\\
\\
\\
S_3 \\
\\
\end{array}
\begin{pmatrix}
* & * & * & 0. & 0 & 0 & 0 & 0 & 0 \\
* & * & * & 0 & 0 & 0 & 0 & 0 & 0 \\
* & * & * & 0 & 0 & 0 & 0 & 0 & 0 \\
0 & 0 & 0 & * & * & * & 0 & 0 & 0 \\
0 & 0 & 0 & * & * & * & 0 & 0 & 0 \\
0 & 0 & 0 & * & * & * & 0 & 0 & 0 \\
0 & 0 & 0 & 0 & 0 & 0 & * & * & * \\
0 & 0 & 0 & 0 & 0 & 0 & * & * & * \\
0. & 0 & 0 & 0 & 0 & 0 & * & * & * \\
\end{pmatrix}
\begin{array}{c}
\\
\text{T} \\
\text{E} \\
\text{R} \\
\\
\text{M} \\
\\
\end{array}
$$

If we can partition the documents into r clusters, $T_1, T_2, \ldots, T_r$, one for each topic, we can take the average of each cluster and that should be a good approximation to the corresponding column of B. It would also suffice to find the sets S_l of terms, since from them we could read off the sets T_l of topics. We now formally state the document generation process under the Pure Topic Assumption and the associated clustering problem. Note that under the Pure Topics Assumption, the distribution $\mathcal{D}$ over columns of C is specified by the probability that we pick each topic to be the only topic of a document. Let $\alpha_1, \alpha_2, \ldots, \alpha_r$ be these probabilities.

Document Generation Process under Pure Topics Assumption

- Intialize all a_{ij} to zero.
- For each document do

  - Select a topic from the distribution given by $\{\alpha_1, \alpha_2, \ldots, \alpha_r\}$.
  - Select m words according to the distribution for the selected topic.
  - For each selected word add $1/m$ to the document-term entry of the matrix A.

Definition 9.2 (**Clustering Problem**) *Given A generated as above and the number of topics r, partition the documents $\{1, 2, \ldots, n\}$ into r clusters $T_1, T_2, \ldots, T_r$, each specified by a topic.*

Approximate Version *Partition the documents into r clusters, where at most εn of the $j \in \{1, 2, \ldots, n\}$ are misclustered.*

The approximate version of Definition 9.2 suffices, since we are taking the average of the document vectors in each cluster j and returning the result as our approximation to column j of B. Note that even if we clustered perfectly, the average will only approximate the column of B. We now show how we can find the term clusters S_l, which then can be used to solve the Clustering Problem.

Construct a graph G on d vertices, with one vertex per term, and put an edge between two vertices if they co-occur in any document. By the separability assumption, we know that there are no edges between vertices belonging to different S_l. This means that if each S_l is a connected component in this graph, then we will be done. Note that we need to assume $m \geq 2$ (each document has at least two words), since if all documents have just one word, there will be no edges in the graph at all and the task is hopeless.

Let us now focus on a specific topic l and ask how many documents n_l we need so that with high probability S_l is a connected component. One annoyance here is that some words may have very low probability and not become connected to the rest of S_l. On the other hand, words of low probability cannot cause much harm, since they are unlikely to be the only words in a document, and so it doesn't matter that much if we fail to cluster them. We make this argument formal here.

Let $\gamma < 1/3$ and define $\varepsilon = \gamma^m$. Consider a partition of S_l into two subsets of terms W and $\overline{W}$ that each have probability mass at least γ in the distribution of terms in topic l. Suppose that for every such partition there is at least one edge between W and $\overline{W}$. This would imply that the largest connected component $\hat{S}_l$ in S_l must have probability mass at least $1 - \gamma$. If $\hat{S}_l$ had probability mass between γ and $1 - \gamma$, then using $W = \hat{S}_l$ would violate the assumption about partitions with mass greater than γ having an edge between them. If the largest partition $\hat{S}_l$ had probability mass less than γ, then one could create a union of connected components W that violates the assumption. Since $\text{Prob}(\hat{S}_l) \geq 1 - \gamma$, the probability that a new random document of topic l contains only words not in $\hat{S}_l$ is at most $\gamma^m = \varepsilon$. Thus, if we can prove the statement about partitions, we will be able to correctly cluster nearly all new random documents.

To prove the statement about partitions, fix some partition of S_l into W and $\overline{W}$ that each have probability mass at least γ. The probability that m words are all in W or $\overline{W}$ is at most $\text{Prob}(W)^m + \text{Prob}(\overline{W})^m$. Thus the probability that none of n_l documents creates an edge between W and $\overline{W}$ is

$$\left(\text{Prob}(W)^m + \text{Prob}(\overline{W})^m\right)^{n_l} \leq \left(\gamma^m + (1-\gamma)^m\right)^{n_l}$$
$$\leq \left((1-\gamma/2)^m\right)^{n_l}$$
$$\leq e^{-\gamma m n_l/2}$$

where the first inequality is due to convexity and the second is a calculation. Since there are at most 2^d different possible partitions of S_l into W and $\overline{W}$, the union bound ensures at most a δ probability of failure by having

$$2^d e^{-\gamma m n_l/2} \leq \delta.$$

This in turn is satisfied for

$$m n_l \geq \frac{2}{\gamma}\left(d \ln 2 + \ln \frac{1}{\delta}\right).$$

This proves the following result.

Lemma 9.1 *If $n_l m \geq \frac{2}{\gamma}(d \ln 2 + \ln \frac{1}{\delta})$, then with probability at least $1 - \delta$, the largest connected component in S_l has probability mass at least $1 - \gamma$. This in turn implies that the probability to fail to correctly cluster a new random document of topic l is at most $\varepsilon = \gamma^{1/m}$.*

9.3. Nonnegative Matrix Factorization

We saw in Section 9.1, while the expected value $E(A|B, C)$ equals BC, the variance can be high. Write

$$A = BC + N,$$

where N stands for noise. In topic modeling, N can be high. But it will be useful to first look at the problem when there is no noise. This can be thought of as the limiting case as the number of words per document goes to infinity.

Suppose we have the exact equations $A = BC$ where A is the given matrix with non-negative entries and all column sums equal to 1. Given A and the number of topics r, can we find B and C such that $A = BC$ where B and C have nonnegative entries? This is called the Nonnegative Matrix Factorization (NMF) problem and has applications besides topic modeling. If B and C are allowed to have negative entries, we can use Singular Value Decomposition on A using the top r singular vectors of A.

Before discussing NMF, we will take care of one technical issue. In topic modeling, besides requiring B and C to be nonnegative, we have additional constraints stemming from the fact that frequencies of terms in one particular topic are nonnegative reals summing to 1, and that the fractions of each topic that a particular document is on are also nonnegative reals summing to 1. All together, the constraints are:

1. $A = BC$.
2. The entries of B and C are all nonnegative.
3. Columns of both B and C sums to 1.

It will suffice to ensure the first two conditions.

Lemma 9.2 *Let A be a matrix with nonnegaitve elements and columns summing to 1. The problem of finding a factorization BC of A satisfying the three conditions above is reducible to the NMF problem of finding a factorization BC satisfying conditions (1) and (2).*

Proof Suppose we have a factorization BC that satisfies (1) and (2) of a matrix A whose columns each sum to 1. We can multiply the kth column of B by a positive real number and divide the kth row of C by the same real number without violating $A = BC$. By doing this, we may assume that each column of B sums to 1. Now we have $a_{ij} = \sum_k b_{ik} c_{kj}$, which implies $\sum_i a_{ij} = \sum_{i,k} b_{ik} c_{kj} = \sum_k c_{kj}$, the sum of the jth column of C, $\sum_i a_{ij}$, is 1. Thus the columns of C sum to 1, giving (3). ∎

Given an $d \times n$ matrix A and an integer r, the exact NMF problem is to determine whether there exists a factorization of A into BC where B is an $d \times r$ matrix with non-negative entries and C is $r \times n$ matrix with nonnegative entries and if so, find such a factorization.[3]

Nonnegative matrix factorization is a general problem, and there are many heuristic algorithms to solve the problem. In general, they suffer from one of two problems. They could get stuck at local optima that are not solutions, or they could take exponential time. In fact, the NMF problem is NP-hard. In practice, often r is much smaller than n and d. We show first that while the NMF problem as formulated above is a nonlinear problem in $r(n + d)$ unknowns (the entries of B and C), it can be reformulated as a nonlinear problem with just $2r^2$ unknowns under the simple non-degeneracy assumption that A has rank r. This, in turn, allows for an algorithm that runs in polynomial time when r is a constant.

Lemma 9.3 *If A has rank r, then the NMF problem can be formulated as a problem with $2r^2$ unknowns. Using this, the exact NMF problem can be solved in polynomial time if r is constant.*

Proof If $A = BC$, then each row of A is a linear combination of the rows of C. So the space spanned by the rows of A is contained in the space spanned by the rows of the $r \times n$ matrix C. The latter space has dimension at most r, while the former has dimension r by assumption. So they must be equal. Thus every row of C must be a linear combination of the rows of A. Choose any set of r independent rows of A to form a $r \times m$ matrix A_1. Then $C = SA_1$ for some $r \times r$ matrix S. By analogous reasoning, if A_2 is a $n \times r$ matrix of r independent columns of A, there is a $r \times r$ matrix T such that $B = A_2 T$. Now we can easily cast NMF in terms of unknowns S and T:

$$A = A_2 T S A_1 \quad ; \quad (SA_1)_{ij} \geq 0 \quad ; \quad (A_2 T)_{kl} \geq 0 \quad \forall i, j, k, l.$$

It remains to solve the nonlinear problem in $2r^2$ variables. There is a classical algorithm that solves such problems in time exponential only in r^2 (polynomial

---

[3] B's columns form a "basis" in which A's columns can be expressed as nonnegative linear combinations, the "coefficients" being given by matrix C.

in the other parameters). In fact, there is a logical theory, called the Theory of Reals, of which this is a special case, and any problem in this theory can be solved in time exponential in the number of variables. We do not give details here. ∎

9.4. NMF with Anchor Terms

An important case of NMF, which can be solved efficiently, is the case where there are *anchor terms*. An anchor term for a topic is a term that occurs in the topic and does not occur in any other topic. For example, the term "batter" may be an anchor term for the topic "baseball" and "election" for the topic "politics." Consider the case that each topic has an anchor term. This assumption is weaker than the separability assumption of Section 9.2, which says that all terms are anchor terms.

In matrix notation, the assumption that each topic has an anchor term implies that for each column of the term-topic matrix B, there is a row whose sole non-zero entry is in that column.

Definition 9.3 (Anchor Term) *For each $j = 1, 2, \ldots r$, there is an index i_j such that*

$$b_{i_j,j} \neq 0 \quad and \quad \forall k \neq j \ \ b_{i_j,k} = 0 .$$

In this case, it is easy to see that each row of the topic-document matrix C has a scalar multiple of it occurring as a row of the given term-document matrix A.

$$\begin{pmatrix} 0.3 \times \mathbf{c_4} \\ \\ A \\ \\ 0.2 \times \mathbf{c_2} \end{pmatrix} = \begin{matrix} \text{election} \\ \\ \\ \\ \text{batter} \end{matrix} \begin{pmatrix} 0 & 0 & 0 & 0.3 \\ \\ & & B & \\ \\ 0 & 0.2 & 0 & 0 \end{pmatrix} \begin{pmatrix} \leftarrow \mathbf{c_1} \rightarrow \\ \leftarrow \mathbf{c_2} \rightarrow \\ \\ \leftarrow \mathbf{c_4} \rightarrow \end{pmatrix} .$$

If there is a NMF of A, there is one in which no row of C is a nonnegative linear combination of other rows of C. If some row of C is a nonnegative linear combination of the other rows of C, then eliminate that row of C as well as the corresponding column of B and suitably modify the other columns of B maintaining $A = BC$. For example, if

$$c_5 = 4 \times c_3 + 3 \times c_6,$$

delete row 5 of C, add 4 times column 5 of B to column 3 of B, add 3 times column 5 of B to column 6 of B, and delete column 5 of B. After repeating this, each row of C is positively independent of the other rows of C, i.e., it cannot be expressed as a nonnegative linear combination of the other rows.

If $A = BC$ is a NMF of A and there are rows in A that are positive linear combinations of other rows, the rows can be removed and the corresponding rows of B removed to give a NMF $\hat{A} = \hat{B}C$ where $\hat{A}$ and $\hat{B}$ are the matrices A and B with the removed rows. Since there are no rows in $\hat{A}$ that are linear combinations of other rows of $\hat{A}$, $\hat{B}$ is a diagonal matrix and the rows of $\hat{A}$ are scalar multiples of rows of C. Now set $C = \hat{A}$ and $\hat{B} = I$ and restore the rows to $\hat{B}$ to get B such that $A = BC$.

To remove rows of A that are scalar multiples of previous rows in polynomial time, check if there are real numbers $x_1, x_2, \ldots x_{i-1}, x_{i+1}, \ldots x_n$ such that

$$\sum_{j \neq i} x_j \mathbf{a_j} = \mathbf{a_i} \quad x_j \geq 0.$$

This is a linear program and can be solved in polynomial time. While the algorithm runs in polynomial time, it requires solving one linear program per term. An improved method, not presented here, solves just one linear program.

9.5. Hard and Soft Clustering

In Section 9.2, we saw that under the assumptions that each document is purely on one topic and each term occurs in only one topic, approximately finding B was reducible to clustering documents according to their topic. Clustering here has the usual meaning of partitioning the set of documents into clusters. We call this *hard clustering*, meaning each data point is to be assigned to a single cluster.

The more general situation is that each document has a mixture of several topics. We may still view each topic as a cluster and each topic vector, i.e., each column of B, as a "cluster center" (Figure 9.1). But now each document belongs fractionally to several clusters, the fractions being given by the column of C corresponding to the document. We may then view $P(:, j) = BC(:, j)$ as the "cluster center" for document j. The document vector $A(:, j)$ is its cluster center plus an offset or noise $N(:, j)$.

Barring ties, each column of C has a largest entry. This entry is the primary topic of document j in topic modeling. Identifying the primary topic of each document is a "hard clustering" problem, which intuitively is a useful step in solving the "soft

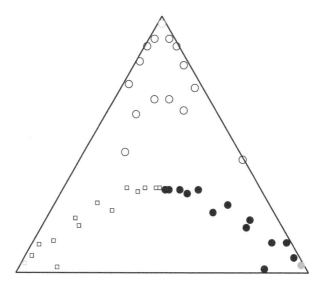

Figure 9.1: Geometry of Topic Modeling. The corners of the triangle are the columns of B. The columns of A for topic 1 are represented by circles, for topic 2 by squares, and for topic 3 by dark circles. Columns of BC (not shown) are always inside the big triangle, but not necessarily the columns of A.

clustering" problem of finding the fraction of each cluster each data point belongs to. "Soft clustering" just refers to finding B and C so that $N = A - BC$ is small. In this sense, soft clustering is equivalent to NMF.

We will see in Sections 9.8 and 9.9 that doing hard clustering to identify the primary topic and using that to solve the soft clustering problem can be carried out under some assumptions. The primary topic of each document is used to find the "catchwords" of each topic, the important words in a weaker sense than anchor words, and then using the catchwords to find the term-topic matrix B and then C. But as stated earlier, the general NMF problem is NP-hard. So, we make some assumptions before solving the problem. For this, we first look at Latent Dirichlet Allocation (LDA), which guides us toward reasonable assumptions.

9.6. The Latent Dirichlet Allocation Model for Topic Modeling

The most widely used model for topic modeling is the Latent Dirichlet Allocation (LDA) model. In this model, the topic weight vectors of the documents, the columns of C, are picked independently from what is known as a Dirichlet distribution. The term-topic matrix B is fixed. It is not random. The Dirichlet distribution has a parameter μ called the "concentration parameter," which is a real number in $(0, 1)$, typically set to $1/r$. For each vector $\mathbf{v}$ with r nonnegative components summing to 1,

$$\text{Prob density (column } j \text{ of } C = \mathbf{v}) = \frac{1}{g(\mu)} \prod_{l=1}^{r} v_l^{\mu-1},$$

where, $g(\mu)$ is the normalizing constant so that the total probability mass is 1. Since $\mu < 1$, if any $v_l = 0$, then the probability density is infinite.

Once C is generated, the Latent Dirichlet Allocation model hypothesizes that the matrix

$$P = BC$$

acts as the probability matrix for the data matrix A, namely

$$E(A|P) = P.$$

Assume the model picks m terms from each document. Each trial is according to the multinomial distribution with probability vector $P(:, j)$; so the probability that the first term we pick to include in the document j is the ith term in the dictionary is p_{ij}. Then, a_{ij} is set equal to the fraction out of m of the number of times term i occurs in document j.

The Dirichlet density favors low v_l, but since the v_l have to sum to 1, there is at least one component that is high. We show that if μ is small, then with high probability the highest entry of the column is typically much larger than the average. So, in each document, one topic, which may be thought as the "primary topic" of the document, gets disproportionately high weight. To prove this, we have to work out some properties of the Dirichlet distribution. The first lemma describes the marginal probability density of each coordinate of a Dirichlet distributed random variable:

Lemma 9.4 *Suppose the joint distribution of $\mathbf{y} = (y_1, y_2, \ldots, y_r)$ is the Dirichlet distribution with concentration parameter μ. Then, the marginal probability density $q(y)$ of y_1 is given by*

$$q(y) = \frac{\Gamma(r\mu + 1)}{\Gamma(\mu)\Gamma((r-1)\mu + 1)} y^{\mu-1}(1-y)^{(r-1)\mu} \, , \ \mu \in (0, 1],$$

where Γ is the Gamma function (see Chapter 12 for the definition).

Proof By definition of the marginal,

$$q(y) = \frac{1}{g(\mu)} y^{\mu-1} \int_{\substack{y_2,y_3,\ldots,y_r \\ y_2+y_3+\cdots+y_r=1-y}} (y_2 \, y_3 \cdots y_r)^{\mu-1} \, dy_2 \, dy_3 \ldots dy_r.$$

Put $z_l = y_l/(1-y)$. With this change of variables,

$$q(y) = \frac{1}{g(\mu)} y^{\mu-1}(1-y)^{(r-1)\mu} \left(\int_{\substack{z_2,z_3,\ldots,z_r \\ z_2+z_3+\cdots+z_r=1-y}} (z_2 z_3 \cdots z_r)^{\mu-1} \, dz_2 \, dz_3 \ldots dz_r \right).$$

The quantity inside the parentheses is independent of y, so for some c we have

$$q(y) = cy^{\mu-1}(1-y)^{(r-1)\mu}.$$

Since $\int_0^1 q(y) \, dy = 1$, we must have

$$c = \frac{1}{\int_0^1 y^{\mu-1}(1-y)^{(r-1)\mu}} = \frac{\Gamma(r\mu + 1)}{\Gamma(\mu)\Gamma((r-1)\mu + 1)}.$$

∎

Lemma 9.5 *Suppose the joint distribution of* $\mathbf{y} = (y_1, y_2, \ldots, y_r)$ *is the Dirichlet distribution with parameter* $\mu \in (0, 1)$. *For* $\zeta \in (0, 1)$,

$$Prob\,(y_1 \geq 1 - \zeta) \geq \frac{0.85\mu\zeta^{(r-1)\mu+1}}{(r-1)\mu + 1}.$$

Hence, for $\mu = 1/r$, *we have* $Prob(y_1 \geq 1 - \zeta) \geq 0.4\zeta^2/r$. *If also,* $\zeta < 0.5$, *then*

$$Prob\left(Max_{l=1}^r y_l \geq 1 - \zeta\right) \geq 0.4\zeta^2.$$

Proof Since $\mu < 1$, we have $y^{\mu-1} > 1$ for $y < 1$ and so $q(y) \geq c(1-y)^{(r-1)\mu}$, so

$$\int_{1-\zeta}^1 q(y) \, dy \geq \frac{c}{(r-1)\mu + 1} \zeta^{(r-1)\mu+1}.$$

To lower bound c, note that $\Gamma(\mu) \leq 1/\mu$ for $\mu \in (0, 1)$. Also, $\Gamma(x)$ is an increasing function for $x \geq 1.5$, so if $(r-1)\mu+1 \geq 1.5$, then $\Gamma(r\mu+1) \geq \Gamma((r-1)\mu+1)$ and in this case, the first assertion of the lemma follows. If $(r-1)\mu+1 \in [1, 1.5]$, then $\Gamma((r-1)\mu + 1) \leq 1$ and $\Gamma(r\mu + 1) \geq \min_{z\in[1,2]} \Gamma(z) \geq 0.85$, so again, the first assertion follows.

If now, $\mu = 1/r$, then $(r-1)\mu+1 < 2$, and so $\zeta^{(r-1)\mu+1}/((r-1)\mu+1) \geq \zeta^2/2$. So the second assertion of the lemma follows easily. For the third assertion, note that $y_l > 1 - \zeta, l = 1, 2, \ldots, r$ are mutually exclusive events for $\zeta < 0.5$ (since at most one y_l can be greater than 1/2), so $Prob\left(\max_{l=1}^r y_l \geq 1 - \zeta\right) = \sum_{l=1}^r Prob(y_l > 1 - \zeta) = rProb(y_1 \geq 1 - \zeta) \geq 0.4\zeta^2$. ∎

For example, from the last lemma, it follows that

1. With high probabilty, a constant fraction of the documents have a primary topic of weight at least 0.6. In expectation, the fraction of documents for which this holds is at least $0.4(0.6)^2$.
2. Also with high probability, a smaller constant fraction of the documents are nearly pure (weight at least 0.95 on a single topic). Take $\zeta = 0.05$.

If the total number of documents, n, is large, there will be many nearly pure documents. Since for nearly pure documents, $c_{l,j} \geq 0.95$, $BC_{:,j} = B(:,j) + \Delta$, where $||\Delta||_1 \leq 0.05$. If we could find the nearly pure documents for a given topic l, then the average of the A columns corresponding to these documents will be close to the average of those columns in the matrix BC (though this is not true for individual columns), and it is intuitively clear that we would be done. We pursue (1) and (2) in the next section, where we see that under these assumptions, plus one more assumption, we can indeed find B.

More generally, the concentration parameter may be different for different topics. We then have $\mu_1, \mu_2, \ldots, \mu_r$ so that

$$\text{Prob density (column } j \text{ of } C = \mathbf{v}) \; \propto \; \prod_{l=1}^{r} v_l^{\mu_l - 1}.$$

The model fitting problem for Latent Dirichlet Allocation given A find the B, the term-topic matrix, is in general NP-hard. There are heuristics, however, which are widely used. Latent Dirichlet Allocation is known to work well in several application areas.

9.7. The Dominant Admixture Model

In this section, we formulate a model with three key assumptions. The first two are motivated by Latent Dirichlet Allocation, respectively by (1) and (2) of the last section. The third assumption is also natural; it is more realistic than the anchor words assumptions discussed earlier. This section is self-contained and no familiarity with Latent Dirichlet Allocation is needed.

We first recall the notation. A is a $d \times n$ data matrix with one document per column, which is the frequency vector of the d terms in that document. m is the number of words in each document. r is the "inner dimension", i.e., B is $d \times r$ and C is $r \times n$. We always index topics by l and l', terms by i, and documents by j.

We give an intuitive description of the model assumptions first and then make formal statements.

1. **Primary Topic** Each document has a primary topic. The weight of the primary topic in the document is high and the weight of each non-primary topic is low.
2. **Pure Document** Each topic has at least one *pure document* that is mostly on that topic.
3. **Catchword** Each topic has at least one *catchword*, which has high frequency in that topic and low frequency in other topics.

In the next section, we state quantitative versions of the assumptions and show that these assumptions suffice to yield a simple polynomial time algorithm to find the primary topic of each document. The primary topic classification can then be used to find B approximately, but this requires a further assumption (4) in Section (9.9) below, which is a robust version of the Pure Document assumption.

Let's provide some intuition for how we are able to do the primary topic classification. By using the primary topic and catchword assumptions, we can show (quantitative version in Claim 9.1 below) that if i is a catchword for topic l, then there is a threshold μ_i, which we can compute for each catchword, so that for each document j with primary topic l, p_{ij} is above μ_i and for each document j whose primary topic is not l, p_{ij} is substantially below μ_i. So, if

1. we were given P, and
2. knew a catchword for each topic and the threshold, we can find the primary topic of each document.

We illustrate the situation in Equation 9.4, where rows $1, 2, \ldots, r$ of P correspond to catchwords for topics $1, 2, \ldots, r$ and we have rearranged columns in order of primary topic. H stands for a high entry and L for a low entry.

$$
P = \begin{pmatrix}
H & H & H & L & L & L & L & L & L & L & L & L \\
L & L & L & H & H & H & L & L & L & L & L & L \\
L & L & L & L & L & L & H & H & H & L & L & L \\
L & L & L & L & L & L & L & L & L & H & H & H \\
\cdot & \cdot & \cdot & \cdot & \cdot & \cdot & \cdot & \cdot & \cdot & \cdot & \cdot & \cdot \\
\cdot & \cdot & \cdot & \cdot & \cdot & \cdot & \cdot & \cdot & \cdot & \cdot & \cdot & \cdot \\
\cdot & \cdot & \cdot & \cdot & \cdot & \cdot & \cdot & \cdot & \cdot & \cdot & \cdot & \cdot \\
\cdot & \cdot & \cdot & \cdot & \cdot & \cdot & \cdot & \cdot & \cdot & \cdot & \cdot & \cdot
\end{pmatrix} \tag{9.4}
$$

We are given A, but not P. While $E(A|P) = P, A$ could be far off from P. In fact, if in column j of P, there are many entries smaller than c/m in A (since we are doing only m multinomial trials), they could all be zeros and so are not a good approximation to the entries of $P(:,j)$. However, if $p_{ij} > c/m$, for a large value c, then $a_{ij} \approx p_{ij}$. Think of tossing a coin m times whose probability of heads is p_{ij}. If $p_{ij} \geq c/m$, then the number of heads one gets is close to $p_{ij}m$. We will assume c larger than $\Omega(\log(nd))$ for catchwords so that for every such i and j we have $p_{ij} \approx a_{ij}$. See the formal catchwords assumption in the next section. This addresses (1), namely $A \approx B$, at least in these rows.

One can ask if this is a reasonable assumption. If m is in the hundreds, the assumption is arguably reasonable. But a weaker and more reasonable assumption would be that there is a set of catchwords, not just one, with total frequency higher than c/m. However, here we use the stronger assumption of a single high-frequency catchword.

(2) is more difficult to address. Let $l(i) = \arg\max_{l'=1}^{r} b_{il'}$. Let T_l be the set of j with primary topic l. Whether or not i is a catchword, the primary topic assumption will imply that p_{ij} does not drop by more than a certain factor α among $j \in T_{l(i)}$. We prove this formally in Claim 9.1 of Section 9.8. That claim also proves that if i is a catchword for topic l, that there is a sharp drop in p_{ij} between $j \in T_l$ and $j \notin T_l$.

But for non-catchwords, there is no guarantee of a sharp fall in p_{ij} between $j \in T_{l(i)}$ and $j \notin T_{l(i)}$. However, we can identify for each i, where the first fall of roughly α

factor from the maximum occurs in row i of A. For catchwords, we show below (9.8) that this happens precisely between $T_{l(i)}$ and $[n] \setminus T_{l(i)}$. For non-catchwords, we show that the fall does not occur among $j \in T_{l(i)}$. So, the minimal sets where the fall occurs are the T_l and we use this to identify them. We call this process Pruning.

9.8. Formal Assumptions

Parameters α, β, ρ and δ are real numbers in $(0, 0.4]$ satisfying

$$\beta + \rho \leq (1 - 3\delta)\alpha. \tag{9.5}$$

(1) **Primary Topic** There is a partition of $[n]$ into $T_1, T_2, \ldots, T_k$ with:

$$c_{lj} \begin{cases} \geq \alpha & \text{for } j \in T_l \\ \leq \beta. & \text{for } j \notin T_l. \end{cases} \tag{9.6}$$

(2) **Pure Document** For each l, there is some j with

$$c_{lj} \geq 1 - \delta.$$

(3) **Catchwords** For each l, there is at least one catchword i satisfying:

$$b_{il'} \leq \rho b_{il} \qquad \qquad \text{for } l' \neq l \tag{9.7}$$

$$b_{il} \geq \mu, \quad \text{where,} \quad \mu = \frac{c \log(10nd/\delta)}{m\alpha^2\delta^2}, \quad c \text{ constant.} \tag{9.8}$$

Let

$$l(i) = \arg \max_{l'=1}^{r} b_{il'}. \tag{9.9}$$

Another way of stating the assumption $b_{il} \geq \mu$ is that the expected number of times term i occurs in topic l among m independent trials is at least $c \log(10nd/\delta)/\alpha^2\delta^2$, which grows only logarithmically in n and d. As stated at the end of the last section, the point of requiring $b_{il} \geq \mu$ for catchwords is so that using the Hoeffding-Chernoff inequality, we can assert that $a_{ij} \approx p_{ij}$. We state the Hoeffding-Chernoff inequality in the form we use it:

Lemma 9.6

$$Prob(|a_{ij} - p_{ij}| \geq \delta\alpha Max(p_{ij}, \mu)/4) \leq \frac{\delta}{10nd}.$$

So, with probability at least $1 - (\delta/10)$,

$$|a_{ij} - p_{ij}| \leq \delta\alpha Max(\mu, p_{ij})/4 \quad \forall i, j$$

simultaneously. After paying the failure probability of $\delta/10$, we henceforth assume that the above holds.

Proof Since a_{ij} is the average of m independent Bernoulli trials, each with expectation p_{ij}, the Hoeffding-Chernoff inequality asserts that

$$Prob\left(|a_{ij} - p_{ij}| \geq \Delta\right) \leq 2\exp\left(-cm Min\left(\frac{\Delta^2}{p_{ij}}, \Delta\right)\right).$$

Plugging in $\Delta = \alpha \delta \text{Max}(p_{ij}, \mu)/4$, the first statement of the lemma follows with some calculation. The second statement is proved by a union bound over the nd possible (i, j) values. ■

Algorithm

1. **Compute Thresholds:** $\mu_i = \alpha(1 - \delta) \max_j a_{ij}$.

2. **Do thresholding:** Define a matrix $\hat{A}$ by

$$\hat{a}_{ij} = \begin{cases} 1 & \text{if } a_{ij} \geq \mu_i \text{ and } \mu_i \geq \mu\alpha\left(1 - \frac{5\delta}{2}\right). \\ 0 & \text{otherwise} . \end{cases}$$

3. **Pruning:** Let $R_i = \{j | \hat{a}_{ij} = 1\}$. If any R_i strictly contains another, set all entries of row i of $\hat{A}$ to zero.

Theorem 9.7 *For $i = 1, 2, \ldots, d$, let $R_i = \{j | \hat{a}_{ij} = 1\}$ at the end of the algorithm. Then, each non-empty $R_i = T_{l(i)}$, with $l(i)$ as in (9.9).*

Proof We start with a lemma that proves the theorem for catchwords. This is the bulk of the work in the proof of the theorem.

Lemma 9.8 *If i is a catchword for topic l, then $R_i = T_l$.*

Proof Assume throughout this proof that i is a catchword for topic l. The proof consists of three claims. The first argues that for $j \in T_l$, p_{ij} is high and for $j \notin T_l, p_{ij}$ is low. The second claim argues the same for a_{ij} instead of p_{ij}. It follows from the Hoeffding-Chernoff inequality, since a_{ij} is just the average of m Bernoulli trials, each with probability p_{ij}. The third claim shows that the threshold computed in the first step of the algorithm falls between the high and the low.

Claim 9.1 *For i, a catchword for topic l,*

$$b_{il} \geq p_{ij} \geq b_{il}\alpha \qquad\qquad for\ j \in T_l$$
$$p_{ij} \leq b_{il}\alpha(1 - 3\delta) \qquad\qquad for\ j \notin T_l.$$

Proof For $j \in T_l$, using (9.6),

$$p_{ij} = \sum_{l'=1}^{r} b_{il'} c_{l',j} \in [b_{il}\alpha, b_{il}],$$

since $b_{il} = \max_{l'} b_{il'}$. For $j \notin T_l$,

$$p_{ij} = b_{il}c_{lj} + \sum_{l' \neq l} b_{il'}c_{l'j} \leq b_{il}c_{lj} + \rho b_{il}(1 - c_{lj}) \leq b_{il}(\beta + \rho) \leq b_{il}\alpha(1 - 3\delta), \quad (9.10)$$

where the first inequality is from (9.7) and the second inequality is because subject to the constraint $c_{lj} \leq \beta$ imposed by the Primary Topic Assumption (9.6), $b_{il}c_{lj} + \rho b_{il}(1 - c_{lj})$ is maximized when $c_{lj} = \beta$. We have also used (9.5). ■

Claim 9.2 *With probability at least* $1 - \delta/10$, *for every* l *and every catchword* i *of* l:

$$a_{ij} \begin{cases} \geq b_{il}\alpha(1 - \delta/4) & \text{for } j \in T_l \\ \leq b_{il}\alpha(1 - (11/4)\delta), & \text{for } j \notin T_l \end{cases}$$

Proof Suppose for some $j \in T_l, a_{ij} < b_{il}\alpha(1 - \delta/4)$. Then, since $p_{ij} \geq b_{il}\alpha$ by Claim (9.1), $|a_{ij} - p_{ij}| \geq \delta\alpha b_{il}/4$ by Claim (9.1). Since i is a catchword, $b_{il} \geq \mu$, and so $|a_{ij} - p_{ij}| \geq \delta\alpha b_{il}/4 \geq (\delta\alpha \text{Max}(p_{ij}, \mu)/4)$, and we get the first inequality of the current claim using Lemma 9.6.

For the second inequality: for $j \notin T_l, p_{ij} \leq b_{il}\alpha(1 - 3\delta)$ by Claim 9.1, and so if this inequality is violated, $|a_{ij} - p_{ij}| \geq b_{il}\alpha\delta/4$, and we get a contradiction to Lemma (9.6). ∎

Claim 9.3 *With probability at least* $1 - \delta$, *for every topic* l *and every catchword* i *of topic* l, *the* μ_i *computed in step 1 of the algorithm satisfies:* $\mu_i \in \big((1 - (5/2)\delta)b_{il}\alpha, \ b_{il}\alpha(1 - \delta/2)\big)$.

Proof If i is a catchword for topic l and j_0 a pure document for l, then

$$p_{ij_0} = \sum_{l'=1}^{k} b_{il'}c_{l'j_0} \geq b_{il}c_{lj_0} \geq (1 - \delta)b_{il}.$$

Applying Lemma 9.6, $a_{ij_0} > (1 - (3/2)\delta)b_{il}$. Thus, μ_i computed in step 1 of the algorithm satisfies $\mu_i > (1 - (3\delta/2))(1 - \delta)b_{il}\alpha \geq (1 - (5/2)\delta)\alpha b_{il}$. Hence, $\hat{a}_{ij}$ is not set to zero for all j. Now, since $p_{ij} \leq b_{il}$ for all j, $a_{ij} \leq (1 + \delta/4)b_{il}$ by Lemma 9.6 implying

$$\mu_i = \text{Max}_j a_{ij}(1 - \delta)\alpha \leq b_{il}(1 + (\delta/4))(1 - \delta)\alpha \leq b_{il}\alpha(1 - \delta/2).$$

∎

Claims 9.2 and 9.3, complete the proof of Lemma 9.8. ∎

The lemma proves Theorem 9.7 for catchwords. Note that since each topic has at least one catchword, for each l, there is some i with $R_i = T_l$.

Suppose i is a non-catchword. Let $a = \max_j a_{ij}$. If $a < \mu(1 - (5\delta/2))$, then $\mu_i < \mu\alpha(1 - (5\delta/2))$ and the entire row of $\hat{A}$ will be set to all zeros by the algorithm, so $R_i = \emptyset$ and there is nothing to prove. Assume that $a \geq \mu(1 - (5\delta/2))$. Let $j_0 = \arg\max_j a_{ij}$. Then $a = a_{ij_0} \geq \mu(1 - (5\delta/2))$. We claim $p_{i,j_0} \geq a(1 - \delta/2)$. If not, $p_{ij_0} < a(1 - \delta/2)$ and

$$|a_{ij_0} - p_{ij_0}| > \max\left(\frac{p_{ij_0}\delta}{4}, \frac{\mu\alpha\delta}{4}\right),$$

which contradicts Lemma 9.6. So,

$$b_{il} \geq p_{ij_0} \geq \mu(1 - 3\delta). \tag{9.11}$$

Let $l = l(i)$. Then

$$a(1 - \delta/2) \leq p_{ij_0} = \sum_{l'=1}^{r} b_{il'}c_{l'j_0} \leq b_{il}.$$

Also, if j_1 is a pure document for topic l, $c_{l,j_1} \geq (1 - \delta)$ so, $p_{i,j_1} \geq b_{il}c_{l,j_1} \geq b_{il}(1 - \delta)$. Now, we claim that

$$a_{i,j_1} \geq b_{il}(1 - (3\delta/2)). \tag{9.12}$$

If not,

$$p_{ij_1} - a_{ij_1} > b_{il}(1 - \delta) - b_{il}(1 - (3\delta/2)) = b_{il}(\delta/2) \geq \max\left(\frac{\mu\delta}{4}, \frac{p_{ij_1}\delta}{4}\right),$$

contradicting Lemma 9.6. So (9.12) holds, and thus,

$$a \geq b_{il}(1 - (3\delta/2)). \tag{9.13}$$

Now, for all $j \in T_l$, $p_{ij} \geq b_{il}c_{lj} \geq a(1 - \delta/2)\alpha$. So, by applying Lemma 9.6 again, for all $j \in T_l$,

$$a_{ij} \geq a(1 - \delta)\alpha.$$

By step 1 of the algorithm, $\mu_i = a(1 - \delta)\alpha$, so $a_{ij} \geq \mu_i$ for all $j \in T_l$. So, either $R_i = T_l$ or $T_l \subsetneq R_i$. In the latter case, the pruning step will set $\hat{a}_{ij} = 0$ for all j, since topic l has some catchword i_0 for which $R_{i_0} = T_l$ by Lemma 9.8. ∎

9.9. Finding the Term-Topic Matrix

For this, we need an extra assumption, which we first motivate. Suppose as in Section 9.8, we assume that there is a single pure document for each topic. In terms of the Figure 9.1 of three topics, this says that there is a column of P close to each vertex of the triangle. But the corresponding column of A can be very far from this. So, even if we were told which document is pure for each topic, we cannot find the column of B. However, if we had a large number of nearly pure documents for each topic, since the corresponding columns of A are independent even conditioned on P, the average of these columns gives us a good estimate of the column of B. We also note that there is a justification for assuming the existence of a number of documents which are nearly pure for each topic based on the Latent Dirichlet Allocation model (see (2) of Section 9.6). The assumption is:

Assumption (4): Set of Pure Documents For each l, there is a set W_l of at least δn documents with

$$c_{lj} \geq 1 - \frac{\delta}{4} \; \forall j \in W_l.$$

If we could find the set of pure documents for each topic with possibly a small fraction of errors, we could average them. The major task of this section is to state and prove an algorithm that does this. For this, we use the primary topic classification, $T_1, T_2, \ldots, T_r$ from the last section. We know that a for catchword i of topic l, the maximum value of $p_{ij}, j = 1, 2, \ldots, n$ occurs for a pure document, and indeed if the assumption above holds, the set of $\delta n/4$ documents with the top $\delta n/4$ values of p_{ij} should be all pure documents. But to make use of this, we need to know the catchword, which we are not given. To discover them, we use another property of catchwords. If i is a catchword for topic l, then on $T_{l'}, l' \neq l$, the values of p_{ij} are (substantially) lower. So we know that if i is a catchword of topic l, then it has the following property.

Property: $\delta n/4^{th}$ maximum value among $p_{ij}, j \in T_l$ is substantially higher than the $\delta n/4^{th}$ maximum value among $p_{ij}, j \in T_{l'}$ for any $l' \neq l$.

We can computationally recognize the property for A (not P) and on the lines of Lemma 9.6, we can show that it holds essentially for A if and only if it holds for P.

But then, we need to prove a converse of the statement above, namely we need to show that if the property holds for i and l, then i is a catchword for topic l. Since catchwords are not necessarily unique, this is not quite true. But we will prove that any i satisfying the property for topic l does have $b_{il'} < \alpha b_{il} \; \forall l' \neq l$ (Lemma 9.11) and so acts essentially like a catchword. Using this, we will show that the $\delta n/4$ documents among all documents with the highest values of a_{ij} for an i satisfying the property, will be nearly pure documents on topic l in Lemma 9.12 and use this to argue that their average gives a good approximation to column l of B (Theorem 9.13).

The extra steps in the Algorithm: (By the theorem, the $T_l, l = 1, 2, \ldots, r$ are now known.)

1. For $l = 1, 2, \ldots, r$, and for $i = 1, 2, \ldots, d$, let $g(i, l)$ be the $(1 - (\delta/4))^{l;l;th}$ fractile of $\{A_{ij} : j \in T_l\}$. [4]

2. For each l, choose an $i(l)$, (we will prove there is at least 1) such that
$$g(i(l), l) \geq (1 - (\delta/2))\mu \; ; \; g(i(l), l') \leq (1 - 2\delta) \, \alpha \, g(i(l), l) \; \forall l' \neq l. \qquad (9.14)$$

3. Let R_l be the set of $\delta n/4$ j's among $j = 1, 2, \ldots, n$ with the highest $A_{i(l),j}$.

4. Return $\tilde{B}_{\cdot,l} = \frac{1}{|R_l|} \sum_{j \in R_l} A_{\cdot,j}$ as our approximation to $B_{\cdot,l}$.

Lemma 9.9 $i(l)$ *satisfying (9.14) exists for each l.*

Proof Let i be a catchword for l. Then, since, $\forall j \in W_l$, $p_{ij} \geq b_{il}c_{lj} \geq b_{il}(1 - (\delta/4))$ and $b_{il} \geq \mu$, we have $a_{ij} \geq b_{il}(1 - (\delta/2))$ and so $g(i, l) \geq (1 - (\delta/2))b_{il} \geq (1 - (\delta/2))\mu$, by Lemma 9.6. For $j \notin T_l$,
$$a_{ij} \leq b_{il}\alpha(1 - (5\delta/2))$$
by Claim 1.2 and so $g(i, l') \leq b_{il}\alpha(1 - (5\delta/2))$. So $g(i, l)$ satisfies both the requirements of step 2 of the algorithm. ∎

Fix attention on one l. Let $i = i(l)$. Let
$$\rho_i = \max_{k=1}^{r} b_{ik}.$$

Lemma 9.10 $\rho_i \geq \left(1 - \frac{3}{4}\delta\right)\mu$.

Proof We have $p_{ij} = \sum_{k=1}^{r} b_{ik}c_{kj} \leq \rho_i$ for all i. So, $a_{ij} \leq \rho_i + \frac{\alpha\delta}{4}\max(\mu, \rho_i)$, from Lemma 9.6. So, either, $\rho_i \geq \mu$ whence the lemma clearly holds or $\rho_i < \mu$ and
$$\forall j, \; a_{ij} \leq \rho_i + \frac{\alpha\delta}{4}\mu \; \forall j \implies g(i, l) \leq \rho_i + (\alpha\delta/4)\mu.$$

---

[4] The γth fractile of a set S of real numbers is the largest real number a so that at least $\gamma|S|$ elements of S are each greter than or equal to a.

By definition of $i(l), g(i, l) \geq (1 - (\delta/2))\mu$, so

$$\rho_i + \frac{\alpha\delta}{4}\mu \geq (1 - (\delta/2))\mu,$$

from which the lemma follows.

Lemma 9.11 $b_{ik} \leq \alpha b_{il}$ for all $k \neq l$.

Proof Suppose not. Let

$$l' = \arg\max_{k:k\neq l} b_{ik}.$$

We have $b_{il'} > \alpha b_{il}$ and

$$\rho_i = \text{Max}(b_{il}, b_{il'}) < \frac{b_{il'}}{\alpha}. \tag{9.15}$$

Since for $j \in W_{l'}$, at most $\delta/4$ weight is put on topics other than l',

$$\forall j \in W_{l'}, \; p_{ij} \leq b_{il'}\left(1 - \frac{\delta}{4}\right) + \frac{\delta}{4}\rho_i < b_{il'}\left(1 - \frac{\delta}{4} + \frac{\delta}{4\alpha}\right). \tag{9.16}$$

Also, for $j \in W_{l'}$,

$$p_{ij} \geq b_{il'}c_{l'j} \geq b_{il'}\left(1 - \frac{\delta}{4}\right). \tag{9.17}$$

By Lemma 9.6,

$$\forall j \in W_{l'}, a_{ij} \geq p_{ij} - \frac{\alpha\delta}{4}\max(\mu, p_{ij})$$

$$\geq b_{il'}\left(1 - \frac{\delta}{4}\right) - \frac{\alpha\delta}{4}\frac{\rho_i}{1 - (3\delta/4)} \quad \text{by Lemma 9.10}$$

$$\geq b_{il'}\left(1 - \frac{3}{4}\delta\right), \tag{9.18}$$

using (9.15) and $\delta \leq 0.4$. From (9.18), it follows that

$$g(i, l') \geq b_{il'}\left(1 - \frac{3}{4}\delta\right). \tag{9.19}$$

Since $p_{ij} \leq \rho_i$ for all j, using Lemma 9.10,

$$\forall j, a_{ij} \leq \rho_i + (\alpha\delta/4)\text{Max}(\mu, p_{ij}) \leq \rho_i\left(1 + \frac{\alpha\delta}{4}\frac{1}{1 - (3\delta/4)}\right) < b_{il'}\frac{1 + (5\delta/6)}{\alpha},$$

by (9.15); this implies

$$g(i, l) \leq \frac{b_{il'}(1 + (5\delta/6))}{\alpha}. \tag{9.20}$$

Now, the definition of $i(l)$ implies

$$g(i, l') \leq g(i, l)\alpha(1 - 2\delta) \leq b_{il'}(1 + (5\delta/6))\alpha(1 - 2\delta)/\alpha \leq b_{il'}(1 - \delta)$$

contradicting (9.19) and proving Lemma 9.11.

——— **292** ———

Lemma 9.12 *For each $j \in R_l$ of step 3 of the algorithm, we have*

$$c_{lj} \geq 1 - 2\delta.$$

Proof Let $J = \{j : c_{lj} < 1 - 2\delta\}$. Take a $j \in J$. We argue that $j \notin R_l$.

$$p_{ij} \leq b_{il}(1 - 2\delta) + 2\delta\alpha b_{il} \leq b_{il}(1 - 1.2\delta),$$

by Lemma 9.11 using $\alpha \leq 0.4$. So for $j \in J$, we have

$$a_{ij} \leq b_{il}(1 - 1.2\delta) + \frac{\alpha\delta}{4} \max(\mu, b_{il}) < b_{il}(1 - \delta).$$

But

$$\forall j \in W_l, p_{ij} \geq b_{il}\left(1 - \frac{\delta}{4}\right) \implies a_{ij} \geq b_{il}(1 - \delta) \implies g(i, l) \geq b_{il}(1 - \delta).$$

So for no $j \in J$ is $a_{ij} \geq g(i, l)$, and hence no $j \in J$ belong sto R_l.

Theorem 9.13 *Assume*

$$n \geq \frac{cd}{m\delta^3} \ ; \ m \geq \frac{c}{\delta^2}.$$

For all $l, 1 \leq l \leq r$, the $\hat{\mathbf{b}}_{.l}$ returned by step 4 of the Algorithm satisfies

$$||\mathbf{b}_{.l} - \hat{\mathbf{b}}_{.l}||_1 \leq 6\delta.$$

Proof Recall that $BC = P$. Let $V = A - P$. From Lemma 9.12, we know that for each $j \in R_l, c_{lj} \geq 1 - 2\delta$. So

$$P_{.j} = (1 - \gamma)B_{.l} + \mathbf{v},$$

where $\gamma \leq 2\delta$ and $\mathbf{v}$ is a combination of other columns of B with $||\mathbf{v}||_1 \leq \gamma \leq 2\delta$. Thus, we have that

$$\left\|\frac{1}{|R_l|}\sum_{j \in R_l}\mathbf{p}_{.j} - \mathbf{b}_{.l}\right\|_1 \leq 2\delta. \tag{9.21}$$

So it suffices now to show that

$$\left\|\frac{1}{|R_l|}\sum_{j \in R_l}\mathbf{p}_{.j} - \mathbf{a}_{.l}\right\|_1 \leq 2\delta. \tag{9.22}$$

Note that for an individual $j \in R_l, ||\mathbf{a}_{.j} - \mathbf{p}_{.j}||_1$ can be almost 2. For example, if each $\mathbf{p}_{i,j} = 1/d$, then A_{ij} would be $1/m$ for a random subset of m j's and zero for the rest. What we exploit is that when we average over $\Omega(n)$ j's in R_l, the error is small. For this, the independence of $\mathbf{a}_{.j}, j \in R_l$ would be useful. But they are not necessarily independent, there being conditioning on the fact that they all belong to R_l. But there is a simple way around this conditioning. Namely, we prove (9.22) with very high probability for each $R \subseteq [n], |R| = \delta n/4$ and then just take the union bound over all $\binom{n}{(\delta n/4)}$ such subsets.

We know that $E\left(\mathbf{a}_{.j}\right) = \mathbf{p}_{.j}$. Now consider the random variable x defined by

$$x = \frac{1}{|R|} \left\| \sum_{j \in R} \mathbf{v}_{.j} \right\|_1 .$$

x is a function of $m|R|$ independent random variables, namely the choice of $m|R|$ terms in the $|R|$ documents. Changing any one changes x by at most $1/m|R|$. So the Bounded Difference Inequality from probability (also known as McDiarmid's inequality) implies that

$$\text{Prob}\left(|x - Ex| > \delta\right) \le 2\exp\left(-\delta^2 \delta mn/8\right). \tag{9.23}$$

We also have to bound $E(x)$.

$$E(x) = \frac{1}{|R|} E\left(\|\sum_{j \in R} V_{.j}\|_1 \right) = \frac{1}{|R|} \sum_{i=1}^{d} E\left| \sum_{j \in R} v_{ij} \right|$$

$$\le \frac{1}{|R|} \sum_{i=1}^{d} \sqrt{E\left[\left(\sum_{j \in R} v_{ij} \right)^2 \right]} \quad \text{Jensen's inequality:} E(y) \le \sqrt{E(y^2)}$$

$$= \frac{1}{|R|} \sum_{i=1}^{d} \sqrt{\sum_{j \in R} E(v_{ij}^2)} \quad \text{since } \{v_{ij}, j \in R\} \text{are indep. and var adds up}$$

$$\le \frac{\sqrt{d}}{|R|} \left(\sum_{i=1}^{d} \sum_{j \in R} E(v_{ij}^2) \right)^{1/2} \quad \text{Chauchy-Schwartz}$$

$$= \frac{\sqrt{d}}{|R|} \sqrt{\sum_{j} \sum_{i=1}^{d} E(v_{ij}^2)} \le \frac{\sqrt{d}}{\sqrt{m\delta n}} \le \delta,$$

since $E(v_{ij}^2) = p_{ij}/m$ and $\sum_i p_{ij} = 1$ and by hypothesis, $n \ge cd/m\delta^3$. Using this along with (9.23), we see that for a single $R \subseteq \{1, 2, \ldots, n\}$ with $|R| = \delta n/4$,

$$\text{Prob}\left(\left\| \frac{1}{|R|} \sum_{j \in R} \mathbf{v}_{.j} \right\|_1 \ge 2\delta \right) \le 2\exp\left(-c\delta^3 mn\right),$$

which implies using the union bound that

$$\text{Prob}\left(\exists R, |R| = \frac{\delta n}{4} : \left\| \frac{1}{|R|} \sum_{j \in R} \mathbf{v}_{.j} \right\|_1 \ge 2\delta \right) \le 2\exp\left(-c\delta^3 mn + c\delta n\right) \le \delta,$$

because the number of R is $\binom{n}{(\delta n/4)} \le (cn/\delta n)^{\delta n/4} \le \exp(c\delta n)$ and $m \ge c/\delta^2$ by hypothesis. This completes the proof of the theorem. ∎

9.10. Hidden Markov Models

A *hidden Markov model* (HMM) consists of a finite set of states with a transition between each pair of states. There is an initial probability distribution α on the states and a transition probability a_{ij} associated with the transition from state i to state j. Each state also has a probability distribution $p(O, i)$ giving the probability of outputting the symbol O in state i. A transition consists of two components. A state transition to a new state followed by the output of a symbol. The HMM starts by selecting a start state according to the distribution α and outputting a symbol.

Example An example of an HMM with two states q and p and two output symbols h and t is illustrated below.

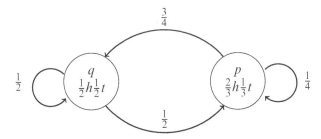

The initial distribution is $\alpha(q) = 1$ and $\alpha(p) = 0$. At each step a change of state occurs followed by the output of heads or tails with probability determined by the new state. ∎

We consider three problems in increasing order of difficulty. First, given an HMM, what is the probability of a given output sequence? Second, given an HMM and an output sequence, what is the most likely sequence of states? And third, knowing that the HMM has at most n states and given an output sequence, what is the most likely HMM? Only the third problem concerns a "hidden" Markov model. In the other two problems, the model is known and the questions can be answered in polynomial time using dynamic programming. There is no known polynomial time algorithm for the third question.

How Probable Is an Output Sequence?
Given an HMM, how probable is the output sequence $O = O_0 O_1 O_2 \cdots O_T$ of length $T + 1$? To determine this, calculate for each state i and each initial segment of the sequence of observations, $O_0 O_1 O_2 \cdots O_t$ of length $t+1$, the probability of observing $O_0 O_1 O_2 \cdots O_t$ ending in state i. This is done by a dynamic programming algorithm starting with $t = 0$ and increasing t. For $t = 0$ there have been no transitions. Thus, the probability of observing O_0 ending in state i is the initial probability of starting in state i times the probability of observing O_0 in state i. The probability of observing $O_0 O_1 O_2 \cdots O_t$ ending in state i is the sum of the probabilities over all states j of observing $O_0 O_1 O_2 \cdots O_{t-1}$ ending in state j times the probability of going from state j to state i and observing O_t. The time to compute the probability of a sequence of length T when there are n states is $O(n^2 T)$. The factor n^2 comes from the calculation for each time unit of the contribution from each possible previous state to the probability of each possible current state. The space complexity is $O(n)$, since one only needs to remember the probability of reaching each state for the most recent value of t.

Algorithm to Calculate the Probability of the Output Sequence

The probability, $\text{Prob}(O_0 O_1 \cdots O_T, i)$ of the output sequence $O_0 O_1 \cdots O_T$ ending in state i, is given by

$$\text{Prob}(O_0, i) = \alpha(i) p(O_0, i)$$

and for $t = 1$ to T,

$$\text{Prob}(O_0 O_1 \cdots O_t, i) = \sum_j \text{Prob}(O_0 O_1 \cdots O_{t-1}, j) a_{ij} p(O_{t+1}, i).$$

Example What is the probability of the sequence hhht by the HMM in the above two-state example?

$t = 3$	$\frac{3}{32}\frac{1}{2}\frac{1}{2} + \frac{5}{72}\frac{3}{4}\frac{1}{2} = \frac{19}{384}$	$\frac{3}{32}\frac{1}{2}\frac{1}{3} + \frac{5}{72}\frac{1}{4}\frac{1}{3} = \frac{37}{64\times27}$
$t = 2$	$\frac{1}{8}\frac{1}{2}\frac{1}{2} + \frac{1}{6}\frac{3}{4}\frac{1}{2} = \frac{3}{32}$	$\frac{1}{8}\frac{1}{2}\frac{1}{3} + \frac{1}{6}\frac{1}{4}\frac{1}{3} = \frac{5}{72}$
$t = 1$	$\frac{1}{2}\frac{1}{2}\frac{1}{2} = \frac{1}{8}$	$\frac{1}{2}\frac{1}{2}\frac{1}{3} = \frac{1}{6}$
$t = 0$	$\frac{1}{2}$	0
	q	p

For $t = 0$, the q entry is $1/2$, since the probability of being in state q is one and the probability of outputting heads is $\frac{1}{2}$. The entry for p is zero, since the probability of starting in state p is zero. For $t = 1$, the q entry is $\frac{1}{8}$, since for $t = 0$ the q entry is $\frac{1}{2}$ and in state q the HMM goes to state q with probability $\frac{1}{2}$ and outputs heads with probability $\frac{1}{2}$. The p entry is $\frac{1}{6}$, since for $t = 0$ the q entry is $\frac{1}{2}$ and in state q the HMM goes to state p with probability $\frac{1}{2}$ and outputs heads with probability $\frac{2}{3}$. For $t = 2$, the q entry is $\frac{3}{32}$, which consists of two terms. The first term is the probability of ending in state q at $t = 1$ times the probability of staying in q and outputting h. The second is the probability of ending in state p at $t = 1$ times the probability of going from state p to state q and outputting h.

From the table, the probability of producing the sequence hhht is $\frac{19}{384} + \frac{37}{1728} = 0.0709$. ∎

The Most Likely Sequence of States – the Viterbi Algorithm

Given an HMM and an observation $O = O_0 O_1 \cdots O_T$, what is the most likely sequence of states? The solution is given by the Viterbi algorithm, which is a slight modification to the dynamic programming algorithm just given for determining the probability of an output sequence. For $t = 0, 1, 2, \ldots, T$ and for each state i, we calculate the probability of the most likely sequence of states to produce the output $O_0 O_1 O_2 \cdots O_t$ ending in state i as follows. For each state j, we have already computed the probability of the most likely sequence producing $O_0 O_1 O_2 \cdots O_{t-1}$ ending in state j, and we multiply this by the probability of the transition from j to i producing O_t. We then select the j for which this product is largest. Note that in the previous example, we added the probabilities of each possibility together.

Now we take the maximum and also record where the maximum came from. The time complexity is $O(n^2 T)$ and the space complexity is $O(nT)$. The space complexity bound is argued as follows. In calculating the probability of the most likely sequence of states that produces $O_0 O_1 \ldots O_t$ ending in state i, we remember the previous state j by putting an arrow with edge label t from i to j. At the end, we can find the most likely sequence by tracing backward as is standard for dynamic programming algorithms.

Example For the earlier example what is the most likely sequence of states to produce the output hhht?

$t = 3$	$\max\{\frac{1}{48}\frac{1}{2}\frac{1}{2}, \frac{1}{24}\frac{3}{4}\frac{1}{2}\} = \frac{1}{64}$ q or p	$\max\{\frac{3}{48}\frac{1}{2}\frac{1}{3}, \frac{1}{24}\frac{1}{4}\frac{1}{3}\} = \frac{1}{96}$ q
$t = 2$	$\max\{\frac{1}{8}\frac{1}{2}\frac{1}{2}, \frac{1}{6}\frac{3}{4}\frac{1}{2}\} = \frac{3}{48}$ p	$\max\{\frac{1}{8}\frac{1}{2}\frac{2}{3}, \frac{1}{6}\frac{1}{4}\frac{2}{3}\} = \frac{1}{24}$ q
$t = 1$	$\frac{1}{2}\frac{1}{2}\frac{1}{2} = \frac{1}{8}$ q	$\frac{1}{2}\frac{1}{2}\frac{2}{3} = \frac{1}{6}$ q
$t = 0$	$\frac{1}{2}$ q	0 p
	q	p

Note that the two sequences of states, $qqpq$ and $qpqq$, are tied for the most likely sequences of states. ∎

Determining the Underlying Hidden Markov Model

Given an n-state HMM, how do we adjust the transition probabilities and output probabilities to maximize the probability of an output sequence $O_1 O_2 \cdots O_T$? The assumption is that T is much larger than n.[5] There is no known computationally efficient method for solving this problem. However, there are iterative techniques that converge to a local optimum.

Let a_{ij} be the transition probability from state i to state j and let $b_j(O_k)$ be the probability of output O_k given that the HMM is in state j. Given estimates for the HMM parameters, a_{ij} and b_j, and the output sequence O, we can improve the estimates by calculating for each time step the probability that the HMM goes from state i to state j and outputs the symbol O_k, conditioned on O being the output sequence.

Given estimates for the HMM parameters, a_{ij} and b_j, and the output sequence O, the probability $\delta_t(i, j)$ of going from state i to state j at time t is given by the probability of producing the output sequence O and going from state i to state j at time t divided by the probability of producing the output sequence O:

$$\delta_t(i,j) = \frac{\alpha_t(i)a_{ij}b_j(O_{t+1})\beta_{t+1}(j)}{p(O)}.$$

The probability $p(O)$ is the sum over all pairs of states i and j of the numerator in the above formula for $\delta_t(i, j)$. That is,

$$p(O) = \sum_i \sum_j \alpha_t(j)a_{ij}b_j(O_{t+1})\beta_{t+1}(j).$$

---

[5]If $T \leq n$, then one can just have the HMM be a linear sequence that outputs $O_1 O_2 \ldots O_T$ with probability 1.

a_{ij}	transition probability from state i to state j
$b_j(O_{t+1})$	probability of O_{t+1} given that the HMM is in state j at time $t+1$
$\alpha_t(i)$	probability of seeing $O_0 O_1 \cdots O_t$ and ending in state i at time t
$\beta_{t+1}(j)$	probability of seeing the tail of the sequence $O_{t+2} O_{t+3} \cdots O_T$ given state j at time $t+1$
$\delta(i,j)$	probability of going from state i to state j at time t given the sequence of outputs O
$s_t(i)$	probability of being in state i at time t given the sequence of outputs O
$p(O)$	probability of output sequence O

The probability of being in state i at time t is given by

$$s_t(i) = \sum_{j=1}^{n} \delta_t(i,j).$$

Summing $s_t(i)$ over all time periods gives the expected number of times state i is visited, and the sum of $\delta_t(i,j)$ over all time periods gives the expected number of times edge i to j is traversed.

Given estimates of the HMM parameters $a_{i,j}$ and $b_j(O_k)$, we can calculate by the above formulas estimates for

1. $\sum_{i=1}^{T-1} s_t(i)$, the expected number of times state i is visited and departed from
2. $\sum_{i=1}^{T-1} \delta_t(i,j)$, the expected number of transitions from state i to state j

Using these estimates we can obtain new estimates of the HMM parameters

$$\overline{a_{ij}} = \frac{\text{expected number of transitions from state } i \text{ to state } j}{\text{expected number of transitions out of state } i} = \frac{\sum_{t=1}^{T-1} \delta_t(i,j)}{\sum_{t=1}^{T-1} s_t(i)}$$

$$\overline{b_j(O_k)} = \frac{\text{expected number of times in state } j \text{ observing symbol } O_k}{\text{expected number of times in state } j} = \frac{\displaystyle\sum_{\substack{t=1 \\ \text{subject to} \\ O_t = O_k}}^{T-1} s_t(j)}{\sum_{t=1}^{T-1} s_t(j)}$$

By iterating the above formulas we can arrive at a local optimum for the HMM parameters $a_{i,j}$ and $b_j(O_k)$.

9.11. Graphical Models and Belief Propagation

A graphical model is a compact representation of a probability distribution over n variables $x_1, x_2, \ldots, x_n$. It consists of a graph, directed or undirected, whose vertices correspond to variables that take on values from some set. In this chapter, we consider the case where the set of values the variables take on is finite, although graphical models are often used to represent probability distributions with continuous variables. The edges of the graph represent relationships or constraints between the variables.

In the directed model, it is assumed that the directed graph is acyclic. This model represents a joint probability distribution that factors into a product of conditional probabilities:

$$p(x_1, x_2, \ldots, x_n) = \prod_{i=1}^{n} p(x_i | \text{parents of } x_i).$$

The directed graphical model is called a *Bayesian* or *belief network* and appears frequently in the artificial intelligence and the statistics literature.

The undirected graphical model, called a *Markov random field*, can also represent a joint probability distribution of the random variables at its vertices. In many applications the Markov random field represents a function of the variables at the vertices that is to be optimized by choosing values for the variables.

A third model called the *factor model* is akin to the Markov random field, but here the dependency sets have a different structure. In the following sections we describe all these models in more detail.

9.12. Bayesian or Belief Networks

A *Bayesian network* (Figure 9.2) is a directed acyclic graph where vertices correspond to variables and a directed edge from y to x represents a conditional probability $p(x|y)$. If a vertex x has edges into it from $y_1, y_2, \ldots, y_k$, then the conditional probability is $p(x \mid y_1, y_2, \ldots, y_k)$. The variable at a vertex with no in edges has an unconditional probability distribution. If the value of a variable at some vertex is known, then the variable is called *evidence*. An important property of a Bayesian network is that the joint probability is given by the product over all nodes of the conditional probability of the node conditioned on all its immediate predecessors.

In the example of Figure 9.1, a patient is ill and sees a doctor. The doctor ascertains the symptoms of the patient and the possible causes such as whether the patient was in contact with farm animals, whether he had eaten certain foods, or whether the patient has an hereditary predisposition to any diseases. Using the above Bayesian

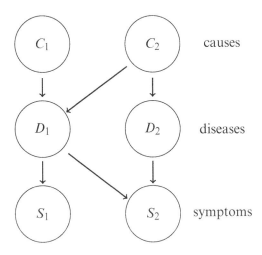

Figure 9.2: A Bayesian network

network where the variables are true or false, the doctor may wish to determine one of two things: what the marginal probability of a given disease is; or what the most likely set of diseases is. In determining the most likely set of diseases, we are given a T or F assignment to the causes and symptoms and ask what assignment of T or F to the diseases maximizes the joint probability. This latter problem is called the *maximum a posteriori probability* (MAP).

Given the conditional probabilities and the probabilities $p(C_1)$ and $p(C_2)$ in Figure 9.1, the joint probability $p(C_1, C_2, D_1, \ldots)$ can be computed easily for any combination of values of $C_1, C_2, D_1, \ldots$. However, we might wish to find the value of the variables of highest probability (MAP) or we might want one of the marginal probabilities $p(D_1)$ or $p(D_2)$. The obvious algorithms for these two problems require evaluating the probability $p(C_1, C_2, D_1, \ldots)$ over exponentially many input values or summing the probability $p(C_1, C_2, D_1, \ldots)$ over exponentially many values of the variables other than those for which we want the marginal probability. In certain situations, when the joint probability distribution can be expressed as a product of factors, a belief propagation algorithm can solve the maximum a posteriori problem or compute all marginal probabilities quickly.

9.13. Markov Random Fields

The Markov random field model arose first in statistical mechanics where it was called the Ising model. It is instructive to start with a description of it. The simplest version of the Ising model consists of n particles arranged in a rectangular $\sqrt{n} \times \sqrt{n}$ grid. Each particle can have a spin that is denoted ± 1. The energy of the whole system depends on interactions between pairs of neighboring particles. Let x_i be the spin, ± 1, of the ith particle. Denote by $i \sim j$ the relation that i and j are adjacent in the grid. In the Ising model, the energy of the system is given by

$$f(x_1, x_2, \ldots, x_n) = \exp\left(c \sum_{i \sim j} |x_i - x_j|\right).$$

The constant c can be positive or negative. If $c < 0$, then energy is lower if many adjacent pairs have opposite spins and if $c > 0$ the reverse holds. The model was first used to model probabilities of spin configurations in physical materials.

In most computer science settings, such functions are mainly used as objective functions that are to be optimized subject to some constraints. The problem is to find the minimum energy set of spins under some constraints on the spins. Usually the constraints just specify the spins of some particles. Note that when $c > 0$, this is the problem of minimizing $\sum_{i \sim j} |x_i - x_j|$ subject to the constraints. The objective function is convex, and so this can be done efficiently. If $c < 0$, however, we need to minimize a concave function for which there is no known efficient algorithm. The minimization of a concave function in general is NP-hard. Intuitively, this is because the set of inputs for which $f(x)$ is less than some given value can be non-convex or even consist of many disconnected regions.

A second important motivation comes from the area of vision. It has to to do with reconstructing images. Suppose we are given noisy observations of the intensity of light at individual pixels, $x_1, x_2, \ldots, x_n$, and wish to compute the true values, the true intensities, of these variables $y_1, y_2, \ldots, y_n$. There may be two sets of constraints, the first stipulating that the y_i should generally be close to the corresponding x_i, and the second, a term correcting possible observation errors, stipulating that y_i should generally be close to the values of y_j for $j \sim i$. This can be formulated as

$$\min_{\mathbf{y}} \left(\sum_i |x_i - y_i| + \sum_{i \sim j} |y_i - y_j| \right),$$

where the values of x_i are constrained to be the observed values. The objective function is convex and polynomial time minimization algorithms exist. Other objective functions using say sum of squares instead of sum of absolute values can be used, and there are polynomial time algorithms as long as the function to be minimized is convex.

More generally, the correction term may depend on all grid points within distance 2 of each point rather than just immediate neighbors. Even more generally, we may have n variables $y_1, y_2, \ldots y_n$ with the value of some of them already specified and subsets $S_1, S_2, \ldots S_m$ of these variables constrained in some way. The constraints are accumulated into one objective function that is a product of functions $f_1, f_2, \ldots, f_m$, where function f_i is evaluated on the variables in subset S_i. The problem is to minimize $\prod_{i=1}^{m} f_i(y_j, j \in S_i)$ subject to constrained values. Note that the vision example had a sum instead of a product, but by taking exponentials we can turn the sum into a product as in the Ising model.

In general, the f_i are not convex; indeed they may be discrete. So the minimization cannot be carried out by a known polynomial time algorithm. The most used forms of the Markov random field involve S_i, which are cliques of a graph. So we make the following definition.

A *Markov Random Field* consists of an undirected graph and an associated function that factorizes into functions associated with the cliques of the graph. The special case when all the factors correspond to cliques of size 1 or 2 is of interest.

9.14. Factor Graphs

Factor graphs arise when we have a function f of a variables $\mathbf{x} = (x_1, x_2, \ldots, x_n)$ that can be expressed as $f(\mathbf{x}) = \prod_\alpha f_\alpha(\mathbf{x}_\alpha)$ where each factor depends only on some small number of variables $\mathbf{x}_\alpha$. The difference from Markov random fields is that the variables corresponding to factors do not necessarily form a clique. Associate a bipartite graph where one set of vertices correspond to the factors and the other set to the variables. Place an edge between a variable and a factor if the factor contains that variable. See Figure 9.3.

9.15. Tree Algorithms

Let $f(\mathbf{x})$ be a function that is a product of factors. When the factor graph is a tree, there are efficient algorithms for solving certain problems. With slight modifications, the algorithms presented can also solve problems where the function is the sum of terms rather than a product of factors.

The first problem is called *marginalization* and involves evaluating the sum of f over all variables except one. In the case where f is a probability distribution, the algorithm computes the marginal probabilities, and thus the word "marginalization."

---

301 ———

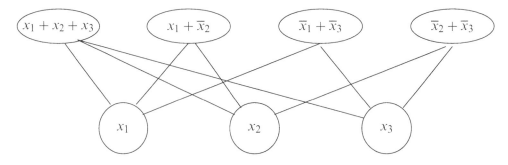

Figure 9.3: The factor graph for the function $f(x_1, x_2, x_3) = (x_1 + x_2 + x_3)(x_1 + \bar{x}_2)(x_1 + \bar{x}_3)(\bar{x}_2 + \bar{x}_3)$.

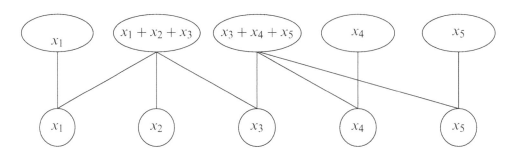

Figure 9.4: The factor graph for the function $f = x_1 (x_1 + x_2 + x_3) (x_3 + x_4 + x_5) x_4 x_5$.

The second problem involves computing the assignment to the variables that maximizes the function f. When f is a probability distribution, this problem is the maximum a posteriori probability or MAP problem.

If the factor graph is a tree (such as in Figure 9.4), then there exists an efficient algorithm for solving these problems. Note that there are four problems: the function f is either a product or a sum, and we are either marginalizing or finding the maximizing assignment to the variables. All four problems are solved by essentially the same algorithm, and we present the algorithm for the marginalization problem when f is a product. Assume we want to "sum out" all the variables except x_1, leaving a function of x_1.

Call the variable node associated with some variable x_i node x_i. First, make the node x_1 the root of the tree. It will be useful to think of the algorithm first as a recursive algorithm and then unravel the recursion. We want to compute the product of all factors occurring in the subtree rooted at the root with all variables except the root-variable summed out. Let g_i be the product of all factors occurring in the subtree rooted at node x_i with all variables occurring in the subtree except x_i summed out. Since this is a tree, x_1 will not reoccur anywhere except the root. Now, the grandchildren of the root are variable nodes, and suppose inductively, each grandchild x_i of the root has already computed its g_i. It is easy to see that we can compute g_1 as follows.

Each grandchild x_i of the root passes its g_i to its parent, which is a factor node. Each child of x_1 collects all its children's g_i, multiplies them together with its own factor, and sends the product to the root. The root multiplies all the products it gets from its children and sums out all variables except its own variable, namely here x_1.

Unraveling the recursion is also simple, with the convention that a leaf node just receives 1, product of an empty set of factors, from its children. Each node waits until it receives a message from each of its children. After that, if the node is a variable node, it computes the product of all incoming messages, and sums this product function over all assignments to the variables except for the variable of the node. Then, it sends the resulting function of one variable out along the edge to its parent. If the node is a factor node, it computes the product of its factor function along with incoming messages from all the children and sends the resulting function out along the edge to its parent.

The reader should prove that the following invariant holds assuming the graph is a tree:

Invariant The message passed by each variable node to its parent is the product of all factors in the subtree under the node with all variables in the subtree except its own summed out.

Consider the following example where

$$f = x_1 (x_1 + x_2 + x_3) (x_3 + x_4 + x_5) x_4 x_5$$

and the variables take on values 0 or 1. Consider marginalizing f by computing

$$f(x_1) = \sum_{x_2 x_3 x_4 x_5} x_1 (x_1 + x_2 + x_3) (x_3 + x_4 + x_5) x_4 x_5.$$

In this case the factor graph is a tree as shown in Figure 9.4. The factor graph as a rooted tree, and the messages passed by each node to its parent are shown in Figure 9.5. If instead of computing marginals, one wanted the variable assignment that maximizes the function f, one would modify the above procedure by replacing the summation by a maximization operation. Obvious modifications handle the situation where $f(\mathbf{x})$ is a sum of products:

$$f(\mathbf{x}) = \sum_{x_1, \dots, x_n} g(\mathbf{x}).$$

9.16. Message Passing in General Graphs

The simple message passing algorithm in the last section gives us the one variable function of x_1 when we sum out all the other variables. For a general graph that is not a tree, we formulate an extension of that algorithm. But unlike the case of trees, there is no proof that the algorithm will converge, and even if it does, there is no guarantee that the limit is the marginal probability. This has not prevented its usefulness in some applications.

First, lets ask a more general question, just for trees. Suppose we want to compute for each i the one-variable function of x_i when we sum out all variables $x_j, j \neq i$. Do we have to repeat what we did for x_1 once for each x_i? Luckily, the answer is no. It will suffice to do a second pass from the root to the leaves of essentially the same message passing algorithm to get *all* the answers. Recall that in the first pass, each edge of the tree has sent a message up from the child to the parent. In the second pass, each edge will send a message down from the parent to the child. We start with the root and

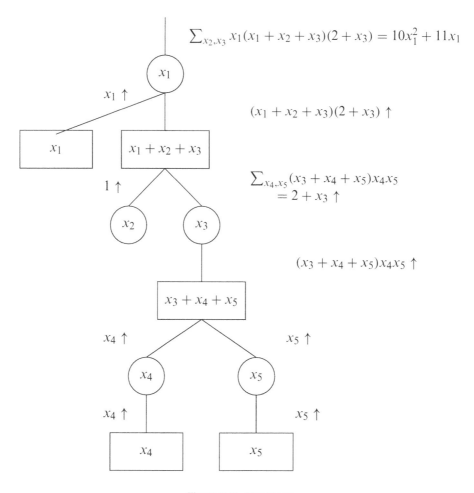

Figure 9.5: Messages.

work downward for this pass. Each node waits until its parent has sent it a message before sending messages to each of its children. The rules for messages are:

Rule 1 The message from a factor node v to a child x_i, which is the variable node x_i, is the product of all messages received by v in both passes from all nodes other than x_i times the factor at v itself.

Rule 2 The message from a variable node x_i to a factor node child, v, is the product of all messages received by x_i in both passes from all nodes except v, with all variables except x_i summed out. The message is a function of x_i alone.

At termination, when the graph is a tree, if we take the product of all messages received in both passes by a variable node x_i and sum out all variables except x_i in this product, what we get is precisely the entire function marginalized to x_i. We do not give the proof here. But the idea is simple. We know from the first pass that the product of the messages coming to a variable node x_i from its children is the product of all factors in the subtree rooted at x_i. In the second pass, we claim that the message from the parent v to x_i is the product of all factors which are not in the subtree rooted at x_i which one can show either directly or by induction working from the root downward.

We can apply the same rules 1 and 2 to any general graph. We do not have child and parent relationships and it is not possible to have the two synchronous passes as before. The messages keep flowing, and one hopes that after some time, the messages will stabilize, but nothing like that is proven. We state the algorithm for general graphs now:

Rule 1 At each unit of time, each factor node v sends a message to each adjacent node x_i. The message is the product of all messages received by v at the previous step except for the one from x_i multiplied by the factor at v itself.

Rule 2 At each time, each variable node x_i sends a message to each adjacent node v. The message is the product of all messages received by x_i at the previous step except the one from v, with all variables except x_i summed out.

9.16.1. Graphs with a Single Cycle

The message passing algorithm gives the correct answers on trees and on certain other graphs. One such situation is graphs with a single cycle that we treat here. We switch from the marginalization problem to the MAP problem, as the proof of correctness is simpler for the MAP problem. Consider the network in Figure 9.6a with a single cycle. The message passing scheme will count some evidence multiply. The local evidence at A will get passed around the loop and will come back to A. Thus, A will count the local evidence multiple times. If all evidence is multiply counted in equal amounts, then there is a possibility that though the numerical values of the marginal probabilities (beliefs) are wrong, the algorithm still converges to the correct maximum a posteriori assignment.

Consider the unwrapped version of the graph in Figure 9.6b. The messages that the loopy version will eventually converge to, assuming convergence, are the same

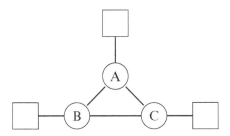

(a) A graph with a single cycle

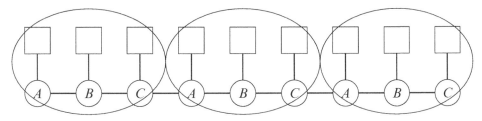

(b) Segment of an unrolled graph

Figure 9.6: Unwrapping a graph with a single cycle.

messages that occur in the unwrapped version provided that the nodes are sufficiently far in from the ends. The beliefs in the unwrapped version are correct for the unwrapped graph, since it is a tree. The only question is, how similar are they to the true beliefs in the original network.

Write $p(A, B, C) = e^{\log p(A,B,C)} = e^{J(A,B,C)}$ where $J(A, B, C) = \log p(A, B, C)$. Then the probability for the unwrapped network is of the form $e^{kJ(A,B,C)+J'}$ where the J' is associated with vertices at the ends of the network where the beliefs have not yet stabilized and the $kJ(A, B, C)$ comes from k inner copies of the cycle where the beliefs have stabilized. Note that the last copy of J in the unwrapped network shares an edge with J' and that edge has an associated Ψ. Thus, changing a variable in J has an impact on the value of J' through that Ψ. Since the algorithm maximizes $J_k = kJ(A, B, C) + J'$ in the unwrapped network for all k, it must maximize $J(A, B, C)$. To see this, set the variables A, B, C so that J_k is maximized. If $J(A, B, C)$ is not maximized, then change A, B, and C to maximize $J(A, B, C)$. This increases J_k by some quantity that is proportional to k. However, two of the variables that appear in copies of $J(A, B, C)$ also appear in J' and thus J' might decrease in value. As long as J' decreases by some finite amount, we can increase J_k by increasing k sufficiently. As long as all Ψ's are non-zero, J', which is proportional to $\log \Psi$, can change by at most some finite amount. Hence, for a network with a single loop, assuming that the message passing algorithm converges, it converges to the maximum a posteriori assignment.

9.16.2. Belief Update in Networks with a Single Loop

In the previous section, we showed that when the message-passing algorithm converges, it correctly solves the MAP problem for graphs with a single loop. The message-passing algorithm can also be used to obtain the correct answer for the marginalization problem. Consider a network consisting of a single loop with variables $x_1, x_2, \ldots, x_n$ and evidence $y_1, y_2, \ldots, y_n$ as shown in Figure 9.7. The x_i and y_i can be represented by vectors having a component for each value x_i can take on. To simplify the discussion assume the x_i take on values $1, 2, \ldots, m$.

Let m_i be the message sent from vertex i to vertex $i + 1 \mod n$. At vertex $i + 1$ each component of the message m_i is multiplied by the evidence y_{i+1} and the constraint function Ψ. This is done by forming a diagonal matrix D_{i+1} where the diagonal elements are the evidence and then forming a matrix M_i whose jk^{th} element is $\Psi(x_{i+1} = j, x_i = k)$. The message m_{i+1} is $M_i D_{i+1} m_i$. Multiplication by the diagonal matrix D_{i+1} multiplies the components of the message m_i by the associated evidence. Multiplication by the matrix M_i multiplies each component of the vector by the appropriate value of Ψ and sums over the values producing message m_{i+1}. Once the message has traveled around the loop, the new message m_1' is given by

$$m_1' = M_n D_1 M_{n-1} D_n \cdots M_2 D_3 M_1 D_2 m_1.$$

Let $M = M_n D_1 M_{n-1} D_n \cdots M_2 D_3 M_1 D_2 m_1$. Assuming that M's principal eigenvalue is unique, the message passing will converge to the principal vector of M. The rate of convergences depends on the ratio of the first and second eigenvalues.

An argument analogous to the above concerning the messages going clockwise around the loop applies to messages moving counter-clockwise around the loop.

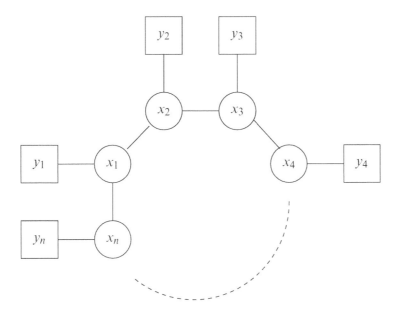

Figure 9.7: A Markov random field with a single loop.

To obtain the estimate of the marginal probability $p(x_1)$, one multiples component-wise the two messages arriving at x_1 along with the evidence y_1. This estimate does not give the true marginal probability, but the true marginal probability can be computed from the estimate and the rate of convergences by linear algebra.

9.16.3. Maximum Weight Matching

We have seen that the belief propagation algorithm converges to the correct solution in trees and graphs with a single cycle. It also correctly converges for a number of problems. Here we give one example, the maximum weight matching problem where there is a unique solution.

We apply the belief propagation algorithm to find the maximal weight matching (MWM) in a complete bipartite graph. If the MWM in the bipartite graph is unique, then the belief propagation algorithm will converge to it.

Let $G = (V_1, V_2, E)$ be a complete bipartite graph where $V_1 = \{a_1, \ldots, a_n\}$, $V_2 = \{b_1, \ldots, b_n\}$, and $(a_i, b_j) \in E$, $1 \le i, j \le n$. Let $\pi = \{\pi(1), \ldots, \pi(n)\}$ be a permutation of $\{1, \ldots, n\}$. The collection of edges $\{(a_1, b_{\pi(1)}), \ldots, (a_n, b_{\pi(n)})\}$ is called a *matching*, which is denoted by π. Let w_{ij} be the weight associated with the edge (a_i, b_j). The weight of the matching π is $w_\pi = \sum_{i=1}^{n} w_{i\pi(i)}$. The maximum weight matching π^* is $\pi^* = \arg\max_\pi w_\pi$.

The first step is to create a factor graph of constraints corresponding to the MWM problem. Each edge of the bipartite graph is represented by a variable c_{ij} that takes on the value zero or 1. The value 1 means that the edge is present in the matching; the value zero means that the edge is not present in the matching. A set of constraints is used to force the set of edges to be a matching. The constraints are of the form $\sum_j c_{ij} = 1$ and $\sum_i c_{ij} = 1$. Any 0,1 assignment to the variables c_{ij} that satisfies all of

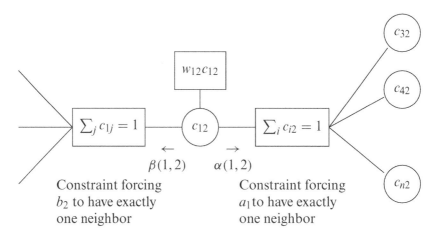

Figure 9.8: Portion of factor graph for the maximum weight matching problem.

the constraints defines a matching. In addition, we have constraints for the weights of the edges.

We now construct a factor graph, a portion of which is shown in Figure 9.8. Associated with the factor graph is a function $f(c_{11}, c_{12}, \ldots)$ consisting of a set of terms for each c_{ij} enforcing the constraints and summing the weights of the edges of the matching. The terms for c_{12} are

$$-\lambda \left| \left(\sum_i c_{i2} \right) - 1 \right| - \lambda \left| \left(\sum_j c_{1j} \right) - 1 \right| + w_{12}c_{12}$$

where λ is a large positive number used to enforce the constraints when we maximize the function. Finding the values of $c_{11}, c_{12}, \ldots$ that maximize f finds the maximum weighted matching for the bipartite graph.

If the factor graph was a tree, then the message from a variable node x to its parent is a message $g(x)$ that gives the maximum value for the subtree for each value of x. To compute $g(x)$, one sums all messages into the node x. For a constraint node, one sums all messages from subtrees and maximizes the sum over all variables except the variable of the parent node subject to the constraint. The message from a variable x consists of two pieces of information, the value $p(x = 0)$ and the value $p(x = 1)$. This information can be encoded into a linear function of x:

$$[p(x = 1) - p(x = 0)]x + p(x = 0).$$

Thus, the messages are of the form $ax + b$. To determine the MAP value of x once the algorithm converges, sum all messages into x and take the maximum over $x = 1$ and $x = 0$ to determine the value for x. Since the arg maximum of a linear form $ax+b$ depends only on whether a is positive or negative and since maximizing the output of a constraint depends only on the coefficient of the variable, we can send messages consisting of just the variable coefficient.

To calculate the message to c_{12} from the constraint that node b_2 has exactly one neighbor, add all the messages that flow into the constraint node from the $c_{i2}, i \neq 1$ nodes and maximize subject to the constraint that exactly one variable has value 1.

If $c_{12} = 0$, then one of $c_{i2}, i \neq 1$, will have value 1 and the message is $\max_{i \neq 1} \alpha(i, 2)$. If $c_{12} = 1$, then the message is zero. Thus, we get

$$- \max_{i \neq 1} \alpha(i, 2)\, x + \max_{i \neq 1} \alpha(i, 2)$$

and send the coefficient $- \max_{i \neq 1} \alpha(i, 2)$. This means that the message from c_{12} to the other constraint node is $\beta(1, 2) = w_{12} - \max_{i \neq 1} \alpha(i, 2)$.

The alpha message is calculated in a similar fashion. If $c_{12} = 0$, then one of c_{1j} will have value one and the message is $\max_{j \neq 1} \beta(1, j)$. If $c_{12} = 1$, then the message is zero. Thus, the coefficient $- \max_{j \neq 1} \alpha(1, j)$ is sent. This means that $\alpha(1, 2) = w_{12} - \max_{j \neq 1} \alpha(1, j)$.

To prove convergence, we unroll the constraint graph to form a tree with a constraint node as the root. In the unrolled graph a variable node such as c_{12} will appear a number of times that depends on how deep a tree is built. Each occurrence of a variable such as c_{12} is deemed to be a distinct variable.

Lemma 9.14 *If the tree obtained by unrolling the graph is of depth k, then the messages to the root are the same as the messages in the constraint graph after k-iterations.*

Proof Straightforward. ∎

Define a matching in the tree to be a set of vertices so that there is exactly one variable node of the match adjacent to each constraint. Let Λ denote the vertices of the matching. Heavy circles in Figure 9.9 represent the nodes of the above tree that are in the matching Λ.

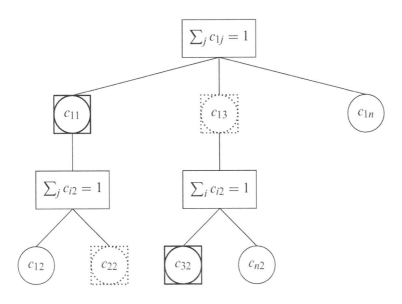

Figure 9.9: Tree for MWM problem.

Let Π be the vertices corresponding to maximum weight matching edges in the bipartite graph. Recall that vertices in the above tree correspond to edges in the bipartite graph. The vertices of Π are denoted by dotted circles in the above tree.

Consider a set of trees where each tree has a root that corresponds to one of the constraints. If the constraint at each root is satisfied by the edge of the MWM, then we have found the MWM. Suppose that the matching at the root in one of the trees disagrees with the MWM. Then there is an alternating path of vertices of length $2k$ consisting of vertices corresponding to edges in Π and edges in Λ. Map this path onto the bipartite graph. In the bipartite graph the path will consist of a number of cycles plus a simple path. If k is large enough there will be a large number of cycles, since no cycle can be of length more than $2n$. Let m be the number of cycles. Then $m \geq \frac{2k}{2n} = \frac{k}{n}$.

Let π^* be the MWM in the bipartite graph. Take one of the cycles and use it as an alternating path to convert the MWM to another matching. Assuming that the MWM is unique and that the next closest matching is ε less, $W_{\pi*} - W_{\pi} > \varepsilon$ where π is the new matching.

Consider the tree matching. Modify the tree matching by using the alternating path of all cycles and the left over simple path. The simple path is converted to a cycle by adding two edges. The cost of the two edges is at most 2w* where w* is the weight of the maximum weight edge. Each time we modify Λ by an alternating cycle, we increase the cost of the matching by at least ε. When we modify Λ by the left over simple path, we increase the cost of the tree matching by $\varepsilon - 2w*$, since the two edges that were used to create a cycle in the bipartite graph are not used. Thus,

$$\text{weight of } \Lambda \text{ - weight of } \Lambda' \geq \frac{k}{n}\varepsilon - 2w*,$$

which must be negative, since Λ' is optimal for the tree. However, if k is large enough, this becomes positive, an impossibility, since Λ' is the best possible. Since we have a tree, there can be no cycles, and as messages are passed up the tree, each subtree is optimal, and hence the total tree is optimal. Thus the message-passing algorithm must find the maximum weight matching in the weighted complete bipartite graph assuming that the maximum weight matching is unique. Note that applying one of the cycles that makes up the alternating path decreased the bipartite graph match but increases the value of the tree. However, it does not give a higher tree matching, which is not possible, since we already have the maximum tree matching. The reason for this is that the application of a single cycle does not result in a valid tree matching. One must apply the entire alternating path to go from one matching to another.

9.17. Warning Propagation

Significant progress has been made using methods similar to belief propagation in finding satisfying assignments for 3-CNF formulas. Thus, we include a section on a version of belief propagation, called warning propagation, that is quite effective in finding assignments. Consider a factor graph for a SAT problem (Figure 9.10). Index the variables by i, j, and k and the factors by a, b, and c. Factor a sends a message m_{ai} to each variable i that appears in the factor a called a warning. The warning is 0 or 1 depending on whether or not factor a believes that the value assigned to i is

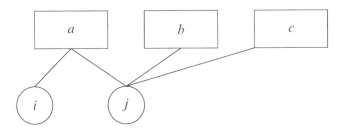

Figure 9.10: Warning propagation.

required for a to be satisfied. A factor a determines the warning to send to variable i by examining all warnings received by other variables in factor a from factors containing them.

For each variable j, sum the warnings from factors containing j that warn j to take value T and subtract the warnings that warn j to take value F. If the difference says that j should take value T or F and this value for variable j does not satisfy a, and this is true for all j, then a sends a warning to i that the value of variable i is critical for factor a.

Start the warning propagation algorithm by assigning 1 to a warning with probability 1/2. Iteratively update the warnings. If the warning propagation algorithm converges, then compute for each variable i the local field h_i and the contradiction number c_i. The local field h_i is the number of clauses containing the variable i that sent messages that i should take value T minus the number that sent messages that i should take value F. The contradiction number c_i is 1 if variable i gets conflicting warnings and 0 otherwise. If the factor graph is a tree, the warning propagation algorithm converges. If one of the warning messages is 1, the problem is unsatisfiable; otherwise it is satisfiable.

9.18. Correlation between Variables

In many situations one is interested in how the correlation between variables drops off with some measure of distance. Consider a factor graph for a 3-CNF formula. Measure the distance between two variables by the shortest path in the factor graph. One might ask if one variable is assigned the value true, what is the percentage of satisfying assignments of the 3-CNF formula in which the second variable also is true. If the percentage is the same as when the first variable is assigned false, then we say that the two variables are uncorrelated. How difficult it is to solve a problem is likely to be related to how fast the correlation decreases with distance.

Another illustration of this concept is in counting the number of perfect matchings in a graph. One might ask what is the percentage of matching in which some edge is present and ask how correlated this percentage is with the presences or absence of edges at some distance d. One is interested in whether the correlation drops off with distance. To explore this concept we consider the Ising model studied in physics.

As mentioned earlier, the Ising or ferromagnetic model is a pairwise random Markov field. The underlying graph, usually a lattice, assigns a value of ± 1, called spin, to the variable at each vertex. The probability (Gibbs measure) of a given configuration of spins is proportional to $exp(\beta \sum_{(i,j)\in E} x_i x_j) = \prod_{(i,j)\in E} e^{\beta x_i x_j}$ where $x_i = \pm 1$ is the value associated with vertex i. Thus,

$$p(x_1, x_2, \ldots, x_n) = \frac{1}{Z} \prod_{(i,j) \in E} exp(\beta x_i x_j) = \frac{1}{Z} e^{\beta \sum_{(i,j) \in E} x_i x_j}$$

where Z is a normalization constant.

The value of the summation is simply the difference in the number of edges whose vertices have the same spin minus the number of edges whose vertices have opposite spin. The constant β is viewed as inverse temperature. High temperature corresponds to a low value of β and low temperature corresponds to a high value of β. At high temperature, low β, the spins of adjacent vertices are uncorrelated whereas at low temperature adjacent vertices have identical spins. The reason for this is that the probability of a configuration is proportional to $e^{\beta \sum_{i \sim j} x_i x_j}$. As β is increased, for configurations with a large number of edges whose vertices have identical spins, $e^{\beta \sum_{i \sim j} x_i x_j}$ increases more than for configurations whose edges have vertices with nonidentical spins. When the normalization constant $\frac{1}{Z}$ is adjusted for the new value of β, the highest-probability configurations are those where adjacent vertices have identical spins.

Given the above probability distribution, what is the correlation between two variables x_i and x_j? To answer this question, consider the probability that $x_i = +1$ as a function of the probability that $x_j = +1$. If the probability that $x_i = +1$ is $\frac{1}{2}$ independent of the value of the probability that $x_j = +1$, we say the values are uncorrelated.

Consider the special case where the graph G is a tree. In this case a phase transition occurs at $\beta_0 = \frac{1}{2} \ln \frac{d+1}{d-1}$ where d is the degree of the tree. For a sufficiently tall tree and for $\beta > \beta_0$, the probability that the root has value $+1$ is bounded away from $1/2$ and depends on whether the majority of leaves have value $+1$ or -1. For $\beta < \beta_0$ the probability that the root has value $+1$ is $1/2$ independent of the values at the leaves of the tree.

Consider a height 1 tree of degree d. If i of the leaves have spin $+1$ and $d - i$ have spin -1, then the probability of the root having spin $+1$ is proportional to

$$e^{i\beta - (d-i)\beta} = e^{(2i-d)\beta}.$$

If the probability of a leaf being $+1$ is p, then the probability of i leaves being $+1$ and $d - i$ being -1 is

$$\binom{d}{i} p^i (1-p)^{d-i}.$$

Thus, the probability of the root being $+1$ is proportional to

$$A = \sum_{i=1}^{d} \binom{d}{i} p^i (1-p)^{d-i} e^{(2i-d)\beta}$$

$$= e^{-d\beta} \sum_{i=1}^{d} \binom{d}{i} (pe^{2\beta})^i (1-p)^{d-i} = e^{-d\beta} [pe^{2\beta} + 1 - p]^d$$

and the probability of the root being -1 is proportional to

$$B = \sum_{i=1}^{d} \binom{d}{i} p^i (1-p)^{d-i} e^{-(2i-d)\beta}$$

$$= e^{-d\beta} \sum_{i=1}^{d} \binom{d}{i} p^i \left[(1-p) e^{-2(i-d)\beta} \right]$$

$$= e^{-d\beta} \sum_{i=1}^{d} \binom{d}{i} p^i \left[(1-p) e^{2\beta} \right]^{d-i}$$

$$= e^{-d\beta} \left[p + (1-p) e^{2\beta} \right]^d.$$

The probability of the root being $+1$ is

$$q = \frac{A}{A+B} = \frac{\left[pe^{2\beta} + 1 - p \right]^d}{\left[pe^{2\beta} + 1 - p \right]^d + \left[p + (1-p) e^{2\beta} \right]^d} = \frac{C}{D}$$

where

$$C = \left[pe^{2\beta} + 1 - p \right]^d$$

and

$$D = \left[pe^{2\beta} + 1 - p \right]^d + \left[p + (1-p) e^{2\beta} \right]^d.$$

At high temperature, low β, the probability q of the root of the height 1 tree being $+1$ in the limit as β goes to zero is

$$q = \frac{p + 1 - p}{[p + 1 - p] + [p + 1 - p]} = \frac{1}{2}$$

independent of p. At low temperature, high β,

$$q \approx \frac{p^d e^{2\beta d}}{p^d e^{2\beta d} + (1-p)^d e^{2\beta d}} = \frac{p^d}{p^d + (1-p)^d} = \begin{cases} 0 & p = 0 \\ 1 & p = 1 \end{cases}.$$

q goes from a low probability of $+1$ for p below 1/2 to high probability of $+1$ for p above 1/2.

Now consider a very tall tree. If the p is the probability that a root has value $+1$, we can iterate the formula for the height 1 tree and observe that at low temperature the probability of the root being 1 converges to some value. At high temperature, the probability of the root being 1 is $1/2$ independent of p. At the phase transition, the slope of q at $p=1/2$ is 1. See Figure 9.11.

Now the slope of the probability of the root being 1 with respect to the probability of a leaf being 1 in this height 1 tree is

$$\frac{\partial q}{\partial p} = \frac{D \frac{\partial C}{\partial p} - C \frac{\partial D}{\partial p}}{D^2}.$$

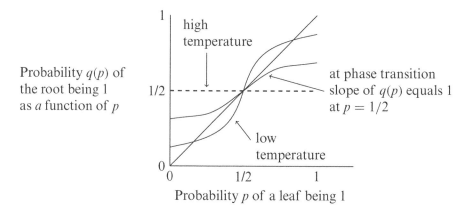

Figure 9.11: Shape of q as a function of p for the height 1 tree and three values of β corresponding to low temperature, the phase transition temperature, and high temperature.

Since the slope of the function $q(p)$ at $p = 1/2$ when the phase transition occurs is 1, we can solve $\frac{\partial q}{\partial p} = 1$ for the value of β where the phase transition occurs. First, we show that $\frac{\partial D}{\partial p}\big|_{p=\frac{1}{2}} = 0$.

$$D = \left[pe^{2\beta} + 1 - p\right]^d + \left[p + (1-p)\,e^{2\beta}\right]^d$$

$$\frac{\partial D}{\partial p} = d\left[pe^{2\beta} + 1 - p\right]^{d-1}\left(e^{2\beta} - 1\right) + d\left[p + (1-p)\,e^{2\beta}\right]^{d-1}\left(1 - e^{2\beta}\right)$$

$$\frac{\partial D}{\partial p}\bigg|_{p=\frac{1}{2}} = \frac{d}{2^{d-1}}\left[e^{2\beta} + 1\right]^{d-1}\left(e^{2\beta} - 1\right) + \frac{d}{2^{d-1}}\left[1 + e^{2\beta}\right]^{d-1}\left(1 - e^{2\beta}\right) = 0$$

Then

$$\frac{\partial q}{\partial p}\bigg|_{p=\frac{1}{2}} = \frac{D\frac{\partial C}{\partial p} - C\frac{\partial D}{\partial p}}{D^2}\bigg|_{p=\frac{1}{2}} = \frac{\frac{\partial C}{\partial p}}{D}\bigg|_{p=\frac{1}{2}} = \frac{d\left[pe^{2\beta} + 1 - p\right]^{d-1}\left(e^{2\beta} - 1\right)}{\left[pe^{2\beta} + 1 - p\right]^d + \left[p + (1-p)\,e^{2\beta}\right]^d}\bigg|_{p=\frac{1}{2}}$$

$$= \frac{d\left[\frac{1}{2}e^{2\beta} + \frac{1}{2}\right]^{d-1}\left(e^{2\beta} - 1\right)}{\left[\frac{1}{2}e^{2\beta} + \frac{1}{2}\right]^d + \left[\frac{1}{2} + \frac{1}{2}e^{2\beta}\right]^d} = \frac{d\left(e^{2\beta} - 1\right)}{1 + e^{2\beta}}$$

Setting

$$\frac{d\left(e^{2\beta} - 1\right)}{1 + e^{2\beta}} = 1$$

And solving for β yields

$$d\left(e^{2\beta} - 1\right) = 1 + e^{2\beta}$$

$$e^{2\beta} = \tfrac{d+1}{d-1}$$

$$\beta = \tfrac{1}{2}\ln\tfrac{d+1}{d-1}$$

To complete the argument, we need to show that q is a monotonic function of p. To see this, write $q = \frac{1}{1+\frac{B}{A}}$. A is a monotonically increasing function of p and B is monotonically decreasing. From this it follows that q is monotonically increasing.

In the iteration going from p to q, we do not get the true marginal probabilities at each level, since we ignored the effect of the portion of the tree above. However, when we get to the root, we do get the true marginal for the root. To get the true marginal's for the interior nodes we need to send messages down from the root.

Note The joint probability distribution for the tree is of the form $e^{\beta \sum_{(ij)\in E} x_i x_j} = \prod_{(i,j)\in E} e^{\beta x_i x_j}$. Suppose x_1 has value 1 with probability p. Then define a function φ, called evidence, such that

$$\varphi(x_1) = \begin{cases} p & \text{for } x_1 = 1 \\ 1-p & \text{for } x_1 = -1 \end{cases}$$
$$= (p - \tfrac{1}{2})x_1 + \tfrac{1}{2}$$

and multiply the joint probability function by φ. Note, however, that the marginal probability of x_1 is not p. In fact, it may be further from p after multiplying the conditional probability function by the function φ.

9.19. Bibliographic Notes

A formal definition of Topic Models described in this chapter as well as the LDA model are from Blei, Ng, and Jordan [BNJ03]; see also [Ble12]. Nonnegative Matrix Factorization has been used in several contexts, for example [DS03]. Anchor terms were defined and used in [AGKM16]. Sections 9.7–9.9 are simplified versions of results from [BBK14].

Good introductions to hidden Markov models, graphical models, Bayesian networks, and belief propagation appear in [Gha01, Bis06]. The use of Markov Random Fields for computer vision originated in the work of Boykov, Veksler, and Zabih [BVZ98], and further discussion appears in [Bis06]. Factor graphs and message-passing algorithms on them were formalized as a general approach (incorporating a range of existing algorithms) in [KFL01]. Message passing in graphs with loops is discussed in [Wei97, WF01].

The use of belief propagation for maximum weighted matching is from [BSS08]. Survey propagation and warning propagation for finding satisfying assignments to k-CNF formulas are described and analyzed in [MPZ02, BMZ05, ACORT11]. For additional relevant papers and surveys, see [FD07, YFW01, YFW03, FK00].

9.20. Exercises

Exercise 9.1 Find a nonnegative factorization of the matrix

$$A = \begin{pmatrix} 4 & 6 & 5 \\ 1 & 2 & 3 \\ 7 & 10 & 7 \\ 6 & 8 & 4 \\ 6 & 10 & 11 \end{pmatrix}$$

Indicate the steps in your method and show the intermediate results.

Exercise 9.2 Find a nonnegative factorization of each of the following matrices.

(1) $\begin{pmatrix} 10 & 9 & 15 & 14 & 13 \\ 2 & 1 & 3 & 3 & 1 \\ 8 & 7 & 13 & 11 & 11 \\ 7 & 5 & 11 & 10 & 7 \\ 5 & 5 & 11 & 6 & 11 \\ 1 & 1 & 3 & 1 & 3 \\ 2 & 2 & 2 & & 2 \end{pmatrix}$
(2) $\begin{pmatrix} 5 & 5 & 10 & 14 & 17 \\ 2 & 2 & 4 & 4 & 6 \\ 1 & 1 & 2 & 4 & 4 \\ 1 & 1 & 2 & 2 & 3 \\ 3 & 3 & 6 & 8 & 10 \\ 5 & 5 & 10 & 16 & 18 \\ 2 & 2 & 4 & 6 & 7 \end{pmatrix}$

(3) $\begin{pmatrix} 4 & 4 & 3 & 3 & 1 & 3 & 4 & 3 \\ 13 & 16 & 13 & 10 & 5 & 13 & 14 & 10 \\ 15 & 24 & 21 & 12 & 9 & 21 & 18 & 12 \\ 7 & 16 & 15 & 6 & 7 & 15 & 10 & 6 \\ 1 & 4 & 4 & 1 & 2 & 4 & 2 & 1 \\ 5 & 8 & 7 & 4 & 3 & 7 & 6 & 4 \\ 3 & 12 & 12 & 3 & 6 & 12 & 6 & 3 \end{pmatrix}$
(4) $\begin{pmatrix} 1 & 1 & 3 & 4 & 4 & 4 & 1 \\ 9 & 9 & 9 & 12 & 9 & 9 & 3 \\ 6 & 6 & 12 & 16 & 15 & 15 & 4 \\ 3 & 3 & 3 & 4 & 3 & 3 & 1 \end{pmatrix}$

Exercise 9.3 Consider the matrix A that is the product of nonnegative matrices B and C.

$$\begin{pmatrix} 12 & 22 & 41 & 35 \\ 19 & 20 & 13 & 48 \\ 11 & 14 & 16 & 29 \\ 14 & 16 & 14 & 36 \end{pmatrix} = \begin{pmatrix} 10 & 1 \\ 1 & 9 \\ 3 & 4 \\ 2 & 6 \end{pmatrix} \begin{pmatrix} 1 & 2 & 4 & 3 \\ 2 & 2 & 1 & 5 \end{pmatrix}$$

Which rows of A are approximate positive linear combinations of other rows of A? Find an approxiamte nonnegative factorization of A

Exercise 9.4 Consider a set of vectors S in which no vector is a positive linear combination of the other vectors in the set. Given a set T containing S along with a number of elements from the convex hull of S find the vectors in S. Develop an efficient method to find S from T that does not require linear programming.

> **Hint.** The points of S are vertices of the convex hull of T. The Euclidean length of a vector is a convex function, and so its maximum over a polytope is attained at one of the vertices. Center the set and find the the maximum length vector in T. This will be one element of S.

Exercise 9.5 Define the nonnegative column rank of a $m \times n$ matrix A to be the minimum number of vectors in m space with the property that every column of A can be expressed as a nonnegative linear combination of these vectors.

1. Show that the nonnegative column rank of A is at least the rank of A.
2. Construct a $3 \times n$ matrix whose nonnegative column rank is n. Hint: Take the plane $x + y = z = 1$ in three-dimensional space; draw a circle in the plane and take n points on the circle.
3. Show that the nonnegative column rank need not be the same as the nonnegative row rank.
4. Read/look up a paper of Vavasis showing that the computation of nonnegative rank is NP-hard.

Exercise 9.6 What happens to the Topic Modeling problem when m, the number of words in a document, goes to infinity? Argue that the Idealized Topic Modeling problem of Section 9.2 is easy to solve when m goes to infinity.

Exercise 9.7 Suppose $\mathbf{y} = (y_1, y_2, \ldots, y_r)$ is jointly distributed according to the Dirichlet distribution with parameter $\mu = 1/r$. Show that the expected value of $max_{l=1}^{r} y_l$ is greater than 0.1. Hint: Lemma 9.6

Exercise 9.8 Suppose there are s documents in a collection that are all nearly pure for a particular topic: i.e., in each of these documents, that topic has weight at least $1 - \delta$. Suppose someone finds and hands to you these documents. Then their average is an approximation to the topic vector. In terms of s, m and δ compute an upper bound on the error of approximation.

Exercise 9.9 Two topics and two words. Toy case of the "Dominant Admixture Model." Suppose in a topic model, there are just two words and two topics; word 1 is a "key word" of topic 1 and word 2 is a key word of topic 2 in the sense:

$$b_{11} \geq 2b_{12} \quad ; \quad b_{21} \leq \frac{1}{2}b_{22}.$$

Suppose each document has one of the two topics as a dominant topic in the sense:

$$\text{Max}(c_{1j}, c_{2j}) \geq 0.75.$$

Also suppose

$$\left|(A - BC)_{ij}\right| \leq 0.1 \quad \forall i, j.$$

Show that there are two real numbers μ_1 and μ_2 such that each document j with dominant topic 1 has $a_{1j} \geq \mu_1$ and $a_{2j} < \mu_2$ and each document j' with dominant topic 2 has $a_{2j'} \geq \mu_2$ and $a_{1j'} < \mu - 1$.

Exercise 9.10 What is the probability of heads occurring after a sufficiently long sequence of transitions in the two-state Viterbi algorithm example in the text of the most likely sequence of states?

Exercise 9.11 Find optimum parameters for a three-state HMM and given output sequence. Note the HMM must have a strong signature in the output sequence or we probably will not be able to find it.

	1	2	3		A	B
1	$\frac{1}{2}$	$\frac{1}{4}$	$\frac{1}{4}$	1	$\frac{3}{4}$	$\frac{1}{4}$
2	$\frac{1}{4}$	$\frac{1}{4}$	$\frac{1}{2}$	2	$\frac{1}{4}$	$\frac{3}{4}$
3	$\frac{1}{3}$	$\frac{1}{3}$	$\frac{1}{3}$	3	$\frac{1}{3}$	$\frac{2}{3}$

Exercise 9.12 In the Ising model for a tree of degree 1, a chain of vertices, is there a phase transition where the correlation between the value at the root and the value at the leaves becomes independent? Work out mathematically what happens.

CHAPTER TEN

Other Topics

10.1. Ranking and Social Choice

Combining feedback from multiple users to rank a collection of items is an important task. We rank movies, restaurants, web pages, and many other items. Ranking has become a multi-billion-dollar industry as organizations try to raise the position of their web pages in the results returned by search engines to relevant queries. Developing a method of ranking that cannot be easily gamed by those involved is an important task.

A ranking of a collection of items is defined as a complete ordering. For every pair of items a and b, either a is preferred to b or b is preferred to a. Furthermore, a ranking is transitive in that $a > b$ and $b > c$ implies $a > c$.

One problem of interest in ranking is that of combining many individual rankings into one global ranking. However, merging ranked lists in a meaningful way is nontrivial as the following example illustrates.

Example Suppose there are three individuals who rank items a, b, and c as illustrated in the following table.

individual	first item	second item	third item
1	a	b	c
2	b	c	a
3	c	a	b

Suppose our algorithm tried to rank the items by first comparing a to b and then comparing b to c. In comparing a to b, two of the three individuals prefer a to b, and thus we conclude a is preferable to b. In comparing b to c, again two of the three individuals prefer b to c, and we conclude that b is preferable to c. Now by transitivity one would expect that the individuals would prefer a to c, but such is not the case: only one of the individuals prefers a to c, and thus c is preferable to a. We come to the illogical conclusion that a is preferable to b, b is preferable to c, and c is preferable to a. ■

Suppose there are a number of individuals or voters and a set of candidates to be ranked. Each voter produces a ranked list of the candidates. From the set of ranked lists can one construct a reasonable single ranking of the candidates? Assume the method of producing a global ranking is required to satisfy the following three axioms.

Non-dictatorship – The algorithm cannot always simply select one individual's ranking to use as the global ranking.

Unanimity – If every individual prefers a to b, then the global ranking must prefer a to b.

Independence of irrelevant alternatives – If individuals modify their rankings but keep the order of a and b unchanged, then the global order of a and b should not change.

Arrow showed that it is not possible to satisfy all three of the above axioms. We begin with a technical lemma.

Lemma 10.1 *For a set of rankings in which each individual ranks an item b either first or last (some individuals may rank b first and others may rank b last), a global ranking satisfying the above axioms must put b first or last.*

Proof Let a, b, and c be distinct items. Suppose to the contrary that b is not first or last in the global ranking. Then there exist a and c where the global ranking puts $a > b$ and $b > c$. By transitivity, the global ranking puts $a > c$. Note that all individuals can move c above a without affecting the order of b and a or the order of b and c since b was first or last on each list. Thus, by independence of irrelevant alternatives, the global ranking would continue to rank $a > b$ and $b > c$ even if all individuals moved c above a, since that would not change the individuals relative order of a and b or the individuals relative order of b and c. But then by unanimity, the global ranking would need to put $c > a$, a contradiction. We conclude that the global ranking puts b first or last. ∎

Theorem 10.2 (Arrow) *Any deterministic algorithm for creating a global ranking from individual rankings of three or more elements in which the global ranking satisfies unanimity and independence of irrelevant alternatives is a dictatorship.*

Proof Let a, b, and c be distinct items. Consider a set of rankings in which every individual ranks b last. By unanimity, the global ranking must also rank b last. Let the individuals, one by one, move b from bottom to top leaving the other rankings in place. By unanimity, the global ranking must eventually move b from the bottom all the way to the top. When b first moves, it must move all the way to the top by Lemma 10.1.

Let v be the first individual whose change causes the global ranking of b to change. We argue that v is a dictator. First, we argue that v is a dictator for any pair ac not involving b. We will refer to the three rankings of v in Figure 10.1. The first ranking of v is the ranking prior to v moving b from the bottom to the top and the second is the ranking just after v has moved b to the top. Choose any pair ac where a is above c in v's ranking. The third ranking of v is obtained by moving a above b in the second ranking so that $a > b > c$ in v's ranking. By independence of irrelevant alternatives, the global ranking after v has switched to the third ranking puts $a > b$, since all individual ab votes are the same as in the first ranking, where the global ranking placed $a > b$. Similarly $b > c$ in

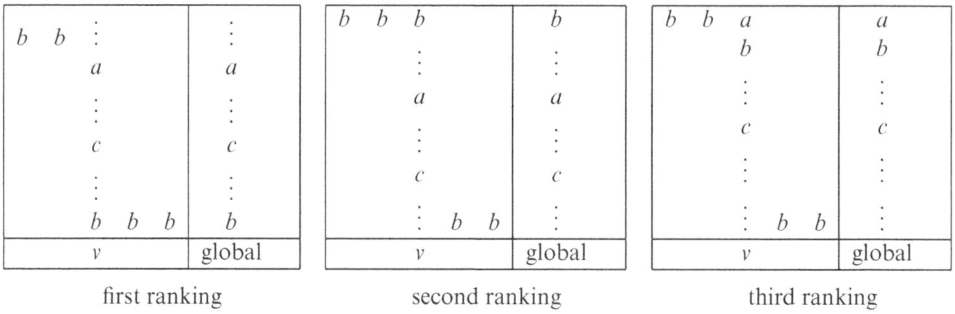

Figure 10.1: The three rankings that are used in the proof of Theorem 10.2.

the global ranking, since all individual bc votes are the same as in the second ranking, in which b was at the top of the global ranking. By transitivity the global ranking must put $a > c$, and thus the global ranking of a and c agrees with v.

Now all individuals except v can modify their rankings arbitrarily while leaving b in its extreme position, and by independence of irrelevant alternatives, this does not affect the global ranking of $a > b$ or of $b > c$. Thus, by transitivity, this does not affect the global ranking of a and c. Next, all individuals except v can move b to any position without affecting the global ranking of a and c.

At this point we have argued that independent of other individuals' rankings, the global ranking of a and c will agree with v's ranking. Now v can change its ranking arbitrarily, provided it maintains the order of a and c, and by independence of irrelevant alternatives the global ranking of a and c will not change and hence will agree with v. Thus, we conclude that for all a and c, the global ranking agrees with v independent of the other rankings except for the placement of b. But other rankings can move b without changing the global order of other elements. Thus, v is a dictator for the ranking of any pair of elements not involving b.

Note that v changed the relative order of a and b in the global ranking when it moved b from the bottom to the top in the previous argument. We will use this in a moment.

To show that individual v is also a dictator over every pair ab, repeat the construction showing that v is a dictator for every pair ac not involving b only this time place c at the bottom. There must be an individual v_c who is a dictator for any pair such as ab not involving c. Since both v and v_c can affect the global ranking of a and b independent of each other, it must be that v_c is actually v. Thus, the global ranking agrees with v no matter how the other voters modify their rankings. ■

10.1.1. Randomization

An interesting randomized algorithm that satisfies unanimity and independence of irrelevant alternatives is to pick a random individual and use that individual's ranking as the output. This is called the "random dictator" rule because it is a randomization over dictatorships. An analogous scheme in the context of voting would be to select a winner with probability proportional to the number of votes for that candidate, because this is the same as selecting a random voter and telling that voter to determine the winner. Note that this method has the appealing property that as a voter, there is never any reason to strategize, e.g., voting for candidate a rather than your preferred candidate b because you think b is unlikely to win and you don't want to throw away your vote. With this method, you should always vote for your preferred candidate.

10.1.2. Examples

Borda Count: Suppose we view each individual's ranking as giving each item a score: putting an item in last place gives it one point, putting it in second-to-last place gives it two points, third-to-last place is three points, and so on. In this case, one simple way to combine rankings is to sum up the total number of points received by each item and then sort by total points. This is called the extended Borda Count method.

Let's examine which axioms are satisfied by this approach. It is easy to see that it is a non-dictatorship. It also satisfies unanimity: if every individual prefers a to b, then every individual gives more points to a than to b, and so a will receive a higher total than b. By Arrow's theorem, the approach must fail independence of irrelevant alternatives, and indeed this is the case. Here is a simple example with three voters and four items $\{a, b, c, d\}$ where the independence of irrelevant alternatives axiom fails:

individual	ranking
1	*abcd*
2	*abcd*
3	*bacd*

In this example, a receives 11 points and is ranked first, b receives 10 points and is ranked second, c receives 6 points and is ranked third, and d receives 3 points and is ranked fourth. However, if individual 3 changes his ranking to *bcda*, then this reduces the total number of points received by a to 9, and so b is now ranked first overall. Thus, even though individual 3's relative order of b and a did not change, and indeed no individual's relative order of b and a changed, the global order of b and a did change.

Hare Voting An interesting system for voting is to have everyone vote for their favorite candidate. If some candidate receives a majority of the votes, he or she is declared the winner. If no candidate receives a majority of votes, the candidate with the fewest votes is dropped from the slate and the process is repeated.

The Hare system implements this method by asking each voter to rank all the candidates. Then one counts how many voters ranked each candidate as number one. If no candidate receives a majority, the candidate with the fewest number one votes is dropped from each voters ranking. If the dropped candidate was number one on some voters' list, then the number-two candidate becomes that voter's number-one choice. The process of counting the number-one rankings is then repeated.

We can convert the Hare voting system into a ranking method in the following way. Whichever candidate is dropped first is put in last place, whichever is dropped second is put in second-to-last place, and so on, until the system selects a winner, which is put in first place. The candidates remaining, if any, are placed between the first-place candidate and the candidates who were dropped, in an order determined by running this procedure recursively on just those remaining candidates.

As with Borda Count, the Hare system also fails to satisfy independence of irrelevant alternatives. Consider the following situation in which there are 21 voters that fall into four categories. Voters within a category rank individuals in the same order.

Category	Number of voters in category	Preference order
1	7	abcd
2	6	bacd
3	5	cbad
4	3	dcba

The Hare system would first eliminate d, since d gets only three rank one votes. Then it would eliminate b, since b gets only six rank one votes whereas a gets seven and c gets eight. At this point a is declared the winner, since a has thirteen votes to c's eight votes. So, the final ranking is *acbd*.

Now assume that Category 4 voters who prefer b to a move b up to first place. This keeps their order of a and b unchanged, but it reverses the global order of a and b. In particular, d is first eliminated, since it gets no rank one votes. Then c with five votes is eliminated. Finally, b is declared the winner with 14 votes, so the final ranking is *bacd*.

Interestingly, Category 4 voters who dislike a and have ranked a last could prevent a from winning by moving a up to first. Ironically this results in eliminating d, then c with five votes, and declaring b the winner with 11 votes. Note that by moving a up, category 4 voters were able to deny a the election and get b to win, whom they prefer over a.

10.2. Compressed Sensing and Sparse Vectors

Define a *signal* to be a vector x of length d, and define a *measurement* of x to be a dot product of x with some known vector a_i. If we wish to uniquely reconstruct x without any assumptions, then d linearly independent measurements are necessary and sufficient. Given $b = Ax$ where A is known and invertible, we can reconstruct x as $x = A^{-1}b$. In the case where there are fewer than d independent measurements and the rank of A is less than d, there will be multiple solutions. However, if we knew that x is sparse with $s \ll d$ non-zero elements, then we might be able to reconstruct x with far fewer measurements using a matrix A with $n \ll d$ rows. See Figure 10.2. In particular, it turns out that a matrix A whose columns are nearly orthogonal, such as a matrix of random Gaussian entries, will be especially well-suited to this task. This is the idea of compressed sensing. Note that we cannot make the columns of A be completely orthogonal, since A has more columns than rows.

Compressed sensing has found many applications, including reducing the number of sensors needed in photography, using the fact that images tend to be sparse in the wavelet domain, and in speeding up magnetic resonance imaging in medicine.

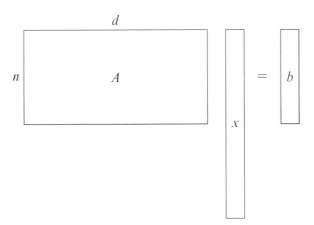

Figure 10.2: $A\mathbf{x} = \mathbf{b}$ has a vector space of solutions but possibly only one sparse solution. If the columns of A are unit length vectors that are pairwise nearly orthogonal, then the system has a unique sparse solution.

10.2.1. Unique Reconstruction of a Sparse Vector

A vector is said to be s-sparse if it has at most s non-zero elements. Let $\mathbf{x}$ be a d-dimensional, s-sparse vector with $s \ll d$. Consider solving $A\mathbf{x} = \mathbf{b}$ for $\mathbf{x}$ where A is an $n \times d$ matrix with $n < d$. The set of solutions to $A\mathbf{x} = \mathbf{b}$ is a subspace. However, if we restrict ourselves to sparse solutions, under certain conditions on A there is a unique s-sparse solution. Suppose that there were two s-sparse solutions, $\mathbf{x}_1$ and $\mathbf{x}_2$. Then $\mathbf{x}_1 - \mathbf{x}_2$ would be a $2s$-sparse solution to the homogeneous system $A\mathbf{x} = \mathbf{0}$. A $2s$-sparse solution to the homogeneous equation $A\mathbf{x} = \mathbf{0}$ requires that some $2s$ columns of A be linearly dependent. Unless A has $2s$ linearly dependent columns, there can be only one s-sparse solution.

The solution to the reconstruction problem is simple. If the matrix A has at least $2s$ rows and the entries of A were selected at random from a standard Gaussian, then with probability one, no set of $2s$ columns will be linearly dependent. We can see this by noting that if we first fix a subset of $2s$ columns and then choose the entries at random, the probability that this specific subset is linearly dependent is the same as the probability that $2s$ random Gaussian vectors in a $2s$-dimensional space are linearly dependent, which is zero.[1] So, taking the union bound over all $\binom{d}{2s}$ subsets, the probability that any one of them is linearly dependent is zero.

The above argument shows that if we choose $n = 2s$ and pick entries of A randomly from a Gaussian, with probability 1 there will be a unique s-sparse solution. Thus, to solve for $\mathbf{x}$ we could try all $\binom{d}{s}$ possible locations for the non-zero elements in $\mathbf{x}$ and aim to solve $A\mathbf{x} = \mathbf{b}$ over just those s columns of A: any one of these that gives a solution will be the correct answer. However, this takes time $\Omega(d^s)$, which is exponential in s. We turn next to the topic of efficient algorithms, describing a polynomial-time optimization procedure that will find the desired solution when n is sufficiently large and A is constructed appropriately.

---

[1] This can be seen by selecting the vectors one at a time. The probability that the ith new vector lies fully in the lower-dimensional subspace spanned by the previous $i - 1$ vectors is zero, and so by the union bound the overall probability is zero.

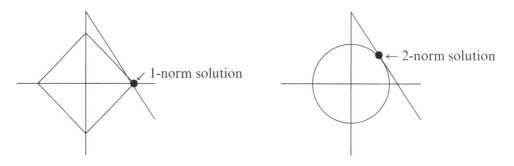

Figure 10.3: Illustration of minimum 1-norm and 2-norm solutions.

10.2.2. Efficiently Finding the Unique Sparse Solution

To find a sparse solution to $A\mathbf{x} = \mathbf{b}$, one would like to minimize the zero norm $\|\mathbf{x}\|_0$ over $\{\mathbf{x}|A\mathbf{x} = \mathbf{b}\}$, i.e., minimize the number of non-zero entries. This is a computationally hard problem. There are techniques to minimize a convex function over a convex set, but $\|\mathbf{x}\|_0$ is not a convex function, and with no further assumptions, it is NP-hard. With this in mind, we use the 1-norm as a proxy for the zero-norm and minimize the 1-norm $\|\mathbf{x}\|_1 = \sum_i |x_i|$ over $\{\mathbf{x}|A\mathbf{x} = \mathbf{b}\}$. Although this problem appears to be nonlinear, it can be solved by linear programming by writing $\mathbf{x} = \mathbf{u} - \mathbf{v}, \mathbf{u} \geq 0$, and $\mathbf{v} \geq 0$, and minimizing the linear function $\sum_i u_i + \sum_i v_i$ subject to $A\mathbf{u}-A\mathbf{v} = \mathbf{b}, \mathbf{u} \geq 0$, and $\mathbf{v} \geq 0$. See Figure 10.3 for an illustration of minimum 1-norm solutions and how they can be sparser than minimum 2-norm solutions.

We now show if the columns of the n by d matrix A are unit length almost orthogonal vectors with pairwise dot products in the range $(-\frac{1}{2s}, \frac{1}{2s})$ that minimizing $\|\mathbf{x}\|_1$ over $\{\mathbf{x}|A\mathbf{x} = \mathbf{b}\}$ recovers the unique s-sparse solution to $A\mathbf{x} = \mathbf{b}$. The ij^{th} element of the matrix $A^T A$ is the cosine of the angle between the ith and j^{th} columns of A. If the columns of A are unit length and almost orthogonal, $A^T A$ will have ones on its diagonal and all off diagonal elements will be small. By Theorem 2.8, if A has $n = s^2 \log d$ rows and each column is a random unit-length n-dimensional vector, with high probability all pairwise dot products will have magnitude less than $\frac{1}{2s}$ as desired.[2] Here, we use $s^2 \log d$, a larger value of n compared to the existence argument in Section 10.2.1, but now the algorithm is computationally efficient.

Let $\mathbf{x}_0$ denote the unique s-sparse solution to $A\mathbf{x} = \mathbf{b}$ and let $\mathbf{x}_1$ be a solution of smallest possible one-norm. Let $\mathbf{z} = \mathbf{x}_1 - \mathbf{x}_0$. We now prove that $\mathbf{z} = \mathbf{0}$ implying that $\mathbf{x}_1 = \mathbf{x}_0$. First, $A\mathbf{z} = A\mathbf{x}_1 - A\mathbf{x}_0 = \mathbf{b} - \mathbf{b} = \mathbf{0}$. This implies that $A^T A\mathbf{z} = \mathbf{0}$. Since each column of A is unit length, the matrix $A^T A$ has ones on its diagonal. Since every pair of distinct columns of A has dot product in the range $(-\frac{1}{2s}, \frac{1}{2s})$, each off-diagonal entry in $A^T A$ is in the range $(-\frac{1}{2s}, \frac{1}{2s})$. These two facts imply that unless $\mathbf{z} = \mathbf{0}$, every entry in $\mathbf{z}$ must have absolute value less than $\frac{1}{2s}\|\mathbf{z}\|_1$. If the jth entry in $\mathbf{z}$ had absolute value greater than or equal to $\frac{1}{2s}\|\mathbf{z}\|_1$, it would not be possible for the jth entry of $A^T A\mathbf{z}$ to equal 0 unless $\|\mathbf{z}\|_1 = 0$.

---

[2]Note that the roles of "n" and "d" are reversed here compared to Theorem 2.8.

Finally let S denote the support of $\mathbf{x_0}$, where $|S| \leq s$. We now argue that $\mathbf{z}$ must have at least half of its ℓ_1 norm inside of S, i.e., $\sum_{j \in S} |z_j| \geq \frac{1}{2} ||\mathbf{z}||_1$. This will complete the argument because it implies that the average value of $|z_j|$ for $j \in S$ is at least $\frac{1}{2s} ||\mathbf{z}||_1$, which as shown above is only possible if $||\mathbf{z}||_1 = 0$. Let t_{in} denote the sum of the absolute values of the entries of $\mathbf{x_1}$ in the set S, and let t_{out} denote the sum of the absolute values of the entries of $\mathbf{x_1}$ outside of S. So, $t_{in} + t_{out} = ||\mathbf{x_1}||_1$. Let t_0 be the 1-norm of $\mathbf{x_0}$. Since $\mathbf{x_1}$ is the minimum 1-norm solution, $t_0 \geq t_{in} + t_{out}$, or equivalently $t_0 - t_{in} \geq t_{out}$. But $\sum_{j \in S} |z_j| \geq t_0 - t_{in}$ and $\sum_{j \notin S} |z_j| = t_{out}$. This implies that $\sum_{j \in S} |z_j| \geq \sum_{j \notin S} |z_j|$, or equivalently, $\sum_{j \in S} |z_j| \geq \frac{1}{2} ||\mathbf{z}||_1$, which as noted above implies that $||\mathbf{z}||_1 = 0$, as desired. ■

To summarize, we have shown the following theorem and corollary.

Theorem 10.3 *If matrix A has unit-length columns $\mathbf{a_1}, \ldots, \mathbf{a_d}$ and the property that $|\mathbf{a_i} \cdot \mathbf{a_j}| < \frac{1}{2s}$ for all $i \neq j$, then if the equation $A\mathbf{x} = \mathbf{b}$ has a solution with at most s non-zero coordinates, this solution is the unique minimum 1-norm solution to $A\mathbf{x} = \mathbf{b}$.*

Corollary 10.4 *For some absolute constant c, if A has n rows for $n \geq cs^2 \log d$ and each column of A is chosen to be a random unit-length n-dimensional vector, then with high probability A satisfies the conditions of Theorem 10.3, and therefore if the equation $A\mathbf{x} = \mathbf{b}$ has a solution with at most s non-zero coordinates, this solution is the unique minimum 1-norm solution to $A\mathbf{x} = \mathbf{b}$.*

The condition of Theorem 10.3 is often called *incoherence* of the matrix A. Other more involved arguments show that it is possible to recover the sparse solution using 1-norm minimization for a number of rows n as small as $O(s \log(ds))$.

10.3. Applications

10.3.1. Biological

There are many areas where linear systems arise in which a sparse solution is unique. One is in plant breeding. Consider a breeder who has a number of apple trees and for each tree observes the strength of some desirable feature. He wishes to determine which genes are responsible for the feature so he can crossbreed to obtain a tree that better expresses the desirable feature. This gives rise to a set of equations $A\mathbf{x} = \mathbf{b}$ where each row of the matrix A corresponds to a tree and each column to a position on the genone. See Figure 10.4. The vector $\mathbf{b}$ corresponds to the strength of the desired feature in each tree. The solution $\mathbf{x}$ tells us the position on the genone corresponding to the genes that account for the feature. It would be surprising if there were two small independent sets of genes that accounted for the desired feature. Thus, the matrix should have a property that allows only one sparse solution.

10.3.2. Low-Rank Matrices

Suppose L is a low-rank matrix that has been corrupted by noise. That is, $A = L + R$. If the R is Gaussian, then principal component analysis will recover L from A. However, if L has been corrupted by several missing entries or several entries have a large

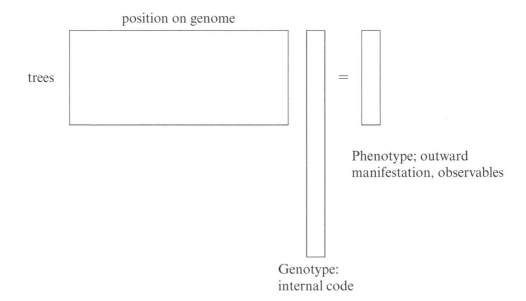

position on genome

trees

Phenotype; outward
manifestation, observables

Genotype:
internal code

Figure 10.4: The system of linear equations used to find the internal code for some observable phenomenon.

noise added to them and become outliers, then principal component analysis may be far off. However, if L is low rank and R is sparse, then L can be recovered effectively from $L + R$. To do this, find the L and R that minimize $\|L\|_* + \lambda \|R\|_1$.[3] Here the nuclear norm $\|L\|_*$ is the 1-norm of the vector of singular values of L and $\|R\|_1$ is the entrywise 1-norm $\sum_{ij} |r_{ij}|$. A small value of $\|L\|_*$ indicates a sparse vector of singular values and hence a low-rank matrix. Minimizing $\|L\|_* + \lambda \|R\|_1$ subject to $L + R = A$ is a complex problem and there has been much work on it. Notice that we do not need to know the rank of L or the elements that were corrupted. All we need is that the low-rank matrix L is not sparse and that the sparse matrix R is not low rank. We leave the proof as an exercise.

If A is a small matrix, one method to find L and R by minimizing $\|L\|_* + \|R\|_1$ is to find the singular value decomposition $A = U\Sigma V^T$ and minimize $\|\Sigma\|_1 + \|R\|_1$ subject to $A = L + R$ and $U\Sigma V^T$ being the singular value decomposition of A. This can be done using Lagrange multipliers (section 12.9.1). Write $R = R^+ + R^-$ where $R^+ \geq 0$ and $R^- \geq 0$. Let

$$f(\sigma_i, r_{ij}) = \sum_{i=1}^{n} \sigma_i + \sum_{ij} r_{ij}^+ + \sum_{ij} r_{ij}^-.$$

Write the Lagrange formula

$$l = f(\sigma_i, r_{ij}) + \sigma_i \lambda_i g_i$$

[3]To minimize the absolute value of x, write $x = u - v$ and using linear programming minimize $u + v$ subject to $u \geq 0$ and $v \geq 0$.

where the g_i are the required constraints

1. $r_{ij}^+ \geq 0$
2. $r_{ij}^- \geq 0$
3. $\sigma_i \geq 0$
4. $a_{ij} = l_{ij} + r_{ij}$
5. $u_i^T u_j = \begin{cases} 1 & i = j \\ 0 & i \neq j \end{cases}$

6. $v_i^T v_j = \begin{cases} 1 & i = j \\ 0 & i \neq j \end{cases}$
7. $l_i = \sum u_i \sigma_i v_j^T$

Conditions (5) and (6) ensure that $U \Sigma V^T$ is the svd of some matrix. The solution is obtained when $\nabla(l) = 0$, which can be found by gradient descent using $\nabla^2(l)$.

An example where low-rank matrices that have been corrupted might occur is aerial photographs of an intersection. Given a long sequence of such photographs, they will be the same except for cars and people. If each photo is converted to a vector and the vector used to make a column of a matrix, then the matrix will be low rank corrupted by the traffic. Finding the original low-rank matrix will separate the cars and people from the background.

10.4. An Uncertainty Principle

Given a function $x(t)$, one can represent the function by the composition of sinusoidal functions. Basically one is representing the time function by its frequency components. The transformation from the time representation of a function to it frequency representation is accomplished by a Fourier transform. The Fourier transform of a function $x(t)$ is given by

$$f(\omega) = \int x(t) e^{-2\pi \omega t} dt.$$

Converting the frequency representation back to the time representation is done by the inverse Fourier transformation,

$$x(t) = \int f(\omega) e^{2\pi \omega t} d\omega.$$

In the discrete case, $\mathbf{x} = [x_0, x_1, \ldots, x_{n-1}]$ and $\mathbf{f} = [f_0, f_1, \ldots, f_{n-1}]$. The Fourier transform is $\mathbf{f} = A\mathbf{x}$ with $a_{ij} = \frac{1}{\sqrt{n}} \omega^{ij}$ where ω is the principal n^{th} root of unity. The inverse transform is $\mathbf{x} = B\mathbf{f}$ where $B = A^{-1}$ has the simple form $b_{ij} = \frac{1}{\sqrt{n}} \omega^{-ij}$.

There are many other transforms such as the Laplace, wavelets, chirplets, etc. In fact, any non-singular $n \times n$ matrix can be used as a transform.

10.4.1. Sparse Vector in Some Coordinate Basis

Consider $A\mathbf{x} = \mathbf{b}$ where A is a square $n \times n$ matrix. The vectors $\mathbf{x}$ and $\mathbf{b}$ can be considered as two representations of the same quantity. For example, $\mathbf{x}$ might be a discrete time sequence, $\mathbf{b}$ the frequency spectrum of $\mathbf{x}$, and the matrix A the Fourier transform. The quantity **x** can be represented in the time domain by **x** and in the frequency domain by its Fourier transform **b**.

Any orthonormal matrix can be thought of as a transformation, and there are many important transformations other than the Fourier transformation. Consider a transformation A and a signal **x** in some standard representation. Then $\mathbf{y} = A\mathbf{x}$ transforms the signal **x** to another representation **y**. If A spreads any sparse signal **x** out so that the information contained in each coordinate in the standard basis is spread out to all coordinates in the second basis, then the two representations are said to be *incoherent*. A signal and its Fourier transform are one example of incoherent vectors. This suggests that if **x** is sparse, only a few randomly selected coordinates of its Fourier transform are needed to reconstruct **x**. In what follows we show that a signal cannot be too sparse in both its time domain and its frequency domain.

10.4.2. A Representation Cannot Be Sparse in Both Time and Frequency Domains

There is an uncertainty principle that states that a time signal cannot be sparse in both the time domain and the frequency domain. If the signal is of length n, then the product of the number of non-zero coordinates in the time domain and the number of non-zero coordinates in the frequency domain must be at least n. This is the mathematical version of Heisenberg's uncertainty principle. Before proving the uncertainty principle we first prove a technical lemma.

In dealing with the Fourier transform it is convenient for indices to run from 0 to $n-1$ rather than from 1 to n. Let $x_0, x_1, \ldots, x_{n-1}$ be a sequence and let $f_0, f_1, \ldots, f_{n-1}$ be its discrete Fourier transform. Let $i = \sqrt{-1}$. Then $f_j = \frac{1}{\sqrt{n}} \sum_{k=0}^{n-1} x_k e^{-\frac{2\pi i}{n} jk}$, $j = 0, \ldots, n-1$. In matrix form $\mathbf{f} = Z\mathbf{x}$ where $z_{jk} = e^{-\frac{2\pi i}{n} jk}$.

$$
\begin{pmatrix} f_0 \\ f_1 \\ \vdots \\ f_{n-1} \end{pmatrix} = \frac{1}{\sqrt{n}} \begin{pmatrix} 1 & 1 & 1 & \cdots & 1 \\ 1 & e^{-\frac{2\pi i}{n}} & e^{-\frac{2\pi i}{n}2} & \cdots & e^{-\frac{2\pi i}{n}(n-1)} \\ \vdots & \vdots & \vdots & & \vdots \\ 1 & e^{-\frac{2\pi i}{n}(n-1)} & e^{-\frac{2\pi i}{n}2(n-1)} & \cdots & e^{-\frac{2\pi i}{n}(n-1)^2} \end{pmatrix} \begin{pmatrix} x_0 \\ x_1 \\ \vdots \\ x_{n-1} \end{pmatrix}
$$

If some of the elements of **x** are zero, delete the zero elements of **x** and the corresponding columns of the matrix. To maintain a square matrix, let n_x be the number of non-zero elements in **x** and select n_x consecutive rows of the matrix. Normalize the columns of the resulting submatrix by dividing each element in a column by the column element in the first row. The resulting submatrix is a Vandermonde matrix that looks like

$$
\begin{pmatrix} 1 & 1 & 1 & 1 \\ a & b & c & d \\ a^2 & b^2 & c^2 & d^2 \\ a^3 & b^3 & c^3 & d^3 \end{pmatrix}
$$

and is non-singular.

Lemma 10.5 *If $x_0, x_1, \ldots, x_{n-1}$ has n_x non-zero elements, then $f_0, f_1, \ldots, f_{n-1}$ cannot have n_x consecutive zeros.*

$$\frac{1}{3}\begin{pmatrix} 1 & 1 & 1 & 1 & 1 & 1 & 1 & 1 & 1 \\ 1 & z & z^2 & z^3 & z^4 & z^5 & z^6 & z^7 & z^8 \\ 1 & z^2 & z^4 & z^6 & z^8 & z & z^3 & z^5 & z^7 \\ 1 & z^3 & z^6 & 1 & z^3 & z^6 & 1 & z^3 & z^6 \\ 1 & z^4 & z^8 & z^3 & z^7 & z^2 & z^6 & z & z^5 \\ 1 & z^5 & z & z^6 & z^2 & z^7 & z^3 & z^8 & z^4 \\ 1 & z^6 & z^3 & 1 & z^6 & z^3 & 1 & z^6 & z^3 \\ 1 & z^7 & z^5 & z^3 & z & z^8 & z^6 & z^4 & z^2 \\ 1 & z^8 & z^7 & z^6 & z^5 & z^4 & z^3 & z^2 & z \end{pmatrix}\begin{pmatrix} 1 \\ 0 \\ 0 \\ 1 \\ 0 \\ 0 \\ 1 \\ 0 \\ 0 \end{pmatrix} = \frac{1}{3}\begin{pmatrix} 3 \\ 1+z^3+z^6 \\ 1+z^6+z^3 \\ 3 \\ 1+z^3+z^6 \\ 1+z^6+z^3 \\ 3 \\ 1+z^3+z^6 \\ 1+z^6+z^3 \end{pmatrix} = \begin{pmatrix} 1 \\ 0 \\ 0 \\ 1 \\ 0 \\ 0 \\ 1 \\ 0 \\ 0 \end{pmatrix}$$

Figure 10.5: The transform of the sequence 100100100.

Proof Let $i_1, i_2, \ldots, i_{n_x}$ be the indices of the non-zero elements of **x**. Then the elements of the Fourier transform in the range $k = m+1, m+2, \ldots, m+n_x$ are

$$f_k = \frac{1}{\sqrt{n}} \sum_{j=1}^{n_x} x_{i_j} e^{\frac{-2\pi i}{n} k i_j}.$$

Note the use of i as $\sqrt{-1}$ and the multiplication of the exponent by i_j to account for the actual location of the element in the sequence. Normally, if every element in the sequence were included, we would just multiply by the index of summation.

Convert the equation to matrix form by defining $z_{kj} = \frac{1}{\sqrt{n}} \exp(-\frac{2\pi i}{n} k i_j)$ and write $\mathbf{f} = Z\mathbf{x}$ where now **x** is the vector consisting of the non-zero elements of the original **x**. By its definition, $\mathbf{x} \neq 0$. To prove the lemma we need to show that **f** is non-zero. This will be true provided Z is non-singular, since $\mathbf{x} = Z^{-1}\mathbf{f}$. If we rescale Z by dividing each column by its leading entry, we get the Vandermonde determinant, which is non-singular. ∎

Theorem 10.6 *Let n_x be the number of non-zero elements in **x** and let n_f be the number of non-zero elements in the Fourier transform of **x**. Let n_x divide n. Then $n_x n_f \geq n$.*

Proof If **x** has n_x non-zero elements, **f** cannot have a consecutive block of n_x zeros. Since n_x divides n, there are $\frac{n}{n_x}$ blocks each containing at least one non-zero element. Thus, the product of non-zero elements in **x** and **f** is at least n. ∎

The Fourier Transform of Spikes Proves That Above Bound Is Tight

To show that the bound in Theorem 10.6 is tight we show that the Fourier transform of the sequence of length n consisting of $\sqrt{n}$ ones, each one separated by $\sqrt{n}-1$ zeros, is the sequence itself. For example, the Fourier transform of the sequence 100100100 is 100100100. Thus, for this class of sequences, $n_x n_f = n$.

Theorem 10.7 *Let $S\left(\sqrt{n}, \sqrt{n}\right)$ be the sequence of 1's and 0's with $\sqrt{n}$ 1's spaced $\sqrt{n}$ apart. The Fourier transform of $S\left(\sqrt{n}, \sqrt{n}\right)$ is itself.*

—— **329** ——

Proof Consider the columns $0, \sqrt{n}, 2\sqrt{n}, \ldots, \left(\sqrt{n}-1\right)\sqrt{n}$. These are the columns for which $S\left(\sqrt{n}, \sqrt{n}\right)$ has value 1. The element of the matrix Z in the row $j\sqrt{n}$ of column $k\sqrt{n}$, $0 \le k < \sqrt{n}$ is $z^{nkj} = 1$. Thus, the product of these rows of Z times the vector $S\left(\sqrt{n}, \sqrt{n}\right)$ equals $\sqrt{n}$ and the $1/\sqrt{n}$ normalization yields $f_{j\sqrt{n}} = 1$.

For rows whose index is not of the form $j\sqrt{n}$, the row b, $b \ne j\sqrt{n}, j \in \{0, \sqrt{n}, \ldots, \sqrt{n}-1\}$, the elements in row b in the columns $0, \sqrt{n}, 2\sqrt{n}, \ldots,$ $\left(\sqrt{n}-1\right)\sqrt{n}$ are $1, z^b, z^{2b}, \ldots, z^{(\sqrt{n}-1)b}$, and thus $f_b = \frac{1}{\sqrt{n}}\left(1 + z^b + z^{2b} \cdots + z^{(\sqrt{n}-1)b}\right) = \frac{1}{\sqrt{n}}\frac{z^{\sqrt{n}b}-1}{z^b-1} = 0$, since $z^{b\sqrt{n}} = 1$ and $z^b \ne 1$. ∎

10.5. Gradient

The gradient of a function $f(\mathbf{x})$ of d variables, $\mathbf{x} = (x_1, x_2, \ldots, x_d)$, at a point $\mathbf{x_0}$ is denoted $\nabla f(\mathbf{x_0})$. It is a d-dimensional vector with components $\frac{\partial f(\mathbf{x_0})}{\partial x_1}, \frac{\partial f(\mathbf{x_0})}{\partial x_2}, \ldots, \frac{\partial f(\mathbf{x_0})}{\partial x_d}$, where $\frac{\partial f}{\partial x_i}$ are partial derivatives. Without explicitly stating, we assume that the derivatives referred to exist. The rate of increase of the function f as we move from $\mathbf{x_0}$ in a direction $\mathbf{u}$ is $\nabla f(\mathbf{x_0}) \cdot \mathbf{u}$. So the direction of steepest descent is $-\nabla f(\mathbf{x_0})$; this is a natural direction to move to minimize f. But by how much should we move? A large move may overshoot the minimum. See Figure 10.6. A simple fix is to minimize f on the line from $\mathbf{x_0}$ in the direction of steepest descent by solving a one dimensional minimization problem. This gives us the next iterate $\mathbf{x_1}$ and we repeat. We do not discuss the issue of step size any further. Instead, we focus on infinitesimal gradient descent, where the algorithm makes infinitesimal moves in the $-\nabla f(\mathbf{x_0})$ direction. Whenever $\nabla \mathbf{f}$ is not the zero vector, we strictly decrease the function in the direction $-\nabla \mathbf{f}$, so the current point is not a minimum of the function f. Conversely, a point $\mathbf{x}$ where $\nabla \mathbf{f} = \mathbf{0}$ is called a *first-order local optimum* of f. A first-order local optimum may be a local minimum, local maximum, or a saddle point. We ignore saddle points, since numerical error is likely to prevent gradient descent from stoping at a saddle point. In general, local minima do not have to be global minima (see Figure 10.6), and gradient descent may converge to a local minimum that is not a global minimum. When the function f is convex, this is not the case.

A function f of a single variable x is said to be convex if for any two points a and b the line joining $f(a)$ and $f(b)$ is above the curve $f(\cdot)$. A function of many variables is convex if on any line segment in its domain it acts as a convex function of one variable on the line segment.

Definition 10.1 *A function f over a convex domain is a convex function if for any two points $\mathbf{x}$ and $\mathbf{y}$ in the domain and any λ in $[0, 1]$ we have*

$$f(\lambda \mathbf{x} + (1-\lambda)\mathbf{y}) \le \lambda f(\mathbf{x}) + (1-\lambda)f(\mathbf{y}).$$

The function is concave if the inequality is satisfied with $\ge$ instead of $\le$.

Theorem 10.8 *Suppose f is a convex, differentiable function defined on a closed bounded convex domain. Then any first-order local minimum is also a global minimum. Infinitesimal gradient descent always reaches the global minimum.*

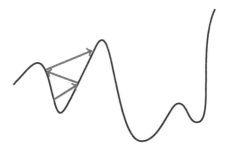

Figure 10.6: Gradient descent overshooting minimum.

Proof We will prove that if $\mathbf{x}$ is a local minimum, then it must be a global minimum. If not, consider a global minimum point $\mathbf{y} \neq \mathbf{x}$. On the line joining $\mathbf{x}$ and $\mathbf{y}$, the function must not go above the line joining $f(\mathbf{x})$ and $f(\mathbf{y})$. This means for an infinitesimal $\varepsilon > 0$, moving distance ε from $\mathbf{x}$ toward $\mathbf{y}$, the function must decrease, so $\triangledown\mathbf{f}(\mathbf{x})$ is not $\mathbf{0}$, contradicting the assumption that $\mathbf{x}$ is a local minimum. ∎

The second derivatives $\frac{\partial^2}{\partial x_i \partial x_j}$ form a matrix, called the Hessian, denoted $H(f(\mathbf{x}))$. The Hessian of f at $\mathbf{x}$ is a symmetric $d \times d$ matrix with ij^{th} entry $\frac{\partial^2 f}{\partial x_i \partial x_j}(\mathbf{x})$. The second derivative of f at $\mathbf{x}$ in the direction $\mathbf{u}$ is the rate of change of the first derivative in the direction $\mathbf{u}$ from $\mathbf{x}$. It is easy to see that it equals

$$\mathbf{u}^T H(f(\mathbf{x}))\mathbf{u}.$$

To see this, note that the second derivative of f along the unit vector $\mathbf{u}$ is

$$\sum_j u_j \frac{\partial}{\partial x_j} (\triangledown f(\mathbf{x}) \cdot \mathbf{u}) = \sum_j u_j \sum_i \frac{\partial}{\partial x_j} \left(u_i \frac{\partial f(\mathbf{x})}{\partial x_i} \right)$$

$$= \sum_{j,i} u_j u_i \frac{\partial^2 f(\mathbf{x})}{\partial x_j \partial x_i}.$$

Theorem 10.9 *Suppose f is a function from a closed convex domain D in $\mathbf{R}^d$ to the reals and the Hessian of f exists everywhere in D. Then f is convex (concave) on D if and only if the Hessian of f is positive (negative) semi-definite everywhere on D.*

Gradient descent requires the gradient to exist. But even if the gradient is not always defined, one can minimize a convex function over a convex domain efficiently, i.e., in polynomial time. Technically, one can only find an approximate minimum, and the time depends on the error parameter as well as the presentation of the convex set. We do not go into these details. But in principle, we can minimize a convex function over a convex domain. We can also maximize a concave function over a concave domain. However, in general, we do not have efficient procedures to maximize a convex function over a convex domain. It is easy to see that at a first-order local minimum of a possibly non-convex function, the gradient vanishes. But second-order local decrease of the function may be possible. The steepest second-order decrease is in the direction of $\pm\mathbf{v}$, where $\mathbf{v}$ is the eigenvector of the Hessian corresponding to the largest absolute valued eigenvalue.

10.6. Linear Programming

Linear programming is an optimization problem that has been carefully studied and is immensely useful. We consider linear programming problem in the following form where A is an $m \times n$ matrix, $m \leq n$, of rank m, $\mathbf{c}$ is $1 \times n$, $\mathbf{b}$ is $m \times 1$, and $\mathbf{x}$ is $n \times 1$:

$$\max \ \mathbf{c} \cdot \mathbf{x} \quad \text{subject to} \quad A\mathbf{x} = \mathbf{b}, \ \mathbf{x} \geq 0.$$

Inequality constraints can be converted to this form by adding slack variables. Also, we can do Gaussian elimination on A and if it does not have rank m, we either find that the system of equations has no solution, whence we may stop; or we can find and discard redundant equations. After this preprocessing, we may assume that A's rows are independent.

The simplex algorithm is a classical method to solve linear programming problems. It is a vast subject and is well discussed in many texts. Here, we will discuss the ellipsoid algorithm, which is in a sense based more on continuous mathematics and is closer to the spirit of this book.

10.6.1. The Ellipsoid Algorithm

The first polynomial time algorithm for linear programming[4] was developed by Khachiyan based on work of Iudin, Nemirovsky, and Shor and is called the *ellipsoid algorithm*. The algorithm is best stated for the seemingly simpler problem of determining whether there is a solution to $A\mathbf{x} \leq \mathbf{b}$ and, if so, finding one. The ellipsoid algorithm starts with a large ball in d-space that is guaranteed to contain the polyhedron $A\mathbf{x} \leq \mathbf{b}$. Even though we do not yet know if the polyhedron is empty or non-empty, such a ball can be found. The algorithm checks if the center of the ball is in the polyhedron; if it is, we have achieved our objective. If not, we know from the Separating Hyperplane Theorem of convex geometry that there is a hyperplane called the *separating hyperplane* through the center of the ball such that the whole polytope lies in one of the half spaces.

We then find an ellipsoid that contains the ball intersected with this half-space. See Figure 10.7. The ellipsoid is guaranteed to contain $Ax \leq b$ as was the ball earlier. If the center of the ellipsoid does not satisfy the inequalities, then again there is a separating hyperplane, and we repeat the process. After a suitable number of steps, either we find a solution to the original $A\mathbf{x} \leq \mathbf{b}$ or we end up with a very small ellipsoid. If the original A and $\mathbf{b}$ had integer entries, one can ensure that the set $A\mathbf{x} \leq \mathbf{b}$, after a slight perturbation that preserves its emptiness/non-emptiness, has a volume of at least some $\epsilon > 0$. If our ellipsoid has shrunk to a volume of less

---

[4]Although there are examples where the simplex algorithm requires exponential time, it was shown by Shanghua Teng and Dan Spielman that the expected running time of the simplex algorithm on an instance produced by taking an arbitrary instance and then adding small Gaussian perturbations to it is polynomial.

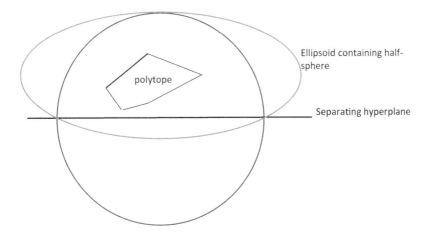

Figure 10.7: Ellipsoid algorithm.

than this ϵ, then there is no solution. Clearly this must happen within $\log_\rho V_0/\epsilon = O(V_0 d/\epsilon)$ steps, where V_0 is an upper bound on the initial volume and ρ is the factor by which the volume shrinks in each step. We do not go into details of how to get a value for V_0, but the important points are that (1) only the logarithm of V_0 appears in the bound on the number of steps, and (2) the dependence on d is linear. These features ensure a polynomial time algorithm.

The main difficulty in proving fast convergence is to show that the volume of the ellipsoid shrinks by a certain factor in each step. Thus, the question can be phrased as: suppose E is an ellipsoid with center $\mathbf{x_0}$ and consider the half-ellipsoid E' defined by

$$E' = \{\mathbf{x} | \mathbf{x} \in E, \ \mathbf{a} \cdot (\mathbf{x} - \mathbf{x_0}) \geq 0\}$$

where $\mathbf{a}$ is some unit length vector. Let $\hat{E}$ be the smallest volume ellipsoid containing E'. Show that

$$\frac{\text{Vol}(\hat{E})}{\text{Vol}(E)} \leq 1 - \rho$$

for some $\rho > 0$. A sequence of geometric reductions transforms this into a simple problem. Translate and then rotate the coordinate system so that $\mathbf{x_0} = 0$ and $\mathbf{a} = (1, 0, 0, \ldots, 0)$. Finally, apply a non-singular linear transformation τ so that $\tau E = B = \{\mathbf{x} | \, |\mathbf{x}| = 1\}$, the unit sphere. The important point is that a non-singular linear transformation τ multiplies the volumes of all sets by $|\det(\tau)|$, so that $\frac{\text{Vol}(\hat{E})}{\text{Vol}(E)} = \frac{\text{Vol}(\tau(\hat{E}))}{\text{Vol}(\tau(E))}$. The following lemma answers the question raised.

Lemma 10.10 *Consider the half-sphere* $B' = \{\mathbf{x} | x_1 \geq 0, \ |\mathbf{x}| \leq 1\}$. *The following ellipsoid* $\hat{E}$ *contains* B':

$$\hat{E} = \left\{ \mathbf{x} \left| \left(\frac{d+1}{d}\right)^2 \left(x_1 - \frac{1}{d+1}\right)^2 + \left(\frac{d^2-1}{d^2}\right)\left(x_2^2 + x_3^2 + \ldots + x_d^2\right) \leq 1 \right. \right\}.$$

Further,

$$\frac{Vol(\hat{E})}{Vol(B)} = \left(\frac{d}{d+1}\right)\left(\frac{d^2}{d^2-1}\right)^{(d-1)/2} \le 1 - \frac{1}{4d}.$$

The proof is left as an exercise (Exercise 10.27).

10.7. Integer Optimization

The problem of maximizing a linear function subject to linear inequality constraints, but with the variables constrained to be integers, is called integer programming.

$$\text{Max } \mathbf{c} \cdot \mathbf{x} \quad \text{subject to } A\mathbf{x} \le \mathbf{b} \text{ with } x_i \text{ integers}$$

This problem is NP-hard. One way to handle the hardness is to relax the integer constraints, solve the linear program in polynomial time, and round the fractional values to integers. The simplest rounding – round each variable that is 1/2 or more to 1, the rest to 0 – yields sensible results in some cases. The vertex cover problem is one of them. The problem is to choose a subset of vertices so that each edge is covered with at least one of its end points in the subset. The integer program is:

$$\text{Min } \sum_i x_i \quad \text{subject to } x_i + x_j \ge 1 \ \forall \text{ edges } (i,j); \quad x_i \text{ integers.}$$

Solve the linear program. At least one variable for each edge must be at least 1/2 and the simple rounding converts it to 1. The integer solution is still feasible. It clearly at most doubles the objective function from the linear programming solution, and since the LP solution value is at most the optimal integer programming solution value, we are within a factor of 2 of the optimal.

10.8. Semi-Definite Programming

Semi-definite programs are special cases of convex programs. Recall that an $n \times n$ matrix A is positive semi-definite if and only if A is symmetric and for all $\mathbf{x} \in \mathbf{R}^n, \mathbf{x}^T A\mathbf{x} \ge 0$. There are many equivalent characterizations of positive semi-definite matrices. We mention one. A symmetric matrix A is positive semi-definite if and only if it can be expressed as $A = BB^T$ for a possibly rectangular matrix B.

A semi-definite program (SDP) is the problem of minimizing a linear function $\mathbf{c}^T \mathbf{x}$ subject to a constraint that $F = F_0 + F_1 x_1 + F_2 x_2 + \cdots + F_d x_d$ is positive semi-definite. Here $F_0, F_1, \ldots, F_d$ are given symmetric matrices.

This is a convex program, since the set of $\mathbf{x}$ satisfying the constraint is a convex set. To see this, note that if $F(\mathbf{x}) = F_0 + F_1 x_1 + F_2 x_2 + \cdots + F_d x_d$ and $F(\mathbf{y}) = F_0 + F_1 y_1 + F_2 y_2 + \cdots + F_d y_d$ are positive semi-definite, then so is $F(\alpha \mathbf{x} + (1-\alpha)\mathbf{y})$ for $0 \le \alpha \le 1$. In principle, SDPs can be solved in polynomial time. It turns out that there are more efficient algorithms for SDPs than general convex programs and that many interesting problems can be formulated as SDPs. We discuss the latter aspect here.

Linear programs are special cases of SDPs. For any vector $\mathbf{v}$, let $\text{diag}(\mathbf{v})$ denote a diagonal matrix with the components of $\mathbf{v}$ on the diagonal. Then it is easy to see that the constraints $\mathbf{v} \geq \mathbf{0}$ are equivalent to the constraint $\text{diag}(\mathbf{v})$ is positive semi-definite. Consider the linear program:

$$\text{Minimize } \mathbf{c}^T\mathbf{x} \text{ subject to } A\mathbf{x} = \mathbf{b}; \quad \mathbf{x} \geq \mathbf{0}.$$

Rewrite $A\mathbf{x} = \mathbf{b}$ as $A\mathbf{x} - \mathbf{b} \geq \mathbf{0}$ and $\mathbf{b} - A\mathbf{x} \geq \mathbf{0}$ and use the idea of diagonal matrices above to formulate this as an SDP.

A second interesting example is that of quadratic programs of the form:

$$\text{Minimize } \frac{\left(\mathbf{c}^T\mathbf{x}\right)^2}{\mathbf{d}^T\mathbf{x}} \text{ subject to } A\mathbf{x} + \mathbf{b} \geq \mathbf{0}.$$

This is equivalent to

$$\text{Minimize } t \text{ subject to } A\mathbf{x} + \mathbf{b} \geq \mathbf{0} \text{ and } t \geq \frac{\left(\mathbf{c}^T\mathbf{x}\right)^2}{\mathbf{d}^T\mathbf{x}}.$$

This is in turn equivalent to the SDP

Minimize t subject to the following matrix being positive semi-definite:

$$\begin{pmatrix} \text{diag}(A\mathbf{x} + \mathbf{b}) & 0 & 0 \\ 0 & t & \mathbf{c}^T\mathbf{x} \\ 0 & \mathbf{c}^T\mathbf{x} & \mathbf{d}^T\mathbf{x} \end{pmatrix}.$$

Application to Approximation Algorithms

An exciting area of application of SDP is in finding near-optimal solutions to some integer problems. The central idea is best illustrated by its early application in a breakthrough due to Goemans and Williamson [GW95] for the maximum cut problem that, given a graph $G(V, E)$, asks for the cut $S, \bar{S}$ maximizing the number of edges going across the cut from S to $\bar{S}$. For each $i \in V$, let x_i be an integer variable assuming values ± 1 depending on whether $i \in S$ or $i \in \bar{S}$ respectively. Then the max-cut problem can be posed as

$$\text{Maximize } \sum_{(i,j) \in E} (1 - x_i x_j) \text{ subject to the constraints } x_i \in \{-1, +1\}.$$

The integrality constraint on the x_i makes the problem NP-hard. Instead replace the integer constraints by allowing the $\mathbf{x_i}$ to be unit length vectors. This enlarges the set of feasible solutions, since ± 1 are just one-dimensional vectors of length 1. The relaxed problem is an SDP and can be solved in polynomial time. To see that it is an SDP, consider $\mathbf{x_i}$ as the rows of a matrix X. The variables of our SDP are not X, but actually $Y = XX^T$, which is a positive semi-definite matrix. The SDP is

$$\text{Maximize } \sum_{(i,j) \in E} (1 - y_{ij}) \text{ subject to } Y \text{ positive semi-definite,}$$

which can be solved in polynomial time. From the solution Y, find X satisfying $Y = XX^T$. Now, instead of a ± 1 label on each vertex, we have vector labels, namely the rows of X. We need to round the vectors to ± 1 to get an S. One natural way to do this is to pick a random vector $\mathbf{v}$ and if for vertex i, $\mathbf{x_i} \cdot \mathbf{v}$ is positive, put i in S, otherwise put it in $\bar{S}$. Goemans and Williamson showed that this method produces a cut guaranteed to be at least 0.878 times the maximum. The 0.878 factor is a big improvement on the previous best factor of 0.5, which is easy to get by putting each vertex into S with probability 1/2.

Application to Machine Learning

As discussed in Chapter 5, kernel functions are a powerful tool in machine learning. They allow one to apply algorithms that learn linear classifiers, such as Perceptron and Support Vector Machines, to problems where the positive and negative examples might have a more complicated separating curve.

More specifically, a kernel K is a function from pairs of examples to reals such that for some implicit function ϕ from examples to $\Re^N$, we have $K(a, a') = \phi(a)^T \phi(a')$. (We are using a and a' to refer to examples, rather than x and x', in order to not conflict with the notation used earlier in this chapter.) Notice that this means that for any set of examples $\{a_1, a_2, \ldots, a_n\}$, the matrix A whose ij entry equals $K(a_i, a_j)$ is positive semi-definite. Specifically, $A = BB^T$ where the ith row of B equals $\phi(a_i)$.

Given that a kernel corresponds to a positive semi-definite matrix, it is not surprising that there is a related use of semi-definite programming in machine learning. In particular, suppose that one does not want to specify up front exactly which kernel an algorithm should use. In that case, a natural idea is instead to specify a space of kernel functions and allow the algorithm to select the best one from that space for the given data. Specifically, given some labeled training data and some unlabeled test data, one could solve for the matrix A over the combined data set that is positive semi-definite (so that it is a legal kernel function) and optimizes some given objective. This objective might correspond to separating the positive and negative examples in the labeled data while keeping the kernel simple so that it does not over-fit. If this objective is linear in the coefficients of A along with possibly additional linear constraints on A, then this is an SDP. This is the high-level idea of kernel learning, first proposed in [LCB+04].

10.9. Bibliographic Notes

Arrow's impossibility theorem, stating that any ranking of three or more items satisfying unanimity and independence of irrelevant alternatives must be a dictatorship, is from [Arr50]. For extensions to Arrow's theorem on the manipulability of voting rules, see Gibbard [Gib73] and Satterthwaite [Sat75]. A good discussion of issues in social choice appears in [Lis13]. The results presented in Section 10.2.2 on compressed sensing are due to Donoho and Elad [DE03] and Gribonval and Nielsen [GN03]. See [Don06] for more details on issues in compressed sensing. The ellipsoid algorithm for linear programming is due to Khachiyan [Kha79] based on work of Shor [Sho70] and Iudin and Nemirovski [IN77]. For more information on the ellipsoid algorithm and on semi-definite programming, see the book of Grötschel, Lovász, and Schrijver [GLS12]. The use of SDPs for approximating the max-cut problem is due to Goemans and Williamson[GW95], and the use of SDPs for learning a kernel function is due to [LCB+04].

10.10. Exercises

Exercise 10.1 Select a method that you believe is good for combining individual rank-ings into a global ranking. Consider a set of rankings where each individual ranks b last. One by one move b from the bottom to the top leaving the other rankings in place. Does there exist a v as in Theorem 10.2 where v is the ranking that causes b to move from the bottom to the top in the global ranking. If not, does your method of combing individual rankings satisfy the axioms of unanimity and independence of irrelevant alternatives.

Exercise 10.2 Show that for the three axioms – non-dictator, unanimity, and inde-pendence of irrelevant alternatives – it is possible to satisfy any two of the three.

Exercise 10.3 Does the axiom of independence of irrelevant alternatives make sense? What if there were three rankings of five items? In the first two rankings, A is number one and B is number two. In the third ranking, B is number one and A is number five. One might compute an average score where a low score is good. A gets a score of $1 + 1 + 5 = 7$ and B gets a score of $2 + 2 + 1 = 5$ and B is ranked number one in the global ranking. Now if the third ranker moves A up to the second position, A's score becomes $1 + 1 + 2 = 4$ and the global ranking of A and B changes even though no individual ordering of A and B changed. Is there some alternative axiom to replace independence of irrelevant alternatives? Write a paragraph on your thoughts on this issue.

Exercise 10.4 Prove that in the proof of Theorem 10.2, the global ranking agrees with column v even if item b is moved down through the column.

Exercise 10.5 Let A be an m by n matrix with elements from a zero mean, unit vari-ance Gaussian. How large must n be for there to be two or more sparse solutions to $Ax = b$ with high probability? You will need to define how small s should be for a solution with at most s non-zero elements to be sparse.

Exercise 10.6 Section 10.2.1 showed that if A is an $n \times d$ matrix with entries selected at random from a standard Gaussian, and $n \geq 2s$, then with probability 1 there will be a unique s-sparse solution to $Ax = b$. Show that if $n \leq s$, then with probability 1 there will *not* be a unique s-sparse solution. Assume $d > s$.

Exercise 10.7 Section 10.2.2 used the fact that $n = O(s^2 \log d)$ rows is sufficient so that if each column of A is a random unit-length n-dimensional vector, then with high probability all pairwise dot products of columns will have magnitude less than $\frac{1}{2s}$. Here, we show that $n = \Omega(\log d)$ rows is necessary as well. To make the notation less confusing for this argument, we will use m instead of d.

Specifically, prove that for $m > 3^n$, it is not possible to have m unit-length n-dimensional vectors such that all pairwise dot products of those vectors are less than $\frac{1}{2}$.

Some hints: (1) note that if two unit-length vectors $\mathbf{u}$ and $\mathbf{v}$ have dot product greater than or equal to $\frac{1}{2}$, then $|\mathbf{u} - \mathbf{v}| \leq 1$ (if their dot product is equal to $\frac{1}{2}$ then $\mathbf{u}, \mathbf{v}$, and the origin form an equilateral triangle). So, it is enough to prove that $m > 3^n$ unit-length vectors in $\mathfrak{R}^n$ cannot all have distance at least 1 from each other; (2) use the fact that the volume of a ball of radius r in $\mathfrak{R}^n$ is proportional to r^n.

Exercise 10.8 Create a random 100-by-100 orthonormal matrix A and a sparse 100-dimensional vector $\mathbf{x}$. Compute $Ax = b$. Randomly select a few coordinates of

b and reconstruct **x** from the samples of **b** using the minimization of 1-norm technique of Section 10.2.2. Did you get **x** back?

Exercise 10.9 Let A be a low-rank $n \times m$ matrix. Let r be the rank of A. Let $\tilde{A}$ be A corrupted by Gaussian noise. Prove that the rank r SVD approximation to $\tilde{A}$ minimizes $|A - \tilde{A}|_F^2$.

Exercise 10.10 Prove that minimizing $\|x\|_0$ subject to $Ax = b$ is NP-complete.

Exercise 10.11 When one wants to minimize $\|x\|_0$ subject to some constraint, the problem is often NP-hard and one uses the 1-norm as a proxy for the 0-norm. To get an insite into this issue consider minimizing $\|x\|_0$ subject to the constraint that x lies in a convex region. For simplicity assume the convex region is a sphere with center more than the radius of the circle from the origin. Explore sparsity of solution when minimizing the 1-norm for values of x in the circular region with regards to location of the center.

Exercise 10.12 Express the matrix

$$
\begin{array}{ccccc}
2 & 17 & 2 & 2 & 2 \\
2 & 2 & 2 & 2 & 2 \\
2 & 2 & 2 & 9 & 2 \\
2 & 2 & 2 & 2 & 2 \\
13 & 2 & 2 & 2 & 2
\end{array}
$$

as the sum of a low rank matrix plus a sparse matrix. To simplify the computation assume you want the low-rank matrix to be symmetric so that its singular valued decomposition will be $V\Sigma V^T$.

Exercise 10.13 Generate 100×100 matrices of rank 20, 40, 60 80, and 100. In each matrix randomly delete 50, 100, 200, or 400 entries. In each case try to recover the original matrix. How well do you do?

Exercise 10.14 Repeat the previous exercise but instead of deleting elements, corrupt the elements by adding a reasonable size corruption to the randomly selected matrix entries.

Exercise 10.15 Compute the Fourier transform of the sequence 1000010000.

Exercise 10.16 What is the Fourier transform of a Gaussian?

Exercise 10.17 What is the Fourier transform of a cyclic shift of a sequence?

Exercise 10.18 Let $S(i,j)$ be the sequence of i blocks each of length j where each block of symbols is a 1 followed by $j - 1$ 0's. The number n = 6 is factorable but not a perfect square. What is Fourier transform of $S(2,3) = 100100$?

Exercise 10.19 Let Z be the n root of unity. Prove that $\{z^{bi} | 0 \le i < n\} = \{z^i | 0 \le i < n\}$ provided that b does not divide n.

Exercise 10.20 Show that if the elements in the second row of the $n \times n$ Vandermonde matrix

$$\begin{pmatrix} 1 & 1 & \cdots & 1 \\ a & b & \cdots & c \\ a^2 & b^2 & \cdots & c^2 \\ \vdots & \vdots & & \vdots \\ a^{n-1} & b^{n-1} & \cdots & c^{n-1} \end{pmatrix}$$

are distinct, then the Vandermonde matrix is non-singular by expressing the determinant of the matrix as an $n - 1$ degree polynomial in a.

Exercise 10.21 Show that the following two statements are equivalent.

1. If the elements in the second row of the $n \times n$ Vandermonde matrix

$$\begin{pmatrix} 1 & 1 & \cdots & 1 \\ a & b & \cdots & c \\ a^2 & b^2 & \cdots & c^2 \\ \vdots & \vdots & & \vdots \\ a^{n-1} & b^{n-1} & \cdots & c^{n-1} \end{pmatrix}$$

are distinct, then the Vandermonde matrix is non-singular.
2. Specifying the value of a polynomial of degree n–1 at n points uniquely determines the polynomial.

Exercise 10.22 Many problems can be formulated as finding $\mathbf{x}$ satisfying $A\mathbf{x} = \mathbf{b}$ where A has more columns than rows and there is a subspace of solutions. If one knows that the solution is sparse but some error in the measurement $\mathbf{b}$ may prevent finding the sparse solution, they might add some residual error to $\mathbf{b}$ and reformulate the problem as solving for $\mathbf{x}$ and $\mathbf{r}$ subject to $A\mathbf{x} = \mathbf{b} + \mathbf{r}$ where $\mathbf{r}$ is the residual error. Discuss the advantages and disadvantages of each of the following three versions of the problem.

1. Set $\mathbf{r} = 0$ and find $\mathbf{x} = argmin \, \|\mathbf{x}\|_1$ satisfying $A\mathbf{x} = \mathbf{b}$
2. Lasso: find $\mathbf{x} = argmin \left(\|\mathbf{x}\|_1 + \alpha \, \|\mathbf{r}\|_2^2 \right)$ satisfying $A\mathbf{x} = \mathbf{b} + \mathbf{r}$
3. find $\underline{x} = argmin \, \|\mathbf{x}\|_1$ such that $\|\mathbf{r}\|_2^2 < \varepsilon$

Exercise 10.23 Let $M = L + R$ where L is a low-rank matrix corrupted by a sparse noise matrix R. Why can we not recover L from M if R is low rank or if L is sparse?

Exercise 10.24

1. Suppose for a univariate convex function f and a finite interval D, $|f''(x)| \leq \delta |f'(x)|$ for every x. Then, what is a good step size to choose for gradient descent? Derive a bound on the number of steps needed to get an approximate minimum of f in terms of as few parameters as possible.
2. Generalize the statement and proof to convex functions of d variables.

Exercise 10.25 Prove that the maximum of a convex function over a polytope is attained at one of its vertices.

Exercise 10.26 Create a convex function and a convex region where the maximization problem has local maximuns.

Exercise 10.27 Prove Lemma 10.10.

Exercise 10.28 Consider the following symmetric matrix A:

$$\begin{pmatrix} 1 & 0 & 1 & 1 \\ 0 & 1 & 1 & -1 \\ 1 & 1 & 2 & 0 \\ 1 & -1 & 0 & 2 \end{pmatrix}$$

Find four vectors $\mathbf{v_1}, \mathbf{v_2}, \mathbf{v_3}, \mathbf{v_4}$ such that $a_{ij} = \mathbf{v_i}^T \mathbf{v_j}$ for all $1 \leq i, j \leq 4$. Also, find a matrix B such that $A = BB^T$.

Exercise 10.29 Prove that if A_1 and A_2 are positive semi-definite matrices, then so is $A_1 + A_2$.

CHAPTER ELEVEN

Wavelets

Given a vector space of functions, one would like an orthonormal set of basis functions that span the space. The Fourier transform provides a set of basis functions based on sines and cosines. Often we are dealing with functions that have finite support, in which case we would like the basis vectors to have finite support. Also we would like to have an efficient algorithm for computing the coefficients of the expansion of a function in the basis.

11.1. Dilation

We begin our development of wavelets by first introducing dilation. A *dilation* is a mapping that scales all distances by the same factor.

A dilation equation is an equation where a function is defined in terms of a linear combination of scaled, shifted versions of itself. For instance,

$$f(x) = \sum_{k=0}^{d-1} c_k f(2x - k).$$

An example of this is $f(x) = f(2x) + f(2x - 1)$, which has a solution $f(x)$ equal to 1 for $0 \leq x < 1$ and is zero elsewhere. The equation is illustrated in the figure below. The solid rectangle is $f(x)$ and the dotted rectangles are $f(2x)$ and $f(2x - 1)$.

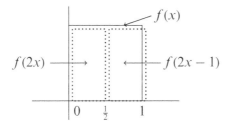

Another example is $f(x) = \frac{1}{2}f(2x) + f(2x-1) + \frac{1}{2}f(2x-2)$. A solution is illustrated in the figure below. The function $f(x)$ is indicated by solid lines. The functions $\frac{1}{2}f(2x), f(2x+1)$, and $\frac{1}{2}f(2x-2)$ are indicated by dotted lines.

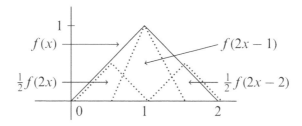

If a dilation equation is of the form $\sum_{k=1}^{d-1} c_k f(2x-k)$, then we say that all dilations in the equation are factor of two reductions.

Lemma 11.1 *If a dilation equation in which all the dilations are a factor of two reduction has a solution, then either the coefficients on the right-hand side of the equation sum to 2 or the integral $\int_{-\infty}^{\infty} f(x)dx$ of the solution is zero.*

Proof Integrate both sides of the dilation equation from $-\infty$ to $+\infty$.

$$\int_{-\infty}^{\infty} f(x)dx = \int_{-\infty}^{\infty} \sum_{k=0}^{d-1} c_k f(2x-k)dx = \sum_{k=0}^{d-1} c_k \int_{-\infty}^{\infty} f(2x-k)dx$$

$$= \sum_{k=0}^{d-1} c_k \int_{-\infty}^{\infty} f(2x)dx = \frac{1}{2}\sum_{k=0}^{d-1} c_k \int_{-\infty}^{\infty} f(x)dx$$

If $\int_{-\infty}^{\infty} f(x)dx \neq 0$, then dividing both sides by $\int_{-\infty}^{\infty} f(x)dx$ gives $\sum_{k=0}^{d-1} c_k = 2$ ∎

The above proof interchanged the order of the summation and the integral. This is valid provided the 1-norm of the function is finite. Also note that there are non-zero solutions to dilation equations in which all dilations are a factor of two reduction where the coefficients do not sum to two such as

$$f(x) = f(2x) + f(2x-1) + f(2x-2) + f(2x-3)$$

or

$$f(x) = f(2x) + 2f(2x-1) + 2f(2x-2) + 2f(2x-3) + f(2x-4).$$

In these examples $f(x)$ takes on both positive and negative values and $\int_{-\infty}^{\infty} f(x) dx = 0$.

11.2. The Haar Wavelet

Let $\phi(x)$ be a solution to the dilation equation $f(x) = f(2x) + f(2x-1)$. The function ϕ is called a *scale function* or *scale vector* and is used to generate the two-dimensional family of functions, $\phi_{jk}(x) = \phi(2^j x - k)$, where j and k are nonnegative integers (see Figure 11.1). Other authors scale $\phi_{jk} = \phi(2^j x - k)$ by $2^{\frac{j}{2}}$ so that the 2-norm,

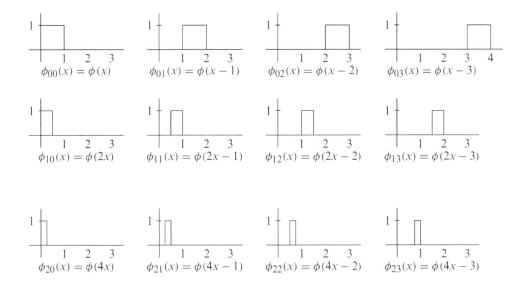

Figure 11.1: Set of scale functions associated with the Haar wavelet.

$\int_{-\infty}^{\infty} \phi_{jk}^2(t)dt$, is 1. However, for educational purposes, simplifying the notation for ease of understanding was preferred.

For a given value of j, the shifted versions, $\{\phi_{jk}|k \geq 0\}$, span a space V_j. The spaces $V_0, V_1, V_2, \ldots$ are larger and larger spaces and allow better and better approximations to a function. The fact that $\phi(x)$ is the solution of a dilation equation implies that for any fixed j, ϕ_{jk} is a linear combination of the $\{\phi_{j+1,k'}|k' \geq 0\}$, and this ensures that $V_j \subseteq V_{j+1}$. It is for this reason that it is desirable in designing a wavelet system for the scale function to satisfy a dilation equation. For a given value of j, the shifted ϕ_{jk} are orthogonal in the sense that $\int_x \phi_{jk}(x)\phi_{jl}(x)dx = 0$ for $k \neq l$.

Note that for each j, the set of functions ϕ_{jk}, $k = 0, 1, 2\ldots$, form a basis for a vector space V_j and are orthogonal. The set of basis vectors ϕ_{jk}, for all j and k, form an over-complete basis and for different values of j are not orthogonal. Since $\phi_{jk}, \phi_{j+1,2k}$, and $\phi_{j+1,2k+1}$ are linearly dependent, for each value of j delete $\phi_{j+1,k}$ for odd values of k to get a linearly independent set of basis vectors. To get an orthogonal set of basis vectors, define

$$\psi_{jk}(x) = \begin{cases} 1 & \frac{2k}{2^j} \leq x < \frac{2k+1}{2^j} \\ -1 & \frac{2k+1}{2^j} \leq x < \frac{2k+2}{2^j} \\ 0 & \text{otherwise} \end{cases}$$

and replace $\phi_{j,2k}$ with $\psi_{j+1,2k}$. Basically, replace the three functions

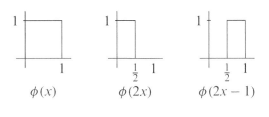

$$\phi(x) \qquad \phi(2x) \qquad \phi(2x-1)$$

by the two functions

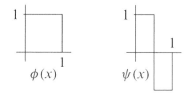

$$\phi(x) \qquad \psi(x)$$

The basis set becomes

$$
\begin{array}{llll}
\phi_{00} & \psi_{10} & & \\
\psi_{20} & \psi_{22} & & \\
\psi_{30} & \psi_{32} & \psi_{34} & \psi_{36} \\
\psi_{40} & \psi_{42} & \psi_{44} & \psi_{46} \quad \psi_{48} \quad \psi_{4,10} \quad \psi_{4,12} \quad \psi_{4,14}
\end{array}
$$

To approximate a function that has only finite support, select a scale vector $\phi(x)$ whose scale is that of the support of the function to be represented. Next approximate the function by the set of scale functions $\phi(2^j x - k), k = 0, 1, \ldots$, for some fixed value of j. The value of j is determined by the desired accuracy of the approximation. Basically the x axis has been divided into intervals of size 2^{-j} and in each interval the function is approximated by a fixed value. It is this approximation of the function that is expressed as a linear combination of the basis functions.

The Haar Wavelet

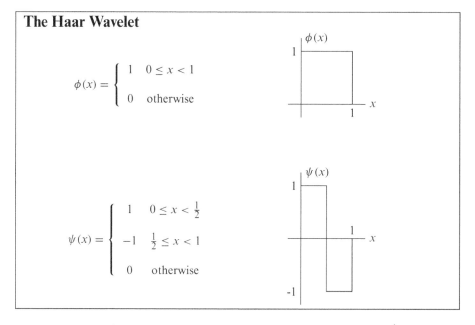

$$
\phi(x) = \begin{cases} 1 & 0 \le x < 1 \\ 0 & \text{otherwise} \end{cases}
$$

$$
\psi(x) = \begin{cases} 1 & 0 \le x < \frac{1}{2} \\ -1 & \frac{1}{2} \le x < 1 \\ 0 & \text{otherwise} \end{cases}
$$

Once the value of j has been selected, the function is sampled at 2^j points, one in each interval of width 2^{-j}. Let the sample values be $s_0, s_1, \ldots$. The approximation to the function is $\sum_{k=0}^{2^j-1} s_k \phi(2^j x - k)$ and is represented by the vector $(s_0, s_1 \ldots, s_{2^j-1})$. The problem now is to represent the approximation to the function using the basis vectors rather than the non-orthogonal set of scale functions $\phi_{jk}(x)$. This is illustrated in the following example.

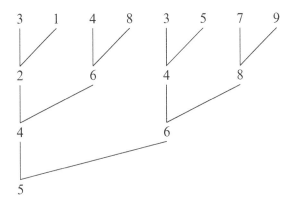

Figure 11.2: Tree of function averages.

To represent the function corresponding to a vector such as (3 1 4 8 3 5 7 9), one needs to find the c_i such that

$$\begin{pmatrix} 3 \\ 1 \\ 4 \\ 8 \\ 3 \\ 5 \\ 7 \\ 9 \end{pmatrix} = \begin{pmatrix} 1 & 1 & 1 & 0 & 1 & 0 & 0 & 0 \\ 1 & 1 & 1 & 0 & -1 & 0 & 0 & 0 \\ 1 & 1 & -1 & 0 & 0 & 1 & 0 & 0 \\ 1 & 1 & -1 & 0 & 0 & -1 & 0 & 0 \\ 1 & -1 & 0 & 1 & 0 & 0 & 1 & 0 \\ 1 & -1 & 0 & 1 & 0 & 0 & -1 & 0 \\ 1 & -1 & 0 & -1 & 0 & 0 & 0 & 1 \\ 1 & -1 & 0 & -1 & 0 & 0 & 0 & -1 \end{pmatrix} \begin{pmatrix} c_1 \\ c_2 \\ c_3 \\ c_4 \\ c_5 \\ c_6 \\ c_7 \\ c_8 \end{pmatrix}.$$

The first column represents the scale function $\phi(x)$ and subsequent columns the ψ's. The tree in Figure 11.2 illustrates an efficient way to find the coefficients representing the vector (3 1 4 8 3 5 7 9) in the basis. Each vertex in the tree contains the average of the quantities of its two children. The root gives the average of the elements in the vector, which is 5 in this example. This average is the coefficient of the basis vector in the first column of the above matrix. The second basis vector converts the average of the eight elements into the average of the first four elements, which is 4, and the last four elements, which is 6, with a coefficient of -1. Working up the tree determines the coefficients for each basis vector.

$$\begin{pmatrix} 3 \\ 1 \\ 4 \\ 8 \\ 3 \\ 5 \\ 7 \\ 9 \end{pmatrix} = 5\begin{pmatrix} 1 \\ 1 \\ 1 \\ 1 \\ 1 \\ 1 \\ 1 \\ 1 \end{pmatrix} - 1\begin{pmatrix} 1 \\ 1 \\ 1 \\ 1 \\ -1 \\ -1 \\ -1 \\ -1 \end{pmatrix} - 2\begin{pmatrix} 1 \\ 1 \\ -1 \\ -1 \\ 0 \\ 0 \\ 0 \\ 0 \end{pmatrix} - 2\begin{pmatrix} 0 \\ 0 \\ 0 \\ 0 \\ 1 \\ 1 \\ -1 \\ -1 \end{pmatrix} + 1\begin{pmatrix} 1 \\ -1 \\ 0 \\ 0 \\ 0 \\ 0 \\ 0 \\ 0 \end{pmatrix} - 2\begin{pmatrix} 0 \\ 0 \\ 1 \\ -1 \\ 0 \\ 0 \\ 0 \\ 0 \end{pmatrix} - 1\begin{pmatrix} 0 \\ 0 \\ 0 \\ 0 \\ 1 \\ -1 \\ 0 \\ 0 \end{pmatrix} - 1\begin{pmatrix} 0 \\ 0 \\ 0 \\ 0 \\ 0 \\ 0 \\ 1 \\ -1 \end{pmatrix}$$

11.3. Wavelet Systems

So far we have explained wavelets using the simple-to-understand Haar wavelet. We now consider general wavelet systems. A wavelet system is built from a basic scaling function $\phi(x)$, which comes from a dilation equation. Scaling and shifting of the basic scaling function gives a two-dimensional set of scaling functions ϕ_{jk} where

$$\phi_{jk}(x) = \phi(2^j x - k).$$

For a fixed value of j, the ϕ_{jk} span a space V_j. If $\phi(x)$ satisfies a dilation equation

$$\phi(x) = \sum_{k=0}^{d-1} c_k \phi(2x - k),$$

then ϕ_{jk} is a linear combination of the $\phi_{j+1,k}$'s, and this implies that $V_0 \subseteq V_1 \subseteq V_2 \subseteq V_3 \ldots$.

11.4. Solving the Dilation Equation

Consider solving a dilation equation

$$\phi(x) = \sum_{k=0}^{d-1} c_k \phi(2x - k)$$

to obtain the scale function for a wavelet system. Perhaps the easiest way is to assume a solution and then calculate the scale function by successive approximation as in the following program for the Daubechies scale function (see Figure 11.3):

$$\phi(x) = \tfrac{1+\sqrt{3}}{4}\phi(2x) + \tfrac{3+\sqrt{3}}{4}\phi(2x - 1) + \tfrac{3-\sqrt{3}}{4}\phi(2x - 2) + \tfrac{1-\sqrt{3}}{4}\phi(2x - 3).$$

The solution will actually be samples of $\phi(x)$ at some desired resolution.

Program Compute-Daubechies:
Insert the coefficients of the dilation equation.

$$c_1 = \tfrac{1+\sqrt{3}}{4} \qquad c_2 = \tfrac{3+\sqrt{3}}{4} \qquad c_3 = \tfrac{3-\sqrt{3}}{4} \qquad c_4 = \tfrac{1-\sqrt{3}}{4}$$

Set the initial approximation to $\phi(x)$ by generating a vector whose components approximate the samples of $\phi(x)$ at equally spaced values of x.

Execute the following loop until the values for $\phi(x)$ converge.

begin

   Calculate $\phi(2x)$ by averaging successive values of $\phi(x)$ together. Fill out the remaining half of the vector representing $\phi(2x)$ with zeros.

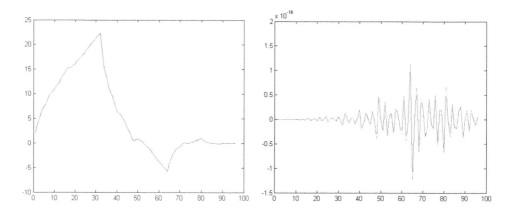

Figure 11.3: Daubechies scale function and associated wavelet.

Calculate $\phi(2x-1), \phi(2x-2)$, and $\phi(2x-3)$ by shifting the contents of $\phi(2x)$ the appropriate distance, discarding the zeros that move off the right end, and adding zeros at the left end.

Calculate the new approximation for $\phi(x)$ using the above values for $\phi(2x-1), \phi(2x-2)$, and $\phi(2x-3)$ in the dilation equation for $\phi(2x)$.

end

The convergence of the iterative procedure for computing is fast if the eigenvectors of a certain matrix are unity.

Another Approach to Solving the Dilation Equation

Consider the dilation equation $\phi(x) = \frac{1}{2}f(2x) + f(2x-1) + \frac{1}{2}f(2x-2)$ and consider continuous solutions with support in $0 \le x < 2$.

$$\phi(0) = \tfrac{1}{2}\phi(0) + \phi(-1) + \phi(-2) = \tfrac{1}{2}\phi(0) + 0 + 0 \qquad\qquad \phi(0) = 0$$

$$\phi(2) = \tfrac{1}{2}\phi(4) + \phi(3) + \phi(2) = \tfrac{1}{2}\phi(2) + 0 + 0 \qquad\qquad \phi(2) = 0$$

$$\phi(1) = \tfrac{1}{2}\phi(2) + \phi(1) + \phi(0) = 0 + \phi(1) + 0 \qquad\qquad \phi(1) \quad \text{arbitrary}$$

Set $\phi(1) = 1$. Then

$$\phi\left(\tfrac{1}{2}\right) = \tfrac{1}{2}\phi(1) + \phi(0) + \tfrac{1}{2}\phi(-1) = \tfrac{1}{2}$$

$$\phi\left(\tfrac{3}{2}\right) = \tfrac{1}{2}\phi(3) + \phi(2) + \tfrac{1}{2}\phi(1) = \tfrac{1}{2} \qquad .$$

$$\phi\left(\tfrac{1}{4}\right) = \tfrac{1}{2}\phi\left(\tfrac{1}{2}\right) + \phi\left(-\tfrac{1}{2}\right) + \tfrac{1}{2}\phi\left(-\tfrac{3}{2}\right) = \tfrac{1}{4}$$

One can continue this process and compute $\phi(\frac{i}{2^j})$ for larger values of j until $\phi(x)$ is approximated to a desired accuracy. If $\phi(x)$ is a simple equation as in this example, one could conjecture its form and verify that the form satisfies the dilation equation.

11.5. Conditions on the Dilation Equation

We would like a basis for a vector space of functions where each basis vector has finite support and the basis vectors are orthogonal. This is achieved by a wavelet system consisting of a shifted version of a scale function that satisfies a dilation equation along with a set of wavelets of various scales and shifts. For the scale function to have a non-zero integral, Lemma 11.1 requires that the coefficients of the dilation equation sum to two. Although the scale function $\phi(x)$ for the Haar system has the property that $\phi(x)$ and $\phi(x-k), k > 0$, are orthogonal, this is not true for the scale function for the dilation equation $\phi(x) = \frac{1}{2}\phi(2x) + \phi(2x-1) + \frac{1}{2}\phi(2x-2)$. The conditions that integer shifts of the scale function be orthogonal and that the scale function has finite support puts additional conditions on the coefficients of the dilation equation. These conditions are developed in the next two lemmas.

Lemma 11.2 *Let*

$$\phi(x) = \sum_{k=0}^{d-1} c_k \phi(2x - k).$$

If $\phi(x)$ and $\phi(x-k)$ are orthogonal for $k \neq 0$ and $\phi(x)$ has been normalized so that $\int_{-\infty}^{\infty} \phi(x)\phi(x-k)dx = \delta(k)$, then $\sum_{i=0}^{d-1} c_i c_{i-2k} = 2\delta(k)$.

Proof Assume $\phi(x)$ has been normalized so that $\int_{-\infty}^{\infty} \phi(x)\phi(x-k)dx = \delta(k)$. Then

$$\int_{x=-\infty}^{\infty} \phi(x)\phi(x-k)dx = \int_{x=-\infty}^{\infty} \sum_{i=0}^{d-1} c_i \phi(2x-i) \sum_{j=0}^{d-1} c_j \phi(2x-2k-j)dx$$

$$= \sum_{i=0}^{d-1}\sum_{j=0}^{d-1} c_i c_j \int_{x=-\infty}^{\infty} \phi(2x-i)\phi(2x-2k-j)dx$$

Since

$$\int_{x=-\infty}^{\infty} \phi(2x-i)\phi(2x-2k-j)dx = \frac{1}{2}\int_{x=-\infty}^{\infty} \phi(y-i)\phi(y-2k-j)dy$$

$$= \frac{1}{2}\int_{x=-\infty}^{\infty} \phi(y)\phi(y+i-2k-j)dy$$

$$= \frac{1}{2}\delta(2k+j-i),$$

$\int_{x=-\infty}^{\infty} \phi(x)\phi(x-k)dx = \sum_{i=0}^{d-1}\sum_{j=0}^{d-1} c_i c_j \frac{1}{2}\delta(2k+j-i) = \frac{1}{2}\sum_{i=0}^{d-1} c_i c_{i-2k}$.
Since $\phi(x)$ was normalized so that

$$\int_{-\infty}^{\infty} \phi(x)\phi(x-k)dx = \delta(k), \text{ it follows that } \sum_{i=0}^{d-1} c_i c_{i-2k} = 2\delta(k). \quad \blacksquare$$

Scale and wavelet coefficients equations

$$\phi(x) = \sum_{k=0}^{d-1} c_k \phi(2x-k) \qquad\qquad \psi(x) = \sum_{k=0}^{d-1} b_k \phi(x-k)$$

$$\int_{-\infty}^{\infty} \phi(x)\phi(x-k)dx = \delta(k) \qquad\qquad \int_{x=-\infty}^{\infty} \phi(x)\psi(x-k) = 0$$

$$\sum_{j=0}^{d-1} c_j = 2 \qquad\qquad\qquad \int_{x=-\infty}^{\infty} \psi(x)dx = 0$$

$$\sum_{j=0}^{d-1} c_j c_{j-2k} = 2\delta(k) \qquad\qquad \int_{x=-\infty}^{\infty} \psi(x)\psi(x-k)dx = \delta(k)$$

$$c_k = 0 \text{ unless } 0 \leq k \leq d-1 \qquad \sum_{i=0}^{d-1} (-1)^k b_i b_{i-2k} = 2\delta(k)$$

$$d \text{ even} \qquad\qquad\qquad \sum_{j=0}^{d-1} c_j b_{j-2k} = 0$$

$$\sum_{j=0}^{d-1} c_{2j} = \sum_{j=0}^{d-1} c_{2j+1} \qquad\qquad \sum_{j=0}^{d-1} b_j = 0$$

$$b_k = (-1)^k c_{d-1-k}$$

One designs wavelet systems so the above conditions are satisfied.

Lemma 11.2 provides a necessary but not sufficient condition on the coefficients of the dilation equation for shifts of the scale function to be orthogonal. One should note that the conditions of Lemma 11.2 are not true for the triangular or piecewise quadratic solutions to

$$\phi(x) = \frac{1}{2}\phi(2x) + \phi(2x - 1) + \frac{1}{2}\phi(2x - 2)$$

and

$$\phi(x) = \frac{1}{4}\phi(2x) + \frac{3}{4}\phi(2x - 1) + \frac{3}{4}\phi(2x - 2) + \frac{1}{4}\phi(2x - 3)$$

which overlap and are not orthogonal.

For $\phi(x)$ to have finite support the dilation equation can have only a finite number of terms. This is proved in the following lemma.

Lemma 11.3 *If $0 \leq x < d$ is the support of $\phi(x)$, and the set of integer shifts, $\{\phi(x - k) | k \geq 0\}$, are linearly independent, then $c_k = 0$ unless $0 \leq k \leq d - 1$.*

Proof If the support of $\phi(x)$ is $0 \leq x < d$, then the support of $\phi(2x)$ is $0 \leq x < \frac{d}{2}$. If

$$\phi(x) = \sum_{k=-\infty}^{\infty} c_k \phi(2x - k),$$

the support of both sides of the equation must be the same. Since the $\phi(x - k)$ are linearly independent, the limits of the summation are actually $k = 0$ to $d - 1$ and

$$\phi(x) = \sum_{k=0}^{d-1} c_k \phi(2x - k).$$

It follows that $c_k = 0$ unless $0 \leq k \leq d - 1$.

The condition that the integer shifts are linearly independent is essential to the proof, and the lemma is not true without this condition. ∎

One should also note that $\sum_{i=0}^{d-1} c_i c_{i-2k} = 0$ for $k \neq 0$ implies that d is even, since for d odd and $k = \frac{d-1}{2}$,

$$\sum_{i=0}^{d-1} c_i c_{i-2k} = \sum_{i=0}^{d-1} c_i c_{i-d+1} = c_{d-1} c_0.$$

For $c_{d-1} c_0$ to be zero either c_{d-1} or c_0 must be zero. Since either $c_0 = 0$ or $c_{d-1} = 0$, there are only $d - 1$ non-zero coefficients. From here on we assume that d is even. If the dilation equation has d terms and the coefficients satisfy the linear equation $\sum_{k=0}^{d-1} c_k = 2$ and the $\frac{d}{2}$ quadratic equations $\sum_{i=0}^{d-1} c_i c_{i-2k} = 2\delta(k)$ for $1 \leq k \leq \frac{d-1}{2}$, then for $d > 2$ there are $\frac{d}{2} - 1$ coefficients that can be used to design the wavelet system to achieve desired properties.

11.6. Derivation of the Wavelets from the Scaling Function

In a wavelet system one develops a mother wavelet as a linear combination of integer shifts of a scaled version of the scale function $\phi(x)$. Let the mother wavelet $\psi(x)$ be given by $\psi(x) = \sum_{k=0}^{d-1} b_k \phi(2x - k)$. One wants integer shifts of the mother wavelet $\psi(x - k)$ to be orthogonal and also for integer shifts of the mother wavelet to be orthogonal to the scaling function $\phi(x)$. These conditions place restrictions on the coefficients b_k, which are the subject matter of the next two lemmas.

Lemma 11.4 (**Orthogonality of $\psi(x)$ and $\psi(x - k)$**) *Let* $\psi(x) = \sum_{k=0}^{d-1} b_k \phi$ $(2x - k)$. *If* $\psi(x)$ *and* $\psi(x - k)$ *are orthogonal for* $k \neq 0$ *and* $\psi(x)$ *has been normalized so that* $\int_{-\infty}^{\infty} \psi(x)\psi(x - k)dx = \delta(k)$, *then*

$$\sum_{i=0}^{d-1} (-1)^k b_i b_{i-2k} = 2\delta(k).$$

Proof Analogous to Lemma 11.2. ∎

Lemma 11.5 (**Orthogonality of $\phi(x)$ and $\psi(x - k)$**) *Let* $\phi(x) = \sum_{k=0}^{d-1} c_k \phi$ $(2x - k)$ *and* $\psi(x) = \sum_{k=0}^{d-1} b_k \phi(2x - k)$. *If* $\int_{x=-\infty}^{\infty} \phi(x)\phi(x - k)dx = \delta(k)$ *and* $\int_{x=-\infty}^{\infty} \phi(x)\psi(x - k)dx = 0$ *for all* k, *then* $\sum_{i=0}^{d-1} c_i b_{i-2k} = 0$ *for all* k.

Proof

$$\int_{x=-\infty}^{\infty} \phi(x)\psi(x - k)dx = \int_{x=-\infty}^{\infty} \sum_{i=0}^{d-1} c_i \phi(2x - i) \sum_{j=1}^{d-1} b_j \phi(2x - 2k - j)dx = 0.$$

Interchanging the order of integration and summation

$$\sum_{i=0}^{d-1}\sum_{j=0}^{d-1} c_i b_j \int_{x=-\infty}^{\infty} \phi(2x - i)\phi(2x - 2k - j)dx = 0.$$

Substituting $y = 2x - i$ yields

$$\frac{1}{2}\sum_{i=0}^{d-1}\sum_{j=0}^{d-1} c_i b_j \int_{y=-\infty}^{\infty} \phi(y)\phi(y - 2k - j + i)dy = 0.$$

Thus,

$$\sum_{i=0}^{d-1}\sum_{j=0}^{d-1} c_i b_j \delta(2k + j - i) = 0.$$

Summing over j gives

$$\sum_{i=0}^{d-1} c_i b_{i-2k} = 0.$$

∎

Lemma 11.5 gave a condition on the coefficients in the equations for $\phi(x)$ and $\psi(x)$ if integer shifts of the mother wavelet are to be orthogonal to the scale function. In addition, for integer shifts of the mother wavelet to be orthogonal to the scale function requires that $b_k = (-1)^k c_{d-1-k}$.

Lemma 11.6 *Let the scale function $\phi(x)$ equal $\sum_{k=0}^{d-1} c_k \phi(2x - k)$ and let the wavelet function $\psi(x)$ equal $\sum_{k=0}^{d-1} b_k \phi(2x - k)$. If the scale functions are orthogonal*

$$\int_{-\infty}^{\infty} \phi(x)\phi(x - k)dx = \delta(k)$$

and the wavelet functions are orthogonal with the scale function

$$\int_{x=-\infty}^{\infty} \phi(x)\psi(x - k)dx = 0$$

for all k, then $b_k = (-1)^k c_{d-1-k}$.

Proof By Lemma 11.5, $\sum_{j=0}^{d-1} c_j b_{j-2k} = 0$ for all k. Separating $\sum_{j=0}^{d-1} c_j b_{j-2k} = 0$ into odd and even indices gives

$$\sum_{j=0}^{\frac{d}{2}-1} c_{2j} b_{2j-2k} + \sum_{j=0}^{\frac{d}{2}-1} c_{2j+1} b_{2j+1-2k} = 0 \qquad (11.1)$$

for all k.

$$
\begin{array}{ll}
c_0 b_0 + c_2 b_2 + c_4 b_4 + \cdots + c_1 b_1 + c_3 b_3 + c_5 b_5 + \cdots = 0 & k = 0 \\
c_2 b_0 + c_4 b_2 + \cdots \qquad\qquad + c_3 b_1 + c_5 b_3 + \cdots = 0 & k = 1 \\
c_4 b_0 + \cdots \qquad\qquad\qquad + c_5 b_1 + \cdots = 0 & k = 2
\end{array}
$$

By Lemmas 11.2 and 11.4, $\sum_{j=0}^{d-1} c_j c_{j-2k} = 2\delta(k)$ and $\sum_{j=0}^{d-1} b_j b_{j-2k} = 2\delta(k)$ and for all k. Separating odd and even terms,

$$\sum_{j=0}^{\frac{d}{2}-1} c_{2j} c_{2j-2k} + \sum_{j=0}^{\frac{d}{2}-1} c_{2j+1} c_{2j+1-2k} = 2\delta(k) \qquad (11.2)$$

and

$$\sum_{j=0}^{\frac{d}{2}-1} b_{2j} b_{2j-2k} + \sum_{j=0}^{\frac{d}{2}-1} (-1)^j b_{2j+1} b_{2j+1-2k} = 2\delta(k) \qquad (11.3)$$

for all k.

$$
\begin{array}{ll}
c_0 c_0 + c_2 c_2 + c_4 c_4 + \cdots + c_1 c_1 + c_3 c_3 + c_5 c_5 + \cdots = 2 & k = 0 \\
c_2 c_0 + c_4 c_2 + \cdots \qquad\qquad + c_3 c_1 + c_5 c_3 + \cdots = 0 & k = 1 \\
c_4 c_0 + \cdots \qquad\qquad\qquad + c_5 c_1 + \cdots = 0 & k = 2
\end{array}
$$

$$b_0b_0 + b_2b_2 + b_4b_4 + \cdots + b_1b_1 - b_3b_3 + b_5b_5 - \cdots = 2 \qquad k = 0$$
$$b_2b_0 + b_4b_2 + \cdots \qquad\qquad - b_3b_1 + b_5b_3 - \cdots = 0 \qquad k = 1$$
$$b_4b_0 + \cdots \qquad\qquad\qquad + b_5b_1 - \cdots = 0 \qquad k = 2$$

Let $C_e = (c_0, c_2, \ldots, c_{d-2})$, $C_o = (c_1, c_3, \ldots, c_{d-1})$, $B_e = (b_0, b_2, \ldots, b_{d-2})$, and $B_o = (b_1, b_3, \ldots, b_{d-1})$. Equations 12.1, 12.2, and 11.3 can be expressed as convolutions[1] of these sequences. Equation 12.1 is $C_e * B_e^R + C_o * B_o^R = 0$, 12.2 is $C_e * C_e^R + C_o * C_o^R = \delta(k)$, and 11.3 is $B_e * B_e^R + B_o * B_o^R = \delta(k)$, where the superscript R stands for reversal of the sequence. These equations can be written in matrix format as

$$\begin{pmatrix} C_e & C_o \\ B_e & B_o \end{pmatrix} * \begin{pmatrix} C_e^R & B_e^R \\ C_o^R & B_o^R \end{pmatrix} = \begin{pmatrix} 2\delta & 0 \\ 0 & 2\delta \end{pmatrix}.$$

Taking the Fourier or z-transform yields

$$\begin{pmatrix} F(C_e) & F(C_o) \\ F(B_e) & F(B_o) \end{pmatrix} \begin{pmatrix} F(C_e^R) & F(B_e^R) \\ F(C_o^R) & F(B_o^R) \end{pmatrix} = \begin{pmatrix} 2 & 0 \\ 0 & 2 \end{pmatrix}$$

where F denotes the transform. Taking the determinant yields

$$\big(F(C_e)F(B_o) - F(B_e)F(C_o)\big)\big(F(C_e)F(B_o) - F(C_o)F(B_e)\big) = 4.$$

Thus $F(C_e)F(B_o) - F(C_o)F(B_e) = 2$ and the inverse transform yields

$$C_e * B_o - C_o * B_e = 2\delta(k).$$

Convolution by C_e^R yields

$$C_e^R * C_e * B_o - C_e^R * B_e * C_o = C_e^R * 2\delta(k).$$

Now $\sum_{j=0}^{d-1} c_j b_{j-2k} = 0$ so $-C_e^R * B_e = C_o^R * B_o$. Thus,

$$C_e^R * C_e * B_o + C_o^R * B_o * C_o = 2C_e^R * \delta(k)$$
$$(C_e^R * C_e + C_o^R * C_o) * B_o = 2C_e^R * \delta(k)$$
$$2\delta(k) * B_o = 2C_e^R * \delta(k)$$
$$C_e = B_o^R$$

Thus, $c_i = 2b_{d-1-i}$ for even i. By a similar argument, convolution by C_0^R yields

$$C_0^R * C_e * B_0 - C_0^R * C_0 * B_e = 2C_0^R \delta(k).$$

Since $C_0^R * B_0 = -C_0^R * B_e$

$$-C_e^R * C_e^R * B_e - C_0^R * C_0 * B_e = 2C_0^R \delta(k)$$
$$-(C_e * C_e^R + C_0^R * C_0) * B_e = 2C_0^R \delta(k)$$
$$-2\delta(k)B_e = 2C_0^R \delta(k)$$
$$-B_e = C_0^R$$

Thus, $c_i = -2b_{d-1-i}$ for all odd i, and hence $c_i = (-1)^i 2b_{d-1-i}$ for all i. ∎

---

[1] The convolution of $(a_0, a_1, \ldots, a_{d-1})$ and $(b_0, b_1, \ldots, b_{d-1})$ denoted $(a_0, a_1, \ldots, a_{d-1}) * (b_0, b_1, \ldots, b_{d-1})$ is the sequence $(a_0 b_{d-1}, a_0 b_{d-2} + a_1 b_{d-1}, a_0 b_{d-3} + a_1 b_{d-2} + a_3 b_{d-1} \ldots, a_{d-1} b_0)$.

11.7. Sufficient Conditions for the Wavelets to Be Orthogonal

Section 11.6 gave necessary conditions on the b_k and c_k in the definitions of the scale function and wavelets for certain orthogonality properties. In this section we show that these conditions are also sufficient for certain orthogonality conditions. One would like a wavelet system to satisfy certain conditions.

1. Wavelets, $\psi_j(2^j x - k)$, at all scales and shifts to be orthogonal to the scale function $\phi(x)$.
2. All wavelets to be orthogonal. That is,

$$\int_{-\infty}^{\infty} \psi_j(2^j x - k)\psi_l(2^l x - m)dx = \delta(j - l)\delta(k - m).$$

3. $\phi(x)$ and $\psi_{jk}, j \leq l$ and all k, to span V_l, the space spanned by $\phi(2^l x - k)$ for all k.

These items are proved in the following lemmas. The first lemma gives sufficient conditions on the wavelet coefficients b_k in the definition

$$\psi(x) = \sum_k b_k \psi(2x - k)$$

for the mother wavelet so that the wavelets will be orthogonal to the scale function. The lemma shows that if the wavelet coefficients equal the scale coefficients in reverse order with alternating negative signs, then the wavelets will be orthogonal to the scale function.

Lemma 11.7 If $b_k = (-1)^k c_{d-1-k}$, then $\int_{-\infty}^{\infty} \phi(x)\psi(2^j x - l)dx = 0$ for all j and l.

Proof Assume that $b_k = (-1)^k c_{d-1-k}$. We first show that $\phi(x)$ and $\psi(x - k)$ are orthogonal for all values of k. Then we modify the proof to show that $\phi(x)$ and $\psi(2^j x - k)$ are orthogonal for all j and k.

Assume $b_k = (-1)^k c_{d-1-k}$. Then

$$\int_{-\infty}^{\infty} \phi(x)\psi(x - k) = \int_{-\infty}^{\infty} \sum_{i=0}^{d-1} c_i\phi(2x - i) \sum_{j=0}^{d-1} b_j\phi(2x - 2k - j)dx$$

$$= \sum_{i=0}^{d-1}\sum_{j=0}^{d-1} c_i(-1)^j c_{d-1-j} \int_{-\infty}^{\infty} \phi(2x - i)\phi(2x - 2k - j)dx$$

$$= \sum_{i=0}^{d-1}\sum_{j=0}^{d-1} (-1)^j c_i c_{d-1-j}\delta(i - 2k - j)$$

$$= \sum_{j=0}^{d-1} (-1)^j c_{2k+j} c_{d-1-j}$$

$$= c_{2k}c_{d-1} - c_{2k+1}c_{d-2} + \cdots + c_{d-2}c_{2k-1} - c_{d-1}c_{2k}$$

$$= 0$$

The last step requires that d be even, which we have assumed for all scale functions.

For the case where the wavelet is $\psi(2^j - l)$, first express $\phi(x)$ as a linear combination of $\phi(2^{j-1}x - n)$. Now for each these terms,

$$\int_{-\infty}^{\infty} \phi(2^{j-1}x - m)\psi(2^j x - k)dx = 0.$$

To see this, substitute $y = 2^{j-1}x$. Then

$$\int_{-\infty}^{\infty} \phi(2^j x - m)\psi(2^j x - k)dx = \frac{1}{2^{j-1}}\int_{-\infty}^{\infty} \phi(y - m)\psi(2y - k)dy$$

which by the previous argument is zero. ∎

The next lemma gives conditions on the coefficients b_k that are sufficient for the wavelets to be orthogonal.

Lemma 11.8 *If $b_k = (-1)^k c_{d-1-k}$, then*

$$\int_{-\infty}^{\infty} \frac{1}{2^j}\psi_j(2^j x - k)\frac{1}{2^k}\psi_l(2^l x - m)dx = \delta(j - l)\delta(k - m).$$

Proof The first level wavelets are orthogonal.

$$\int_{-\infty}^{\infty} \psi(x)\psi(x - k)dx = \int_{-\infty}^{\infty} \sum_{i=0}^{d-1} b_i\phi(2x - i)\sum_{j=0}^{d-1} b_j\phi(2x - 2k - j)dx$$

$$= \sum_{i=0}^{d-1} b_i \sum_{j=0}^{d-1} b_j \int_{-\infty}^{\infty} \phi(2x - i)\phi(2x - 2k - j)dx$$

$$= \sum_{i=0}^{d-1}\sum_{j=0}^{d-1} b_i b_j \delta(i - 2k - j)$$

$$= \sum_{i=0}^{d-1} b_i b_{i-2k}$$

$$= \sum_{i=0}^{d-1} (-1)^i c_{d-1-i}(-1)^{i-2k} c_{d-1-i+2k}$$

$$= \sum_{i=0}^{d-1} (-1)^{2i-2k} c_{d-1-i} c_{d-1-i+2k}$$

Substituting j for $d - 1 - i$ yields

$$\sum_{j=0}^{d-1} c_j c_{j+2k} = 2\delta(k).$$

Example of orthogonality when wavelets are of different scale.

$$\int_{-\infty}^{\infty} \psi(2x)\psi(x-k)dx = \int_{-\infty}^{\infty} \sum_{i=0}^{d-1} b_i\phi(4x-i) \sum_{j=0}^{d-1} b_j\phi(2x-2k-j)dx$$

$$= \sum_{i=0}^{d-1}\sum_{i=0}^{d-1} b_ib_j \int_{-\infty}^{\infty} \phi(4x-i)\phi(2x-2k-j)dx$$

Since $\phi(2x-2k-j) = \sum_{l=0}^{d-1} c_l\phi(4x-4k-2j-l)$,

$$\int_{-\infty}^{\infty} \psi(2x)\psi(x-k)dx = \sum_{i=0}^{d-1}\sum_{j=0}^{d-1}\sum_{l=0}^{d-1} b_ib_jc_l \int_{-\infty}^{\infty} \psi(4x-i)\phi(4x-4k-2j-l)dx$$

$$= \sum_{i=0}^{d-1}\sum_{j=0}^{d-1}\sum_{l=0}^{d-1} b_ib_jc_l\delta(i-4k-2j-l)$$

$$= \sum_{i=0}^{d-1}\sum_{j=0}^{d-1} b_ib_jc_{i-4k-2j}$$

Since $\sum_{j=0}^{d-1} c_jb_{j-2k} = 0$, $\sum_{i=0}^{d-1} b_ic_{i-4k-2j} = \delta(j-2k)$. Thus,

$$\int_{-\infty}^{\infty} \psi(2x)\psi(x-k)dx = \sum_{j=0}^{d-1} b_j\delta(j-2k) = 0.$$

Orthogonality of scale function with wavelet of different scale.

$$\int_{-\infty}^{\infty} \phi(x)\psi(2x-k)dx = \int_{-\infty}^{\infty} \sum_{j=0}^{d-1} c_j\phi(2x-j)\psi(2x-k)dx$$

$$= \sum_{j=0}^{d-1} c_j \int_{-\infty}^{\infty} \phi(2x-j)\psi(2x-k)dx$$

$$= \frac{1}{2}\sum_{j=0}^{d-1} c_j \int_{-\infty}^{\infty} \phi(y-j)\psi(y-k)dy$$

$$= 0$$

If ψ was of scale 2^j, ϕ would be expanded as a linear combination of ϕ of scale 2^j all of which would be orthogonal to ψ. ∎

11.8. Expressing a Function in Terms of Wavelets

Given a wavelet system with scale function ϕ and mother wavelet ψ, we wish to express a function $f(x)$ in terms of an orthonormal basis of the wavelet system. First we will express $f(x)$ in terms of scale functions $\phi_{jk}(x) = \phi(2^jx-k)$. To do this we will build a tree similar to that in Figure 11.2 for the Haar system, except that computing the coefficients will be much more complex. Recall that the coefficients at a level in the tree are the coefficients to represent $f(x)$ using scale functions with the precision of the level.

Let $f(x) = \sum_{k=0}^{\infty} a_{jk}\phi_j(x-k)$ where the a_{jk} are the coefficients in the expansion of $f(x)$ using level j scale functions. Since the $\phi_j(x-k)$ are orthogonal,

$$a_{jk} = \int_{x=-\infty}^{\infty} f(x)\phi_j(x-k)dx.$$

Expanding ϕ_j in terms of ϕ_{j+1} yields

$$a_{jk} = \int_{x=-\infty}^{\infty} f(x) \sum_{m=0}^{d-1} c_m\phi_{j+1}(2x-2k-m)dx$$

$$= \sum_{m=0}^{d-1} c_m \int_{x=-\infty}^{\infty} f(x)\phi_{j+1}(2x-2k-m)dx$$

$$= \sum_{m=0}^{d-1} c_m a_{j+1,2k+m}$$

Let $n = 2k + m$. Now $m = n - 2k$. Then

$$a_{jk} = \sum_{n=2k}^{d-1} c_{n-2k} a_{j+1,n}. \tag{11.4}$$

In construction of the tree similar to that in Figure 11.2, the values at the leaves are the values of the function sampled in the intervals of size 2^{-j}. Equation 11.4 is used to compute values as one moves up the tree. The coefficients in the tree could be used if we wanted to represent $f(x)$ using scale functions. However, we want to represent $f(x)$ using one scale function whose scale is the support of $f(x)$ along with wavelets, which gives us an orthogonal set of basis functions. To do this we need to calculate the coefficients for the wavelets. The value at the root of the tree is the coefficient for the scale function. We then move down the tree calculating the coefficients for the wavelets.

11.9. Designing a Wavelet System

In designing a wavelet system there are a number of parameters in the dilation equation. If one uses d terms in the dilation equation, one degree of freedom can be used to satisfy

$$\sum_{i=0}^{d-1} c_i = 2,$$

which insures the existence of a solution with a non-zero mean. Another $\frac{d}{2}$ degrees of freedom are used to satisfy

$$\sum_{i=0}^{d-1} c_i c_{i-2k} = \delta(k),$$

which insures the orthogonal properties. The remaining $\frac{d}{2} - 1$ degrees of freedom can be used to obtain some desirable properties such as smoothness. Smoothness appears to be related to vanishing moments of the scaling function. Material on the design of systems is beyond the scope of this book and can be found in the literature.

11.10. Applications

Wavelets are widely used in data compression for images and speech, as well as in computer vision for representing images. Unlike the sines and cosines of the Fourier transform, wavelets have spatial locality in addition to frequency information, which can be useful for better understanding the contents of an image and for relating pieces of different images to each other. Wavelets are also being used in power line communication protocols that send data over highly noisy channels.

11.11. Bibliographic Notes

In 1909, Alfred Haar presented an orthonormal basis for functions with finite support. Ingrid Daubechies [Dau90] generalized Haar's work and created the area of wavelets. There are many references on wavelets. Several that maybe be useful are Strang and Nguyen, Wavelets and Filter Banks [SN97], and Burrus, Gopinath, and Guo [BGG97].

11.12. Exercises

Exercise 11.1 Give a solution to the dilation equation $f(x) = f(2x) + f(2x - k)$ satisfying $f(0) = 1$. Assume k is an integer.

Exercise 11.2 Are there solutions to $f(x) = f(2x) + f(2x - 1)$ other than a constant multiple of

$$f(x) = \begin{cases} 1 & 0 \leq x < 1 \\ 0 & \text{otherwise} \end{cases} ?$$

Exercise 11.3 Is there a solution to $f(x) = \frac{1}{2}f(2x) + f(2x - 1) + \frac{1}{2}f(2x - 2)$ with $f(0) = f(1) = 1$ and $f(2) = 0$?

Exercise 11.4 What is the solution to the dilation equation

$$f(x) = f(2x) + f(2x - 1) + f(2x - 2) + f(2x - 3).$$

Exercise 11.5 Consider the dilation equation

$$f(x) = f(2x) + 2f(2x - 1) + 2f(2x - 2) + 2f(2x - 3) + f(2x - 4)$$

1. What is the solution to the dilation equation?
2. What is the value of $\int_{-\infty}^{\infty} f(x)dx$?

Exercise 11.6 What are the solutions to the following families of dilation equations.

1.

$$f(x) = f(2x) + f(2x - 1)$$
$$f(x) = \frac{1}{2}f(2x) + \frac{1}{2}f(2x - 1) + \frac{1}{2}f(2x - 2) + \frac{1}{2}f(2x - 3)$$

$$f(x) = \frac{1}{4}f(2x) + \frac{1}{4}f(2x-1) + \frac{1}{4}f(2x-2) + \frac{1}{4}f(2x-3) + \frac{1}{4}f(2x-4)$$

$$+ \frac{1}{4}f(2x-5) + \frac{1}{4}f(2x-6) + \frac{1}{4}f(2x-7)$$

$$f(x) = \frac{1}{k}f(2x) + \frac{1}{k}f(2x) + \cdots + \frac{1}{k}f(2x)$$

2.

$$f(x) = \frac{1}{3}f(2x) + \frac{2}{3}f(2x-1) + \frac{2}{3}f(2x-2) + \frac{1}{3}f(2x-3)$$

$$f(x) = \frac{1}{4}f(2x) + \frac{3}{4}f(2x-1) + \frac{3}{4}f(2x-2) + \frac{1}{4}f(2x-3)$$

$$f(x) = \frac{1}{5}f(2x) + \frac{4}{5}f(2x-1) + \frac{4}{5}f(2x-2) + \frac{1}{5}f(2x-3)$$

$$f(x) = \frac{1}{k}f(2x) + \frac{k-1}{k}f(2x-1) + \frac{k-1}{k}f(2x-2) + \frac{1}{k}f(2x-3)$$

3.

$$f(x) = \frac{1}{2}f(2x) + \frac{1}{2}f(2x-1) + \frac{1}{2}f(2x-2) + \frac{1}{2}f(2x-3)$$

$$f(x) = \frac{3}{2}f(2x) - \frac{1}{2}f(2x-1) + \frac{3}{2}f(2x-2) - \frac{1}{2}f(2x-3)$$

$$f(x) = \frac{5}{2}f(2x) - \frac{3}{2}f(2x-1) + \frac{5}{2}f(2x-2) - \frac{3}{2}f(2x-3)$$

$$f(x) = \frac{1+2k}{2}f(2x) - \frac{2k-1}{2}f(2x-1) + \frac{1+2k}{2}f(2x-2) - \frac{2k-1}{2}f(2x-3)$$

4.

$$f(x) = \frac{1}{3}f(2x) + \frac{2}{3}f(2x-1) + \frac{2}{3}f(2x-2) + \frac{1}{3}f(2x-3)$$

$$f(x) = \frac{4}{3}f(2x) - \frac{1}{3}f(2x-1) + \frac{5}{3}f(2x-2) - \frac{2}{3}f(2x-3)$$

$$f(x) = \frac{7}{3}f(2x) - \frac{4}{3}f(2x-1) + \frac{8}{3}f(2x-2) - \frac{5}{3}f(2x-3)$$

$$f(x) = \frac{1+3k}{3}f(2x) - \frac{2-3k}{3}f(2x-1) + \frac{2+3k}{3}f(2x-2) - \frac{1-3k}{3}f(2x-3)$$

Exercise 11.7

1. What is the solution to the dilation equation $f(x) = \frac{1}{2}f(2x) + \frac{3}{2}f(2x-1)$? Hint: Write a program to see what the solution looks like.
2. How does the solution change when the equation is changed to $f(x) = \frac{1}{3}f(2x) + \frac{5}{3}f(2x-1)$?
3. How does the solution change if the coefficients no longer sum to 2 as in $f(x) = f(2x) + 3f(2x-1)$?

Exercise 11.8 If $f(x)$ is frequency limited by 2π, prove that

$$f(x) = \sum_{k=0}^{\infty} f(k) \frac{\sin(\pi(x-k))}{\pi(x-k)}.$$

Hint: Use the Nyquist sampling theorem, which states that a function frequency limited by 2π is completely determined by samples spaced one unit apart. Note that this result means that

$$f(k) = \int_{-\infty}^{\infty} f(x) \frac{\sin(\pi(x-k))}{\pi(x-k)} dx.$$

Exercise 11.9 Compute an approximation to the scaling function that comes from the dilation equation

$$\phi(x) = \frac{1+\sqrt{3}}{4}\phi(2x) + \frac{3+\sqrt{3}}{4}\phi(2x-1) + \frac{3-\sqrt{3}}{4}\phi(2x-2) + \frac{1\sqrt{3}}{4}\phi(2x-3).$$

Exercise 11.10 Consider $f(x)$ to consist of the semicircle $(x-\frac{1}{2})^2 + y^2 = \frac{1}{4}$ and $y \geq 0$ for $0 \leq x \leq 1$ and 0 otherwise.

1. Using precision $j = 4$ find the coefficients for the scale functions and the wavelets for D_4 defined by the dilation equation

$$\phi(x) = \frac{1+\sqrt{3}}{4}\phi(2x) + \frac{3+\sqrt{3}}{4}\phi(2x-1) + \frac{3-\sqrt{3}}{4}\phi(2x-2) + \frac{1\sqrt{3}}{4}\phi(2x-3)$$

2. Graph the approximation to the semicircle for precision $j = 4$.

Exercise 11.11 What is the set of all solutions to the dilation equation

$$\phi(x) = \frac{1+\sqrt{3}}{4}\phi(2x) + \frac{3+\sqrt{3}}{4}\phi(2x-1) + \frac{3-\sqrt{3}}{4}\phi(2x-2) + \frac{1\sqrt{3}}{4}\phi(2x-3)?$$

Exercise 11.12 Prove that if scale functions defined by a dilation equation are orthogonal, then the sum of the even coefficients must equal the sum of the odd coefficients in the dilation equation. That is, $\sum_{k} c_{2k} = \sum_{k} c_{2k+1}$.

CHAPTER TWELVE

Background Material

12.1. Definitions and Notation

12.1.1. Integers

$$\underbrace{\ldots, -3, -2, -1, \overbrace{0, \underbrace{1, 2, 3, \ldots}_{\text{positive integers}}}^{\text{nonnegative integers}}}_{\textit{integers}}$$

12.1.2. Substructures

A substring of a string is a contiguous string of symbols from the original string. A subsequence of a sequence is a sequence of elements from the original sequence in order but not necessarily contiguous. With subgraphs there are two possible definitions. We define a subgraph of a graph to be a subset of the vertices and a subset of the edges of the graph induced by the vertices. An induced subgraph is a subset of the vertices and all the edges of the graph induced by the subset of vertices.

12.1.3. Asymptotic Notation

We introduce the big O notation here. A motivating example is analyzing the running time of an algorithm. The running time may be a complicated function of the input length n such as $5n^3 + 25n^2 \ln n - 6n + 22$. Asymptotic analysis is concerned with the behavior as $n \to \infty$ where the higher-order term $5n^3$ dominates. Further, the coefficient 5 of $5n^3$ is not of interest, since its value varies depending on the machine model. So we say that the function is $O(n^3)$. The big O notation applies to functions on the positive integers taking on positive real values.

Definition 12.1 *For functions f and g from the natural numbers to the positive reals, $f(n)$ is $O(g(n))$ if there exists a constant $c > 0$ such that for all n, $f(n) \leq cg(n)$.* ∎

---

asymptotic upper bound
$f(n)$ is $O(g(n))$ if for all n, $f(n) \leq cg(n)$ for some constant $c > 0$. $\leq$

asymptotic lower bound
$f(n)$ is $\Omega(g(n))$ if for all n, $f(n) \geq cg(n)$ for some constant $c > 0$. $\geq$

asymptotic equality
$f(n)$ is $\Theta(g(n))$ if it is both $O(g(n))$ and $\Omega(g(n))$. $=$

$f(n)$ is $o(g(n))$ if $\lim\limits_{n\to\infty} \frac{f(n)}{g(n)} = 0$. $<$

$f(n) \sim g(n)$ if $\lim\limits_{n\to\infty} \frac{f(n)}{g(n)} = 1$. $=$

$f(n)$ is $\omega(g(n))$ **if** $\lim\limits_{n\to\infty} \frac{f(n)}{g(n)} = \infty$. $>$

Thus, $f(n) = 5n^3 + 25n^2 \ln n - 6n + 22$ is $O(n^3)$. The upper bound need not be tight. For example, in this case, $f(n)$ is also $O(n^4)$. Note that in our definition we require $g(n)$ to be strictly greater than 0 for all n.

To say that the function $f(n)$ grows at least as fast as $g(n)$, one uses a notation Omega. For positive real valued f and g, $f(n)$ is $\Omega(g(n))$ if there exists a constant $c > 0$ such that for all $n, f(n) \geq cg(n)$. If $f(n)$ is both $O(g(n))$ and $\Omega(g(n))$, then $f(n)$ is $\Theta(g(n))$. Theta is used when the two functions have the same asymptotic growth rate.

Many times one wishes to bound the low-order terms. To do this, a notation called little o is used. We say $f(n)$ is $o(g(n))$ if $\lim\limits_{n\to\infty} \frac{f(n)}{g(n)} = 0$. Note that $f(n)$ being $O(g(n))$ means that asymptotically $f(n)$ does not grow faster than $g(n)$, whereas $f(n)$ being $o(g(n))$ means that asymptotically $f(n)/g(n)$ goes to zero. If $f(n) = 2n + \sqrt{n}$, then $f(n)$ is $O(n)$, but in bounding the lower-order term, we write $f(n) = 2n + o(n)$. Finally, we write $f(n) \sim g(n)$ if $\lim\limits_{n\to\infty} \frac{f(n)}{g(n)} = 1$ and say $f(n)$ is $\omega(g(n))$ if $\lim\limits_{n\to\infty} \frac{f(n)}{g(n)} = \infty$. The difference between $f(n)$ being $\Theta(g(n))$ and $f(n) \sim g(n)$ is that in the first case $f(n)$ and $g(n)$ may differ by a multiplicative constant factor. We also note here that formally, $O(g(n))$ is a set of functions, namely the set of functions f such that $f(n)$ is $O(g(n))$; that is, "$f(n)$ is $O(g(n))$" formally means that $f(n) \in O(g(n))$.

12.2. Useful Relations

Summations

$$\sum_{i=0}^{n} a^i = 1 + a + a^2 + \cdots = \frac{1 - a^{n+1}}{1 - a}, \quad a \neq 1$$

$$\sum_{i=0}^{\infty} a^i = 1 + a + a^2 + \cdots = \frac{1}{1 - a}, \quad |a| < 1$$

$$\sum_{i=0}^{\infty} ia^i = a + 2a^2 + 3a^3 \cdots = \frac{a}{(1 - a)^2}, \quad |a| < 1$$

$$\sum_{i=0}^{\infty} i^2 a^i = a + 4a^2 + 9a^3 \cdots = \frac{a(1+a)}{(1-a)^3}, \quad |a| < 1$$

$$\sum_{i=1}^{n} i = \frac{n(n+1)}{2}$$

$$\sum_{i=1}^{n} i^2 = \frac{n(n+1)(2n+1)}{6}$$

$$\sum_{i=1}^{\infty} \frac{1}{i^2} = \frac{\pi^2}{6}$$

We prove one equality:

$$\sum_{i=0}^{\infty} i a^i = a + 2a^2 + 3a^3 \cdots = \frac{a}{(1-a)^2}, \text{ provided } |a| < 1.$$

Proof Write $S = \sum_{i=0}^{\infty} i a^i$. So,

$$aS = \sum_{i=0}^{\infty} i a^{i+1} = \sum_{i=1}^{\infty} (i-1) a^i.$$

Thus,

$$S - aS = \sum_{i=1}^{\infty} i a^i - \sum_{i=1}^{\infty} (i-1) a^i = \sum_{i=1}^{\infty} a^i = \frac{a}{1-a},$$

from which the equality follows. The sum $\sum_i i^2 a^i$ can also be done by an extension of this method (left to the reader). Using generating functions, we will see another proof of both these equalities by derivatives.

$$\sum_{i=1}^{\infty} \frac{1}{i} = 1 + \tfrac{1}{2} + \left(\tfrac{1}{3} + \tfrac{1}{4} \right) + \left(\tfrac{1}{5} + \tfrac{1}{6} + \tfrac{1}{7} + \tfrac{1}{8} \right) + \cdots \geq 1$$

$$+ \tfrac{1}{2} + \tfrac{1}{2} + \cdots \text{ and thus diverges.}$$

The summation $\sum_{i=1}^{n} \frac{1}{i}$ grows as $\ln n$, since $\sum_{i=1}^{n} \frac{1}{i} \approx \int_{x=1}^{n} \frac{1}{x} \, dx$. In fact, $\lim_{n \to \infty} \left(\sum_{i=1}^{n} \frac{1}{i} - \ln(n) \right) = \gamma$ where $\gamma \cong 0.5772$ is Euler's constant. Thus, $\sum_{i=1}^{n} \frac{1}{i} \cong \ln(n) + \gamma$ for large n.

Truncated Taylor series
If all the derivatives of a function $f(x)$ exist, then we can write

$$f(x) = f(0) + f'(0)x + f''(0)\frac{x^2}{2} + \cdots .$$

The series can be truncated. In fact, there exists some y between 0 and x such that

$$f(x) = f(0) + f'(y)x.$$

Also, there exists some z between 0 and x such that

$$f(x) = f(0) + f'(0)x + f''(z)\frac{x^2}{2}$$

and so on for higher derivatives. This can be used to derive inequalities. For example, if $f(x) = \ln(1 + x)$, then its derivatives are

$$f'(x) = \frac{1}{1+x} \; ; f''(x) = -\frac{1}{(1+x)^2} \; ; f'''(x) = \frac{2}{(1+x)^3}.$$

For any x, $f''(x) < 0$ and thus $f(x) \leq f(0) + f'(0)x$, hence $\ln(1 + x) \leq x$, which also follows from the inequality $1 + x \leq e^x$. Also using

$$f(x) = f(0) + f'(0)x + f''(0)\frac{x^2}{2} + f'''(z)\frac{x^3}{3!}$$

for $x > -1$, $f'''(x) > 0$, and so for $x > -1$,

$$\ln(1 + x) > x - \frac{x^2}{2}.$$

Exponentials and Logs

$$a^{\log b} = b^{\log a}$$

$$e^x = 1 + x + \frac{x^2}{2!} + \frac{x^3}{3!} + \cdots \qquad e \approx 2.718 \qquad \frac{1}{e} \approx 0.3679.$$

Setting $x = 1$ in the equation $e^x = 1 + x + \frac{x^2}{2!} + \frac{x^3}{3!} + \cdots$ yields $e = \sum_{i=0}^{\infty} \frac{1}{i!}$.

$$\lim_{n \to \infty} \left(1 + \frac{a}{n}\right)^n = e^a$$

$$\ln(1 + x) = x - \frac{1}{2}x^2 + \frac{1}{3}x^3 - \frac{1}{4}x^4 \cdots \qquad |x| < 1$$

The above expression with $-x$ substituted for x gives rise to the approximations

$$\ln(1 - x) < -x$$

which also follows from $1 - x \leq e^{-x}$, since $\ln(1 - x)$ is a monotone function for $x \in (0, 1)$.

For $0 < x < 0.69$, $\ln(1 - x) > -x - x^2$.

Trigonometric Identities

$$e^{ix} = \cos(x) + i\sin(x)$$
$$\cos(x) = \frac{1}{2}\left(e^{ix} + e^{-ix}\right)$$
$$\sin(x) = \frac{1}{2i}\left(e^{ix} - e^{-ix}\right)$$
$$\sin(x \pm y) = \sin(x)\cos(y) \pm \cos(x)\sin(y)$$
$$\cos(x \pm y) = \cos(x)\cos(y) \mp \sin(x)\sin(y)$$
$$\cos(2\theta) = \cos^2\theta - \sin^2\theta = 1 - 2\sin^2\theta$$
$$\sin(2\theta) = 2\sin\theta\cos\theta$$
$$\sin^2\frac{\theta}{2} = \frac{1}{2}(1 - \cos\theta)$$
$$\cos^2\frac{\theta}{2} = \frac{1}{2}(1 + \cos\theta)$$

Gaussian and Related Integrals

$$\int x e^{ax^2} dx = \frac{1}{2a} e^{ax^2}$$

$$\int \frac{1}{a^2+x^2} dx = \frac{1}{a} \tan^{-1} \frac{x}{a} \text{ thus } \int_{-\infty}^{\infty} \frac{1}{a^2+x^2} dx = \frac{\pi}{a}$$

$$\int_{-\infty}^{\infty} e^{-\frac{a^2 x^2}{2}} dx = \frac{\sqrt{2\pi}}{a} \text{ thus } \frac{a}{\sqrt{2\pi}} \int_{-\infty}^{\infty} e^{-\frac{a^2 x^2}{2}} dx = 1$$

$$\int_{0}^{\infty} x^2 e^{-ax^2} dx = \frac{1}{4a} \sqrt{\frac{\pi}{a}}$$

$$\int_{0}^{\infty} x^{2n} e^{-\frac{x^2}{a^2}} dx = \sqrt{\pi} \frac{1 \cdot 3 \cdot 5 \cdots (2n-1)}{2^{n+1}} a^{2n-1} = \sqrt{\pi} \frac{(2n)!}{n!} \left(\frac{a}{2}\right)^{2n+1}$$

$$\int_{0}^{\infty} x^{2n+1} e^{-\frac{x^2}{a^2}} dx = \frac{n!}{2} a^{2n+2}$$

$$\int_{-\infty}^{\infty} e^{-x^2} dx = \sqrt{\pi}$$

To verify $\int_{-\infty}^{\infty} e^{-x^2} dx = \sqrt{\pi}$, consider $\left(\int_{-\infty}^{\infty} e^{-x^2} dx\right)^2 = \int_{-\infty}^{\infty} \int_{-\infty}^{\infty} e^{-(x^2+y^2)} dx dy$. Let $x = r\cos\theta$ and $y = r\sin\theta$. The Jacobian of this transformation of variables is

$$J(r,\theta) = \begin{vmatrix} \frac{\partial x}{\partial r} & \frac{\partial x}{\partial \theta} \\ \frac{\partial y}{\partial r} & \frac{\partial y}{\partial \theta} \end{vmatrix} = \begin{vmatrix} \cos\theta & -r\sin\theta \\ \sin\theta & r\cos\theta \end{vmatrix} = r$$

Thus,

$$\left(\int_{-\infty}^{\infty} e^{-x^2} dx\right)^2 = \int_{-\infty}^{\infty} \int_{-\infty}^{\infty} e^{-(x^2+y^2)} dx dy = \int_{0}^{\infty} \int_{0}^{2\pi} e^{-r^2} J(r,\theta) dr d\theta$$

$$= \int_{0}^{\infty} e^{-r^2} r dr \int_{0}^{2\pi} d\theta$$

$$= -2\pi \left[\frac{e^{-r^2}}{2}\right]_{0}^{\infty} = \pi$$

Thus, $\int_{-\infty}^{\infty} e^{-x^2} dx = \sqrt{\pi}$.

The integral $\int_{1}^{\infty} x^r dx$ converges if $r \leq -1-\epsilon$ and diverges if $r \geq -1+\epsilon$

$$\int_{1}^{\infty} x^r dx = \frac{1}{r+1} x^{r+1} \Big|_{1}^{\infty} = \begin{cases} -\frac{1}{\epsilon} \frac{1}{x^\epsilon} \Big|_{1}^{\infty} = \frac{1}{\epsilon} & r = 1-\epsilon \\ \\ -\frac{1}{\epsilon} x^\epsilon \Big|_{1}^{\infty} = -\infty & r = 1+\epsilon \end{cases}$$

Thus $\sum_{i=1}^{\infty} \frac{1}{i^{1+\epsilon}}$ converges, since $\sum_{i=2}^{\infty} \frac{1}{i} < \int_{1}^{\infty} x^r dx$, and $\sum_{i=1}^{\infty} \frac{1}{i^{1-\epsilon}}$ diverges, since $\sum_{i=1}^{\infty} \frac{1}{i} > \int_{1}^{\infty} x^r dx$.

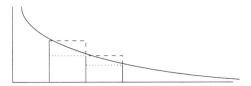

Miscellaneous Integrals

$$\int_{x=0}^{1} x^{\alpha-1}(1-x)^{\beta-1} dx = \frac{\Gamma(\alpha)\Gamma(\beta)}{\Gamma(\alpha+\beta)}$$

For definition of the Gamma function, $\Gamma(x)$, see Section 12.3.

Binomial Coefficients

The binomial coefficient $\binom{n}{k} = \frac{n!}{(n-k)!k!}$ is the number of ways of choosing k items from n. When choosing $d+1$ items from a set of $n+1$ items for $d < n$ one can either choose the first item and then choose d out of the remaining n or not choose the first item and then choose $d+1$ out of the remaining n. Therefore, for $d < n$,

$$\binom{n}{d} + \binom{n}{d+1} = \binom{n+1}{d+1}.$$

The observation that the number of ways of choosing k items from $2n$ equals the number of ways of choosing i items from the first n and choosing $k-i$ items from the second n summed over all $i, 0 \leq i \leq k$ yields the identity

$$\sum_{i=0}^{k} \binom{n}{i}\binom{n}{k-i} = \binom{2n}{k}.$$

Setting $k = n$ in the above formula and observing that $\binom{n}{i} = \binom{n}{n-i}$ yields

$$\sum_{i=0}^{n} \binom{n}{i}^2 = \binom{2n}{n}.$$

More generally, $\sum_{i=0}^{k} \binom{n}{i}\binom{m}{k-i} = \binom{n+m}{k}$ by a similar derivation.

12.3. Useful Inequalities

$1 + x \leq e^x$ for all real x.

One often establishes an inequality such as $1 + x \leq e^x$ by showing that the difference of the two sides, namely $e^x - (1 + x)$, is always positive. This can be done by taking derivatives. The first and second derivatives are $e^x - 1$ and e^x. Since e^x is always positive, $e^x - 1$ is monotonic and $e^x - (1 + x)$ is convex. Since $e^x - 1$ is monotonic, it can be zero only once and is zero at $x = 0$. Thus, $e^x - (1 + x)$ takes on its minimum at $x = 0$ where it is zero, establishing the inequality.

$(1 - x)^n \geq 1 - nx$ for $0 \leq x \leq 1$

Let $g(x) = (1 - x)^n - (1 - nx)$. We establish $g(x) \geq 0$ for x in $[0, 1]$ by taking the derivative.

$$g'(x) = -n(1 - x)^{n-1} + n = n\big(1 - (1 - x)^{n-1}\big) \geq 0$$

for $0 \leq x \leq 1$. Thus, g takes on its minimum for x in $[0, 1]$ at $x = 0$ where $g(0) = 0$ proving the inequality.

$1 + x \leq e^x$ for all real x

$(1 - x)^n \geq 1 - nx$ for $0 \leq x \leq 1$

$(x + y)^2 \leq 2x^2 + 2y^2$

Triangle Inequality $\quad |\mathbf{x} + \mathbf{y}| \leq |\mathbf{x}| + |\mathbf{y}|$.

Cauchy-Schwartz Inequality $\quad |\mathbf{x}||\mathbf{y}| \geq \mathbf{x}^T \mathbf{y}$

Young's Inequality For positive real numbers p and q where $\frac{1}{p} + \frac{1}{q} = 1$ and positive reals x and y,

$$xy \leq \frac{1}{p}x^p + \frac{1}{q}y^q.$$

Hölder's inequality For positive real numbers p and q with $\frac{1}{p} + \frac{1}{q} = 1$,

$$\sum_{i=1}^{n} |x_i y_i| \leq \left(\sum_{i=1}^{n} |x_i|^p\right)^{1/p} \left(\sum_{i=1}^{n} |y_i|^q\right)^{1/q}.$$

Jensen's inequality For a convex function f, for $\alpha_1 + \ldots + \alpha_n = 1, \alpha_i \geq 0$,

$$f\left(\sum_{i=1}^{n} \alpha_i x_i\right) \leq \sum_{i=1}^{n} \alpha_i f(x_i),$$

$(x + y)^2 \leq 2x^2 + 2y^2$

The inequality follows from $(x + y)^2 + (x - y)^2 = 2x^2 + 2y^2$.

Lemma 12.1 *For any nonnegative reals* $a_1, a_2, \ldots, a_n$ *and any* $\rho \in [0, 1]$, $\left(\sum_{i=1}^{n} a_i\right)^\rho \leq \sum_{i=1}^{n} a_i^\rho$.

Proof We will see that we can reduce the proof of the lemma to the case when only one of the a_i is non-zero and the rest are zero. To this end, suppose a_1 and a_2 are both positive and, without loss of generality, assume $a_1 \geq a_2$. Add an infinitesimal positive amount ϵ to a_1 and subtract the same amount from a_2. This does not alter the left-hand side. We claim it does not increase the right hand side. To see this, note that

$$(a_1 + \epsilon)^\rho + (a_2 - \epsilon)^\rho - a_1^\rho - a_2^\rho = \rho(a_1^{\rho-1} - a_2^{\rho-1})\epsilon + O(\epsilon^2),$$

and since $\rho - 1 \leq 0$, we have $a_1^{\rho-1} - a_2^{\rho-1} \leq 0$, proving the claim. Now by repeating this process, we can make $a_2 = 0$ (at that time a_1 will equal the sum of the original a_1 and a_2). Now repeating on all pairs of a_i, we can make all but one of them zero, and in the process the left-hand side remains the same and the right-hand side has not increased. So it suffices to prove the inequality at the end, which clearly holds. This method of proof is called the variational method. ∎

The Triangle Inequality

For any two vectors $\mathbf{x}$ and $\mathbf{y}$, $|\mathbf{x} + \mathbf{y}| \leq |\mathbf{x}| + |\mathbf{y}|$. This can be seen by viewing $\mathbf{x}$ and $\mathbf{y}$ as two sides of a triangle; equality holds if and only if the angle α between $\mathbf{x}$ and $\mathbf{y}$ is 180 degrees. Formally, by the law of cosines, we have $|\mathbf{x} + \mathbf{y}|^2 = |\mathbf{x}|^2 + |\mathbf{y}|^2 - 2|\mathbf{x}||\mathbf{y}|\cos(\alpha) \leq |\mathbf{x}|^2 + |\mathbf{y}|^2 + 2|\mathbf{x}||\mathbf{y}| = (|\mathbf{x}| + |\mathbf{y}|)^2$. The inequality follows by taking square roots.

Stirling Approximation

$$n! \cong \left(\frac{n}{e}\right)^n \sqrt{2\pi n} \qquad \binom{2n}{n} \cong \frac{1}{\sqrt{\pi n}} 2^{2n}$$

$$\sqrt{2\pi n}\frac{n^n}{e^n} < n! < \sqrt{2\pi n}\frac{n^n}{e^n}\left(1 + \frac{1}{12n - 1}\right)$$

We prove the inequalities, except for constant factors. Namely, we prove that

$$1.4 \left(\frac{n}{e}\right)^n \sqrt{n} \leq n! \leq e\left(\frac{n}{e}\right)^n \sqrt{n}.$$

Write $\ln(n!) = \ln 1 + \ln 2 + \cdots + \ln n$. This sum is approximately $\int_{x=1}^n \ln x \, dx$. The indefinite integral $\int \ln x \, dx = (x \ln x - x)$ gives an approximation, but without the $\sqrt{n}$ term. To get the $\sqrt{n}$, differentiate twice and note that $\ln x$ is a concave function. This means that for any positive x_0,

$$\frac{\ln x_0 + \ln(x_0 + 1)}{2} \leq \int_{x=x_0}^{x_0+1} \ln x \, dx,$$

since for $x \in [x_0, x_0 + 1]$, the curve $\ln x$ is always above the spline joining $(x_0, \ln x_0)$ and $(x_0 + 1, \ln(x_0 + 1))$. Thus,

$$\ln(n!) = \frac{\ln 1}{2} + \frac{\ln 1 + \ln 2}{2} + \frac{\ln 2 + \ln 3}{2} + \cdots + \frac{\ln(n-1) + \ln n}{2} + \frac{\ln n}{2}$$

$$\leq \int_{x=1}^n \ln x \, dx + \frac{\ln n}{2} = [x \ln x - x]_1^n + \frac{\ln n}{2}$$

$$= n \ln n - n + 1 + \frac{\ln n}{2}.$$

Thus, $n! \leq n^n e^{-n} \sqrt{n}e$. For the lower bound on $n!$, start with the fact that for any $x_0 \geq 1/2$ and any real ρ

$$\ln x_0 \geq \frac{1}{2}(\ln(x_0 + \rho) + \ln(x_0 - \rho)) \quad \text{implies} \quad \ln x_0 \geq \int_{x=x_0-0.5}^{x_0+.5} \ln x \, dx.$$

Thus,

$$\ln(n!) = \ln 2 + \ln 3 + \cdots + \ln n \geq \int_{x=1.5}^{n+.5} \ln x \, dx,$$

from which one can derive a lower bound with a calculation.

Stirling Approximation for the Binomial Coefficient

$$\binom{n}{k} \leq \left(\frac{en}{k}\right)^k$$

Using the Stirling approximation for $k!$,

$$\binom{n}{k} = \frac{n!}{(n-k)!\,k!} \leq \frac{n^k}{k!} \cong \left(\frac{en}{k}\right)^k.$$

The Gamma Function

For $a > 0$,

$$\Gamma(a) = \int_0^\infty x^{a-1} e^{-x} dx$$

$\Gamma\left(\frac{1}{2}\right) = \sqrt{\pi}$, $\quad \Gamma(1) = \Gamma(2) = 1$, and for $n \geq 2$, $\quad \Gamma(a) = (a-1)\Gamma(a-1)$.

To prove $\Gamma(a) = (a-1)\Gamma(a-1)$ use integration by parts.

$$\int f(x) g'(x) \, dx = f(x) g(x) - \int f'(x) g(x) \, dx$$

Write $\Gamma(a) = \int_{x=0}^\infty f(x)g'(x) \, dx$, where, $f(x) = x^{a-1}$ and $g'(x) = e^{-x}$. Thus,

$$\Gamma(a) = \int_0^\infty x^{a-1} e^{-x} dx = [f(x)g(x)]_{x=0}^\infty + \int_{x=0}^\infty (a-1)x^{a-2} e^{-x} \, dx$$

$$= \lim_{x \to \infty} x^{a-1} e^{-x} + (a-1)\Gamma(a-1) = (a-1)\Gamma(a-1),$$

as claimed.

Cauchy-Schwartz Inequality

$$\left(\sum_{i=1}^n x_i^2\right) \left(\sum_{i=1}^n y_i^2\right) \geq \left(\sum_{i=1}^n x_i y_i\right)^2$$

In vector form, $|\mathbf{x}||\mathbf{y}| \geq \mathbf{x}^T \mathbf{y}$, the inequality states that the dot product of two vectors is at most the product of their lengths. The Cauchy-Schwartz inequality is a special case of Hölder's inequality with $p = q = 2$.

Young's Inequality

For positive real numbers p and q where $\frac{1}{p} + \frac{1}{q} = 1$ and positive reals x and y,

$$\frac{1}{p}x^p + \frac{1}{q}y^q \geq xy.$$

The left-hand side of Young's inequality, $\frac{1}{p}x^p + \frac{1}{q}y^q$, is a convex combination of x^p and y^q, since $\frac{1}{p}$ and $\frac{1}{q}$ sum to 1. $\ln(x)$ is a concave function for $x > 0$, and so the ln of the convex combination of the two elements is greater than or equal to the convex combination of the ln of the two elements,

$$\ln\left(\frac{1}{p}x^p + \frac{1}{q}y^p\right) \geq \frac{1}{p}\ln(x^p) + \frac{1}{q}\ln(y^q) = \ln(xy).$$

Since for $x \geq 0$, $\ln x$ is a monotone increasing function, $\frac{1}{p}x^p + \frac{1}{q}y^q \geq xy$.

Hölder's Inequality

For positive real numbers p and q with $\frac{1}{p} + \frac{1}{q} = 1$,

$$\sum_{i=1}^{n} |x_i y_i| \leq \left(\sum_{i=1}^{n} |x_i|^p\right)^{1/p} \left(\sum_{i=1}^{n} |y_i|^q\right)^{1/q}.$$

Let $x_i' = x_i / \left(\sum_{i=1}^{n} |x_i|^p\right)^{1/p}$ and $y_i' = y_i / \left(\sum_{i=1}^{n} |y_i|^q\right)^{1/q}$. Replacing x_i by x_i' and y_i by y_i' does not change the inequality. Now $\sum_{i=1}^{n} |x_i'|^p = \sum_{i=1}^{n} |y_i'|^q = 1$, so it suffices to prove $\sum_{i=1}^{n} |x_i' y_i'| \leq 1$. Apply Young's inequality to get $|x_i' y_i'| \leq \frac{|x_i'|^p}{p} + \frac{|y_i'|^q}{q}$. Summing over i, the right-hand side sums to $\frac{1}{p} + \frac{1}{q} = 1$, finishing the proof.

For $a_1, a_2, \ldots, a_n$ real and k a positive integer,

$$(a_1 + a_2 + \cdots + a_n)^k \leq n^{k-1}(|a_1|^k + |a_2|^k + \cdots + |a_n|^k).$$

Using Hölder's inequality with $p = k$ and $q = k/(k-1)$,

$$|a_1 + a_2 + \cdots + a_n| \leq |a_1 \cdot 1| + |a_2 \cdot 1| + \cdots + |a_n \cdot 1|$$

$$\leq \left(\sum_{i=1}^{n} |a_i|^k\right)^{1/k} (1 + 1 + \cdots + 1)^{(k-1)/k},$$

from which the current inequality follows.

Arithmetic and Geometric Means

The arithmetic mean of a set of nonnegative reals is at least their geometric mean. For $a_1, a_2, \ldots, a_n > 0$,

$$\frac{1}{n}\sum_{i=1}^{n} a_i \geq \sqrt[n]{a_1 a_2 \cdots a_n}.$$

Assume that $a_1 \geq a_2 \geq \ldots \geq a_n$. We reduce the proof to the case when all the a_i are equal using the variational method. In this case the inequality holds with equality. Suppose $a_1 > a_2$. Let ε be a positive infinitesimal. Add ε to a_2 and subtract ε from a_1

to get closer to the case when they are equal. The left-hand side $\frac{1}{n} \sum_{i=1}^{n} a_i$ does not change.

$$(a_1 - \varepsilon)(a_2 + \varepsilon)a_3 a_4 \cdots a_n = a_1 a_2 \cdots a_n + \varepsilon(a_1 - a_2)a_3 a_4 \cdots a_n + O(\varepsilon^2)$$
$$> a_1 a_2 \cdots a_n$$

for small enough $\varepsilon > 0$. Thus, the change has increased $\sqrt[n]{a_1 a_2 \cdots a_n}$. So if the inequality holds after the change, it must hold before. By continuing this process, one can make all the a_i equal.

Approximating Sums by Integrals

For monotonic decreasing $f(x)$,

$$\int\limits_{x=m}^{n+1} f(x)dx \leq \sum_{i=m}^{n} f(i) \leq \int\limits_{x=m-1}^{n} f(x)dx.$$

See Figure 12.1. Thus,

$$\int\limits_{x=2}^{n+1} \frac{1}{x^2} dx \leq \sum_{i=2}^{n} \frac{1}{i^2} = \frac{1}{4} + \frac{1}{9} + \cdots + \frac{1}{n^2} \leq \int\limits_{x=1}^{n} \frac{1}{x^2} dx,$$

and hence $\frac{3}{2} - \frac{1}{n+1} \leq \sum_{i=1}^{n} \frac{1}{i^2} \leq 2 - \frac{1}{n}$.

Jensen's Inequality

For a convex function f,

$$f\left(\frac{1}{2}(x_1 + x_2)\right) \leq \frac{1}{2}(f(x_1) + f(x_2)).$$

(See Figure 12.2.) More generally, for any convex function f,

$$f\left(\sum_{i=1}^{n} \alpha_i x_i\right) \leq \sum_{i=1}^{n} \alpha_i f(x_i),$$

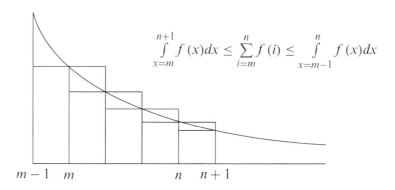

$$\int\limits_{x=m}^{n+1} f(x)dx \leq \sum_{i=m}^{n} f(i) \leq \int\limits_{x=m-1}^{n} f(x)dx$$

$m-1$ m n $n+1$

Figure 12.1: Approximating sums by integrals.

—— **370** ——

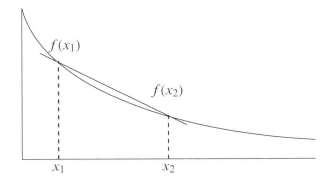

Figure 12.2: For a convex function f, $f\left(\frac{x_1+x_2}{2}\right) \leq \frac{1}{2}\left(f(x_1) + f(x_2)\right)$.

where $0 \leq \alpha_i \leq 1$ and $\sum_{i=1}^{n} \alpha_i = 1$. From this, it follows that for any convex function f and random variable x,

$$E\left(f\left(x\right)\right) \geq f\left(E\left(x\right)\right).$$

We prove this for a discrete random variable x taking on values $a_1, a_2, \ldots$ with $\text{Prob}(x = a_i) = \alpha_i$:

$$E(f(x)) = \sum_i \alpha_i f(a_i) \geq f\left(\sum_i \alpha_i a_i\right) = f(E(x)).$$

Example Let $f\left(x\right) = x^k$ for k an even positive integer. Then, $f''(x) = k(k-1)x^{k-2}$ which, since $k-2$ is even, is nonnegative for all x implying that f is convex. Thus,

$$E\left(x\right) \leq \sqrt[k]{E\left(x^k\right)},$$

since $t^{\frac{1}{k}}$ is a monotone function of t, $t > 0$. It is easy to see that this inequality does not necessarily hold when k is odd; indeed for odd k, x^k is not a convex function. ∎

Tails of Gaussians

For bounding the tails of Gaussian densities, the following inequality is useful. The proof uses a technique useful in many contexts. For $t > 0$,

$$\int_{x=t}^{\infty} e^{-x^2}\, dx \leq \frac{e^{-t^2}}{2t}.$$

In proof, first write: $\int_{x=t}^{\infty} e^{-x^2}\, dx \leq \int_{x=t}^{\infty} \frac{x}{t} e^{-x^2}\, dx$, using the fact that $x \geq t$ in the range of integration. The latter expression is integrable in closed form, since $d(e^{-x^2}) = (-2x)e^{-x^2}\, dx$ yielding the claimed bound.

A similar technique yields an upper bound on

$$\int_{x=\beta}^{1} (1 - x^2)^\alpha\, dx,$$

for $\beta \in [0, 1]$ and $\alpha > 0$. Just use $(1 - x^2)^\alpha \leq \frac{x}{\beta}(1 - x^2)^\alpha$ over the range and integrate the last expression.

$$\int_{x=\beta}^{1} (1 - x^2)^\alpha dx \leq \int_{x=\beta}^{1} \frac{x}{\beta}(1 - x^2)^\alpha dx = \frac{-1}{2\beta(\alpha + 1)}(1 - x^2)^{\alpha+1}\Big|_{x=\beta}^{1}$$
$$= \frac{(1 - \beta^2)^{\alpha+1}}{2\beta(\alpha + 1)}$$

12.4. Probability

Consider an experiment such as flipping a coin, whose outcome is determined by chance. To talk about the outcome of a particular experiment, we introduce the notion of a *random variable* whose value is the outcome of the experiment. The set of possible outcomes is called the *sample space*. If the sample space is finite, we can assign a probability of occurrence to each outcome. In some situations where the sample space is infinite, we can assign a probability of occurrence. The probability $p(i) = \frac{6}{\pi^2}\frac{1}{i^2}$ for i an integer greater than or equal to one is such an example. The function assigning the probabilities is called a *probability distribution function*.

In many situations, a probability distribution function does not exist. For example, for the uniform probability on the interval [0,1], the probability of any specific value is zero. What we can do is define a *probability density function $p(x)$* such that

$$\text{Prob}(a < x < b) = \int_a^b p(x)dx.$$

If x is a continuous random variable for which a density function exists, then the *cumulative distribution function $f(a)$* is defined by

$$f(a) = \int_{-\infty}^{a} p(x)dx,$$

which gives the probability that $x \leq a$.

12.4.1. Sample Space, Events, and Independence

There may be more than one relevant random variable in a situation. For example, if one tosses n coins, there are n random variables, $x_1, x_2, \ldots, x_n$, taking on values 0 and 1, a 1 for heads and a 0 for tails. The set of possible outcomes, the sample space, is $\{0, 1\}^n$. An *event* is a subset of the sample space. The event of an odd number of heads, consists of all elements of $\{0, 1\}^n$ with an odd number of 1's.

Let A and B be two events. The joint occurrence of the two events is denoted by $(A \wedge B)$. The *conditional probability* of event A given that event B has occurred is denoted by $\text{Prob}(A|B)$ and is given by

$$\text{Prob}(A|B) = \frac{\text{Prob}(A \wedge B)}{\text{Prob}(B)}.$$

Events A and B are *independent* if the occurrence of one event has no influence on the probability of the other. That is, $\text{Prob}(A|B) = \text{Prob}(A)$ or equivalently,

$\text{Prob}(A \wedge B) = \text{Prob}(A)\text{Prob}(B)$. Two random variables x and y are *independent* if for every possible set A of values for x and every possible set B of values for y, the events x in A and y in B are independent.

A collection of n random variables $x_1, x_2, \ldots, x_n$ is *mutually independent* if for all possible sets $A_1, A_2, \ldots, A_n$ of values of $x_1, x_2, \ldots, x_n$,

$$\text{Prob}(x_1 \in A_1, x_2 \in A_2, \ldots, x_n \in A_n) = \text{Prob}(x_1 \in A_1)\text{Prob}(x_2 \in A_2) \cdots \text{Prob}(x_n \in A_n).$$

If the random variables are discrete, it would suffice to say that for any values $a_1, a_2, \ldots, a_n$

$$\text{Prob}(x_1 = a_1, x_2 = a_2, \ldots, x_n = a_n) = \text{Prob}(x_1 = a_1)\text{Prob}(x_2 = a_2) \cdots \text{Prob}(x_n = a_n).$$

Random variables $x_1, x_2, \ldots, x_n$ are pairwise independent if for any a_i and a_j, $i \neq j$, $\text{Prob}(x_i = a_i, x_j = a_j) = \text{Prob}(x_i = a_i)\text{Prob}(x_j = a_j)$. An example of random variables x_1, x_2, x_3 that are pairwise independent but not mutually independent would be if x_1 and x_2 are the outcomes of independent fair coin flips, and x_3 is a $\{0, 1\}$-valued random variable that equals 1 when $x_1 = x_2$.

If (x, y) is a random vector and one normalizes it to a unit vector $\left(\frac{x}{\sqrt{x^2+y^2}}, \frac{y}{\sqrt{x^2+y^2}} \right)$, the coordinates are no longer independent, since knowing the value of one coordinate uniquely determines the absolute value of the other.

12.4.2. Linearity of Expectation

An important concept is that of the expectation of a random variable. The *expected value*, $E(x)$, of a random variable x is $E(x) = \sum_x xp(x)$ in the discrete case and $E(x) = \int_{-\infty}^{\infty} xp(x)dx$ in the continuous case. The expectation of a sum of random variables is equal to the sum of their expectations. The linearity of expectation follows directly from the definition and does not require independence.

12.4.3. Union Bound

Let $A_1, A_2, \ldots, A_n$ be events. The actual probability of the union of events is given by Boole's formula,

$$\text{Prob}(A_1 \cup A_2 \cup \cdots A_n) = \sum_{i=1}^{n} \text{Prob}(A_i) - \sum_{ij} \text{Prob}(A_i \wedge A_j)$$
$$+ \sum_{ijk} \text{Prob}(A_i \wedge A_j \wedge A_k) - \cdots$$

Often we only need an upper bound on the probability of the union and use

$$\text{Prob}(A_1 \cup A_2 \cup \cdots A_n) \leq \sum_{i=1}^{n} \text{Prob}(A_i).$$

This upper bound is called the *union bound*.

12.4.4. Indicator Variables

A useful tool is that of an indicator variable that takes on value 0 or 1 to indicate whether some quantity is present or not. The indicator variable is useful in determining the expected size of a subset. Given a random subset of the integers $\{1, 2, \ldots, n\}$, the expected size of the subset is the expected value of $x_1 + x_2 + \cdots + x_n$ where x_i is the indicator variable that takes on value 1 if i is in the subset.

> **Example** Consider a random permutation of n integers. Define the indicator function $x_i = 1$ if the ith integer in the permutation is i. The expected number of fixed points is given by
>
> $$E\left(\sum_{i=1}^{n} x_i\right) = \sum_{i=1}^{n} E(x_i) = n\frac{1}{n} = 1.$$
>
> Note that the x_i are not independent. However, linearity of expectation still applies. ∎

> **Example** Consider the expected number of vertices of degree d in a random graph $G(n, p)$. The number of vertices of degree d is the sum of n indicator random variables, one for each vertex, with value 1 if the vertex has degree d. The expectation is the sum of the expectations of the n indicator random variables, and this is just n times the expectation of one of them. Thus, the expected number of degree d vertices is $n\binom{n}{d}p^d(1-p)^{n-d}$. ∎

12.4.5. Variance

In addition to the expected value of a random variable, another important parameter is the variance. The *variance* of a random variable x, denoted var(x) or often $\sigma^2(x)$, is $E(x - E(x))^2$ and measures how close to the expected value the random variable is likely to be. The *standard deviation* σ is the square root of the variance. The units of σ are the same as those of x.

By linearity of expectation

$$\sigma^2 = E(x - E(x))^2 = E(x^2) - 2E(x)E(x) + E^2(x) = E(x^2) - E^2(x).$$

For the probability distribution Prob$(x = i) = \frac{6}{\pi^2}\frac{1}{i^2}$ $E(x) = \infty$. The probability distributions Prob$(x = i) = c\frac{1}{i^3}$ and Prob$(x_i = 2^i) = \frac{1}{4^i}$ have finite expectation but infinite variance.

12.4.6. Variance of the Sum of Independent Random Variables

In general, the variance of the sum is not equal to the sum of the variances. However, if x and y are independent, then $E(xy) = E(x)E(y)$ and

$$var(x + y) = var(x) + var(y).$$

To see this,

$$var(x + y) = E((x + y)^2) - E^2(x + y)$$
$$= E(x^2) + 2E(xy) + E(y^2) - E^2(x) - 2E(x)E(y) - E^2(y).$$

From independence, $2E(xy) - 2E(x)E(y) = 0$ and

$$var(x + y) = E(x^2) - E^2(x) + E(y^2) - E^2(y)$$
$$= var(x) + var(y).$$

More generally, if $x_1, x_2, \ldots, x_n$ are pairwise independent random variables, then

$$var(x_1 + x_2 + \cdots + x_n) = var(x_1) + var(x_2) + \cdots + var(x_n).$$

For the variance of the sum to be the sum of the variances requires only pairwise independence not full independence.

12.4.7. Median

One often calculates the average value of a random variable to get a feeling for the magnitude of the variable. This is reasonable when the probability distribution of the variable is Gaussian, or has a small variance. However, if there are outliers, then the average may be distorted by outliers. An alternative to calculating the expected value is to calculate the median, the value for which half of the probability is above and half is below.

12.4.8. The Central Limit Theorem

Let $s = x_1 + x_2 + \cdots + x_n$ be a sum of n independent random variables where each x_i has probability distribution

$$x_i = \begin{cases} 0 \text{ with probability } 0.5 \\ 1 \text{ with probability } 0.5 \end{cases}.$$

The expected value of each x_i is $1/2$ with variance

$$\sigma_i^2 = \left(\frac{1}{2} - 0\right)^2 \frac{1}{2} + \left(\frac{1}{2} - 1\right)^2 \frac{1}{2} = \frac{1}{4}.$$

The expected value of s is $n/2$, and since the variables are independent, the variance of the sum is the sum of the variances and hence is $n/4$. How concentrated s is around its mean depends on the standard deviation of s, which is $\frac{\sqrt{n}}{2}$. For $n = 100$, the expected value of s is 50 with a standard deviation of 5, which is 10% of the mean. For $n = 10,000$, the expected value of s is 5,000 with a standard deviation of 50, which is 1% of the mean. Note that as n increases, the standard deviation increases, but the ratio of the standard deviation to the mean goes to zero. More generally, if x_i are independent and identically distributed, each with standard deviation σ, then the standard deviation of $x_1 + x_2 + \cdots + x_n$ is $\sqrt{n}\sigma$. So, $\frac{x_1 + x_2 + \cdots + x_n}{\sqrt{n}}$ has standard deviation σ. The central limit theorem makes a stronger assertion that in fact $\frac{x_1 + x_2 + \cdots + x_n}{\sqrt{n}}$ has Gaussian distribution with standard deviation σ.

Theorem 12.2 *Suppose $x_1, x_2, \ldots, x_n$ is a sequence of identically distributed independent random variables, each with mean μ and variance σ^2. The distribution of the random variable*

$$\frac{1}{\sqrt{n}} (x_1 + x_2 + \cdots + x_n - n\mu)$$

converges to the distribution of the Gaussian with mean 0 and variance σ^2.

12.4.9. Probability Distributions

The Gaussian or Normal Distribution

The normal distribution is

$$\frac{1}{\sqrt{2\pi}\,\sigma} e^{-\frac{1}{2}\frac{(x-m)^2}{\sigma^2}}$$

where m is the mean and σ^2 is the variance. The coefficient $\frac{1}{\sqrt{2\pi}\,\sigma}$ makes the integral of the distribution be 1. If we measure distance in units of the standard deviation σ from the mean, then the standard normal distribution $\phi(x)$ with mean zero and variance 1 is

$$\phi(x) = \frac{1}{\sqrt{2\pi}} e^{-\frac{1}{2}x^2}.$$

Standard tables give values of the integral

$$\int_0^t \phi(x)dx,$$

and from these values one can compute probability integrals for a normal distribution with mean m and variance σ^2.

General Gaussians

So far we have seen spherical Gaussian densities in $\mathbf{R}^d$. The word "spherical" indicates that the level curves of the density are spheres. If a random vector $\mathbf{y}$ in $\mathbf{R}^d$ has a spherical Gaussian density with zero mean, then y_i and y_j, $i \neq j$, are independent. However, in many situations the variables are correlated. To model these Gaussians, level curves that are ellipsoids rather than spheres are used.

For a random vector $\mathbf{x}$, the covariance of x_i and x_j is $E((x_i - \mu_i)(x_j - \mu_j))$. We list the covariances in a matrix called the *covariance matrix*, denoted Σ.[1] Since $\mathbf{x}$ and $\boldsymbol{\mu}$ are column vectors, $(\mathbf{x} - \boldsymbol{\mu})(\mathbf{x} - \boldsymbol{\mu})^T$ is a $d \times d$ matrix. Expectation of a matrix or vector means componentwise expectation:

$$\Sigma = E\big((\mathbf{x} - \boldsymbol{\mu})(\mathbf{x} - \boldsymbol{\mu})^T\big).$$

The general Gaussian density with mean $\boldsymbol{\mu}$ and positive definite covariance matrix Σ is

$$f(\mathbf{x}) = \frac{1}{\sqrt{(2\pi)^d \det(\Sigma)}} \exp\left(-\frac{1}{2}(\mathbf{x} - \boldsymbol{\mu})^T \Sigma^{-1} (\mathbf{x} - \boldsymbol{\mu})\right).$$

To compute the covariance matrix of the Gaussian, substitute $\mathbf{y} = \Sigma^{-1/2}(\mathbf{x} - \boldsymbol{\mu})$. Noting that a positive definite symmetric matrix has a square root:

$$E((\mathbf{x} - \boldsymbol{\mu})(\mathbf{x} - \boldsymbol{\mu})^T = E(\Sigma^{1/2}\mathbf{y}\mathbf{y}^T\Sigma^{1/2})$$
$$= \Sigma^{1/2}\big(E(\mathbf{y}\mathbf{y}^T)\big)\Sigma^{1/2} = \Sigma.$$

The density of $\mathbf{y}$ is the unit variance, zero mean Gaussian, thus $E(yy^T) = I$.

---

[1] Σ is the standard notation for the covariance matrix. We will use it sparingly so as not to confuse with the summation sign.

Bernoulli Trials and the Binomial Distribution

A Bernoulli trial has two possible outcomes, called success or failure, with probabilities p and $1-p$, respectively. If there are n independent Bernoulli trials, the probability of exactly k successes is given by the *binomial distribution*:

$$B(n,p) = \binom{n}{k} p^k (1-p)^{n-k}.$$

The mean and variance of the binomial distribution $B(n,p)$ are np and $np(1-p)$, respectively. The mean of the binomial distribution is np, by linearity of expectations. The variance is $np(1-p)$, since the variance of a sum of independent random variables is the sum of their variances.

Let x_1 be the number of successes in n_1 trials and let x_2 be the number of successes in n_2 trials. The probability distribution of the sum of the successes, $x_1 + x_2$, is the same as the distribution of $x_1 + x_2$ successes in $n_1 + n_2$ trials. Thus, $B(n_1, p) + B(n_2, p) = B(n_1 + n_2, p)$.

When p is a constant, the expected degree of vertices in $G(n,p)$ increases with n. For example, in $G(n, \frac{1}{2})$, the expected degree of a vertex is $(n-1)/2$. In many applications, we will be concerned with $G(n,p)$ where $p = d/n$, for d a constant; i.e., graphs whose expected degree is a constant d independent of n. Holding $d = np$ constant as n goes to infinity, the binomial distribution

$$\text{Prob}(k) = \binom{n}{k} p^k (1-p)^{n-k}$$

approaches the Poisson distribution

$$\text{Prob}(k) = \frac{(np)^k}{k!} e^{-np} = \frac{d^k}{k!} e^{-d}.$$

To see this, assume $k = o(n)$ and use the approximations $n - k \cong n$, $\binom{n}{k} \cong \frac{n^k}{k!}$, and $\left(1 - \frac{1}{n}\right)^{n-k} \cong e^{-1}$ to approximate the binomial distribution by

$$\lim_{n \to \infty} \binom{n}{k} p^k (1-p)^{n-k} = \frac{n^k}{k!} \left(\frac{d}{n}\right)^k \left(1 - \frac{d}{n}\right)^n = \frac{d^k}{k!} e^{-d}.$$

Note that for $p = \frac{d}{n}$, where d is a constant independent of n, the probability of the binomial distribution falls off rapidly for $k > d$, and is essentially zero for all but some finite number of values of k. This justifies the $k = o(n)$ assumption. Thus, the Poisson distribution is a good approximation.

Poisson Distribution

The Poisson distribution describes the probability of k events happening in a unit of time when the average rate per unit of time is λ. Divide the unit of time into n segments. When n is large enough, each segment is sufficiently small so that the probability of two events happening in the same segment is negligible. The Poisson distribution gives the probability of k events happening in a unit of time and can be derived from the binomial distribution by taking the limit as $n \to \infty$.

Let $p = \frac{\lambda}{n}$. Then

$$\text{Prob}(k \text{ successes in a unit of time}) = \lim_{n \to \infty} \binom{n}{k} \left(\frac{\lambda}{n}\right)^k \left(1 - \frac{\lambda}{n}\right)^{n-k}$$

$$= \lim_{n \to \infty} \frac{n(n-1)\cdots(n-k+1)}{k!} \left(\frac{\lambda}{n}\right)^k \left(1 - \frac{\lambda}{n}\right)^n \left(1 - \frac{\lambda}{n}\right)^{-k}$$

$$= \lim_{n \to \infty} \frac{\lambda^k}{k!} e^{-\lambda}.$$

In the limit, as n goes to infinity, the binomial distribution $p(k) = \binom{n}{k}p^k (1 - p)^{n-k}$ becomes the Poisson distribution $p(k) = e^{-\lambda}\frac{\lambda^k}{k!}$. The mean and the variance of the Poisson distribution have value λ. If x and y are both Poisson random variables from distributions with means λ_1 and λ_2, respectively, then $x + y$ is Poisson with mean $m_1 + m_2$. For large n and small p, the binomial distribution can be approximated with the Poisson distribution.

The binomial distribution with mean np and variance $np(1 - p)$ can be approximated by the normal distribution with mean np and variance $np(1 - p)$. The central limit theorem tells us that there is such an approximation in the limit. The approximation is good if both np and $n(1 - p)$ are greater than 10 provided k is not extreme. Thus,

$$\binom{n}{k} \left(\frac{1}{2}\right)^k \left(\frac{1}{2}\right)^{n-k} \cong \frac{1}{\sqrt{\pi n/2}} e^{-\frac{(n/2-k)^2}{\frac{1}{2}n}}.$$

This approximation is excellent provided k is $\Theta(n)$. The Poisson approximation

$$\binom{n}{k} p^k (1 - p)^k \cong e^{-np} \frac{(np)^k}{k!}$$

is off for central values and tail values even for $p = 1/2$. The approximation

$$\binom{n}{k} p^k (1 - p)^{n-k} \cong \frac{1}{\sqrt{\pi pn}} e^{-\frac{(pn-k)^2}{pn}}$$

is good for $p = 1/2$ but is off for other values of p.

Generation of Random Numbers According to a Given Probability Distribution

Suppose one wanted to generate a random variable with probability density $p(x)$ where $p(x)$ is continuous. Let $P(x)$ be the cumulative distribution function for x and let u be a random variable with uniform probability density over the interval [0,1]. Then the random variable $x = P^{-1}(u)$ has probability density $p(x)$.

Example For a Cauchy density function the cumulative distribution function is

$$P(x) = \int_{t=-\infty}^{x} \frac{1}{\pi} \frac{1}{1 + t^2} dt = \frac{1}{2} + \frac{1}{\pi} \tan^{-1}(x).$$

Setting $u = P(x)$ and solving for x yields $x = \tan\left(\pi\left(u - \frac{1}{2}\right)\right)$. Thus, to generate a random number $x \geq 0$ using the Cauchy distribution, generate u, $0 \leq u \leq 1$,

—— **378** ——

uniformly and calculate $x = \tan\left(\pi\left(u - \frac{1}{2}\right)\right)$. The value of x varies from $-\infty$ to ∞ with $P(0) = 1/2$. ∎

12.4.10. Bayes Rule and Estimators

Bayes Rule

Bayes rule relates the conditional probability of A given B to the conditional probability of B given A:

$$\text{Prob}(A|B) = \frac{\text{Prob}(B|A)\,\text{Prob}(A)}{\text{Prob}(B)}.$$

Suppose one knows the probability of A and wants to know how this probability changes if we know that B has occurred. Prob(A) is called the *prior probability*. The conditional probability Prob($A|B$) is called the *posterior probability* because it is the probability of A after we know that B has occurred.

The example below illustrates that if a situation is rare, a highly accurate test will often give the wrong answer.

Example Let A be the event that a product is defective and let B be the event that a test says a product is defective. Let Prob($B|A$) be the probability that the test says a product is defective assuming the product is defective, and let Prob$\left(B|\bar{A}\right)$ be the probability that the test says a product is defective if it is not actually defective.

What is the probability Prob($A|B$) that the product is defective if the test says it is defective? Suppose Prob(A) = 0.001, Prob($B|A$) = 0.99, and Prob$\left(B|\bar{A}\right)$ = 0.02. Then

$$\text{Prob}(B) = \text{Prob}(B|A)\,\text{Prob}(A) + \text{Prob}\left(B|\bar{A}\right)\text{Prob}\left(\bar{A}\right)$$
$$= 0.99 \times 0.001 + 0.02 \times 0.999$$
$$= 0.02087$$

and

$$\text{Prob}(A|B) = \frac{\text{Prob}(B|A)\,\text{Prob}(A)}{\text{Prob}(B)} \approx \frac{0.99 \times 0.001}{0.0210} = 0.0471.$$

Even though the test fails to detect a defective product only 1% of the time when it is defective and claims that it is defective when it is not only 2% of the time, the test is correct only 4.7% of the time when it says a product is defective. This comes about because of the low frequencies of defective products. ∎

The words "prior," "a posteriori," and "likelihood" come from Bayes theorem.

$$\text{a posteriori} = \frac{\text{likelihood} \times \text{prior}}{\text{normalizing constant}}$$
$$\text{Prob}(A|B) = \frac{\text{Prob}(B|A)\,\text{Prob}(A)}{\text{Prob}(B)}$$

The a posteriori probability is the conditional probability of A given B. The likelihood is the conditional probability Prob($B|A$).

Unbiased Estimators

Consider n samples $x_1, x_2, \ldots, x_n$ from a Gaussian distribution of mean μ and variance σ^2. For this distribution, $m = \frac{x_1 + x_2 + \cdots + x_n}{n}$ is an unbiased estimator of μ, which means that $E(m) = \mu$ and $\frac{1}{n} \sum_{i=1}^{n} (x_i - \mu)^2$ is an unbiased estimator of σ^2. However, if μ is not known and is approximated by m, then $\frac{1}{n-1} \sum_{i=1}^{n} (x_i - m)^2$ is an unbiased estimator of σ^2.

Maximum Likelihood Estimation (MLE)

Suppose the probability distribution of a random variable x depends on a parameter r. With slight abuse of notation, since r is a parameter rather than a random variable, we denote the probability distribution of x as $p(x|r)$. This is the likelihood of observing x if r was in fact the parameter value. The job of the maximum likelihood estimator (MLE) is to find the best r after observing values of the random variable x. The likelihood of r being the parameter value given that we have observed x is denoted $L(r|x)$. This is again not a probability, since r is a parameter, not a random variable. However, if we were to apply Bayes' rule as if this was a conditional probability, we get

$$L(r|x) = \frac{\text{Prob}(x|r)\text{Prob}(r)}{\text{Prob}(x)}.$$

Now, assume $\text{Prob}(r)$ is the same for all r. The denominator $\text{Prob}(x)$ is the absolute probability of observing x and is independent of r. So to maximize $L(r|x)$, we just maximize $\text{Prob}(x|r)$. In some situations, one has a prior guess as to the distribution $\text{Prob}(r)$. This is then called the "prior," and in that case, we call $\text{Prob}(x|r)$ the posterior, which we try to maximize.

> **Example** Consider flipping a coin 100 times. Suppose 62 heads and 38 tails occur. What is the maximum likelihood value of the probability of the coin to come down heads when the coin is flipped? In this case, it is $r = 0.62$. The probability that we get 62 heads if the unknown probability of heads in one trial is r is
>
> $$\text{Prob}(62 \text{ heads}|r) = \binom{100}{62} r^{62}(1 - r)^{38}.$$
>
> This quantity is maximized when $r = 0.62$. To see this take the derivative with respect to r of $r^{62}(1 - r)^{38}$ The derivative is zero at $r = 0.62$ and the second derivative is negative indicating a maximum. Thus, $r = 0.62$ is the maximum likelihood estimator of the probability of heads in a trial. ∎

12.5. Bounds on Tail Probability

12.5.1. Chernoff Bounds

Markov's inequality bounds the probability that a nonnegative random variable exceeds a value a.

$$p(x \geq a) \leq \frac{E(x)}{a}$$

or

$$p(x \geq aE(x)) \leq \frac{1}{a}.$$

If one also knows the variance, σ^2, then using Chebyshev's inequality one can bound the probability that a random variable differs from its expected value by more than a standard deviations. Let $m = E(x)$. Then Chebyshev's inequality states that

$$p(|x - m| \geq a\sigma) \leq \frac{1}{a^2}.$$

If a random variable s is the sum of n independent random variables $x_1, x_2, \ldots, x_n$ of finite variance, then better bounds are possible. Here we focus on the case where the n independent variables are binomial. In the next section we consider the more general case where we have independent random variables from any distribution that has a finite variance.

Let $x_1, x_2, \ldots, x_n$ be independent random variables where

$$x_i = \begin{cases} 0 & \text{Prob } 1 - p \\ 1 & \text{Prob } p \end{cases}.$$

Consider the sum $s = \sum_{i=1}^{n} x_i$. Here the expected value of each x_i is p and by linearity of expectation, the expected value of the sum is $m = np$. Chernoff bounds bound the probability that the sum s exceeds $(1 + \delta)m$ or is less than $(1 - \delta)m$. We state these bounds as Theorems 12.3 and 12.4 below and give their proofs.

Theorem 12.3 *For any $\delta > 0, Prob\left(s > (1 + \delta)m\right) < \left(\frac{e^\delta}{(1+\delta)^{(1+\delta)}}\right)^m.$*

Theorem 12.4 *Let $0 < \gamma \leq 1$, then $Prob\left(s < (1 - \gamma)m\right) < \left(\frac{e^{-\gamma}}{(1+\gamma)^{(1+\gamma)}}\right)^m <$*
$e^{-\frac{\gamma^2 m}{2}}.$

Proof (Theorem 12.3) For any $\lambda > 0$, the function $e^{\lambda x}$ is monotone. Thus,

$$\text{Prob}\left(s > (1 + \delta)m\right) = \text{Prob}\left(e^{\lambda s} > e^{\lambda(1+\delta)m}\right).$$

$e^{\lambda x}$ is nonnegative for all x, so we can apply Markov's inequality to get

$$\text{Prob}\left(e^{\lambda s} > e^{\lambda(1+\delta)m}\right) \leq e^{-\lambda(1+\delta)m} E(e^{\lambda s}).$$

Since the x_i are independent,

$$E\left(e^{\lambda s}\right) = E\left(e^{\lambda \sum_{i=1}^{n} x_i}\right) = E\left(\prod_{i=1}^{n} e^{\lambda x_i}\right) = \prod_{i=1}^{n} E\left(e^{\lambda x_i}\right)$$

$$= \prod_{i=1}^{n} \left(e^\lambda p + 1 - p\right) = \prod_{i=1}^{n} \left(p(e^\lambda - 1) + 1\right).$$

Using the inequality $1 + x < e^x$ with $x = p(e^\lambda - 1)$ yields

$$E\left(e^{\lambda s}\right) < \prod_{i=1}^{n} e^{p(e^\lambda - 1)}.$$

Thus, for all $\lambda > 0$,

$$\text{Prob}\left(s > (1+\delta)m\right) \leq \text{Prob}\left(e^{\lambda s} > e^{\lambda(1+\delta)m}\right)$$
$$\leq e^{-\lambda(1+\delta)m} E\left(e^{\lambda s}\right)$$
$$\leq e^{-\lambda(1+\delta)m} \prod_{i=1}^{n} e^{p(e^{\lambda}-1)}.$$

Setting $\lambda = \ln(1+\delta)$,

$$\text{Prob}\left(s > (1+\delta)m\right) \leq \left(e^{-\ln(1+\delta)}\right)^{(1+\delta)m} \prod_{i=1}^{n} e^{p(e^{\ln(1+\delta)}-1)}$$
$$\leq \left(\frac{1}{1+\delta}\right)^{(1+\delta)m} \prod_{i=1}^{n} e^{p\delta}$$
$$\leq \left(\frac{1}{(1+\delta)}\right)^{(1+\delta)m} e^{np\delta}$$
$$\leq \left(\frac{e^{\delta}}{(1+\delta)^{(1+\delta)}}\right)^{m}.$$

To simplify the bound of Theorem 12.3, observe that

$$(1+\delta)\ln(1+\delta) = \delta + \frac{\delta^2}{2} - \frac{\delta^3}{6} + \frac{\delta^4}{12} - \cdots.$$

Therefore,

$$(1+\delta)^{(1+\delta)} = e^{\delta + \frac{\delta^2}{2} - \frac{\delta^3}{6} + \frac{\delta^4}{12} - \cdots}$$

and hence,

$$\frac{e^{\delta}}{(1+\delta)^{(1+\delta)}} = e^{-\frac{\delta^2}{2} + \frac{\delta^3}{6} - \cdots}.$$

Thus, the bound simplifies to

$$\text{Prob}\left(s < (1+\delta)m\right) \leq e^{-\frac{\delta^2}{2}m + \frac{\delta^3}{6}m - \cdots}.$$

For small δ, the probability drops exponentially with δ^2.

When δ is large, another simplification is possible. First,

$$\text{Prob}\left(s > (1+\delta)m\right) \leq \left(\frac{e^{\delta}}{(1+\delta)^{(1+\delta)}}\right)^{m} \leq \left(\frac{e}{1+\delta}\right)^{(1+\delta)m}.$$

If $\delta > 2e - 1$, substituting $2e - 1$ for δ in the denominator yields

$$\text{Prob}(s > (1+\delta)m) \leq 2^{-(1+\delta)m}.$$

Theorem 12.3 gives a bound on the probability of the sum being significantly greater than the mean. We now prove Theorem 12.4, bounding the probability that the sum will be significantly less than its mean.

Proof (Theorem 12.4) For any $\lambda > 0$,

$$\text{Prob}\big(s < (1 - \gamma)m\big) = \text{Prob}\big(-s > -(1 - \gamma)m\big) = \text{Prob}\big(e^{-\lambda s} > e^{-\lambda(1-\gamma)m}\big).$$

Applying Markov's inequality,

$$\text{Prob}\big(s < (1 - \gamma)m\big) < \frac{E(e^{-\lambda x})}{e^{-\lambda(1-\gamma)m}} < \frac{\prod_{i=1}^{n} E(e^{-\lambda X_i})}{e^{-\lambda(1-\gamma)m}}.$$

Now,

$$E(e^{-\lambda x_i}) = pe^{-\lambda} + 1 - p = 1 + p(e^{-\lambda} - 1) + 1.$$

Thus,

$$\text{Prob}(s < (1 - \gamma)m) < \frac{\prod_{i=1}^{n} [1 + p(e^{-\lambda} - 1)]}{e^{-\lambda(1-\gamma)m}}.$$

Since $1 + x < e^x$,

$$\text{Prob}\big(s < (1 - \gamma)m\big) < \frac{e^{np(e^{-\lambda}-1)}}{e^{-\lambda(1-\gamma)m}}.$$

Setting $\lambda = \ln \frac{1}{1-\gamma}$

$$\text{Prob}\big(s < (1 - \gamma)m\big) < \frac{e^{np(1-\gamma-1)}}{(1 - \gamma)^{(1-\gamma)m}}$$

$$< \left(\frac{e^{-\gamma}}{(1 - \gamma)^{(1-\gamma)}}\right)^m.$$

But for $0 < \gamma \leq 1$, $(1 - \gamma)^{(1-\gamma)} > e^{-\gamma + \frac{\gamma^2}{2}}$. To see this, note that

$$(1 - \gamma) \ln (1 - \gamma) = (1 - \gamma)\left(-\gamma - \frac{\gamma^2}{2} - \frac{\gamma^3}{3} - \cdots\right)$$

$$= -\gamma - \frac{\gamma^2}{2} - \frac{\gamma^3}{3} - \cdots + \gamma^2 + \frac{\gamma^3}{2} + \frac{\gamma^4}{3} + \cdots$$

$$= -\gamma + \left(\gamma^2 - \frac{\gamma^2}{2}\right) + \left(\frac{\gamma^3}{2} - \frac{\gamma^3}{3}\right) + \cdots$$

$$= -\gamma + \frac{\gamma^2}{2} + \frac{\gamma^3}{6} + \cdots$$

$$\geq -\gamma + \frac{\gamma^2}{2}.$$

It then follows that

$$\text{Prob}\big(s < (1 - \gamma)m\big) < \left(\frac{e^{-\gamma}}{(1 - \gamma)^{(1-\gamma)}}\right)^m < e^{-\frac{m\gamma^2}{2}}.$$

12.5.2. More General Tail Bounds

The main purpose of this section is to state the Master Tail bounds theorem of Chapter 2 (with more detail), give a proof of it, and derive the other tail inequalities mentioned in the table in that chapter. Recall that Markov's inequality bounds the tail probability of a nonnegative random variable x based only on its expectation. For $a > 0$,

$$\text{Prob}(x > a) \leq \frac{E(x)}{a}.$$

As a grows, the bound drops off as $1/a$. Given the second moment of x, recall that Chebyshev's inequality, which does not assume x is a nonnegative random variable, gives a tail bound falling off as $1/a^2$:

$$\text{Prob}(|x - E(x)| \geq a) \leq \frac{E\big((x - E(x))^2\big)}{a^2}.$$

Higher moments yield bounds by applying either of these two theorems. For example, if r is a nonnegative even integer, then x^r is a nonnegative random variable even if x takes on negative values. Applying Markov's inequality to x^r,

$$\text{Prob}(|x| \geq a) = \text{Pr}(x^r \geq a^r) \leq \frac{E(x^r)}{a^r},$$

a bound that falls off as $1/a^r$. The larger the r, the greater the rate of fall, but a bound on $E(x^r)$ is needed to apply this technique.

For a random variable x that is the sum of a large number of independent random variables, $x_1, x_2, \ldots, x_n$, one can derive bounds on $E(x^r)$ for high even r. There are many situations where the sum of a large number of independent random variables arises. For example, x_i may be the amount of a good that the ith consumer buys, the length of the ith message sent over a network, or the indicator random variable of whether the ith record in a large database has a certain property. Each x_i is modeled by a simple probability distribution. Gaussian, exponential probability density (at any $t > 0$ is e^{-t}), or binomial distributions are typically used – in fact, they are used respectively in the three examples here. If the x_i have 0-1 distributions, then the Chernoff bounds described in Section 12.5.1 can be used to bound the tails of $x = x_1 + x_2 + \cdots + x_n$. But exponential and Gaussian random variables are not bounded, so the proof technique used in Section 12.5.1 does not apply. However, good bounds on the moments of these two distributions are known. Indeed, for any integer $s > 0$, the sth moment for the unit variance Gaussian and the exponential are both at most $s!$.

Given bounds on the moments of individual x_i, the following theorem proves moment bounds on their sum. We use this theorem to derive tail bounds not only for sums of 0-1 random variables but also for Gaussians, exponentials, Poisson, etc.

The gold standard for tail bounds is the central limit theorem for independent, identically distributed random variables $x_1, x_2, \cdots, x_n$ with zero mean and $\text{Var}(x_i) = \sigma^2$ that states as $n \to \infty$ the distribution of $x = (x_1 + x_2 + \cdots + x_n)/\sqrt{n}$ tends to the Gaussian density with zero mean and variance σ^2. Loosely, this says that in the limit, the tails of $x = (x_1 + x_2 + \cdots + x_n)/\sqrt{n}$ are bounded by that of a Gaussian with variance σ^2. But this theorem is only in the limit, whereas we prove a bound that applies for all n.

In the following theorem, x is the sum of n independent, not necessarily identically distributed, random variables $x_1, x_2, \ldots, x_n$, each of zero mean and variance at most σ^2. By the central limit theorem, in the limit the probability density of x goes to that of the Gaussian with variance at most $n\sigma^2$. In a limit sense, this implies an upper bound of $ce^{-a^2/(2n\sigma^2)}$ for the tail probability $\Pr(|x| > a)$ for some constant c. The following theorem assumes bounds on higher moments, and asserts a quantitative upper bound of $3e^{-a^2/(12n\sigma^2)}$ on the tail probability, not just in the limit, but for every n. We will apply this theorem to get tail bounds on sums of Gaussian, binomial, and power law distributed random variables.

Theorem 12.5 *Let* $x = x_1 + x_2 + \cdots + x_n$, *where* $x_1, x_2, \ldots, x_n$ *are mutually independent random variables with zero mean and variance at most* σ^2. *Suppose* $a \in [0, \sqrt{2}n\sigma^2]$ *and* $s \le n\sigma^2/2$ *is a positive even integer and* $|E(x_i^r)| \le \sigma^2 r!$, *for* $r = 3, 4, \ldots, s$. *Then,*

$$\text{Prob}\,(|x_1 + x_2 + \cdots x_n| \ge a) \le \left(\frac{2sn\sigma^2}{a^2}\right)^{s/2}.$$

If further, $s \ge a^2/(4n\sigma^2)$, *then we also have*

$$\text{Prob}\,(|x_1 + x_2 + \cdots x_n| \ge a) \le 3e^{-a^2/(12n\sigma^2)}.$$

Proof We first prove an upper bound on $E(x^r)$ for any even positive integer r and then use Markov's inequality as discussed earlier. Expand $(x_1 + x_2 + \cdots + x_n)^r$.

$$(x_1 + x_2 + \cdots + x_n)^r = \sum \binom{r}{r_1, r_2, \ldots, r_n} x_1^{r_1} x_2^{r_2} \cdots x_n^{r_n}$$

$$= \sum \frac{r!}{r_1! r_2! \cdots r_n!} x_1^{r_1} x_2^{r_2} \cdots x_n^{r_n}$$

where the r_i range over all nonnegative integers summing to r. By independence,

$$E(x^r) = \sum \frac{r!}{r_1! r_2! \cdots r_n!} E(x_1^{r_1}) E(x_2^{r_2}) \cdots E(x_n^{r_n}).$$

If in a term, any $r_i = 1$, the term is zero, since $E(x_i) = 0$. Assume henceforth that $(r_1, r_2, \ldots, r_n)$ runs over sets of non-zero r_i summing to r where each non-zero r_i is at least 2. There are at most $r/2$ non-zero r_i in each set. Since $|E(x_i^{r_i})| \le \sigma^2 r_i!$,

$$E(x^r) \le r! \sum_{(r_1, r_2, \ldots, r_n)} \sigma^{2(\text{ number of non-zero } r_i \text{ in set})}.$$

Collect terms of the summation with t non-zero r_i for $t = 1, 2, \ldots, r/2$. There are $\binom{n}{t}$ subsets of $\{1, 2, \ldots, n\}$ of cardinality t. Once a subset is fixed as the set of t values of i with non-zero r_i, set each of the $r_i \ge 2$. That is, allocate two to each of the r_i and then allocate the remaining $r - 2t$ to the t r_i arbitrarily. The number of such allocations is just $\binom{r-2t+t-1}{t-1} = \binom{r-t-1}{t-1}$. So,

$$E(x^r) \le r! \sum_{t=1}^{r/2} f(t), \quad \text{where} \quad f(t) = \binom{n}{t}\binom{r-t-1}{t-1}\sigma^{2t}.$$

Thus $f(t) \leq h(t)$, where $h(t) = \frac{(n\sigma^2)^t}{t!} 2^{r-t-1}$. Since $t \leq r/2 \leq n\sigma^2/4$, we have

$$\frac{h(t)}{h(t-1)} = \frac{n\sigma^2}{2t} \geq 2.$$

So, we get

$$E(x^r) = r! \sum_{t=1}^{r/2} f(t) \leq r! \, h(r/2) \left(1 + \frac{1}{2} + \frac{1}{4} + \cdots \right) \leq \frac{r!}{(r/2)!} 2^{r/2} (n\sigma^2)^{r/2}.$$

Applying Markov inequality,

$$\mathrm{Prob}(|x| > a) = \mathrm{Prob}(|x|^r > a^r) \leq \frac{r! \, (n\sigma^2)^{r/2} 2^{r/2}}{(r/2)! \, a^r} = g(r) \leq \left(\frac{2rn\sigma^2}{a^2}\right)^{r/2}.$$

This holds for all $r \leq s, r$ even and applying it with $r = s$, we get the first inequality of the theorem.

We now prove the second inequality. For even $r, g(r)/g(r-2) = \frac{4(r-1)n\sigma^2}{a^2}$, and so $g(r)$ decreases as long as $r - 1 \leq a^2/(4n\sigma^2)$. Taking r to be the largest even integer less than or equal to $a^2/(6n\sigma^2)$, the tail probability is at most $e^{-r/2}$, which is at most $e \cdot e^{-a^2/(12n\sigma^2)} \leq 3 \cdot e^{-a^2/(12n\sigma^2)}$, proving the theorem. ∎

12.6. Applications of the Tail Bound

Chernoff Bounds

Chernoff bounds deal with sums of Bernoulli random variables. Here we apply Theorem 12.5 to derive these.

Theorem 12.6 *Suppose $y_1, y_2, \ldots, y_n$ are independent 0-1 random variables with $E(y_i) = p$ for all i. Let $y = y_1 + y_2 + \cdots + y_n$. Then for any $c \in [0, 1]$,*

$$\mathrm{Prob}\big(|y - E(y)| \geq cnp\big) \leq 3e^{-npc^2/8}.$$

Proof Let $x_i = y_i - p$. Then, $E(x_i) = 0$ and $E(x_i^2) = E(y - p)^2 = p$. For $s \geq 3$,

$$\begin{aligned}
|E(x_i^s)| &= \big|E(y_i - p)^s\big| \\
&= \big|p(1-p)^s + (1-p)(0-p)^s\big| \\
&= \big|p(1-p)\big((1-p)^{s-1} + (-p)^{s-1}\big)\big| \\
&\leq p.
\end{aligned}$$

Apply Theorem 12.5 with $a = cnp$. Noting that $a < \sqrt{2} \, np$ completes the proof. ∎

Section (12.5.1) contains a different proof that uses a standard method based on moment-generating functions and gives a better constant in the exponent.

Power Law Distributions

The power law distribution of order k where k is a positive integer is

$$f(x) = \frac{k-1}{x^k} \quad \text{for} \quad x \geq 1.$$

If a random variable x has this distribution for $k \geq 4$, then

$$\mu = E(x) = \frac{k-1}{k-2} \quad \text{and} \quad \text{Var}(x) = \frac{k-1}{(k-2)^2(k-3)}.$$

Theorem 12.7 *Suppose $x_1, x_2, \ldots, x_n$ are i.i.d, each distributed according to the Power Law of order $k \geq 4$ (with $n > 10k^2$). Then, for $x = x_1 + x_2 + \cdots + x_n$, and any $\varepsilon \in (1/(2\sqrt{nk}), 1/k^2)$, we have*

$$Pr\left(|x - E(x)| \geq \varepsilon E(x)\right) \leq \left(\frac{4}{\varepsilon^2(k-1)n}\right)^{(k-3)/2}.$$

Proof For integer s, the sth moment of $x_i - E(x_i)$, namely $E((x_i - \mu)^s)$, exists if and only if $s \leq k-2$. For $s \leq k-2$,

$$E((x_i - \mu)^s) = (k-1) \int_1^\infty \frac{(y-\mu)^s}{y^k} dy.$$

Using the substitution of variable $z = \mu/y$,

$$\frac{(y-\mu)^s}{y^k} = y^{s-k}(1-z)^s = \frac{z^{k-s}}{\mu^{k-s}}(1-z)^s.$$

As y goes from 1 to ∞, z goes from μ to 0, and $dz = -\frac{\mu}{y^2}dy$. Thus,

$$E((x_i - \mu)^s) = (k-1) \int_1^\infty \frac{(y-\mu)^s}{y^k} dy$$

$$= \frac{k-1}{\mu^{k-s-1}} \int_0^1 (1-z)^s z^{k-s-2} dz + \frac{k-1}{\mu^{k-s-1}} \int_1^\mu (1-z)^s z^{k-s-2} dz.$$

The first integral is just the standard integral of the beta function and its value is $\frac{s!(k-2-s)!}{(k-1)!}$. To bound the second integral, note that for $z \in [1, \mu]$, $|z-1| \leq \frac{1}{k-2}$ and

$$z^{k-s-2} \leq \left(1 + \left(1/(k-2)\right)\right)^{k-s-2} \leq e^{(k-s-2)/(k-2)} \leq e.$$

So, $\left|E((x_i - \mu)^s)\right| \leq \frac{(k-1)s!\,(k-2-s)!}{(k-1)!} + \frac{e(k-1)}{(k-2)^{s+1}}$

$$\leq s!\,\text{Var}(y)\left(\frac{1}{k-4} + \frac{e}{3!}\right) \leq s!\,\text{Var}(x).$$

Now, apply the first inequality of Theorem 12.5 with s of that theorem set to $k-2$ or $k-3$, whichever is even. Note that $a = \varepsilon E(x) \leq \sqrt{2}n\sigma^2$ (since $\varepsilon \leq 1/k^2$). The present theorem follows by a calculation. ∎

12.7. Eigenvalues and Eigenvectors

Let A be an $n \times n$ real matrix. The scalar λ is called an eigenvalue of A if there exists a non-zero vector $\mathbf{x}$ satisfying the equation $A\mathbf{x} = \lambda\mathbf{x}$. The vector $\mathbf{x}$ is called the eigenvector of A associated with λ. The set of all eigenvectors associated with a given eigenvalue form a subspace as seen from the fact that if $A\mathbf{x} = \lambda\mathbf{x}$ and $A\mathbf{y} = \lambda\mathbf{y}$, then for any scalars c and d, $A(c\mathbf{x} + d\mathbf{y}) = \lambda(c\mathbf{x} + d\mathbf{y})$. The equation $A\mathbf{x} = \lambda\mathbf{x}$ has a nontrivial solution only if $\det(A - \lambda I) = 0$. The equation $\det(A - \lambda I) = 0$ is called the *characteristic* equation and has n not necessarily distinct roots.

Matrices A and B are similar if there is an invertible matrix P such that $A = P^{-1}BP$.

Theorem 12.8 *If A and B are similar, then they have the same eigenvalues.*

Proof Let A and B be similar matrices. Then there exists an invertible matrix P such that $A = P^{-1}BP$. For an eigenvector $\mathbf{x}$ of A with eigenvalue λ, $A\mathbf{x} = \lambda\mathbf{x}$, which implies $P^{-1}BP\mathbf{x} = \lambda\mathbf{x}$ or $B(P\mathbf{x}) = \lambda(P\mathbf{x})$. So, $P\mathbf{x}$ is an eigenvector of B with the same eigenvalue λ. Since the reverse also holds, the theorem follows. ■

Even though two similar matrices, A and B, have the same eigenvalues, their eigenvectors are in general different.

The matrix A is *diagonalizable* if A is similar to a diagonal matrix.

Theorem 12.9 *A is diagonalizable if and only if A has n linearly independent eigenvectors.*

Proof **(only if)** Assume A is diagonalizable. Then there exists an invertible matrix P and a diagonal matrix D such that $D = P^{-1}AP$. Thus, $PD = AP$. Let the diagonal elements of D be $\lambda_1, \lambda_2, \ldots, \lambda_n$ and let $\mathbf{p}_1, \mathbf{p}_2, \ldots, \mathbf{p}_n$ be the columns of P. Then $AP = [A\mathbf{p}_1, A\mathbf{p}_2, \ldots, A\mathbf{p}_n]$ and $PD = [\lambda_1\mathbf{p}_1, \lambda_2\mathbf{p}_2, \ldots, \lambda_n\mathbf{p}_n]$. Hence, $A\mathbf{p}_i = \lambda_i\mathbf{p}_i$. That is, the λ_i are the eigenvalues of A and the $\mathbf{p}_i$ are the corresponding eigenvectors. Since P is invertible, the $\mathbf{p}_i$ are linearly independent.

(if) Assume that A has n linearly independent eigenvectors $\mathbf{p}_1, \mathbf{p}_2, \ldots, \mathbf{p}_n$ with corresponding eigenvalues $\lambda_1, \lambda_2, \ldots, \lambda_n$. Then $A\mathbf{p}_i = \lambda_i\mathbf{p}_i$, and reversing the above steps,

$$AP = \left[A\mathbf{p}_1, A\mathbf{p}_2, \ldots, A\mathbf{p}_n\right] = \left[\lambda_1\mathbf{p}_1, \lambda_2\mathbf{p}_2, \ldots \lambda_n\mathbf{p}_n\right] = PD.$$

Thus, $AP = PD$. Since the $\mathbf{p}_i$ are linearly independent, P is invertible, and hence $A = PDP^{-1}$. Thus, A is diagonalizable. ■

It follows from the proof of the theorem that if A is diagonalizable and has eigenvalue λ with multiplicity k, then there are k linearly independent eigenvectors associated with λ.

A matrix P is *orthogonal* if it is invertible and $P^{-1} = P^T$. A matrix A is *orthogonally diagonalizable* if there exists an orthogonal matrix P such that $P^{-1}AP = D$ is diagonal. If A is orthogonally diagonalizable, then $A = PDP^T$ and $AP = PD$. Thus, the columns of P are the eigenvectors of A and the diagonal elements of D are the corresponding eigenvalues.

If P is an orthogonal matrix, then P^TAP and A are both representations of the same linear transformation with respect to different bases. To see this, note that if $\mathbf{e}_1, \mathbf{e}_2, \ldots, \mathbf{e}_n$ is the standard basis, then a_{ij} is the component of $A\mathbf{e}_j$ along the direction $\mathbf{e}_i$, namely $a_{ij} = \mathbf{e}_i{}^T A\mathbf{e}_j$. Thus, A defines a linear transformation by specifying the image under the transformation of each basis vector. Denote by $\mathbf{p_j}$ the jth column of P. It is easy to see that $(P^T A P)_{ij}$ is the component of $A\mathbf{p_j}$ along the direction $\mathbf{p_i}$, namely $(P^T A P)_{ij} = \mathbf{p_i}^T A \mathbf{p_j}$. Since P is orthogonal, the $\mathbf{p_j}$ form a basis of the space and so $P^T A P$ represents the same linear transformation as A, but in the basis $p_1, p_2, \ldots, p_n$.

Another remark is in order. Check that

$$A = PDP^T = \sum_{i=1}^{n} d_{ii} \mathbf{p_i} \mathbf{p_i}^T.$$

Compare this with the singular value decomposition where

$$A = \sum_{i=1}^{n} \sigma_i \mathbf{u_i} \mathbf{v_i}^T,$$

the only difference being that $\mathbf{u_i}$ and $\mathbf{v_i}$ can be different, and indeed if A is not square, they will certainly be.

12.7.1. Symmetric Matrices

For an arbitrary matrix, some of the eigenvalues may be complex. However, for a symmetric matrix with real entries, all eigenvalues are real. The number of eigenvalues of a symmetric matrix, counting multiplicities, equals the dimension of the matrix. The set of eigenvectors associated with a given eigenvalue form a vector space. For a non-symmetric matrix, the dimension of this space may be less than the multiplicity of the eigenvalue. Thus, a non-symmetric matrix may not be diagonalizable. However, for a symmetric matrix, the eigenvectors associated with a given eigenvalue form a vector space of dimension equal to the multiplicity of the eigenvalue. Thus, all symmetric matrices are diagonalizable. The above facts for symmetric matrices are summarized in the following theorem.

Theorem 12.10 (Real Spectral Theorem) *Let A be a real symmetric matrix. Then*

1. *The eigenvalues, $\lambda_1, \lambda_2, \ldots, \lambda_n$, are real, as are the components of the corresponding eigenvectors, $\mathbf{v_1}, \mathbf{v_2}, \ldots, \mathbf{v_n}$.*
2. *(Spectral Decomposition) A is orthogonally diagonalizable, and indeed*

$$A = VDV^T = \sum_{i=1}^{n} \lambda_i \mathbf{v_i} \mathbf{v_i}^T,$$

where V is the matrix with columns $\mathbf{v_1}, \mathbf{v_2}, \ldots, \mathbf{v_n}$, $|\mathbf{v_i}| = 1$ and D is a diagonal matrix with entries $\lambda_1, \lambda_2, \ldots, \lambda_n$.

Proof $A\mathbf{v_i} = \lambda_i \mathbf{v_i}$ and $\mathbf{v_i}^c A \mathbf{v_i} = \lambda_i \mathbf{v_i}^c \mathbf{v_i}$. Here the c superscript means conjugate transpose. Then

$$\lambda_i = \mathbf{v_i}^c A \mathbf{v_i} = (\mathbf{v_i}^c A \mathbf{v_i})^{cc} = (\mathbf{v_i}^c A^c \mathbf{v_i})^c = (\mathbf{v_i}^c A \mathbf{v_i})^c = \lambda_i^c$$

and hence λ_i is real.

Since λ_i is real, a non-trivial solution to $(A - \lambda_i I)\,\mathbf{x} = 0$ has real components.

Let P be a real symmetric matrix such that $P\mathbf{v_1} = \mathbf{e_1}$ where $\mathbf{e_1} = (1, 0, 0, \ldots, 0)^T$ and $P^{-1} = P^T$. We will construct such a P shortly. Since $A\mathbf{v_1} = \lambda_1 \mathbf{v_1}$,

$$PAP^T \mathbf{e_1} = PA\mathbf{v_1} = \lambda P\mathbf{v_1} = \lambda_1 \mathbf{e_1}.$$

The condition $PAP^T \mathbf{e_1} = \lambda_1 \mathbf{e_1}$ plus symmetry implies that $PAP^T = \begin{pmatrix} \lambda_1 & 0 \\ 0 & A' \end{pmatrix}$ where A' is $n - 1$ by $n - 1$ and symmetric. By induction, A' is orthogonally diagonalizable. Let Q be the orthogonal matrix with $QA'Q^T = D'$, a diagonal matrix. Q is $(n-1) \times (n-1)$. Augment Q to an $n \times n$ matrix by putting 1 in the $(1, 1)$ position and 0 elsewhere in the first row and column. Call the resulting matrix R. R is orthogonal too.

$$R\begin{pmatrix} \lambda_1 & 0 \\ 0 & A' \end{pmatrix} R^T = \begin{pmatrix} \lambda_1 & 0 \\ 0 & D' \end{pmatrix} \implies RPAP^T R^T = \begin{pmatrix} \lambda_1 & 0 \\ 0 & D' \end{pmatrix}.$$

Since the product of two orthogonal matrices is orthogonal, this finishes the proof of (2) except it remains to construct P. For this, take an orthonormal basis of space containing $\mathbf{v_1}$. Suppose the basis is $\{\mathbf{v_1}, \mathbf{w_2}, \mathbf{w_3}, \ldots\}$ and V is the matrix with these basis vectors as its columns. Then $P = V^T$ will do. ∎

Theorem 12.11 (The fundamental theorem of symmetric matrices) *A real matrix A is orthogonally diagonalizable if and only if A is symmetric.*

Proof **(if)** Assume A is orthogonally diagonalizable. Then there exists P such that $D = P^{-1}AP$. Since $P^{-1} = P^T$, we get

$$A = PDP^{-1} = PDP^T,$$

which implies

$$A^T = (PDP^T)^T = PDP^T = A,$$

and hence A is symmetric.
(only if) Already proved. ∎

Note that a non-symmetric matrix may not be diagonalizable, it may have eigenvalues that are not real, and the number of linearly independent eigenvectors corresponding to an eigenvalue may be less than its multiplicity. For example, the matrix

$$\begin{pmatrix} 1 & 1 & 0 \\ 0 & 1 & 1 \\ 1 & 0 & 1 \end{pmatrix}$$

has eigenvalues 2, $\frac{1}{2} + i\frac{\sqrt{3}}{2}$, and $\frac{1}{2} - i\frac{\sqrt{3}}{2}$. The matrix $\begin{pmatrix} 1 & 2 \\ 0 & 1 \end{pmatrix}$ has characteristic equation $(1 - \lambda)^2 = 0$ and thus has eigenvalue 1 with multiplicity 2 but has only one linearly independent eigenvector associated with the eigenvalue 1, namely $\mathbf{x} = c\begin{pmatrix} 1 \\ 0 \end{pmatrix}$ $c \neq 0$. Neither of these situations is possible for a symmetric matrix.

12.7.2. Relationship between SVD and Eigen Decomposition

The singular value decomposition exists for any $n \times d$ matrix whereas the eigenvalue decomposition exists only for certain square matrices. For symmetric matrices the decompositions are essentially the same.

The singular values of a matrix are always positive, since each singular value is the length of the vector of projections of the rows to the corresponding singular vector. Given a symmetric matrix, the eigenvalues can be positive or negative. If A is a symmetric matrix with eigenvalue decomposition $A = V_E D_E V_E^T$ and singular value decomposition $A = U_S D_S V_S^T$, what is the relationship between D_E and D_S, between V_E and V_S, and between U_S and V_E? Observe that if A can be expressed as $Q D Q^T$ where Q is orthonormal and D is diagonal, then $AQ = QD$. That is, each column of Q is an eigenvector and the elements of D are the eigenvalues. Thus, if the eigenvalues of A are distinct, then Q is unique up to a permutation of columns. If an eigenvalue has multiplicity k, then the space spanning the k columns is unique. In the following we will use the term *essentially unique* to capture this situation. Now $AA^T = U_S D_S^2 U_S^T$ and $A^T A = V_S D_S^2 V_S^T$. By an argument similar to the one above, U_S and V_S are essentially unique and are the eigenvectors or negatives of the eigenvectors of A and A^T. The eigenvalues of AA^T or $A^T A$ are the squares of the eigenvalues of A. If A is not positive semi-definite and has negative eigenvalues, then in the singular value decomposition $A = U_S D_S V_S$, some of the left singular vectors are the negatives of the eigenvectors. Let S be a diagonal matrix with $\pm 1's$ on the diagonal depending on whether the corresponding eigenvalue is positive or negative. Then $A = (U_S S)(S D_S) V_S$ where $U_S S = V_E$ and $S D_S = D_E$.

12.7.3. Extremal Properties of Eigenvalues

In this section we derive a min max characterization of eigenvalues that implies that the largest eigenvalue of a symmetric matrix A has a value equal to the maximum of $\mathbf{x}^T A \mathbf{x}$ over all vectors $\mathbf{x}$ of unit length. That is, the largest eigenvalue of A equals the 2-norm of A. If A is a real symmetric matrix, there exists an orthogonal matrix P that diagonalizes A. Thus,

$$P^T A P = D$$

where D is a diagonal matrix with the eigenvalues of A, $\lambda_1 \geq \lambda_2 \geq \cdots \geq \lambda_n$, on its diagonal. Rather than working with A, it is easier to work with the diagonal matrix D. This will be an important technique that will simplify many proofs.

Consider maximizing $\mathbf{x}^T A \mathbf{x}$ subject to the conditions,

1. $\sum_{i=1}^{n} x_i^2 = 1$
2. $\mathbf{r}_i^T \mathbf{x} = 0, \quad 1 \leq i \leq s$,

where the r_i are any set of non-zero vectors. We ask: Over all possible sets $\{r_i | 1 \leq i \leq s\}$ of s vectors, what is the minimum value assumed by this maximum?

Theorem 12.12 (Min max theorem) *For a symmetric matrix A,* $\min\limits_{r_1,\ldots,r_s} \max\limits_{\substack{\mathbf{x} \\ r_i \perp \mathbf{x}}} (\mathbf{x}^t A \mathbf{x}) = \lambda_{s+1}$ *where the minimum is over all sets $\{r_1, r_2, \ldots, r_s\}$ of s non-zero vectors and the maximum is over all unit vectors x orthogonal to the s non-zero vectors.*

Proof A is orthogonally diagonalizable. Let P satisfy $P^T P = I$ and $P^T A P = D$, D diagonal. Let $\mathbf{y} = P^T \mathbf{x}$. Then $\mathbf{x} = P\mathbf{y}$ and

$$\mathbf{x}^T A \mathbf{x} = \mathbf{y}^T P^T A P \mathbf{y} = \mathbf{y}^T D \mathbf{y} = \sum_{i=1}^{n} \lambda_i y_i^2.$$

Since there is a one-to-one correspondence between unit vectors $\mathbf{x}$ and $\mathbf{y}$, maximizing $\mathbf{x}^T A \mathbf{x}$ subject to $\sum x_i^2 = 1$ is equivalent to maximizing $\sum_{i=1}^{n} \lambda_i y_i^2$ subject to $\sum y_i^2 = 1$. Since $\lambda_1 \geq \lambda_i, 2 \leq i \leq n, \mathbf{y} = (1, 0, \ldots, 0)$ maximizes $\sum_{i=1}^{n} \lambda_i y_i^2$ at λ_1. Then $\mathbf{x} = P\mathbf{y}$ is the first column of P and is the first eigenvector of A. Similarly λ_n is the minimum value of $\mathbf{x}^T A \mathbf{x}$ subject to the same conditions.

Now consider maximizing $\mathbf{x}^T A \mathbf{x}$ subject to the conditions,

1. $\sum x_i^2 = 1$
2. $\mathbf{r}_i^T \mathbf{x} = 0,$

where the $\mathbf{r}_i$ are any set of non-zero vectors. We ask over all possible choices of s vectors what is the minimum value assumed by this maximum:

$$\min_{\mathbf{r}_1,\ldots,\mathbf{r}_s} \; \max_{\substack{\mathbf{x} \\ \mathbf{r}_i^T \mathbf{x}=0}} \; \mathbf{x}^T A \mathbf{x}.$$

As above, we may work with $\mathbf{y}$. The conditions are

1. $\sum y_i^2 = 1$
2. $\mathbf{q}_i^T \mathbf{y} = 0$ where, $\mathbf{q}_i^T = \mathbf{r}_i^T P.$

Consider any choice for the vectors $\mathbf{r}_1, \mathbf{r}_2, \ldots, \mathbf{r}_s$. This gives a corresponding set of $\mathbf{q}_i$. The $\mathbf{y}_i$ therefore satisfy s linear homogeneous equations. If we add $y_{s+2} = y_{s+3} = \cdots y_n = 0$, we have $n-1$ homogeneous equations in n unknowns $y_1, \ldots, y_n$. There is at least one solution that can be normalized so that $\sum y_i^2 = 1$. With this choice of $\mathbf{y}$,

$$\mathbf{y}^T D \mathbf{y} = \sum \lambda_i y_i^2 \geq \lambda_{s+1},$$

since coefficients greater than or equal to $s+1$ are zero. Thus, for any choice of $\mathbf{r_i}$ there will be a $\mathbf{y}$ such that

$$\max_{\substack{\mathbf{y} \\ \mathbf{r}_i^T \mathbf{y}=0}} (\mathbf{y}^T P^T A P \mathbf{y}) \geq \lambda_{s+1},$$

and hence

$$\min_{\mathbf{r}_1,\mathbf{r}_2,\ldots,\mathbf{r}_s} \; \max_{\substack{\mathbf{y} \\ \mathbf{r}_i^T \mathbf{y}=0}} (\mathbf{y}^T P^T A P \mathbf{y}) \geq \lambda_{s+1}.$$

However, there is a set of s constraints for which the minimum is less than or equal to λ_{s+1}. Fix the relations to be $y_i = 0, \; 1 \leq i \leq s$. There are s equations in n unknowns, and for any $\mathbf{y}$ subject to these relations,

$$\mathbf{y}^T D \mathbf{y} = \sum_{s+1}^{n} \lambda_i y_i^2 \leq \lambda_{s+1}.$$

Combining the two inequalities, min max $\mathbf{y}^T D \mathbf{y} = \lambda_{s+1}$. ∎

The above theorem tells us that the maximum of $\mathbf{x}^T A \mathbf{x}$ subject to the constraint that $|\mathbf{x}|^2 = 1$ is λ_1. Consider the problem of maximizing $\mathbf{x}^T A \mathbf{x}$ subject to the additional restriction that $\mathbf{x}$ is orthogonal to the first eigenvector. This is equivalent to maximizing $\mathbf{y}^t P^t A P \mathbf{y}$ subject to $\mathbf{y}$ being orthogonal to $(1,0,...,0)$, i.e., the first component of $\mathbf{y}$ being 0. This maximum is clearly λ_2 and occurs for $\mathbf{y} = (0,1,0,\ldots,0)$. The corresponding $\mathbf{x}$ is the second column of P or the second eigenvector of A.

Similarly, the maximum of $\mathbf{x}^T A \mathbf{x}$ for $\mathbf{p_1}^T \mathbf{x} = \mathbf{p_2}^T \mathbf{x} = \cdots \mathbf{p_s}^T \mathbf{x} = 0$ is λ_{s+1} and is obtained for $\mathbf{x} = \mathbf{p_{s+1}}$.

12.7.4. Eigenvalues of the Sum of Two Symmetric Matrices

The min max theorem is useful in proving many other results. The following theorem shows how adding a matrix B to a matrix A changes the eigenvalues of A. The theorem is useful for determining the effect of a small perturbation on the eigenvalues of A.

Theorem 12.13 *Let A and B be $n \times n$ symmetric matrices. Let $C = A + B$. Let $\alpha_i, \beta_i,$ and γ_i denote the eigenvalues of $A, B,$ and C respectively, where $\alpha_1 \geq \alpha_2 \geq \ldots \alpha_n$ and similarly for β_i, γ_i. Then $\alpha_s + \beta_1 \geq \gamma_s \geq \alpha_s + \beta_n$.*

Proof By the min max theorem we have

$$\alpha_s = \min_{\mathbf{r_1},\ldots,\mathbf{r_{s-1}}} \max_{\substack{\mathbf{x} \\ \mathbf{r_i} \perp \mathbf{x}}} (\mathbf{x}^T A \mathbf{x}).$$

Suppose $\mathbf{r_1}, \mathbf{r_2}, \ldots, \mathbf{r_{s-1}}$ attain the minimum in the expression. Then using the min max theorem on C,

$$
\begin{aligned}
\gamma_s &\leq \max_{\mathbf{x} \perp \mathbf{r_1},\mathbf{r_2},\ldots\mathbf{r_{s-1}}} \left(\mathbf{x}^T (A + B) \mathbf{x} \right) \\
&\leq \max_{\mathbf{x} \perp \mathbf{r_1},\mathbf{r_2},\ldots\mathbf{r_{s-1}}} (\mathbf{x}^T A \mathbf{x}) + \max_{\mathbf{x} \perp \mathbf{r_1},\mathbf{r_2},\ldots\mathbf{r_{s-1}}} (\mathbf{x}^T B \mathbf{x}) \\
&\leq \alpha_s + \max_{\mathbf{x}} (\mathbf{x}^T B \mathbf{x}) \leq \alpha_s + \beta_1.
\end{aligned}
$$

Therefore, $\gamma_s \leq \alpha_s + \beta_1$.

An application of the result to $A = C + (-B)$ gives $\alpha_s \leq \gamma_s - \beta_n$. The eigenvalues of $-B$ are minus the eigenvalues of B, and thus $-\beta_n$ is the largest eigenvalue. Hence $\gamma_s \geq \alpha_s + \beta_n$ and combining inequalities yields $\alpha_s + \beta_1 \geq \gamma_s \geq \alpha_s + \beta_n$. ∎

Lemma 12.14 *Let A and B be $n \times n$ symmetric matrices. Let $C = A + B$. Let $\alpha_i, \beta_i,$ and γ_i denote the eigenvalues of $A, B,$ and C, respectively, where $\alpha_1 \geq \alpha_2 \geq \ldots \alpha_n$ and similarly for β_i, γ_i. Then $\gamma_{r+s-1} \leq \alpha_r + \beta_s$.*

— **393** —

Proof There is a set of $r - 1$ relations such that over all $\mathbf{x}$ satisfying the $r - 1$ relationships

$$max(\mathbf{x}^T A \mathbf{x}) = \alpha_r.$$

And a set of $s - 1$ relations such that over all $\mathbf{x}$ satisfying the $s - 1$ relationships

$$\max(\mathbf{x}^T B \mathbf{x}) = \beta_s.$$

Consider $\mathbf{x}$ satisfying all these $r + s - 2$ relations. For any such $\mathbf{x}$,

$$\mathbf{x}^T C \mathbf{x} = \mathbf{x}^T A \mathbf{x} + \mathbf{x}^T B \mathbf{x} \mathbf{x} \le \alpha_r + \beta_s,$$

and hence over all the $\mathbf{x}$

$$\max(\mathbf{x}^T C \mathbf{x}) \le \alpha_s + \beta_r$$

Taking the minimum over all sets of $r + s - 2$ relations,

$$\gamma_{r+s-1} = \min \max(\mathbf{x}^T C \mathbf{x}) \le \alpha_r + \beta_s.$$

■

12.7.5. Norms

A set of vectors $\{\mathbf{x_1}, \ldots, \mathbf{x_n}\}$ is *orthogonal* if $\mathbf{x_i}^T \mathbf{x_j} = 0$ for $i \ne j$ and is *orthonormal* if in addition $|\mathbf{x_i}| = 1$ for all i. A matrix A is *orthonormal* if $A^T A = I$. If A is a square orthonormal matrix, then rows as well as columns are orthogonal. In other words, if A is square orthonormal, then A^T is also. In the case of matrices over the complexes, the concept of an orthonormal matrix is replaced by that of a unitary matrix. A^* is the conjugate transpose of A if $a_{ij}^* = \bar{a}_{ji}$ where a_{ij}^* is the ij^{th} entry of A^* and $\bar{a}_{ij}^*$ is the complex conjugate of the ij^{th} element of A. A matrix A over the field of complex numbers is **unitary** if $AA^* = I$.

Norms
A **norm** on $\mathbf{R}^n$ is a function $f : \mathbf{R}^n \to \mathbf{R}$ satisfying the following three axioms:

1. $f(\mathbf{x}) \ge 0$,
2. $f(\mathbf{x} + \mathbf{y}) \le f(\mathbf{x}) + f(\mathbf{y})$, and
3. $f(\alpha \mathbf{x}) = |\alpha| f(\mathbf{x})$.

A norm on a vector space provides a distance function where

$$\text{distance}(\mathbf{x}, \mathbf{y}) = norm(\mathbf{x} - \mathbf{y}).$$

An important class of norms for vectors is the p-norms defined for $p > 0$ by

$$|\mathbf{x}|_p = (|\mathbf{x_1}|^p + \cdots + |\mathbf{x_n}|^p)^{\frac{1}{p}}.$$

Important special cases are

$$|\mathbf{x}|_0 = \text{ the number of non-zero entries (not quite a norm: fails \#3)}$$
$$|\mathbf{x}|_1 = |x_1| + \cdots + |x_n|$$
$$|\mathbf{x}|_2 = \sqrt{|x_1|^2 + \cdots + |x_n|^2}$$
$$|\mathbf{x}|_\infty = \max |x_i|.$$

Lemma 12.15 *For any* $1 \leq p < q, |\mathbf{x}|_q \leq |\mathbf{x}|_p$.

Proof

$$|\mathbf{x}|_q^q = \sum_i |x_i|^q.$$

Let $a_i = |x_i|^q$ and $\rho = p/q$. Using Jensen's inequality (see Section 12.3) that for any non-negative reals $a_1, a_2, \ldots, a_n$ and any $\rho \in (0, 1)$, we have $\left(\sum_{i=1}^n a_i\right)^\rho \leq \sum_{i=1}^n a_i^\rho$, the lemma is proved. ∎

There are two important matrix norms, the matrix p-norm

$$||A||_p = \max_{|\mathbf{x}|=1} ||A\mathbf{x}||_p$$

and the Frobenius norm

$$||A||_F = \sqrt{\sum_{ij} a_{ij}^2}.$$

Let $\mathbf{a_i}$ be the ith column of A. Then $||A||_F^2 = \sum_i \mathbf{a_i}^T \mathbf{a_i} = tr\left(A^T A\right)$. A similar argument on the rows yields $||A||_F^2 = tr\left(AA^T\right)$. Thus, $||A||_F^2 = tr\left(A^T A\right) = tr\left(AA^T\right)$.

If A is symmetric and rank k,

$$||A||_2^2 \leq ||A||_F^2 \leq k\,||A||_2^2.$$

12.7.6. Important Norms and Their Properties

Lemma 12.16 $||AB||_2 \leq ||A||_2\,||B||_2$

Proof $||AB||_2 = \max_{|\mathbf{x}|=1} |AB\mathbf{x}|$. Let $\mathbf{y}$ be the value of $\mathbf{x}$ that achieves the maximum and let $\mathbf{z} = B\mathbf{y}$. Then

$$||AB||_2 = |AB\mathbf{y}| = |A\mathbf{z}| = \left|A\frac{\mathbf{z}}{|\mathbf{z}|}\right| |\mathbf{z}|.$$

But $\left|A\frac{\mathbf{z}}{|\mathbf{z}|}\right| \leq \max_{|\mathbf{x}|=1} |A\mathbf{x}| = ||A||_2$ and $|\mathbf{z}| \leq \max_{|\mathbf{x}|=1} |B\mathbf{x}| = ||B||_2$. Thus $||AB||_2 \leq ||A||_2\,||B||_2$. ∎

Let Q be an orthonormal matrix.

Lemma 12.17 *For all* $\mathbf{x}$, $|Q\mathbf{x}| = |\mathbf{x}|$.

Proof $|Q\mathbf{x}|_2^2 = \mathbf{x}^T Q^T Q\mathbf{x} = \mathbf{x}^T \mathbf{x} = |\mathbf{x}|_2^2$. ∎

Lemma 12.18 $||QA||_2 = ||A||_2$

Proof For all $\mathbf{x}, |Q\mathbf{x}| = |\mathbf{x}|$. Replacing $\mathbf{x}$ by $A\mathbf{x}$, $|QA\mathbf{x}| = |A\mathbf{x}|$, and thus $\max_{|\mathbf{x}|=1} |QA\mathbf{x}| = \max_{|\mathbf{x}|=1} |A\mathbf{x}|$ ∎

Lemma 12.19 $||AB||_F^2 \leq ||A||_F^2 ||B||_F^2$

Proof Let $\mathbf{a_i}$ be the ith column of A and let $\mathbf{b_j}$ be the jth column of B. By the Cauchy-Schwartz inequality, $\|\mathbf{a_i}^T\mathbf{b_j}\| \leq \|\mathbf{a_i}\| \|\mathbf{b_j}\|$. Thus, $||AB||_F^2 = \sum_i \sum_j |\mathbf{a_i}^T\mathbf{b_j}|^2 \leq \sum_i \sum_j \|\mathbf{a_i}\|^2 \|\mathbf{b_j}\|^2 = \sum_i \|\mathbf{a_i}\|^2 \sum_j \|\mathbf{b_j}\|^2 = ||A||_F^2 ||B||_F^2$. ∎

Lemma 12.20 $||QA||_F = ||A||_F$

Proof $||QA||_F^2 = \text{Tr}(A^T Q^T Q A) = \text{Tr}(A^T A) = ||A||_F^2.$ ∎

Lemma 12.21 *For real, symmetric matrix A with eigenvalues $\lambda_1 \geq \lambda_2 \geq \ldots$,* $||A||_2^2 = \max(\lambda_1^2, \lambda_n^2)$ *and* $||A||_F^2 = \lambda_1^2 + \lambda_2^2 + \cdots + \lambda_n^2$

Proof Suppose the spectral decomposition of A is PDP^T, where P is an orthogonal matrix and D is diagonal. We saw that $||P^T A||_2 = ||A||_2$. Applying this again, $||P^T A P||_2 = ||A||_2$. But, $P^T A P = D$, and clearly for a diagonal matrix D, $||D||_2$ is the largest absolute value diagonal entry from which the first equation follows. The proof of the second is analogous. ∎

If A is real and symmetric and of rank k then $||A||_2^2 \leq ||A||_F^2 \leq k ||A||_2^2$.

Theorem 12.22 $||A||_2^2 \leq ||A||_F^2 \leq k ||A||_2^2$

Proof It is obvious for diagonal matrices that $||D||_2^2 \leq ||D||_F^2 \leq k ||D||_2^2$. Let $D = Q^t A Q$ where Q is orthonormal. The result follows immediately since for Q orthonormal, $||QA||_2 = ||A||_2$ and $||QA||_F = ||A||_F$. ∎

Real and symmetric are necessary for some of these theorems. This condition was needed to express $\Sigma = Q^T A Q$. For example, in Theorem 12.22, suppose A is the $n \times n$ matrix,

$$A = \begin{pmatrix} 1 & 1 & \\ 1 & 1 & \\ \vdots & \vdots & 0 \\ 1 & 1 & \end{pmatrix}.$$

$||A||_2 = 2$ and $||A||_F = \sqrt{2n}$. But A is rank 2 and $||A||_F > 2 ||A||_2$ for $n > 8$.

Lemma 12.23 *Let A be a symmetric matrix. Then* $||A||_2 = \max\limits_{|\mathbf{x}|=1} |\mathbf{x}^T A \mathbf{x}|$.

Proof By definition, the 2-norm of A is $||A||_2 = \max\limits_{|\mathbf{x}|=1} |A\mathbf{x}|$. Thus,

$$||A||_2 = \max_{|\mathbf{x}|=1} |A\mathbf{x}| = \max_{|\mathbf{x}|=1} \sqrt{\mathbf{x}^T A^T A \mathbf{x}} = \sqrt{\lambda_1^2} = \lambda_1 = \max_{|\mathbf{x}|=1} \left|\mathbf{x}^T A \mathbf{x}\right|.$$

∎

The 2-norm of a matrix A is greater than or equal to the 2-norm of any of its columns. Let $\mathbf{a_u}$ be a column of A.

Lemma 12.24 $|a_u| \leq \|A\|_2$

Proof Let e_u be the unit vector with a 1 in position u and all other entries zero. Note $\lambda = \max_{|x|=1} |Ax|$. Let $\mathbf{x} = \mathbf{e_u}$ where $\mathbf{a_u}$ is row u. Then $|\mathbf{a_u}| = |A\mathbf{e_u}| \leq \max_{|\mathbf{x}|=1} |A\mathbf{x}| = \lambda$. ∎

12.7.7. Additional Linear Algebra

Lemma 12.25 *Let A be an $n \times n$ symmetric matrix. Then* $\det(A) = \lambda_1 \lambda_2 \cdots \lambda_n$.

Proof The $\det(A - \lambda I)$ is a polynomial in λ of degree n. The coefficient of λ^n will be ± 1 depending on whether n is odd or even. Let the roots of this polynomial be $\lambda_1, \lambda_2, \ldots, \lambda_n$. Then $\det(A - \lambda I) = (-1)^n \prod_{i=1}^n (\lambda - \lambda_i)$. Thus,

$$\det(A) = \det(A - \lambda I)|_{\lambda=0} = (-1)^n \prod_{i=1}^n (\lambda - \lambda_i)\bigg|_{\lambda=0} = \lambda_1 \lambda_2 \cdots \lambda_n.$$

∎

The trace of a matrix is defined to be the sum of its diagonal elements. That is, $\text{tr}(A) = a_{11} + a_{22} + \cdots + a_{nn}$.

Lemma 12.26 $tr(A) = \lambda_1 + \lambda_2 + \cdots + \lambda_n$.

Proof Consider the coefficient of λ^{n-1} in $\det(A - \lambda I) = (-1)^n \prod_{i=1}^n (\lambda - \lambda_i)$. Write

$$A - \lambda I = \begin{pmatrix} a_{11} - \lambda & a_{12} & \cdots \\ a_{21} & a_{22} - \lambda & \cdots \\ \vdots & \vdots & \vdots \end{pmatrix}.$$

Calculate $\det(A - \lambda I)$ by expanding along the first row. Each term in the expansion involves a determinant of size $n - 1$, which is a polynomial in λ of deg $n - 2$ except for the principal minor which is of deg $n - 1$. Thus the term of deg $n - 1$ comes from

$$(a_{11} - \lambda)(a_{22} - \lambda) \cdots (a_{nn} - \lambda)$$

and has coefficient $(-1)^{n-1}(a_{11} + a_{22} + \cdots + a_{nn})$. Now

$$(-1)^n \prod_{i=1}^n (\lambda - \lambda_i) = (-1)^n (\lambda - \lambda_1)(\lambda - \lambda_2) \cdots (\lambda - \lambda_n)$$

$$= (-1)^n \left(\lambda^n - (\lambda_1 + \lambda_2 + \cdots + \lambda_n)\lambda^{n-1} + \cdots \right)$$

Therefore, equating coefficients $\lambda_1 + \lambda_2 + \cdots + \lambda_n = a_{11} + a_{22} + \cdots + a_{nn} = tr(A)$

Note that $(tr(A))^2 \neq tr(A^2)$. For example, $A = \begin{pmatrix} 1 & 0 \\ 0 & 2 \end{pmatrix}$ has trace 3, $A^2 = \begin{pmatrix} 1 & 0 \\ 0 & 4 \end{pmatrix}$ has trace 5 $\neq 9$. However $tr(A^2) = \lambda_1^2 + \lambda_2^2 + \cdots + \lambda_n^2$. To see this, observe that $A^2 = (V^T D V)^2 = V^T D^2 V$. Thus, the eigenvalues of A^2 are the squares of the eigenvalues for A. ∎

Alternative proof that $tr(A) = \lambda_1 + \lambda_2 + \cdots + \lambda_n$: Suppose the spectral decomposition of A is $A = PDP^T$. We have

$$\text{tr}(A) = tr(PDP^T) = \text{tr}(DP^T P) = \text{tr}(D) = \lambda_1 + \lambda_2 + \cdots + \lambda_n.$$

Lemma 12.27 *If A is $n \times m$ and B is a $m \times n$ matrix, then $tr(AB) = tr(BA)$.*

Proof

$$\text{tr}(AB) = \sum_{i=1}^{n} \sum_{j=1}^{m} a_{ij} b_{ji} = \sum_{j=1}^{m} \sum_{i=1}^{n} b_{ji} a_{ij} = \text{tr}(BA)$$

∎

Pseudo Inverse

Let A be an $n \times m$ rank r matrix and let $A = U \Sigma V^T$ be the singular value decomposition of A. Let $\Sigma' = diag(\frac{1}{\sigma_1}, \ldots, \frac{1}{\sigma_r}, 0, \ldots, 0)$ where $\sigma_1, \ldots, \sigma_r$ are the non-zero singular values of A. Then $A' = V \Sigma' U^T$ is the pseudo inverse of A. It is the unique X that minimizes $\|AX - I\|_F$.

Second Eigenvector

Suppose the eigenvalues of a matrix are $\lambda_1 \geq \lambda_2 \geq \cdots$. The second eigenvalue, λ_2, plays an important role for matrices representing graphs. It may be the case that $|\lambda_n| > |\lambda_2|$.

Why is the second eigenvalue so important? Consider partitioning the vertices of a regular degree d graph $G = (V, E)$ into two blocks of equal size so as to minimize the number of edges between the two blocks. Assign value $+1$ to the vertices in one block and -1 to the vertices in the other block. Let $\mathbf{x}$ be the vector whose components are the ± 1 values assigned to the vertices. If two vertices, i and j, are in the same block, then x_i and x_j are both $+1$ or both -1 and $(x_i - x_j)^2 = 0$. If vertices i and j are in different blocks, then $(x_i - x_j)^2 = 4$. Thus, partitioning the vertices into two blocks so as to minimize the edges between vertices in different blocks is equivalent to finding a vector $\mathbf{x}$ with coordinates ± 1 of which half of its coordinates are $+1$ and half of which are -1 that minimizes

$$E_{cut} = \frac{1}{4} \sum_{(i,j) \in E} (x_i - x_j)^2.$$

Let A be the adjacency matrix of G. Then

$$\mathbf{x}^T A \mathbf{x} = \sum_{ij} a_{ij} x_i x_j = 2 \sum_{edges} x_i x_j$$

$$= 2 \times \begin{pmatrix} \text{number of edges} \\ \text{within components} \end{pmatrix} - 2 \times \begin{pmatrix} \text{number of edges} \\ \text{between components} \end{pmatrix}$$

$$= 2 \times \begin{pmatrix} \text{total number} \\ \text{of edges} \end{pmatrix} - 4 \times \begin{pmatrix} \text{number of edges} \\ \text{between components} \end{pmatrix}$$

Maximizing $\mathbf{x}^T A \mathbf{x}$ over all $\mathbf{x}$ whose coordinates are ± 1 and half of whose coordinates are $+1$ is equivalent to minimizing the number of edges between components.

Since finding such an $\mathbf{x}$ is computationally difficult, one thing we can try to do is replace the integer condition on the components of $\mathbf{x}$ and the condition that half of the components are positive and half of the components are negative with the conditions $\sum_{i=1}^{n} x_i^2 = 1$ and $\sum_{i=1}^{n} x_i = 0$. Then finding the optimal $\mathbf{x}$ gives us the second eigenvalue, since it is easy to see that the first eigenvector is along $\mathbf{1}$:

$$\lambda_2 = \max_{\mathbf{x} \perp \mathbf{v}_1} \frac{\mathbf{x}^T A \mathbf{x}}{\sum x_i^2}.$$

Actually we should use $\sum_{i=1}^{n} x_i^2 = n$, not $\sum_{i=1}^{n} x_i^2 = 1$. Thus, $n\lambda_2$ must be greater than $2 \times \begin{pmatrix} \text{total number} \\ \text{of edges} \end{pmatrix} - 4 \times \begin{pmatrix} \text{number of edges} \\ \text{between components} \end{pmatrix}$, since the maximum is taken over a larger set of $\mathbf{x}$. The fact that λ_2 gives us a bound on the minimum number of cross edges is what makes it so important.

12.7.8. Distance between Subspaces

Suppose S_1 and S_2 are two subspaces. Choose a basis of S_1 and arrange the basis vectors as the columns of a matrix X_1; similarly choose a basis of S_2 and arrange the basis vectors as the columns of a matrix X_2. Note that S_1 and S_2 can have different dimensions. Define the square of the distance between two subspaces by

$$dist^2(S_1, S_2) = dist^2(X_1, X_2) = ||X_1 - X_2 X_2^T X_1||_F^2.$$

Since $X_1 - X_2 X_2^T X_1$ and $X_2 X_2^T X_1$ are orthogonal,

$$\|X_1\|_F^2 = \left\|X_1 - X_2 X_2^T X_1\right\|_F^2 + \left\|X_2 X_2^T X_1\right\|_F^2,$$

and hence

$$dist^2(X_1, X_2) = \|X_1\|_F^2 - \left\|X_2 X_2^T X_1\right\|_F^2.$$

Intuitively, the distance between X_1 and X_2 is the Frobenius norm of the component of X_1, not in the space spanned by the columns of X_2.

If X_1 and X_2 are one-dimensional unit length vectors, $dist^2(X_1, X_2)$ is the sine squared of the angle between the spaces.

Example Consider two subspaces in four dimensions,

$$X_1 = \begin{pmatrix} \frac{1}{\sqrt{2}} & 0 \\ 0 & \frac{1}{\sqrt{3}} \\ \frac{1}{\sqrt{2}} & \frac{1}{\sqrt{3}} \\ 0 & \frac{1}{\sqrt{3}} \end{pmatrix} \qquad X_2 = \begin{pmatrix} 1 & 0 \\ 0 & 1 \\ 0 & 0 \\ 0 & 0 \end{pmatrix}$$

Here

$$dist^2\,(X_1, X_2) = \left\| \begin{pmatrix} \frac{1}{\sqrt{2}} & 0 \\ 0 & \frac{1}{\sqrt{3}} \\ \frac{1}{\sqrt{2}} & \frac{1}{\sqrt{3}} \\ 0 & \frac{1}{\sqrt{3}} \end{pmatrix} - \begin{pmatrix} 1 & 0 \\ 0 & 1 \\ 0 & 0 \\ 0 & 0 \end{pmatrix} \begin{pmatrix} 1 & 0 & 0 & 0 \\ 0 & 1 & 0 & 0 \end{pmatrix} \begin{pmatrix} \frac{1}{\sqrt{2}} & 0 \\ 0 & \frac{1}{\sqrt{3}} \\ \frac{1}{\sqrt{2}} & \frac{1}{\sqrt{3}} \\ 0 & \frac{1}{\sqrt{3}} \end{pmatrix} \right\|_F^2$$

$$= \left\| \begin{pmatrix} 0 & 0 \\ 0 & 0 \\ \frac{1}{\sqrt{2}} & \frac{1}{\sqrt{3}} \\ 0 & \frac{1}{\sqrt{3}} \end{pmatrix} \right\|_F^2 = \frac{7}{6}.$$

In essence, we projected each column vector of X_1 onto X_2 and computed the Frobenius norm of X_1 minus the projection. The Frobenius norm of each column is the sin squared of the angle between the original column of X_1 and the space spanned by the columns of X_2. ∎

12.7.9. Positive Semi-Definite Matrix

A square symmetric matrix is positive semi-definite if for all $\mathbf{x}$, $\mathbf{x}^T A \mathbf{x} \geq 0$. There are actually three equivalent definitions of positive semi-definite:

1. for all $\mathbf{x}$, $\mathbf{x}^T A \mathbf{x} \geq 0$
2. all eigenvalues are nonnegative
3. $A = B^T B$

We will prove (1) implies (2), (2) implies (3), and (3) implies (1).

1. (1) implies (2) If λ_i were negative, select $\mathbf{x} = \mathbf{v_i}$. Then $v_i^T (A v_i) = v_i^T (\lambda_i v_i) = \lambda_i < 0$.
2. (2) implies (3) $A = VDV^T = VD^{\frac{1}{2}}D^{\frac{1}{2}}V^T = B^T B$.
3. (3) implies (1) $\mathbf{x}^T A \mathbf{x} = (\mathbf{x}B)^T B\mathbf{x} \geq 0$.

12.8. Generating Functions

A sequence $a_0, a_1, \ldots,$ can be represented by a generating function $g(x) = \sum_{i=0}^{\infty} a_i x^i$. The advantage of the generating function is that it captures the entire sequence in a closed form that can be manipulated as an entity. For example, if $g(x)$ is the generating function for the sequence $a_0, a_1, \ldots,$ then $x\frac{d}{dx}g(x)$ is the generating function for the sequence $0,\ a_1,\ 2a_2,\ 3a_3, \ldots$ and $x^2 g''(x) + x g'(x)$ is the generating function for the sequence for $0,\ a_1,\ 4a_2,\ 9a_3, \ldots$

Example The generating function for the sequence $1, 1, \ldots$ is $\sum_{i=0}^{\infty} x^i = \frac{1}{1-x}$. The generating function for the sequence $0, 1, 2, 3, \ldots$ is

$$\sum_{i=0}^{\infty} i x^i = \sum_{i=0}^{\infty} x \frac{d}{dx} x^i = x \frac{d}{dx} \sum_{i=0}^{\infty} x^i = x \frac{d}{dx} \frac{1}{1-x} = \frac{x}{(1-x)^2}.$$

∎

Example If A can be selected 0 or 1 times and B can be selected 0, 1, or 2 times and C can be selected 0, 1, 2, or 3 times, in how many ways can five objects be selected? Consider the generating function whose i coefficient is the number of ways to select i objects. The generating function for the number of ways of selecting objects, selecting only A's is $1 + x$, only B's is $1 + x + x^2$, and only C's is $1 + x + x^2 + x^3$. The generating function when selecting A's, B's, and C's is the product.

$$(1 + x)(1 + x + x^2)(1 + x + x^2 + x^3) = 1 + 3x + 5x^2 + 6x^3 + 5x^4 + 3x^5 + x^6$$

The coefficient of x^5 is 3 and hence we can select five objects in three ways: ABBCC, ABCCC, or BBCCC. ∎

The Generating Functions for the Sum of Random Variables

Let $f(x) = \sum_{i=0}^{\infty} p_i x^i$ be the generating function for an integer valued random variable where p_i is the probability that the random variable takes on value i. Let $g(x) = \sum_{i=0}^{\infty} q_i x^i$ be the generating function of an independent integer valued random variable where q_i is the probability that the random variable takes on the value i. The sum of these two random variables has the generating function $f(x)g(x)$. This is because the coefficient of x^i in the product $f(x)g(x)$ is $\sum_{k=0}^{i} p_k q_{k-i}$, and this is also the probability that the sum of the random variables is i. Repeating this, the generating function of a sum of independent nonnegative integer valued random variables is the product of their generating functions.

12.8.1. Generating Functions for Sequences Defined by Recurrence Relationships

Consider the Fibonacci sequence

$$0, 1, 1, 2, 3, 5, 8, 13, 21, 34, 55, 89, \ldots$$

defined by the recurrence relationship

$$f_0 = 0 \qquad f_1 = 1 \qquad f_i = f_{i-1} + f_{i-2} \quad i \geq 2$$

Multiply each side of the recurrence by x^i and sum i from 2 to infinity.

$$\sum_{i=2}^{\infty} f_i x^i = \sum_{i=2}^{\infty} f_{i-1} x^i + \sum_{i=2}^{\infty} f_{i-2} x^i$$
$$f_2 x^2 + f_3 x^3 + \cdots = f_1 x^2 + f_2 x^3 + \cdots + f_0 x^2 + f_1 x^3 + \cdots$$
$$= x(f_1 x + f_2 x^2 + \cdots) + x^2(f_0 + f_1 x + \cdots) \qquad (12.1)$$

Let

$$f(x) = \sum_{i=0}^{\infty} f_i x^i. \qquad (12.2)$$

Substituting (12.2) into (12.1) yields

$$f(x) - f_0 - f_1 x = x(f(x) - f_0) + x^2 f(x)$$
$$f(x) - x = x f(x) + x^2 f(x)$$
$$f(x)(1 - x - x^2) = x.$$

Thus, $f(x) = \frac{x}{1-x-x^2}$ is the generating function for the Fibonacci sequence.

Note that generating functions are formal manipulations and do not necessarily converge outside some region of convergence. Consider the generating function $f(x) = \sum_{i=0}^{\infty} f_i x^i = \frac{x}{1-x-x^2}$ for the Fibonacci sequence. Using $\sum_{i=0}^{\infty} f_i x^i$,

$$f(1) = f_0 + f_1 + f_2 + \cdots = \infty$$

and using $f(x) = \frac{x}{1-x-x^2}$,

$$f(1) = \frac{1}{1-1-1} = -1.$$

Asymptotic Behavior

To determine the asymptotic behavior of the Fibonacci sequence, write

$$f(x) = \frac{x}{1-x-x^2} = \frac{\frac{\sqrt{5}}{5}}{1-\phi_1 x} + \frac{-\frac{\sqrt{5}}{5}}{1-\phi_2 x}$$

where $\phi_1 = \frac{1+\sqrt{5}}{2}$ and $\phi_2 = \frac{1-\sqrt{5}}{2}$ are the reciprocals of the two roots of the quadratic $1-x-x^2 = 0$.

Then

$$f(x) = \frac{\sqrt{5}}{5}\left(1 + \phi_1 x + (\phi_1 x)^2 + \cdots - \left(1 + \phi_2 x + (\phi_2 x)^2 + \cdots\right)\right).$$

Thus,

$$f_n = \frac{\sqrt{5}}{5}\left(\phi_1^n - \phi_2^n\right).$$

Since $\phi_2 < 1$ and $\phi_1 > 1$, for large n, $f_n \cong \frac{\sqrt{5}}{5}\phi_1^n$. In fact, since $f_n = \frac{\sqrt{5}}{5}\left(\phi_1^n - \phi_2^n\right)$ is an integer and $\phi_2 < 1$, it must be the case that $f_n = \lfloor f_n + \frac{\sqrt{5}}{2}\phi_2^n \rfloor$. Hence, $f_n = \lfloor \frac{\sqrt{5}}{5}\phi_1^n \rfloor$ for all n.

Means and Standard Deviations of Sequences

Generating functions are useful for calculating the mean and standard deviation of a sequence. Let z be an integral valued random variable where p_i is the probability that z equals i. The expected value of z is given by $m = \sum_{i=0}^{\infty} i p_i$. Let $p(x) = \sum_{i=0}^{\infty} p_i x^i$ be the generating function for the sequence $p_1, p_2, \ldots$. The generating function for the sequence $p_1, 2p_2, 3p_3, \ldots$ is

$$x\frac{d}{dx}p(x) = \sum_{i=0}^{\infty} i p_i x^i.$$

Thus, the expected value of the random variable z is $m = xp'(x)|_{x=1} = p'(1)$. If p was not a probability function, its average value would be $\frac{p'(1)}{p(1)}$, since we would need to normalize the area under p to 1.

The variance of z is $E(z^2) - E^2(z)$ and can be obtained as follows:

$$x^2 \frac{d}{dx} p(x) \bigg|_{x=1} = \sum_{i=0}^{\infty} i(i-1)x^i p(x) \bigg|_{x=1}$$

$$= \sum_{i=0}^{\infty} i^2 x^i p(x) \bigg|_{x=1} - \sum_{i=0}^{\infty} i x^i p(x) \bigg|_{x=1}$$

$$= E(z^2) - E(z).$$

Thus, $\sigma^2 = E(z^2) - E^2(z) = E(z^2) - E(z) + E(z) - E^2(z) = p''(1) + p'(1) - \left(p'(1)\right)^2$.

12.8.2. The Exponential Generating Function and the Moment Generating Function

Besides the ordinary generating function there are a number of other types of generating functions. One of these is the exponential generating function. Given a sequence $a_0, a_1, \ldots$, the associated *exponential generating function* is $g(x) = \sum_{i=0}^{\infty} a_i \frac{x^i}{i!}$.

Moment Generating Functions

The kth moment of a random variable x around the point b is given by $E((x-b)^k)$. Usually the word "moment" is used to denote the moment around the value 0 or around the mean. In the following, we use moment to mean the moment about the origin.

The *moment generating function* of a random variable x is defined by

$$\Psi(t) = E(e^{tx}) = \int_{-\infty}^{\infty} e^{tx} p(x) dx.$$

Replacing e^{tx} by its power series expansion $1 + tx + \frac{(tx)^2}{2!} \cdots$ gives

$$\Psi(t) = \int_{-\infty}^{\infty} \left(1 + tx + \frac{(tx)^2}{2!} + \cdots\right) p(x) dx.$$

Thus, the kth moment of x about the origin is $k!$ times the coefficient of t^k in the power series expansion of the moment generating function. Hence, the moment generating function is the exponential generating function for the sequence of moments about the origin.

The moment generating function transforms the probability distribution $p(x)$ into a function $\Psi(t)$ of t. Note $\Psi(0) = 1$ and is the area or integral of $p(x)$. The moment generating function is closely related to the *characteristic function*, which is obtained by replacing e^{tx} by e^{itx} in the above integral where $i = \sqrt{-1}$, and is related to the *Fourier transform*, which is obtained by replacing e^{tx} by e^{-itx}.

$\Psi(t)$ is closely related to the Fourier transform and its properties are essentially the same. In particular, $p(x)$ can be uniquely recovered by an inverse transform from $\Psi(t)$. More specifically, if all the moments m_i are finite and the sum $\sum_{i=0}^{\infty} \frac{m_i}{i!} t^i$ converges absolutely in a region around the origin, then $p(x)$ is uniquely determined.

The Gaussian probability distribution with zero mean and unit variance is given by $p(x) = \frac{1}{\sqrt{2\pi}} e^{-\frac{x^2}{2}}$. Its moments are given by

$$u_n = \frac{1}{\sqrt{2\pi}} \int_{-\infty}^{\infty} x^n e^{-\frac{x^2}{2}} dx$$

$$= \begin{cases} \frac{n!}{2^{\frac{n}{2}}(\frac{n}{2})!} & \text{n even} \\ 0 & \text{n odd} \end{cases}$$

To derive the above, use integration by parts to get $u_n = (n-1)u_{n-2}$ and combine this with $u_0 = 1$ and $u_1 = 0$. The steps are as follows. Let $u = e^{-\frac{x^2}{2}}$ and $v = x^{n-1}$. Then $u' = -xe^{-\frac{x^2}{2}}$ and $v' = (n-1)x^{n-2}$. Now $uv = \int u'v + \int uv'$ or

$$e^{-\frac{x^2}{2}} x^{n-1} = \int x^n e^{-\frac{x^2}{2}} dx + \int (n-1) x^{n-2} e^{-\frac{x^2}{2}} dx.$$

From which

$$\int x^n e^{-\frac{x^2}{2}} dx = (n-1) \int x^{n-2} e^{-\frac{x^2}{2}} dx - e^{-\frac{x^2}{2}} x^{n-1}$$

$$\int_{-\infty}^{\infty} x^n e^{-\frac{x^2}{2}} dx = (n-1) \int_{-\infty}^{\infty} x^{n-2} e^{-\frac{x^2}{2}} dx.$$

Thus, $u_n = (n-1)u_{n-2}$.

The moment generating function is given by

$$g(s) = \sum_{n=0}^{\infty} \frac{u_n s^n}{n!} = \sum_{\substack{n=0 \\ n \text{ even}}}^{\infty} \frac{n!}{2^{\frac{n}{2}} \frac{n}{2}!} \frac{s^n}{n!} = \sum_{i=0}^{\infty} \frac{s^{2i}}{2^i i!} = \sum_{i=0}^{\infty} \frac{1}{i!} \left(\frac{s^2}{2}\right)^i = e^{\frac{s^2}{2}}.$$

For the general Gaussian, the moment generating function is

$$g(s) = e^{su + \left(\frac{\sigma^2}{2}\right)s^2}.$$

Thus, given two independent Gaussians with mean u_1 and u_2 and variances σ_1^2 and σ_2^2, the product of their moment generating functions is

$$e^{s(u_1+u_2) + (\sigma_1^2 + \sigma_2^2)s^2},$$

the moment generating function for a Gaussian with mean $u_1 + u_2$ and variance $\sigma_1^2 + \sigma_2^2$. Thus, the convolution of two Gaussians is a Gaussian and the sum of two random variables that are both Gaussian is a Gaussian random variable.

12.9. Miscellaneous

12.9.1. Lagrange Multipliers

Lagrange multipliers are used to convert a constrained optimization problem into an unconstrained optimization. Suppose we wished to maximize a function $f(\mathbf{x})$

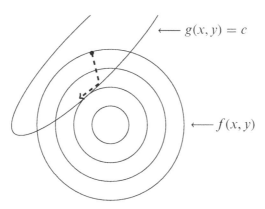

Figure 12.3: In finding the minimum of $f(x, y)$ within the ellipse, the path head toward the minimum of $f(x, y)$ until it hits the boundary of the ellipse and then follows the boundary of the ellipse until the tangent of the boundary is in the same direction as the contour line of $f(x, y)$.

subject to a constraint $g(\mathbf{x}) = c$. The value of $f(\mathbf{x})$ along the constraint $g(\mathbf{x}) = c$ might increase for a while and then start to decrease. At the point where $f(\mathbf{x})$ stops increasing and starts to decrease, the contour line for $f(\mathbf{x})$ is tangent to the curve of the constraint $g(\mathbf{x}) = c$. (See Figure 12.3.) Stated another way, the gradient of $f(\mathbf{x})$ and the gradient of $g(\mathbf{x})$ are parallel.

By introducing a new variable λ we can express the condition by $\nabla_{\mathbf{x}} f = \lambda \nabla_{\mathbf{x}} g$ and $g = c$. These two conditions hold if and only if

$$\nabla_{\mathbf{x}\lambda} \Big(f(\mathbf{x}) + \lambda \left(g(\mathbf{x}) - c \right) \Big) = 0.$$

The partial with respect to λ establishes that $g(\mathbf{x}) = c$. We have converted the constrained optimization problem in x to an unconstrained problem with variables $\mathbf{x}$ and λ.

12.9.2. Finite Fields

For a prime p and integer n there is a unique finite field with p^n elements. In Section 8.6 we used the field $GF(2^n)$, which consists of polynomials of degree less than n with coefficients over the field $GF(2)$. In $GF(2^8)$,

$$(x^7 + x^5 + x) + (x^6 + x^5 + x^4) = x^7 + x^6 + x^4 + x.$$

Multiplication is modulo an irreducible polynomial. Thus,

$$(x^7 + x^5 + x)(x^6 + x^5 + x^4) = x^{13} + x^{12} + x^{11} + x^{11} + x^{10} + x^9 + x^7 + x^6 + x^5$$
$$= x^{13} + x^{12} + x^{10} + x^9 + x^7 + x^6 + x^5$$
$$= x^6 + x^4 + x^3 + x^2 \qquad \mod x^8 + x^4 + x^3 + x + 1$$

Division of $x^{13} + x^{12} + x^{10} + x^9 + x^7 + x^6 + x^5$ by $x^8 + x^4 + x^3 + x + 1$ is illustrated below.

$$
\begin{array}{l}
\qquad\qquad\quad x^{13} \; +x^{12} \; +x^{10} \; +x^9 \qquad\quad +x^7 \; +x^6 \; +x^5 \\
-x^5(x^8 + x^4 + x^3 + x + 1) = \; x^{13} \qquad\qquad\quad +x^9 \; +x^8 \qquad +x^6 \; +x^5 \\
\hline
\qquad\qquad\qquad\qquad\qquad x^{12} \; +x^{10} \qquad\qquad +x^8 \; +x^7 \\
-x^4(x^8 + x^4 + x^3 + x + 1) = \qquad x^{12} \qquad\qquad\qquad +x^8 \; +x^7 \qquad +x^5 \; +x^4 \\
\hline
\qquad\qquad\qquad\qquad\qquad\qquad\quad x^{10} \qquad\qquad\qquad +x^5 \quad x^4 \\
-x^2(x^8 + x^4 + x^3 + x + 1) = \qquad\qquad x^{10} \qquad\qquad x^6 \; +x^5 \qquad x^3 \quad x^2 \\
\hline
\qquad\qquad\qquad\qquad\qquad\qquad\qquad\qquad\qquad\qquad x^6 \qquad\qquad +x^4 \; +x^3 \; +x^2
\end{array}
$$

12.9.3. Application of Mean Value Theorem

The mean value theorem states that if $f(x)$ is continuous and differentiable on the interval $[a, b]$, then there exists $c, a \le c \le b$ such that $f'(c) = \frac{f(b)-f(a)}{b-a}$. That is, at some point between a and b the derivative of f equals the slope of the line from $f(a)$ to $f(b)$. See Figure 12.4.

One application of the mean value theorem is with the Taylor expansion of a function. The Taylor expansion about the origin of $f(x)$ is

$$f(x) = f(0) + f'(0)x + \frac{1}{2!}f''(0)x^2 + \frac{1}{3!}f'''(0)x^3 + \cdots \qquad (12.3)$$

By the mean value theorem there exists $c,\ 0 \le c \le x$, such that $f'(c) = \frac{f(x)-f(0)}{x}$ or $f(x) - f(0) = xf'(c)$. Thus

$$xf'(c) = f'(0)x + \frac{1}{2!}f''(0)x^2 + \frac{1}{3!}f'''(0)x^3 + \cdots$$

and

$$f(x) = f(0) + xf'(c).$$

One could apply the mean value theorem to $f'(x)$ in

$$f'(x) = f'(0) + f''(0)x + \frac{1}{2!}f'''(0)x^2 + \cdots$$

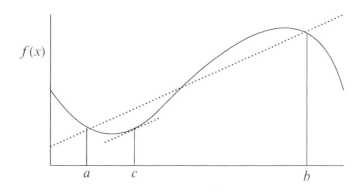

Figure 12.4: Illustration of the mean value theorem.

Then there exists d, $0 \le d \le x$ such that

$$xf''(d) = f''(0)x + \frac{1}{2!}f'''(0)x^2 + \cdots$$

Integrating

$$\frac{1}{2}x^2 f''(d) = \frac{1}{2!}f''(0)x + \frac{1}{3!}f'''(0)x^3 + \cdots$$

Substituting into Eq. (12.3),

$$f(x) = f(0) + f'(0)x + \frac{1}{2}x^2 f''(d).$$

12.10. Exercises

Exercise 12.1 What is the difference between saying $f(n)$ is $O\left(n^3\right)$ and $f(n)$ is $o\left(n^3\right)$?

Exercise 12.2 If $f(n) \sim g(n)$, what can we say about $f(n) + g(n)$ and $f(n) - g(n)$?

Exercise 12.3 What is the difference between $\sim$ and Θ?

Exercise 12.4 If $f(n)$ is $O(g(n))$, does this imply that $g(n)$ is $\Omega(f(n))$?

Exercise 12.5 What is $\lim\limits_{k \to \infty} \left(\frac{k-1}{k-2}\right)^{k-2}$.

Exercise 12.6 Select a, b, and c uniformly at random from $[0, 1]$. The probability that $b < a$ is $1/2$. The probability that $c < a$ is $1/2$. However, the probability that both b and c are less than a is $\frac{1}{3}$ not $1/4$. Why is this? Note that the six possible permutations abc, acb, bac, cab, bca, and cba are all equally likely. Assume that a, b, and c are drawn from the interval $(0,1]$. Given that $b < a$, what is the probability that $c < a$?

Exercise 12.7 Let $A_1, A_2, \ldots, A_n$ be events. Prove that $\text{Prob}(A_1 \cup A_2 \cup \cdots A_n) \le \sum_{i=1}^{n} \text{Prob}(A_i)$.

Exercise 12.8 Give an example of three random variables that are pairwise independent but not fully independent.

Exercise 12.9 Give examples of nonnegative valued random variables with median $>>$ mean. Can we have median $<<$ mean?

Exercise 12.10 Consider n samples $x_1, x_2, \ldots, x_n$ from a Gaussian distribution of mean μ and variance σ. For this distribution $m = \frac{x_1 + x_2 + \cdots + x_n}{n}$ is an unbiased estimator of μ. If μ is known, then $\frac{1}{n}\sum_{i=1}^{n}(x_i - \mu)^2$ is an unbiased estimator of σ^2. Prove that if we approximate μ by m, then $\frac{1}{n-1}\sum_{i=1}^{n}(x_i - m)^2$ is an unbiased estimator of σ^2.

Exercise 12.11 Given the distribution $\frac{1}{\sqrt{2\pi}3}e^{-\frac{1}{2}\left(\frac{x}{3}\right)^2}$, what is the probability that $x > 1$?

Exercise 12.12 $e^{-\frac{x^2}{2}}$ has value 1 at $x = 0$ and drops off very fast as x increases. Suppose we wished to approximate $e^{-\frac{x^2}{2}}$ by a function $f(x)$ where

$$f(x) = \begin{cases} 1 & |x| \le a \\ 0 & |x| > a \end{cases}.$$

What value of a should we use? What is the integral of the error between $f(x)$ and $e^{-\frac{x^2}{2}}$?

Exercise 12.13 Consider two sets of red and black balls, with the number of red and black balls in each set shown in the table below.

	red	black
Set 1	40	60
Set 2	50	50

Randomly draw a ball from one of the sets. Suppose that it turns out to be red. What is the probability that it was drawn from Set 1?

Exercise 12.14 Why cannot one prove an analogous type of theorem that states $p(x \leq a) \leq \frac{E(x)}{a}$?

Exercise 12.15 Compare the Markov and Chebyshev bounds for the following probability distributions:

1. $p(x) = \begin{cases} 1 & x = 1 \\ 0 & \text{otherwise} \end{cases}$

2. $p(x) = \begin{cases} 1/2 & 0 \leq x \leq 2 \\ 0 & \text{otherwise} \end{cases}$

Exercise 12.16 Let s be the sum of n independent random variables $x_1, x_2, \ldots, x_n$ where for each i

$$x_i = \begin{cases} 0 & \text{Prob} \quad p \\ 1 & \text{Prob} \quad 1-p \end{cases}$$

1. How large must δ be if we wish to have $Prob\big(s < (1-\delta)m\big) < \varepsilon$?
2. If we wish to have $Prob\big(s > (1+\delta)m\big) < \varepsilon$?

Exercise 12.17 What is the expected number of flips of a coin until a head is reached? Assume p is probability of a head on an individual flip. What is value if p=1/2?

Exercise 12.18 Given the joint probability

P(A,B)	A=0	A=1
B=0	1/16	1/8
B=1	1/4	9/16

1. What is the marginal probability distribution of A? of B?
2. What is the conditional probability of $B = 1$ given $A = 1$?

Exercise 12.19 Consider independent random variables x_1, x_2, and x_3, each equal to zero with probability $\frac{1}{2}$. Let $S = x_1 + x_2 + x_3$ and let F be event that $S \in \{1, 2\}$. Conditioning on F, the variables x_1, x_2, and x_3 are still each zero with probability $\frac{1}{2}$. Are they still independent?

Exercise 12.20 Consider rolling two dice A and B. What is the probability that the sum S will add to 9? What is the probability that the sum will be 9 if the roll of A is 3?

Exercise 12.21 Write the generating function for the number of ways of producing change using only pennies, nickels, and dimes. In how many ways can you produce 23 cents?

Exercise 12.22 A dice has six faces, each face of the dice having one of the numbers 1 though 6. The result of a role of the dice is the integer on the top face. Consider two roles of the dice. In how many ways can an integer be the sum of two rolls of the dice?

Exercise 12.23 If a(x) is the generating function for the sequence $a_0, a_1, a_2, \ldots$, for what sequence is a(x)(1-x) the generating function?

Exercise 12.24 How many ways can one draw n $a's$ and $b's$ with an even number of $a's$?

Exercise 12.25 Find the generating function for the recurrence $a_i = 2a_{i-1} + i$ where $a_0 = 1$.

Exercise 12.26 Find a closed form for the generating function for the infinite sequence of prefect squares 1, 4, 9, 16, 25, ...

Exercise 12.27 Given that $\frac{1}{1-x}$ is the generating function for the sequence $1, 1, \ldots$, for what sequence is $\frac{1}{1-2x}$ the generating function?

Exercise 12.28 Find a closed form for the exponential generating function for the infinite sequence of prefect squares 1, 4, 9, 16, 25, ...

Exercise 12.29 Prove that the L_2 norm of $(a_1, a_2, \ldots, a_n)$ is less than or equal to the L_1 norm of $(a_1, a_2, \ldots, a_n)$.

Exercise 12.30 Prove that there exists a y, $0 \le y \le x$, such that $f(x) = f(0) + f'(y)x$.

Exercise 12.31 Show that the eigenvectors of a matrix A are not a continuous function of changes to the matrix.

Exercise 12.32 What are the eigenvalues of the two graphs shown below? What does this say about using eigenvalues to determine if two graphs are isomorphic?

Exercise 12.33 Let A be the adjacency matrix of an undirected graph G. Prove that eigenvalue λ_1 of A is at least the average degree of G.

Exercise 12.34 Show that if A is a symmetric matrix and λ_1 and λ_2 are distinct eigenvalues then their corresponding eigenvectors x_1 and x_2 are orthogonal.

Exercise 12.35 Show that a matrix is rank k if and only if it has k non-zero eigenvalues and eigenvalue 0 of rank n-k.

Exercise 12.36 Prove that maximizing $\frac{x^T A x}{x^T x}$ is equivalent to maximizing $x^T A x$ subject to the condition that x be of unit length.

Exercise 12.37 Let A be a symmetric matrix with smallest eigenvalue $\lambda_{\min}$. Give a bound on the largest element of A^{-1}.

Exercise 12.38 Let A be the adjacency matrix of an n vertex clique with no self loops. Thus, each row of A is all ones except for the diagonal entry which is zero. What is the spectrum of A.

Exercise 12.39 Let A be the adjacency matrix of an undirect graph G. Prove that the eigenvalue λ_1 of A is at least the average degree of G.

Exercise 12.40 We are given the probability distribution for two random vectors x and y and we wish to stretch space to maximize the expected distance between them. Thus, we will multiply each coordinate by some quantity a_i. We restrict $\sum_{i=1}^{d} a_i^2 = d$. Thus, if we increase some coordinate by $a_i > 1$, some other coordinate must shrink. Given random vectors $x = (x_1, x_2, \ldots, x_d)$ and $y = (y_1, y_2, \ldots, y_d)$, how should we select a_i to maximize $E\left(|x - y|^2\right)$? The a_i stretch different coordinates. Assume

$$y_i = \begin{cases} 0 & \frac{1}{2} \\ 1 & \frac{1}{2} \end{cases}$$

and that x_i has some arbitrary distribution.

Exercise 12.41 Maximize x+y subject to the constraint that $x^2 + y^2 = 1$.

References

[AB15]   Pranjal Awasthi and Maria-Florina Balcan. Center based clustering: A foundational perspective. In Christian Hennig, Marina Meila, Fionn Murtagh, and Roberto Rocci, editors, *Handbook of Cluster Analysis*. CRC Press, 2015.

[ABC$^+$08]   Reid Andersen, Christian Borgs, Jennifer T. Chayes, John E. Hopcroft, Vahab S. Mirrokni, and Shang-Hua Teng. Local computation of pagerank contributions. *Internet Mathematics*, 5(1):23–45, 2008.

[ACORT11]   Dimitris Achlioptas, Amin Coja-Oghlan, and Federico Ricci-Tersenghi. On the solution-space geometry of random constraint satisfaction problems. *Random Structures & Algorithms*, 38(3):251–268, 2011.

[AF]   David Aldous and James Fill. *Reversible Markov Chains and Random Walks on Graphs*. This should be: www.stat.berkeley.edu/~aldous/RWG/book.html.

[AGKM16]   Sanjeev Arora, Rong Ge, Ravindran Kannan, and Ankur Moitra. Computing a nonnegative matrix factorization – provably. *SIAM Journal on Comput.*, 45(4): 1582–1611, 2016.

[AK05]   Sanjeev Arora and Ravindran Kannan. Learning mixtures of separated nonspherical Gaussians. *Annals of Applied Probability*, 15(1A):69–92, 2005. Preliminary version in ACM Symposium on Theory of Computing (STOC) 2001.

[Alo86]   Noga Alon. Eigenvalues and expanders. *Combinatorica*, 6:83–96, 1986.

[AM05]   Dimitris Achlioptas and Frank McSherry. On spectral learning of mixtures of distributions. In *Conference on Learning Theory (COLT)*, pages 458–469, 2005.

[AMS96]   Noga Alon, Yossi Matias, and Mario Szegedy. The space complexity of approximating the frequency moments. In *Proceedings of the Twenty-Eighth Annual ACM Symposium on Theory of Computing*, pages 20–29. ACM, 1996.

[AN72]   Krishna Athreya and P. E. Ney. *Branching Processes*, volume 107. Springer, 1972.

[AP03]   Dimitris Achlioptas and Yuval Peres. The threshold for random k-SAT is 2^k (ln 2 - o(k)). In *ACM Symposium on Theory of Computing (STOC)*, pages 223–231, 2003.

[Aro11]   Sanjeev Arora, Elad Hazan, and Satyen Kale. The multiplicative weights update method: a meta-algorithm and applications. *Theory of Computing*, 8(1):121–164, 2012.

[Arr50]   Kenneth J. Arrow. A difficulty in the concept of social welfare. *Journal of Political Economy*, 58(4):328–346, 1950.

[AS08]   Noga Alon and Joel H. Spencer. *The Probabilistic Method*. Third edition. Wiley-Interscience Series in Discrete Mathematics and Optimization. John Wiley & Sons Inc., 2008.

[AV07]   David Arthur and Sergei Vassilvitskii. k-means++: The advantages of careful seeding. In *Proceedings of the Eighteenth Annual ACM-SIAM Symposium on*

Discrete Algorithms, pages 1027–1035. Society for Industrial and Applied Mathematics, 2007.

[BA]   Albert-László Barabási and Réka Albert. Emergence of scaling in random networks. *Science*, 286(5439):509–512, 1999.

[BB10]   Maria-Florina Balcan and Avrim Blum. A discriminative model for semi-supervised learning. *Journal of the ACM*, 57(3):19:1–19:46, 2010.

[BBB+13]   Maria-Florina Balcan, Christian Borgs, Mark Braverman, Jennifer Chayes, and Shang-Hua Teng. Finding endogenously formed communities. In *Proceedings of the Twenty-Fourth Annual ACM-SIAM Symposium on Discrete Algorithms*, pages 767–783. Society for Industrial and Applied Mathematics, 2013.

[BBG13]   Maria-Florina Balcan, Avrim Blum, and Anupam Gupta. Clustering under approximation stability. *Journal of the ACM (JACM)*, 60(2):8, 2013.

[BBIS16]   Tomáš Balyo, Armin Biere, Markus Iser, and Carsten Sinz. SAT race 2015. *Artificial Intelligence*, 241:45–65, 2016.

[BBK14]   Trapit Bansal, Chiranjib Bhattacharyya, and Ravindran Kannan. A provable SVD-based algorithm for learning topics in dominant admixture corpus. In *Advances in Neural Information Processing Systems 27 (NIPS)*, pages 1997–2005, 2014.

[BBL09]   Maria-Florina Balcan, Alina Beygelzimer, and John Langford. Agnostic active learning. *Journal of Computer and System Sciences*, 75(1):78–89, 2009. Special Issue on Learning Theory. An earlier version appeared in International Conference on Machine Learning 2006.

[BBV08]   Maria-Florina Balcan, Avrim Blum, and Santosh Vempala. A discriminative framework for clustering via similarity functions. In *Proceedings of the Fortieth Annual ACM Symposium on Theory of Computing*, pages 671–680. ACM, 2008.

[BEHW87]   Anselm Blumer, Andrzej Ehrenfeucht, David Haussler, and Manfred K. Warmuth. Occam's razor. *Information Processing Letters*, 24:377–380, 1987.

[BEHW89]   Anselm Blumer, Andrzej Ehrenfeucht, David Haussler, and Manfred K. Warmuth. Learnability and the Vapnik-Chervonenkis dimension. *Journal of the Association for Computing Machinery*, 36(4):929–965, 1989.

[Ben09]   Yoshua Bengio. Learning deep architectures for AI. *Foundations and Trends in Machine Learning*, 2(1):1–127, 2009.

[BGG97]   C. Sidney Burrus, Ramesh A. Gopinath, and Haitao Guo. *Introduction to Wavelets and Wavelet Transforms: A Primer*. Pearson, 1997.

[BGMZ97]   Andrei Z. Broder, Steven C. Glassman, Mark S. Manasse, and Geoffrey Zweig. Syntactic clustering of the web. *Computer Networks and ISDN Systems*, 29(8–13): 1157–1166, 1997.

[BGV92]   Bernhard E. Boser, Isabelle M. Guyon, and Vladimir N. Vapnik. A training algorithm for optimal margin classifiers. In *Proceedings of the fifth annual workshop on computational learning theory*, pp. 144–152. ACM, 1992.

[Bis06]   Christopher M. Bishop. *Pattern Recognition and Machine Learning*. Springer, 2006.

[Ble12]   David M. Blei. Probabilistic topic models. *Communications of the ACM*, 55(4): 77–84, 2012.

[BLG14]   Maria-Florina Balcan, Yingyu Liang, and Pramod Gupta. Robust hierarchical clustering. *Journal of Machine Learning Research*, 15(1):3831–3871, 2014.

[Blo62]   Hans-Dieter Block. The perceptron: A model for brain functioning. *Reviews of Modern Physics*, 34:123–135, 1962. Reprinted in *Neurocomputing*, Anderson and Rosenfeld.

[BM98]   Avrim Blum and Tom Mitchell. Combining labeled and unlabeled data with co-training. In *Conference on Learning Theory (COLT)*. Morgan Kaufmann Publishers, 1998.

REFERENCES

[BM02] Peter L. Bartlett and Shachar Mendelson. Rademacher and Gaussian complexities: Risk bounds and structural results. *Journal of Machine Learning Research*, 3:463–482, 2002.

[BM07] Avrim Blum and Yishay Mansour. From external to internal regret. *Journal of Machine Learning Research*, 8:1307–1324, 2007.

[BMPW98] Sergey Brin, Rajeev Motwani, Lawrence Page, and Terry Winograd. What can you do with a web in your pocket? *Data Engineering Bulletin*, 21:37–47, 1998.

[BMZ05] Alfredo Braunstein, Marc Mézard, and Riccardo Zecchina. Survey propagation: An algorithm for satisfiability. *Random Structures & Algorithms*, 27(2):201–226, 2005.

[BNJ03] David M. Blei, Andrew Y. Ng, and Michael I. Jordan. Latent dirichlet allocation. *Journal of Machine Learning Research*, 3:993–1022, 2003.

[Bol01] Béla Bollobás. *Random Graphs*. Cambridge, Cambridge University Press, 2001.

[BSS08] Mohsen Bayati, Devavrat Shah, and Mayank Sharma. Max-product for maximum weight matching: Convergence, correctness, and lp duality. *IEEE Transactions on Information Theory*, 54(3):1241–1251, 2008.

[BT87] Béla Bollobás and Andrew Thomason. Threshold functions. *Combinatorica*, 7(1):35–38, 1987.

[BU14] Maria-Florina Balcan and Ruth Urner. *Active Learning – Modern Learning Theory*, pages 1–6. Springer Berlin Heidelberg, Berlin, Heidelberg, 2014.

[BVZ98] Yuri Boykov, Olga Veksler, and Ramin Zabih. Markov random fields with efficient approximations. In *Computer vision and pattern recognition, 1998. Proceedings. 1998 IEEE computer society conference on*, pages 648–655. IEEE, 1998.

[CBFH+97] Nicolo Cesa-Bianchi, Yoav Freund, David Haussler, David P. Helmbold, Robert E. Schapire, and Manfred K. Warmuth. How to use expert advice. *Journal of the ACM*, 44(3):427–485, 1997.

[CD10] Kamalika Chaudhuri and Sanjoy Dasgupta. Rates of convergence for the cluster tree. In *Advances in Neural Information Processing Systems*, pages 343–351, 2010.

[CF86] Ming-Te Chao and John V. Franco. Probabilistic analysis of two heuristics for the 3-satisfiability problem. *SIAM J. Comput.*, 15(4):1106–1118, 1986.

[CGTS99] Moses Charikar, Sudipto Guha, Éva Tardos, and David B. Shmoys. A constant-factor approximation algorithm for the k-median problem (extended abstract). In *Proceedings of the thirty-first annual ACM symposium on Theory of computing*, STOC '99, pages 1–10, New York, NY, USA, 1999. ACM.

[CHK+01] Duncan S. Callaway, John E. Hopcroft, Jon M. Kleinberg, M. E. J. Newman, and Steven H. Strogatz. Are randomly grown graphs really random? *Phys. Rev. E*, 64(Issue 4), 2001.

[Chv92] Vašek Chvátal and Bruce Reed. Mick gets some (the odds are on his side)(satisfiability). In *Proceedings of the 33rd Annual Symposium on Foundations of Computer Science*, pp. 620–627. IEEE, 1992.

[CLMW11] Emmanuel J. Candès, Xiaodong Li, Yi Ma, and John Wright. Robust principal component analysis? *J. ACM*, 58(3):11, 2011.

[CR08] Kamalika Chaudhuri and Satish Rao. Learning mixtures of product distributions using correlations and independence. In *COLT*, pages 9–20, 2008.

[CSZ06] Olivier Chapelle, Bernhard Schölkopf and Alexander Zien, editors. *Semi-Supervised Learning*. MIT Press, Cambridge, MA, 2006.

[CV95] Corinna Cortes and Vladimir Vapnik. Support-vector networks. *Machine Learning*, 20(3):273 – 297, 1995.

[Das11] Sanjoy Dasgupta. Two faces of active learning. *Theor. Comput. Sci.*, 412(19): 1767–1781, April 2011.

[Dau90] Ingrid Daubechies. The wavelet transform, time-frequency localization and signal analysis. *IEEE Trans. Information Theory*, 36(5):961–1005, 1990.

[DE03] David L. Donoho and Michael Elad. Optimally sparse representation in general (nonorthogonal) dictionaries via ℓ_1 minimization. *Proceedings of the National Academy of Sciences*, 100(5):2197–2202, 2003.

[DFK91] Martin Dyer, Alan Frieze, and Ravindran Kannan. A random polynomial time algorithm for approximating the volume of convex bodies. *Journal of the Association for Computing Machinery*, 38:1–17, 1991.

[DFK$^+$99] Petros Drineas, Alan M. Frieze, Ravindran Kannan, Santosh Vempala, and V. Vinay. Clustering in large graphs and matrices. In *SODA*, pages 291–299, 1999.

[DG99] Sanjoy Dasgupta and Anupam Gupta. An elementary proof of the Johnson-Lindenstrauss lemma. *International Computer Science Institute, Technical Report*, 22(1):1–5, 1999.

[DHKS05] Anirban Dasgupta, John E. Hopcroft, Jon M. Kleinberg, and Mark Sandler. On learning mixtures of heavy-tailed distributions. In *FOCS*, pages 491–500, 2005.

[DKM06a] Petros Drineas, Ravindran Kannan, and Michael W Mahoney. Fast Monte Carlo algorithms for matrices I: Approximating matrix multiplication. *SIAM Journal on Computing*, 36(1):132–157, 2006.

[DKM06b] Petros Drineas, Ravindran Kannan, and Michael W. Mahoney. Fast Monte Carlo algorithms for matrices II: Computing a low-rank approximation to a matrix. *SIAM Journal on Computing*, 36(1):158–183, 2006.

[Don06] David L. Donoho. Compressed sensing. *IEEE Transactions on Information Theory*, 52(4):1289–1306, 2006.

[DS84] Peter G. Doyle and J. Laurie Snell. *Random walks and electric networks*, volume 22 of *Carus Mathematical Monographs*. Mathematical Association of America, Washington, DC, 1984.

[DS03] David L. Donoho and Victoria Stodden. When does non-negative matrix factorization give a correct decomposition into parts? In *Advances in Neural Information Processing Systems 16 (NIPS)*, pages 1141–1148, 2003.

[DS07] Sanjoy Dasgupta and Leonard J. Schulman. A probabilistic analysis of em for mixtures of separated, spherical gaussians. *Journal of Machine Learning Research*, 8:203–226, 2007.

[DTD06] David Donoho, Yaakov Tsaig, and David L. Donoho. Compressed sensing. *IEEE Trans. Inf. Theory*, pages 1289–1306, 2006.

[ER60] Paul Erdös and Alfred Rényi. On the evolution of random graphs. *Publication of the Mathematical Institute of the Hungarian Academy of Sciences*, 5:17–61, 1960.

[EVL10] Adam N. Elmachtoub and Charles F. Van Loan. From random polygon to ellipse: An eigenanalysis. *SIAM Review*, 52(1):151–170, 2010.

[FCMR08] Maurizio Filippone, Francesco Camastra, Francesco Masulli, and Stefano Rovetta. A survey of kernel and spectral methods for clustering. *Pattern recognition*, 41(1):176–190, 2008.

[FD07] Brendan J. Frey and Delbert Dueck. Clustering by passing messages between data points. *Science*, 315(5814):972–976, 2007.

[Fel68] William Feller. *An Introduction to Probability Theory and Its Applications*, volume 1. Wiley, January 1968.

[FK99] Alan M. Frieze and Ravindan Kannan. Quick approximation to matrices and applications. *Combinatorica*, 19(2):175–220, 1999.

[FK00] Brendan J. Frey and Ralf Koetter. Exact inference using the attenuated max-product algorithm. *Advanced Mean Field Methods: Theory and Practice*, pp. 213–228, MIT Press, 2000.

[FK15] A. Frieze and M. Karoński. *Introduction to Random Graphs*. Cambridge University Press, Cambridge, 2015.

[FKV04] Alan Frieze, Ravindran Kannan, and Santosh Vempala. Fast Monte Carlo algorithms for finding low-rank approximations. *Journal of the ACM (JACM)*, 51(6):1025–1041, 2004.

[FŁP+51] Kazimierz Florek, Jan Łukaszewicz, Julian Perkal, Hugo Steinhaus, and Stefan Zubrzycki. Sur la liaison et la division des points d'un ensemble fini. In *Colloquium Mathematicae*, volume 2, pages 282–285, 1951.

[FM85] Philippe Flajolet and G. Nigel Martin. Probabilistic counting algorithms for data base applications. *Journal of Computer and System Sciences*, 31(2):182–209, 1985.

[Fri99] Ehud Friedgut and Jean Bourgain. Sharp thresholds of graph properties and the k-sat problem. *Journal of the American Mathematical Society*, 12(4):1017–1054, 1999.

[FS96] Alan M. Frieze and Stephen Suen. Analysis of two simple heuristics on a random instance of k-sat. *J. Algorithms*, 20(2):312–355, 1996.

[FS97] Yoav Freund and Robert E. Schapire. A decision-theoretic generalization of on-line learning and an application to boosting. *Journal of Computer and System Sciences*, 55(1):119–139, 1997.

[GEB15] Leon A. Gatys, Alexander S. Ecker, and Matthias Bethge. A neural algorithm of artistic style. *CoRR*, abs/1508.06576, 2015.

[Gha01] Zoubin Ghahramani. An introduction to hidden Markov models and Bayesian networks. *International Journal of Pattern Recognition and Artificial Intelligence*, 15(1):9–42, 2001.

[Gib73] Allan Gibbard. Manipulation of voting schemes: A general result. *Econometrica*, 41:587–601, 1973.

[GKL+15] Jacob R. Gardner, Matt J. Kusner, Yixuan Li, Paul Upchurch, Kilian Q. Weinberger, and John E. Hopcroft. Deep manifold traversal: Changing labels with convolutional features. *CoRR*, abs/1511.06421, 2015.

[GKP94] Ronald L. Graham, Donald E. Knuth, and Oren Patashnik. *Concrete mathematics – a foundation for computer science (2nd ed.)*. Addison-Wesley, 1994.

[GKSS08] Carla P. Gomes, Henry A. Kautz, Ashish Sabharwal, and Bart Selman. Satisfiability solvers. *Foundations of Artificial Intelligence*, 3:89–134, 2008.

[GLS12] Martin Grötschel, László Lovász, and Alexander Schrijver. *Geometric Algorithms and Combinatorial Optimization*, volume 2. Springer Science & Business Media, 2012.

[GN03] Rémi Gribonval and Morten Nielsen. Sparse decompositions in "incoherent" dictionaries. In *Proceedings of the 2003 International Conference on Image Processing, ICIP 2003, Barcelona, Catalonia, Spain, September 14–18, 2003*, pages 33–36, 2003.

[Gon85] Teofilo F. Gonzalez. Clustering to minimize the maximum intercluster distance. *Theoretical Computer Science*, 38:293–306, 1985.

[GvL96] Gene H. Golub and Charles F. van Loan. *Matrix computations (3rd ed.)*. Johns Hopkins University Press, Baltimore, 1996.

[GW95] Michel X. Goemans and David P. Williamson. Improved approximation algorithms for maximum cut and satisfiability problems using semidefinite programming. *Journal of the ACM (JACM)*, 42(6):1115–1145, 1995.

[HBB10] Matthew D. Hoffman, David M. Blei, and Francis R. Bach. Online learning for latent dirichlet allocation. In *NIPS*, pages 856–864, 2010.

[HLSH18] Kun He, Yingru Li, Sucheta Soundarajan, and John E. Hopcroft. Hidden community detection in social networks. *Information Science*, 425:92–106, 2018.

[HMMR15] Christian Hennig, Marina Meila, Fionn Murtagh, and Roberto Rocci. *Handbook of Cluster Analysis*. CRC Press, 2015.

REFERENCES

[HSB+15] Kun He, Yiwei Sun, David Bindel, John E. Hopcroft, and Yixuan Li. Detecting overlapping communities from local spectral subspaces. In *2015 IEEE International Conference on Data Mining, ICDM 2015, Atlantic City, NJ, USA, November 14–17, 2015*, pages 769–774, 2015.

[HSC+15] Kun He, Sucheta Soundarajan, Xuezhi Cao, John E. Hopcroft, and Menglong Huang. Revealing multiple layers of hidden community structure in networks. *CoRR*, abs/1501.05700, 2015.

[IN77] David B. Yudin and Arkadi S. Nemirovskii. Informational complexity and efficient methods for solving complex extremal problems. *Matekon*, 13(3):25–45, 1977.

[Jai10] Anil K. Jain. Data clustering: 50 years beyond k-means. *Pattern Recognition Letters*, 31(8):651–666, 2010.

[Jer98] Mark Jerrum. Mathematical foundations of the Markov chain Monte Carlo method. In Dorit Hochbaum, editor, *Approximation Algorithms for NP-hard Problems*, PWS Publishing Co., 1998.

[JKLP93] Svante Janson, Donald E. Knuth, Tomasz Luczak, and Boris Pittel. The birth of the giant component. *Random Struct. Algorithms*, 4(3):233–359, 1993.

[JLR00] Svante Janson, Tomasz Łuczak, and Andrzej Ruciński. *Random Graphs*. John Wiley and Sons, 2000.

[Joa99] Thorsten Joachims. Transductive inference for text classification using support vector machines. In *International Conference on Machine Learning*, pages 200–209, 1999.

[Kan09] Ravindran Kannan. A new probability inequality using typical moments and concentration results. In *FOCS*, pages 211–220, 2009.

[Kar90] Richard M. Karp. The transitive closure of a random digraph. *Random Structures and Algorithms*, 1(1):73–94, 1990.

[KFL01] Frank R. Kschischang, Brendan J. Frey, and Hans-Andrea Loeliger. Factor graphs and the sum-product algorithm. *IEEE Transactions on Information Theory*, 47(2):498–519, 2001.

[Kha79] Leonid G. Khachiyan. A polynomial algorithm in linear programming. *Akademiia Nauk SSSR, Doklady*, 244:1093–1096, 1979.

[KK10] Amit Kumar and Ravindran Kannan. Clustering with spectral norm and the k-means algorithm. In *Foundations of Computer Science (FOCS), 2010 51st Annual IEEE Symposium on*, pages 299–308. IEEE, 2010.

[Kle99] Jon M. Kleinberg. Authoritative sources in a hyperlinked environment. *Journal of the ACM*, 46(5):604–632, 1999.

[Kle00] Jon M. Kleinberg. The small-world phenomenon: An algorithm perspective. In *STOC*, pages 163–170, 2000.

[Kle02] Jon M. Kleinberg. An impossibility theorem for clustering. In *NIPS*, pages 446–453, 2002.

[KS13] Michael Krivelevich and Benny Sudakov. The phase transition in random graphs: A simple proof. *Random Struct. Algorithms*, 43(2):131–138, 2013.

[KV95] Michael Kearns and Umesh Vazirani. *An Introduction to Computational Learning Theory*. MIT Press, Cambridge, MA, 1995.

[KV09] Ravindran Kannan and Santosh Vempala. Spectral algorithms. *Foundations and Trends in Theoretical Computer Science*, 4(3–4):157–288, 2009.

[KVV04] Ravindran Kannan, Santosh Vempala, and Adrian Vetta. On clusterings: Good, bad and spectral. *J. ACM*, 51(3):497–515, May 2004.

[LCB+04] Gert R. G. Lanckriet, Nello Cristianini, Peter Bartlett, Laurent El Ghaoui, and Michael I. Jordan. Learning the kernel matrix with semidefinite programming. *Journal of Machine Learning Research*, 5(Jan):27–72, 2004.

[LHBH15] Yixuan Li, Kun He, David Bindel, and John E. Hopcroft. Uncovering the small community structure in large networks: A local spectral approach. In *Proceedings of the 24th International Conference on World Wide Web, WWW 2015, Florence, Italy, May 18–22, 2015*, pages 658–668, 2015.

[Lis13] Christian List. Social choice theory. In Edward N. Zalta, editor, *The Stanford Encyclopedia of Philosophy*. Metaphysics Research Lab, Stanford University, winter 2013 edition, 2013.

[Lit87] Nick Littlestone. Learning quickly when irrelevant attributes abound: A new linear-threshold algorithm. In *28th Annual Symposium on Foundations of Computer Science*, pages 68–77. IEEE, 1987.

[Liu01] Jun Liu. *Monte Carlo Strategies in Scientific Computing*. Springer, 2001.

[Llo82] Stuart Lloyd. Least squares quantization in PCM. *IEEE Transactions on Information Theory*, 28(2):129–137, 1982.

[LW94] Nick Littlestone and Manfred K. Warmuth. The weighted majority algorithm. *Information and Computation*, 108(2):212–261, 1994.

[Mat10] Jiří Matoušek. *Geometric discrepancy*, volume 18 of *Algorithms and Combinatorics*. Springer-Verlag, Berlin, 2010. An illustrated guide, revised paperback reprint of the 1999 original.

[McS01] Frank McSherry. Spectral partitioning of random graphs. In *FOCS*, pages 529–537, 2001.

[MG82] Jayadev Misra and David Gries. Finding repeated elements. *Science of Computer Programming*, 2(2):143–152, 1982.

[Mit97] Tom M. Mitchell. *Machine Learning*. McGraw-Hill, New York, 1997.

[MM02] Gurmeet Singh Manku and Rajeev Motwani. Approximate frequency counts over data streams. In *Proceedings of the 28th International Conference on Very Large Data Bases*, pages 346–357. VLDB Endowment, 2002.

[MP69] Marvin Minsky and Seymour Papert. *Perceptrons: An Introduction to Computational Geometry*. MIT Press, Cambridge, MA, 1969.

[MPZ02] Marc Mézard, Giorgio Parisi, and Riccardo Zecchina. Analytic and algorithmic solution of random satisfiability problems. *Science*, 297(5582):812–815, 2002.

[MR95a] Michael Molloy and Bruce A. Reed. A critical point for random graphs with a given degree sequence. *Random Struct. Algorithms*, 6(2/3):161–180, 1995.

[MR95b] Rajeev Motwani and Prabhakar Raghavan. *Randomized Algorithms*. Cambridge University Press, Cambridge, 1995.

[MR99] Rajeev Motwani and Prabhakar Raghavan. Randomized algorithms. In *Algorithms and Theory of Computation Handbook*, pages 15-1–15-23. CRC, Boca Raton, FL, 1999.

[MU05] Michael Mitzenmacher and Eli Upfal. *Probability and Computing – Randomized Algorithms and Probabilistic Analysis*. Cambridge University Press, Cambridge, 2005.

[MV10] Ankur Moitra and Gregory Valiant. Settling the polynomial learnability of mixtures of gaussians. In *FOCS*, pages 93–102, 2010.

[Nov62] Albert B.J. Novikoff. On convergence proofs on perceptrons. In *Proceedings of the Symposium on the Mathematical Theory of Automata, Vol. XII*, pages 615–622, 1962.

[OHM06] Robert Orsi, Uwe Helmke, and John B. Moore. A Newton-like method for solving rank constrained linear matrix inequalities. *Automatica*, 42(11):1875–1882, 2006.

[Pal85] Edgar M. Palmer. *Graphical evolution*. Wiley-Interscience Series in Discrete Mathematics. John Wiley & Sons Ltd., Chichester, 1985. An introduction to the theory of random graphs, A Wiley-Interscience Publication.

[Par98] Beresford N. Parlett. *The symmetric eigenvalue problem*, volume 20 of *Classics in Applied Mathematics*. Society for Industrial and Applied Mathematics (SIAM), Philadelphia, PA, 1998. Corrected reprint of the 1980 original.

[per10] David Asher Levin, Yuval Peres, and Elizabeth Lee Wilmer. *Markov Chains and Mixing Times*. American Mathematical Society, Providence, RI, 2010.

[RFP10] Benjamin Recht, Maryam Fazel, and Pablo A. Parrilo. Guaranteed minimum-rank solutions of linear matrix equations via nuclear norm minimization. *SIAM Review*, 52(3):471–501, 2010.

[RV99] Ravindran Kannan and V. Vinay. *Analyzing the Structure of Large Graphs*. Bonn, Rheinische Friedrich-Wilhelms-Universität Bonn, 1999.

[Sat75] Mark A. Satterthwaite. Strategy-proofness and arrows conditions: Existence and correspondence theorems for voting procedures and social welfare functions. *Journal of Economic Theory*, 10:187–217, 1975.

[Sch90] Robert E. Schapire. Strength of weak learnability. *Machine Learning*, 5:197–227, 1990.

[Sho70] Naum Z. Shor. Convergence rate of the gradient descent method with dilatation of the space. *Cybernetics and Systems Analysis*, 6(2):102–108, 1970.

[SJ89] Alistair Sinclair and Mark Jerrum. Approximate counting, uniform generation and rapidly mixing markov chains. *Information and Computation*, 82:93–133, 1989.

[Sly10] Allan Sly. Computational transition at the uniqueness threshold. In *FOCS*, pages 287–296, 2010.

[SN97] Gilbert Strang and Truong Q. Nguyen. *Wavelets and filter banks*. Wellesley-Cambridge Press, 1997.

[SS01] Bernhard Scholkopf and Alexander J. Smola. *Learning with Kernels: Support Vector Machines, Regularization, Optimization, and Beyond*. MIT Press, Cambridge, MA, 2001.

[SSBD14] Shai Shalev-Shwartz and Shai Ben-David. *Understanding Machine Learning: From Theory to Algorithms*. Cambridge University Press, Cambridge, 2014.

[ST04] Daniel A. Spielman and Shang-Hua Teng. Smoothed analysis of algorithms: Why the simplex algorithm usually takes polynomial time. *J. ACM*, 51(3):385–463, 2004.

[STBWA98] John Shawe-Taylor, Peter L. Bartlett, Robert C. Williamson, and Martin Anthony. Structural risk minimization over data-dependent hierarchies. *IEEE Transactions on Information Theory*, 44(5):1926–1940, 1998.

[SWY75] Gerard Salton, Anita Wong, and Chung-Shu Yang. A vector space model for automatic indexing. *Communications of the ACM*, 18(11):613–620, 1975.

[Thr96] Sebastian Thrun. *Explanation-Based Neural Network Learning: A Lifelong Learning Approach*. Kluwer Academic Publishers, Boston, MA, 1996.

[TM95] Sebastian Thrun and Tom M. Mitchell. Lifelong robot learning. *Robotics and Autonomous Systems*, 15(1–2):25–46, 1995.

[Val84] Leslie G. Valiant. A theory of the learnable. In *STOC*, pages 436–445, 1984.

[Val13] Leslie Valiant. *Probably Approximately Correct: Nature's Algorithms for Learning and Prospering in a Complex World*. Basic Books, New York, 2013.

[Vap82] Vladimir N. Vapnik. *Estimation of Dependences Based on Empirical Data*. Springer-Verlag, New York, 1982.

[Vap98] Vladimir N. Vapnik. *Statistical Learning Theory*. John Wiley and Sons Inc., New York, 1998.

[VC71] Vladimir N. Vapnik and Alexey Chervonenkis. On the uniform convergence of relative frequencies of events to their probabilities. *Theory of Probability and its Applications*, 16(2):264–280, 1971.

REFERENCES

[Vem04] Santosh Vempala. *The Random Projection Method*. DIMACS, 2004.

[VW02] Santosh Vempala and Grant Wang. A spectral algorithm for learning mixtures of distributions. *Journal of Computer and System Sciences*, pages 113–123, 2002.

[War63] Joe H. Ward. Hierarchical grouping to optimize an objective function. *Journal of the American Statistical Association*, 58(301):236–244, 1963.

[Wei97] Yair Weiss. Belief propagation and revision in networks with loops. Technical Report A.I. Memo No. 1616, MIT, 1997.

[WF01] Yair Weiss and William T. Freeman. On the optimality of solutions of the max-product belief-propagation algorithm in arbitrary graphs. *IEEE Transactions on Information Theory*, 47(2):736–744, 2001.

[Wil06] Herbert S. Wilf. *Generatingfunctionology*. A. K. Peters Series. A. K. Peters, 2006.

[Wis69] David Wishart. Mode analysis: A generalization of nearest neighbor which reduces chaining effects. *Numerical Taxonomy*, 76(282–311):17, 1969.

[WS98] Duncan J. Watts and Steven H. Strogatz. Collective dynamics of 'small-world' networks. *Nature*, 393 (6684), 1998.

[WW96] Edmund Taylor Whittaker and George Neville Watson. *A course of modern analysis*. Cambridge Mathematical Library. Cambridge University Press, Cambridge, 1996. An introduction to the general theory of infinite processes and of analytic functions; with an account of the principal transcendental functions, reprint of the fourth (1927) edition.

[YFW01] Jonathan S. Yedidia, William T. Freeman, and Yair Weiss. Bethe free energy, Kikuchi approximations, and belief propagation algorithms. *IEEE Transactions on Information Theory*, 51(7):2282–2312, 2005.

[YFW03] Jonathan S. Yedidia, William T. Freeman, and Yair Weiss. Understanding belief propagation and its generalizations. *Exploring Artificial Intelligence in the New Millennium*, 8:236–239, 2003.

[ZGL03] Xiaojin Zhu, Zoubin Ghahramani, and John Lafferty. Semi-supervised learning using gaussian fields and harmonic functions. In *Proc. 20th International Conference on Machine Learning*, pages 912–912, 2003.

[Zhu06] Xiaojin Zhu. Semi-supervised learning literature survey. 2006. Computer Sciences TR 1530 University of Wisconsin–Madison.

Index

2-universal, 162
4-way independence, 168

Affinity matrix, 201
Algorithm
    greedy k-clustering, 189
    k-means, 185
    singular value decomposition, 39
Almost surely, 223
Anchor Term, 281
Aperiodic, 63
Arithmetic mean, 369

Bad pair, 225
Bayes rule, 379
Bayesian, 299
Bayesian network, 299
Belief Network, 299
belief propagation, 298
Bernoulli trials, 377
Best fit, 29
Bigoh, 360
Binomial distribution, 218
    approximated by Poisson, 377
Boosting, 146
Branching process, 241
Breadth-first search, 230

Cartesian coordinates, 9
Cauchy-Schwartz inequality, 366, 368
Central Limit Theorem, 375
Characteristic equation, 388
Characteristic function, 403
Chebyshev's inequality, 5
Chernoff bounds, 380
Clustering, 182
    k-center criterion, 189
    k-means, 185
    Social networks, 208
    Sparse Cuts, 202

CNF
    CNF-sat, 248
Cohesion, 204
Combining expert advice, 143
Commute time, 88
Conditional probability, 372
Conductance, 81
Coordinates
    Cartesian, 9
    polar, 9
Coupon collector problem, 90
Cumulative distribution function, 372
Current
    probabilistic interpretation, 84
Cycles, 236
    emergence, 235
    number of, 235

Data streams
    counting frequent elements, 165
    frequency moments, 160
    frequent element, 165
    majority element, 165
    number of distinct elements, 161
    number of occurrences of an element, 164
    second moment, 166
Degree distribution, 218
    power law, 218
Depth-first search, 232
Diagonalizable, 388
Diameter of a graph, 225, 238
Diameter two, 236
dilation, 341
Disappearance of isolated vertices, 236
Discovery time, 85
Distance
    total variation, 68
Distribution
    vertex degree, 216
Document ranking, 49

Effective resistance, 88
Eigenvalue, 387
Eigenvector, 42, 388
Electrical network, 81
Erdös Rényi, 215
Error-correcting codes, 167
Escape probability, 85
Euler's constant, 91
Event, 372
Expander, 75
Expected degree
    vertex, 215
Expected value, 373
Exponential generating function, 403
Extinct families
    size, 245
Extinction probability, 241, 243

Finite fields, 405
First-moment method, 223
Fourier transform, 328, 403
Frequency domain, 328

G(n,p), 215
Gamma function, 10, 368
Gaussian, 15, 376, 404
    fitting to data, 20
    tail, 371
Gaussians
    sparating, 18
General tail bounds, 384
Generating function, 241
    component size, 256
    for sum of two variables, 242
Generating functions, 400
Generating points in the unit ball, 13
Geometric mean, 369
Giant component, 216, 223, 227, 232, 236
Gibbs sampling, 70
Graph
    connecntivity, 235
    resistance, 91
Graphical model, 298
Greedy
    k-clustering, 189
Growth models, 254
    with preferential attachment, 260
    without preferential attachment, 254

Haar wavelet, 342
Harmonic function, 82
Hash function
    universal, 162
Heavy tail, 218
Hidden Markov model, 295

Hidden structure, 209
Hitting time, 85, 96
Hölder's inequality, 366, 369

Immortality probability, 243
Incoherent, 325, 328
Increasing property, 223, 239
    unsatisfiability, 248
Independence
    limited way, 167
Independent, 372
Indicator random variable, 226
    of triangle, 221
Indicator variable, 374
Ising model, 311
Isolated vertices, 227, 236
    number of, 228

Jensen's inequality, 370
Johnson–Lindenstrauss lemma, 16, 17

k-clustering, 189
k-means clustering algorithm, 185
Kernel methods, 201
Kirchhoff's law, 83
Kleinberg, 262

Lagrange, 404
Laplacian, 57
Law of large numbers, 4, 6
Learning, 109
Linearity of expectation, 220, 373
Lloyd's algorithm, 185
Local algorithm, 262
Long-term probabilities, 65

m-fold, 240
Markov chain, 63
    state, 67
Markov Chain Monte Carlo, 64
Markov random field, 301
Markov's inequality, 5
Matrix
    multiplication
        by sampling, 170
    diagonalizable, 388
    similar, 388
Maximum-cut problem, 51
Maximum likelihood estimation, 380
Maximum likelihood estimator, 20
Maximum principle, 82
MCMC, 64
Mean value theorem, 406
Median, 375
Metropolis–Hastings algorithm, 68

Mixing time, 65
Model
    random graph, 215
Molloy Reed, 253
Moment generating function, 403
Mutually independent, 373

Nearest neighbor problem, 18
Nonuniform Random Graphs, 252
Normalized conductance, 65, 73
Number of triangles in $G(n, p)$, 221

Ohm's law, 83
Orthonormal, 394

Page rank, 95
    personalized, 98
Persistent, 63
Phase transition, 222
    CNF-sat, 248
    non-finite components, 258
Poisson distribution, 377
Polar coordinates, 9
Polynomial interpolation, 167
Positive semidefinite, 400
Power iteration, 49
Power law distribution, 218
Power method, 39
Power-law distribution, 252
Principle component analysis, 44
Probability density function, 372
Probability distribution function, 372
Psuedo random, 168
Pure-literal heuristic, 249

Queue, 249
    arrival rate, 250

Radon, 121
Random graph, 215
Random projection, 16
    theorem, 17
Random variable, 372
Random walk
    Eucleadean space, 92
    in three dimensions, 93
    in two dimensions, 92
    on lattice, 92
    undirected graph, 85
    web, 95
Rapid Mixing, 67
Real spectral theorem, 389
Replication, 240

Resistance, 81, 91
    efffective, 84
Restart, 95
    value, 95
Return time, 95

Sample space, 372
Sampling
    length squared, 171
Satisfying assignments
    expected number of, 248
Scale function, 342
Scale vector, 342
Second moment method, 221, 223, 224
Sharp threshold, 223
Similar matrices, 388
Singular value decomposition, 29
Singular vector, 31
    first, 32
    left, 34
    right, 34
    second, 32
Six-degrees separation, 262
Sketch
    matrix, 173
Sketches
    documents, 177
Small world, 261
Smallest-clause heuristic, 249
Spam, 97
Spectral clustering, 190
Stanley Milgram, 261
State, 67
Stirling approximation, 367
Streaming model, 159
Symmetric matrices, 389

Tail bounds, 380, 384
Tail of Gaussian, 371
Taylor series, 362
Threshold, 222
    CNF-sat, 246
    diameter $O(\ln n)$, 239
    disappearance of isolated vertices, 227
    emergence of cycles, 235
    emergence of diameter two, 225
    giant component plus isolated vertices, 237
Time domain, 328
Total variation distance, 68
Trace, 397
Triangle inequality, 366
Triangles, 220

Union bound, 373
Unit clause heuristic, 249

Unitary matrix, 394
Unsatisfiability, 248

Variance, 374
variational method, 367
VC-dimension, 118
    convex polygons, 121
    finite sets, 121
    half spaces, 121
    intervals, 120
    pairs of intervals, 121

rectangles, 120
spheres, 122
Viterbi algorithm, 296
Voltage
    probabilistic interpretation, 83

Wavelet, 341
World Wide Web, 95

Young's inequality, 366, 369